# A Frequency Dictionary
# of French

*A Frequency Dictionary of French* is an invaluable tool for all learners of French, providing a list of the 5000 most frequently used words in the language.

Based on a 23-million-word corpus of French which includes written and spoken material both from France and overseas, this dictionary provides the user with detailed information for each of the 5000 entries, including English equivalents, a sample sentence, its English translation, usage statistics, and an indication of register variation.

Users can access the top 5000 words either through the main frequency listing or through an alphabetical index. Throughout the frequency listing there are thematically organized lists of the top words from a variety of key topics such as sports, weather, clothing, and family terms.

An engaging and highly useful resource, the *Frequency Dictionary of French* will enable students of all levels to get the most out of their study of French vocabulary.

**Deryle Lonsdale** is Associate Professor in the Linguistics and English Language Department at Brigham Young University (Provo, Utah). **Yvon Le Bras** is Associate Professor of French and Department Chair of the French and Italian Department at Brigham Young University (Provo, Utah).

# Routledge Frequency Dictionaries

**Other books in the series:**
*A Frequency Dictionary of Mandarin Chinese*
*A Frequency Dictionary of German*
*A Frequency Dictionary of Portuguese*
*A Frequency Dictionary of Spanish*
*A Frequency Dictionary of Arabic* (forthcoming)

# A Frequency Dictionary
# of  French

*Core vocabulary for learners*

**Deryle Lonsdale  and Yvon Le Bras**

Routledge
Taylor & Francis Group

LONDON AND NEW YORK

First published 2009
by Routledge
2 Park Square, Milton Park, Abingdon, Oxon OX14 4RN

Simultaneously published in the USA and Canada
by Routledge
270 Madison Ave, New York, NY 10016

*Routledge is an imprint of the Taylor & Francis Group, an informa business*

Typeset in Parisine by Swales & Willis, Exeter, Devon
Printed and bound in Great Britain
by CPI Antony Rowe, Chippenham, Wiltshire

*British Library Cataloguing in Publication Data*
A catalogue record for this book is available from the British Library

*Library of Congress Cataloging in Publication Data*
Lonsdale, Deryle.
   A frequency dictionary of French : core vocabulary for learners / Deryle Lonsdale,
   Yvon Le Bras.
     p. cm.
   Includes index.
   1. French language—Word frequency—Dictionaries. I. Lonsdale, Deryle. II. Title.
   PC2691.L66 2009
   443'.21—dc19    2008042400

ISBN10: 0–415–77531–0 (pbk)
ISBN10: 0–415–77530–2 (hbk)
ISBN10: 0–203–88304–7 (ebk)

ISBN13: 978–0–415–77531–1 (pbk)
ISBN13: 978–0–415–77530–4 (hbk)
ISBN13: 978–0–203–88304–4 (ebk)

# Contents

# Thematic vocabulary lists

# Series preface

There is a growing consensus that frequency information has a role to play in language learning. Data derived from corpora allows the frequency of individual words and phrases in a language to be determined. That information may then be incorporated into language learning. In this series, the frequency of words in large corpora is presented to learners to allow them to use frequency as a guide in their learning. In providing such a resource, we are both bringing students closer to real language (as opposed to textbook language, which often distorts the frequencies of features in a language, see Ljung 1990) and providing the possibility for students to use frequency as a guide for vocabulary learning. In addition we are providing information on differences between frequencies in spoken and written language as well as, from time to time, frequencies specific to certain genres.

Why should one do this? Nation (1990) has shown that the 4,000 – 5,000 most frequent words account for up to 95 per cent of a written text and the 1,000 most frequent words account for 85 per cent of speech. While Nation's results were for English, they do at least present the possibility that, by allowing frequency to be a general guide to vocabulary learning, one task facing learners – to acquire a lexicon which will serve them well on most occasions most of the time – could be achieved quite easily. While frequency alone may never act as the sole guide for a learner, it is nonetheless a very good guide, and one which may produce rapid results. In short, it seems rational to prioritize learning the words one is likely to hear and use most often. That is the philosophy behind this series of dictionaries.

The information in these dictionaries is presented in a number of formats to allow users to access the data in different ways. So, for example, if you would prefer not to simply drill down through the word frequency list, but would rather focus on verbs, the part of speech index will allow you to focus on just the most frequent verbs. Given that verbs typically account for 20 per cent of all words in a language, this may be a good strategy. Also, a focus on function words may be equally rewarding – 60 per cent of speech in English is composed of a mere 50 function words.

We also hope that the series provides information of use to the language teacher. The idea that frequency information may have a role to play in syllabus design is not new (see, for example, Sinclair and Renouf 1988). However, to date it has been difficult for those teaching languages other than English to use frequency information in syllabus design because of a lack of data. While English has long been well provided with such data, there has been a relative paucity of such material for other languages. This series aims to provide such information so that the benefits of the use of frequency information in syllabus design can be explored for languages other than English.

We are not claiming, of course, that frequency information should be used slavishly. It would be a pity if teachers and students failed to notice important generalizations across the lexis presented in these dictionaries. So, for example, where one pronoun is more frequent than another, it would be problematic if a student felt they had learned all pronouns when they had learned only the most frequent pronoun. Our response to such issues in this series is to provide indexes to the data from a number of perspectives. So, for example, a student working down the frequency list who encounters a pronoun can switch to the part of speech list to see what other pronouns there are in the dictionary and what their frequencies are. In short, by using the lists in combination a student or teacher should be able to focus on specific words and groups of words. Such a use of the data presented here is to be encouraged.

Tony McEnery and Paul Rayson
Lancaster, 2005

# References

**Ljung, M. (1990)**
*A Study of TEFL Vocabulary*. Stockholm: Almqvist & Wiksell International.

**Nation, I.S.P. (1990)**
*Teaching and Learning Vocabulary*. Boston: Heinle and Heinle.

**Sinclair, J.M. and Renouf, A. (1988)**
"A Lexical Syllabus for Language Learning". In R. Carter and M. McCarthy (eds) *Vocabulary and Language Teaching* London: Longman, pp. 140–158.

# Acknowledgments

We are first and foremost grateful to Mark Davies for proposing that we undertake this work, and for his occasional guidance and suggestions throughout its duration. This work also would not have been possible without the help of our able and hard-working student research assistants at Brigham Young University: Fritz Abélard, Amy Berglund, Katharine Chamberlin, and Ben Sparks.

The first author would like to thank his French instructors throughout his formative years, particularly France Levasseur-Ouimet and Gérard Guénette. He also acknowledges the inspiring influence of past colleagues in translation and lexicography including Greg Garner, Benoît Thouin, Brian Harris, Robert Good, Alain Danik, and Claude Bédard. He dedicates this book to his parents, to his wonderfully supportive wife Daniela, and to Walter H. Speidel whose own pioneering work in corpus-based computerized lexicography stands as an example for all of us who work in this field.

The second author wishes to thank Philippe Hamon, Bernard Quemada, and Réal Ouellet, his professors at the University of Rennes, the University of Paris III, and Laval University, who instilled in him the desire to study and teach the French language and literature. He dedicates this book to his parents and especially to his wife Hoa for her continued support and encouragement in his professional endeavors.

# Abbreviations

| Categories | | Example | |
|---|---|---|---|
| *adj* | adjective | 1026 | **lourd** *adj* heavy |
| *adv* | adverb | 1071 | **certainement** *adv* certainly |
| *conj* | conjunction | 528 | **puisque** *conj* since |
| *det* | determiner | 214 | **votre** *det* your |
| *intj* | interjection | 889 | **euh** *intj* er, um, uh |
| *n* | noun | 802 | **absence** *nf* absence |
| *nadj* | noun/adjective | 4614 | **insensé** *nadj* insane |
| *prep* | preposition | 389 | **parmi** *prep* among |
| *pro* | pronoun | 522 | **lui-même** *pro* himself |
| *v* | verb | 1014 | **confirmer** *v* to confirm |

| Features on categories | | Example | |
|---|---|---|---|
| *f* | feminine | 1011 | **armée** *nf* army |
| *i* | invariable | 1324 | **après-midi** *nmi* afternoon |
| *m* | masculine | 707 | **signe** *nm* sign |
| *pl* | plural | 3654 | **dépens** *nmpl* expense |
| *(f)* | no distinct feminine | 3770 | **apte** *adj*(f) capable |
| *(pl)* | no distinct plural | 3901 | **croix** *nf*(pl) cross |

# Introduction

## The value of a frequency dictionary for French

Today French is the second most taught and widespread second language globally, behind English. Yet, surprisingly, there is no current corpus-based frequency dictionary of the French language. The present dictionary is meant to address this shortcoming, and is part of a series that includes other highly useful dictionaries for Spanish (Davies, 2006) and Portuguese (Davies & Preto-Bay, 2008). As such it is similar in intent, approach, structure, and content to its predecessors. As noted below, some modifications have also been made to make it more usable for English speakers, who do constitute the largest group of speakers on the planet.

The purpose for this book is to prepare students of French for the words that they are most likely to encounter in the "real world". It is meant to help alleviate the phenomenon encountered all too often in dictionaries and language primers where word lists are introduced based on intuitive or unverifiable notions of which words might conceivably be most useful for students to acquire, and in which order. The dictionary is designed primarily as a reference work which could be used in concert with standard classroom curricular materials or used on an individual study basis. Ideas on how to carry out this integration have been noted in the previous dictionaries noted above.

## Contents of the dictionary

This is first and foremost a frequency dictionary. The principal information concerns the 5,000 most frequent words in French as determined in the process described below. This information is arranged in three different formats: (i) a main frequency listing, which begins with the most frequent word (with associated information) followed by the next most frequent word, and so forth; (ii) an alphabetical index of these words, and (iii) a frequency listing of the words organized by part of speech, and (iv) thematic lists grouping some of the words into related semantic classes. Each of the entries in the main frequency listing contains the word itself, its part(s) of speech (e.g. noun, verb, adjective, etc.), a context reflecting its actual usage previously in French, an English translation of that context, and summary statistical information about the usage of that word. Some or all of this information is likely to be highly useful for language learners in different settings.

The vocabulary itself was derived from a corpus, or body, of French texts. The corpus we collected was assembled specifically for this work and totals millions of words, half of them reflecting transcriptions of spoken French and the other half written French texts. Since the dictionary is focused primarily on frequency and usage, the words do not have associated with them any pronunciation guides, etymological history, or domain-specific usage information. The dictionary is also focused on single words, which is a crucial but not exclusive consideration in language learning; to extensively address fixed word expressions such as collocations and idioms would be beyond the scope of this dictionary.

The dictionary, then, is designed as an instrument for helping students acquire a core vocabulary of French words in various ways, including based on their observed frequency in recent French language usage. The versatility in its organization should presumably allow its use in a wide range of language learning scenarios.

## Previous frequency dictionaries for French

French dictionaries are plentiful and widely varied in content, so one might wonder whether another dictionary is necessary. A short survey of existing dictionaries should suffice to illustrate why this one was developed.

Two landmark frequency dictionaries have been produced for French. One (Henmon 1924) was based on 400,000 words of text, and the other (Juilland et al. 1970) derives from a study of 500,000 words.

Information on the words contained in those lists, though, was minimal, and the ability to handle more sizable corpora has since – of course – been vastly improved with computer technology.

Other word reference lists have been developed largely for scholarly purposes and hence not very accessible to the average learner. Brunet (1981) focuses on development of French vocabulary over time based on the superb Trésor de la Langue Française (Imbs 1971-1994). Beauchemin *et al.* (1992) focus only on the French spoken in Quebec. All of these resources require some effort to use effectively.

Some lexical resources are at the disposal of French language learners through the Internet, such as the ARTFL FRANTEXT and TLFi resources. The subscription costs and on-line access methods are sometimes less practical than having a reasonably sized dictionary like this one at one's fingertips.

Finally, some helpful recent beginner dictionaries exist, though each has its own limitations. Recent ones by Oxford University Press (2006), Living Language (Lazare 1992), and Dover Publications (Buxbaum 2001) list from 1001 to 20,000 "most useful" words but give no rationale for how they were selected. Another venerable work by Gougenheim (1958) lists 3500 basic French words with related information including definitions, but which are entirely in French and hence challenging for the beginner.

Our dictionary seeks to combine the best from this tradition of French lexical research while at the same time avoiding these shortcomings. Its presentation design and the rationale and methodology for selecting the contents reflect what we believe to be the state of the art in corpus research, text processing, and lexicography.

## The corpus and its annotation

Our dictionary is derived from a corpus of some 23,000,000 French words that have been assembled from a wide variety of sources. As mentioned above, half of this total reflects a collection of transcriptions from oral or spoken French, while the other half reflects French in its textual or written form. Reflecting a desire to make our dictionary a modern representation of the French language, we have included no materials that date before the year 1950.

We did not try to proportion our data based on geographical region or demographics, but we did try to achieve some balance across genres; however, this balance is not perfect. It is also important to note that some of our content from particular sources was exhaustive whereas in other cases it was selectively or randomly sampled; in other words, only parts of the material were used because there was too much content and hence the risk of skewing coverage of particular areas.

The spoken text portion of the corpus was made up of approximately 11.5 million words. These words were pulled from such various forms such as transcripts of governmental debates/hearings, telephone calls, and face-to-face dialogues. There were also transcripts of interviews with writers, entertainment figures, business leaders, athletes, academicians and other media personnel. And finally we made use of movie scripts/subtitles and theatrical plays.

The written text portion of the corpus was also made up of roughly 11.5 million words. This part of the corpus was assembled from newswire stories, daily and weekly newspapers, newsletters, bulletins, business correspondence, and technical manuals. Magazines such as popular science and other technical publications were used. We also targeted different genres of literature such as fiction/nonfiction essays, memoirs, novels and more.

Table 1 gives a more detailed listing of the composition of the corpus.

### Corpus standardization and annotation

Collection of the corpus involved much work in what has been called corpus standardization or text preprocessing. Given the wide range of sources for the corpus, they involved many different file types, character encodings, and formatting conventions. For example, the documents used a wide range of character representations and formats such as EBCDIC, MACROMAN, ISO, UTF-8, and HTML. In many cases unneeded material such as images, advertisements, or templatic information had to be stripped out, a process called document scrubbing.

Each type of transcription or text document was then processed so that the paragraphs, sentences, words, and characters were identified and encoded in a standard way to enable further processing, a process called tokenization. The scrubbing and tokenization processes involve linguistic issues that had to be addressed, such as deciding on how to break up

*Table 1* Composition of 23 million word French corpus

| | Approx. # of words | Type | Sources |
|---|---|---|---|
| **Spoken** | | | |
| | 175,000 | Conversations | [3] |
| | 3,750,000 | Canadian Hansard | [4] |
| | 3,020,000 | Misc. interviews/transcripts | [5] |
| | 1,000,000 | European Union parliamentary debates | [6] |
| | 855,000 | Telephone conversations | [7] |
| | 470,000 | Theatre dialogue/monologue | [8] |
| | 2,230,000 | Film subtitles | [9] |
| TOTAL | 11,500,000 | | |
| | | | |
| **Written** | | | |
| | 3,000,000 | Newswire stories | [10] |
| | 2,015,000 | Newspaper stories | [11] |
| | 4,734,000 | Literature (fiction, non-fiction) | [12] |
| | 434,000 | Popular science magazine articles | [13] |
| | 1,317,000 | Newsletters, tech reports, user manuals | [14] |
| TOTAL | 11,500,000 | | |
| | | | |
| GRAND TOTAL | 23,000,000 | | |

[3]  The French portion of the C-ORAL-ROM corpus (Cresti & Moneglia 2005).

[4]  Aligned Hansards of the 36th Parliament of Canada; for more information consult
http://www.isi.edu/natural-language/download/hansard/.

[5]  Miscellaneous transcripts of interviews with various business, political, artistic, and academic personalities mined from hundreds of Internet sites. Many were from media sites such as French television studios (e.g. www.tf1.fr and www.france2.fr), publishing houses (www.lonergan.fr), popular culture websites (e.g. www.evene.fr), and business information portals (e.g. http://www.journaldunet.com).

[6]  A small random sampling from the French portion of the Multilingual Corpora for Cooperation (MLCC) corpus. See resource W0023 at www.elda.fr.

[7]  Aligned transcribed training data from the ESTER Phase 2 evaluation campaign; downloaded from
http://www.irisa.fr/metiss/guig/ester/.

[8]  A small random sampling of extracts from theatrical works posted at various sites including www.leproscenium.fr.

[9]  Selected portions of several film subtitles from Jörg Tiedemann's OPUS corpus; downloaded from
http://urd.let.rug.nl/tiedeman/OPUS/OpenSubtitles.php.

[10]  A tiny random sampling of stories from the French GigaWord corpus; for more information see
http://www.ldc.upenn.edu/Catalog/CatalogEntry.jsp?catalogId=LDC2006T17.

[11]  A sampling from newspaper articles on the Internet from journalism sites throughout the French-speaking world
(e.g. www.lemonde.fr, www.ledevoir.com).

[12]  Samples and complete short works of fiction and non-fiction works from various publishing houses
(e.g. www.edition-grasset.fr, www.lonergan.fr) and Web virtual libraries (e.g. www.gutenberg.org).

[13]  A variety of articles from popular science magazine sites on the Internet
(e.g. www.pourlascience.com, www.larecherche.com, etc.).

[14]  A variety of technical report and newsletter articles including weather bulletins, user manuals, business newsletters, and banking correspondence. Some of these materials are sampled from the French portions of the European Corpus Initiative
(see http://wwww.ldc.upenn.edu/Catalog/CatalogEntry.jsp?catalogId=LDC2006T17.

words separated by hyphens (dis-moi vs. week-end) and apostrophes (l'homme vs. aujourd'hui). Some documents had accented upper letters whereas others did not, so the process of case folding – or reducing capitalized words to their lower-case form – was also nontrivial. Many special symbols including degree signs, ellipsis punctuation, currency symbols, bullets, and dots also required standardization. To perform all of this work we used several file conversion programs as well as our own Perl scripts, Unix tools (e.g. make, awk, grep, sort, uniq, join, comm), and SGML/HTML/XML parsers.

Once the corpus was standardized, it was then necessary for us to assign to each word its part of speech; in other words, whether it functions as a noun, a verb, an adjective, and so forth. Currently there are about a dozen different part of speech taggers for the French language, each with its own theoretical framework, implementation approach, and set of tag encodings to flag the relevant parts of speech for each word. In this work we installed and tested several of these taggers. In our case we found that each tagger had its own strengths and weaknesses and that by combining several of them and merging the results in a postprocessing stage we could create our own tagging procedure and tagset to produce the best results for our purpose. We also performed a certain amount of editing and correcting tagging results by hand for the most common tagging errors, though for the entire corpus a thorough examination of each word would have been prohibitively time-consuming and costly.

It was also necessary to perform a morphological analysis of each word in the corpus to find its base form, or lemma. For example, the second word in the sentence "Je suis heureux." is a verb conjugation of the verb "être", which is its base form or lemma. Similarly, pronouns with regular inflections (e.g. "il" to "ils"), adjectives, and determiners with variant forms were combined together. The lemmatization process was necessary for our frequency computations, to be described below. Various lemmatization programs exist for French, and in fact some of them perform both part of speech tagging and lemmatization at the same time. In this stage, too, there were challenges that we had to overcome. For example, many words are morphologically ambiguous, having several possible lemmas, such as the verb form "suis" having both "être" and "suivre" as possible lemmas,

depending on the particular instance. Another difficulty is deciding when non-finite forms (i.e. past and present participles and infinitives) function more as verbs or as other parts of speech (especially nouns, adjectives). Again we found that combining some of the most popular programs and postprocessing the results ended up being the most helpful for our purposes.

*Target vocabulary identification and description*

With the whole corpus standardized and annotated, it was possible to compute word frequencies and identify the most-used words. Counting words in a corpus can be done in several ways. We have chosen to collapse all of the variant forms of the same word and sum them up together. For example, the word "pour" is a conjunction or preposition and occurs in two other forms across the corpus: "Pour" and "POUR". Summing up all occurrences of the variant forms of this word we arrive at a total count of 151,709. Similarly, plural forms of nouns are normally reduced to their singular form, verb conjugations are reduced to their infinitive form, and inflected adjectives are reduced to the masculine singular form, as is done in other French dictionaries. For example, throughout the corpus there are 25 different forms of the verb "déterminer" including inflections and variant forms such as "déterminerait", "détermine", "déterminons", and "Déterminez"; all of these were combined with their counts into the infinitive form.

Our target vocabulary list is thus formed from the top 5000 scoring lemmas in the corpus. In identifying these top 5000 lemmas, some items (such as proper nouns and punctuation) were rejected. However, one more refinement was necessary in identifying the top 5000 words. Experience in corpus linguistics has shown that the raw frequency count for all variants of a word turns out not to be the best measure of its usefulness. Consideration must be made of how widely a word is spread across the different parts of a corpus.

Exactly quantifying how widely a word is spread across a document or corpus has been a thorny problem in corpus linguistics. If a given word occurs very frequently in one part of the corpus (e.g. the spoken part) but not elsewhere, it might be desirable to discount that word's raw frequency so that it becomes a little less "important" in comparison to other less-frequent words. Literally dozens of approaches have been taken over the last decades to come up with workable solutions. One of the most promising, and the one used in the compilation of this book, is called the "deviation of proportions", or DP (Gries, 2008).

The DP measure looks at the proportion of a term's occurrence across various "slices" of a corpus, taking into account the size of each slice. Each word's final calculation involves three steps: (i) summing up all of the occurrences of that word's for each slice and normalizing it against that word's overall frequency in the whole corpus, called the "observed proportion"; (ii) normalizing each corpus slice with respect to the size of the whole corpus, called the "expected proportion"; (iii) computing the absolute difference between observed and expected proportions, summing them up, and dividing by 2. The result is a measure between 0 and 1, where 0 means the word is distributed evenly across the corpus slices and 1 means it is restricted to narrow parts of the corpus.

While helpful in describing word distribution across a corpus, the DP measure is only one metric, and for the purposes of this dictionary it was necessary to combine it with the raw frequency. Thus we computed, for each lemma, its frequency divided by its DP. The result determined the ranking of each lemma and hence its final appearance and relative order in the top 5000 words in the vocabulary. For example, all forms of the word "avoir" sum up to a frequency of 405,020 and its DP score is 0.11533. Its ranking score is thus 405020/0.115363, or 3,510,831.029. This is the sixth highest score among all of the lemmas, so this word places sixth in the ranked list.

Finally, the DP values are somewhat unwieldy as long numbers behind a decimal point. To solve this problem we mapped these values to a much more intuitive set of integers ranging from about 27 to 100. These numbers are called dispersion codes. The mathematical calculation for obtaining a dispersion code from its corresponding DP measure involves an exponential function: $100*exp^{-DP}$. Values approaching 100 indicate that the word is quite evenly distributed across the corpus; values below 50 indicate words that are limited to only certain narrow portions of the corpus.

Though these computations are somewhat technical, the general intuition is that the words

in this dictionary are ranked by the summed frequency of all of their variant forms, tempered by how well they are spread across various portions of the corpus.

Once the terms were identified, additional information had to be collected to construct the associated entries.

*Developing associated information*

Providing parts of speech was done through a combination of automatic and manual methods. The values were derived from (i) the part of speech tags provided from the lemmatization process described above; (ii) popular lexical databases for French lexical information (e.g. BDLEX[1]); and (iii) hand-editing of the merged and accumulated results.

Glossing the terms was a completely manual effort. An intuitive effort was made to give as much of the core meaning(s) as possible while at the same time avoiding the temptation to be exhaustive.

The next stage involved finding a suitable usage context for each word. In each case the usage context comes from the corpus itself, so that it represents an illustration of natural French, the way a French-speaking person would use the word. Equally important was the need to find contexts that were clear, short, self-contained, and indicative of the core meaning of the word. Ideally, the contexts should also contain as few words as possible that are not covered in the dictionary elsewhere. To find the contexts, a computer-generated list of possible contexts was prepared for each word, and then scored automatically according to these criteria. We then manually chose from among these lists the best context for each word.

Like glossing, generating English translations for the usage contexts was also a human effort. Each context was taken in isolation and, often using the English glosses that had been prepared, a translation was entered manually. Some texts already had English translations from previous work and hence could have been extracted manually using word-alignment techniques, but we purposely chose to not use these techniques so as to assure that the translations were "fresh" in each instance.

---

[1] See http://www.irit.fr/PERSONNEL/SAMOVA/decalmes/IHMPT/ress_ling.v1/rbdlex_en.php.

Finally, we compiled the thematic lists. In each case the content of the list was done using a combination of automatic and manual techniques. For semantic subject areas (e.g. food and weather terms) hierarchical lexical databases (e.g. French WordNet[2]) were used to locate the terms' position in a taxonomy of semantic field areas. A parallel effort of hand-selecting relevant terms was also carried out, and the results were merged together.

All of these results have been combined into a comprehensive database (we used both mySQL and Microsoft Access) that enables versatile retrieval of relevant information.

In conclusion, this dictionary is calibrated to the learners' needs, and organized in such a way that is easy for the reader. Corpus linguistics is at the core of the effort, but a wide array of human skills and computational linguistic techniques were vital in the process.

## The main frequency index

The frequency index is the main portion of this dictionary: it contains a ranked list of the top 5000 lemmas in French, starting with the highest-scoring one and progressing to the lowest-scoring word. Each entry has the following information:

> ranked score (1, 2, 3…), headword, part(s) of speech, English gloss, sample context, English translation of sample context, dispersion value, raw frequency total, indication of register variation

For example, here is the entry for the word "aimer":

> **242   aimer** *v* to like, love
> • tu sais que je t'aime
>   *you know I love you*
>   71 | 10085 –n

This entry shows that the word (and all of its related forms) ranks 242nd among all French words in terms of combined frequency and dispersion. The part-of-speech code shows that it's a verb. Two possible English glosses are "to like" and "to love". One context from the corpus is shown, which uses one of

the related forms of this verb: "aime". An English translation for the usage context then appears. Next, the number "71" flags the dispersion value for the word on a scale from 27 to 100; the word and its forms are reasonably evenly spread across the corpus. The number "10085" indicates the raw frequency, or how many times the word and its related forms occur in the corpus. Finally, a register code –n indicates that this word is noticeably infrequent in nonfiction.

Here are some additional notes for the items appearing in the entries.

### The part(s) of speech

Several categories have been combined to increase readability. For example, *nadj* signifies a word that can be either a noun or an adjective. Marking for major features is also provided, such as for gender (*nm* for masculine, *nf* for feminine), number (*pl* for non-distinct plurals), and invariable words that don't inflect (e.g. *adji*). Some nouns have both genders. In this dictionary participles that have drifted semantically from their core meaning, or that have acquired a status that makes them more like adjectives or nouns, have been listed separately. Examples of such words include "reçu (receipt)", "fabricant (manufacturer)", and "âgé (old)".

### The English gloss

The gloss is meant to be indicative only – it's not a complete listing of all possibilities. This is not an exhaustive bilingual dictionary. Many of these words also participate in idioms, fixed expressions, collocations, or multi-word expressions. These meanings are not included in the glosses since the focus is on single words. The glosses are written in standard American English. In certain parts of the dictionary (e.g. in the thematic lists) only shortened forms of the glosses are used.

### The French usage context

As noted above, all of the usage contexts come from the corpus itself. In selecting them the goal was to find contexts that illustrate clearly the core meaning of the word as concisely as possible. Contexts will sometimes unavoidably include words that are not in the top 5000 words, as well as occasional idiomatic usages. The contexts are taken verbatim, with only very infrequent correction (e.g. spelling errors). Capitalization is (for the most part) neutralized to improve readability. Sometimes the contexts are not always grammatically correct, especially when taken

---

[2] See http://www.illc.uva.nl/EuroWordNet/.

from a spoken language transcript where speech errors, non-standard usage, and non-prescribed forms are common (e.g. "j'sais pas" vs. "je ne sais pas"). Finally, the contexts reflect real-world usage, and hence may not always be factually or politically correct. No editorial endorsement or philosophical conclusions should be ascribed to the authors on the basis of the contexts used.

### The English translation of the context
Translations are rendered into American English, with it attendant spelling and vocabulary choices. An attempt was made to project the register, style, and structure. of the source context into its translation. However, translations were focused more on meaning than structure, so some translations are fairly loose and sometimes creative. On occasion a translation may involve a word whose part of speech is different than its related word appearing in the English gloss. Since the glosses are only meant to be indicative and not exhaustive, the translations may involve words not shown in the glosses, but usually the relationship is readily apparent. Sometimes idiomatic usages or collocations may be used in a translation to show how flexibly the word can be used. It is important to note that the contexts were translated in standalone fashion. Since the context was isolated from its surrounding material before translation, reference of pronouns, articles, etc. is not guaranteed to perfect match the meanings in the source documents. For example, a context "Je lui téléphone" might either be translated "I'm telephoning him" or "I'm telephoning her". Clearly one translation would be most appropriate to the context when viewed in its original source file, but to supply such is not necessarily our intention here.

### The statistical and register information
The last line of each entry has two numbers divided by a vertical bar. The first is the dispersion value discussed above. The second is the raw frequency count for all of the variants of the entry's headword. Some words also have a register code that specifies the word's distribution across registers. The three registers and their codes are spoken (±s), literature (±l), and non-fiction (±n). A positive value for some register means that the word occurs in the top 5% of

the expected frequencies for the words in that register, when compared against the other two registers. Conversely, a negative value means that the word occurs in the bottom 5% of the expected frequencies for the words in that register. For example the first-person pronoun "je" has a −n register code, indicating that it occurs comparatively very infrequently in the nonfiction register. On the other hand, a very imagery-laden descriptive adverb like "brusquement" has the codes +l and −s, meaning that it is very infrequent in spoken language but very frequent in literature.

## Thematic vocabulary ("call-out boxes")
A number of thematically-grouped words are given in tables that are placed throughout the frequency index. These include lists of terms for such semantic classes as animals, body parts, foods, colors, nationalities, and professions. Other tables give data on grammatical questions (e.g. use of the pronoun "se"), word length, and variation of word usage across the three registers (spoken, literature, and nonfiction). When glosses appear in these lists, they may only represent a portion of the glosses given in the main frequency list. In addition, sometimes words are ambiguous in their meaning; for example, the word "poisson (fish)" is both an animal and a food. In cases where the word's usage exhibits a clear preference for one sense over another, it will only appear in the list associated with the preferred sense. In other cases, though, where no clear preference exists, the word may appear in both relevant thematic lists.

## Alphabetical and part of speech indexes
The alphabetical index gives an alphabetical listing of all of the words listed in the previous section. Each entry in this chapter includes: (1) the lemma (2) the part of speech (3) a basic English equivalent, and (4) the word's score in this dictionary.

The part of speech index gives a listing of the words from the frequency index, this time arranged by "parts of speech". Each category lists the lemmas by their score in decreasing frequency of occurrence. The alphabetical index can be used to link a given word with its score.

# References

**Beauchemin, N., Margel, P., and Théoret, M.
1992.** *Dictionnaire de fréquence des mots du français parlé au Québec: fréquence, dispersion, usage, écart réduit.* New York: P. Lang.

**Brunet, É. 1981.**
*Le vocabulaire français de 1789 à nos jours d'après les données du Trésor de la langue française.* Paris: Champion. (Travaux de linguistique quantitative, 46).

**Buxbaum, M.O. 2001.**
*1001 Most Useful French Words.* Mineola, NY: Dover Publications.

**Davies, M. 2006.**
*Frequency Dictionary of Spanish: Core Vocabulary for Learners.* New York: Routledge.

**Davies, M. and Preto-Bay, A.M.R. 2008.**
*Frequency Dictionary of Portuguese: Core Vocabulary for Learners.* New York: Routledge.

**Galarneau, A. 2002.**
Les dictionnaires de langue française. Dictionnaires d'apprentissage. Dictionnaires spécialisés de la langue. Dictionnaires de spécialité. *International Journal of Lexicography* (15)3:246–248.

**Gougenheim, G. 1958.**
*Dictionnaire fondamental de la langue française.* Paris: Librairie Marcel Didier.

**Gries, S.T. forthcoming.**
Dispersions and adjusted frequencies in corpora. *International Journal of Corpus Linguistics.*

**Henmon, V.A.C. 1924.**
*A French word book based on a count of 400,000 running words.* Madison, WI: University of Wisconsin.

**Imbs, P. 1971–1994.**
*Trésor de la langue française.* Paris: CNRS, Gallimard.

**Juilland, A., Brodin, D., and Davidovitch, C. 1970.**
*Frequency Dictionary of French Words.* La Haye, Paris: Mouton.

**Lazare, L 1992.**
*French Learner's Dictionary.* New York: Living Language.

# Frequency index

**rank frequency (501, 502 . . .)**, **headword**, *part of speech*, English equivalent
• sample sentence
range count | raw frequency total, indication of major register variation

**1 le** *det, pro* the; him, her, it, them
• vive la politique, vive l'amour – *long live politics, long live love*
89 | 2359662

**2 de** *det, prep* of, from, some, any
• il ne rêve que d'argent et de plaisirs – *he only dreams of money and pleasure*
88 | 1665907

**3 un** *adj, det, nm, pro* a, an, one
• je me suis cassé un ongle – *I broke one of my fingernails*
95 | 421500

**4 à** *prep* to, at, in
• ils restent à l'école le plus longtemps possible – *they remain at school as long as possible*
93 | 557546

**5 être** *nm,v* to be; being
• tout le monde veut être beau – *everybody wants to be beautiful*
91 | 514562

**6 et** *conj* and
• et les larmes se remirent à couler – *and the tears started flowing again*
93 | 364443

**7 en** *adv,prep,pro* in, by
• je suis retournée en Espagne en septembre – *I returned to Spain in September*
94 | 242952

**8 avoir** *nm,v* to have
• on était six donc tu peux pas avoir une conversation – *there were six of us so you can't have a conversation*
89 | 405020

**9 que** *adv,conj,pro* that, which, who, whom
• c'est un soldat. mais que fait-il ici? – *it's a soldier. but what's he doing here?*
88 | 348428

**10 pour** *prep* for, in order to
• elle jouait pour gagner – *she played to win*
93 | 151709

**11 dans** *prep* in, into, from
• je reviendrai dans dix minutes – *I will return in 10 minutes*
93 | 161033

**12 ce** *det,pro* this, that
• je ne déteste pas cet homme – *I do not detest this man*
87 | 307421

**13 il** *pro* he, it
• allez voir s'il est blessé – *go see if he is injured*
86 | 251585

**14 qui** *pro* who, whom
• je ne sais pas à qui m'adresser – *I don't know who to talk to*
89 | 160867

**15 ne** *adv* not
• nous ne faisons pas du très bon travail – *we are not doing very good work*
86 | 195309

**16 sur** *adj,prep* on, upon
• t'avais une chance sur un million – *you had one chance in a million*
92 | 97798

## 1 Animals

**animal** 1002 M animal

**poisson** 1616 M fish

**chien** 1744 M dog

**cheval** 2220 M horse

**oiseau** 2435 M bird

**bête** 2591 F beast

**vache** 2768 F cow

**chat** 3138 M cat

**monstre** 3353 M monster

**virus** 3382 M virus

**bœuf** 3914 M ox

**loup** 3927 M wolf

**porc** 4036 M pig

**mouton** 4175 M sheep

**rat** 4290 M rat

**poule** 4321 F hen

**souris** 4328 F mouse

**singe** 4739 M monkey

**ours** 4800 M bear

**bétail** 4842 M livestock

**cochon** 4947 M pig

**canard** 5295 M duck

**lion** 5413 M lion

**serpent** 5574 M snake

**puce** 5788 F flea

**lapin** 5833 M rabbit

**papillon** 5979 M butterfly

**dragon** 6054 M dragon

**chèvre** 6074 F nanny goat

**saumon** 6287 M salmon

**moule** 6520 F mussel

**17 se** *pro* oneself, himself, herself, itself, themselves
- avec ce traité, le Japon se rapproche des Etats-Unis – *with this treaty, Japan brings itself closer to the U.S.*
88 | 144707

**18 pas** *adv,nm(pl)* not, n't; footstep
- non, ne touchez pas! – *no, don't touch it!*
83 | 161746

**19 plus** *adv* more, no more
- il est considérablement plus jeune que moi – *he's considerably younger than I am*
90 | 85987

**20 pouvoir** *nm,v* can, to be able to
- tu peux jouer de la guitare électrique – *you can play electric guitar*
90 | 78074

**21 par** *prep* by
- il s'y trouvait par hasard – *he found himself there by accident*
87 | 99628

**22 je** *pro* I
- je suis contente de vous revoir – *I am happy to see you again*
73 | 227259-n

**23 avec** *prep* with
- vous voulez aller au ciné avec moi? – *do you want to go to a movie with me?*
91 | 66056

**24 tout** *adv,det,nadj,pro* all, very
- comme vous voyez, tout est propre – *as you see, everything is clean*
86 | 95071

**25 faire** *nm,v* to do, make
- qu'est-ce qu'il fait? – *what's he doing?*
85 | 99587

**26 son** *det,nm* his, her, its; sound; bran
- un ami ingénieur du son m'aide pour les arrangements – *a sound engineer friend of mine helped me with the arrangements*
81 | 116681

**27 mettre** *v* to put, place
- je peux me mettre à votre table? – *may I sit at your table?*
96 | 19654

**28 autre** *det,nadj(f),pro* other
- il y a un autre problème – *there's another problem*
91 | 40519

**29 on** *pro* one, we
- on tire et on pose les questions ensuite – *we shoot first and ask questions later*
80 | 87982

**30 mais** *adv,conj,intj* but
- je ne suis pas riche, mais je connais la vérité – *I'm not rich, but I know the truth*
83 | 69661

**31 nous** *pro* we, us
- nous devons nous défendre nous-mêmes – *we must defend ourselves*
78 | 89100

**32 comme** *adv,conj* like, as
- Tony et moi, on est comme des frères – *Tony and I, we're like brothers*
87 | 49608

**33 ou** *conj* or
- il en reste du café ou pas? – *is there some coffee left or not?*
86 | 49714

**34 si** *adv,conj,nmi* if, whether
- aujourd'hui, notre économie va si mal – *today our economy is going so poorly*
87 | 46439

**35 leur** *det,adj(f),pro* them, their, theirs
- l'énergie solaire assurait leur survie – *solar energy assured their survival*
87 | 39904

**36 y** *adv,nmi,pro* there
- c'est certain qu'on va y aller – *it's for certain that we'll be going there*
83 | 55889

**37 dire** *nm,v* to say
- je décrochais le téléphone sans rien dire à personne – *I picked up the telephone receiver without saying anything to anyone*
77 | 66657-n

**38 elle** *pro* she, her
- j'étais fou amoureux. elle m'aimait bien – *I was head-over-heels in love. she loved me a lot*
78 | 66136

**39 devoir** *nm,v* to have to, owe; duty
- je dois travailler sans la moindre entrave – *I must work without the least bit of hindrance*
83 | 46491

**40 avant** *adji,adv,nm,prep* before
- tu vas te pencher en avant – *you're going to lean forward*
94 | 14109

**41 deux** *det,nmi* two
- il prend le train deux fois par semaine pour affaires – *he takes the train on business twice per week*
87 | 31727

**42 même** *adj(f),adv,pro* same, even, self
- ils ne s'excusent même pas – *they don't even excuse themselves*
85 | 37784

**43 prendre** *v* to take
- elle lui prit la main – *she took him by the hand*
90 | 24323

**44 aussi** *adv,conj* too, also, as
- je rêvais aussi de beaucoup voyager – *I also dreamed of traveling a lot*
88 | 26219

**45 celui** *pro* that, the one, he, him
- tu es celui que je respecte le plus – *you're the one I respect the most*
87 | 28015

**46 donner** *v* to give
- j'aurais donné ma vie pour lui – *I would have given my life for him*
90 | 19581

**47 bien** *adji,adv,nm* well
- tout va bien maintenant – *everything's going well now*
81 | 39477

**48 où** *adv,pro* where
- on ne dit pas où il vit – *they aren't saying where he lives*
87 | 27126

**49 fois** *nf(pl)* time, times
- lève la main une fois – *raise your hand one time*
92 | 15724

**50 vous** *pro* you
- ici, vous avez une personnalité publique – *here, you are a public personality*
65 | 77127-n +s

**51 encore** *adv* again, yet
- tu as encore menti à ta femme – *you lied once again to your wife*
89 | 19772

**52 nouveau** *adj,nm* new
- il a construit une nouvelle vie ici – *he made a new life for himself here*
88 | 22005

**53 aller** *nm,v* to go
- tu devrais aller te coucher, tu as l'air vanné – *you should go to bed, you look wiped out*
73 | 50452

**54 cela** *pro* that, it
- cela demande de l'intégrité et du courage – *that requires integrity and courage*
73 | 50891-n +s

**55 entre** *prep* between
- je marche entre les maisons – *I'm walking between the houses*
86 | 23028

**56 premier** *det,nadj* first
- est-elle la première épouse, la deuxième? – *is she the first wife, the second one?*
84 | 27061

**57 vouloir** *nm,v* to want
- tu veux faire ton chemin. c'est bien – *you want to continue on your way. that's OK*
79 | 36467

**58 déjà** *adv* already
- les rues étaient déjà pleines de monde – *the streets were already full of people*
93 | 11298

**59 grand** *adv,nadj* great, big, tall
- tu es plus grand que je pensais – *you're taller than I thought*
87 | 21583

**60 mon** *det* my
- t'aurais pu rencontrer mon copain – *you could've met my buddy*
70 | 55084-n

**61 me** *pro* me, to me, myself
- reviens me voir dans cinq ou six ans – *come back to see me in five or six years*
65 | 63357-n

**62 moins** *adji(pl),adv,nm(pl),prep* less
- il avait moins d'excuses encore que ses complices – *he had even less excuses than his accomplices did*
90 | 14730

**63 aucun** *det,adj,pro* none, either, neither, not any
- trop d'argent et aucun goût – *too much money and no taste*
93 | 9641

**64 lui** *pro* him, her
- mais j'ai confiance qu'en lui – *but I have confidence in him*
75 | 38286

**65 temps** *nm(pl)* time
- sur le plan spirituel, le temps n'existe pas – *on the spiritual level, time does not exist*
86 | 20420

**66 très** *adv* very
- j'ai été bonne? très, très bonne – *was I good? very, very good*
82 | 26324

**67 savoir** *nm,v* to know
- je ne savais plus quoi dire – *I didn't know what to say any more*
78 | 32739

**68 falloir** *v* to take, require, need
- il ne faut pas être raciste, point – *there's no need to be a racist, at all*
84 | 22844

**69 voir** *v* to see
- je tenais seulement à te voir pour te dire ... bonne chance – *I just wanted to see you to say ... good luck*
78 | 30907

**70 quelque** *adv,adj,det* some
- il restera pour quelques mois – *he will stay for a few months*
86 | 18939

**71 sans** *prep* without
- je fais plus jeune sans maquillage – *I look younger without makeup*
81 | 25099

**72 raison** *nf* reason
- elle a raison, tu sais – *she's right, you know*
92 | 9506

**73 notre** *det* our
- notre ville a le sens de la communauté – *our city has a sense of community*
78 | 29713

**74 dont** *pro* whose, of which
- on a tout ce dont tu rêvais en ville – *everything you dreamed about is available in town*
86 | 17841

**75 non** *adv,nmi* no, not
- non, je ne peux pas parler maintenant – *no, I can't talk now*
81 | 24848

**76 an** *nm* year
- j'avais un an à la mort de mon père – *I was one year old when my father died*
82 | 22241

**77 monde** *nm* world, people
• notre ultime but est de reconstruire le monde – *our ultimate goal is to remake the world*
87 | 15475

**78 jour** *nm* day
• un jour, je retrouverais mes vrais parents – *one day, I would find my real parents*
86 | 17641

**79 monsieur** *nm* mister, sir, gentleman
• comment allez-vous , monsieur? – *how are you, sir?*
67 | 45411

**80 demander** *v* to ask for
• j'ai un service à vous demander – *I would like to ask you to do something for me*
86 | 16076

**81 alors** *adv* then, so
• et alors? vous revenez quand? – *so? when are you coming back ?*
84 | 18443

**82 après** *adv,prep* after
• il a succombé à ses blessures peu après – *he shortly thereafter succumbed to his wounds*
83 | 17733

**83 trouver** *v* to find
• j'ai trouvé du sang. sur le siège avant – *I found some blood. on the front seat*
85 | 16036

**84 personne** *nf,pro* person, people, anybody, anyone, nobody
• il ne parlait à personne en particulier – *he was speaking to nobody in particular*
84 | 16218

**85 rendre** *v* to render, return, yield, give up
• je m'y rendis à 4 heures du matin – *I went there at 4 o'clock in the morning*
90 | 10226

**86 part** *nf* share
• je voudrais vous faire part de quelques données – *I want to share some data with you*
91 | 8971

**87 dernier** *nadj* last
• c'est le dernier endroit où vous auriez dû vous rencontrer – *that's the last place you should have met*
83 | 17524

**88 venir** *v* to come
• venez rencontrer les autres – *come meet the others*
81 | 19776

**89 pendant** *adj,prep,nm* during; pendant
• où t'étais pendant tout ce temps? – *where were you all of this time?*
91 | 8413

**90 passer** *v* to pass
• nous sommes passées devant la maison de ma grand-mère – *we went past the front of my grandmother's place*
83 | 17070

**91 peu** *adv* little
• un secret se dévoile peu à peu – *a secret unfolds little by little*
81 | 18830

**92 lequel** *pro* who, whom, which
• il y a bien des points sur lesquels je voudrais faire des commentaires – *there are many points on which I would like to comment*
87 | 12507

**93 suite** *nf* result, follow-up, rest
• deux, trois et ainsi de suite – *two, three, and so on*
93 | 5964

**94 bon** *adj,adv,intj,nm* good
• ce n'est pas le bon moment – *it's not a good time*
81 | 18375

**95 comprendre** *v* to understand
• je comprends que vous soyez fâché – *I understand that you're upset*
87 | 12482

**96 depuis** *adv,prep* since, for
• je le connais depuis le lycée – *I have known him since high school*
83 | 16243

**97 point** *adv,nm* point; at all
• je suis d'accord avec ce point de vue – *I'm in agreement with that point of view*
85 | 13938

**98 ainsi** *adv* thus
• qu'est-ce qui le pousse à agir ainsi? – *what drives him to act that way?*
86 | 12358

**99 heure** *nf* hour
• a quelle heure sont-ils partis? – *at what time did they leave?*
85 | 13215

**100 rester** *v* to stay
• le temps qu'il te reste, trouve une solution – *in the remaining time, find a solution*
86 | 11942

**101 seul** *adj* alone, only
• parler tout seul était signe d'aliénation – *talking to oneself was a sign of loneliness*
84 | 13542

**102 année** *nf* year
• il devait se présenter l'année suivante – *he had to show up the next year*
81 | 16316

**103 toujours** *adv* always
• tu es toujours en retard – *you're always late*
81 | 15106

**104 tenir** *v* to hold
• c'est une porte de sécurité. tiens ça – *it's a security door. hold this*
85 | 12229

**105 porter** *nm,v* to wear, carry
• il a porté le maillot jaune un jour – *he wore the yellow jersey one day*
89 | 8044

**106 parler** *nm,v*  to speak
- je sais de quoi je parle – *I know what I'm talking about*
77 | 18598-n

**107 fort** *adv,adj,nm*  strong
- c'est une femme forte – *she is a strong woman*
90 | 6811

**108 montrer** *v*  to show
- c'est une étrange façon de montrer votre reconnaissance – *that's a strange way to show your gratitude*
92 | 5634

**109 là** *adv,intj*  there, here
- je n'étais pas passé par là – *I hadn't passed by there*
73 | 21735-n

**110 certain** *adj,det,nm,pro*  certain, sure
- certains ont affirmé que le gouvernement était trop faible – *some contend that the government was too weak*
79 | 16317

**111 fin** *adj,adv,nf,nm*  end; gist; clever person
- la fin est importante en toutes choses – *the ending is important in everything*
85 | 10595

**112 tu** *pro*  you
- a ma place, tu ne le ferais pas – *in my position, you would not do it*
54 | 42483-n +s

**113 continuer** *v*  to continue
- tu continues de m'impressionner – *you continue to impress me*
91 | 6377

**114 pays** *nm(pl)*  country
- ils vivent dans ce beau pays – *they live in this beautiful country*
74 | 19496

**115 trois** *det,nmi*  three
- les trois chasseurs étaient en pleine lumière – *the three hunters were directly in the light*
83 | 12562

**116 penser** *nm,v*  to think
- je pense que vous le connaissez bien – *I think you know him very well*
78 | 16338-n

**117 lieu** *nm*  place
- je suis né dans un lieu public – *I was born in a public place*
89 | 7344

**118 partie** *nf*  part
- il garde la majeure partie de cet argent – *he's keeping most of that money*
85 | 10177

**119 quand** *adv,conj*  when
- tu aurais dû me tuer quand tu en as eu l'occasion – *you should have killed me when you had the chance*
75 | 18704

**120 suivre** *v*  to follow
- les autres, suivez-moi! – *everybody else, follow me!*
89 | 7251

**121 contre** *adv,nm,prep*  against
- je vois, tu es en colère contre moi – *I see you're angry with me*
78 | 15564

**122 sous** *prep*  under
- juste sous ton nez – *right under your nose*
84 | 10840

**123 côté** *nm*  side
- il s'arrête à côté du fauteuil – *he stops beside the armchair*
89 | 7002

**124 ensemble** *adv,nm*  together
- on n'a jamais été si bien ensemble – *we've never gotten along so well together*
90 | 6055

**125 chose** *adj(f),nf*  thing
- les choses pourraient bien changer à l'avenir – *things could change in the future*
75 | 18086-n

**126 enfant** *nm,nf,adj(f)*  child
- mes enfants sont en vie – *my children are alive*
85 | 9836

**127 cause** *nf*  cause
- ces hallucinations ont une cause – *these hallucinations have a cause*
91 | 5353

**128 politique** *nadj(f)*  politics; political
- elle se spécialise en sciences politiques – *her specialty is political science*
77 | 15972

**129 place** *nf*  room, space, square, place
- je n'aimerais pas être à votre place – *I wouldn't want to be in your stead*
87 | 8092

**130 seulement** *adv*  only
- on va seulement rester quelques jours, ma chérie – *we're only going to stay a few days, my dear*
88 | 7546

**131 moi** *nm,pro*  me
- tu sors avec moi ce soir? – *are you going out with me tonight?*
63 | 27118-n

**132 vie** *nf*  life
- je suis sûr qu'elle est en vie – *I'm sure she's alive*
80 | 13285

**133 connaître** *v*  to know
- je le connaissais depuis vingt ans – *I had known him for twenty years*
83 | 10612

**134 jusque** *adv,prep*  to, up to, until
- ils me poursuivirent jusque dans la rue – *they followed me right into the street*
85 | 9482

**135 croire** *v*  to believe
- je n'arrive pas à y croire – *I just can't believe it*
77 | 15044-n

**136 homme** *nm* man
- l'homme est plus important que l'État –
*man is more important than country*
76 | 15266

**137 cas** *nm(pl)* case
- en tout cas, moi, je ne l'ai pas – *in any case,
I don't have it*
80 | 12096

**138 petit** *nadj* small, little
- ce petit drogué n'a pas tort – *this little drug
addict isn't wrong*
76 | 15029

**139 commencer** *v* to begin, start
- il est important que ces entretiens
commencent immédiatement – *it's
important that these meetings start
immediately*
88 | 6996

**140 compter** *v* to count
- je peux compter sur toi – *I can count on you*
89 | 6072

**141 fait** *adj,nm* done, fact
- dans les faits, il a raison – *factually, he is
correct*
80 | 12241

**142 tel** *adj,det,pro* such
- je vais m'abstenir d'employer un tel langage
– *I'm going to refrain from using such
language*
84 | 9491

**143 droit** *adj,adv,nm* right
- elle a le droit de tout savoir – *she has the
right to know everything*
78 | 13566

**144 question** *nf* question
- je suis gêné de répondre à cette question –
*I'm embarrassed to answer this question*
68 | 20584+s

**145 donc** *conj* so, then, therefore, thus
- nous avons donc dû faire les calculs
nous-mêmes – *we had to do the
calculations ourselves*
74 | 15588

**146 quel** *det,adj,pro* which, what
- quel livre cherchiez-vous? – *which book are
you looking for?*
80 | 11958

**147 général** *nadj* general
- voici quelques conseils généraux – *here are
a few general pieces of advice*
82 | 10245

**148 moment** *nm* moment
- arrête de parler pour un moment – *stop
talking for a moment*
82 | 10053

**149 entendre** *v* to hear
- j'ai entendu la nouvelle – *I heard the news*
81 | 10290

**150 beaucoup** *adv* much, a lot of, many
- il est en mesure de révéler beaucoup de
choses – *he's in a position to reveal many
things*
78 | 12421

**151 chaque** *det,adj* each
- chaque entreprise doit avoir sa propre
organisation – *every company must have its
own organization*
86 | 7202

**152 jeune** *nadj(f)* young
- le gouvernement cherche à exploiter les
jeunes – *the government is trying to exploit
young people*
83 | 9357

**153 travail** *nm* work
- je ne prenais pas mon travail au sérieux – *I
wasn't taking my work seriously*
78 | 11952

**154 femme** *nf* woman, wife
- je vous déclare maintenant mari et femme
– *I now declare you husband and wife*
78 | 12016

**155 attendre** *v* to wait
- ma mère m'attend dans la grande salle –
*my mother awaits me in the large room*
82 | 9327

**156 remettre** *v* to deliver, replace, set, put
- on s'est remis à marcher – *we resumed
walking*
93 | 3181

**157 appeler** *v* to call
- comment s'appelle-t-il? – *what's his name?*
83 | 8899

**158 permettre** *v* to allow
- vous permettez que j'utilise votre téléphone?
– *would you allow me to use your telephone?*
78 | 11760

**159 occuper** *v* to occupy
- sa main droite était occupée à tenir la petite
valise – *his right hand was busy holding the
small suitcase*
92 | 3921

**160 gouvernement** *nm* government
- le gouvernement a augmenté les impôts –
*the government increased taxes*
58 | 25743+s

**161 eux** *pro* them
- c'est eux qui comptent – *they are the ones
who matter*
87 | 6631

**162 devenir** *nm,v* to become
- je suis très heureux que vous deveniez ma
voisine – *I'm very happy you've become my
neighbor*
82 | 8933

**163 partir** *v* to leave
- il est parti à présent – *he is gone for the
moment*
83 | 8299

**164 plan** *adj,nm* plan
- achetez donc un plan de la ville – *so buy a
map of the city*
87 | 5978

**165 décider** *v* to decide
- j'ai décidé d'écrire un roman – *I decided to
write a novel*
88 | 5533

**166 soit** *adv,conj* either...or
- il a pas le choix: soit il est une star soit il est rien – *he doesn't have a choice: either he's a star or he's nothing*
84 | 7623

**167 ici** *adv* here
- moi je reste ici – *I'm going to stay here*
77 | 11898

**168 rien** *adv,nm,pro* nothing
- moi, je n'en sais rien – *I don't know anything about it*
69 | 16549

**169 cours** *nfpl,nm(pl)* course
- ils organisaient des petits cours et des séminaires – *they organized short courses and seminars*
82 | 8559

**170 affaire** *nf* business, matter
- occupe-toi de tes affaires – *mind your own business*
80 | 9899

**171 nom** *nm* name
- quel est son nom? – *what is his name?*
85 | 6836

**172 famille** *nf* family
- il provient sûrement d'une excellente famille – *he surely comes from an excellent family*
87 | 5986

**173 effet** *nm* effect
- il s'agit, en effet, d'une question cruciale – *it is, indeed, a crucial question*
83 | 8142

**174 arriver** *v* to arrive, happen
- cela ne m'était pas arrivé depuis – *that hasn't happened to me since*
79 | 10070

**175 possible** *adj(f)* possible
- nous avons donc deux scénarios possibles – *so we have two possible scenarios*
86 | 6178

**176 car** *conj,nm* because; bus
- c'est dommage, car tu vas perdre un gros client – *it's too bad, because you're going to lose a major customer*
81 | 8864

**177 servir** *v* to serve
- il m'a servi une coupe de champagne – *he served me a glass of champagne*
89 | 4942

**178 mois** *nm(pl)* month
- il a écrit ce livre en deux mois – *he wrote this book in two months*
82 | 8318

**179 jamais** *adv* never
- je jure de ne plus jamais te contacter – *I swear I will never contact you again*
73 | 12997

**180 sembler** *v* to seem
- le processus semble irréversible – *the process seems irreversible*
83 | 7471

**181 tant** *adv* so much, so many
- mais vous avez tant à enseigner – *but you have so much to teach*
84 | 7284

**182 vers** *nm(pl),prep* toward; verse
- un tram se dirige vers toi. monte dedans – *a tram is approaching you. get on it*
77 | 10203

**183 besoin** *nm* need
- nous avons vraiment besoin d'aide – *we really need some help*
82 | 7899

**184 revenir** *v* to come back
- je sais qu'elle ne reviendra jamais – *I know she will never return*
85 | 6514

**185 dès** *prep* from, as soon
- on me fera signe dès que vous descendrez – *they'll wave to me as soon as you get down there*
89 | 4537

**186 moyen** *adj,nm* means, way; medium
- il songeait aux moyens de profiter de sa victoire – *he was dreaming of a way to profit from his victory*
81 | 8104

**187 groupe** *nm* group
- on va commencer avec le premier groupe – *we'll start with the first group*
76 | 10535

**188 problème** *nm* problem
- nous avons osé soulever le problème – *we dared raise the problem*
76 | 10795+s

**189 rapport** *nm* relationship, report
- je propose que le rapport du comité soit adopté – *I move that the committee's report be adopted*
75 | 11146

**190 peut-être** *adv* perhaps, maybe
- j'ai peut-être une idée – *I might have an idea*
79 | 9067

**191 vue** *nf* view
- la vue est belle, de cette fenêtre – *the view from this window is pretty*
87 | 5172

**192 maintenant** *adv* now
- je ne peux pas partir maintenant – *I can't leave now*
78 | 9309+s

**193 pourquoi** *adv,conj,nmi* why
- pourquoi tu ne m'invites pas? – *why don't you invite me?*
74 | 11128-n +s

**194 meilleur** *nadj* better, best
- j'apprends à être un meilleur mari – *I'm learning to be a better husband*
87 | 5030

**195 trop** *adv* too much, too many
- la vie est trop courte. essayez d'être heureuse – *life is too short. try to be happy*
78 | 9356

## 2  Body

| | | |
|---|---|---|
| **tête** 343 F head | **peau** 2122 F skin | **poitrine** 4168 F breast |
| **voix** 414 F voice | **cheveu** 2296 M hair | **gorge** 4194 F throat |
| **main** 418 F hand | **sac** 2343 M sac | **crâne** 4314 M skull |
| **œil** 474 M eye | **organe** 2417 M organ | **coude** 4404 M elbow |
| **esprit** 538 M mind | **jambe** 2472 F leg | **poumon** 4679 M lung |
| **sein** 563 M bosom | **épaule** 2494 F shoulder | **poil** 4723 M hair |
| **cœur** 568 M heart | **nez** 2661 M nose | **foie** 4817 M liver |
| **pied** 626 M foot | **tissu** 2696 M tissue | **talon** 5049 M heel |
| **langue** 712 F tongue | **dent** 2784 F tooth | **barbe** 5053 F beard |
| **sang** 1126 M blood | **cadavre** 2892 M corpse | **veine** 5263 F vein |
| **bras** 1253 M arm | **lèvre** 2927 F lip | **cuisse** 5292 F thigh |
| **visage** 1292 M face | **cul** 2949 M ass | **rein** 5493 M kidney |
| **côte** 1385 F rib (also coast) | **genou** 2967 M knee | **muscle** 5860 M muscle |
| **dos** 1672 M back | **gueule** 3015 F mouth | **fesse** 6087 F buttock |
| **front** 1729 M forehead | **ventre** 3150 M belly | **estomac** 6209 F stomach |
| **figure** 1825 F face (also figure) | **chair** 3260 F flesh | **ongle** 6275 F fingernail |
| **bouche** 1838 F mouth | **pouce** 3298 M thumb | **cheville** 6313 F ankle |
| **oreille** 1884 F ear | **cou** 3820 M neck | **sourcil** 6344 M eyebrow |
| **doigt** 1938 M finger | **poing** 3889 M fist | **moustache** 6360 F moustache |
| **cerveau** 1990 M brain | **joue** 3932 F cheek | **hormone** 6434 F hormone |
| | **os** 4092 M bone | **tumeur** 6450 F tumor |

**196 laisser** *v*  to leave
- il va nous laisser tranquilles – *he'll leave us alone*
- 77 | 9854

**197 ordre** *nm*  order
- ce sont des scientifiques de premier ordre – *they are first-rate scientists*
- 86 | 5610

**198 devant** *adv,nm,prep*  in front, ahead
- une fumée montait devant nous sur l'horizon – *smoke billowed ahead of us on the horizon*
- 81 | 7783

**199 recevoir** *v*  to receive
- il n'a plus reçu de lettres de moi – *he didn't receive any more letters from me*
- 82 | 7201

**200 répondre** *v*  to answer
- j'aimerais y répondre par une autre question – *I would like to respond to it with another question*
- 83 | 6672

**201 vivre** *nm,v*  to live
- aucune Marocaine ne vit seule dans le quartier – *no Moroccan woman lives alone in the neighborhood*
- 80 | 8023

**202 long** *adv,nadj*  long, lengthy
- l'éducation sur le long terme paiera, j'en

suis convaincu – *long-term education pays off, I'm convinced of that*
82 | 6947

**203 service** *nm*  service
- je faisais mon service militaire – *I was doing my military service*
- 75 | 10131

**204 ministre** *nm,nf*  minister
- les ministres se sont réunis dans la nuit – *the ministers met during the night*
- 57 | 20107-l

**205 face** *nf*  front, side, face
- on s'est trouvés face à face – *we found ourselves face to face*
- 85 | 5438

**206 chez** *prep*  at, with
- elle ira peut être vivre définitivement chez lui – *she might go live with him permanently*
- 78 | 8646

**207 te** *pro*  you, to you, from you
- je vais t'emmener chez un médecin – *I'm going to take you to a doctor*
- 51 | 23312-n +s

**208 rappeler** *v*  to recall, call back
- je ne me rappelle pas avoir été aussi heureux – *I don't remember having been that happy*
- 86 | 4966

**209 présenter** *v* to present
- papa je te présente Claire – *daddy, this is Claire*
79 | 8243

**210 accepter** *v* to accept
- j'accepte avec plaisir votre aimable invitation – *I accept with pleasure your kind invitation*
87 | 4705

**211 agir** *v* to act
- c'est le moment d'agir – *now is the time to act*
78 | 8418

**212 simple** *nadj(f)* simple
- on préférerait une réponse simple – *we would prefer a simple answer*
90 | 3579

**213 plusieurs** *det,adj,pro* several
- il y a plusieurs formes d'humour – *there are several types of humor*
80 | 7714

**214 votre** *det* your
- permettez-moi de vous parler dans votre langue – *allow me to speak to you in your language*
64 | 15483-n +s

**215 important** *nadj* important
- c'est une question extrêmement importante – *it's an extremely important question*
75 | 9564

**216 présent** *nadj* present
- il est trop tard pour dîner à présent – *it's too late to have supper now*
86 | 5151

**217 mieux** *adji(pl),adv,nm* better
- je ne vous ai jamais mieux aimée – *I have never loved you more*
82 | 6736

**218 poser** *v* to put, pose, ask
- je ne me posais plus de questions – *I didn't ask myself any more questions*
84 | 5949

**219 jouer** *v* to play
- les enfants jouent dehors – *the children are playing outside*
83 | 6092

**220 mot** *nm* word
- je ne crois pas un mot sorti de ta petite bouche – *I don't believe a single word from your little mouth*
81 | 7191

**221 reconnaître** *v* to recognize
- Joseph reconnut le chant de la grive – *Joseph recognized the thrush's song*
85 | 5513

**222 force** *nf* force
- parle-moi de ces forces surnaturelles – *talk to me of these supernatural forces*
80 | 7546

**223 situation** *nf* situation
- dans des situations aussi difficiles, il faut trancher – *in such difficult situations, drastic measures must be taken*
79 | 7616

**224 offrir** *v* to offer
- alors, je vous offre la vie éternelle – *so I offer you eternal life*
87 | 4365

**225 près** *adv,prep* near, nearby, close by
- il y a un siège vide près de vous – *there's an empty seat near you*
81 | 6660

**226 choisir** *v* to choose
- c'est maintenant le moment de choisir – *now is the moment to choose*
89 | 3731

**227 national** *nadj* national
- il y avait l'intérêt national français – *the national interests of the French were involved*
74 | 9570

**228 projet** *nm* project
- le gouvernement ne financerait aucun projet touchant cette pratique – *the government would not fund any project involving this practice*
60 | 16661+s

**229 ni** *conj* nor
- je ne mange pas de viandes, ni de produits laitiers – *I don't eat meat or dairy products*
77 | 8528

**230 puis** *adv* then, so
- elle a tenté de me tuer, puis elle m'a chassée – *she tried to kill me, then she chased me*
72 | 10366

**231 toucher** *nm,v* to touch
- il lui touche l'épaule – *he touches her shoulder*
88 | 4032

**232 train** *nm* train
- je pris le train pour un aller-retour vers la mer – *I took the train on a round-trip outing to the sea*
90 | 3198

**233 aujourd'hui** *adv* today
- je peux, aujourd'hui encore, en réciter – *even today I can still recite some of them*
73 | 9905

**234 comment** *adv,conj,intj,nmi* how
- voyons un peu comment les choses se sont passées – *let's take a look at how things unfolded*
72 | 10133+s

**235 surtout** *adv,nm* especially, above all
- j'ai surtout besoin d'argent – *what I need above all is money*
83 | 5548

**236 gens** *nmpl* people
- des gens sont venus me voir – *people came to see me*
70 | 11090-n +s

**237 propre** *nadj(f)* clean, proper
- la pétasse était propre, mec – *the woman was clean, man*
85 | 5012

**238 grâce** *nf* thanks, grace, favour
- je ne vous demande aucune grâce – *I'm not asking you for any favors*
90 | 3271

**239 idée** *nf* idea
- que pensez-vous de cette idée? – *what do you think of this idea?*
81 | 6128

**240 selon** *prep* according to
- tout est prêt selon vos désirs – *everything's ready according to your wishes*
68 | 11561

**241 région** *nf* region
- la région a connu une cinquantaine de massacres – *the region has experienced some fifty massacres*
78 | 7352

**242 aimer** *v* to like, love
- tu sais que je t'aime – *you know I love you*
71 | 10085-n

**243 sens** *nm(pl)* sense, meaning
- il manquait un sens à donner à ma vie – *there was a lack of meaning in my life*
82 | 5836

**244 retrouver** *v* to find, recall
- je te retrouve dehors – *I'll find you outside*
84 | 5166

**245 semaine** *nf* week
- ma pièce se jouait cette semaine – *my play was showing that week*
79 | 6831

**246 également** *adv* also, too, as well, equally
- reculer est également hors de question – *backing down is also not an option*
74 | 9011

**247 ci** *adv,pro* this one, here
- et celui-ci? oui, il est vraiment super – *and this one here? yes, he's really great*
83 | 5303

**248 façon** *nf* way, manner
- c'est une façon de voir, je suppose – *it's a way of looking at it, I guess*
75 | 8326

**249 nombre** *nm* number
- il existe un nombre infini de réponses possibles – *there are an infinite number of possible answers*
78 | 7158

**250 perdre** *v* to lose
- vous avez perdu votre mère, mademoiselle? – *did you lose your mother, miss?*
82 | 5728

**251 français** *nadj(pl)* French
- il faut leur parler en français – *you need to speak to them in French*
71 | 9969

**252 expliquer** *v* to explain
- je vous en prie, expliquez-moi tout – *I beg you, explain everything to me*
82 | 5749

**253 quatre** *det,nmi* four
- nous sommes quatre étudiants dans la maison – *we're four students sharing a house*
80 | 6272

**254 compte** *nm* account, count
- cette ville a eu son compte de désastres – *this city has had its fair share of disasters*
81 | 5923

**255 considérer** *v* to consider
- la présidence considère cela comme une priorité majeure – *the presidency considers that a major priority*
85 | 4591

**256 lorsque** *conj* when
- que se passe-t-il lorsque nous manquons de sucre? – *what happens when we lack sugar?*
74 | 8682

**257 ouvrir** *v* to open
- s'il vous plaît, ouvrez les yeux – *please open your eyes*
83 | 5254

**258 gagner** *v* to win, earn
- que le meilleur gagne – *may the best man win*
88 | 3492

**259 exemple** *nm* example
- ces exemples sont encore bien pauvres – *these examples are still very weak*
73 | 8876

**260 ville** *nf* city
- nous étions de la même ville – *we were from the same city*
81 | 5914

**261 économique** *nadj(f)* economic, economical
- le rétablissement économique de l'Asie est plus rapide que prévu – *Asian economic recovery is faster than projected*
77 | 7421

**262 mesure** *nf* measure
- écrire me libère dans une certaine mesure – *writing liberates me to a certain extent*
70 | 9966

**263 histoire** *nf* history, story
- on a raconté d'amusantes histoires – *we told funny stories*
80 | 6193

**264 haut** *adv,nadj* top, high
- voilà qui vous lancera dans la haute société – *that's who will launch you into high society*
84 | 4897

**265 ensuite** *adv* next
- ensuite il va au restaurant – *then he's going to the restaurant*
88 | 3533

**266 guerre** *nf* war
- c'est nul, la guerre! – *war is nothing!*
77 | 6897

**267 loi** *nf* law
- je vais voter contre le projet de loi – *I'm going to vote against the bill*
53 | 17361+s

**268 président** *nm* president
- j'ai rencontré le président des Etats-Unis – *I met the president of the U.S.*
63 | 12235

269 **exister** *v* to exist
- le risque n'existe plus – *there is no more risk*
83 | 5074

270 **sûr** *adj* sure
- tu m'attends? bien sûr, poupée – *will you wait for me? of course, doll*
78 | 6629

271 **refuser** *v* to refuse
- attendez . . . vous refusez d'obéir? – *wait . . . you refuse to obey?*
87 | 3714

272 **plutôt** *adv* rather
- ce jet vole plutôt bas – *this jet is flying rather low*
83 | 4794

273 **bureau** *nm* office, desk
- il veut vous voir dans son bureau immédiate-ment – *he wants to see you in his office immediately*
91 | 2518

274 **mauvais** *adv,nadj(pl)* bad, wrong
- il constitue un pas dans la mauvaise direction – *it constitutes a step in the wrong direction*
88 | 3425

275 **quant** *adv* as for
- les vents tempêtueux ont modifié la situation quant aux avalanches – *the stormy winds changed the avalanche situation*
89 | 2911

276 **mort** *adj,nf* dead; death
- la mort ne m'effraye pas – *death doesn't frighten me*
71 | 8855

277 **mal** *adji,adv,nm* bad
- autrement dit, la journée a plutôt mal commencé – *in other words, the day started out rather badly*
77 | 6809

278 **lire** *nf,v* to read; lira
- je ne voulais pas lire mes poèmes – *I didn't want to read my poems*
80 | 5707

279 **réussir** *v* to succeed
- il ne réussit pas à vendre un seul dessin – *he can't manage to sell even one drawing*
89 | 2822

280 **marché** *nm* market
- le marché des maisons est resté stable – *the housing market has remained stable*
74 | 7783

281 **condition** *nf* condition
- l'unité de la condition humaine – *the unity of the human condition*
80 | 5589

282 **international** *nadj* international
- elle jouit également d'une excellente réputation internationale – *she also has an excellent international reputation*
70 | 9001

283 **changer** *v* to change
- ensemble, ils ont changé beaucoup de choses – *together, they changed many things*
82 | 5082

284 **oui** *adv,nmi* yes
- oui, oui, je sais! – *yes, yes, I know*
62 | 12295n +s

285 **public** *nadj* public, audience
- je dois beaucoup au public – *I owe a lot to the public*
78 | 6074

286 **humain** *nadj* human
- vous savez, on est humains, nous aussi – *you know, we are also human*
81 | 5151

287 **souvent** *adv* often
- mais alors souvent en fin de soirée c'est la fête – *well, often the night ends with a party*
79 | 5945

288 **cinq** *det,nm(pl)* five
- j'ai cinq minutes, je dois rencontrer quelqu'un à midi – *I have five minutes—I have to meet someone at noon*
77 | 6263

289 **système** *nm* system
- j'ai décrit le système idéal – *I described the ideal system*
65 | 10450

290 **travailler** *v* to work
- nous devons travailler ensemble – *we have to work together*
76 | 6761

291 **jeu** *nm* game
- nous n'entrons pas dans le jeu de la politique – *we don't enter into the political fray*
85 | 3874

292 **vrai** *adv,nadj* true
- ah, oui, c'est vrai – *oh, yes, that's right*
73 | 7846

293 **représenter** *v* to represent
- il représente bien le sport français – *he represents French sports very well*
80 | 5385

294 **madame** *nf* madam, lady
- et je suis au service de madame – *I'm at your service, ma'am*
71 | 8195

295 **société** *nf* society
- on vit dans une société où tout s'accélère – *we live in a society where everything is accelerating*
73 | 7615

296 **difficile** *nadj(f)* difficult
- c'est difficile, monsieur, très difficile d'être un homme – *sir, it's difficult—very difficult—to be a man*
84 | 4116

297 **quoi** *pro* what
- je ne sais pas de quoi vous parlez – *I don't know what you're talking about*
63 | 10985-n +s

**298 entreprise** *nf* enterprise, business
• j'ai moi-même l'esprit d'entreprise
– *I myself have an entrepreneurial
spirit*
72 | 7912

**299 coup** *nm* coup, blow, knock, stroke
• je lui donne juste un coup de main. je le lui
dois – *I'm just giving him a helping hand. I
owe it to him*
77 | 6123

**300 or** *conj,nm* gold; hence, thus
• je ne suis pas chercheuse d'or – *I'm not a
gold-digger*
87 | 3245

**301 social** *nadj* social
• elle a une dimension sociale autant que
biologique – *it has a social dimension as
much as a biological one*
71 | 8096

**302 assurer** *v* to assure, insure
• le contrat assure une pension à l'époux
survivant – *the contract guarantees a
pension to the surviving spouse*
77 | 6044

**303 essayer** *v* to try
• je vais essayer de vous convaincre – *I'll try to
convince you*
79 | 5341

**304 juste** *adv,nadj(f)* just, only; fair
• vous êtes juste et impartial, comme
toujours – *you're fair and impartial, as
always*
79 | 5294

**305 étranger** *nadj* foreigner; foreign
• la situation est bien différente à l'étranger –
*the situation is very different abroad*
76 | 6272

**306 empêcher** *v* to prevent
• cela n'aurait évidemment rien empêché –
*apparently that wouldn't have prevented
anything*
89 | 2705

**307 million** *nm* million
• un quart de million d'articles ont été
distribués – *a quarter million articles were
distributed*
69 | 8380

**308 manière** *nf* manner, way
• de cette manière, nous serons ensemble –
*this way, we will be together*
80 | 5094

**309 sortir** *v* to go out, leave
• sortez ou j'appelle la police – *get out of here
or I'll call the police*
73 | 7005

**310 prix** *nm(pl)* price; prize
• il y a un prix pour les gagnants – *there is a
prize for the winners*
78 | 5543

**311 terme** *nm* term, deadline
• l'éducation sur le long terme paiera –
*education will pay off in the long term*
77 | 5905

**312 longtemps** *adv* a long time, a long while
• pendant longtemps il ne bougea pas de son
lit – *for a long while he didn't move from his
bed*
84 | 3743

**313 reprendre** *v* to resume, recover, start again,
take back
• on peut les arrêter, leur reprendre cette ville
– *we can arrest them, take back this city
from them*
84 | 3867

**314 courant** *adj,nm* current
• je suis au courant, il a téléphoné – *I'm
aware of it, he telephoned*
89 | 2490

**315 intérêt** *nm* interest
• l'avenir ne présente guère d'intérêt – *the
future is hardly interesting*
77 | 5773

**316 mener** *v* to lead
• la police mène une enquête pour arrêter les
assaillants – *the police are leading an
investigation to arrest the attackers*
85 | 3622

**317 information** *nf* information
• ces dirigeants ont décidé de taire ces
informations – *these leaders decided to
suppress this information*
73 | 6966

**318 détail** *nm* detail
• vous devriez tout me raconter en détails –
*you should tell me everything in minute detail*
92 | 1765

**319 appartenir** *v* to belong
• cet argent n'appartient pas au gouvernement – *this money does not belong to the
government*
91 | 1920

**320 liberté** *nf* liberty, freedom
• on se bat pour la liberté d'expression –
*we're fighting for freedom of expression*
86 | 3350

**321 assez** *adv* enough
• les journées ne sont plus assez longues –
*the days are no longer long enough*
77 | 5630

**322 risquer** *v* to risk
• un avocat ne viendra pas risquer sa vie – *a
lawyer won't come here to risk his life*
88 | 2752

**323 chacun** *pro* each
• ils ont chacun leurs intérêts, leurs passions
– *they each have their own interests,
passions*
84 | 3785

**324 concerner** *v* to concern
• en ce qui me concerne, je voudrais te
féliciter – *for my part, I would like to
congratulate you*
70 | 7875

**325 maison** *nf* house
• elle est revenue habiter à la maison – *she
came back to live at home*
76 | 5803

**326 d'abord** *adv* first of all
- je voudrais d'abord savoir quel métier tu exerces – *I would first of all like to know what you do for a living*
83 | 3844

**327 apprendre** *v* to learn
- où as-tu appris le métier? – *where did you learn your trade?*
83 | 4035

**328 niveau** *nm* level
- ce niveau de collaboration ne sera pas maintenu – *this level of cooperation will not be maintained*
71 | 7236

**329 rencontrer** *v* to meet
- il rencontrera le pape au Vatican vendredi – *he will meet the Pope at the Vatican on Friday*
82 | 4103

**330 ton** *det,nm* your; tone
- le ton était donné – *the tone was sounded*
57 | 12083-n +s

**331 œuvre** *nf* work, task
- peu d'auteurs font référence à son œuvre – *few authors cite his work*
84 | 3754

**332 créer** *v* to create
- des malentendus nous créent des problèmes terribles – *misunderstandings create horrible problems for us*
77 | 5446

**333 état** *nm* state
- la police était en état d'alerte maximum – *the police were in a full state of emergency*
74 | 6400

**334 obtenir** *v* to get, obtain
- j'essaierai d'obtenir la réponse pour demain – *I will try to get the answer for tomorrow*
79 | 5088

**335 clair** *adv,nadj* clear
- la nuit était froide et claire, sous la lune – *the night was cold and clear, under the moon*
86 | 3080

**336 chercher** *v* to look for
- je ne cherche pas la richesse – *I am not seeking riches*
76 | 5694

**337 entrer** *v* to enter, go in, come in
- faut trouver le moyen d' entrer dans le sous-sol – *gotta find the way to enter into the basement*
83 | 3800

**338 proposer** *v* to propose
- le jeune Français propose une promenade au parc – *the young Frenchman proposed a stroll through the park*
73 | 6484

**339 apporter** *v* to bring
- je vous ai apportée des fleurs de mon jardin – *I brought you flowers from my garden*
84 | 3624

**340 programme** *nm* program
- utilisons ce programme comme il se doit – *let's use this program the way it should be*
69 | 7525

**341 loin** *adv,nm* far
- tu es venu de si loin – *you came from so far away*
80 | 4677

**342 ligne** *nf* line
- il ne compte qu'une seule ligne de texte – *it only has a single line of text*
80 | 4557

**343 tête** *nf* head
- ma tête me gratte – *my head is itchy*
71 | 6952

**344 libre** *adj(f)* free
- demain je suis libre toute la journée – *tomorrow I'm free all day*
87 | 2703

**345 utiliser** *v* to use
- il utilisait une sorte de rasoir – *he was using some type of razor*
68 | 7709

**346 atteindre** *v* to reach
- leur fortune atteindrait des milliards – *their fortune would reach billions*
82 | 3980

**347 tenter** *v* to tempt, try
- il tente de sortir de l'Italie – *he tried to leave Italy*
85 | 3186

**348 tard** *adv* late
- retournez au lit, il est tard – *go back to bed, it's late*
82 | 3996

**349 enfin** *adv* at last, finally
- elle avait enfin la réponse – *she finally got the answer*
74 | 5989

**350 différent** *adj* different
- c'est un bruit complètement différent – *it's a completely different noise*
75 | 5696

**351 sorte** *nf* sort, kind
- la boisson est une sorte de drogue – *liquor is a kind of drug*
79 | 4741

**352 cependant** *adv,conj* however
- cette sécurité se trouve cependant menacée – *this security is, however, threatened*
81 | 4220

**353 sujet** *nm* subject, topic
- je cherchais un sujet de mémoire – *I was looking for a thesis topic*
73 | 6227

**354 importer** *v* to import; to be important
- il importait de ne pas répéter l'erreur – *it's important to not repeat the mistake*
86 | 3055

**355 action** *nf* action
- le président devrait éviter des actions irréfléchies – *the president should avoid rash actions*
78 | 4997

**356 relation** *nf* relationship
- il y a là une relation intéressante à explorer – *now there is an interesting relationship to explore*
81 | 4222

**357 recherche** *nf* research, search
- la recherche en santé peut se révéler extrêmement bénéfique – *health research can be extremely beneficial*
77 | 5132

**358 livre** *nm,nf* book
- je me mis à feuilleter les livres – *I began paging through the books*
70 | 7124

**359 ajouter** *v* to add
- il ajouta à sa lettre une note – *he added a note to his letter*
74 | 5987

**360 ailleurs** *adv* elsewhere, somewhere else
- les négociations décisives se tiennent ailleurs – *the decisive negotiations are taking place elsewhere*
84 | 3382

**361 vraiment** *adv* truly, really, very
- très mauvais, c'est pas vraiment sexy – *very bad, it's not really sexy*
70 | 7077-n +s

**362 doute** *nm* doubt
- il n'y a sans doute rien à voir – *without a doubt, there's nothing to see*
80 | 4304

**363 reste** *nm* rest
- c'est tout. le reste, je m'en fous – *that's all. for the rest, I couldn't give a sh\*t*
87 | 2607

**364 début** *nm* beginning
- je l'ai expliqué au début de mon discours – *I explained it at the beginning of my talk*
77 | 5096

**365 présence** *nf* presence
- j'ai besoin de sa présence; elle est mon ange – *I need to be in her presence; she is my angel*
88 | 2475

**366 nombreux** *adj(pl)* numerous
- j'ai participé à de nombreux débats de ce genre – *I have participated in numerous debates of this kind*
78 | 4678

**367 produire** *v* to product
- nous devons produire quelque chose sur les terres en jachère – *we must produce something with the fallow lands*
81 | 4014

**368 préparer** *v* to prepare
- je vous prépare à manger? – *should I prepare you some food?*
89 | 2223

**369 forme** *nf* form
- les électrons ne sont plus sous forme de gaz – *the electrons are no longer in the form of gas*
79 | 4533

**370 décision** *nf* decision
- parfois, vos décisions nous déçoivent – *sometimes your decisions disappoint us*
73 | 5924

**371 rôle** *nm* role
- il joue un rôle actif sur la scène internationale – *he plays an active role in the international scene*
79 | 4354

**372 dix** *det,nmi* ten
- je patiente depuis dix minutes – *I have been patiently waiting for ten minutes*
81 | 3871

**373 produit** *nm* product
- de nouveaux marchés s'ouvrent ainsi aux produits français – *new markets are thus opening to French products*
79 | 4492

**374 américain** *nadj* American
- c'est la voie que les Américains ont choisie – *it's the path that the Americans have chosen*
60 | 9762

**375 minute** *nf* minute
- vous ne pouvez pas attendre deux minutes – *you can't wait two minutes*
81 | 4025

**376 relever** *v* to raise
- elle relevait la tête pour croiser mon regard – *she lifted up her head to catch me looking at her*
89 | 2219

**377 autant** *adv* as much, as many
- il a une bonne raison pour tarder autant – *he has a good reason for being so late*
84 | 3276

**378 peuple** *nm* people
- ma vengeance va s'abattre sur votre peuple! – *my vengeance will smite your people!*
84 | 3206

**379 second** *adj,det,nm* second
- j'ai écrit la seconde partie du roman avant la première – *I wrote the second part of the novel before the first*
84 | 3301

**380 prochain** *nadj* next
- je vous offre 50% sur votre billet prochain – *I'll offer you 50% off your next ticket*
76 | 5091

**381 particulier** *nadj* particular, peculiar; person
- j'ai un regard un peu particulier – *I have a somewhat peculiar look*
78 | 4643

**382 écrire** *v* to write
- c'est pour cela que j'écris – *that's why I'm writing*
70 | 6496

## 3 Food

This list includes foods, drinks, and other ingestible substances (e.g. tobacco) as well as other words related to serving and obtaining food.

| | | |
|---|---|---|
| **eau** 475 F water | **tranche** 2692 F slice | **pâte** 3641 F pasta |
| **fruit** 896 M fruit | **déjeuner** 2724 M lunch | **baie** 3719 F berry |
| **poisson** 1616 M fish | **pain** 2802 M bread | **orange** 3912 F orange |
| **café** 1886 M coffee | **aliment** 2845 M food | **bœuf** 3914 M beef |
| **plat** 2167 M dish | **pomme** 2847 F apple | **porc** 4036 M pork |
| **nourriture** 2285 F food | **cigarette** 2855 F cigarette | **beurre** 4112 M butter |
| **vin** 2309 M wine | **repas** 2948 M meal | **mouton** 4175 M sheep |
| **restaurant** 2336 M restaurant | **bouteille** 2979 F bottle | **poulet** 4222 M chicken |
| **huile** 2340 F oil | **bar** 3012 M bar | **sel** 4276 M salt |
| **dîner** 2365 M dinner | **légume** 3117 F vegetable | **poule** 4321 F hen |
| **tabac** 2393 M tobacco | **bière** 3152 F beer | **fromage** 4475 M cheese |
| **alcool** 2465 M alcohol | **sucre** 3258 M sugar | **chocolat** 4556 M chocolate |
| **lait** 2507 M milk | **blé** 3265 M wheat | **soupe** 4563 F soup |
| **glace** 2580 F ice | **spécialité** 3356 F specialty | **crème** 4748 F cream |
| **cuisine** 2618 F cooking | **menu** 3470 M menu | **gâteau** 4845 M cake |
| **viande** 2625 F meat | **thé** 3517 M tea | **céréale** 4983 F cereal |
| **œuf** 2685 M egg | **liquide** 3520 F liquid | **cocktail** 4992 M cocktail |
| | **herbe** 3562 F herb | **riz** 5012 M rice |

383 **position** nf  position
• ils ne changent pas de position à ce sujet – they aren't changing positions on this subject
78 | 4628

384 **développement** nm  development
• nous allons poursuivre le développement de nos activités – we will pursue the development of our activities
74 | 5540

385 **défendre** v  to defend, forbid
• je pensais que je pouvais me défendre – I thought I could defend myself
87 | 2412

386 **chef** nm  head, leader, chief
• vous surestimez le pouvoir des chefs d'Etat – you overestimate the power of the heads of state
71 | 6263

387 **économie** nf  economy
• les exportations sont le moteur de notre économie – exports are what drive our economy
76 | 4973

388 **effort** nm  effort
• ils doivent faire un effort pour nous comprendre – they have to make an effort to understand us
83 | 3239

389 **parmi** prep  among
• il y en a un parmi vous qui est un démon – one among you is a demon
84 | 3165

390 **membre** nm  member
• j'espère que tous les membres seront présents – I hope that all the members will be present
67 | 7128

391 **tirer** v  to pull, fire
• à mon ordre, tirez sur ce câble – when I give the word, pull on this cable
79 | 4267

392 **ancien** adj,nm  ancient; former
• je dis merci à tous les anciens combattants – I thank all the combat veterans
73 | 5545

393 **beau** adj,nm  handsome, fine, right
• ce sont là de belles paroles, mais des paroles creuses – those are pretty words, but empty ones
71 | 6210

394 **plein** adv,nadj,prep  full
• l'église est pleine – the church is full
81 | 3694

395 **juger** v  to judge
• ce n'est pas à moi de juger ça – it's not my place to judge that
84 | 3077

**396 éviter** *v* to avoid
- on ne peut évidemment pas l'éviter – *we obviously can't avoid that*
86 | 2608

**397 soir** *nm* evening
- il est environ neuf heures du soir – *it's about nine o'clock in the evening*
70 | 6293

**398 personnel** *nadj* personnel, personal
- vous semblez vous inspirer de votre vie personnelle pour écrire – *you seem to draw inspiration from your own personal life in writing*
81 | 3741

**399 titre** *nm* title
- ils nous accuseront à juste titre – *they are rightly accusing us*
79 | 4197

**400 parti** *nadj* party
- il n'y a qu'un parti à blâmer – *there's only one party to blame*
66 | 7249

**401 objet** *nm* objective; object
- Mathias remit l'objet dans sa poche – *Mathias returned the object into his pocket*
81 | 3622

**402 unique** *adj(f)* unique
- j'ai longtemps cru que tu étais unique – *I have long believed that you were unique*
89 | 1936

**403 souhaiter** *v* to wish
- l'équipage vous souhaite un bon voyage – *the crew wishes you a pleasant voyage*
81 | 3680

**404 afin** in order to, so that
- fixer des cordes afin de descendre en rappel – *set some ropes so that you can rappel down*
76 | 4800

**405 peine** *nf* effort, trouble
- mes jambes ne me soutenaient qu'à peine – *my legs barely kept me standing*
78 | 4273

**406 malgré** *prep* despite, in spite of
- nous serons bons amis malgré tout – *we will be good friends in spite of it all*
85 | 2886

**407 période** *nm,nf* period
- j'étais amoureuse pendant une brève période de ma vie – *I was in love for a brief period of my life*
79 | 4197

**408 engager** *v* to hire, involve
- nous sommes engagés dans un travail de réflexion – *we're involved in some reflective thinking*
83 | 3182

**409 réaliser** *v* to realize, achieve
- je réaliserai ton rêve – *I will achieve your dream*
82 | 3399

**410 parfois** *adv* sometimes
- il est parfois sage d'être un peu fou – *sometimes it's wise to be a little bit crazy*
83 | 3241

**411 lors** *adv* at the time of
- je vous ai vu lors de votre dernière visite – *I saw you at the time of our last visit*
69 | 6429

**412 sérieux** *nadj(pl)* serious
- mon thème est sérieux, mais mon texte est rigolo – *my topic is serious, but my text is comical*
89 | 2052

**413 aider** *v* to help, assist
- bonjour, je peux vous aider? – *hello, can I help you?*
76 | 4636+s

**414 voix** *nf(pl)* voice
- viens, me dit-elle d'une voix brève – *come, she said in a curt voice*
66 | 7218

**415 terminer** *v* to finish, end,
- va terminer ton petit déjeuner – *go finish your breakfast*
85 | 2717

**416 base** *nf* base
- les matériaux de base sont toujours les mêmes – *the basic materials are always the same*
78 | 4223

**417 espérer** *v* to hope
- j'espère obtenir une réponse claire – *I hope to obtain a clear response*
80 | 3893

**418 main** *nf* hand
- nous avons marché main dans la main – *we walked hand-in-hand*
67 | 6915+l

**419 gros** *adv,nadj(pl)* big
- ce n'était pas un gros chien – *it wasn't a large dog*
80 | 3786

**420 arrêter** *v* to stop, arrest
- les deux dirigeants ont été arrêtés par la police – *the two leaders were arrested by the police*
73 | 5457

**421 retour** *nm* return
- votre retour pose énormément de problèmes – *your return causes huge problems*
81 | 3592

**422 prêt** *adj,nm* ready
- le dîner est prêt! – *supper is ready!*
80 | 3721

**423 occasion** *nf* chance, opportunity
- quand l'occasion se présentera, elle reviendra souvent – *when the opportunity arises, she'll return often*
81 | 3484

**424 député** *nm* deputy, parliamentary delegate
- j'ai écouté plusieurs interventions des députés – *I heard several deputies' speeches*
48 | 12395-l -n +s

**425 regarder** *v* to look, watch
- je regarde les reportages depuis ce matin – *I've been watching news reports since this morning*
62 | 7977-n

**426 plupart** most, the majority
- la plupart des jeux vidéo violents sont japonais – *most violent video games are Japanese*
85 | 2633

**427 deuxième** *det,nm,nf* second
- tout le monde a besoin d'une deuxième opinion – *everybody needs a second opinion*
78 | 4024

**428 résultat** *nm* result, follow-up
- nous avons pu constater les résultats hier – *we were able to notice the results yesterday*
72 | 5458

**429 écouter** *v* to listen to
- je pouvais l'écouter pendant des heures – *I could listen to him for hours*
78 | 4164

**430 terre** *nf* earth, world, soil, land
- que la paix soit sur terre, dès maintenant – *may peace reign on the earth henceforth*
78 | 4037

**431 valoir** *v* to be worth
- c'est fini. ça vaut pas la peine – *it's over. it's not worth it*
85 | 2640

**432 dollar** *nm* dollar
- tu veux combien? 10 dollars – *you want how much? 10 dollars*
63 | 7528-l

**433 intérieur** *nadj* interior, inside
- je sentais mon cœur battre à l'intérieur – *I felt my heart beating within me*
80 | 3574

**434 page** *nm,nf* page
- j'écrivis les premières pages d'un roman – *I was writing the first pages of a novel*
79 | 3726

**435 confiance** *nf* confidence, trust
- je ne peux pas lui faire confiance – *I can't trust him*
86 | 2373

**436 choix** *nm(pl)* choice
- elle n'a pas d'autres choix que de rester – *she has no other choice but to stay*
84 | 2819

**437 prévoir** *v* to foresee, anticipate
- son mandat présidentiel est prévu pour s'achever en 2007 – *his presidential mandate is due to expire in 2007*
71 | 5428

**438 chance** *nf* luck; chance
- c'est notre dernière chance – *it's our last chance*
82 | 3195

**439 notamment** *adv* notably
- on ignore notamment si des gendarmes figurent parmi les victimes – *at the moment it's unsure whether policemen are among the victims*
71 | 5570

**440 type** *nm* type; guy
- ce type de pêche est en cours d'abandon – *this type of fishing is disappearing*
72 | 5213

**441 but** *nm* goal, aim, objective, purpose
- notre premier but est toujours de respecter l'intégrité de la famille – *our primary objective is to always respect the integrity of the family*
84 | 2734

**442 matin** *nm* morning
- ce matin, je me suis réveillée tôt – *this morning I woke up early*
74 | 4793

**443 grave** *adv,nadj(f),nm* serious, grave
- ce n'est peut-être pas si grave que ça – *maybe it's not quite that serious*
85 | 2606

**444 prise** *nf* grip, hold, seizure, catch
- il y a souvent des prises de becs entre les deux – *there were frequent squabbles between the two of them*
85 | 2561

**445 européen** *nadj* European
- vous avez fait une tournée européenne – *you toured around Europe*
57 | 9055-l

**446 étude** *nf* study
- il existe une vie après les études – *there is life after school*
72 | 5119

**447 principe** *nm* principle
- tel est le premier principe de l'existentialisme – *that is the main principle of existentialism*
77 | 4156

**448 remplacer** *v* to replace
- tu dois être prêt à nous remplacer, le cas échéant – *you must be ready to replace us, if need be*
91 | 1429

**449 avancer** *v* to advance, move forward
- c'est moi qui ai avancé les fonds – *I'm the one who advanced the funds*
88 | 1999

**450 six** *det,nmi* six
- elle était enceinte de six mois – *she was six months pregnant*
78 | 3894

**451 nécessaire** *nadj(f)* necessary, required
- je ne pense pas qu'il soit nécessaire de la distribuer – *I don't think it will be necessary to distribute it*
73 | 4920

**452 activité** *nf* activity
- certains sont impliqués dans des activités terroristes – *some of them are implicated in terrorist activities*
78 | 3850

**453 valeur** *nf* value, worth
- on a payé dix fois sa valeur – *we paid ten times what it was worth*
72 | 5031

**454 marquer** *v* to mark
- cet épisode tragique marque la fin d'une aventure – *this tragic episode marks the end of an adventure*
86 | 2281

**455 entier** *nadj* whole, full
- le monde entier est contre nous – *the whole world is against us*
86 | 2212

**456 réponse** *nf* answer, response
- il donne une réponse claire à cette question – *he gives a clear answer to that question*
72 | 5034

**457 aide** *nm,nf* help, assistance
- j'ai besoin d'un peu d'aide – *I need a little help*
75 | 4309

**458 principal** *nadj* principal
- trouver le rôle principal s'est révélé assez problématique – *finding the lead role turned out to be a problem*
74 | 4477

**459 élever** *v* to grow, lift, raise
- des murmures s'élevèrent autour de lui – *murmuring arose all around him*
78 | 3830

**460 pourtant** *adv* yet, nonetheless, nevertheless
- pourtant cette perspective aussi m'effrayait – *yet this outlook also frightened me*
77 | 4017

**461 commission** *nf* commission
- on a mis cette commission enplace pour revoir cette question importante – *we have set up this commission to review this important question*
56 | 8906l +s

**462 cesser** *v* to cease, stop
- on ne doit pas cesser de poser des questions – *we should never stop asking questions*
83 | 2712

**463 poursuivre** *v* to pursue
- je poursuis cette criminelle – *I'm pursuing this criminal*
78 | 3625

**464 maintenir** *v* to maintain
- ce principe sera maintenu – *this principle will be maintained*
85 | 2339

**465 époque** *nf* era, period
- ils ont vécu à la même époque – *they lived in the same time period*
81 | 3128

**466 exprimer** *v* to express
- encore une fois, j'exprime ma frustration – *once again, I express my frustration*
81 | 3066

**467 ami** *nadj* friend
- je te présente mon ami – *this is my friend*
71 | 5135

**468 bas** *adv,nadj(pl),nm(pl)* low; stockings
- elle ajouta presque à voix basse, comme quelqu'un qui parle dans l'obscurité – *she spoke in a low voice, like someone speaking from obscurity*
81 | 3141

**469 imposer** *v* to impose
- on leur impose des changements très rapides – *rapid change is being imposed upon them*
78 | 3668

**470 moitié** *nf* half
- pendant la moitié de la nuit, je pleurai – *during half the night, I cried*
89 | 1682

**471 avenir** *nm* future
- je me sens très optimiste pour l'avenir – *I feel very optimistic about the future*
80 | 3167

**472 argent** *nm* money; silver
- bon, c'est son argent que je veux – *well, it's his money that I want*
72 | 4779

**473 mise** *nf* putting, placing
- il annonce en effet la mise en place d' une police fédérale européenne – *he is indeed announcing putting in place a European federal police*
79 | 3412

**474 œil** *nm* eye
- ferme les yeux, et respire – *close your eyes and breathe*
62 | 7013+l

**475 eau** *nf* water
- faites chauffer une casserole d'eau – *heat up a pan of water*
79 | 3367

**476 sauf** *adj,prep* except; safe
- tout le monde rit sauf elle – *everyone's laughing except her*
89 | 1706

**477 école** *nf* school
- je n'aimais pas aller à l'école – *I didn't like to go to school*
83 | 2671

**478 sécurité** *nf* security, safety
- ils se sentaient plus en sécurité dans la rue qu'à la maison – *he felt safer in the streets than at home*
67 | 5670

**479 milieu** *nm* middle
- elle hésita au milieu de la route – *she paused in the middle of the road*
78 | 3571

**480 lettre** *nf* letter
- il écrivit une lettre de neuf pages – *he wrote a nine-page letter*
80 | 3244

**481 presque** *adv* almost
- il y a presque 10 millions de lignes téléphoniques – *there are almost 10 million telephone lines*
77 | 3680

**482 attention** *nf* attention
- il se lève pour attirer notre attention – *he stood up to attract our attention*
82 | 2741

**483 cadre** *nm* frame, executive
- cette enquête s'inscrit dans le cadre d'une autre – *this inquiry takes place in the framework of another*
74 | 4274

**484 futur** *nadj* future
- un futur sans guerre, c'est cool, hein? – *a future without wars—cool, eh?*
88 | 1823

**485 mouvement** *nm* movement
- il me serra la main d'un mouvement presque inconscient – *he shook my hand with an almost unconscious movement*
74 | 4226

**486 former** *v* to form
- ils ne parviennent pas à former un groupe – *they didn't manage to form a group*
85 | 2331

**487 conduire** *v* to lead, drive
- conduisons-la à l'hôpital – *let's drive her to the hospital*
84 | 2505

**488 règle** *nf* rule
- ce jeu fonctionne avec une règle très simple – *this game follows one very simple rule*
80 | 3012

**489 poste** *nm,nf* post, position; post office
- le chef de poste haussa les épaules – *the station chief shrugged his shoulders*
83 | 2627

**490 demande** *nf* request, demand
- la demande des consommateurs a créé un marché – *consumer demand has created a market*
77 | 3633

**491 centre** *nm* center
- l'amour et ses conséquences sont au centre de ce roman – *love and its consequences are the focus of this novel*
69 | 5072

**492 acte** *nm* act
- c'était un acte de guerre – *it was an act of war*
85 | 2158

**493 disparaître** *v* to disappear, vanish
- l'avion a subitement disparu des écrans – *the airplane suddenly disappeared from the screens*
84 | 2444

**494 priver** *v* to deprive
- je ne me serais pas privée de sommeil à cause de vous – *I wouldn't lose any sleep over you*
83 | 2563

**495 constituer** *v* to constitute
- le djihad et le sacrifice constituent donc un devoir – *jihad and sacrifice are thus a duty*
76 | 3789

**496 accord** *nm* agreement
- le gouvernement fédéral a signé un accord – *the federal government signed an agreement*
66 | 5739

**497 milliard** *nm* billion, thousand million
- le déficit budgétaire a atteint 226,3 milliards de francs – *the budget deficit reached 226.3 billion francs*
61 | 6724-l

**498 lier** *v* to link, join
- c'est le premier décès lié à l'épidémie – *it's the first death linked to the epidemic*
82 | 2624

**499 obliger** *v* to require, force, oblige
- tu ne peux pas m'obliger à rester! – *you can't force me to stay!*
88 | 1707

**500 craindre** *v* to fear, be afraid of
- il ne craignait rien – *he was afraid of nothing*
88 | 1679

**501 passé** *nadj,prep* past
- j'étais prisonnier de mon passé – *I was a prisoner of my past*
87 | 1843

**502 âge** *nm* age
- il a simplement demandé mon âge – *he simply asked my age*
84 | 2274

**503 déclarer** *v* to declare
- il déclare que cette méthode était utile à l'époque – *he declared that this method was useful at that time*
63 | 6208

**504 oublier** *v* to forget
- je ne t'oublierai jamais – *I will never forget you*
75 | 3841

**505 propos** *nm(pl)* remark
- ces propos ne sont pas les miens – *these are not my own words*
77 | 3535

**506 troisième** *det,nm,nf* third
- la troisième et dernière tentative fut la bonne – *the third and final attempt succeeded*
81 | 2775

**507 quitter** *v* to leave
- vous êtes priés de quitter l'hôpital sans précipitation – *please leave the hospital immediately*
76 | 3644

**508 bout** *nm* bit, tip, end
- ils marchèrent en silence jusqu'au bout de la rue – *they walked in silence to the end of the street*
79 | 3216

**509 population** *nf* population
- une partie de la population s'enfonce dans la précarité – *part of the population is sliding into precariousness*
73 | 4303

**510 toi** *nm,pro* you, yourself
- on est là, toi et moi, deux types ordinaires – *here we are, you and me, two ordinary guys*
52 | 8956-n +s

**511 responsable** *nadj(f)* responsible
- je ne suis pas le seul responsable – *I'm not the only one responsible*
69 | 4952

**512 route** *nf* road
- le reste de la route était en construction – *the rest of the road was under construction*
79 | 3214

**513 tôt** *adji,adv* early
- plus tôt on partira, mieux ce sera – *the sooner we leave, the better it will be*
85 | 2124

**514 lancer** *nm,v* to throw, launch
- je lance des mots au hasard – *I toss out words at random*
76 | 3557

**515 limite** *nf* limit
- elle atteint les limites de ses possibilités – *she's reaching the limit of her possibilities*
86 | 1994

**516 fonction** *nf* function
- vous êtes relevé de vos fonctions – *you are relieved of your functions*
70 | 4808

**517 emploi** *nm* employment, work, use
- leur emploi exige qu'ils fournissent leurs propres outils – *their work requires use of their own tools*
66 | 5590

**518 objectif** *adj,nm* objective, aim, goal; lens
- je ne me suis jamais fixé d'objectifs précis – *I never set definite goals for myself*
74 | 3962

**519 paraître** *v* to appear
- il paraît qu'il est à la bibliothèque maintenant – *it appears that he's at the library now*
75 | 3805

**520 journal** *nm* newspaper, paper
- je vais acheter le journal pour ma mère – *I'm going to buy the newspaper for my mother*
78 | 3296

**521 annoncer** *v* to announce
- l'année 1993 s'annonce donc difficile – *1993 is hence showing to be a difficult year*
63 | 6147

**522 lui-même** *pro* himself
- il ne s'est pas sauvé lui-même – *he didn't save himself*
76 | 3563

**523 tour** *nm,nf* tower; turn; tour
- je passais ma vie à faire le tour du monde – *I spent my life touring the world*
75 | 3738

**524 voilà** *prep* right, there, here
- tiens, c'est pour toi. voilà – *here, this is for you. take it*
68 | 5135-n

**525 volonté** *nf* will
- par ta seule volonté, tu peux le faire – *with your willpower alone, you can do it*
84 | 2345

**526 envoyer** *v* to send
- les deux femmes envoyèrent la lettre – *the two women sent the letter*
74 | 3946

**527 partager** *v* to share
- je ne peux pas te partager – *I can't share you*
83 | 2458

**528 puisque** *conj* since
- je ne lui répondais pas puisque j'étais muet – *I didn't answer him since I was a mute*
82 | 2615

**529 établir** *v* to establish
- avant d'attaquer, établissons les règles – *before we attack, let's establish the ground rules*
74 | 3929

**530 changement** *nm* change
- nous savons qu'il faut effectuer des changements – *we know that changes must be made*
79 | 3154

**531 garder** *v* to keep
- je la gardais dans mes bras – *I held her in my arms*
78 | 3200

**532 réalité** *nf* reality
- c'est un rêve devenu réalité pour plusieurs – *for several it's a dream come true*
79 | 3021

**533 interdire** *v* to forbid, prohibit, ban
- je m'interdis d'écrire et de prononcer votre nom – *I forbid myself to write or speak your name*
87 | 1798

**534 finir** *v* to finish
- je dois finir de nettoyer les droïdes – *I have to finish cleaning the droids*
71 | 4563

**535 placer** *nm,v* to place
- la famille a été placée en détention – *the family was placed in detention*
84 | 2297

**536 sentir** *v* to feel, smell
- tu ne sens pas son parfum? – *you don't smell her perfume?*
66 | 5339-n

**537 payer** *v* to pay
- c'est moi qui paie votre salaire – *I'm the one who pays your salary*
74 | 3957

**538 esprit** *nm* mind, spirit
- t'as l'esprit vif, toi – *you've got a quick mind*
76 | 3547

**539 domaine** *nm* domain, field
- là, nous sommes dans le domaine de l'expérience mystique – *there we enter the realm of mystical experiences*
73 | 4152

**540 diriger** *v* to lead, direct
- nous ne sommes dirigés que par nos désirs – *we are only led by our desires*
85 | 2084

**541 noter** *v* to note, notice
- tu as tout noté? – *did you note everything?*
85 | 2109

**542 nature** *nf* nature
- vous venez de découvrir votre vraie nature – *you have just discovered your true nature*
82 | 2571

**543 régime** *nm* regime
- Pravda, la voix de l'ancien régime communiste, ferme ses portes – *Pravda, the voice of the former communist regime, is shutting down*
66 | 5302

**544 charger** *v* to load, charge
- le juge chargé du dossier refuse de convoquer le maire – *the judge assigned to the case refuses to summon the mayor*
81 | 2662

**545 court** *adj,adv,nm* short
- j'inscris mes objectifs long terme, court terme – *I wrote my short-term and long-term goals*
83 | 2356

**546 parent** *nadj* parent
- il faudrait que je te présente mes parents – *I will have to introduce you to my parents*
82 | 2454

**547 tomber** *v* to fall
- il s'arrêta, tomba à genoux pour remercier Dieu – *he stopped, fell to his knees to thank God*
73 | 3963

**548 départ** *nm* departure
- on avait les heures de départ et les heures d'arrivée – *we had the departure and arrival times*
77 | 3382

**549 mondial** *adj* world, global
- nous vivons dans une économie mondiale qui évolue très rapidement – *we live in a rapidly evolving global economy*
72 | 4138

**550 entraîner** *v* to carry along, train
- tu es trop jeune pour t'entraîner – *you're too young to receive training*
85 | 2097

**551 disposer** *v* to arrange, set
- la France dispose d'unités navales basées à Djibouti – *France has naval units based in Djibouti*
80 | 2817

**552 parole** *nf* word
- je regrette mes paroles, moi aussi – *I regret my words too*
75 | 3677

**553 fond** *nm* bottom
- le fond des cœurs ne change pas – *the deepest part of the heart doesn't change*
78 | 3073

**554 publique** *adj,nf* public
- la morale publique ne peut être sacrifiée au progrès – *public morals can't be sacrificed for progress*
74 | 3815

**555 faux** *adv,adj(pl),nm(pl),nf(pl)* false; scythe
- ce ne sont pas là de fausses accusations – *these aren't false accusations*
86 | 1845

**556 genre** *nm* type, kind, sort
- je dénonce ce genre de choses – *I denounce this type of thing*
76 | 3469

**557 retenir** *v* to retain, hold back, remember
- depuis ma blessure, je ne retiens rien – *since my injury I can't remember anything*
86 | 1781

**558 communauté** *nf* community
- la communauté internationale l'a en grande partie rejeté – *the international community largely rejected it*
68 | 4811

**559 intéresser** *v* to interest, involve
- leur avis ne m'intéresse pas – *their advice doesn't interest me*
81 | 2515

**560 c'est-à-dire** *adv* in other words
- il s'agit de vivre, c'est-à-dire d'avancer – *it's about living, or in other words about progressing*
78 | 3100

**561 corps** *nm(pl)* body
- tout mon corps en était secoué – *my whole body was shaken*
76 | 3472

**562 matière** *nf* matter, subject, material
- la matière est parfaite pour les peaux sensibles – *the material is perfect for sensitive skin*
73 | 3945

**563 sein** *nm* breast, bosom
- le cancer du sein est rare chez l'homme – *breast cancer is rare in men*
80 | 2759

**564 difficulté** *nf* difficulty
- j'avais quelque difficulté à lui parler – *it was somewhat difficult for me to talk to him*
81 | 2576

# 4 Clothing

**bas** 468 M **stockings** (also low)

**complet** 965 M **suit** (also complete)

**poche** 1940 F **pocket**

**vêtement** 2383 M **garment**

**robe** 2864 F **dress**

**chapeau** 2908 M **hat**

**manche** 3437 F **sleeve**

**chaussure** 3638 F **shoe**

**manteau** 3746 M **coat**

**chemise** 3892 F **shirt**

**bouton** 4462 M **button**

**ceinture** 4538 F **belt**

**pantalon** 4670 M **trousers**

**botte** 5353 F **boot**

**gant** 5587 M **glove**

**maillot** 5609 M **jersey**

**veste** 5721 F **jacket**

**jupe** 5871 F **skirt**

**mouchoir** 6732 M **handkerchief**

**cravate** 6806 F **necktie**

**foulard** 7078 M **scarf**

**habillement** 7408 M **clothing**

**vestiaire** 8094 M **cloakroom**

**bonnet** 8169 M **bonnet**

**blouse** 8869 F **blouse**

**lingerie** 9086 F **lingerie**

**tablier** 9153 M **apron**

**bague** 9410 F **ring**

**sabot** 9607 M **clog**

**bretelles** 9631 F **suspenders**

**veston** 9685 M **jacket**

**tee-shirt** 9795 M **T-shirt**

**t-shirt** 9813 M **T-shirt**

**slip** 9839 M **underpants**

**badge** 9984 M **badge**

---

**565 parvenir** *v* to reach, achieve
- je suis content d'être parvenu au bout – *I am happy to have reached the end*
84 | 2133

**566 secteur** *nm* sector
- la police a décrété le secteur «zone interdite» – *the police declared the area off-limits*
67 | 4928

**567 appel** *nm* call
- il a reçu des appels téléphoniques menaçants – *he received menacing telephone calls*
65 | 5345+n

**568 cœur** *nm* heart
- j'aimerais vous féliciter du fond du cœur – *I would like to congratulate you from the depths of my heart*
72 | 4042

**569 père** *nm* father
- je suis père célibataire – *I'm an unwed father*
65 | 5263

**570 organisation** *nf* organisation
- plus grande devient l'organisation, plus il y a de règles – *the bigger the organization grows, the more rules there are*
72 | 4077

**571 unité** *nf* unity; unit
- vous partez inspecter nos unités de désinfection – *you are leaving to inspect our disinfection units*
81 | 2536

**572 noir** *nadj* black
- seule la police roule en noir et blanc? – *only the police drive black-and-white vehicles?*
74 | 3652

**573 événement** *nm* event
- je me souviens de ces événements avec précision – *I remember those events in great detail*
83 | 2300

**574 double** *nadj(f)* double
- on parle beaucoup de la double peine pour les délinquants étrangers – *there's much talk about doubling sentences for foreign delinquents*
90 | 1303

**575 convaincre** *v* to convince
- c'est bon, tu m'as convaincue – *OK, you convinced me*
86 | 1742

**576 nation** *nf* nation
- elle bouscule sérieusement les droits des nations – *it is seriously undermining the rights of nations*
76 | 3343

**577 conseil** *nm* advice, counsel, council
- les militaires ont formé un Conseil de salut national – *the military formed a National Salvation Council*
76 | 3399

**578 soutenir** *v* to sustain, support
- nous avons été nombreux à soutenir son innocence – *many of us supported his innocence*
80 | 2732

**579 paix** *nf(pl)* peace
- laissez ma famille en paix – *leave my family in peace*
73 | 3783

**580 nuit** *nf* night
- je n'ai pas dormi cette nuit – *I didn't sleep last night*
67 | 4874

**581 partout** *adv* everywhere
- je t'ai cherché partout – *I looked everywhere for you*
83 | 2191

**582 direction** *nf* direction, management
- je n'osais aller dans cette direction – *I didn't dare go in this direction*
79 | 2847

**583 manquer** *v* to miss
- la Chine manque d'argent, et manque de savants – *China lacks money and scholars*
79 | 2767

**584 actuel** *adj* current, present
- les gens ont peur du gouvernement actuel – *people fear the current government*
72 | 3949

**585 opposer** *v* to oppose
- comment peut-il maintenant s'y opposer? – *how could he oppose it now?*
80 | 2654

**586 signifier** *v* to mean
- cela ne signifiait rien pour moi – *that didn't mean anything to me*
87 | 1615

**587 journée** *nf* day
- j'ai attendu toute la journée pour te voir – *I waited all day to see you*
72 | 3849

**588 d'ailleurs** *adv* moreover, besides, for that matter
- je n'entends d'ailleurs pas le tenir secret – *besides, I don't intend to keep it a secret*
77 | 3086

**589 traiter** *v* to treat, handle, deal with
- deux chapitres, enfin, traitent de la question – *two chapters, at last, address the issue*
78 | 2860

**590 indiquer** *v* to indicate, signal
- le contrôleur indique qu'il est prêt – *the controller signals readiness*
61 | 5804+n

**591 tuer** *v* to kill
- les fusils, ça tue – *rifles kill*
64 | 5298

**592 technique** *nadj(f)* technique, technics, technical
- parlons un peu de votre technique – *let's talk a little about your technique*
78 | 2856

**593 rapidement** *adv* quickly, rapidly
- ils ont passé rapidement dans l'histoire – *they disappeared quickly into history*
85 | 1894

**594 autour** *adv,nm* around
- je t'emmènerai autour du monde – *I'll take you around the world*
77 | 3008

**595 réduire** *v* to reduce
- tu réduis les aliments graisseux et le chocolat – *you reduce your intake of fatty foods and chocolate*
73 | 3705

**596 d'après** according to
- qui a bâti les pyramides d'après vous? – *according to you, who built the pyramids?*
90 | 1183

**597 préférer** *v* to prefer
- préférez-vous que j'appelle la police? – *would you prefer that I call the police?*
83 | 2174

**598 rue** *nf* street
- je me promenais dans les rues, seule – *I strolled alone down the streets*
76 | 3185

**599 riche** *nadj(f)* rich
- elle est jolie, riche, mince ... et amoureuse de mon mari – *she is cute, rich, thin ... and in love with my husband*
87 | 1522

**600 bref** *adj,adv,nm* brief
- le rapport était bref et précis – *the report was brief and precise*
87 | 1603

**601 nommer** *v* to call, name, appoint
- ses membres sont nommés par le premier ministre – *its members are appointed by the prime minister*
86 | 1644

**602 violence** *nf* violence
- la violence a fait six nouveaux morts – *the violence killed six people*
81 | 2461

**603 siècle** *nm* century
- le XXe siècle a fait plus de martyrs chrétiens – *the 20th century created more Christian martyrs*
76 | 3105

**604 article** *nm* article
- vous m'avez convaincue de finir l'article – *you convinced me to finish the article*
65 | 4867+s

**605 durer** *v* to last
- voilà quinze jours que ça dure – *this has lasted two weeks*
86 | 1693

**606 qualité** *nf* quality
- Renaud est quelqu'un d'une grande qualité humaine – *Renaud is someone with great human qualities*
76 | 3052

**607 gauche** *nadj(f)* left
- elle écrit de gauche à droite – *she writes from left to right*
79 | 2604

**608 solution** *nf* solution
- il n'existe pas de solution miracle – *there's no miracle solution*
76 | 3043

**609 voie** *nf* road, lane, route, track, way
- il a toujours suivi sa voie, ton père – *your father has always followed his own way*
69 | 4187

**610 capable** *adj(f)* able, capable
• je ne suis pas capable de répondre à votre question – *I'm not capable of responding to your question*
85 | 1869

**611 canadien** *nadj* Canadian
• 75 p. 100 des Canadiens et des Canadiennes sont en bonne santé mentale – *75% of male and female Canadians are in good mental health*
47 | 8624-l -n +s

**612 erreur** *nf* mistake, error
• certaines erreurs ont été commises – *certain mistakes were made*
79 | 2704

**613 livrer** *v* to deliver
• je pensais te faire livrer un plat chaud – *I thought I would have a hot plate delivered to you*
89 | 1257

**614 auprès** *adv* nearby, close to
• il avait beaucoup de succès auprès des femmes – *he had much success with women*
83 | 2114

**615 simplement** *adv* simply
• c'est tout simplement inacceptable – *it's just simply unacceptable*
76 | 3132

**616 souvenir** *nm,v* memory; to remember
• je ne veux me souvenir de rien – *I don't remember anything*
73 | 3468

**617 conséquence** *nf* consequence
• il y a donc des conséquences extrêmement sérieuses – *hence there are extremely serious consequences*
79 | 2598

**618 large** *adj(f),adv,nm* wide, width
• tes yeux sont devenus plus larges – *your eyes got wider*
83 | 2025

**619 contraire** *nadj(f)* opposite, contrary
• mais le contraire est vrai aussi – *but the opposite is also true*
80 | 2529

**620 succès** *nm(pl)* success
• le succès prouve que mes livres avaient du mérite – *the success proves that my books were worthwhile*
82 | 2210

**621 élément** *nm* element
• trois éléments d'information présentent un intérêt particulier – *three items of information are particularly interesting*
75 | 3181

**622 local** *nadj* local
• nous respectons l'autonomie de chaque groupe local – *we respect the autonomy of each local group*
67 | 4422

**623 été** *nm* summer
• l'été constitue le pic de la consommation d'essence – *summer is the peak season for gas consumption*
89 | 1233

**624 inviter** *v* to invite
• un soir, ils m'invitent à dîner – *one night, they invite me to supper*
84 | 1951

**625 extérieur** *nadj* exterior
• la porte extérieure s'ouvre – *the outer door opens*
81 | 2269

**626 pied** *nm* foot
• tu n'iras pas assez vite à pied – *you won't get there as fast on foot*
74 | 3304

**627 mission** *nf* mission
• si quelqu'un apprend notre mission, on échoue – *if anyone learns about our mission, we'll fail*
81 | 2259

**628 débat** *nm* debate
• il voulait simplement contribuer au débat – *he simply wanted to contribute to the debate*
61 | 5373+s

**629 fille** *nf* girl, daughter
• c'est une jeune fille de seize ans – *she's a young girl of sixteen years*
65 | 4669

**630 répéter** *v* to repeat
• ce rêve se répète sans cesse – *this dream keeps repeating*
81 | 2225

**631 texte** *nm* text
• je donne un texte et l'artiste intervient comme il veut – *I give a text and the artist adapts it as necessary*
70 | 3929

**632 profiter** *v* to take advantage, profit
• je profitais de ces derniers jours de vraies vacances – *I took advantage of these last days of real vacation*
84 | 1822

**633 chambre** *nf* bedroom, chamber
• avant d'entrer dans la chambre de mon fils j'entrai dans la mienne – *before going into my son's bedroom I went into my own*
73 | 3447

**634 création** *nf* creation
• nous nous battons depuis la création de notre parti – *we have been fighting since the creation of our party*
78 | 2716

**635 prouver** *v* to prove
• je n'ai rien besoin de prouver à qui que ce soit – *I have no need to prove anything to anybody at all*
89 | 1279

**636 acheter** *v* to buy
• achetez vos billets à un revendeur agréé – *buy your tickets from an approved reseller*
83 | 2047

**637 justice** *nf* justice
- vous rendrez la justice de manière impartiale – *you will render justice in an impartial way*
70 | 3840

**638 production** *nf* production
- ce serait une maison de production plutôt qu'une société – *it would be a factory rather than a company*
70 | 3841

**639 ignorer** *v* to ignore
- j'ignorais pourquoi il jurait comme ça – *I didn't know why he was swearing like that*
85 | 1706

**640 directeur** *nadj* director
- j'ai reçu un mot du directeur – *I received a note from the director*
75 | 3074

**641 santé** *nf* health
- il est en bonne santé – *he's in good health*
62 | 5116+s

**642 souffrir** *v* to suffer
- elle n'a pas souffert, elle s'est endormie – *she didn't suffer, she fell asleep*
83 | 1934

**643 précis** *nadj(pl)* precise
- c'est à cet instant précis que je suis devenu adulte – *at that precise moment I became an adult*
85 | 1684

**644 fixer** *v* to fix, arrange, set
- nous avons fixé une date limite – *we set a deadline*
82 | 2105

**645 mère** *adj,nf* mother
- peut-être que tous les enfants déçoivent leur mère – *perhaps all children disappoint their mother*
65 | 4595

**646 croissance** *nf* growth
- les taux de croissance ont été importants – *the growth rates were substantial*
78 | 2657

**647 risque** *nm* risk
- vous prenez de sacrés risques – *you're taking huge risks*
81 | 2236

**648 arme** *nf* weapon
- je suis un trafiquant d'armes – *I'm an arms dealer*
73 | 3294

**649 estimer** *v* to estimate; to consider, deem
- j'estime que cela est inadmissible – *I consider this to be inexcusable*
65 | 4560

**650 endroit** *nm* place, spot
- on aime vraiment cet endroit – *we really like this place*
79 | 2442

**651 comité** *nm* committee
- les délibérations des comités peuvent être enregistrées – *committee deliberations may be recorded*
56 | 6128+s

**652 impossible** *nadj(f)* impossible
- je peux te rendre la vie impossible – *I can make life impossible for you*
84 | 1823

**653 preuve** *nf* proof
- vous nous donnez les preuves, et nous vous protégeons à vie – *you give us the proof, and we'll protect you for the rest of your life*
79 | 2495

**654 véritable** *adj(f)* real, true
- les véritables coupables restaient en liberté – *the true guilty parties remained free*
81 | 2210

**655 amener** *v* to bring
- on pourrait les amener à changer leurs habitudes – *we could bring them to change their habits*
83 | 1943

**656 viser** *v* to aim
- quel but visez-vous en thérapie bioénergétique? – *what's your goal with biofeedback therapy?*
70 | 3695

**657 retirer** *v* to remove, withdraw
- j'aimerais qu'il retire ce qu'il a dit – *I want him to take back what he said*
84 | 1815

**658 total** *nadj* total
- Ming, c'est l'anarchiste total – *Ming is the absolute anarchist*
76 | 2793

**659 image** *nf* picture, image
- certains films contiennent des images fameuses – *some films contain famous images*
74 | 3088

**660 date** *nf* date
- c'est la vraie date de ton anniversaire – *that's the real date of your birthday*
82 | 1979

**661 travers** *nm(pl)* breadth, across; fault, amiss
- le héros se promenait à travers le monde – *the hero walked across the world*
78 | 2617

**662 contrôle** *nm* control
- la situation est complètement sous contrôle – *the situation is completely under control*
71 | 3598

**663 énorme** *adj(f)* enormous
- je pense que c'est un énorme effort – *I think it's an enormous effort*
87 | 1415

**664 conserver** *v* to keep, preserve
- cette petite note, je la conserve comme un trésor – *this little note I keep like a treasure*
88 | 1252

**665 réel** *nadj* real
- nous avons toutefois un problème réel – *we still have a real problem*
78 | 2535

**666 campagne** *nf* countryside
- les gens allaient dormir à la campagne – *people were going into the countryside to sleep*
80 | 2229

**667 naître** *v* to be born
- il était né lui-même dans une famille de onze enfants – *he himself was born into a family of eleven children*
80 | 2310

**668 accorder** *v* to grant
- les banques ont cessé d'accorder des prêts – *the banks stopped granting loans*
74 | 3069

**669 tourner** *v* to turn
- je trouvai un commutateur et le tournai – *I found a switch and turned it*
74 | 3100

**670 participer** *v* to participate
- elle a participé à la création du Mouvement – *she participated in creation of the Movement*
73 | 3262

**671 vieux** *adj(pl),nm(pl)* old
- ça fait trop longtemps, mon vieil ami – *it has been too long, my old friend*
66 | 4194

**672 rapide** *nadj(f)* fast, quick
- elle parle d'une voix rapide et menue – *she talks in a rapid and small voice*
86 | 1458

**673 respecter** *v* to respect
- j'avais le pouvoir. j'étais respecté – *I had power. I was respected*
76 | 2726

**674 passage** *nm* passage, way
- je lirai seulement un petit passage – *I will only read a short passage*
82 | 1976

**675 essentiel** *nadj* essential
- ils sont tous désignés comme employés essentiels – *they are all designated essential employees*
80 | 2225

**676 adopter** *v* to adopt
- j'hésite pour ma part à adopter l'idée – *I for one hesitate to adopt the idea*
58 | 5500+s

**677 subir** *v* to undergo, be subjected to, suffer
- certaines autres ont subi de terribles ravages – *certain others suffered terrible ravages*
86 | 1533

**678 environ** *adv,prep,nm* about, thereabouts, or so
- mon père et ma mère sont mariés depuis environ 60 ans – *my father and mother have been married for about 60 years*
71 | 3450

**679 expérience** *nf* experience
- ça va te donner de l'expérience – *this will give you experience*
76 | 2734

**680 admettre** *v* to admit
- je dois admettre que je suis toujours célibataire – *I must admit that I'm still single*
85 | 1565

**681 découvrir** *v* to discover
- la sœur a découvert la fenêtre cassée – *the sister discovered the broken window*
78 | 2535

**682 couvrir** *v* to cover
- il était couvert de taches de sang – *he was covered by blood stains*
86 | 1477

**683 assister** *v* to attend; to assist, help
- il assista à la dernière répétition – *he attended the last rehearsal*
87 | 1402

**684 sénateur** *nm* senator
- les honorables sénateurs ont été si généreux – *the honorable senators were very generous*
44 | 8224-l -n +s

**685 dépasser** *v* to pass, go beyond
- personne ne dépasse son potentiel – *no one exceeds his potential*
82 | 1991

**686 affirmer** *v* to affirm, maintain, declare, allege
- ce témoin a affirmé avoir vu trois hommes – *this witness alleged to have seen three men*
65 | 4373

**687 soumettre** *v* to submit
- de retour chez eux, elle l'a soumis à un ultime test – *back at their place, she put him to the final test*
83 | 1905

**688 financier** *nadj* financial, financier
- j'ai aussi travaillé dans le monde financier – *I also worked in the financial sector*
67 | 3986

**689 processus** *nm(pl)* process
- j'ai été renseigné à chaque étape du processus – *I was kept informed at each stage of the process*
72 | 3316

**690 militaire** *nadj(f)* military
- la justice militaire me donne le droit à un avocat – *the military code of justice grants me the right to an attorney*
65 | 4334

**691 frais** *adj(pl),nm(pl)* cool, fresh; fee, expense
- on me paie mes frais de déplacement – *my travel expenses are being covered*
85 | 1563

**692 industrie** *nf* industry
- le tourisme est une industrie saisonnière – *tourism is a seasonal industry*
68 | 3801

**693 apparaître** *v* to appear
- son nom apparaissait dans une autre liste – *her name appeared on another list*
79 | 2342

**694 responsabilité** *nf* responsibility
- il porte la seule responsabilité – *he alone is responsible*
74 | 2969

**695 réserver** *v* to reserve, keep
- je veux ce que l'avenir me réserve – *I want what the future is keeping from me*
  88 | 1222

**696 porte** *nf* door
- veuillez fermer la porte derrière vous – *please close the door after you*
  68 | 3897

**697 victime** *nf* victim
- nos prières vont aux victimes – *our prayers go out to the victims*
  70 | 3561

**698 territoire** *nm* territory
- c'est eux autres qui occupent le territoire – *they are the ones who are occupying the territory*
  78 | 2415

**699 pauvre** *nadj(f)* poor
- vous êtes idiote, ma pauvre femme, comme toujours – *you're an idiot, my poor woman, as always*
  78 | 2485

**700 taux** *nm(pl)* rate
- les taux d'intérêt ont notablement haussé – *interest rates have risen appreciably*
  62 | 4761

**701 organiser** *v* to organize
- on pensait t'organiser une fête d'anniversaire – *we were thinking of organizing a birthday party for you*
  77 | 2578

**702 posséder** *v* to possess, own, have
- je possède les coupures de presse vous concernant – *I have the press clippings about you*
  85 | 1587

**703 matériel** *nadj* material, equipment
- nous avons déjà du nouveau matériel en chantier – *we already have new equipment on the construction site*
  88 | 1241

**704 cent** *det,nm* one hundred, cent
- aucun des cinq cents voyageurs n'a été blessé – *none of the five hundred travelers was injured*
  64 | 4457

**705 constater** *v* to note, notice; to establish, certify
- je constate de ce fait – *I notice that fact*
  78 | 2435

**706 prononcer** *v* to pronounce
- je ne devrais même pas prononcer ces mots – *I should not even pronounce those words*
  82 | 1978

**707 signe** *nm* sign
- cependant, il y a des signes encourageants – *yet there are encouraging signs*
  84 | 1723

**708 blanc** *adj,nm* white
- tu es donc noir à rayures blanches. dilemme résolu – *so you are black with white stripes. dilemma resolved*
  73 | 3024

**709 origine** *nf* origin, source
- la guérilla n'est pas à l'origine de la violence – *the insurgency isn't the source of the violence*
  76 | 2621

**710 vendre** *v* to sell
- non, vous ne pouvez pas vendre votre bétail – *no, you may not sell your livestock*
  80 | 2125

**711 vite** *adv* fast, quickly
- déployez les sentinelles ... vite! – *dispatch the guards ... quick!*
  73 | 3088

**712 langue** *nf* language, tongue
- tu maîtrises bien la langue – *you're mastering the language well*
  75 | 2804

**713 dangereux** *adj(pl)* dangerous
- ce type est dangereux – *this guy is dangerous*
  85 | 1488

**714 déplacer** *v* to move, displace
- nous nous déplaçons librement entre les deux pays – *we travel freely between the two countries*
  91 | 887

**715 importance** *nf* importance
- cela n'a pas d'importance – *that isn't important*
  78 | 2423

**716 suffire** *v* to be sufficient, suffice
- bon, ça suffit – *OK, that's enough*
  78 | 2401

**717 espoir** *nm* hope
- hélas, ce n'était qu'un espoir – *alas, it was only a hope*
  82 | 1897

**718 davantage** *adv* more
- nous sentons tous que nous devons travailler davantage – *we sense that we must work more*
  78 | 2311

**719 saisir** *v* to take hold of, grab
- le reflet du miroir saisit son regard – *the mirror's reflection captured her face*
  80 | 2177

**720 énergie** *nf* energy
- l'énergie est le pivot de notre économie – *energy is the lynchpin of our society*
  81 | 2029

**721 réseau** *nm* network
- ce réseau peut me servir à établir des contacts – *this network might help me establish contacts*
  59 | 4984+n

**722 mourir** *v* to die
- ma foi, je meurs de faim – *goodness, I'm dying of hunger*
  68 | 3726

**723 faible** *nadj(f)* weak
- je devenais de plus en plus faible – *I became progressively weaker*
  75 | 2665

**724 employer** *v* to use, employ
- vous en employez beaucoup, de ces intellos gonflants – *you sure employ a lot of these stuffy eggheads*
84 | 1611

**725 possibilité** *nf* possibility
- il va avoir la possibilité d'influencer son passé – *he will be able to influence his past*
74 | 2804

**726 spécial** *adj* special
- je fais rien de spécial – *I'm not doing anything special*
79 | 2201

**727 accompagner** *v* to accompany
- que Dieu vous accompagne – *may God be with you*
85 | 1563

**728 actuellement** *adv* at present, at the moment
- je suis très seul actuellement – *I'm very alone at the moment*
74 | 2776

**729 union** *nf* union
- cette définition devrait comprendre les unions homosexuelles et lesbiennes – *this definition should include homosexual and lesbian unions*
67 | 3788

**730 supposer** *v* to suppose, assume
- je suppose qu'ils ont peur – *I imagine they are afraid*
82 | 1878

**731 fournir** *v* to provide, supply
- elle ne souhaitait fournir aucun effort – *she didn't want to provide any efforts*
74 | 2815

**732 ceci** *pro* this
- tout ceci est votre création – *this is all your creation*
81 | 1915

**733 exiger** *v* to require, demand
- une vie publique exige de nombreux sacrifices – *public life requires many sacrifices*
81 | 1958

**734 intervenir** *v* to intervene
- il doit intervenir sur le marché – *he must intervene in the market*
75 | 2734

**735 fils** *nm(pl)* son
- votre fils est en entraînement pour devenir soldat – *your son is in training to become a soldier*
71 | 3142

**736 d'accord** *intj* okay, alright
- je m'en occupe, d'accord? – *I'll take care of it, OK?*
62 | 4443+s

**737 discuter** *v* to discuss, debate; to question
- personne ne discute ses ordres – *nobody questions his orders*
80 | 2088

**738 différence** *nf* difference
- il y a une différence entre les pommes et les hommes – *there's a difference between men and apples*
79 | 2132

**739 protéger** *v* to protect
- je suis ici pour te protéger, pas les cookies – *I'm here to protect you, not the cookies*
75 | 2595

**740 abandonner** *v* to give up, abandon
- la propriété semblait abandonnée – *the property seemed abandoned*
83 | 1726

**741 avis** *nm(pl)* opinion, mind
- j'ai changé d'avis – *I changed my mind*
66 | 3768+s

**742 battre** *v* to beat, hit
- ne nous battons pas l'un contre l'autre – *let's not fight against each other*
66 | 3724

**743 pire** *nadj(f)* worse, worst
- c'est le pire jour de ma vie! – *it's the worst day of my life!*
85 | 1495

**744 adresser** *v* to address
- ces bourses s'adressent à des étudiants – *these scholarships are intended for students*
78 | 2195

**745 préciser** *v* to state, specify, clarify
- je préciserai seulement deux choses – *I will only specify two things*
67 | 3620+n

**746 intervention** *nf* intervention; talk
- je suis favorable aux interventions extérieures – *I'm in favor of outside intervention*
76 | 2432

**747 attirer** *v* to attract
- les attentats récents ont attiré trop d'attention – *the recent attacks have attracted too much attention*
85 | 1389

**748 demeurer** *v* to remain, live
- les crimes économiques demeurent largement impunis – *white-collar crimes remain largely unpunished*
80 | 1961

**749 chiffre** *nm* figure, number
- j'ignore si ce chiffre est exact – *I don't know if this figure is exact*
70 | 3246

**750 consacrer** *v* to devote, consecrate
- j'ai consacré beaucoup de temps à la recherche – *I consecrated much time to research*
79 | 2104

**751 remplir** *v* to fill, fulfill
- une voisine passerait, le panier rempli de poires – *a neighbor would walk by, her basket full of pears*
85 | 1481

# 5 Transportation

**train** 232 M train

**rue** 598 F street

**voie** 609 F road

**voiture** 881 F car

**transport** 935 M transportation

**bateau** 1287 M boat

**port** 1304 M harbor

**avion** 1409 M plane

**navire** 1416 M ship

**vol** 1531 M flight

**véhicule** 1959 M vehicule

**aéroport** 2113 M airport

**automobile** 2407 F automobile

**camion** 2542 M truck

**gare** 2581 F train station

**hélicoptère** 2978 M helicopter

**routier** 3101 M truck driver

**missile** 3452 M missile

**ballon** 3692 M ball

**sous-marin** 3777 M submarine

**autoroute** 3794 F freeway

**transit** 3848 M transit

**bus** 4027 M bus

**vapeur** 4111 M steamship

**autobus** 4216 M bus

**taxi** 4235 M taxi

**jet** 4454 M jet

**auto** 4494 F car

**vélo** 4594 M bicycle

**rail** 4697 M rail

**navette** 4814 F shuttle

**boulevard** 4821 M boulevard

**garage** 4881 M garage

**wagon** 5008 M wagon

**fusée** 5894 F rocket

**ascenseur** 5961 M elevator

---

**752 divers** *adj(pl),det* diverse, various
- des formes très diverses surgissent sous vos yeux – *widely varying patterns dance before your eyes*
- 78 | 2176

**753 appliquer** *v* to apply
- il faut que la loi soit appliquée – *the law must be applied*
- 68 | 3463

**754 frapper** *v* to hit, strike, knock
- je n'ai pas frappé vraiment fort – *I didn't knock very loudly*
- 80 | 2033

**755 peur** *nf* fear
- maman, j'ai peur! – *mommy, I'm afraid!*
- 70 | 3193

**756 parlement** *nm* parliament
- il faut élargir le rôle du Parlement européen – *we need to enlarge the role of the European Parliament*
- 55 | 5296-l +s

**757 fermer** *v* to close, shut
- je vais fermer les yeux maintenant – *I'm going to close my eyes now*
- 79 | 2035

**758 forcer** *v* to force
- on peut me forcer à venir, pas à parler – *I can be forced to come, not to speak*
- 86 | 1310

**759 lutte** *nf* struggle, fight, conflict
- tu as mené une lutte acharnée – *you fought an unrelenting battle*
- 80 | 1962

**760 naturel** *nadj* natural
- c'est un sentiment tout à fait naturel – *it's a perfectly natural feeling*
- 81 | 1894

**761 air** *nm* air, appearance
- tu as l'air fatigué – *you seem tired*
- 61 | 4450+l

**762 auteur** *nm,nf* author
- chez cet auteur schizophrène cohabitent deux personnages – *two personalities live together in this schizophrenic author*
- 73 | 2737

**763 opération** *nf* operation
- les opérations militaires continuent du côté serbe – *Serbian military operations continue*
- 67 | 3612

**764 heureux** *nadj(pl)* happy, lucky, fortunate
- je n'étais pas heureuse non plus – *I wasn't happy either*
- 73 | 2834-n

**765 crise** *nf* crisis
- plus la crise est grande, plus elle est grave – *the bigger the crisis, the worse it is*
- 70 | 3131

**766 numéro** *nm* number
- donnez votre numéro à mon assistant – *give your number to my assistant*
- 70 | 3208

**767 résoudre** *v* to solve, resolve
- ça va résoudre tous nos problèmes – *that will resolve all of our problems*
- 85 | 1367

**768 publier** *v* to publish
- j'ai publié un livre – *I published a book*
- 71 | 2987

**769 instant** *adj,nm* instant, moment
- je suis à vous dans un instant – *I'll be with you in a moment*
- 69 | 3227

**770 toutefois** *adv,conj* however
- toutefois, l'industrie connaît des problèmes réels – *however, the industry is experiencing real problems*
71 | 3054

**771 pousser** *v* to push
- je ne t'ai jamais poussée à te marier – *I never pushed you to marry me*
79 | 2060

**772 quelqu'un** *pro* somebody, someone
- il vaudrait mieux le demander au quelqu'un – *it would be better to ask someone about it*
71 | 3014-n +s

**773 discours** *nm(pl)* speech, talk, discourse
- j'ai écouté ce discours avec intérêt – *I listened intently to this talk*
71 | 2956

**774 banque** *nf* bank
- j'ai obtenu auprès d'une banque un prêt personnel habitat de 90 000 euros – *I got a housing loan from a bank for 90,000 euros*
68 | 3437

**775 compagnie** *nf* company
- des compagnies pétrolières russes ont signé plusieurs accords – *Russian oil companies signed several agreements*
75 | 2473

**776 reposer** *v* to rest
- on peut se reposer, maintenant – *we can rest, now*
87 | 1222

**777 opinion** *nf* opinion
- notre opinion et notre politique doivent être crédibles – *our opinion and our politics must be believable*
81 | 1838

**778 classe** *nf* class
- nous étions dans la même classe d'anglais – *we were in the same English class*
78 | 2115

**779 particulièrement** *adv* particularly
- ce sont là des problèmes particulièrement délicats – *those are particularly delicate questions*
76 | 2401

**780 commun** *nadj* common
- il a quelque chose de commun avec d'autres problèmes que nous vivons – *it has something in common with the other problems we're experiencing*
81 | 1795

**781 satisfaire** *v* to satisfy
- ils ne satisfont pas aux conditions requises – *they won't satisfy the required conditions*
86 | 1265

**782 intention** *nf* intention
- je l'ai fait avec les meilleures intentions – *I did it with the best intentions*
78 | 2120

**783 autorité** *nf* authority
- elle prit mon bras avec autorité – *she took my arm with authority*
65 | 3730

**784 anglais** *nadj(pl)* English
- où as-tu appris l'anglais? – *where did you learn English?*
82 | 1669

**785 échange** *nm* exchange
- on discute, on échange des idées – *we discuss, we exchange ideas*
82 | 1741

**786 feu** *adj(f),nm* fire
- réchauffez-vous près du feu – *warm yourself by the fire*
74 | 2612

**787 neuf** *det,adj,nmi* nine; new
- on devait avoir des vêtements neufs! – *we should have new clothes!*
75 | 2513

**788 observer** *v* to observe, watch
- observez votre propre famille, vous serez édifié – *watch your family and you'll be uplifted*
82 | 1701

**789 capacité** *nf* capacity, ability
- il ne faut pas sous-estimer la capacité de lecture des jeunes – *one must not underestimate the reading abilities of young people*
75 | 2509

**790 désigner** *v* to designate
- ce mot désigne plusieurs réalités bien distinctes – *this word designates several very distinct realities*
85 | 1413

**791 dépendre** *v* to depend
- les femmes ne dépendent plus autant des hommes – *women don't depend on men as much any more*
81 | 1772

**792 message** *nm* message
- il me semble que le message est clair – *it seems to me that the message is clear*
50 | 5890+n -s

**793 construire** *v* to build, construct
- nous avons dû construire une digue – *we had to construct a dike*
81 | 1773

**794 scène** *nf* scene
- la scène ressemble à un énorme feu de forêt – *the scene resembled an enormous forest fire*
76 | 2355

**795 durant** *prep* during, for
- j'ai travaillé sur ce problème durant toute ma carrière – *I have worked on this problem for my entire career*
79 | 2002

**796 secret** *nadj* secret
- j'en connais tous les secrets – *I know all the relevant secrets*
80 | 1867

**797 plaisir** *nm* pleasure
- quel plaisir d'avoir des parents cultivés – *what a pleasure to have cultured relatives*
74 | 2544-n

**798 dossier** *nm* file, record; case
- le gouvernement s'occupe activement du dossier des hélicoptères – *the government is actively pursuing the helicopter affair*
74 | 2532

**799 proposition** *nf* proposition, proposal
- sa proposition soulève certaines questions – *his proposal raises certain issues*
63 | 3905+s

**800 combien** *adv,conj* how much, how many
- tu pèses combien maintenant? – *how much do you weigh now?*
77 | 2211-n +s

**801 nul** *adj,det,pro* nil, null
- les préservatifs c'est nul. ils marchent pas – *condoms are crap. they don't work*
82 | 1649

**802 absence** *nf* absence
- l'absence de punition les pousse au crime – *the absence of punishment pushed them to crime*
83 | 1524

**803 cher** *adj,adv* expensive
- j'ai payé cher pour le savoir – *I paid dearly to find out about that*
77 | 2163

**804 plaire** *v* to please
- réponds, s'il te plaît – *answer me, please*
72 | 2758-n

**805 derrière** *adv,nm,prep* last; behind
- Mathieu s'abrita derrière le pilier – *Mathieu took shelter behind the pillar*
72 | 2684

**806 connaissance** *nf* knowledge
- nous serons heureux d'en prendre connaissance – *we will be happy to learn about it*
79 | 1969

**807 immédiatement** *adv* immediately
- les enfants, partez immédiatement – *children, leave immediately*
85 | 1309

**808 entrée** *nf* entrance
- à l'entrée de son couloir, je me suis arrêté – *at the entrance to the hallway, I stopped*
74 | 2515

**809 signer** *v* to sign
- tu voulais que je signe les papiers – *you wanted me to sign papers*
76 | 2246

**810 révéler** *v* to reveal
- je veux que tu révèles tout ça au monde – *I want you to reveal everything to the world*
83 | 1492

**811 couper** *v* to cut
- je me suis coupé. comment? sur mon couteau – *I cut myself. how? on my knife*
80 | 1839

**812 salle** *nf* room
- dans la salle, rien de plus qu'un murmure – *in the room there was nothing more than a murmur*
79 | 1970

**813 pièce** *nf* piece, part, component; room
- ces gens vont vous mettre en pièces – *these people are going to tear you to pieces*
77 | 2159

**814 équipe** *nf* team
- depuis mercredi nos équipes travaillent 24 h sur 24 h – *since Wednesday our teams have been working around the clock*
67 | 3258

**815 situer** *v* to situate, locate
- je me situe quelque part entre les deux – *I find myself somewhere between the two*
76 | 2260

**816 souligner** *v* to underline, stress
- j'ai deux points à souligner – *I have two points to stress*
65 | 3574

**817 source** *nf* source, spring
- un bon journaliste ne révèle jamais ses sources – *a good journalist never reveals his sources*
70 | 2917

**818 respect** *nm* respect
- il salua avec beaucoup de respect – *he saluted with deep respect*
80 | 1802

**819 crime** *nm* crime
- un crime motivé par la haine – *a hate crime*
78 | 1978

**820 précédent** *nadj* precedent; previous
- le manège précédent a été construit en 1950 – *the previous merry-go-round was built in 1950*
75 | 2383

**821 installer** *v* to install
- t'as bien installé son micro? – *did you set up his microphone correctly?*
81 | 1705

**822 facile** *adj(f)* easy
- il n'y avait rien de plus facile – *nothing was easier*
79 | 1853

**823 augmenter** *v* to increase, raise
- les dépenses à la consommation augmentent – *consumer spending is rising*
71 | 2761

**824 réunir** *v* to gather, reunite, raise
- je sais comment réunir l'argent – *I know how to raise money*
78 | 1998

**825 impression** *nf* impression
- oui, c'est l'impression que j'ai eue – *yes, that's the impression I had*
82 | 1549

**826 octobre** *nm* October
- il sortira en français au mois d'octobre – *it will hit the shelves in French in October.*
75 | 2283

**827 médecin** *nm* physician, doctor
- j'ai besoin d'un médecin – *I need a doctor*
82 | 1614

**828 fédéral** *nadj* federal
- le gouvernement fédéral a contribué au problème – *the federal government contributed to the problem*
54 | 5018-l +s

**829 police** *nf* police
- la police poursuit une bande de criminels très dangereux – *the police are pursuing a very dangerous gang of criminals*
65 | 3532

**830 coût** *nm* cost
- les coûts de production seront réduits – *production costs will be reduced*
73 | 2501

**831 formation** *nf* training
- je suis toujours dans ma période de formation – *I'm still in my training stage*
72 | 2632

**832 contrat** *nm* contract
- j'ai rompu le contrat. je l'ai trompé – *I broke the contract. I didn't honor it*
81 | 1701

**833 normal** *adj* normal
- j'ai une vie plutôt normale, avec un mari, des enfants – *I have a rather normal life, with a husband, children*
77 | 2091

**834 attitude** *nf* attitude
- il est difficile de changer les attitudes – *it's difficult to change attitudes*
84 | 1356

**835 faute** *nf* mistake, error, fault
- vous comprendrez combien vos fautes sont graves – *you will understand how serious your errors are*
81 | 1715

**836 série** *nf* series
- on a interrompu la série pendant 15 ans – *we interrupted the series for 15 years*
73 | 2501

**837 lever** *v* to lift, raise
- je t'en prie, lève-toi – *please, get up*
68 | 3095+l

**838 proche** *adv,nadj(f),prep* nearby, close
- nous n'avions pas de famille proche – *we didn't have any close relatives*
75 | 2300

**839 direct** *nadj* direct
- on parle toujours des émissions en direct – *they always talk about live broadcasts*
79 | 1885

**840 imaginer** *v* to imagine
- j'imagine qu'elle a des documents – *I imagine she has the documents*
77 | 2042

**841 figurer** *v* to represent, appear
- parmi les signataires, figurent 42 maires – *among the signatories appeared 42 mayors*
72 | 2602

**842 pratique** *nadj(f)* practice, practical
- les résultats pratiques obtenus sont-ils très probants? – *are the practical results very convincing?*
76 | 2127

**843 finalement** *adv* finally, eventually
- finalement, la porte s'ouvrit – *finally, the door opened*
79 | 1874

**844 allemand** *nadj* German
- un type fume une cigarette allemande, l'air pensif – *a guy smokes a German cigarette, with a pensive air*
71 | 2755-s

**845 pression** *nf* pressure
- cette pression fait partie de la négociation – *this pressure is part of the negotiation*
78 | 1929

**846 accès** *nm(pl)* access
- voici les codes d'accès – *there are the access codes*
70 | 2791

**847 champ** *nm* field, realm
- dans le champ administratif, il peut y avoir des incertitudes – *in the administrative realm, uncertainties can exist*
80 | 1785

**848 film** *nm* film
- j'ai vu tous les films d'action – *I saw all the action films*
64 | 3542

**849 charge** *nf* to charge, load
- l'arbre plie sous la charge – *the tree collapsed under the weight*
77 | 2039

**850 envisager** *v* to view, contemplate
- je ne pouvais pas envisager que son état fût grave – *I couldn't imagine that her condition was serious*
80 | 1721

**851 commune** *nf* locality; common, joint
- il s'agit là d'une responsabilité commune – *now that's a joint responsibility*
68 | 3093

**852 ressource** *nf* resource
- le nœud intermédiaire dispose des ressources nécessaires – *the intermediate node has the necessary resources*
66 | 3228

**853 monter** *v* to go up, rise, assemble
- j'ai monté et descendu cinq étages – *I went up and down five floors*
71 | 2707

**854 promettre** *v* to promise
- s'il promet quelque chose, il tient parole – *if he promises something, he keeps his word*
81 | 1653

**855 motion** *nf* motion
- la motion définitive était validée par Nicolas Sarkozy – *the final motion was ratified by Nicolas Sarkozy*
44 | 6425-l -n +s

**856 concentrer** *v* to concentrate
- je me concentre plus sur ma condition physique – *I'm concentrating on my physical condition*
89 | 867

857 **exactement** *adv* exactly
- la pièce ne paraissait pas exactement sombre – *the room didn't appear exactly dark*
  80 | 1732

858 **composer** *v* to compose, dial
- il avait juste besoin de composer mon numéro – *all he needed to do was dial my number*
  83 | 1482

859 **chemin** *nm* path, way
- le chemin pour rentrer me semblait interminable – *the road home seemed never-ending*
  78 | 1973

860 **zone** *nf* zone, area
- vous pouvez venir, j'ai sécurisé la zone – *you can come here – I've secured the area*
  70 | 2805

861 **province** *nf* province
- l'armée française abandonne une de nos provinces – *the French army is abandoning one of our provinces*
  55 | 4597+s

862 **élection** *nf* election
- l'élection présidentielle en Russie est prévue l'été prochain – *the Russian presidential elections are slated for next summer*
  66 | 3255

863 **usage** *nm* use, usage
- il avait perdu l'usage de la mémoire immédiate – *he had lost the use of short-term memory*
  85 | 1230

864 **conflit** *nm* conflict
- ils se préparent à un éventuel conflit – *they're preparing for a possible conflict*
  75 | 2205

865 **hors** *adv,prep* except, outside
- ils s'installèrent hors de la ville – *they moved in outside the city*
  80 | 1716

866 **enquête** *nf* inquiry, enquiry, investigation
- cela coûte cher de faire enquête sur les activités criminelles – *criminal investigations are costly*
  71 | 2658

867 **terrain** *nm* ground, terrain
- vous combattez sur un terrain qui s'enfonce – *you're fighting on shaky ground*
  79 | 1820

868 **mars** *nm(pl)* March; Mars
- la date est fixée au 1er mars 2004 – *the date is set for March 1, 2004*
  63 | 3557+n

869 **tellement** *adv* so much
- vous êtes tellement différente des autres femelles – *you are so different from other females*
  77 | 2006-n

870 **espace** *nm,nf* space
- je m'invente un espace magique pour moi tout seul – *I'm inventing a magic space just for myself*
  78 | 1864

871 **demain** *adv,nm* tomorrow
- je te verrai demain matin – *I'll see you tomorrow morning*
  71 | 2586

872 **hier** *adv* yesterday
- tu nous as manqué, hier soir – *we missed you last night*
  65 | 3313-n +s

873 **confier** *v* to entrust
- je te confie ce garçon. rends-moi un homme – *I entrust you with this boy. return a man to me*
  86 | 1162

874 **remarquer** *v* to remark; to notice, point out
- ils ont fait remarquer que ces jeunes avaient été pris – *they pointed out that these youths were taken*
  79 | 1758

875 **égard** *nm* consideration, respect, regard
- rien n'est prévu à cet égard – *nothing has been planned in this regard*
  68 | 2926

876 **supérieur** *nadj* superior
- je suis votre supérieur ecclésiastique – *I'm your religious superior*
  74 | 2307

877 **huit** *det,nmi* eight
- il a presque huit ans – *he's almost eight years old*
  73 | 2434

878 **condamner** *v* to condemn
- le mousquetaire est seul. et condamné à la solitude – *the musketeer is alone. and condemned to loneliness*
  76 | 2091

879 **capital** *nadj* major, chief, principal; capital, assets
- ils ont pris une décision capitale en renonçant à leur statut – *they took a major decision in renouncing their status*
  72 | 2479

880 **lien** *nm* link, bond
- sachez que nos liens ne sont pas rompus – *understand that our bonds are not broken*
  80 | 1705

881 **voiture** *nf* car
- mettez votre voiture dans le parking – *put your car in the parking lot*
  72 | 2509

882 **discussion** *nf* discussion
- j'ai eu une discussion avec elle – *I had a discussion with her*
  75 | 2161

883 **limiter** *v* to limit
- les freins limitent les transactions informatisées – *the blocking mechanism limits computerized transactions*
  75 | 2198

**884 justifier** *v* to justify
- ça ne justifie pas la mesure extrême – *that doesn't justify the extreme measures taken*
83 | 1418

**885 agent** *nm,nf* agent
- notre partenaire est un agent immobilier – *our partner is a real estate agent*
79 | 1806

**886 sentiment** *nm* feeling
- elle connaît tes sentiments pour elle? – *does she know your feelings for her?*
76 | 2117

**887 tâche** *nf* task
- nous déciderons à qui reviendra cette tâche agréable – *we will decide who will get this pleasant task*
85 | 1250

**888 directement** *adv* directly
- son action s'exerce directement ou par intermédiaire – *his actions are taken personally or by an intermediary*
81 | 1606

**889 euh** *intj* er, um, uh
- il faut euh avoir euh une intention particulière – *you um have to have um a particular intention*
39 | 7099-l -n +s

**890 raconter** *v* to tell
- je ne raconte plus de blagues – *I don't tell jokes any more*
71 | 2555

**891 décembre** *nm* December
- c'était un samedi après-midi de décembre – *it was a Saturday afternoon in December*
70 | 2658

**892 développer** *v* to develop
- l'embryon vit, grandit et se développe – *the embryo lives, grows, and develops*
70 | 2601

**893 honorable** *adj(f)* honorable
- c'est un but honorable – *it's an honorable goal*
46 | 5863-l -n +s

**894 contact** *nm* contact
- je ne veux plus perdre contact avec toi – *I don't want to lose contact with you any more*
81 | 1573

**895 conclure** *v* to conclude
- il vous reste une minute pour conclure – *you have one minute to conclude*
75 | 2085

**896 fruit** *nm* fruit
- allez manger des fruits – *go eat fruit*
89 | 844

**897 ouvert** *adj* open
- je suis très ouvert à cette suggestion – *I'm very open to this suggestion*
84 | 1287

**898 investissement** *nm* investment
- ce sont là des investissements importants – *those are important investments*
69 | 2755

**899 insister** *v* to insist
- elle insistait pour m'accompagner, je refusai – *she insisted on accompanying me, I refused*
85 | 1205

**900 avantage** *nm* advantage
- je désirais cet avantage pour mon fils – *I wanted this advantage for my son*
79 | 1697

**901 garde** *nm,nf* guard
- on a fait venir le garde du corps – *they had the bodyguard come*
76 | 1991

**902 historique** *nadj(f)* historical
- c'est également devenu un lieu historique – *it has also become a historical site*
80 | 1643

**903 probablement** *adv* probably
- il est probablement mort à ce moment-là – *that's probably when he died*
81 | 1491

**904 voyage** *nm* trip, journey
- le ferry fera plusieurs voyages – *the ferry will make many trips*
79 | 1681

**905 sept** *det,nmi* seven
- il était sept heures, exactement – *it was exactly seven o'clock*
66 | 3077

**906 marche** *nf* walk, step, march
- mais enfin il arrêta brusquement leur marche – *finally he abruptly stopped their march*
77 | 1916

**907 vérité** *nf* truth
- provoqué à la vérité, je répondrai au défi – *pushed to the truth, I will answer the challenge*
71 | 2480

**908 commercial** *nadj* commercial
- la Chine est un partenaire commercial important – *China is an important commercial partner*
72 | 2332

**909 critique** *nadj(f)* criticism, critic, critical
- cette critique est légitime – *this criticism is legitimate*
75 | 2028

**910 ministère** *nm* ministry
- des représentants de divers ministères y ont pris part – *representatives from various ministries took part*
62 | 3417

**911 baisser** *v* to lower, turn down, bend down
- la jeune femme baisse encore un peu plus la tête – *the young woman bows her head a little lower*
80 | 1568

**912 somme** *nm,nf* amount, sum; nap
- pourquoi n'ont-ils pas mentionné ces sommes? – *why didn't they mention these sums?*
83 | 1313

**913 culture** *nf* culture
• la culture permet d'ouvrir les esprits –
*culture enables the opening of minds*
70 | 2555

**914 cacher** *v* to hide
• je ne vous cache rien du tout – *I am not
hiding anything at all from you*
76 | 1970

**915 prêter** *v* to lend
• le gouvernement devrait prêter l'oreille –
*the government should pay attention*
86 | 1056

**916 définir** *v* to define
• tout dépend de la manière dont on définit le
concept – *everything depends on how we
define the concept*
70 | 2551

**917 client** *nm* client
• le client contrôle toujours la destination
de la marchandise – *the customer
always controls the destination of the
goods*
80 | 1600

**918 exposer** *v* to display, exhibit, expose
• en m'exposant, vous me condamnez! –
*by exposing me, you're condemning me!*
85 | 1119

**919 progrès** *nm(pl)* progress
• mes fils font des progrès – *my sons are
making progress*
80 | 1545

**920 secrétaire** *nm,nf* secretary
• mais voilà, ma secrétaire accouche cet après-
midi – *so there you go, my secretary is
delivering a baby this afternoon*
64 | 3219

**921 mer** *nf* sea
• il les a laissés en pleine mer – *he left them
in the middle of the sea*
76 | 1909

**922 rapporter** *v* to bring back, report
• je t'ai rapporté ton livre – *I brought back
your book*
80 | 1583

**923 appuyer** *v* to lean, support
• nous avons toujours appuyé l'unité
nationale – *we have always supported
national unity*
65 | 3090

**924 liste** *nf* list
• j'aimerais avoir une liste de ces témoins –
*I'd like to have a list of these witnesses*
75 | 1976

**925 rentrer** *v* to go in, come in, come back, return
• je ne t'avais pas entendu rentrer – *I hadn't
heard you come in*
68 | 2709

**926 mémoire** *nm,nf* memory
• cette soirée restera gravée dans nos
mémoires – *this evening will remain
engraven in our memory*
77 | 1868

**927 caractère** *nm* nature, character
• mais c'est un caractère difficile – *but he's a
difficult character*
69 | 2630

**928 détruire** *v* to destroy
l'environnement a été entièrement
détruit – *the environment was completely
destroyed*
82 | 1402

**929 civil** *nadj* civil; civilian
• la protection des citoyens et des civils
est une cause excellente – *the protection
of citizens and civilians is an excellent
cause*
71 | 2379

**930 nécessité** *nf* necessity, need
• nous sommes conscients de la nécessité de
réduire ces cotisations – *we're aware of the
need to reduce these subscriptions*
80 | 1517

**931 juin** *nm* June
• deux pays ont signé en juin un accord – *two
countries signed an agreement in June*
67 | 2844

**932 danger** *nm* danger
• le cyclisme est en danger de mort – *cycling
is in danger of dying out*
71 | 2346

**933 complexe** *nadj(f)* complex
• les problèmes et les solutions sont
complexes – *the problems and solutions are
complex*
83 | 1289

**934 commerce** *nm* trade, commerce
• nous ne sommes pas contre le commerce
équitable – *we aren't against equitable
commerce*
70 | 2479

**935 transport** *nm* transportation
• il nous faut un transport plus rapide – *we
need a faster means of transportation*
72 | 2261

**936 attente** *nf* wait
• six mois d'attente, c'est beaucoup trop long
– *six years of waiting, that's much too long*
83 | 1252

**937 institution** *nf* institution
• nous devons réformer ces institutions – *we
must reform these institutions*
74 | 2102

**938 défense** *nf* defense
• je me porte à la défense de la personne
responsable – *I'm here to help defend the
person responsible*
74 | 2086

**939 janvier** *nm* January
• j'irai en Californie en janvier prochain – *I'll
be going to California next January*
66 | 2908+n

**940 échapper** *v* to escape
• on ne peut pas y échapper – *you can't
escape it*
81 | 1434

## 6 Family

| | | |
|---|---|---|
| **enfant** 126 MF child | **époux** 1953 M male spouse | **grand-mère** 3883 F grandmother |
| **femme** 154 F wife | **maman** 2168 F mommy | |
| **famille** 172 F family | **bébé** 2271 MF baby | **tante** 3891 F aunt |
| **parent** 546 M parent | **papa** 2458 M daddy | **héritier** 3955 M heir |
| **père** 569 M father | **aîné** 2786 M eldest | **jumeau** 4357 M twin |
| **fille** 629 F daughter | **ancêtre** 3067 MF ancestor | **parrain** 6013 M godfather |
| **mère** 645 F mother | **cousin** 3387 M cousin | **grands-parents** 6062 M grandparents |
| **fils** 735 M son | **oncle** 3628 M uncle | |
| **frère** 1043 M brother | **descendant** 3656 M descendant | **petits-enfants** 6267 M grandchildren |
| **mariage** 1210 M marriage | | **petit-fils** 6280 M grandson |
| **sœur** 1558 F sister | **grand-père** 3748 M grandfather | **épouse** 8240 F female spouse |
| **mari** 1589 M husband | | |

941 **négociation** nf negotiation
• il se présente à la table de négociation – *he shows up at the negotiation table*
65 | 2961

942 **franc** adj,adv,adj,nm frank; franc
• le vétérinaire avait un regard franc – *the veterinarian had a candid look*
55 | 4157+n -s

943 **mai** nm May
• elle avait disparu le 30 mai dernier – *she had disappeared last May 30*
68 | 2694

944 **septembre** nm September
• elle est née un 22 septembre – *she was born on September 22*
69 | 2515

945 **environnement** nm environment
• nous rejetons la nécessité de protéger notre environnement – *we reject the need to protect our environment*
64 | 3082

946 **séparer** v to separate
• ce sont deux mondes séparés qui ont des interfaces – *they are two separate worlds that have interfaces*
80 | 1478

947 **réaction** nf reaction
• j'estime que leur réaction est naturelle – *I judge their reaction to be normal*
82 | 1383

948 **disposition** nf arrangement, disposition
• elle tenait de notre père une disposition mélancolique – *she got a melancholy disposition from our father's side*
64 | 3055

949 **positif** nadj positive
• les réactions des téléspectateurs sont très positives – *the reactions of the viewers were very positive*
78 | 1665

950 **scientifique** nadj(f) scientific
• le nom scientifique de ma maladie ne l'intéressait pas – *he wasn't interested in the scientific name of my disease*
75 | 1986

951 **papier** nm paper
• ils veulent juste voir nos papiers – *they just wanted to see our papers*
74 | 2030

952 **expression** nf expression
• cette expression a un sens extrêmement simple – *this expression has an extremely simple meaning*
80 | 1473

953 **protection** nf protection
• on voudrait créer des aires de protection marines – *they wanted to create marine conservation areas*
68 | 2584

954 **indépendant** nadj independent
• il est indépendant financièrement, cultivé et cinglé – *he's financially independent, cultivated, and nuts*
77 | 1757

955 **carte** nf card
• j'ai reçu votre carte – *I received your card*
81 | 1401

956 **association** nf association
• l'association a vocation à être une entreprise – *the association's goal is to become a company*
73 | 2107

957 **régler** v to pay, adjust, settle
• vous ne réglerez rien avec l'argent – *you won't settle anything with the money*
77 | 1792

958 **modèle** nm model
• votre styliste va nous proposer trois modèles – *your stylist is going to show us three models*
73 | 2111

**959 commander** *v* to order, command
- il a commandé plusieurs exemplaires du guide de référence – *he ordered several copies of the reference guide*
76 | 1858

**960 étudier** *v* to study
- j'ai étudié la situation avant de venir ici – *I studied the situation before coming here*
73 | 2094

**961 déterminer** *v* to determine, find out, specify
- il faut plutôt déterminer si le contrat était juste – *rather we should determine out whether the contract was accurate*
72 | 2240

**962 budget** *nm* budget
- il paraît assez douteux que le budget soit rejeté – *it seems rather unlikely that the budget would be rejected*
59 | 3511+s

**963 fonder** *v* to found, set
- il a fondé la société – *he founded the company*
80 | 1449

**964 structure** *nf* structure
- une structure bien déterminée est choisie – *a well specified structure is chosen*
74 | 2034

**965 complet** *adj,nm* full, complete; suit
- je veux un rapport complet sur mon bureau, demain – *I want a complete report on my desk tomorrow*
79 | 1578

**966 exercer** *v* to exercise, exert, practise, carry out
- j'ai également exercé diverses fonctions dans ce secteur – *I also carried out various roles in this sector*
77 | 1774

**967 amour** *nm* love
- rien ne pourrait détruire mon amour pour toi – *nothing could destroy my love for you*
63 | 3071+l -n

**968 manifester** *v* to show, demonstrate, display
- il avait manifesté son hostilité contre elle – *he displayed his hostility toward her*
82 | 1310

**969 menacer** *v* to threaten
- ils ont menacé de l'incarcérer et de le torturer – *they threatened to imprison and torture him*
75 | 1903

**970 conseiller** *nm,v* adviser, to advise
- je lui conseille de consulter le dictionnaire – *I advised her to consult the dictionary*
79 | 1595

**971 réunion** *nf* meeting
- j'ai moi-même participé à diverses réunions de la troïka – *I even attended several of the trilateral meetings*
69 | 2433

**972 opposition** *nf* opposition
- il est membre de l'opposition officielle – *he is a member of the official opposition*
62 | 3175

**973 maladie** *nf* illness, disease
- ce n'est pas une maladie psychiatrique – *it's not a psychiatric illness*
74 | 1981

**974 outre** *adv,prep* besides
- il a en outre publié deux ouvrages – *he also published two works*
73 | 2107

**975 tandis** while
- il pria tandis que l'océan gelait – *he prayed while the ocean froze over*
74 | 1984-s

**976 construction** *nf* construction, building
- son rôle dans la construction du produit final – *his role in building the final product*
76 | 1829

**977 bande** *nf* band, strip
- Le Chili est une longue et étroite bande de terre – *Chile is a long and narrow strip of land*
70 | 2394

**978 signal** *nm* signal
- on va perdre le signal – *we're going to lose the signal*
42 | 5779-l +n -s

**979 voisin** *nadj* neighbor
- je l'expédie chez le petit voisin – *I sent him to the little neighbor's house*
79 | 1560

**980 réforme** *nf* reform
- les réformes continuent, et ces pays progressent – *the reforms continue, and these countries are progressing*
68 | 2517

**981 rejeter** *v* to reject
- je rejette l'argument invoqué fréquemment aujourd'hui – *I reject the argument invoked often today*
72 | 2132

**982 novembre** *nm* November
- rappelez-vous où vous étiez le 1er novembre? – *do you remember where you were on November 1st?*
70 | 2344

**983 fonds** *nm(pl)* funds
- cela vient des fonds publics – *this comes from public funds*
62 | 3199-l

**984 coûter** *v* to cost
- cette décision va coûter des milliards de dollars – *this decision will cost billions of dollars*
81 | 1334

**985 reprise** *nf* resumption, renewal; time
- elle l'a prouvé à maintes reprises – *she proved it many times*
72 | 2146

**986 presse** *nf* press
- la presse aime bien les grands titres – *the press really likes dramatic headlines*
63 | 2991

**987 rouge** *nadj(f)* red
• le sang a séché, le rouge est devenu brun –
  *the blood dried, red turning to brown*
75 | 1898

**988 majorité** *nf* majority
• la grande majorité n'en faisait rien – *the
  great majority didn't do anything about it*
70 | 2294

**989 autoriser** *v* to authorize
• aucun fait n'autorise cette accusation de
  jalousie – *no fact licenses this accusation of
  jealousy*
74 | 1994

**990 effectuer** *v* to carry out, undergo
• elle avait effectué trois jours de prison – *she
  had served three days of prison time*
71 | 2238

**991 bord** *nm* edge, side
• voyant un banc au bord du trottoir je m'y
  assis – *seeing a bench alongside the sidewalk
  I sat down*
75 | 1885

**992 central** *nadj* central
• elle habitait dans le quartier central de la
  ville – *she lived in the city's central
  neighborhood*
66 | 2736

**993 procédure** *nf* procedure
• pour cela, il existe une procédure spéciale –
  *for that, a special procedure exists*
60 | 3288

**994 faveur** *nf* favor
• je me prononcerai en faveur des amendements – *I will declare myself in favor of the
  amendments*
70 | 2272

**995 éducation** *nf* education
• l'éducation est devenue obligatoire –
  *education has become mandatory*
74 | 1954

**996 officiel** *nadj* official
• ils doivent fournir une réponse honnête et
  officielle – *they have to provide an honest
  and official response*
68 | 2546

**997 document** *nm* document
• je suis un document vivant! – *I'm a living
  document!*
66 | 2742

**998 aspect** *nm* aspect
• il a oublié quelques aspects de la gastronomie – *he forgot some aspects of
  gastronomie*
75 | 1877

**999 retourner** *v* to return, go back
• je ne retournerai pas sur la Terre – *I will not
  return to Earth*
71 | 2209

**1000 professionnel** *nadj* professional
• il est entré dans la vie professionnelle voilà
  huit ans – *he entered professional life eight
  years ago*
73 | 2067

**1001 auparavant** *adv* beforehand
• je n'ai jamais vu cela auparavant – *I've
  never seen that before*
85 | 1047

**1002 animal** *nadj* animal
• le singe aussi est un animal familier – *the
  monkey is also a familiar animal*
81 | 1364

**1003 utile** *adj(f)* useful
• l'hypocrisie, pour être utile, doit se cacher –
  *hypocrisy, to be useful, must be hidden*
83 | 1173

**1004 inscrire** *v* to register, write down
• j'inscrivis mon nom sur la fiche – *I wrote
  down my name on the card*
78 | 1595

**1005 concurrence** *nf* competition
• Pékin est en concurrence avec Paris –
  *Peking is in competition with Paris*
77 | 1713

**1006 déclaration** *nf* declaration
• nous devons répondre à cette déclaration –
  *we must respond to this declaration*
65 | 2782

**1007 rejoindre** *v* to rejoin, reunite
• allez, rejoignez votre famille – *go, rejoin
  your family*
81 | 1321

**1008 mille** *det,nm,nmi* a thousand
• leur culture a duré quelque vingt mille ans –
  *their culture lasted some twenty thousand
  years*
59 | 3431

**1009 absolument** *adv* absolutely
• cela ne veut absolument rien dire – *that
  means absolutely nothing at all*
75 | 1829+s

**1010 prison** *nf* prison
• les prisons sont la solution à la délinquance
  juvénile – *prisons are the solution to juvenile
  deliquence*
73 | 2014

**1011 armée** *nf* army
• l'armée fait retraite, sans avoir combattu –
  *the army retreats, without having fought*
63 | 2921

**1012 revenu** *nm* income
• les hauts revenus ne verront pas la
  différence – *high-income people will not see
  the difference*
61 | 3119

**1013 complètement** *adv,nm* completely
• le ciel est complètement couvert – *the sky is
  completely overcast*
79 | 1513

**1014 confirmer** *v* to confirm
• cette information n'a pas été confirmée –
  *this information was not confirmed*
71 | 2163

**1015 salaire** *nm* salary, wage
• beaucoup de travailleurs gagnent le salaire
  minimum – *many workers earn minimum
  wage*
80 | 1390

**1016 lecture** *nf* reading
- elle consacrait son temps à la lecture – *she consecrated her time to reading*
- 70 | 2252

**1017 contribuer** *v* to contribute
- la consommation de drogues illicites contribue à la criminalité – *illegal drug use contributes to crime*
- 73 | 1990

**1018 attaquer** *v* to attack
- il est temps d'attaquer le mal à la racine – *it's time to attack evil at its roots*
- 78 | 1580

**1019 table** *nf* table
- la bouteille est là sur la table – *the bottle is there on the table*
- 72 | 2116

**1020 remonter** *v* to go back up
- notre dernière participation remontait au génocide rwandais – *our last participation goes back to the Rwandan genocide*
- 83 | 1140

**1021 certes** *adv* indeed, certainly, of course
- le rapport ne fournit certes pas de solution miracle – *the report certainly doesn't provide the miraculous solution*
- 79 | 1477

**1022 avril** *nm* April
- je suis né le 10 avril – *I was born on April 10th*
- 68 | 2434

**1023 autrement** *adv* differently, something else, otherwise
- les Américains ont décidé d'agir autrement – *the Americans decided to act otherwise*
- 81 | 1309

**1024 ferme** *adj(f),adv,nf* farm; firm
- les parents doivent parfois se montrer fermes – *parents should sometimes stand firm*
- 78 | 1538

**1025 désormais** *adv* from now on, henceforth
- c'est désormais chose faite – *it's henceforth a done deal*
- 71 | 2158

**1026 lourd** *adj* heavy
- nous avons accepté une lourde partie de la responsabilité – *we have accepted a heavy part of the responsibility*
- 79 | 1502

**1027 susciter** *v* to arouse, provoke
- une femme qui a étudié la théologie suscite toujours quelque méfiance – *a woman who has studied theology still arouses some suspicion*
- 83 | 1133

**1028 république** *nf* republic
- je rêve d'une république indépendante, libre et démocratique – *I dream of an independent, free, democratic republic*
- 69 | 2278

**1029 dur** *adv,nadj* hard
- il va traverser des moments très durs – *he will pass through very difficult times*
- 76 | 1688

**1030 application** *nf* application
- l'accord sera mis en application – *the agreement will be enacted*
- 67 | 2530

**1031 lutter** *v* to struggle, fight
- je me préoccupe de lutter contre la pauvreté – *I'm busy fighting against poverty*
- 85 | 1004

**1032 profit** *nm* profit, benefit
- j'ai toujours profit à l'écouter – *I always benefit from listening to her*
- 80 | 1394

**1033 contenir** *v* to contain
- ce livre contient donc un message – *so this book contains a message*
- 70 | 2243

**1034 déposer** *v* to deposit, put down
- pourquoi ne dépose-t-il pas ses bagages? – *why doesn't he set down his luggage?*
- 70 | 2204

**1035 modifier** *v* to modify, adjust
- nous pouvons modifier nos paramètres – *we can adjust our parameters*
- 61 | 3119

**1036 communication** *nf* communication
- aucun moyen de communication n'a été fermé par le gouvernement – *no means of communication was cut off by the government*
- 66 | 2583

**1037 jugement** *nm* judgement
- il faut que son jugement s'exerce très très très rapidement – *his judgment must be exercised very very very quickly*
- 84 | 1097

**1038 manque** *nm* lack
- c'est aussi un manque de respect – *it's also a lack of respect*
- 84 | 1091

**1039 échec** *adji,nm* failure
- l'objectif central est de combattre l'échec scolaire – *the main goal is to fight failure in schools*
- 80 | 1385

**1040 traverser** *v* to cross, traverse
- c'est suicidaire de traverser seul la galaxie entière – *it's suicidal to traverse the whole galaxy alone*
- 80 | 1403

**1041 transformer** *v* to transform
- cela s'est transformé en un match physique – *it was transformed into a physical contest*
- 81 | 1253

**1042 engagement** *nm* agreement, commitment
- mon premier engagement fut de nature politique – *my first appointment was political in nature*
- 73 | 1929

**1043 frère** *nm* brother
- tu es mon frère, et je t'aime – *you're my brother, and I love you*
73 | 1973

**1044 mardi** *nm* Tuesday
- des manifestations se sont déroulées mardi – *protests took place Tuesday*
53 | 3902-l +n -s

**1045 rencontre** *nm* meeting
- le matin, je vais à la rencontre du soleil – *in the morning I go to meet the sun*
68 | 2353

**1046 vote** *nm* vote
- le vote aura lieu aujourd'hui – *the vote will take place today*
59 | 3238-l +s

**1047 renvoyer** *v* to send back, dismiss
- il devrait renvoyer le signal de libération au réseau – *he had to send the liberation signal to the network*
81 | 1315

**1048 regretter** *v* to regret
- tous étaient violents. peu regrettaient leurs actes – *everybody was violent. few regretted their acts*
82 | 1232

**1049 espèce** *nf* species
- c'est une espèce en voie de disparition – *that's an endangered species*
76 | 1707

**1050 recommandation** *nf* recommendation
- nous avons fait neuf recommandations précises – *we made nine specific recommendations*
49 | 4421-l +n

**1051 consister** *v* to consist
- en quoi consiste ton travail? – *what does your job consist of?*
78 | 1488

**1052 réagir** *v* to react
- tu réagis comme une enfant – *you're reacting like a child*
84 | 1061

**1053 surprendre** *v* to surprise
- mon garçon, parfois tu me surprends – *my son, sometimes you surprise me*
83 | 1124

**1054 circonstance** *nf* circumstance
- les circonstances ne sont pas idéales – *the circumstances are less than ideal*
82 | 1179

**1055 témoin** *nm* witness
- j'ai des témoins. ma femme a été enlevée – *I have witnesses. my wife was kidnapped*
78 | 1481

**1056 améliorer** *v* to improve
- la situation semblait s'améliorer – *the situation seemed to improve*
69 | 2231

**1057 administration** *nf* administration
- les administrations précédentes ont perdu toute autorité – *the preceding administrations have lost all authority*
70 | 2200

**1058 réfléchir** *v* to reflect
- j'ai réfléchi à la question – *I thought about the question*
79 | 1461

**1059 lumière** *nf* light
- elle était juste heureuse de voir la lumière du jour – *she was happy to see daylight again*
68 | 2304

**1060 vert** *nadj* green
- il avait 23 ans, des yeux vert émeraude – *he was twenty-three years old, with emerald green eyes*
79 | 1459

**1061 apprécier** *v* to appreciate
- ils n'apprécient pas le spectacle – *they don't appreciate the show*
84 | 1031

**1062 combat** *nm* fight, combat
- nous devons nous préparer pour le grand combat – *we must prepare for the big battle*
75 | 1759

**1063 sensible** *nadj(f)* sensitive
- je dois avoir touché une corde sensible – *I must have touched a sensitive nerve*
83 | 1121

**1064 étudiant** *nadj* student
- les dames serviront à boire aux étudiants – *the ladies served drinks to the students*
69 | 2237

**1065 vitesse** *nf* speed
- accélérez en vitesse d'attaque – *accelerate to attack speed*
84 | 1027

**1066 malade** *nadj(f)* ill, sick
- ton père est malade, il aimerait te voir – *your father is sick, he wants to see you*
78 | 1478

**1067 portée** *nf* range, reach, scope
- Linux est à présent à la portée du grand public – *Linux is now within reach of the general public*
91 | 570

**1068 élève** *nm,nf* pupil, student
- ils ont été mes élèves – *they were my students*
82 | 1167

**1069 contrôler** *v* to control, check, inspect, monitor
- c'est la volonté du propriétaire de contrôler ce qui se passe chez lui – *it's up to the owner to decide whether to check up on what's happening at his house*
78 | 1511

**1070 merci** *intj,nm,nf* thank you; favor
- merci pour la bière – *thanks for the beer*
54 | 3729-n +s

**1071 certainement** *adv* certainly
- ce n'est certainement pas nous qui ferons cela – *we are certainly not the ones to do that*
76 | 1660

**1072 visite** *nf* visit
- je reviendrais bien ici, en visite – *I would gladly come back here on a visit*
69 | 2229

**1073 assemblée** *nf* assembly, meeting
- la direction organisa une assemblée générale – *management organized a general meeting*
70 | 2157

**1074 émission** *nf* transmission, broadcasting, programme
- une émission de télé passe, les écrits restent – *a TV show disappears, but writings persist*
59 | 3210-l

**1075 arrivée** *nf* arrival
- on annonçait notre arrivée dans le quartier – *our arrival was noised about in the neighborhood*
67 | 2352

**1076 puissance** *nf* power
- la Chine est une puissance importante sur la scène mondiale – *China is an important power on the global scene*
67 | 2340-s

**1077 partenaire** *nm,nf* partner
- nous pourrions être amis! partenaires. frères d'arme – *we could be friends, partners, brothers in arms*
77 | 1552

**1078 contenter** *v* to satisfy, please
- tu te contenteras d'être le chauffeur – *you will be satisfied to be the driver*
86 | 860

**1079 perte** *nf* loss
- c'était une perte de temps d'aller chez le médecin – *it was a waste of time to go see the doctor*
75 | 1724

**1080 libéral** *nadj* liberal
- nous avons maintenant un gouvernement libéral – *we now have a liberal government*
54 | 3706+s

**1081 citoyen** *nadj* citizen
- les gouvernements doivent représenter tous les citoyens – *governments must represent every citizen*
67 | 2352+s

**1082 citer** *v* to quote
- j'aimerais citer quatre paragraphes – *I would like to cite four paragraphs*
75 | 1698

**1083 influence** *nf* influence
- la France perdit de son influence – *France lost her influence*
79 | 1356

**1084 camp** *nm* camp
- on n'a jamais bombardé nos camps – *our camps were never bombed*
76 | 1636

**1085 établissement** *nm* establishment, organization
- l'établissement de systèmes de contrôle est important – *it's important to establish verification systems*
69 | 2135

**1086 vendredi** *nm* Friday
- vendredi en quinze, on prend le train – *two weeks from Friday we take the train*
53 | 3709-l +n -s

**1087 avance** *nf* advance
- j'arrivai au cours en avance – *I arrived to class early*
81 | 1237

**1088 destiner** *v* to intend, be used
- ce programme n'est pas destiné aux informaticiens – *this program is not meant for computer scientists*
75 | 1692

**1089 causer** *v* to cause
- tout ceci a causé une certaine frustration – *this all caused some frustration*
82 | 1169

**1090 nord** *adji,nm* north
- les tensions raciales ont explosé dans le nord – *racial tensions have exploded in the north*
59 | 3095

**1091 lundi** *nm* Monday
- il quitte l'hôpital ce lundi – *he leaves the hospital this Monday*
53 | 3736-l +n -s

**1092 maître** *nm* master
- je suis le maître de ta vie et de ta mort – *I am the master of your life and of your death*
72 | 1907

**1093 interroger** *v* to question, interrogate
- on doit vous interroger sur ces événements – *you should be questioned about these events*
74 | 1726

**1094 conférence** *nf* conference
- un certain nombre de séminaires et de conférences ont été organisés – *several seminars and a conference were organized*
71 | 1953

**1095 provoquer** *v* to provoke
- je ne veux pas provoquer de révolte – *I don't want to provoke a revolution*
70 | 2066

**1096 vente** *nf* sale
- je m'oppose à la taxe de vente – *I'm opposed to the sales tax*
68 | 2201

**1097 ramener** *v* to bring back, return, take back
- je me demandais, tu pourrais me ramener chez moi? – *I was wondering, could you take me back home?*
79 | 1389

**1098 soldat** *nm* soldier
- voilà nos petits soldats qui sont venus nous aider – *here come our little soldiers to help us out*
67 | 2339

**1099 collègue** *nm,nf* colleague
- je remercie mon collègue pour sa contribution d'hier – *I thank my colleague for his contribution yesterday*
54 | 3593-l -n +s

**1100 concevoir** *v* to conceive
- j'ai alors conçu le projet – *then I conceived the project*
82 | 1104

**1101 procéder** *v* to proceed
- j'ai procédé à l'arrestation – *I proceeded with the arrest*
76 | 1578

**1102 poids** *nm(pl)* weight
- c'est comme un énorme poids posé sur votre poitrine – *it's like an enormous weight placed on your chest*
83 | 1075

**1103 voici** *prep* here is, here are, this is, these are
- voici le résultat de l'essai – *here's the result of the test*
76 | 1575

**1104 acquérir** *v* to acquire
- ce mot a acquis une connotation très particulière – *this word has acquired a very particular connotation*
82 | 1154

**1105 moindre** *adj(f)* lesser, least, slightest
- il n'avait absolument pas la moindre idée – *he didn't have the slightest clue*
76 | 1583

**1106 convenir** *v* to agree, be suitable
- seul un partenaire de même philosophie pourra leur convenir – *only a partner with the same outlook will be agreeable to them*
69 | 2090

**1107 logique** *nadj(f)* logic, logical
- je ne suis pas la logique de l'argument – *I don't follow the logic behind the argument*
77 | 1464

**1108 examiner** *v* to examine
- ils ont fini d'examiner la maison – *they finished examining the house*
65 | 2430

**1109 soin** *nm* care
- tu peux prendre soin de toi toute seule – *you can take care of yourself alone*
64 | 2549+s

**1110 mesurer** *v* to measure
- il mesure un mètre soixante-huit – *he's one meter sixty-eight tall*
75 | 1602

**1111 traitement** *nm* treatment, salary, wage
- vous acceptez d'être soumis au traitement – *you accept to undergo the treatment*
69 | 2079

**1112 jeudi** *nm* Thursday
- le jugement de jeudi pourrait influencer une autre affaire – *Thursday's judgment could influence another matter*
52 | 3762-l +n -s

**1113 impliquer** *v* to imply, implicate
- je suis désolé de t'avoir impliqué – *I'm sorry I had you implicated*
77 | 1482

**1114 science** *nf* science
- la psychanalyse est une science du vivant – *psychoanalysis is one of the life sciences*
75 | 1657

**1115 individu** *nm* individual
- ce type d'individu n'a rien à faire en prison – *this type of individual doesn't belong in prison*
77 | 1436

**1116 donnée** *nf* fact, datum
- tout en travaillant, il nota les données sur son carnet – *while working he jotted down data in his notebook*
60 | 2902+n

**1117 demi** *adj,adv,nm* half
- rentrer déjeuner à midi et demi tous les jours – *come back for lunch at 12:30 every day*
81 | 1197

**1118 combattre** *v* to fight
- nous avons combattu pour chaque détail – *we fought for every detail*
86 | 849

**1119 violent** *nadj* violent
- évitez de recourir à des moyens trop violents – *avoid relying on overly violent means*
82 | 1100

**1120 comporter** *v* to comprise, include; to behave
- tâche de bien te comporter – *try to be well-behaved*
80 | 1245

**1121 suivant** *nadj,prep* following
- les 20 jours suivants, ils meurent de faim – *in the 20 days that followed, they starve to death*
64 | 2537

**1122 mériter** *v* to deserve, merit
- tout le monde mérite d'avoir sa chance – *everyone deserves a chance*
80 | 1255

**1123 emprunter** *v* to borrow
- tout ce que tu as emprunté s'évanouira en fumée – *everything you borrowed will vanish in smoke*
90 | 558

**1124 conscience** *nf* conscience, consciousness
- j'acquérais une conscience plus attentive des autres – *I acquired a more attentive conscience than most*
72 | 1806

**1125 traduire** *v* to translate
- elle peut être traduite dans un langage mathématique précis – *it can be translated into a precise mathematical language*
78 | 1400

**1126 sang** *nm* blood
- il y a du sang dans vos cheveux – *there's blood in your hair*
71 | 1924

**1127 millier** *nm* thousand
- des milliers d'entre eux refusent de partir – *thousands of them are refusing to leave*
71 | 1873

**1128 emporter** *v* to take, remove
- il n'emporte rien avec lui, pas même une chemise – *he doesn't take anything with him, not even a shirt*
80 | 1258

## 7 Materials

| | | |
|---|---|---|
| **or** 300 M gold | **acier** 3306 M steel | **marbre** 5817 M marble |
| **argent** 472 M money | **carton** 3827 M cardboard | **ciment** 5940 M cement |
| **papier** 951 M paper | **béton** 4146 M concrete | **soie** 5997 F silk |
| **fer** 1621 M iron | **plomb** 4193 M lead | **brique** 6044 F brick |
| **pierre** 1767 F stone | **bijou** 4301 M jewel | **cuivre** 6201 M copper |
| **pétrole** 2157 M crude oil | **boue** 4507 F mud | **cristal** 6208 M crystal |
| **plastique** 2191 F plastic | **coton** 4516 M cotton | **aluminium** 6232 M aluminium |
| **huile** 2340 F oil | **diamant** 4706 M diamond | **perle** 6271 F perl |
| **tissu** 2696 M fabric | **textile** 4785 M textile | **ivoire** 6559 M ivory |
| **métal** 2793 M metal | **plutonium** 5285 M plutonium | **paille** 6564 F straw |
| **uranium** 2844 M uranium | | **radium** 8714 M radium |
| **charbon** 2935 M coal | **caoutchouc** 5784 M rubber | **granit** 9926 M granite |
| **matériau** 3205 M material | | |

**1129 initiative** *nf* initiative
- nombreuses furent les critiques contre ces initiatives – *numerous criticisms were leveled against these initiatives*
64 | 2461

**1130 nucléaire** *adj(f)* nuclear
- une attaque nucléaire? c'est une possibilité – *a nuclear attack? it's possible*
70 | 1980

**1131 industriel** *nadj* industrial
- les sociétés industrielles de ce temps mobilisent – *industrial societies of this time are mobilizing*
66 | 2296

**1132 vif** *nadj* lively
- les agents du mal étaient brûlés vifs – *the instigators of evil were burned alive*
79 | 1265

**1133 exact** *adj* exact, correct
- l'histoire est une science exacte – *history is an exact science*
84 | 968

**1134 exception** *nf* exception
- vous ne pouvez pas faire une exception? – *can't you make an exception?*
84 | 936

**1135 doubler** *v* to double, pass; to dub
- il essaie de nous doubler – *he's trying to drive past us*
90 | 589

**1136 février** *nm* February
- nous devons maintenant attendre jusqu'en février – *we must now wait until February*
65 | 2418+n

**1137 mode** *nm,nf* mode, way, fashion
- on a souvent critiqué le mode de recrute-ment des juges – *recruitment methods for judges are often criticized*
67 | 2204

**1138 tendre** *nadj(f),v* to tighten; to extend, stretch; tender
- il faut parler, tendre la main, dialoguer – *you have to speak, reach out, dialogue*
72 | 1833

**1139 musique** *nf* music
- la musique transforme les gens – *music transforms people*
67 | 2215

**1140 gestion** *nf* management
- et je fournis l'expérience de gestion – *and I have management experience*
63 | 2561-l

**1141 honneur** *nm* honor
- c'est un grand honneur de vous rencontrer – *it's a great honor to meet you*
68 | 2111

**1142 vaste** *adj(f)* vast, immense
- c'est très vaste comme sujet, mais c'est fascinant – *it's a huge subject, but it's fascinating*
82 | 1051

**1143 évoquer** *v* to recall, evoke
- on peut l'écouter des heures évoquer des souvenirs – *you could listen to her for hours evoking memories*
72 | 1800

**1144 fonctionner** *v* to function, work
- le processus fonctionne, et fonctionne bien – *the process works, and works well*
73 | 1748

**1145 étape** *nf* stage, step
- je vais procéder étape par étape – *I'm going to proceed step by step*
71 | 1850

**1146 physique** *nadj(f)* physical, physics
- j'aime aussi beaucoup l'activité physique – *I also really like physical activity*
76 | 1491

**1147 accuser** v to accuse
- de quoi nous accusez-vous? – *what are you accusing us of?*
69 | 2033

**1148 parfaitement** adv perfectly
- votre baladeur fonctionne parfaitement – *your Walkman works perfectly*
82 | 1043

**1149 méthode** nf method, procedure
- j'avais deviné la bonne méthode à suivre – *I guessed the right procedure to follow*
67 | 2207

**1150 professeur** nm,nf professor, teacher
- je serais professeur dans un lycée – *I would be a teacher in a high school*
74 | 1655

**1151 envers** nm(pl),prep towards
- nous respectons nos engagements envers les minorités – *we honor commitments to the minorities*
79 | 1256

**1152 distribuer** v to distribute, give out
- ces valeurs se distribuent selon une courbe en cloche – *these values are distributed along a bell curve*
89 | 647

**1153 existence** nf existence
- je menais une drôle d'existence – *I led a strange life*
74 | 1643

**1154 prétendre** v to pretend
- il prétend avoir un portable – *he claims to have a mobile phone*
78 | 1356

**1155 global** adj global
- l'opération peut être locale ou globale – *the operation can be local or global*
74 | 1653

**1156 dommage** nm damage, harm; too bad
- dommage que les choses aient mal tourné – *too bad things turned out as badly as they did*
86 | 806

**1157 crédit** nm credit
- le gouvernement socialiste voulait mettre le crédit au service de l'économie – *the socialist government wanted to make credit work for the economy*
64 | 2390

**1158 tendance** nf tendency, trend
- les entreprises creés ont tendance à grossir – *the enterprises that were created tend to grow bigger*
74 | 1599

**1159 chaîne** nf chain, channel
- la chaîne a programmé ce divertissement le mardi soir – *the channel scheduled this entertainment for Tuesday night*
72 | 1794

**1160 relatif** nadj relative
- tout est relatif dans la vie – *everything is relative in life*
64 | 2459

**1161 note** nf note, grade
- je prends des notes comme un fou – *I'm taking notes like crazy*
86 | 806

**1162 réserve** nf reserve
- toute ma réserve d'énergie va être gaspillée – *all of my spare energy is about to be wasted*
69 | 2007

**1163 maximum** nadj maximum
- je vais essayer de faire le maximum – *I will try to do my best*
84 | 926

**1164 moteur** nadj motor
- il avait éteint le moteur – *he had stopped the engine*
88 | 695

**1165 version** nf version
- vous avez entendu les deux versions de l'incident – *you have heard both versions of the incident*
81 | 1153

**1166 règlement** nm rule, regulation
- il existe déjà des règlements dans ce secteur – *there is already regulation in this sector*
54 | 3303+s

**1167 couple** nm,nf couple
- le couple qui prie ensemble reste ensemble – *the couple that prays together stays together*
84 | 922

**1168 mercredi** nm Wednesday
- je ne serai payée que mercredi – *I won't be paid until Wednesday*
51 | 3608-l +n -s

**1169 régional** nadj regional
- il existe toujours deux taux régionaux – *there have always been two regional rates*
68 | 2092

**1170 sinon** conj otherwise, or else
- mais n'anticipons pas, sinon nous n'arriverons jamais – *let's not get impatient or we'll never arrive there*
75 | 1552

**1171 entreprendre** v to begin, start, undertake
- la dame blanche entreprend de monter l'escalier – *the white lady undertook to climb the stairs*
82 | 1056

**1172 au-delà** adv,nmi beyond
- la réalité va au-delà des concepts – *reality surpasses concepts*
79 | 1255

**1173 étendre** v to spread out, stretch out
- je me suis étendue sur le sol de ma chambre – *I stretched out on the floor of my bedroom*
79 | 1264

**1174 sortie** nf exit
- il alla chercher Josette à la sortie du théâtre – *he went to look for Josette at the theatre exit*
72 | 1723

**1175 profond** *adv,nadj* deep
- le ciel était d'un bleu profond – *the sky was a dark blue*
76 | 1486

**1176 décrire** *v* to describe
- je n'aurais qu'à décrire ce que je voyais – *all I had to do was describe what I saw*
67 | 2168

**1177 etc** etc., et cetera
- j'ai dormi dans les gares, etc. – *I slept in train stations, etc.*
66 | 2229

**1178 récent** *adj* recent
- quel est votre regard sur les récents déboires? – *what is your opinion of the recent disappointments?*
77 | 1376

**1179 télévision** *nf* television
- elle t'a vu à la télévision – *she saw you on the television*
67 | 2127

**1180 retraite** *nf* retirement, pension
- c'était un rocker à la retraite – *he's a retired rock-n-roll artist*
69 | 1943

**1181 art** *nm* art
- j'ai perdu l'art de convaincre – *I lost the art of convincing*
74 | 1565

**1182 frontière** *nf* border
- il essaie d'atteindre la frontière – *he's trying to reach the border*
70 | 1899

**1183 égal** *nadj* equal
- tout le monde ne sera pas égal devant la loi – *everyone will not be equal before the law*
78 | 1337

**1184 promesse** *nf* promise
- pensez-vous qu'elle va tenir sa promesse? – *do you think she'll keep her promise?*
86 | 774

**1185 entretenir** *v* to maintain
- je n'ai jamais entretenu de relations amicales avec lui – *I never maintained amical relations with him*
82 | 1052

**1186 habiter** *v* to live
- j'ai habité dix ans la France – *I lived in France for ten years*
81 | 1072

**1187 quartier** *nm* district, quarter
- ils vivaient dans les quartiers les plus pauvres – *they lived in the poorest neighborhoods*
74 | 1587

**1188 avocat** *nm* lawyer
- j'étais avocat avant de venir ici – *I was a lawyer before coming here*
73 | 1647

**1189 accueillir** *v* to welcome, greet, accommodate
- on va vers les étrangers pour les accueillir – *we're going to greet the foreigners*
78 | 1285

**1190 libérer** *v* to free, liberate, release
- tous les prisonniers furent libérés sans condition – *all the prisoners were freed unconditionally*
76 | 1462

**1191 vivant** *nadj* alive, living
- si elle est vivante, je te la ramènerai – *if she's alive, I'll bring her back to you*
75 | 1542

**1192 université** *nf* university
- la grève se généralise dans les universités – *the strike is widening in the universities*
71 | 1770

**1193 rire** *nm,v* to laugh
- l'aventure nous fit beaucoup rire – *the adventure made us laugh heartily*
60 | 2664+l -n

**1194 facilement** *adv* easily
- j'ai retrouvé facilement le carton – *I easily located the cardboard box*
86 | 801

**1195 crainte** *nf* fear
- je n'ai absolument pas eu de crainte – *I had absolutely no fear*
85 | 831

**1196 commettre** *v* to commit
- vous avez commis presque tous les crimes informatiques – *you have committed almost every computer crime*
75 | 1495

**1197 précisément** *adv* precisely
- pouvez-vous nous parler plus précisément des personnes que vous suivez? – *can you tell us more precisely about the people you track?*
80 | 1126

**1198 soutien** *nm* support
- elle a manifestement bénéficié d'un large soutien – *she clearly enjoyed widespread support*
70 | 1893

**1199 urgence** *nf* emergency
- prépare-toi pour un atterrissage d'urgence – *prepare yourself for an emergency landing*
77 | 1343

**1200 clé** *nf* key
- je ne trouve pas ma clé – *I can't find my key*
85 | 856

**1201 enlever** *v* to remove
- pouvez-vous enlever votre chapeau? – *can you remove your hat?*
78 | 1251

**1202 jeter** *v* to throw
- c'est moi qui ai jeté le caillou – *I'm the one who threw the stone*
64 | 2304+l

**1203 religieux** *nadj(pl)* religious
- il a l'âme religieuse, pourtant – *still, he has a religious soul*
75 | 1447

**1204 analyse** *nf* analysis
- je ne veux pas faire d'analyse – *I don't want to do any analysis*
79 | 1209

**1205 disponible** *adj(f)* available
- j'utilise des outils disponibles sans restriction – *I use any available tools without restriction*
74 | 1571

**1206 regard** *nm* look, glance
- elle ne posera jamais un regard vers moi – *she will never turn her attention to me*
63 | 2377+l

**1207 prévenir** *v* to prevent, warn; to notify
- je suis à deux doigts de prévenir la police – *I'm within an inch of notifying the police*
81 | 1056

**1208 bientôt** *adv* soon
- bientôt, je vous connaîtrai mieux que vous-même – *soon I will know you better than you do*
72 | 1665

**1209 analyser** *v* to analyse
- il analyse aussi les échecs de la politique – *he also analyzes political failures*
77 | 1309

**1210 mariage** *nm* marriage
- le mariage devait avoir lieu à Paris – *the marriage should have taken place in Paris*
76 | 1414

**1211 couleur** *nf* color
- le vert était censé être la couleur préférée du Prophète – *green is supposed to be the favorite colour of the Prophet*
74 | 1509

**1212 témoigner** *v* to testify
- je pourrai en témoigner, au besoin, dit-elle – *I'll be able to testify of it, if necessary, she said*
82 | 973

**1213 sauver** *v* to rescue, save
- tu m'as sauvé la vie – *you saved my life*
72 | 1689

**1214 parlementaire** *nadj(f)* parliamentary; member of parliament
- les parlementaires ont été agacés par les réactions israéliennes – *the members of parliament were annoyed by the Israeli reactions*
54 | 3189-l +s

**1215 conclusion** *nf* conclusion
- la conclusion du rapporteur semble raisonnable – *the conclusion of the reporter seems reasonable*
75 | 1464

**1216 bleu** *adj,nm* blue
- le soleil a déchiré le voile bleu de la nuit – *the sun tore through the blue veil of the night*
73 | 1573

**1217 dehors** *adv,nm(pl),prep* outside
- dehors il fait froid – *it's cold outside*
73 | 1594

**1218 remercier** *v* to thank
- je vous remercie de m'avoir sauvé la vie – *thank you for saving my life*
68 | 1990-n +s

**1219 actif** *nadj* active
- l'Europe doit donc jouer un rôle actif – *Europe must therefore play an active role*
75 | 1423

**1220 réclamer** *v* to ask for, call for; to claim
- ils ont réclamé leur droit au sens critique – *they reserved the right to be critical*
74 | 1533

**1221 habitude** *nf* habit
- les gens fonctionnent beaucoup par habitude – *people operate a lot through habits*
79 | 1194

**1222 récemment** *adv* recently
- j'ai reçu récemment une lettre – *I recently received a letter*
74 | 1536

**1223 fil** *nm* thread, wire
- Joseph Glidden fait breveter le fil de fer barbelé – *Joseph Glidden is granted a patent for barbed wire*
82 | 964

**1224 collectif** *nadj* collective
- luttons pour nos buts collectifs . . . notre indépendance – *let's fight for our collective goals, our independance*
77 | 1322

**1225 excellent** *adj* excellent
- le café est excellent ici – *the coffee's excellent here*
78 | 1266+s

**1226 moral** *nadj* moral, morale
- ce dossier implique une question morale – *this affair involves an ethical question*
87 | 695

**1227 accident** *nm* accident
- elle est morte d'un accident – *she died from an accident*
75 | 1436

**1228 code** *nm* code
- composez votre code secret – *punch in your secret code*
63 | 2367

**1229 puissant** *nadj* powerful
- son effet est très puissant, ça calme et ça soigne – *its effect is very powerful, calming and soothing*
81 | 1071

**1230 recueillir** *v* to collect, gather
- il a été recueilli par des montagnards – *he was picked up by mountain dwellers*
80 | 1140

**1231 fabriquer** *v* to manufacture, invent, make
- mon métier consiste à fabriquer des livres – *my job involves manufacturing books*
85 | 817

**1232 représentant** *nm* representative
- nous rencontrerons les représentants de divers pays – *we will meet representatives from various countries*
70 | 1801

**1233 rare** *adj(f)* rare
- vous collectionnez les billets particulièrement rares – *you collect particularly rare
  bills*
  78 | 1257

**1234 extraordinaire** *adj(f)* extraordinary
- c'est un homme au talent extraordinaire
  – *he's a man with an extraordinary
  talent*
  83 | 940

**1235 dimanche** *nm* Sunday
- de fortes pluies sont annoncées pour
  dimanche – *heavy rains are forecast for
  Sunday*
  52 | 3265+n -s

**1236 vérifier** *v* to check, verify
- appelle ton contrôleur, vérifie – *call your
  inspector, double-check*
  77 | 1280

**1237 envie** *nf* envy
- elle n'avait envie de parler de rien – *she
  didn't want to talk about anything*
  63 | 2272-n

**1238 enregistrer** *v* to record, check in
- le fonds de l'assurance-emploi enregistre un
  surplus – *unemployment insurance funds
  have recorded a surplus*
  74 | 1518

**1239 moderne** *nadj(f)* modern
- on va utiliser un système plus moderne
  – *we're going to use a more modern
  system*
  77 | 1266

**1240 parc** *nm* park
- Disney va créer un parc à thèmes à Hong
  Kong – *Disney will create a theme park in
  Hong Kong*
  87 | 690

**1241 impôt** *nm* tax
- ils travaillent, ils payent des impôts – *they
  work, they pay taxes*
  54 | 3088-l +s

**1242 sud** *adji,nm* south
- va faire une tentative au pôle sud – *go try to
  reach the south pole*
  58 | 2672

**1243 efficace** *adj(f)* efficient, effective
- mon équipe est compacte et efficace – *my
  team is small and efficient*
  74 | 1454

**1244 intéressant** *adj* interesting
- moi, je vous trouve intéressante – *me, I find
  you interesting*
  71 | 1692+s

**1245 île** *nf* island
- c'est une île qui ne peut être trouvée – *it's
  an island that no one can find*
  75 | 1431

**1246 cité** *nf* city
- la cité était gouvernée par les poètes et les
  philosophes – *the city was ruled by poets
  and philosophers*
  80 | 1109

**1247 carrière** *nf* career
- je vous souhaite une longue carrière à ce
  poste – *I wish you a long career in this
  position*
  78 | 1210

**1248 voter** *v* to vote
- nous serions encore à voter ce soir – *we
  would still be here tonight voting*
  63 | 2260

**1249 traité** *nm* treaty
- il s'agit d'élaborer des traités internationaux
  – *it involves setting up international treaties*
  69 | 1824

**1250 libération** *nf* liberation
- nous exigeons la libération de nos camarades – *we demand the release of our
  comrades*
  63 | 2254

**1251 nourrir** *v* to feed, nourish
- l'inégalité nourrit l'injustice – *inequality
  feeds injustice*
  84 | 810

**1252 sérieusement** *adv* seriously
- il aurait mieux fait d'étudier sérieusement –
  *it would have been better for him to have
  studied seriously*
  87 | 679

**1253 bras** *nm(pl)* arm
- venez dans mes bras – *come to my arms*
  62 | 2315+l

**1254 immédiat** *nadj* immediate
- je n'ai plus de mémoire immédiate – *I have
  no more short-term memory*
  82 | 973

**1255 exceptionnel** *nadj* exceptional
- le plan d'action est exceptionnel – *the plan
  of attack is exceptional*
  86 | 726

**1256 rechercher** *v* to search for
- des dirigeants africains recherchent un
  solution à la crise – *African leaders are
  seeking a solution to the crisis*
  84 | 826

**1257 palestinien** *nm* Palestinian
  les mères palestiniennes veulent que leurs
  enfants grandissent dans la paix –
  *Palestinian mothers want their children to
  grow up in peace*
  50 | 3418-l +n

**1258 lendemain** *nm* next day
- je devais repartir le lendemain – *I had to
  leave the next day*
  73 | 1490

**1259 producteur** *nadj* producer
- les producteurs sont souvent aussi les
  consommateurs – *producers are also often
  consumers*
  73 | 1546

**1260 garantir** *v* to guarantee
- il faut garantir la sécurité du personnel
  – *we have to guarantee the safety of the
  staff*
  72 | 1586

**1261 geste** *nm* gesture
- je fais ces gestes tout en marchant – *I make these gestures while walking*
73 | 1497

**1262 roman** *adj,nm* novel
- j'avais lu des romans, en prose et en vers – *I had read novels, in prose and in verse*
58 | 2652

**1263 augmentation** *nf* increase, rise
- cela constitue une augmentation de 25 p. 100 – *this represents an increase of 25%*
66 | 1973

**1264 facteur** *nm* postman, mailman; factor
- le facteur apportait enfin de gros paquets – *the mailman finally brought large packages*
73 | 1485

**1265 policier** *nadj* policeman
- tous les policiers doivent se présenter à leur sergent – *all the policemen must present themselves to their sergeant*
67 | 1928

**1266 échelle** *nf* ladder, scale
- cette guerre peut être menée à grande échelle – *this war could be waged on a large scale*
80 | 1064

**1267 supplémentaire** *adj(f)* additional
- voilà un exemple supplémentaire – *here's an additional example*
68 | 1882

**1268 pratiquer** *v* to practice
- ils pratiquent vraiment le football que j'aime – *they play the kind of football that I really enjoy*
80 | 1037

**1269 pensée** *nf* thought
- il me poursuit dans mes pensées – *he chases me in my thoughts*
62 | 2304

**1270 extrême** *nadj(f)* extreme
- nous allons affronter un péril extrême – *we're going to face extreme peril*
79 | 1141

**1271 néanmoins** *adv,conj* nevertheless
- avez-vous néanmoins un code de discipline à respecter? – *still, don't you have a code of conduct to follow?*
80 | 1057

**1272 bénéficier** *nm,v* to benefit
- il devient donc impératif de pouvoir bénéficier de plus d'argent – *we must be able to benefit from more money*
72 | 1583

**1273 vingt** *det,nmi* twenty
- elle inventait dix, vingt, cent prétextes – *she dreamed up ten, twenty, a hundred excuses*
65 | 2019

**1274 revoir** *v* to see again, revise
- je disparaîtrai. tu ne me reverras jamais – *I will disappear. you will never see me again*
70 | 1715

**1275 perspective** *nf* perspective, viewpoint
- je me place dans la perspective de mes personnages – *I place myself in the perspective of my characters*
72 | 1579

**1276 défaut** *nm* fault, flaw, shortcoming
- on peut parler de mes défauts si tu veux – *we can talk about my shortcomings if you want*
82 | 924

**1277 précieux** *nadj(pl)* precious
- ta vie m'est aussi précieuse que celle de ma femme – *your life is as precious to me as my wife's*
88 | 582

**1278 retard** *nm* delay
- viens, on va être en retard – *come, we're going to be late*
77 | 1255

**1279 démocratie** *nf* democracy
- nous avons choisi la démocratie comme mode de vie – *we have chosen democracy for a way of life*
70 | 1681

**1280 renforcer** *v* to reinforce, strengthen
- j'œuvrerai pour renforcer nos forces armées – *I will work to reinforce our armed forces*
72 | 1535

**1281 silence** *nm* silence
- ils regardèrent en silence les arbres du petit jardin – *in silence they watched the trees in the little garden*
60 | 2402+I

**1282 troupe** *nf* troup, troop
- il faut remonter le moral des troupes – *the morale of the troops must be boosted again*
72 | 1572

**1283 qualifier** *v* to qualify
- on doit se qualifier pour le tournoi – *we have to qualify for the tournament*
70 | 1643

**1284 absolu** *nadj* absolute
- la mort est un fait absolu – *death is an absolute fact*
81 | 984

**1285 dégager** *v* to free, clear
- la route est dégagée ... mais il faut mettre vos chaînes – *the road is clear ... but you must use chains*
79 | 1099

**1286 stratégie** *nf* strategy
- nous espérons voir une stratégie intégrée – *we hope to see an integrated strategy*
70 | 1695

**1287 bateau** *nm* boat, ship
- un seul bateau de pêche a survécu à la tourmente – *only one fishing boat survived the tempest*
77 | 1196

**1288 printemps** *nm(pl)* spring
- c'est une splendide matinée de printemps – *it's a splendid spring morning*
84 | 787

**1289 course** *nf* race, shopping
- je viens faire des courses, alors je me suis arrêtée ici – *I came shopping, and then I stopped here*
79 | 1108

**1290 exercice** *nm* exercise,
- j'ai fait un exercice avec nos collègues de la presse – *I carried out an exercise with our colleagues in the press*
73 | 1460

**1291 fondamental** *adj* fundamental
je fais une distinction fondamentale – *I'm making a fundamental distinction*
71 | 1621

**1292 visage** *nm* face
- ils avaient de beaux visages tranquilles et las – *they had beautiful, peaceful, weary faces*
57 | 2618+l -n -s

**1293 droite** *nf* right
- elle tourna la tête à droite – *she turned her head to the right*
76 | 1247

**1294 machine** *nf* machine
- il faut arrêter la machine avant de la réparer – *you must stop the machine before repairing it*
77 | 1194

**1295 village** *nm* village
- des dizaines de villages ont été rayés de la carte – *tens of villages were wiped off the map*
72 | 1499

**1296 britannique** *nadj(f)* British
- nous nous inspirons de la tradition britannique – *we draw our inspiration from the British*
60 | 2353

**1297 surveiller** *v* to watch
- je vais te surveiller, je sais où tu habites – *I'm going to watch you, I know where you live*
83 | 826

**1298 édition** *nf* publishing, editing, edition
- c'est la fin de cette première édition d'informations – *that is the end of this early edition of the news*
73 | 1481

**1299 organisme** *nm* organism
- c'est un organisme qui est mi-figue mi-raisin – *it's an organism that's half fig and half grape*
67 | 1835

**1300 leçon** *nf* lesson
- je reçois ma leçon d'armes à six heures – *I get my weapons lesson at six o'clock*
85 | 741

**1301 accomplir** *v* to accomplish
- il vous faut continuer, accomplir votre destinée – *you have to continue, to acomplish your destiny*
80 | 1041

**1302 décevoir** *v* to disappoint
- désolé de t'avoir déçue – *sorry for having disappointed you*
88 | 601

**1303 bataille** *nf* battle
- on obéit à tes ordres et la bataille est gagnée – *we obey your orders and the battle is won*
82 | 911

**1304 port** *nm* harbour, port
- le dernier bateau quitte le port – *the last boat left the port*
80 | 1035

**1305 naissance** *nf* birth
- l'histoire commence avec la naissance d'un enfant étrange – *the story begins with the birth of a strange child*
81 | 974

**1306 majeur** *nadj* major
- c'est un enjeu économique majeur aujourd'hui – *it's a major economic challenge today*
77 | 1178

**1307 froid** *nadj* cold
- dehors il fait froid – *it's cold outside*
72 | 1471

**1308 hôpital** *nm* hospital
- le garçon est mort à l'hôpital – *the boy died at the hospital*
73 | 1413

**1309 circuit** *nm* circuit
- ce circuit doit être libéré selon la procédure normale – *this circuit must be discharged according to the normal procedure*
44 | 3791-l +n -s

**1310 terrible** *adj(f)* terrible, dreadful
- c'était terrible! la situation était terrible – *it was terrible! the situation was horrible*
80 | 997

**1311 degré** *nm* degree
- il n'y a pas de degrés dans la sainteté – *there are no degrees of holiness*
78 | 1147

**1312 exigence** *nf* demand, strictness
- c'est une exigence impossible à respecter – *it's a requirement impossible to meet*
80 | 993

**1313 rêve** *nm* dream
- on attend maintenant que nos rêves se réalisent – *now we're waiting for the fulfillment of our dreams*
70 | 1647

**1314 inspirer** *v* to inspire
- considérons que les livres ont inspiré le tueur – *let's assume that the books inspired the killer*
78 | 1101

**1315 opérer** *v* to operate, carry out
- les grandes sociétés opèrent à l'échelle mondiale – *large companies operate on a global scale*
83 | 830

**1316 entièrement** *adv* entirely, completely
- je suis entièrement d'accord avec vous – *I completely agree with you*
81 | 973

# 8 Time

## General terms:
**temps** 65 M time
**période** 407 F period
**date** 660 F date
**étape** 1145 F stage
**quotidien** 1318 M daily
**durée** 1464 F duration
**fête** 1490 F holiday
**délai** 1522 M delay
**phase** 1754 F phase
**anniversaire** 2043 F
  birthday
**enfance** 2207 F childhood
**congé** 2445 M day off
**week-end** 2475 M weekend
**loisir** 2772 M leisure
**calendrier** 2947 M calendar
**horaire** 3192 M timetable
**intervalle** 3226 M interval
**vieillesse** 4813 F old age

## Units of time (small to large):
**seconde** 1542 F second
**instant** 769 M instant
**moment** 148 M moment
**minute** 375 F minute
**demi-heure** 3338 F half an
  hour
**heure** 99 F hour
**jour** 78 M day
**semaine** 245 F week
**mois** 178 M month
**an** 76 M year

**année** 102 F year
**décennie** 2361 F decade
**vie** 132 F life
**siècle** 603 M century
**époque** 465 F era
**ère** 3079 F era

## Parts of day (morning to night):
**aube** 2728 F dawn
**matin** 442 M morning
**matinée** 3029 F morning
**journée** 587 F day
**midi** 2483 M noon
**après-midi** 1324 M
  afternoon
**soir** 397 M evening
**soirée** 1530 F evening
**veille** 1840 F eve of
**nuit** 580 F night
**minuit** 3453 M midnight
**lendemain** 1258 M next
  day

## Relative time:
**histoire** 263 F history
**passé** 501 M past
**présent** 216 M present
**immédiat** 1254 M
  immediate
**aujourd'hui** 233 M
  today
**demain** 871 M tomorrow
**futur** 484 M future
**avenir** 471 M future

## Seasons:
**printemps** 1288 M
  springtime
**été** 623 M summer
**automne** 1503 M autumn
**hiver** 1586 M winter
**saison** 1667 F season

## Months:
**janvier** 939 M January
**février** 1136 M February
**mars** 868 M March
**avril** 1022 M April
**mai** 943 M May
**juin** 931 M June
**juillet** 1326 M July
**août** 1445 M August
**septembre** 944 M
  September
**octobre** 826 M October
**novembre** 982 M November
**décembre** 891 M December

## Days of week:
**lundi** 1091 M Monday
**mardi** 1044 M Tuesday
**mercredi** 1168 M
  Wednesday
**jeudi** 1112 M Thursday
**vendredi** 1086 M Friday
**samedi** 1355 M Saturday
**dimanche** 1235 M Sunday

---

**1317 chapitre** nm chapter
• il reste un chapitre à écrire – *one chapter remains to be written*
75 | 1310

**1318 quotidien** nadj daily
• elles apportent conseils dans les travaux ménagers quotidiens – *they provide advice through their daily household chores*
65 | 1929

**1319 clairement** adv clearly
• le rapport de force est clairement déséquilibré – *the threat assessment is clearly skewed*
70 | 1620

**1320 joindre** v to join
• je serais très heureux si vous vous joigniez à moi pour dîner – *I would be delighted if you would join me for supper*
80 | 974

**1321 léger** adj light
• d'un pas léger elle sortit de la bibliothèque – *with airy steps she left the library*
75 | 1329

**1322 permanent** adj permanent
• ils vivent dans le climat permanent de la violence – *they live in a permanent setting of violence*
67 | 1792

**1323 juge** *nm,nf* judge
- il reviendra alors au juge de décider – *so it will be up to the judge to decide*
64 | 2031

**1324 après-midi** *nmi* afternoon
- j'ai passé l'après-midi avec des amis – *I spent the afternoon with friends*
67 | 1791

**1325 russe** *nadj(f)* Russian
- la Turquie est une destination privilégiée des touristes russes – *Turkey is a privileged destination for Russian tourists*
60 | 2309+n -s

**1326 juillet** *nm* July
- la réunion s'ouvrit le 17 juillet – *the meeting began on July 17th*
65 | 1960

**1327 ordinaire** *nadj(f)* ordinary
- je suis un type ordinaire, un vrai type normal – *I'm an ordinary guy, a really normal guy*
83 | 811

**1328 candidat** *nm* candidate
- nous avons un candidat que nous soutenons – *we have a candidate who we support*
66 | 1892

**1329 rapprocher** *v* to bring closer, get closer
- j'ai voulu me rapprocher de toi – *I wanted to get closer to you*
84 | 752

**1330 résistance** *nf* resistance
- sa résistance à la sonde mentale est considérable – *his resistance to the mental probe is significant*
74 | 1342

**1331 fier** *adj,v* to rely on; proud
- je suis très fière de mon héritage – *I'm very proud of my heritage*
73 | 1422-n

**1332 justement** *adv* exactly, rightly, precisely
- j'étais justement en train de faire du thé – *I was just making some tea*
70 | 1631-n +s

**1333 habitant** *nm* inhabitant
- les 200.000 habitants ont fui – *the 200,000 inhabitants fled*
69 | 1698

**1334 formule** *nf* formula, expression
- je garderai toujours cette formule – *I will always remember this expression*
80 | 972

**1335 mur** *nm* wall
- il frappe le mur avec son doigt replié – *he knocked on the wall with his knuckle*
67 | 1768+l

**1336 tribunal** *nm* court
- les tribunaux jouent un rôle essentiel – *the courts play an essential role*
63 | 2108

**1337 journaliste** *nm,nf* journalist
- ce journaliste a la double nationalité française et américaine – *this journalist has dual French and American nationality*
64 | 2021

**1338 manger** *nm,v* to eat
- avec votre maladie, vous pouvez manger de la viande? – *with your illness, can you eat meat?*
63 | 2085-n

**1339 soulever** *v* to lift up
- il sourit, tandis que le vent soulevait ses cheveux – *he smiled, the wind tossing his hair*
69 | 1687

**1340 évidemment** *adv* obviously
- en tout cas, évidemment, elles vous connaissent – *in any case, they obviously know you*
70 | 1562

**1341 travailleur** *nadj* worker
- il y avait huit travailleurs pour un retraité – *there were eight workers per retired person*
61 | 2205+s

**1342 résolution** *nf* resolution
- il est important que nous adoptions cette résolution – *it's important that we adopt this resolution*
63 | 2023

**1343 dirigeant** *nadj* leader
- qu'est-il advenu des dirigeants militaires? – *what ever happened to the military leaders?*
63 | 2075

**1344 marque** *nf* brand, mark
- il y a des marques sur les portes – *there are marks on the doors*
83 | 792

**1345 utilisation** *nf* use
- je ne veux pas que l'utilisation des phtalates soit bannie – *I don't want the use of phthalates to be banned*
66 | 1860

**1346 offre** *nf* offer
- il n'y avait aucune offre d'emploi – *there weren't any job offers*
81 | 924

**1347 habituel** *adj* customary, habitual
- ils font leur routine habituelle – *they do their daily routine*
89 | 485

**1348 survivre** *v* to survive
- il ne sait que faire pour survivre – *he doesn't know what to do to survive*
85 | 705

**1349 populaire** *nadj(f)* popular
- j'ignorais que vous étiez si populaire! – *I didn't know you were so popular*
70 | 1573

**1350 constitution** *nf* constitution
- premièrement, nous devons respecter la constitution – *first, we must respect the constitution*
72 | 1431

**1351 participation** *nf* participation
- comment qualifieriez-vous votre participation? – *how would you characterize your participation?*
69 | 1600

**1352 évolution** *nf* evolution
- la rapidité de cette évolution n'est pas surprenante – *the swiftness of this evolution is not surprising*
66 | 1810

**1353 totalement** *adv* totally
- les tribunaux russes sont totalement engorgés – *the Russian court system is totally swamped*
77 | 1162

**1354 gérer** *v* to manage
- nous savons comment gérer l'éducation – *we know how to manage education*
74 | 1307

**1355 samedi** *nm* Saturday
- elle organisera une fête samedi – *she will organize a party on Sunday*
50 | 3090+n -s

**1356 informer** *v* to inform
- je t'informerai dès qu'ils l'auront repéré – *I'll inform you as soon as they locate him*
73 | 1404

**1357 fou** *adj,nm* mad, crazy
- tu es complètement fou – *you are completely crazy*
66 | 1814

**1358 attacher** *v* to attach
- attachez vos ceintures. le spectacle commence – *fasten your sealtbelts. the show is about to begin*
80 | 972

**1359 renouveler** *v* to renew
- nos synapses ne se renouvellent plus passé 20 ans – *our synapses don't regenerate after the age of 20 years*
88 | 556

**1360 asseoir** *v* to sit
- il était assis devant moi – *he was seated in front of me*
59 | 2346+l -n

**1361 oh** *intj* oh
- au secours! oh non! – *help! oh no!*
54 | 2666-n +s

**1362 transfert** *nm* transfer
- le transfert aura lieu sous deux semaines – *the transfer will take place in two weeks*
61 | 2159

**1363 renoncer** *v* to give up, renounce
- elle avait renoncé à me convaincre – *she gave up trying to convince me*
78 | 1085

**1364 roi** *nm* king
- une nuit, le roi lui apparut en rêve – *one night, the king appeared to him in a dream*
68 | 1702

**1365 soi** *nmi,pro* one, oneself, self
- il s'agissait enfin d'être soi, rien que soi – *in the end it was all about being oneself, nothing but oneself*
67 | 1726

**1366 téléphone** *nm* telephone
- les téléphones ne marchent pas – *the telephones don't work*
75 | 1241

**1367 net** *adj,nm* clear; Internet
- les Canadiens veulent des réponses bien nettes – *the Canadians want very clear answers*
75 | 1272

**1368 foi** *nf* faith
- tu as la foi . . . nous avons tous besoin de foi – *you have faith . . . we all need faith*
76 | 1172

**1369 motif** *nm* motive, purpose
- je ne voyais aucun motif de refus – *I didn't see any reason for refusal*
83 | 808

**1370 plaindre** *v* to pity, feel sorry for, complain
- elle ne se plaignait pas; mais elle détestait faire le ménage – *she didn't complain, but she detested housework*
85 | 716

**1371 tradition** *nf* tradition
- il faut s'enraciner dans ses traditions – *you have to be rooted in your traditions*
78 | 1050

**1372 institut** *nm* institute
- à l'institut, j'ai été formée à l'orthophonie – *at the institute I majored in speech therapy*
75 | 1236

**1373 victoire** *nf* victory
- beau match. enfin, une victoire – *nice game. finally, a victory*
66 | 1786

**1374 arrêt** *nm* stop
- l'arrêt cardiaque est un état de mort apparente – *a heart attack is a state of apparent death*
76 | 1176

**1375 concours** *nm(pl)* entrance exam, competition
- vous avez gagné le concours? – *did you win the competition?*
86 | 627

**1376 vis-à-vis** *nmpl,prep* face to face, regarding
- il reprenait sa liberté vis-à-vis de moi – *he regained his freedom from me*
82 | 869

**1377 aboutir** *v* to succeed, end up at
- ce projet n'a pourtant pas abouti – *this project didn't end, however*
80 | 962

**1378 visiter** *v* to visit
- nous allons visiter la maison – *we're going to visit the house*
85 | 690

**1379 elle-même** *pro* herself, itself
- la révolte n'est pas en elle-même un élément de civilisation – *rebellion is not by itself an element of civilization*
71 | 1444

**1380 démocratique** *adj(f)* democratic
- il ne respecte pas le processus démocratique – *he doesn't respect the democratic process*
67 | 1708

**1381 tentative** *nf* attempt
- à la troisième tentative, l'homme part le premier – *on the third attempt, the man left first*
75 | 1253

**1382 largement** *adv* widely
- on doit payer largement sa part d'impôt – *you should pay the bulk of your taxes*
77 | 1129

**1383 échouer** *v* to fail
- tout ce que j'ai tenté a échoué – *everything that I tried to do failed*
87 | 579

**1384 désirer** *v* to desire
- ce que l'on désire, c'est éviter une surpollution – *what we want is to avoid rampant pollution*
75 | 1238

**1385 côte** *nf* coast
- on est basés sur la côte ouest – *we're based on the west coast*
76 | 1140

**1386 génération** *nf* generation
- une nouvelle génération prend le pouvoir – *a new generation takes over*
74 | 1304

**1387 vent** *nm* wind
- dans la rue il faisait du vent – *it was windy in the street*
70 | 1545

**1388 technologie** *nf* technology
- en Chine, on utilise cette technologie depuis plus de 20 ans – *in China this technology has been used for over 20 years*
69 | 1577-l

**1389 inquiéter** *v* to worry, disturb
- et ça, ça m'inquiète un petit peu – *and this, this disturbs me a little bit*
73 | 1334

**1390 dépit** *nm* spite, heartache
- j'ai ressenti un soulagement mêlé de dépit – *I felt relief mixed with spite*
81 | 897

**1391 équilibre** *nm* balance, equilibrium
- j'aperçois une sorte d'équilibre qui peut durer longtemps – *I sense a kind of equilibrium that may endure*
77 | 1124

**1392 inquiet** *nadj* worried, anxious
- tu as l'air inquiet – *you seem anxious*
84 | 721

**1393 obstacle** *nm* obstacle
- j'ai surmonté tous les obstacles – *I overcame all the obstacles*
85 | 699

**1394 réflexion** *nf* reflection
- elle le surprend en pleine réflexion – *she surprised him as he was deep in thought*
74 | 1248

**1395 uniquement** *adv* only
- il a survécu uniquement avec la diète anticancéreuse – *he only survived via the anti-cancer diet*
77 | 1117

**1396 affecter** *v* to affect
- elles n'ont pas été affectées par l'accident – *they weren't affected by the accident*
75 | 1186

**1397 revanche** *nf* revenge; return
- elle, en revanche, m'inspecta avec désinvolture – *she, in return, inspected me with detachment*
70 | 1529

**1398 ressembler** *v* to look like, resemble
- celle-là ressemble à une intellectuel new-yorkaise – *that one looks like she's a New York intellectual*
71 | 1452

**1399 station** *nf* station
- il a traîné dans la station toute la journée – *he lingered in the station all day*
58 | 2343

**1400 supporter** *nm,v* to support, endure
- des fois, je ne supporte pas la vie quotidienne – *sometimes I can't stand daily life*
79 | 1006

**1401 privé** *nadj* private
- c'est une fête privée ... vous ne pouvez pas venir – *it's a private party ... you can't come*
69 | 1562

**1402 catégorie** *nf* category
- les autres catégories de l'entreprise sont concernées par cette démarche – *the other kinds of companies are worried about this process*
74 | 1264

**1403 mine** *nf* mine; appearance, look, mien
- je haussai les épaules et fis mine de rire – *I shrugged my shoulders and feigned laughing*
84 | 726

**1404 législatif** *nadj* legislative
- en 1978, la gauche échoue aux législatives – *in 1978, the left lost in the legislative elections*
59 | 2211-l +s

**1405 ah** *intj* ah, oh
- ah oui? tu commences à m'intéresser – *oh yeah? you're starting to interest me*
57 | 2404-n +s

**1406 propriétaire** *nm,nf* owner
- vous êtes le propriétaire des lieux? – *you're the owner of this property?*
83 | 758

**1407 favoriser** *v* to favor
- cela favorise le commerce et l'investisse-ment – *this favors trade and investment*
75 | 1176

**1408 priorité** *nf* priority
- il faut maintenant donner la priorité aux enfants – *now we must give priority to the children*
70 | 1489

**1409 avion** *nm* plane
- en voiture, en avion, j'aime le mouvement – *in a car, in an airplane, I like motion*
67 | 1704

**1410 minimum** *nadj* minimum
- nos fabricants exigent un délai minimum de 6 semaines – *our manufacturers require at least 6 weeks'notice*
81 | 886

**1411 criminel** *nadj* criminal
- l'incendie peut être d'origine criminelle – *the fire might have a criminal origin*
65 | 1782

**1412 photo** *nf* photo
- je peux voir la photo? – *can I see the photo?*
71 | 1433

**1413 précéder** *v* to precede
- la métaphysique ne doit pas précéder la physique, elle doit la suivre – *metaphysics shouldn't precede physics, it should follow it*
86 | 606

**1414 solide** *nadj(f)* solid
- nous avons une base solide sur laquelle bâtir – *we have a solid foundation on which to build*
82 | 798

**1415 correspondre** *v* to correspond
- j'espère que nous correspondrons – *I hope we'll keep in touch*
68 | 1611

**1416 navire** *nm* ship
- je suis comme le capitaine d'un navire – *I'm like the captain of a ship*
80 | 929

**1417 centaine** *nf* hundred
- la pétition est signée par plusieurs centaines de résidents – *the petition was signed by hundreds of residents*
68 | 1590

**1418 explication** *nf* explanation
- il doit y avoir une explication rationnelle – *there must be a rational explanation*
80 | 900

**1419 transmettre** *v* to forward, transmit
- voilà comment se transmettre les maladies! – *that's how to transmit illnesses!*
65 | 1762

**1420 appareil** *nm* apparatus, device
- place la bobine vierge sur l'appareil – *place the empty reel on the machine*
71 | 1437

**1421 publication** *nf* publication
- vous pouvez parler de vos publications? – *can you talk about your publications?*
81 | 871

**1422 associer** *v* to associate
- le tabagisme n'était pas directement associé au cancer – *smoking was not directly associated with cancer*
70 | 1485

**1423 trait** *nm* line, feature
- mon trait est très fin, comme des cheveux – *I have very fine features, like hair*
72 | 1376

**1424 référence** *nf* reference
- je n'ai pas compris sa référence aux oiseaux – *I didn't understand his reference to the birds*
65 | 1754

**1425 bois** *nm(pl)* wood
- tu attendras dans les bois que la nuit tombe – *you will wait in the woods until nightfall*
72 | 1365

**1426 identifier** *v* to identify
- pouvez-vous identifier cet homme? – *can you identify this man?*
73 | 1274

**1427 symbole** *nm* symbol
- je peux déchiffrer les symboles – *I can decipher the symbols*
86 | 587

**1428 consommation** *nf* consumption
- cela aura un impact sur la consommation – *this will have an impact on consumption*
75 | 1155

**1429 idéal** *nadj* ideal
- j'ai eu une enfance idéale – *I had an ideal childhood*
84 | 702

**1430 chômage** *nm* unemployment
- le chômage chez les jeunes est devenu un grave problème – *unemployment among the youth has become a serious problem*
64 | 1856

**1431 courage** *nm* courage
- j'en ai pas le courage. je suis fatiguée – *I don't have the courage. I'm tired*
79 | 941

**1432 reconnaissance** *nf* recognition, gratitude
- les fêtes musulmanes n'avaient aucune reconnaissance officielle – *Moslem holidays weren't officially recognized at all*
74 | 1217

**1433 entretien** *nm* interview, discussion, maintenance
- je devais réaliser un entretien pour un mensuel – *I had to conduct an interview for a monthly magazine*
66 | 1672

**1434 encourager** *v* to encourage
- allez, encouragez notre petit gars – *go encourage our little guy*
75 | 1188

**1435 kilomètre** *nm* kilometer
- j'ai un jardin à vingt-cinq kilomètres de Paris – *I have a garden 25 kilometers from Paris*
64 | 1845

**1436 dérouler** *v* to unwind, enroll
- la cérémonie aurait dû se dérouler la veille – *the ceremony should have taken place the night before*
75 | 1155

**1437 identité** *nf* identity
- donnez-moi d'abord votre carte d'identité – *first give me your identification card*
75 | 1151

**1438 amendement** *nm* amendment
- la Commission a accepté une partie des amendements – *the commission accepted some of the amendments*
47 | 3107-l -n +s

**1439 signaler** *v* to indicate, signal
- il a signalé que la mission avait joué un rôle important – *he pointed out that the mission played an important role*
71 | 1361

**1440 division** *nf* division
- l'Irak disposait de trois divisions près de la frontière – *Iraq had three divisions close to the border*
78 | 1014

**1441 contexte** *nm* context
- comment tenez-vous compte du contexte social en thérapie? – *how do you account for the social context in therapy?*
68 | 1535

**1442 coupable** *nadj(f)* guilty
- aujourd'hui, tout le monde est coupable – *these days, everybody is guilty*
80 | 920

**1443 favorable** *adj(f)* favorable
- l'évolution a été particulièrement favorable – *the evolution was particularly favorable*
74 | 1217

**1444 obligation** *nf* obligation, bond
- nous avons une obligation morale de redresser les torts du passé – *we have a moral obligation to right the wrongs of the past*
69 | 1523

**1445 août** *nm* August
- je suis né en août – *I was born in August*
65 | 1752+n -s

**1446 attribuer** *v* to award, grant, attribute
- son mari attribuait cette apathie à sa naissance – *her husband attributed this apathy to her birth*
77 | 1069

**1447 courir** *v* to run
- je courus le long des docks – *I ran along the docks*
69 | 1509

**1448 examen** *nm* exam
- on commence par faire un examen clinique – *we'll start by doing a clinical exam*
68 | 1547

**1449 personnage** *nm* character, individual
- les personnages de mes romans me jouent des tours – *the characters in my novels play tricks on me*
61 | 1995

**1450 dénoncer** *v* to denounce
- il s'attacha à dénoncer les abus et la corruption – *he took up the cause of denouncing abuse and corruption*
72 | 1285

**1451 inconnu** *nadj* unknown
- je me réveille dans des endroits inconnus – *I wake up in unknown places*
81 | 849

**1452 échanger** *v* to exchange
- les rebelles échangeront leurs prisonniers – *the rebels will exchange their prisoners*
82 | 800

**1453 montant** *nadj* upright, upwards, sum, total
- on ignore le montant de ce contrat – *we don't know the total amount of this contract*
67 | 1622

**1454 éliminer** *v* to eliminate
- nous sommes aussi parvenus à éliminer le déficit – *we have also achieved elimination of the deficit*
76 | 1095

**1455 ouverture** *nf* opening
- chaque ouverture de magasin crée une vingtaine d'emplois – *every store we open creates about twenty jobs*
69 | 1501

**1456 tableau** *nm* frame, picture, painting, panel
- allez vérifier le tableau d'alerte – *go check the alarm panel*
58 | 2176+n -s

**1457 exclure** *v* to exclude
- le projet de loi exclut ce type de mode de vie – *the bill excludes this type of lifestyle*
79 | 940

**1458 meurtre** *nm* murder
- vous êtes accusé de meurtre! – *you are accused of murder!*
77 | 1023

**1459 exemplaire** *nadj(f)* exemplary; copy
- j'en ai déjà vendu 100.000 exemplaires – *I already sold 100,000 copies of it*
88 | 511

**1460 propriété** *nf* property
- vous êtes sur ma propriété – *you're on my property*
78 | 987

**1461 final** *nadj* final
- je me souviens de la séance finale – *I remember the final showing*
70 | 1436

**1462 site** *nm* site
- combien de sites Internet avez-vous? – *how many websites do you have?*
65 | 1677

**1463 séance** *nf* session, meeting
- elle se souvient d'une séance particulièrement pénible – *she remembers a particularly painful session*
70 | 1418

**1464 durée** *nf* length, duration
- il faudrait alors augmenter la durée du travail – *then we would need to lengthen the work timeframe*
68 | 1543

**1465 élire** *v* to elect
- les chefs sont élus pour représenter leur peuple – *the chiefs are elected to represent their people*
69 | 1465

**1466 baisse** *nf* fall, drop
- il devrait y avoir une baisse d'autres impôts – *there should be a drop in the other taxes*
61 | 1939+n

**1467 inquiétude** *nf* worry, anxiety
- j'entretenais de sérieuses inquiétudes à ce sujet – *I harbored serious anxiety on the project*
79 | 943

**1468 israélien** *nadj* Israeli
- le camp de la paix israélien se divise en deux – *the Israeli peace coalition has split in two*
49 | 2834-l +n

**1469 représentation** *nf* representation
- votre souci est la représentation des femmes – *your concern is for the representation of women*
78 | 968

**1470 pareil** *nadj* similar, likewise; peer, equal
- c'est toujours pareil – *it's always the same*
71 | 1326

**1471 mandat** *nm* term, mandate
- sa présence à un second mandat est inévitable – *his presence in a second term is inevitable*
71 | 1369

**1472 quinze** *det,nmi* fifteen
- David s'arrêta devant une tour de quinze étages – *David stopped in front of a fifteen-story tower*
70 | 1419

**1473 vide** *nadj(f)* empty
- je regrette, le frigo est vide – *I'm sorry, the fridge is empty*
70 | 1376

**1474 statut** *nm* status
- le jeune reste sous statut scolaire – *the young man remains in student status*
75 | 1147

**1475 essai** *nm* attempt, try, test
- ça demanderait un essai et je ne suis pas une spécialiste – *that would require an essay and I'm not a specialist*
54 | 2462+n -s

**1476 sourire** *nm,v* smile, to smile
- alors, pourquoi tu souris? – *so why are you smiling?*
56 | 2274+l -n -s

**1477 italien** *nadj* Italian
- c'est un génie particulier aux italiens – *it's a type of genius that only Italians have*
69 | 1474

**1478 suggérer** *v* to suggest
- je voudrais suggérer de changer les horaires de travail – *I would like to suggest a change in the working hours*
80 | 861

**1479 interrompre** *v* to interrupt
- je n'aime pas qu'on m'interrompe – *I don't like being interrupted*
80 | 875

**1480 au-dessus** *adv* above
- les avocats ne sont pas au-dessus des lois – *lawyers are not above the law*
63 | 1789-s

**1481 agence** *nf* agency
- il a décidé de créer une agence – *he decided to create an agency*
65 | 1712

**1482 usine** *nf* factory
- je rouvre une usine aux États-Unis – *I'm reopening a factory in the U.S.*
76 | 1058

**1483 unir** *v* to unite
- le mariage devrait unir un homme et une femme – *marriage should unite one man and one woman*
76 | 1080

**1484 rang** *nm* rank, row
- nous sommes assis au premier rang – *we sat on the first row*
79 | 915

**1485 employé** *nm* employee
- les patrons veulent des employés qualifiés – *bosses want qualified employees*
68 | 1529+s

**1486 sommet** *nm* summit
- le sommet extraordinaire de Bruxelles n'était pas une fête – *the special summit at Brussels was no picnic*
62 | 1835

**1487 franchir** *v* to get over
- les Huns ont franchi notre frontière nord – *the Huns broke through our northern border*
82 | 778

**1488 évident** *adj* obvious
- ce n'était pas évident pour nous au début – *it wasn't obvious to us at first*
73 | 1215

**1489 comportement** *nm* behavior
- leur comportement agressif et violent ne change pas – *their aggressive and violent behavior is not changing*
73 | 1199

**1490 fête** *nf* holiday, celebration
- c'est une fête privée – *it's a private party*
74 | 1174

**1491 sol** *nm* floor, ground
- nous dormions sur le sol en béton – *we were sleeping on the cement-covered ground*
75 | 1124

**1492 écarter** *v* to separate, move apart, keep away
- les journalistes ont été écartés de l'intérieur du bâtiment – *the reporters were kept away from the building's interior*
80 | 869

**1493 vague** *nadj(f),nf* vague; wave
- ces vagues sont tellement puissantes! – *these waves are so powerful!*
77 | 993

**1494 réduction** *nf* reduction
- il parle aussi des réductions d'impôt – *he's also talking about tax reductions*
62 | 1848

## 9 Sports

| | | |
|---|---|---|
| **jeu** 291 M game | **championnat** 2980 M championship | **plongée** 7479 F diving |
| **but** 441 M goal | **tournoi** 3582 M tournament | **base-ball** 7727 M baseball |
| **lutte** 759 F wrestling | **ballon** 3692 M ball | **marathon** 7736 M marathon |
| **équipe** 814 F team | **saut** 3841 M jump | **athlétisme** 7876 M track and field |
| **course** 1289 F race | **tennis** 3867 M tennis | **coéquipier** 7898 M teammate |
| **exercice** 1290 M exercise | **gagnant** 3886 M winner | **gymnase** 8519 M gymnasium |
| **pêche** 1790 F fishing | **perdant** 4395 M loser | **coach** 8539 M coach |
| **stade** 1967 M stadium (also stage) | **ski** 4571 M ski | **boxe** 8624 F boxing |
| **joueur** 2003 M player | **boule** 4789 F bowling | **footballeur** 8886 M soccer player |
| **sport** 2011 M sport | **golf** 4936 M golf | **slalom** 9528 M slalom |
| **chasse** 2115 F hunting | **piscine** 5510 F pool | **ring** 9572 M boxing ring |
| **champion** 2443 M champion | **hockey** 6048 M hockey | **natation** 9731 F swimming |
| **football** 2602 M soccer | **foot** 6577 M soccer | **patin** 9979 M skate |
| **chasseur** 2879 M hunter | **rugby** 6944 M rugby | |
| | **basket** 7026 M basketball | |

**1495 culturel** *adj* cultural
• la vie culturelle est appauvrie, terne et stagnante – *cultural life is impoverished, dull, and stagnant*
66 | 1592

**1496 coopération** *nf* cooperation
• nous ne bénéficions pas toujours d'une coopération sérieuse de leur part – *we don't always enjoy serious cooperation on their behalf*
64 | 1751

**1497 vertu** *nf* virtue
• la vertu et le vice, tout se confond – *virtue and vice, everything's getting mixed up*
67 | 1557

**1498 d'autant** since
• il lui est d'autant plus facile d'en acquérir d'autres – *it's so much easier for him to buy other ones*
75 | 1120-s

**1499 leader** *nm,nf* leader
• il est très difficile d'être un leader autochtone – *it's difficult to be a native leader*
58 | 2095-l +s

**1500 taille** *nf* size, height
• je l'ai interrogée sur sa taille, sur son âge – *I asked her about her height, her age*
78 | 950

**1501 contenu** *nadj* contents
• il faut réviser la réglementation quant au contenu francophone – *we must revise the regulation of French-speaking content*
75 | 1117

**1502 distance** *nf* distance
• la distance entre les villes est énorme – *the distance between cities is enormous*
76 | 1047

**1503 automne** *nm* fall, autumn
• on dirait un après-midi d'automne – *it felt like an autumn afternoon*
84 | 645

**1504 arrière** *adji,adv,nm* back, rear
• mets tes cheveux en arrière – *put your hair back*
69 | 1407

**1505 vision** *nf* vision, view
• nous avons sur ce sujet une vision commune – *we have a common view on this subject*
71 | 1308

**1506 investir** *v* to invest
• il veut y investir encore plus d'argent – *he wants to invest even more money in it*
69 | 1411

**1507 diminuer** *v* to diminish, decrease
• les investissements en provenance de l'extérieur diminuent – *investments from abroad are decreasing*
73 | 1187

**1508 réfugier** *v* to take refuge
• je m'étais réfugié dans une espèce d'esprit farceur – *I sought refuge in a farcical mindset*
71 | 1318

**1509 entourer** *v*  to surround
- il courut à lui et l'entoura de ses bras – *he ran up to him and held him in his arms*
81 | 805

**1510 juif** *nadj*  Jew, Jewish
- la société se retourne contre les juifs – *society has turned against the Jews*
73 | 1181

**1511 considérable** *adj(f)*  considerable, significant
- nous avons réalisé des progrès considérables – *we achieved considerable progess*
81 | 790

**1512 conduite** *nf*  behavior, driving
- certaines de mes conduites affectaient directement ma mère – *some of my behavior directly affected my mother*
80 | 835

**1513 convention** *nf*  agreement, convention
- la convention relative aux droits de l'enfant – *the convention on children's rights*
71 | 1321

**1514 communiquer** *v*  to communicate
- mes fonctionnaires ont communiqué avec le ministère des finances – *my public servants communicated with the finance minister*
76 | 1031

**1515 prolonger** *v*  to prolong, extend
- quels sont les indicateurs d'une sécheresse prolongée? – *what are the indications of a prolonged drought?*
84 | 628

**1516 verser** *v*  to pour, deposit, shed
- cette conversation sera versée au dossier – *this conversation will be deposited into the record*
70 | 1321

**1517 évidence** *nf*  evidence
- je souhaite que cette évidence pénètre les esprits – *I hope this evidence will provoke minds*
78 | 920

**1518 essentiellement** *adv*  essentially
- votre métier est essentiellement une fonction de médiation – *your trade is essentially a function of mediation*
77 | 990

**1519 démontrer** *v*  to demonstrate
- il ne démontre aucun signe de compassion envers ces travailleurs – *he shows no sign of compassion towards these workers*
76 | 1037

**1520 négatif** *nadj*  negative
- ils n'ont pas totalement une image négative – *they don't have a completely negative image*
78 | 927

**1521 approche** *nf*  approach
- c'est là une approche équilibrée – *that's a balanced approach*
71 | 1266

**1522 délai** *nm*  delay
- je vous demande donc de prolonger le délai – *I therefore ask you to extend the timeframe*
68 | 1442

**1523 accroître** *v*  to increase
- évidemment, cela accroît le climat de tension – *apparently, this increased the tension*
67 | 1502

**1524 bruit** *nm*  noise
- j'entends ce bruit horrible – *I hear this horrible noise*
58 | 2073-s

**1525 humanité** *nf*  humanity
- il ne faut pas renier notre humanité – *we must not deny our humanity*
80 | 842

**1526 radio** *adji,nm,nf*  radio
- j'éteins mon émetteur radio – *I turn off my radio*
63 | 1729

**1527 moi-même** *pro*  myself
- j'aimerais redevenir moi-même – *I would like to become myself again*
73 | 1153-n

**1528 syndicat** *nm*  union
- ça n'appartient pas au syndicat – *that's not up to the union*
65 | 1584

**1529 prudent** *adj*  prudent, careful, cautious
- nous avons été très prudents dans nos demandes – *we were very prudent in our requests*
87 | 526

**1530 soirée** *nf*  evening
- je rentre d'une soirée chez des amis – *I'm going home from an evening at my friends' place*
73 | 1169

**1531 vol** *nm*  flight, theft
- il a pu prendre un autre vol – *he was able to take another flight*
72 | 1211

**1532 marcher** *v*  to walk
- elle se lève et elle marche comme ça – *she gets up and walks like this*
65 | 1583

**1533 tiers** *nadj(pl)*  third
- elle est musulmane du tiers monde – *she is a third-world Moslem*
72 | 1216

**1534 mètre** *nm*  meter
- la zone cible fait seulement 2 mètres de large – *the target zone is only two meters wide*
71 | 1289

**1535 aborder** *v*  to reach, approach
- je voudrais aborder la question sous un autre angle – *I would like to address the issue from another angle*
70 | 1310+s

**1536 occidental** *nadj*  western
- peut-on être moderne sans être occidental? – *can one be modern and not Western?*
71 | 1268

**1537 suffisant** *adj* sufficient
- cette motivation n'est toutefois pas suffisante – *still, these motives aren't enough*
80 | 830

**1538 ciel** *nm* sky
- le ciel est resté bleu au-dessus de Paris – *the sky remained blue over Paris*
60 | 1874+I

**1539 tromper** *v* to deceive
- oups! je me suis trompé – *oops, I made a mistake*
70 | 1324

**1540 modeste** *adj(f)* modest
- ce serait un modeste pas dans la bonne voie – *it would be a modest step in the right direction*
86 | 560

**1541 éloigner** *v* to move away, take away, distance
- il avait besoin de s'éloigner de sa femme – *he needed to distance himself from his wife*
73 | 1143

**1542 seconde** *det,nf* second
- au bout de quelques secondes tout reprend – *after a few seconds everything started over again*
71 | 1269

**1543 malheureusement** *adv* unfortunately
- il y a malheureusement des criminels et des terroristes – *unfortunately there are criminals and terrorists*
72 | 1218+s

**1544 évaluer** *v* to evaluate
- nous évaluons des projets en fonction de leur pertinence – *we evaluate projects based on their relevance*
78 | 910

**1545 extrêmement** *adv* extremely
- ce processus a été extrêmement lent – *this process was extremely slow*
71 | 1259

**1546 interne** *nadj(f)* internal, interior, intern
- chez les internes, sa renommée était moins prestigieuse – *among interns his renown was less prestigious*
75 | 1060

**1547 voire** *adv* even, indeed
- deux, trois cent millions. voire plus – *two, three billion. even more.*
74 | 1104

**1548 témoignage** *nm* testimony
- les contrôleurs aériens étudient les témoignages oculaires – *the air traffic controllers are studying eyewitness testimony*
80 | 828

**1549 messieurs** *nmpl* gentlemen
- je vous remercie, messieurs, madame – *thank you, gentlemen, madam*
67 | 1487

**1550 effectivement** *adv* effectively
- c'est effectivement quelque chose qui nous préoccupe – *indeed that's something we worry about*
67 | 1447+s

**1551 gaz** *nm(pl)* gas
- c'est un gaz mortel sans odeur – *it's a deadly, odorless gas*
76 | 984

**1552 acteur** *nm* actor
- tu es le plus grand acteur au monde – *you're the greatest actor in the world*
71 | 1247

**1553 adapter** *v* to adapt
- il dit savoir s'adapter à toutes les difficultés – *he says he can adapt to any difficulty*
77 | 959

**1554 cour** *nf* yard, court
- ils m'attendaient dans la cour de la Sorbonne – *they waited for me in the courtyard of the Sorbonne*
69 | 1366

**1555 dépense** *nf* expense, expenditure
- nous avons vu les dépenses publiques augmenter – *we saw public expenditures increase*
62 | 1720

**1556 souci** *nm* worry, concern
- nos petits soucis ne sont pas importants – *our little concerns are not important*
80 | 804

**1557 expert** *nadj* expert
- je ne prétends pas être expert en la matière – *I don't pretend to be an expert on the topic*
71 | 1226

**1558 sœur** *nf* sister
- je suis la grande sœur mariée – *I'm the elder married sister*
65 | 1581

**1559 relativement** *adv* relatively
- le trafic était dense mais relativement fluide – *the traffic was heavy but relatively free-flowing*
74 | 1105

**1560 comparer** *v* to compare
- il est important de ne pas se comparer aux autres – *it's important to not compare oneself to others*
79 | 863

**1561 procès** *nm(pl)* trial, proceedings
- un juge recommandait un nouveau procès – *a judge recommended a new trial*
68 | 1384

**1562 provenir** *v* to be from, come from
- la balle provient d'un revolver britannique – *the bullet comes from a British revolver*
74 | 1073

**1563 réellement** *adv* really
- elle ne sait pas qui je suis réellement – *she doesn't know who I really am*
81 | 755

**1564 conscient** *adj* conscious, aware
- nous sommes conscients des exigences économiques – *we are aware of the economic demands*
79 | 837

**1565 céder** *v*  to give up, give way
- l'euro cède quelques fractions face au dollar – *the euro lost some percentage points to the dollar*
76 | 986

**1566 médical** *adj*  medical
- sans aide médicale, je vais mourir – *without medical help, I'll die*
72 | 1190

**1567 diviser** *v*  to divide
- le reste se divisait en trois fractions sensiblement égales – *the rest was divided in three largely equal amounts*
82 | 686

**1568 colère** *nf*  anger
- je me sentis soudain très en colère contre mon père – *I suddenly felt myself angry at my father*
72 | 1188

**1569 patient** *nadj*  patient
- la clinique a beaucoup de patients, mais je peux vous aider – *the clinic has many patients, but I can help you*
79 | 834

**1570 notion** *nf*  notion
- par contre, je n'ai aucune notion de médecine – *on the other hand, I have no clue about medicine*
74 | 1056

**1571 siège** *nm*  seat, bench
- puis je vous conduire à votre siège, monsieur? – *may I help you to your seat, sir?*
70 | 1258

**1572 hausse** *nf*  rise, raise, increase
- il faut s'attendre à une légère hausse des prix – *a slight raise in prices is to be expected*
62 | 1701-l +n

**1573 mécanisme** *nm*  mechanism
- il existe donc un mécanisme pour prévenir la fuite – *thus there is a mechanism to prevent escapes*
73 | 1107

**1574 traditionnel** *adj*  traditional
- il faut maintenir des cultures traditionnelles – *traditional cultures must be maintained*
76 | 954

**1575 quart** *nadj*  quarter
- le train part dans trois quarts d'heure – *the train leaves in three-quarters of an hour*
74 | 1082

**1576 approcher** *v*  to approach
- le gros monsieur s'approche de nous – *the big man is approaching us*
71 | 1199

**1577 trafic** *nm*  traffic, circulation
- le week-end, en revanche, le trafic doit être normal – *on the other hand, during weekends traffic should be normal*
57 | 2000+n -s

**1578 catholique** *nadj(f)*  Catholic
ma sœur était une fervente catholique – *my sister was a devout Catholic*
80 | 791

**1579 foyer** *nm*  home, hearth
- ils ont eu chacun un foyer – *each of them had a home*
83 | 645

**1580 adulte** *nadj(f)*  adult
- je me suis sentie devenir une adulte – *I felt myself becoming an adult*
78 | 883

**1581 reprocher** *v*  to blame, reproach
- nous lui avons reproché d'avoir manqué le sommet – *we blame him for not having reached the summit*
79 | 846

**1582 métier** *nm*  job, occupation, trade
- c'est déjà plus qu'un métier, c'est une profession – *it's more than a job – it's a profession*
69 | 1292

**1583 modification** *nf*  modification
- d'autres modifications sont aussi apportées à la convention – *other changes were also made to the agreement*
56 | 2069+s

**1584 peser** *v*  to weigh
- il pesait lourd sur mon cœur – *it weighed heavily on my heart*
78 | 891

**1585 médias** *nmpl*  media
- les médias vous ont comparée à Oprah Winfrey – *the media has compared you to Oprah Winfrey*
67 | 1390-l

**1586 hiver** *nm*  winter
- tu ne peux pas passer l'hiver ici – *you can't spend the winter here*
80 | 758

**1587 définition** *nf*  definition
- je voudrais savoir quelle est sa définition d'égalité – *I would like to know his definition of equality*
68 | 1373

**1588 spécialiste** *nadj(f)*  specialist
- il y a des spécialistes pour ça – *there are specialists for that*
76 | 941

**1589 mari** *nm*  husband
- je suis un collègue de votre mari – *I'm a colleague of your husband*
65 | 1482

**1590 supprimer** *v*  to remove, withdraw
- supprime ce paragraphe, cela ne changera rien – *delete this paragraph; that won't change anything*
75 | 992

**1591 guère** *adv*  hardly
- mon travail n'avançait guère – *my job was hardly going anywhere*
68 | 1319

**1592 douter** *v*  to doubt
- il n'avait jamais douté de la victoire – *he never doubted victory*
74 | 1026

**1593 ressentir** *v* to feel
- c'est alors qu'il ressentit, dans sa nuque, la douleur – *that's when he felt, on the back of his neck, a sharp pain*
76 | 935

**1594 sexuel** *adj* sexual
- il y a des pervers sexuels partout – *there are sexual perverts everywhere*
76 | 938

**1595 consulter** *v* to consult
- je n'ai pas été consulté – *I was not consulted*
70 | 1219

**1596 renseignement** *nm* information
- je cherche des renseignements sur la femme qui a été tuée – *I'm seeking information on the woman who was killed*
63 | 1605

**1597 âgé** *adj* old
- ces hommes sont tous très âgés maintenant – *these men are all very old now*
68 | 1350

**1598 fonctionnement** *nm* operation, functioning
- laissez-moi vous expliquer le fonction-nement de ce système – *let me explain to you how the system works*
63 | 1601

**1599 garçon** *nm* boy
- c'est un garçon unique – *he's a unique boy*
63 | 1595

**1600 parfait** *nadj* perfect
- je suis en parfaite santé – *I'm in perfect health*
72 | 1161

**1601 résumer** *v* to summarize, sum up
- les résultats obtenus sont résumés dans le tableau – *the results are summarized in the table*
83 | 622

**1602 prévision** *nf* forecast, prediction, expectation
- l'économie mondiale a surpassé toutes les prévisions – *the global economy surpassed all predictions*
79 | 815

**1603 quatrième** *det,nm,nf* fourth
- c'est mon quatrième séjour en France – *it's my fourth stay in France*
76 | 930

**1604 fenêtre** *nf* window
- j'ai sauté par la fenêtre – *I jumped out the window*
58 | 1893+l -s

**1605 incapable** *nadj(f)* incapable, incompetent
- il est incapable de rentrer dans des détails concrets – *he's incapable of delving into concrete details*
82 | 668

**1606 hésiter** *v* to hesitate
- n'hésitez pas à les appeler – *don't hesitate to call them*
75 | 971

**1607 menace** *nf* threat
- la menace terroriste est bien réelle – *the terrorist threat is very real*
74 | 1039

**1608 universel** *nadj* universal
- nous voulons un régime de santé universel – *we want a universal health care system*
77 | 876

**1609 jeunesse** *nf* youth
- c'est la jeunesse que j'aime en eux – *it's their youthfulness that I like*
77 | 883

**1610 voler** *v* to steal, rob
- c'est pas bien de voler – *it's not good to steal*
72 | 1114

**1611 résister** *v* to resist
- j'ai résisté à la mort de ma fille – *I wasn't able to accept the death of my daughter*
81 | 727

**1612 profondément** *adv* profoundly, deeply
- j'en suis profondément heureux – *I am deeply pleased about it*
82 | 691

**1613 séparation** *nf* separation
- la séparation tend à devenir une invasion – *separation tends to turn into invasion*
85 | 535

**1614 inutile** *nadj(f)* useless
- notre travail vous semble inutile – *our work seems useless to you*
79 | 796

**1615 refus** *nm(pl)* refusal
- plusieurs raisons peuvent motiver un refus de visa – *a visa may be refused for several reasons*
79 | 784

**1616 poisson** *nm* fish
- nous pouvons bien survivre sans manger du poisson – *we can survive very well without eating fish*
77 | 904

**1617 révolution** *nf* revolution
- la révolution allemande était sans avenir – *the German revolution had no future*
70 | 1196

**1618 prisonnier** *nadj* prisoner, captive
- je viens demander la libération d'une prisonnière – *I have come to ask for the release of one female prisoner*
73 | 1071

**1619 avouer** *v* to admit
- j'avoue que j'étais encore plutôt naïf – *I admit I was still somewhat naïve*
76 | 950

**1620 saluer** *v* to greet, salute
- tu ne dois pas saluer les gens que tu ne connais pas – *you shouldn't greet people you don't know*
80 | 762

**1621 fer** *nm* iron
- la grille de fer était ouverte – *the iron gate was open*
78 | 834

**1622 familial** *adj* family
- la violence familiale n'est que trop fréquente – *family violence is only too frequent*
76 | 947

**1623 cinéma** *nm* cinema
• il était allé au cinéma voir un film extraordinaire – *he went to the movies and saw an extraordinary film*
69 | 1253

**1624 calcul** *nm* calculation
• une erreur de calcul figurait dans votre facture – *there was a miscalculation in your bill*
76 | 920

**1625 armé** *adj* armed
• ils ont croisé un homme armé – *they came upon an armed man*
69 | 1240

**1626 enseignement** *nm* education, teaching
• c'est dans l'enseignement que j'ai acquis mes cheveux blancs – *teaching is what gave me gray hair*
74 | 1020

**1627 étonnant** *nadj* surprising, amazing, incredible
• il est étonnant de voir combien d'argent on peut obtenir – *it's striking to see how much money one can obtain*
84 | 570

**1628 dizaine** *nf* approximately ten
• il y a des dizaines de milliers de jeunes dans ce pays – *there are tens of thousands of youth in this country*
67 | 1357

**1629 dessus** *adv,nm(pl),prep* above, on top
• je mets mes pieds dessus – *I'm putting my feet on top of it*
71 | 1137

**1630 achever** *v* to complete, finish, end
• pensez-vous réellement que cette guerre s'achèvera – *do you really think that this war will end?*
72 | 1104

**1631 fonctionnaire** *nm,nf* state employee, public servant
• les juges sont aussi des fonctionnaires – *judges are also public servants*
68 | 1293

**1632 instruction** *nf* instruction, direction
• je ne reçois aucune instruction de l'industrie nucléaire – *I don't receive any instruction from the nuclear industry*
69 | 1270

**1633 pratiquement** *adv* practically
• ils ont continué de grimper de manière pratiquement ininterrompue – *they continued with their practically uninterrupted climbing*
78 | 816

**1634 oser** *v* to dare
• ose me dire que tu vas rester ici! – *dare to tell me that you will stay here!*
71 | 1167-n

**1635 rassembler** *v* to gather together
• je rassemblai assez de forces pour me lever – *I summoned enough energy to get up*
77 | 881

**1636 réalisation** *nf* realization, achievement
• un lancement d'opération demande la réalisation d'une action – *launching an operation requires performing some action*
77 | 893

**1637 fiscal** *adj* fiscal
• le régime fiscal n'est pas juste – *the tax system is not fair*
57 | 1878-l +s

**1638 démarche** *nf* walk, process
• la démarche serait trop longue et trop coûteuse – *the process would be too long and too costly*
74 | 985

**1639 corriger** *v* to correct
• je voudrais corriger un petit détail technique – *I would like to correct a small technical detail*
79 | 795

**1640 volume** *nm* volume
• gardez le moral haut et le volume bas – *keep your morale up and your volume down*
73 | 1055

**1641 réussite** *nf* success
• elle est aussi capable de magnifiques réussites – *she's also capable of magnificent successes*
84 | 560

**1642 désir** *nm* desire
• faites attention à vos désirs – *watch out for your desires*
68 | 1286

**1643 pur** *nadj* pure
• l'oxygène pur annihile toute douleur – *pure oxygen obliterates all pains*
70 | 1183

**1644 exportation** *nf* export
• les exportations ont légèrement baissé – *exports dropped slightly*
65 | 1452

**1645 prier** *v* to pray
• je vais prier pour que Dieu vous bénisse – *I'll pray for God to bless you*
65 | 1442-n

**1646 trente** *det,nmi* thirty
• il a été trente ans chez nous – *he lived at our place for thirty years*
68 | 1288

**1647 âme** *nf* soul
• je ne vendrai jamais mon âme au diable – *I will never sell my soul to the devil*
61 | 1676+l

**1648 dominer** *v* to dominate
• la France a dominé l'Europe pendant trois siècles – *France dominated Europe for three centuries*
75 | 974

**1649 autorisation** *nf* authorization, permission, permit
• j'ai besoin d'une autorisation – *I need an authorization*
82 | 655

**1650 instrument** *nm* instrument
- je voulais connaître mieux l'instrument et apprendre des solos – *I want to know the instrument better and learn some solos*
73 | 1034

**1651 indépendance** *nf* independence
- l'île a acquis son indépendance en 1981 – *the island gained its independance in 1981*
74 | 994

**1652 tort** *nm* wrong
- vous aviez raison, j'avais tort – *you were right, I was wrong*
75 | 954

**1653 hauteur** *nf* height
- ceux qui tombent de cette hauteur sont morts – *whoever falls from this height dies*
77 | 860

**1654 critiquer** *v* to criticize
- ils s'arrogent le droit de me critiquer, me juger – *they reserve the right to criticize me, to judge me*
76 | 917

**1655 attaque** *nf* attack
- l'attaque rebelle survient après deux jours – *the rebel attack took place after two days*
61 | 1627

**1656 assurance** *nf* insurance, confidence
- tout mon argent sert à payer l'assurance médicale – *all my money goes to pay medical insurance*
69 | 1201

**1657 déficit** *nm* deficit
- le déficit du extérieur s'est fortement contracté – *the foreign trade deficit dropped sharply*
63 | 1541

**1658 évoluer** *v* to evolve
- la situation évolue cependant dans le bon sens – *but the situation did evolve in the right direction*
72 | 1058

**1659 drogue** *nf* drug
- il parle ouvertement des effets des drogues – *he talks openly about the effects of drugs*
76 | 913

**1660 concret** *nadj* concrete
- que proposez-vous comme solutions concrètes? – *what concrete solutions do you propose?*
76 | 881

**1661 percevoir** *v* to perceive
- il était perçu comme agressif, arrogant et généralement hostile – *he was perceived as aggressive, arrogant, and generally hostile*
76 | 893

**1662 rythme** *nm* rhythm, rate
- le génie génétique progresse à un rythme incroyable – *genetic engineering is progressing at an unbelievable pace*
73 | 1016

**1663 approuver** *v* to approve
- chacun de vos projets a été approuvé – *each of your trips has been approved*
68 | 1249

**1664 douze** *det,nmi* twelve
- on a envoyé des petits de douze ans à la mine – *little twelve-year-olds were sent to the mine*
71 | 1116

**1665 juridique** *adj(f)* legal, judicial
- le système juridique gêne le travail des policiers – *the legal system hinders police work*
66 | 1342-l

**1666 espagnol** *nadj* Spanish
- vous n'êtes pas espagnole, vous – *you're not a Spaniard*
66 | 1362

**1667 saison** *nf* season
- l'automne, c'est la saison du football – *autumn is football season*
69 | 1193

**1668 épreuve** *nf* test, ordeal, trial
- nous mettons peut-être votre patience à l'épreuve – *perhaps we're putting your patience to the test*
73 | 1044

**1669 hypothèse** *nf* hypothesis
- cette hypothèse était tellement invraisemblable – *this hypothesis was so unlikely*
77 | 831

**1670 relier** *v* to connect
- toutes les choses sont reliées. nous le savons – *everything is connected. we know that*
78 | 784

**1671 financement** *nm* financing
- le financement de cet achat est assuré – *the financing of this purchase is assured*
65 | 1391-l

**1672 dos** *nm(pl)* back
- il est couché sur le dos, les bras en croix – *he's lying on his back, arms crossed*
68 | 1232

**1673 consommateur** *nm* consumer, customer
- les consommateurs en ressentent directement les avantages – *consumers feel the advantages directly*
69 | 1210

**1674 soviétique** *nadj(f)* Soviet
- une sonde spatiale soviétique se pose sur Vénus – *a Soviet space probe is sitting on Venus*
73 | 1009

**1675 volontaire** *nadj(f)* volunteer; voluntary
- je me porte volontaire pour sortir – *I hereby volunteer to go outside*
82 | 632

**1676 négocier** *v* to negotiate
- l'Israël veut dicter et non pas négocier – *Israel wants to dictate, not negotiate*
73 | 1033

**1677 finance** *nf* finance
- je n'ai pas étudié la finance mais j'étais un guerrier dans l'âme – *I didn't study finance but I was a warrior at heart*
58 | 1743

## 10  Natural features and plants

| | | |
|---|---|---|
| **monde** 77 M world | **canal** 1919 M canal | **bassin** 3032 M basin |
| **courant** 314 M current | **arbre** 2111 M tree | **col** 3054 M mountain |
| **nature** 542 F nature | **branche** 2140 F branch | **souffle** 3120 M breath |
| **passage** 674 M passage | **satellite** 2200 M satellite | **lac** 3121 M lake |
| **feu** 786 M fire | **rivière** 2223 F river | **montée** 3215 F ascent |
| **mer** 921 F sea | **fleur** 2305 F flower | **poussière** 3236 F dust |
| **lumière** 1059 F light | **continent** 2388 M continent | **sable** 3263 M sand |
| **île** 1245 F island | **écho** 2400 M echo | **rive** 3314 F shore |
| **côte** 1385 F coast | **électricité** 2469 F electricity | **lune** 3346 F moon |
| **réflexion** 1394 F reflection | **flux** 2501 M flow | **quai** 3354 M embankment |
| **bois** 1425 M wood | **racine** 2593 F root | **cap** 3532 M cape |
| **sol** 1491 M ground | **plante** 2702 F plant | **baie** 3719 F bay |
| **forêt** 1724 F forest | **étoile** 2776 F star | **banc** 3724 M bench |
| **massif** 1760 M massif | **plateau** 2803 M plateau | **golfe** 4024 M gulf |
| **chute** 1761 F fall | **vallée** 2856 F valley | **gorge** 4194 F gorge |
| **pierre** 1767 F stone | **pente** 2873 F slope | **boue** 4507 F mud |
| **planète** 1875 F planet | **fleuve** 2893 M river | **jungle** 4891 F jungle |
| **pointe** 1907 F point | **colline** 2937 F hill | **plaine** 5056 F plain |

**1678 rêver** *v* to dream
• j'ai rêvé de toi – *I dreamed about you*
71 | 1119

**1679 indien** *nadj* Indian
• la police fédérale indienne va enquêter – *the Indian federal police is going to investigate*
70 | 1166

**1680 quantité** *nf* quantity
• ces services existent en quantités limitées – *these services are available in limited quantities*
76 | 899

**1681 définitif** *nadj* definitive, final
• je n'ai pas pris de décision définitive à ce sujet – *I haven't taken a final decision on this subject*
79 | 751

**1682 persuader** *v* to convince, persuade
• il était persuadé que j'avais un talent – *he was convinced I had a talent*
82 | 635

**1683 interpréter** *v* to interpret
• ces résultats sont évidemment à interpréter avec prudence – *these results are clearly to be interpreted carefully*
82 | 639

**1684 annuel** *adj* annual
• l'inflation annuelle a augmenté à 4.1 % – *annual inflation grew by 4.1%*
70 | 1155

**1685 commentaire** *nm* comment, remark
• j'ai été très impressionné des commentaires que j'ai reçus – *I'm very impressed by the comments I have received*
72 | 1072

**1686 marier** *v* to marry
• il veut se marier avec moi – *he wants to marry me*
71 | 1082

**1687 spectacle** *nm* sight, show
• ça va être un spectacle d'enfer – *that will be a hellish spectacle*
73 | 987

**1688 pari** *nm* bet
• je n'ai jamais fait le pari de quoi que ce soit – *I have never bet on anything*
47 | 2459-I

**1689 célèbre** *adj(f)* famous
• elle était une musicienne célèbre dans notre pays – *she was a famous musician in our country*
78 | 773

**1690 ouest** *adji,nm* west
• le vent arrive toujours de l'ouest – *the wind always blows from the west*
65 | 1375

**1691 sexe** *nm* sex
• je ne sais pas, le sexe n'a peut-être rien à voir – *I don't know, perhaps sex doesn't have anything to do with it*
77 | 851

**1692 eh** *intj*  hey, uh
- eh bien, j'ai changé d'avis – *well, I have changed my mind*
60 | 1647-n +s

**1693 recours** *nm(pl)*  resort, recourse
- vous disiez qu'on a eu recours à des injonctions – *you were saying we can resort to injunctions*
72 | 1048

**1694 accent** *nm*  accent
- son accent est tellement mignon – *her accent is so cute*
82 | 633

**1695 introduire** *v*  to introduce
- on l'avait introduit dans une chambre – *he was taken into a room*
74 | 946

**1696 communiste** *nadj(f)*  communist
- les communistes ont toujours une certaine influence – *the communists still have some influence*
70 | 1118

**1697 concert** *nm*  concert
- ce soir, on va à un concert – *tonight we're going to a concert*
80 | 692

**1698 couverture** *nf*  blanket
- la couverture de neige a fortement fondu – *the blanket of snow melted drastically*
76 | 885

**1699 religion** *nf*  religion
- l'Islam est une religion de paix et de tolérance – *Islam is a religion of peace and tolerance*
72 | 1038

**1700 appui** *nm*  support
- sa loyauté et son appui me manqueront – *I'll miss his loyalty and his support*
69 | 1185

**1701 théâtre** *nm*  theater
- ils allaient au café, au théâtre, au cinéma – *they went to the café, the theatre, the movies*
70 | 1107

**1702 saint** *nadj*  saint, holy
- je priais devant la statue de la Sainte Vierge – *I was praying before the statue of the Holy Virgin*
68 | 1222

**1703 conséquent** *nadj*  logical, rational, consistent
- il semble, par conséquent, que nous soyons face à une contradiction – *consequently it seems that we are facing a contradiction*
68 | 1221

**1704 équipement** *nm*  equipment
- nous avons le meilleur équipement possible – *we have the best possible equipment*
52 | 2096-l +n -s

**1705 descendre** *v*  to go down, come down
- personne n'entre, personne ne descend du train – *nobody gets on or off the train*
60 | 1607

**1706 patron** *nm*  boss
- je veux parler avec ton patron – *I want to speak with your boss*
69 | 1169

**1707 marge** *nf*  margin
- il y avait une marge d'incertitude considérable – *there was a substantial margin of uncertainty*
73 | 971

**1708 abri** *nm*  shelter
- mettons-nous à l'abri – *let's take shelter*
82 | 613

**1709 recette** *nf*  recipe
- il n'y a pas de recette secrète – *there's no secret recipe*
76 | 859

**1710 généralement** *adv*  generally
- les conditions sont généralement favorables – *the conditions are generally favorable*
72 | 1044

**1711 vigueur** *nf*  vigor
- le nouveau programme sera en vigueur dès juillet prochain – *the new program will take effect starting next July*
70 | 1136

**1712 baser** *v*  to base
- cette loi se base sur trois principes – *this law is based on three principles*
75 | 906

**1713 soleil** *nm*  sun
- ces lunettes de soleil valent 100 millions de dollars? – *these sunglasses are worth 100 million dollars?*
61 | 1531+l

**1714 électoral** *adj*  electoral
- les campagnes électorales sont affaire de pouvoir – *electoral campaigns involve power*
65 | 1339

**1715 ennemi** *nadj*  enemy
- s'il est l'ennemi de notre ennemi, c'est un ami – *the enemy of our enemy is our friend*
69 | 1155

**1716 bourse** *nf*  purse, scholarship
- j'ai réussi à obtenir une bourse pour ma deuxième année – *I managed to obtain a scholarship for my second year*
66 | 1286

**1717 dimension** *nf*  dimension
- nous connaissions un univers à trois dimensions – *we experienced a three-dimensional universe*
70 | 1096

**1718 déployer** *v*  to deploy, open
- des chars d'assaut israéliens ont été déployés – *Israeli assault vehicles were deployed*
78 | 781

**1719 dialogue** *nm*  dialogue
- nous avons voulu proposer un dialogue sur ces trois sujets – *we wanted to propose a dialogue on these three topics*
67 | 1237

**1720 thème** *nm* theme, topic
• vous pouvez choisir un thème – *you can choose a topic*
69 | 1154

**1721 circuler** *v* to drive, circulate
• elle peut désormais circuler librement – *she can henceforth circulate freely*
84 | 520

**1722 porte-parole** *nmi* spokesperson, spokes-woman, spokesman
• je ne me sens porte-parole de personne – *I don't feel like I'm anybody's spokesman*
52 | 2033-l +n -s

**1723 présentation** *nf* presentation
• j'ai écouté avec intérêt la présentation de mon collègue – *I listened with interest to the presentation of my colleague*
71 | 1073

**1724 forêt** *nf* forest
• de ma fenêtre, on voyait la forêt – *from my window you could see the forest*
80 | 674

**1725 outil** *nm* tool
• ça m'a donné les outils pour atteindre mes buts – *that gave me the wherewithal to achieve my goals*
70 | 1126

**1726 vacance** *nf* vacancy; vacation
• moi, j'ai interrompu mes vacances – *as for me, I had to interrupt my vacation*
79 | 742

**1727 suffisamment** *adv* sufficiently
• je ne l'ai pas dit suffisamment – *I haven't said it enough*
76 | 843

**1728 défi** *nm* challenge
• tu es peut-être venu me lancer un défi – *maybe you came to challenge me*
74 | 923

**1729 front** *nm* front, forehead
• le moustique vibrait autour de son front – *the mosquito buzzed around his forehead*
66 | 1271

**1730 suspendre** *v* to suspend, postpone
• il faut suspendre la séance pour quelques instants – *the hearing will have to be suspended for a little while*
75 | 874

**1731 calme** *nadj(f)* calm
• le temps est désormais très calme – *the weather has since been very calm*
65 | 1353

**1732 montagne** *nf* mountain
• il atteignit le sommet de la grande montagne – *he reached the summit of the great mountain*
76 | 840

**1733 sévère** *adj(f)* severe
• ils sont contrôlés de façon sévère, de façon méticuleuse – *they are strictly, meticulously controlled*
82 | 606

**1734 apparemment** *adv* apparently
• apparemment, ces moulins tournent encore – *apparently, these mills are still turning*
81 | 631

**1735 présidence** *nf* presidency
• vous devez comprendre que la présidence a une mission – *you must understand that the presidency has a mission*
61 | 1512-l

**1736 magasin** *nm* store
• il travaillait dans un petit magasin en face – *he worked in a little shop across the street*
80 | 695

**1737 commissaire** *nm,nf* superintendent, commissioner
• excusez-moi, je vois que le commissaire vient d'arriver – *excuse me, I see the commissioner has just arrived*
67 | 1241

**1738 écrivain** *nm* writer
• ma chérie, devenir écrivain est tout aussi dur – *my dear, becoming a writer is just as hard*
66 | 1270

**1739 monétaire** *adj(f)* monetary
• le travailleur désire une élévation de salaire monétaire – *the worker wants an increase in monetary salary*
57 | 1747

**1740 ouvrage** *nm* work
• il s'agit du seul ouvrage de référence sur le sujet – *it's the only reference work on the subject*
67 | 1244

**1741 réputation** *nf* reputation
• nous sommes fiers de notre réputation – *we're proud of our reputation*
87 | 426

**1742 cabinet** *nm* cabinet, agency, office
• les députés ministériels sont les membres du Cabinet – *the deputy ministers are Cabinet ministers*
78 | 742

**1743 écart** *nm* space, gap
• elle est un peu à l'écart de la route – *it's a little bit off the road*
79 | 702

**1744 chien** *nm* dog
• notre mère avait peur des chiens – *our mother was afraid of dogs*
63 | 1388

**1745 surveillance** *nf* surveillance, monitoring
• les caméras de surveillance l'ont bien vue – *the surveillance cameras sure saw it*
75 | 881

**1746 indispensable** *adj(f)* essential
• le gouvernement français estime cette opération indispensable – *the French government deems this operation essential*
77 | 807

**1747 conversation** *nf* conversation
• notre conversation a duré deux heures – *our conversation lasted two hours*
66 | 1269

**1748 surface** *nf* surface
• les eaux de surface sont très chaudes – *the surface water is very hot*
74 | 913

**1749 féliciter** *v* to congratulate
• je voulais te féliciter pour cette victoire – *I wanted to congratulate you on this victory*
63 | 1420+s

**1750 sûrement** *adv* surely
• quelqu'un a sûrement besoin d'aide – *someone surely needs help*
75 | 867-n

**1751 bombe** *nf* bomb
• une vingtaine de bombes sont tombées sur la capitale – *some twenty bombs fell on the capital*
71 | 1049

**1752 efficacité** *nf* efficiency, effectiveness
• les chercheurs pourront vérifier l'efficacité du traitement – *the researchers will be able to verify the effectiveness of the treatment*
69 | 1114

**1753 euro** *nm* euro
• à 21 euros, ce n'est pas très cher – *at 21 euros, it's not very expensive*
52 | 1995-l +n

**1754 phase** *nf* phase
• toute maladie est une phase de guérison – *each sickness is a phase of healing*
67 | 1204

**1755 confusion** *nf* confusion, mix-up
• j'ai cru mourir de confusion – *I thought I would die from confusion*
84 | 512

**1756 précision** *nf* precision
• il faut une certaine précision dans la loi – *the law must have some degree of precision*
77 | 800

**1757 compétence** *nf* competence
• nous voulons qu'ils acquièrent les compétences nécessaires – *we want them to acquire the necessary competency*
64 | 1327+s

**1758 bilan** *nm* balance sheet, outcome
• pouvez-vous proposer un bilan de ces épreuves? – *can you suggest an outcome for these tests?*
66 | 1272

**1759 immense** *adj(f)* immense
• nous vivons dans un territoire immense – *we live in an immense territory*
73 | 946

**1760 massif** *nadj* massive
• une faillite institutionnelle massive se produit – *a massive institutional failure took place*
72 | 971

**1761 chute** *nf* fall
• quelques mois après la chute du mur de Berlin, en avril 1990 – *a few months after the fall of the Berlin wall, in April 1990*
67 | 1220

**1762 constant** *adj* constant
• vous travailliez tous de façon constante – *you all work in a consistent manner*
82 | 604

**1763 sain** *adj* healthy, sane
• si vous menez une vie saine, vos réduisez vos risques – *if you live a healthy life, you reduce your risks*
85 | 468

**1764 intégrer** *v* to integrate
• l'art est une tentative pour intégrer le mal – *art is an attempt to integrate evil*
71 | 1036

**1765 aérien** *adj* aerial
• les renforts aériens arrivent – *air support is arriving*
65 | 1299

**1766 contrairement** *adv* contrary
• contrairement à une idée couramment répandue – *contrary to a commonly held idea*
78 | 723

**1767 pierre** *nf* stone
• on nous lance des pierres par la fenêtre – *they were throwing stones out the window at us*
65 | 1278

**1768 socialiste** *nadj(f)* socialist
• les pays que nous appelons socialistes aujourd'hui ne le sont pas du tout – *countries that we call socialist today really aren't at all*
63 | 1367

**1769 fortement** *adv* strongly
• encore une fois, j'insiste fortement – *again, I strongly insist*
73 | 917

**1770 régulier** *adj* regular
• travaillez-vous avec des clients réguliers – *do you work with regular clients?*
85 | 484

**1771 boîte** *nf* box
• elle va vérifier plusieurs fois sa boîte aux lettres – *she went several times to look in her mailbox*
77 | 776

**1772 financer** *v* to finance
• il a déjà financé des films en Europe – *he has already financed films in Europe*
67 | 1200

**1773 théorie** *nf* theory
• je crois me souvenir de tes théories – *I think I remember your theories*
66 | 1244

**1774 hôtel** *nm* hotel
• il change d'hôtel chaque soir – *he changes hotels every night*
70 | 1051

**1775 nier** *v* to deny
• vous ne pouvez pas le nier et les autres non plus – *you can't deny it, neither can the others*
79 | 680

**1776 phénomène** *nm* phenomenon
- je suis un phénomène, non? – *I'm a phenomenon, right?*
67 | 1192

**1777 là-bas** *adv* over there, out there
- il y a deux mecs là-bas qui vous cherchent – *there are two guys over there looking for you*
69 | 1100-n

**1778 étonner** *v* to astonish, amaze
- évidemment, ça a étonné tout le monde – *evidently this stunned the whole world*
72 | 957

**1779 totalité** *nf* totality, entirety
- toute totalité, paradoxalement, est restrictive – *entirety is, paradoxically, restrictive*
82 | 571

**1780 sort** *nm* fate, curse
- le sort de la pièce était entre mes mains – *the outcome of the play was in my hands*
81 | 608

**1781 accéder** *v* to access, reach, attain
- j'ai besoin d'accéder à ces données – *I need to access this data*
83 | 540

**1782 église** *nf* church
- vous allez toujours à l'église? – *do you still go to church?*
72 | 978

**1783 récupérer** *v* to get back, recover, recuperate
- nous avons récupéré vos armes – *we recovered your weapons*
81 | 625

**1784 doter** *v* to endow, provide
- vous êtes dotée d'un superbe vocabulaire – *you're endowed with a superb vocabulary*
75 | 833

**1785 contribution** *nf* contribution
- nous reconnaissons leur contribution dans le domaine médical – *we recognize their contribution to the medical domain*
68 | 1138

**1786 profondeur** *nf* depth
- ce serait sous-estimer la profondeur de la crise – *that would be to underestimate the gravity of the crisis*
84 | 521

**1787 émettre** *v* to emit, issue
- ce sont eux qui émettent le plus de CO2 – *that's what emits the most carbon dioxide*
54 | 1850+n -s

**1788 test** *nm* test
- j'ai eu un test de Q. I. cette année – *I had an IQ test this year*
71 | 1003-l

**1789 vice-président** *nm* vice-president
- le vice-président sortant a passé la nuit dans sa résidence – *the outgoing vice-president spent the night in his residence*
61 | 1444-l +s

**1790 pêche** *nf* fishing; peach
- tu viens à la pêche cet après-midi? – *are you coming fishing this afternoon?*
55 | 1791+s

**1791 découverte** *nf* discovery
- cette découverte l'amusa toute la soirée – *this discovery kept her happy all evening*
74 | 882

**1792 potentiel** *nadj* potential
- elle a vraiment un bon potentiel! – *she really has great potential!*
76 | 813

**1793 agricole** *adj(f)* agricultural, farming
- les subventions agricoles sont des taxes – *farm subsidies are taxes*
60 | 1520

**1794 intellectuel** *nadj* intellectual
- je crois que la vie intellectuelle changerait profondément – *I think that intellectual life would change dramatically*
68 | 1134

**1795 essence** *nf* gas, petrol
- ta moto n'a plus d'essence – *your motorbike ran out of gas*
80 | 659

**1796 pencher** *v* to lean, tilt
- vous penchez à gauche, ça tourne à gauche – *lean to the left and it turns to the left*
69 | 1104

**1797 artiste** *nadj(f)* artist
- l'artiste refait le monde à son compte – *the artist remakes the world according to his own fashion*
68 | 1118

**1798 coin** *nm* corner
- ils vivent peut-être ici, au coin de la rue – *maybe they live here, on the street corner*
68 | 1111

**1799 tension** *nf* tension
- parler pour briser la tension – *say something to break the tension*
69 | 1068

**1800 don** *nm* gift
- elle a le don de communiquer avec la musique – *she has the gift of communication through music*
75 | 850

**1801 uniforme** *adj(f),nm* uniform, steady, regular
- vous ne portiez pas d'uniforme, quoique armé – *you weren't wearing a uniform, even though you were armed*
84 | 503

**1802 fidèle** *nadj(f)* faithful
- tes hommes te sont fidèles – *your men are faithful to you*
76 | 806

**1803 grève** *nf* strike
- nous allons faire grève demain – *we're going on strike tomorow*
64 | 1287

**1804 achat** *nm* purchase
- il est devenu responsable des achats – *he became the purchasing agent*
73 | 902

**1805 mentionner** *v* to mention
- ces points ont déjà été mentionnés par le rapporteur – *these points were already mentioned by the reporter*
62 | 1376+s

**1806 exécution** *nf* execution, accomplishment
- dans sa cellule, avant l'exécution, il en refuse les secours – *in his cell, before the execution, he refuses help*
82 | 557

**1807 distinguer** *v* to distinguish
- c'est cela qui nous distingue des orientaux – *that's what distinguishes us from the Orientals*
71 | 975

**1808 exploiter** *v* to exploit
- les Américains veulent exploiter notre pétrole – *the Americans want to exploit our oil*
78 | 703

**1809 administratif** *nadj* administrative
- j'occupe actuellement un poste administratif – *I currently hold an administrative position*
75 | 822

**1810 effectif** *nadj* effective; size, workforce
- Volkswagen supprime un quart de ses effectifs aux Etats-Unis – *Volkswagen is eliminating a quarter of its workforce in the U.S.*
69 | 1082

**1811 communautaire** *adj(f)* community, communal
- une intervention au niveau communautaire ne se justifiait pas – *community intervention was not justified*
56 | 1664-l +s

**1812 individuel** *adj* individual
- la religion se fait sur une base individuelle – *religion happens at an individual level*
76 | 807

**1813 faciliter** *v* to make easier, facilitate
- je voudrais faciliter votre décision – *I would like to facilitate your decision*
76 | 806

**1814 original** *nadj* original
- dire que la ville était belle était original – *to say that the city was beautiful was quite a stretch*
81 | 604

**1815 surprise** *nf* surprise
- j'étais plutôt content, c'était la bonne surprise – *I was rather pleased – that was a nice surprise*
79 | 687

**1816 veiller** *v* to look after, stay up
- ne veille pas trop tard, cela use les yeux – *don't stay up too late, it wears out your eyes*
69 | 1060

**1817 dette** *nf* debt
- je vais régler ma dette – *I'm going to take care of my debt*
66 | 1202

**1818 capitale** *nf* capital
- nous ne sommes pas la capitale de l'État mais nous grandissons – *we're not the state capital but we're growing*
57 | 1627

**1819 maintien** *nm* holding, maintaining
- le maintien de la paix ne se limite plus – *maintaining peace has no limits*
70 | 1041

**1820 chanter** *v* to sing
- il chantait la mélodie – *he sang the melody*
66 | 1212-n

**1821 pension** *nf* pension; room and board, boarding school
- elle ira directement du camp en pension – *she'll go directly from the camp to a boarding school*
53 | 1822+s

**1822 revue** *nf* review, magazine, journal
- la revue n'a pas publié les résultats des travaux – *the journal didn't publish the results of the work*
77 | 751

**1823 clore** *v* to close
- pour moi, le sujet est clos – *for me, the subject is moot*
79 | 684

**1824 neige** *nf* snow
- ils ne peuvent plus pelleter la neige – *they can't shovel snow any more*
49 | 2030+n -s

**1825 figure** *nf* face; figure
- sa figure était maigre et pâle, un peu effrayante – *his face was lean and pale, somewhat frightening*
60 | 1454-s

**1826 masse** *nf* mass
- l'entreprise doit atteindre une masse critique – *the company must achieve critical mass*
71 | 973

**1827 susceptible** *adj(f)* sensitive, touchy
- oh! ce que vous pouvez être susceptible mon ami – *gee, can you ever be touchy, my friend*
80 | 640

**1828 étroit** *adj* narrow, tight
- ils demeurèrent quelques instants dans l'étroit couloir – *they lingered for a few moments in the narrow corridor*
75 | 810

**1829 goût** *nm* taste
- le goût n'a rien à voir avec l'appétit – *taste has nothing to do with appetite*
67 | 1157

**1830 prestation** *nf* benefit
- de nombreuses prestations ont été éliminées – *numerous benefits were eliminated*
51 | 1903-l +s

**1831 régner** *v* to reign
- un silence de mort règne dans la salle – *a deathly silence filled the room*
78 | 695

**1832 catastrophe** *nf* catastrophe, disaster
- les agriculteurs subissent déjà beaucoup de catastrophes naturelles – *farmers are already suffering from many natural disasters*
80 | 627

**1833 ressortir** *v* to go out again, come out again, take out again
- sur un fond noir, les couleurs ressortaient mieux – *on a black background the colors showed up better*
83 | 530

**1834 exploitation** *nf* operation, exploitation
- il s'agit d'une exploitation intellectuelle de l'enfant – *it's all about intellectual exploitation of children*
63 | 1289+n

**1835 manifestation** *nf* demonstration, event
- on en attendait des manifestations spectaculaires – *a spectacular event was expected*
63 | 1327

**1836 dormir** *v* to sleep
- je ne faisais que dormir sur la plage – *all I did was sleep on the beach*
57 | 1579-n

**1837 lit** *nm* bed
- je sautai joyeusement du lit – *I jumped joyfully out of the bed*
58 | 1528+l -n

**1838 bouche** *nf* mouth
- des mots sortirent mécaniquement de ma bouche – *words left my mouth automatically*
60 | 1465+l

**1839 excuse** *nf* excuse, apology
- tu pouvais t'inventer une meilleure excuse – *you could have come up with a better excuse*
83 | 520

**1840 veille** *nf* the day before, the eve of, night watch
- on s'était fiancés la veille – *we were engaged the night before*
69 | 1056

**1841 content** *adj* glad, pleased, happy
- elles étaient très contentes d'y aller – *they were very happy to go there*
66 | 1152-n

**1842 rassurer** *v* to reassure, calm down
- le premier travail consiste à rassurer le gosse – *the first task is to calm the kid down*
79 | 655

**1843 triste** *adj(f)* sad
- ouais, ouais, ne sois pas triste pour ça – *yeah, yeah, don't be sad about that*
72 | 910

**1844 latin** *nadj* Latin
- l'anglais est encore plus latin que le français – *English is more Latin than French is*
78 | 687

**1845 classique** *nadj(f)* classic
- j'ai étudié la musique classique – *I studied classical music*
72 | 916

**1846 alliance** *nf* alliance
- nous reconnaissons nos obligations envers l'alliance – *we recognize our duty to the alliance*
75 | 791

**1847 préoccupation** *nf* worry, concern
- je pense que c'est une préoccupation que nous partageons – *I think it's a concern we share*
64 | 1265+s

**1848 trace** *nf* trace, mark, track
- l'histoire humaine laisse d'éternelles traces – *human history is leaving behind eternal footprints*
76 | 747

**1849 logement** *nm* accommodation
- ils ont trouvé un logement et fait venir leur famille – *they found a place to live and had their family come*
63 | 1270

**1850 langage** *nm* language
- je parle le langage de la passion – *I speak the language of passion*
70 | 974

**1851 plainte** *nf* moan, groan, complaint
- quand cette femme a porté plainte, sa vie a été menacée – *when this woman filed a complaint, her life was threatened*
72 | 926

**1852 chaud** *adv,nadj* warm, hot
- il y a du café chaud dans le coffre sous la banquette – *there's hot coffee in the box under the bench*
69 | 1046

**1853 taire** *v* to keep quiet
- oh, tais toi, tu n'as pas honte – *oh, shut up, you have no shame*
59 | 1474+l -n

**1854 émotion** *nf* emotion, feeling
- je fis de mon émotion un événement – *I turned my emotions into a spectacle*
79 | 653

**1855 judiciaire** *adj(f)* judiciary
- nous devons préserver l'indépendance du pouvoir judiciaire – *we must preserve the judiciary's independance*
63 | 1274-l

**1856 progresser** *v* to progress
- nous avons pas mal progressé à ce sujet – *we have progressed quite well on this topic*
67 | 1120+n

**1857 secours** *nm(pl)* help, aid, assistance
- une jeune fille appelait au secours – *a young girl was crying for help*
69 | 1007

**1858 confronter** *v* to confront
- elle est confrontée à des défis plus nombreux – *she was confronted by numerous challenges*
74 | 820

**1859 strict** *adj* strict, absolute
- ce serait son strict devoir – *this would be his strict duty*
85 | 447

# 11  Weather

| | | |
|---|---|---|
| **frais** 691 **cool** | **atmosphère** 2493 F atmosphere | **brouillard** 4452 M **fog** |
| **froid** 1307 **cold** | **glace** 2580 F **ice** | **météo** 4574 F **weather forecast** |
| **vent** 1387 M **wind** | **tempête** 2695 F **storm** | **inondation** 4677 F **flood** |
| **vague** 1493 F **wave** | **chaleur** 2773 F **heat** | **orage** 4788 M **thunderstorm** |
| **front** 1729 M **front** (also **forehead**) | **température** 2924 F temperature | **humide** 4841 **humid** |
| **neige** 1824 F **snow** | **rayon** 2926 M **ray** | **nuageux** 5429 **cloudy** |
| **chaud** 1852 **hot** | **nuage** 3219 M **cloud** | **torrent** 6506 M **torrent** |
| **climat** 2006 M **climate** | **gel** 4122 M **frost** | **pluvieux** 6682 **rainy** |
| **pluie** 2217 F **rain** | **avalanche** 4426 F avalanche | **humidité** 7559 F **humidity** |
| **sec** 2313 **dry** | | **ensoleillé** 7852 **sunny** |

1860 **club** nm club
- j'arrivais dans un club qui avait gagné deux championnats – I joined a club that had won two championships
67 | 1100

1861 **ouvrier** nadj worker
- l'Allemand a toujours été bon ouvrier – the German has always been a hard worker
71 | 935

1862 **souffrance** nf suffering
- je connais les souffrances du monde – I know the sufferings of the world
78 | 671

1863 **observation** nf observation
- j'ai trouvé l'observation astucieuse – I found the observation astute
64 | 1214

1864 **rétablir** v to restore, re-establish
- parfois, j'ai envie de rétablir quelques vérités – sometimes I want to re-establish some truths
76 | 740

1865 **immeuble** nadj(f) building
- j'habite dans cet immeuble – I live in this building
79 | 656

1866 **passion** nf passion
- lirait-il avec passion les journaux? – would he read newspapers with passion?
65 | 1170+l

1867 **rupture** nf break, rupture
- il y a eu rupture des négociations, reprise des négociations – negotiations broke down, then restarted
81 | 569

1868 **office** nm office, bureau
- il perd son emploi à l'office des jardins – he lost his job at the gardening office
72 | 899

1869 **compliquer** v to complicate
- le système actuel s'avère-t-il compliqué – the current system proves too complicated
84 | 473

1870 **assumer** v to assume
- les autorités font assumer la responsabilité des troubles – the authorities will assume responsibility for the confusion
74 | 808

1871 **partiel** nadj partial
- elle travaille à temps partiel – she works part-time
77 | 712

1872 **éprouver** v to feel, experience
- je n'éprouvais aucune hâte à procéder – I didn't feel any need to continue
71 | 916

1873 **rendez-vous** nm(pl) appointment
- oui, nous avions un rendez-vous clandestin – yes, we had a secret rendez-vous
74 | 828

1874 **argument** nm argument
- j'ai entendu des arguments peu convaincants – I heard fairly unconvincing arguments
69 | 1029

1875 **planète** nf planet
- toute la planète est fatiguée de ce conflit – the whole planet is tired of this conflict
75 | 784

1876 **maire** nm mayor
- il a fait 3 mandats comme maire – he filled three terms as mayor
71 | 916

1877 **délicat** nadj delicate, fine, gentle
- c'est toujours délicat d'embaucher des amies! – it's always tricky to hire girlfriends
81 | 576

1878 **attentat** nm attack, assassination attempt
- il s'agit d'un attentat de la guérilla – it was a guerilla attack
50 | 1897+n -s

**1879  boire** *nm,v*  to drink
- vous boirez quelque chose? – *would you like something to drink?*
59 | 1457-n

**1880  richesse** *nf*  wealth, richness
- ce sera mon passeport pour la richesse, l'indépendance – *this will be my passport to riches, independence*
79 | 650

**1881  caisse** *nf*  till, cash desk
- tu vas passer à la caisse! – *you must go to the cashier!*
68 | 1040

**1882  hasard** *nm*  chance, luck
- on ne laissait rien au hasard – *nothing was left to chance*
71 | 940

**1883  héros** *nm(pl)*  hero
- un héros lui aurait sauvé la vie – *a hero would have saved her life*
75 | 765

**1884  oreille** *nf*  ear
- il s'introduisit un doigt dans l'oreille – *he stuck a finger in his ear*
67 | 1101

**1885  incident** *adj,nm*  incident
- fort heureusement, l'incident n'a pas fait de victime – *very fortunately, the incident was without victims*
73 | 868

**1886  café** *nm*  coffee, café
- Amélie est serveuse dans un café de Montmartre – *Amélie is a waitress in a Montmartre café*
66 | 1124

**1887  annonce** *nf*  announcement
- il n'y a pas eu d'annonce à ce sujet – *there was no announcement concerning this*
70 | 983

**1888  régulièrement** *adv*  regularly
- elle a promis de venir régulièrement – *she promised to come regularly*
78 | 666

**1889  pont** *nm*  bridge
- il fallait jeter un pont entre l'Est et l'Ouest – *a bridge had to be built between the East and the West*
77 | 707

**1890  foutre** *v,nm*  to f*ck, shove off
- va te faire foutre – *go f*ck yourself*
56 | 1577-n +s

**1891  apercevoir** *v*  to see, notice
- on aperçoit la sortie du tunnel – *you can see the exit of the tunnel*
66 | 1134+l

**1892  refléter** *v*  to reflect
- la pièce d'eau reflétait la majestueuse façade d'un palais de pierre – *the ornamental pool reflected the majestic facade of a stone palace*
76 | 740

**1893  bouger** *v*  to move, shift, budge
- je reste là. je ne bouge pas – *I'll stay here. I won't budge*
62 | 1273-n

**1894  foule** *nf*  crowd
- il y a foule chez toi, ce soir – *there's a crowd at your place tonight*
73 | 833

**1895  chrétien** *nadj*  Christian
la moitié des habitants sont de confession chrétienne – *half of the inhabitants are Christians*
73 | 861

**1896  isoler** *v*  to isolate, insulate
- il se sentait isolé, isolé psychologiquement – *he felt isolated, psychologically alone*
83 | 500

**1897  norme** *nf*  norm, standard
- nous appliquons désormais les normes d'hygiène – *from now on we are applying hygiene standards*
67 | 1059

**1898  égalité** *nf*  equality
- l'égalité des hommes et des femmes est garantie – *equality for men and women is guaranteed*
70 | 958

**1899  tenue** *nf*  dress, outfit
- il est rare qu'on me complimente sur ma tenue – *rarely do I receive compliments on my outfit*
78 | 666

**1900  animer** *v*  to lead, conduct, animate
- le vin suscitait des conversations animées – *the wine gave rise to animated conversations*
76 | 731

**1901  statistique** *nf*  statistics, statistical
- je suis tombé sur une statistique très intéressante – *I came across an interesting statistic*
75 | 770

**1902  piste** *nf*  track, trail
- c'est là où la piste s'arrête – *that's where the trail ends*
76 | 730

**1903  préserver** *v*  to preserve
- dans le bocal, mes larmes préservent le cœur de mon fils – *inside the jar, my tears preserved my son's heart*
78 | 673

**1904  hommage** *nm*  homage, tribute
- il a ensuite rendu hommage au président – *then he paid homage to the president*
77 | 679

**1905  inférieur** *nadj*  inferior
- il déclare qu'elle lui est inférieure en amitié – *he declares that she is less loving than he*
61 | 1326+n -s

**1906  match** *nm*  match, game
- je n'avais pas gagné un match depuis deux mois – *I hadn't won a match in two months*
54 | 1652

**1907 pointe** *nf* point, tip
- la longue pointe de mon parapluie était comme un doigt – *the long tip of my umbrella was like a finger*
80 | 594

**1908 gouvernemental** *adj* governmental
on va alléger l'appareil gouvernemental – *we're going to lighten the governmental apparatus*
61 | 1299-I

**1909 exécuter** *v* to execute, carry out
- je suis ici pour exécuter vos ordres – *I'm here to carry out your orders*
79 | 613

**1910 tragédie** *nf* tragedy
- la tragédie a commencé. Hitler a attaqué l'URSS – *the tragedy began. Hitler invaded the Soviet Union*
83 | 490

**1911 distribution** *nf* distribution
- j'ai participé à un programme de distribution de petits déjeuners – *I participated in a breakfast distribution program*
71 | 908

**1912 scandale** *nm* scandal, uproar
- il y aurait eu un petit scandale dans le famille – *there was a little scandal in the family*
80 | 580

**1913 irakien** *nadj* Iraqi
- Hussein est totalement coupé de la population irakienne – *Hussein is totally cut off from the Iraqi population*
48 | 1943-I

**1914 chinois** *nadj(pl)* Chinese
- la main-d'œuvre chinoise a contribué de façon importante au développement économique – *Chinese manpower contributed greatly to economic development*
66 | 1089

**1915 bénéfice** *nm* benefit, profit
- l'entreprise fait des bénéfices – *the company is making profits*
66 | 1097

**1916 billet** *nm* ticket
- j'ai pas de billet pour le match de demain – *I don't have a ticket for tomorrow's game*
76 | 732

**1917 choc** *nm* shock, clash
- elle est en état de choc – *she's in a state of shock*
79 | 599

**1918 proportion** *nf* proportion
- la fréquence des agressions atteint des proportions alarmantes – *the frequency of attacks is reaching alarming proportions*
82 | 517

**1919 canal** *nm* canal, channel
- l'utilisation du canal sémaphore est suspendue – *the use of a semaphore channel is discontinued*
46 | 2077+n -s

**1920 briser** *v* to break
- vous m'avez brisé le cœur – *you broke my heart*
76 | 707

**1921 destruction** *nf* destruction
- votre salut est sa destruction – *your salvation is his destruction*
73 | 816

**1922 reculer** *v* to move back, back up
- ils ne reculent devant rien – *they don't back down from anything*
72 | 878

**1923 critère** *nm* criterion, criteria
- selon quels critères ces traits sont-ils sélectionnés? – *according to what criteria were these features selected?*
67 | 1068-I

**1924 gardien** *nadj* guardian, keeper
- nous sommes les gardiens de cette planète – *we are the guardians of this planet*
80 | 590

**1925 adresse** *nf* address
- on a une adresse Internet – *we have an Internet address*
52 | 1725+n -s

**1926 réception** *nf* reception
- les mêmes invités étaient présents à chaque réception – *the same invited guests were at each reception*
43 | 2196-I +n -s

**1927 conservateur** *nadj* conservative
- dans les auteurs, y a un conservateur – *among the authors, there is a conservative one*
61 | 1280-I

**1928 ouais** *intj* yeah
- j'aime mon job. ouais, bien sûr – *I like my job. yeah, of course*
43 | 2215-I -n +s

**1929 transporter** *v* to transport, carry
- il transporta des milliers d'hommes ici – *it transported thousands of men here*
77 | 673

**1930 brûler** *v* to burn
- je sais que Lucy brûlait d'une passion secrète pour vous – *I know Lucy was burning up with a secret passion for you*
70 | 911

**1931 manœuvre** *nm,nf* manoeuvre
- nous étions trois soldats à faire la manœuvre – *three of us soldiers participated in the manoeuvre*
81 | 551

**1932 monnaie** *nf* currency, coin, change
- aujourd'hui, nous avons une monnaie stable – *today we have a stable currency*
66 | 1079

**1933 transmission** *nf* transmission
- cette transmission est vraiment excellente – *this transmission is really excellent*
47 | 1982-I +n -s

**1934 quelconque** *adj(f)*  any, some
- est-ce qu'on a un vase quelconque? – *do we have some kind of vase?*
  77 | 669

**1935 courrier** *nm*  mail, post
- il y a peut-être du courrier – *maybe there's mail*
  86 | 383

**1936 grandir** *v*  to grow, increase, expand
- je ne grandis plus … je grossis – *I'm not growing any taller … just stouter*
  80 | 566

**1937 élaborer** *v*  to work out, develop
- cette vision a été élaborée avant le 11 septembre – *this vision was developed before September 11*
  69 | 950

**1938 doigt** *nm*  finger
- il tapait du doigt sur la table, à coups secs – *he tapped his finger on the table repeatedly*
  62 | 1241+l

**1939 illustrer** *v*  to illustrate
- cette manifestation illustre les craintes des citoyens – *this protest shows the citizens' fears*
  78 | 647

**1940 poche** *nf*  pocket
- je n'ai rien dans les poches – *I don't have anything in my pockets*
  68 | 996+l

**1941 affronter** *v*  to confront, face
- j'ai dû affronter la terrible réalité – *I had to confront the terrible reality*
  76 | 719

**1942 éclater** *v*  to burst, explode
- quand la guerre a éclaté, tout était perdu – *when war broke out, everything was lost*
  73 | 818

**1943 honte** *nf*  shame
- n'aie pas honte de tes origines – *don't be ashamed of your origins*
  71 | 868-n

**1944 faiblesse** *nf*  weakness
- c'est là ma faiblesse et ma force – *therein lies my weakness and my strength*
  77 | 685

**1945 fédération** *nf*  federation
- les fonctionnaires étaient convoqués par leurs fédérations – *the bureaucrats were called together by their federations*
  62 | 1212-l

**1946 presser** *v*  to squeeze, press
- ils ont laissé un soldat chargé de presser le détonateur – *they left a soldier with the order to press the detonator*
  74 | 761

**1947 mêler** *v*  to mingle, mix
- la fiction se mêle constamment à l'autobiographie – *fiction constantly gets mixed in with autobiography*
  75 | 747

**1948 bonheur** *nm*  happiness
- aujourd'hui, ce bonheur n'est plus que souvenir – *today this happiness is merely a memory*
  63 | 1195+l

**1949 formuler** *v*  to formulate
- je veux formuler un commentaire général – *I want to make a general comment*
  73 | 794

**1950 crier** *v*  to shout, scream, cry out
- ils se meurent. ils crient au secours – *they're dying. they cry out for help*
  62 | 1240+l

**1951 pauvreté** *nf*  poverty
- ils vivent dans la pauvreté – *they live in poverty*
  60 | 1305+s

**1952 bâtiment** *nm*  building
- il travaillait au deuxième étage du bâtiment – *he worked on the second floor of the building*
  70 | 906

**1953 époux** *nm(pl)*  husband, spouse
- je suis fier de l'avoir choisi comme époux – *I'm proud of having chosen him for a husband*
  72 | 843

**1954 médicament** *nm*  medicine, drug, medication
- je crois en les médicaments génériques peu coûteux – *I believe in cheap generic medications*
  72 | 832

**1955 firme** *nf*  firm
- il gérait les fonds de la firme – *he managed the firm's funds*
  59 | 1351+l -s

**1956 élargir** *v*  to widen, expand
- nous devons élargir nos horizons – *we have to expand our horizons*
  76 | 694

**1957 électeur** *nm*  elector, voter
- je remercie également les électeurs de ma circonscription – *I also thank the voters in my district*
  62 | 1231

**1958 plonger** *v*  to dive
- chaque matin, je plonge dans la mer – *every morning I take a dip in the sea*
  75 | 713

**1959 véhicule** *nm*  vehicle
- sortez du véhicule. vous aussi – *exit the vehicle. you too*
  70 | 914

**1960 fuir** *v*  to flee
- j'aggravai ma situation en voulant fuir – *I worsened my situation by wanting to flee*
  73 | 801

**1961 chercheur** *nadj*  researcher
- même si vous êtes un bon chercheur, la compétition est rude – *even if you're a good researcher, competition is fierce*
  66 | 1048

**1962 varier** *v* to vary, change
- on aime varier les plaisirs. varier, c'est bon – *we like to vary our pleasures. change is good*
76 | 694

**1963 personnalité** *nf* personality
- il était brillant et avait une riche personnalité – *he was brilliant and had a rich personality*
70 | 881

**1964 inventer** *v* to invent
- je n'ai pas pu inventer un tel souvenir – *I couldn't have invented such a memory*
72 | 833

**1965 principalement** *adv* principally, mainly, primarily
- c'est sur les femmes principalement qu'elle a exercé une grande influence – *it's primarily with women that she wields great influence*
77 | 639

**1966 prudence** *nf* prudence, care, caution
- la prudence est la meilleure attitude à adopter – *caution is the best policy*
80 | 568

**1967 stade** *nm* stadium, stage
- leurs recherches sont encore au stade préliminaire – *their research is still at the preliminary stage*
70 | 881

**1968 liaison** *nf* liaison, connection
- les liaisons ferroviaires ont été interrompues – *railroad connections were interrupted*
55 | 1518+n -s

**1969 consultation** *nf* consultation
- après consultation confidentielle des professeurs – *after confidential consultation with the professors*
63 | 1145+s

**1970 québécois** *nadj(pl)* Quebecker, Quebecer, Québécois
- il existe un marché pour le produit québécois en France – *there's a market for Quebecois products in France*
50 | 1729-l -n +s

**1971 ordonner** *v* to ordain, organize, order
- soldat, je vous ordonne d'avancer ces catapultes – *soldier, I order you to move these catapults forward*
78 | 605

**1972 bonjour** *nm* hello
- voilà ma petite fille. bonjour, ma chérie. viens par ici – *there's my little girl. hello, dear. come here*
47 | 1871-n +s

**1973 morale** *nf* ethics; moral
- la morale judéo-chrétienne me paraît l'une des plus belles – *to me the Judeo-Christian ethic seems among the finest*
72 | 819

**1974 contester** *v* to contest, question
- l'art conteste le réel – *art questions reality*
75 | 709

**1975 nécessairement** *adv* necessarily
- le bien n'est pas nécessairement beau – *what's good is not necessarily beautiful*
75 | 707

**1976 détermination** *nf* determination, resolution
- il peut avoir sans doute des déterminations égoïstes – *he certainly could have selfish resolve*
77 | 642

**1977 congrès** *nm(pl)* congress, conference
- c'est lui qui préside le congrès – *he's who presides over the conference*
65 | 1077

**1978 semblable** *nadj(f)* similar
- nous avons vu un cas semblable ici – *we have seen a similar case here*
72 | 817

**1979 préoccuper** *v* to worry, preoccupy
- il nous faut sans doute nous préoccuper de l'avenir de nos enfants – *we need to be concerned about the future of our children*
66 | 1031+s

**1980 dépôt** *nm* deposit, depot
- voici le mandat de dépôt du détenu – *here's the incarceration order for the prisoner*
70 | 883

**1981 considération** *nf* consideration
- j'aimerais que vous preniez en considération ma suggestion – *I would like you take my suggestion under consideration*
68 | 964

**1982 multiplier** *v* to multiply
- nous sommes maintenant en train de multiplier le danger nucléaire – *we're currently multiplying nuclear risks*
73 | 766

**1983 dame** *intj,nf* lady
- une belle rose pour une belle dame – *a beautiful rose for a beautiful lady*
66 | 1033

**1984 joie** *nf* joy
- je ne ressens ni peine ni joie – *I feel neither pain nor joy*
65 | 1054+l

**1985 durable** *adj(f)* durable, long-lasting
- la transgenèse promeut une agriculture durable – *hybrid crops encourage durable agriculture*
76 | 682

**1986 faim** *nf* hungry
- je commence à avoir faim – *I'm starting to feel hungry*
73 | 760

**1987 excuser** *v* to excuse
- excusez moi de vous interrompre monsieur – *excuse me for interrupting, sir*
60 | 1279-n +s

**1988 recommander** *v* to recommend
- je ne lui recommandai même pas la prudence – *I didn't even recommend caution to him*
64 | 1095

**1989 concept** *nm* concept
- ce concept me réjouit, il est plein d'espoir – *I delight in this concept, it's full of hope*
67 | 974

**1990 cerveau** *nm* brain
- à la naissance, le cerveau humain est loin d'être complètement développé – *at birth, the human brain is far from completely developed*
77 | 650

**1991 truc** *nm* trick; thingamajig
- je peux avoir un truc à grignoter? – *can I have something to snack on?*
53 | 1566-n +s

**1992 allié** *nadj* allied; ally
- la guerre sera gagnée par les Alliés – *the war will be won by the Allies*
70 | 859

**1993 scolaire** *adj(f)* school, educational, academic
- je veux juste finir l'année scolaire avec mes amis – *I just want to finish the school year with my friends*
70 | 869

**1994 arabe** *nadj(f)* Arabic, Arab
- le monde arabe devient bipolaire – *the Arab world is becoming bipolar*
61 | 1231

**1995 diffuser** *v* to diffuse, broadcast
- nos stations diffusent une émission quotidienne – *our stations broadcast a daily program*
63 | 1147

**1996 budgétaire** *adj(f)* budgetary
- la situation budgétaire nous place dans une position critique – *the budgetary situation puts us in a critical position*
61 | 1224-l

**1997 inquiétant** *adj* worrying, disturbing
- la puissance iranienne est inquiétante – *Iranian power is disturbing*
86 | 368

**1998 inclure** *v* to include
- n'incluez pas une extension de fichier – *don't include a file extension*
68 | 941-l

**1999 style** *nm* style
- faut que je change de style – *I've gotta change my style*
69 | 892

**2000 combler** *v* to fill, fill in, fulfill
- les gens tentent de combler ce vide, pierre par pierre – *people try to fill up the void, stone by stone*
82 | 474

**2001 ombre** *nm,nf* shade, shadow
- il vivait dans son ombre et ne cherchait qu'à lui complaire – *he lived in her shadow and only sought to please her*
62 | 1167+l -s

**2002 annuler** *v* to cancel
- il a dû annuler un voyage – *he had to cancel a trip*
74 | 720

**2003 joueur** *nadj* player
- j'étais même le meilleur joueur de l'équipe – *I was even the best player on the team*
61 | 1196

**2004 bloquer** *v* to block
- ils nous disent que nous bloquons le progrès – *they say we're blocking progress*
70 | 849

**2005 interprétation** *nf* interpretation
- vous pouvez être en désaccord avec mon interprétation – *you can disagree with my interpretation*
70 | 852

**2006 climat** *nm* climate
- pour rétablir le climat de confiance, il faut gagner le respect – *to reestablish the climate of trust, respect must be gained*
79 | 558

**2007 séjour** *nm* stay
- notre séjour s'achève. nous partons demain – *our visit is over. we leave tomorrow*
79 | 561

**2008 guider** *v* to guide
- voilà les convictions qui guident mes pas – *these are the convictions that guide my footsteps*
83 | 447

**2009 spécialiser** *v* to specialize
- la main-d'œuvre spécialisée vieillit – *specialized manpower is ageing*
73 | 757

**2010 bien?** *adv* well
- bon ... ben il va falloir que je m'y mette – *OK, well I will have to get busy with it*
51 | 1633+s

**2011 sport** *adji,nm* sport
- le sport est le meilleur remède physique et mental – *sports are the best physical and mental cure*
67 | 973

**2012 amélioration** *nf* improvement
- il faut prévoir que l'amélioration sera lente – *you have to expect the improvement to be slow*
64 | 1081-l

**2013 douleur** *nf* pain
- je comprends votre douleur et combien ceci est pénible – *I feel your pain and how difficult this is*
70 | 880

**2014 issue** *nf* exit, outcome
- nous fondons nos espoirs sur une issue positive au référendum – *our hopes rest on a positive outcome in the referendum*
63 | 1118

**2015 généreux** *adj(pl)* generous
- il était généreux dans ses activités bénévoles – *he was generous in his charitable activities*
82 | 480

**2016 absent** *nadj* absent
- il a été absent trois heures – *he was absent for three hours*
81 | 504

**2017 talent** *nm* talent
- votre frère a beaucoup de talent – *your brother has a lot of talent*
76 | 669

**2018 normalement** *adv* normally
- normalement, je suis un chien très gentil – *normally, I'm a very gentle dog*
75 | 689

**2019 remarque** *nf* remark
- par cette remarque je n'accuse personne – *by making that remark I don't accuse anyone*
58 | 1309

**2020 détourner** *v* to redirect
- pour rentrer, il suffit de détourner l'attention du gardien – *to gain entry you just have to distract the security guard*
74 | 738

**2021 raisonnable** *adj(f)* reasonable, fair
- soyez raisonnable, rentrez vous reposer – *be reasonable—go home and rest*
73 | 758

**2022 suprême** *nadj(f)* supreme
- certains ont fait le sacrifice suprême – *some made the supreme sacrifice*
67 | 983

**2023 éventuel** *nadj* possible
- ce serait peut-être un éventuel projet pour vous – *that might be a possible project for you*
66 | 1002

**2024 blesser** *v* to hurt
- le premier avait été légèrement blessé, le second était sorti indemne – *the first was lightly injured, the second escaped unharmed*
61 | 1193

**2025 orientation** *nf* orientation, trend
- je suis d'orientation homosexuelle – *I have a homosexual orientation*
71 | 828

**2026 grec** *nadj* Greek
- il utilisait deux mots grecs – *he used two Greek words*
70 | 854

**2027 secondaire** *nadj(f)* secondary
- quels types d'effets secondaires pourraient survenir? – *what kind of secondary effects could take place?*
77 | 625

**2028 reporter** *nm,nf,v* to report; to postpone
- nous pourrions avoir à reporter certaines choses – *we might have to delay certain things*
71 | 808

**2029 partisan** *nadj* partisan, supporter
- je ne suis pas un ardent partisan – *I'm not an ardent supporter*
69 | 903

**2030 cinquième** *det,nm,nf* fifth
- il s'agissait de la cinquième médaille olympique de sa carrière – *it was the fifth Olympic medal of his career*
79 | 565

**2031 distinction** *nf* distinction
- il y a une distinction sémantique importante à faire – *there's an important semantic distinction to be made*
80 | 543

**2032 impact** *nm* impact
- ses paroles ont un impact épouvantable – *her words have a deadful impact*
71 | 807-I

**2033 magazine** *nm* magazine
- on fait semblant de lire un magazine – *we pretend to read a magazine*
74 | 702

**2034 compléter** *v* to complete
- cela complète notre présentation, mesdames et messieurs – *that completes our presentation, ladies and gentlemen*
78 | 582

**2035 mérite** *nm* merit
- mon mérite était nul – *I had nothing going for me*
78 | 595

**2036 naturellement** *adv* naturally
- elle va naturellement sortir avec des garçons – *naturally she will date guys*
72 | 789

**2037 collaboration** *nf* collaboration
- c'est cette collaboration qui a mené aux progrès – *this collaboration is what is leading to progress*
69 | 898

**2038 procurer** *v* to get, bring
- j'ignore comment vous vous êtes procuré cette carte – *I don't know how you got that card*
80 | 528

**2039 officier** *nm,nf,v* officer; officiate
- il craint de perdre ses meilleurs officiers – *he fears losing his best officers*
73 | 745

**2040 remarquable** *adj(f)* remarkable, outstanding
- c'est remarquable, ce qui peut être fait – *it's remarkable, what can be done*
81 | 490

**2041 efforcer** *v* endeavor
- nous nous efforçons de contenir ce fléau – *we are endeavoring to contain this plague*
78 | 580

**2042 tragique** *nadj(f)* tragic
- c'est tragique, elles sont mortes – *tragically, they died*
83 | 437

**2043 anniversaire** *nadj(f)* anniversary, birthday
- j'ai un cadeau d'anniversaire pour toi – *I have a birthday present for you*
73 | 739

**2044 issu** *adj* descended from
- Hugh était issu d'une famille de cinq garçons – *Hugh came from a family of five boys*
71 | 804

## 12 Professions

This table lists the most frequently occurring professions, functions, and offices from the corpus.

**ministre** 204 MF **minister**

**président** 268 M **president**

**chef** 386 M **leader**

**aide** 457 MF **aide**

**cadre** 483 M **executive**

**directeur** 640 M **director**

**sénateur** 684 M **senator**

**financier** 688 M **financier**

**militaire** 690 M **military**

**auteur** 762 MF **author**

**autorité** 783 F **authority**

**médecin** 827 M **physician**

**garde** 901 MF **guard**

**critique** 909 M **critic**

**client** 917 M **client**

**soldat** 1098 M **soldier**

**professeur** 1150 MF professor

**avocat** 1188 M **lawyer**

**religieux** 1203 M **religious**

**représentant** 1232 M representative

**producteur** 1259 M producer

**facteur** 1264 M **mailman**

**juge** 1323 MF **judge**

**candidat** 1328 M **candidate**

**journaliste** 1337 MF journalist

**travailleur** 1341 M **worker**

**dirigeant** 1343 M **leader**

**propriétaire** 1406 MF **owner**

**criminel** 1411 M **criminal**

**leader** 1499 MF **leader**

**interne** 1546 MF **intern**

**acteur** 1552 M **actor**

**fonctionnaire** 1631 MF public

**patron** 1706 M **boss**

**porte-parole** 1722 M spokesperson

**commissaire** 1737 MF commissioner

**écrivain** 1738 M **writer**

**vice-président** 1789 M vice-president

**artiste** 1797 NF **artist**

**ouvrier** 1861 N **worker**

**maire** 1876 M **mayor**

**gardien** 1924 M guardian

**électeur** 1957 M **elector**

**chercheur** 1961 M researcher

**officier** 2039 MF **officer**

**infirmier** 2049 M **nurse**

**gouverneur** 2089 MF governor

**lecteur** 2100 M **reader**

**marin** 2101 M **sailor**

**salarié** 2119 M **employee**

**docteur** 2176 M **doctor**

---

**2045 poursuite** *nf* chase, pursuit
- je suis parti à la poursuite de mon rêve – *I left to pursue my dream*
- 72 | 780

**2046 nôtre** *nadj(f)* ours, our own
- j'aurais aimé qu'il soit des nôtres – *I would have preferred him to be on our side*
- 80 | 522

**2047 éclairer** *v* to light up
- vous êtes là pour que je vous éclaire – *you're here so that I can enlighten you*
- 71 | 792

**2048 consommer** *v* to eat, consume, drink, use, consummate
- nous consommons des aliments génétiquement modifiés – *we consume genetically modified food*
- 84 | 390

**2049 infirmier** *nadj* nurse
- un infirmier lui est venu en aide – *a male nurse came to his aid*
- 85 | 368

**2050 caractéristique** *nadj(f)* characteristic
- il est toutefois caractéristique qu'aucune décision définitive n'a été prise – *it is nevertheless characteristic that no definitive decision was taken*
- 54 | 1452+n -s

**2051 dépenser** *v* to spend
- j'ai dépensé beaucoup d'argent pour elle – *I spent a lot of money on her*
- 63 | 1103+s

**2052 censé** *adj* supposed
- elle est censé donner une réponse – *she is supposed to give a response*
- 75 | 664

**2053 fuite** *nf* escape
- l'assassin prend la fuite à cheval – *the assassin is fleeing on horseback*
- 76 | 626

**2054 conviction** *nf* conviction, belief
- vous avez agi selon vos convictions – *you acted according to your convictions*
- 78 | 564

**2055 nettement** *adv* clearly, distinctly
- il savait nettement ce qu'il devait et voulait faire – *he knew clearly what he needed to do and wanted to do*
- 75 | 662

**2056 détenir** *v* to hold, detain
- je ne prétends pas détenir la vérité – *I don't pretend to have the whole truth*
- 64 | 1051

**2057 évaluation** *nf* evaluation
- il faudrait procéder à une évaluation avant de le faire – *we'll have to carry out an evaluation before doing it*
70 | 837

**2058 installation** *nf* installation, setup
- on accordera une très grande importance aux installations – *the installations will be very important for us*
72 | 766

**2059 innocent** *nadj* innocent
- l'essentiel est qu'ils soient innocents – *the important thing is that they are innocent*
79 | 537

**2060 fameux** *adj(pl)* famous
- voici l'un de nos plus fameux sadiques – *here is one of our most famous sadists*
76 | 633

**2061 cultiver** *v* to cultivate, grow
- elle cultive le goût des petits plaisirs – *she cultivates a taste for simple pleasures*
86 | 335

**2062 doux** *adv,nadj(pl)* soft, sweet
- le soleil était doux et chaud – *the sunshine was soft and hot*
64 | 1046+l

**2063 gouverner** *v* to govern, rule, steer, helm
- il a été élu pour gouverner – *he was elected to govern*
84 | 410

**2064 jouir** *v* to enjoy
- elle jouit du respect et de l'admiration des gens – *she enjoys people's respect and admiration*
76 | 624

**2065 parcourir** *v* to cover, travel
- il parcourut son courrier – *he went through his mail*
80 | 513

**2066 bloc** *nm* block
- ici, nous avons un bloc de béton – *here, we have a cement block*
74 | 675

**2067 électrique** *adj(f)* electric
- je n'aime pas tous ces appareils électriques – *I don't like all of these electrical devices*
74 | 688

**2068 seuil** *nm* doorstep, threshold
- a peine le seuil franchi elle s'arrêtait – *barely crossing the threshold, she stopped*
69 | 863

**2069 croissant** *nadj* growing, crescent, crescent-shape
- la compétition avec les Etats-Unis ira croissant – *competition with the U.S. will be growing*
79 | 530

**2070 classer** *v* to classify, file, grade, rate
- vous devenez plus difficile à classer – *you're becoming more difficult to pigeonhole*
82 | 437

**2071 audience** *nf* audience, hearing
- l'audience a été suspendue jusqu'à mercredi – *the hearing was suspended until Wednesday*
68 | 893

**2072 multiple** *nadj(f)* multiple
- il s'oppose aux multiples procédures d'extradition – *he opposes multiple extradition proceedings*
69 | 854

**2073 minorité** *nf* minority
- il y a une minorité francophone appréciable dans la région – *there's a sizable French-speaking minority in the region*
72 | 754

**2074 phrase** *nf* sentence, phrase
- je vomissais les phrases dans un très grand désordre – *I spewed out the phrases in chaotic fashion*
64 | 1015

**2075 provisoire** *adj(f)* temporary, provisional
- son fils était maintenu en détention provisoire – *his son was held in temporary confinement*
76 | 613

**2076 hein** *intj* eh, huh
- c'est un bon club, hein? – *this is a good club, eh?*
46 | 1761-n +s

**2077 disparition** *nf* disappearance
- les condors sont en voie de disparition – *condors are becoming extinct*
79 | 531

**2078 dynamique** *nadj(f)* dynamic
- le marché reste très dynamique jusqu'à présent – *the markets remain very volatile at present*
73 | 710

**2079 renverser** *v* to knock down, turn over, overturn
- tout le container est renversé, tout est mélangé – *the whole container was overturned, everything is mixed up*
80 | 505

**2080 trouble** *adj(f),nm* turmoil, agitation, blurred, cloudy, trouble
- la cause de ces troubles reste mal connue – *the cause of these troubles remains relatively unknown*
77 | 588

**2081 désoler** *v* to upset, sadden
- je suis tellement désolé. désolé pour tout – *I am so sorry. sorry for everything*
50 | 1593-n +s

**2082 accélérer** *v* to speed up, accelerate
- les événements pourraient donc s'accélérer – *the events could thus accelerate*
77 | 579

**2083 littérature** *nf* literature
- je crois que la littérature africaine se porte bien – *I think that African literature is faring very well*
60 | 1179

**2084 résider** *v*  to reside
- c'est là que réside l'avenir de nos enfants – *that's where the future of our children lies*
  80 | 515

**2085 adolescent** *nm*  teenager, adolescent
- nous étions alors de jeunes adolescents – *we were young teenagers at the time*
  76 | 619

**2086 dessiner** *v*  to draw, design
- je ne sais pas dessiner. c'est une frustration – *I don't know how to draw. it's frustrating*
  71 | 789

**2087 rompre** *v*  to break
- il a rompu avec les Frères musulmans – *he left the Muslim Brotherhood*
  76 | 622

**2088 agriculture** *nf*  agriculture
- nous devons continuer de pratiquer une agriculture scientifique – *we must continue to practice scientific agriculture*
  58 | 1233-l

**2089 gouverneur** *nm,nf*  governor
- le rôle du nouveau gouverneur de l'île est si important – *the role of the island's new governor is so important*
  69 | 826

**2090 aventure** *nf*  adventure
- un voyage en auto est une véritable aventure – *a car trip is a real adventure*
  70 | 793

**2091 armer** *v*  to arm
- l'Iran est en train de s'armer – *Iran is arming itself*
  75 | 636

**2092 volet** *nm*  shutter
- fermez bien les volets, il y aura de la tempête – *close the shutters tightly, a storm is coming*
  81 | 475

**2093 bâtir** *v*  to build
- nous pouvons continuer à bâtir une nation basée sur la tolérance – *we can continue to forge a nation based on tolerance*
  77 | 596

**2094 prime** *nadj(f),nf*  free gift, premium, bonus
- ils extorquent chaque jour une prime de protection – *every day they extort protection money*
  77 | 581

**2095 résulter** *v*  to result
- il en est résulté une tragédie humaine énorme – *an enormous human tragedy was the result*
  69 | 820

**2096 occupation** *nf*  occupation, pastime
- lire et faire l'amour sont ses occupations préférées – *reading and making love are his favorite pastimes*
  70 | 800

**2097 japonais** *nadj(pl)*  Japanese
- l'économie japonaise ne se porte pas si mal – *the Japanese economy is faring rather well*
  64 | 992+n

**2098 emmener** *v*  to take
- maman et papa ont dû l'emmener à l'hôpital – *mommy and daddy had to take him to the hospital*
  65 | 980

**2099 alimentaire** *adj(f)*  food
- l'épidémie met en péril la sécurité alimentaire – *the epidemic is threatening food safety*
  69 | 815

**2100 lecteur** *nm*  reader
- j'espère ne pas perdre des lecteurs – *I hope to not lose any readers*
  61 | 1122

**2101 marin** *nadj*  sea, marine, sailor
- la plupart des marins ont perdu leur emploi – *most sailors have lost their jobs*
  80 | 499

**2102 intermédiaire** *nadj(f)*  intermediate, intermediary
- le fait d'avoir des intermédiaires me dérange – *having intermediaries bothers me*
  66 | 923

**2103 vœu** *nm*  vow, wish, will
- j'ai rendu mes voeux de moine – *I took my vows as a monk*
  84 | 386

**2104 dresser** *v*  to draw up, put up, raise
- trois portes se dressaient maintenant devant lui – *now three doors stood before him*
  72 | 731

**2105 conception** *nf*  conception
- c'est notre conception de la politesse – *it's our idea of politeness*
  69 | 821

**2106 afficher** *v*  to display
- ils ont affiché ma photo dans tous les bâtiments – *they posted my photo in all the buildings*
  68 | 855

**2107 fragile** *adj(f)*  fragile, delicate, frail
- une bulle de savon semblerait moins fragile – *a soap bubble would seem to be less fragile*
  83 | 413

**2108 satisfaction** *nf*  satisfaction
- il rougit de satisfaction modeste – *he blushes with modest satisfaction*
  78 | 554

**2109 survenir** *v*  to occur, take place, appear
- trop d' événements néfastes sont survenus cette année – *too many harmful events took place this year*
  73 | 686

**2110 publicité** *nf*  advertising, advertisement, publicity
- même la mauvaise publicité peut être bonne – *even bad publicity can be good*
  71 | 753

**2111 arbre** *nm*  tree
- je fais tailler mes arbres pour donner de l'ombre – *I trim my trees so they'll give shade*
  64 | 992+l

**2112 univers** *nm(pl)* universe
• on connaît à peine notre univers – *we barely know our universe*
67 | 891

**2113 aéroport** *nm* airport
• il faut qu'on parte pour l'aéroport – *we have to leave for the airport*
65 | 948-l

**2114 sauter** *v* to jump
• je saute la barrière, je tombe – *I jump over the barrier and fall down*
65 | 936

**2115 chasse** *nf* chase, hunt, hunting
• la chasse et la pêche y sont une tradition – *hunting and fishing are a tradition over there*
81 | 448

**2116 collège** *nm* secondary school, college
• je n'ai jamais été au collège, j'étais trop pauvre – *I never went to college; I was too poor*
75 | 642

**2117 garantie** *nf* guarantee
• je ne puis vous donner cette garantie – *I can't give you this guarantee*
73 | 697

**2118 morceau** *nm* piece, bit
• je les ai notées sur un morceau de papier – *I jotted them down on a piece of paper*
71 | 736

**2119 salarié** *nadj* wage-earning, employee
• on doit protéger les salariés contre tout licenciement abusif – *employees are supposed to be protected from any abusive firings*
57 | 1231-l +n

**2120 discipline** *nf* discipline
• il n'y a pas de démocratie sans ordre et discipline – *there's no democracy without order and discipline*
73 | 696

**2121 explosion** *nf* explosion
• une autre explosion a eu lieu presque au même moment – *another explosion happened at almost the same instant*
61 | 1075

**2122 peau** *nf* skin
• elles ont la peau blanche – *they have white skin*
65 | 935

**2123 commande** *nf* order, control
• dès ce jour nous vous passons commande pour cet ouvrage – *from this day on we order that work from you*
53 | 1387+n -s

**2124 orienter** *v* to position, give advice, direct, orientate
• il orientera les antennes à 140 degrés – *he will position the antennas at 140 degrees*
78 | 545

**2125 reproduire** *v* to reproduce, repeat
• malheureusement, ces situations se reproduiront – *unfortunately, these situations will arise again*
82 | 422

**2126 paragraphe** *nm* paragraph
• j'aimerais lire son dernier paragraphe – *I would like to read its last paragraph*
59 | 1161-l +s

**2127 radical** *nadj* radical
• il faudra des changements radicaux – *what it will take is radical change*
74 | 658

**2128 transférer** *v* to transfer
• le trafic est transféré d'un ou de plusieurs canaux sémaphores – *the traffic is routed through one or more signal channels*
72 | 710

**2129 diffusion** *nf* diffusion, spreading, circulation
• la diffusion débridée d'armes crée de nouvelles menaces – *rampant arms proliferation is spawning new threats*
70 | 780

**2130 spécialement** *adv* especially, particularly
• vous aimez les chats? pas spécialement – *you like cats? not particularly*
86 | 320

**2131 croître** *v* to grow, increase
• les bureaucraties ont tendance à croître et à s'étendre – *bureaucracies tend to grow and spread*
81 | 455

**2132 tolérer** *v* to tolerate, access, put up, bear, endure
• je te tolère car c'est bien de te tolérer – *I tolerate you because it's good to tolerate you*
87 | 295

**2133 copie** *nf* copy, replica, paper
• j'en ai fait une copie – *I made a copy of it*
84 | 381

**2134 enseigner** *v* to teach
• j'ai enseigné les mathématiques et les finances – *I taught mathematics and finance*
70 | 778

**2135 rédiger** *v* to write, draw up
• l'année suivante, j'ai rédigé mon mémoire – *the next year I wrote my dissertation*
74 | 661

**2136 magnifique** *adj(f)* magnificent
• cet endroit est magnifique – *this place is magnificent*
74 | 642

**2137 initial** *adj* initial
• au succès initial a succédé une stabilisation – *after initial success there was a stabilization*
62 | 1024

**2138 indice** *nm* indication, sign, clue
• cet indice était d'ailleurs inutile – *this clue was in fact useless*
61 | 1065+n -s

**2139 promotion** *nf* promotion, advertising
• on a un budget pour de la promotion – *we have an advertising budget*
70 | 770+s

**2140 branche** *nf* branch
- la situation économique de la branche s'est légèrement détériorée – *the economic situation of the branch deteriorated somewhat*
70 | 778-s

**2141 section** *nf* section
- il y a aussi une section en français – *there's also a French section*
62 | 1032

**2142 chanson** *nf* song
- je pense que toutes les chansons sont plaisantes à chanter – *I think that all songs are fun to sing*
60 | 1106-n +s

**2143 pair** *adj,nm* peer, pair, even
- l'histoire de la musique va de pair avec l'histoire politique – *music history goes hand-in-hand with political history*
86 | 321

**2144 contraindre** *v* to compel, force
- on ne peut les contraindre à comparaître – *they can't be compelled to appear*
73 | 685

**2145 trancher** *v* to cut, sever, settle, decide
- ils tranchent avec l'éclat du ciel – *they stand out clearly with the brilliance of heaven*
84 | 371

**2146 réformiste** *nadj(f)* reformist
- les réformistes adoraient suivre l'évolution de la dette – *the reformists love to follow the debt's progress*
44 | 1765-l -n +s

**2147 retarder** *v* to delay, hold up
- j'ai été retardé par un embouteillage, un accident – *I was delayed by a traffic jam, an accident*
80 | 463

**2148 réjouir** *v* to delight, rejoice
- Dieu me pardonnera peut-être de me réjouir de ma mort – *perhaps God will forgive me for rejoicing in my death*
75 | 614

**2149 punir** *v* to punish
- si je t'ai offensé, punis-moi – *if I offended you, punish me*
83 | 403

**2150 repartir** *v* to set off again, start up again
- hélas, je repars demain par le premier train – *alas, I leave tomorrow on the first train*
74 | 647

**2151 cellule** *nf* cell
- j'ai aidé à bâtir ces cellules – *I helped build these cells*
65 | 936

**2152 déclencher** *v* to trigger, release, unleash
- on ignore ce qui a déclenché la violence – *we're unsure who unleashed the violence*
68 | 812+n

**2153 uni** *nadj* united
- votre famille est unie, je le sens – *your family is united, I can feel it*
62 | 1037

**2154 connexion** *nf* connection
- il y a donc une connexion profonde entre science et technologie – *hence there's a deep connection between science and technology*
40 | 1952-l +n -s

**2155 écouler** *v* to sell, run off, flow out
- le jus s'écoule librement, sans contact avec la peau – *the juice flows out freely, without touching the peel*
77 | 563

**2156 option** *nf* option
- il ne leur reste donc qu'une option – *so they only have one option left*
67 | 860

**2157 pétrole** *nm* crude oil, petroleum
- elle alluma une lampe à pétrole – *she lit an oil lamp*
64 | 943

**2158 laboratoire** *nm* laboratory
- les gros laboratoires n'ont pas toujours cette éthique-là – *the big laboratories don't always have that ethical outlook*
69 | 796

**2159 étrange** *nadj(f)* strange, odd
- j'ai fait un rêve étrange – *I had a strange dream*
68 | 819

**2160 coucher** *nm,v* to lie down, sleep
- lavez-les, nourrissez-les. couchez-les – *wash them, feed them. put them to bed*
57 | 1192+l -n

**2161 département** *nm* department
- nous avons encore un département de relation publique – *we still have a public relations department*
64 | 965

**2162 génie** *nm* genius
- notre fils est un génie – *our son is a genius*
72 | 712

**2163 profession** *nf* profession
- vous faites honte à votre profession! – *you're a disgrace to your profession!*
78 | 520

**2164 rumeur** *nf* rumour
- après plusieurs années de rumeurs, le scandale a éclaté – *after years of rumors, the scandal broke*
76 | 590

**2165 mien** *nadj,pro* mine
- le mien avait fonctionné sur 20 ans – *mine worked for 20 years*
62 | 1021+l -n

**2166 drôle** *adj(f),nm* funny, strange
- je ne trouve pas ça drôle – *I don't find that funny*
63 | 975-n

**2167 plat** *adj,nm* dish, flat
- un plat avec cinq choix de dessert – *a plate with five dessert choices*
71 | 710

**2168 maman** *nf* mom
- je suis ta maman et tu peux tout me dire –
  *I'm your mommy, and you can tell me
  everything*
  54 | 1292-n

**2169 incertitude** *nf* uncertainty
- cette incertitude est pesante pour nous –
  *this uncertainty is unsettling for us*
  81 | 447

**2170 célébrer** *v* to celebrate
- nous venons célébrer le mariage de mon
  frère – *we just celebrated the marriage
  of my brother*
  78 | 526

**2171 dignité** *nf* dignity
- il est toujours difficile de maintenir dignité
  et humour – *it's always hard to retain both
  dignity and humor*
  78 | 523

**2172 légitime** *nadj(f)* legitimate
- il l'aura l'autorité légitime de le faire
  – *he will have the legitimate authority to
  do so*
  77 | 539

**2173 philosophie** *nf* philosophy
- j'ai fait des études de philosophie – *I studied
  philosophy*
  62 | 991

**2174 verre** *nm* glass
- prenez un verre avec moi – *have a drink
  with me*
  59 | 1129

**2175 spécifique** *adj(f)* specific
- il n'y a pas d'heure spécifique – *there's not a
  specific time*
  63 | 987

**2176 docteur** *nm* doctor
- le docteur ne nous laissa aucun espoir – *the
  doctor didn't give us any hope*
  68 | 806

**2177 hausser** *v* to raise
- il faudra hausser les cotisations –
  *subscriptions will have to be raised*
  71 | 721

**2178 fréquence** *nf* frequency
- toutes les fréquences sont bloquées – *all of
  the frequencies are blocked*
  43 | 1787-l +n -s

**2179 urgent** *adj* urgent
- il est urgent de remettre l'église au milieu du
  village – *it's urgent to put the church back
  into a village setting*
  71 | 718

**2180 trou** *nm* hole
- au mur, il y a un trou blanc – *in the wall
  there's a white hole*
  69 | 782

**2181 stratégique** *adj(f)* strategic
- il est très stratégique pour la région – *it's
  very strategic for the region*
  72 | 698

**2182 mental** *nadj* mental
- il sentait que ses facultés mentales étaient
  diminuées – *he felt that his mental
  capacities were diminished*
  77 | 534

**2183 éditeur** *nm* publisher, editor
- j'ai mis un mot chez l'éditeur – *I wrote a
  letter to the editor*
  70 | 759

**2184 provincial** *nadj* provincial
- les municipalités sont de juridiction
  provinciale – *the municipalities are under
  provincial jurisdiction*
  49 | 1482-n +s

**2185 casser** *v* to break
- j'ai cassé une bouteille de bière – *I broke a
  beer bottle*
  66 | 856

**2186 probable** *adj(f)* probable, likely
- il est probable que le visa sera refusé – *the
  visa will probably be refused*
  78 | 511

**2187 signature** *nf* signature
- j'ai besoin de votre signature pour
  l'emmener – *I need your signature to bring
  her along*
  73 | 660

**2188 forcément** *adv* without question, inevitably
- les deux ne sont pas forcément liées – *the
  two aren't necessarily connected*
  69 | 768

**2189 conformément** *adv* in accordance
- le débat se déroulera conformément au
  règlement – *the debate unfolded according
  to regulations*
  56 | 1204

**2190 croiser** *v* to cross
- ce sont deux histoires qui se croisent –
  *these are two stories that intersect*
  74 | 617

**2191 plastique** *nadj(f)* plastic
- on devait jouer avec un poulet en plastique
  – *we had to play with a plastic chicken*
  88 | 256

**2192 autonome** *nadj(f)* autonomous, independent
- mon corps est autonome. il ne m'écoute pas
  – *my body is autonomous. it doesn't obey
  me*
  78 | 522

**2193 héritage** *nm* heritage
- je leur laisserais cet héritage – *I will leave
  them this heritage*
  87 | 291

**2194 voyager** *v* to travel
- ça m'apprendra à voyager en classe éco –
  *that'll teach me to travel in economy
  class*
  80 | 449

**2195 électronique** *nadj(f)* electronic
- un message électronique m'informe que
  le code est erroné – *an electronic message
  tells me that the code is incorrect*
  69 | 779

**2196 parallèle** *nadj(f)* parallel, similar
• vous mettriez son conservatisme en parallèle avec sa ferveur catholique? – *you would link his conservatism and his Catholic fervor?*
78 | 516

**2197 répartir** *v* to distribute, spread out, share out, divide up
• ils se répartissent en trois grands groupes – *they spread out into three big groups*
80 | 451

**2198 courageux** *nadj(pl)* courageous
• une femme moderne, courageuse, sensible – *a modern, courageous, sensible woman*
88 | 246

**2199 réveiller** *v* to wake up
• j'ai pas envie de réveiller mon copain – *I don't want to wake up my friend*
61 | 1006

**2200 satellite** *nm* satellite
• on aurait sûrement des images satellites animées – *we must surely have animated satellite imagery*
51 | 1379-l +n -s

**2201 ordinateur** *nadj* computer
• l'ordinateur est un outil tellement merveilleux – *the computer is such a marvelous tool*
70 | 727-l

**2202 fondé** *adj,nm,nf* founded, justified; agent, clerk
• ce régime admirable est fondé sur l'honnêteté – *this admirable regime is founded on honesty*
76 | 572

**2203 blessé** *nadj* injured
• les blessés ont été transportés dans sept hôpitaux – *the injured were transported to seven hospitals*
52 | 1356+n

**2204 municipal** *adj* municipal
• les élus municipaux méritent notre respect – *elected municipal representatives deserve our respect*
73 | 653

**2205 salut** *intj,nm* salute, hi, bye
• salut, ma chérie – *hi, dear*
56 | 1199-n +s

**2206 songer** *v* to dream
• ne songez pas à quitter le pays – *don't even dream of leaving the country*
66 | 859+l -n

**2207 enfance** *nf* childhood
• depuis ma tendre enfance, je rêve de ce jour – *since early childhood I have been dreaming of this day*
69 | 745

**2208 là-dessus** *adv* on top, about it
• j'aimerais connaître son opinion là-dessus – *I would like to know her opinion on the topic*
72 | 684-n +s

**2209 merveilleux** *adj(pl)* marvellous, wonderful
• je vous souhaite une merveilleuse journée – *I wish you a wonderful day*
73 | 645-n

**2210 sien** *nadj* his, hers
• la patrie vit les meilleurs des siens mourir en la défendant – *the motherland saw her best die in her defense*
68 | 778+l

**2211 commenter** *v* to comment
• laissez moi une chance de commenter ce que vous avez dit – *let me have a chance to comment on what you said*
74 | 607

**2212 inciter** *v* to incite, encourage
• cela incitera les compagnies à poursuivre leurs recherches – *this will encourage companies to pursue research*
75 | 574

**2213 prière** *nf* prayer
• alors, fais correctement ta prière – *then pray correctly*
78 | 506

**2214 nécessiter** *v* to require, necessitate
• des situations extraordinaires nécessitent un acte extraordinaire – *extraordinary situations require extraordinary action*
73 | 634

**2215 urbain** *adj* urban
• je vis en milieu urbain – *I live in an urban setting*
75 | 568

**2216 musée** *nm* museum
• je suis allé faire un tour au musée – *I took a look through the museum*
76 | 556

**2217 pluie** *nf* rain
• les jours de pluie, nous restions à la maison – *on rainy days we stayed inside the house*
67 | 814

**2218 précaution** *nf* precaution
• t'as pris tes précautions? – *have you taken precautions?*
81 | 424

**2219 anticiper** *v* to anticipate, foresee, look or think ahead
• je n'avais pas anticipé une telle reprise – *I didn't anticipate such a recovery*
81 | 425

**2220 cheval** *nm* horse
• Napoléon lui-même est tombé de son cheval – *Napoleon himself even fell off his horse*
66 | 853

**2221 communiqué** *nm* communiqué, release, statement
• le communiqué a été distribué aux journalistes – *the communiqué was distributed to the journalists*
52 | 1335-l +n -s

**2222 suicide** *nm* suicide
• arrêt cardiaque, suicide, on ne savait pas – *heart attack, suicide, we didn't know*
83 | 379

**2223 rivière** *nf* river
• laissez la rivière faire son travail – *let the river do its work*
84 | 356

## 13  Creating nouns – 1

This table lists some of the most commonly used suffixes used to form nouns in French. Many of them are cognate with English words.

### -eur (all are M)

**directeur** 640 director
**sénateur** 684 senator
**auteur** 762 author
**professeur** 1150 professor
**moteur** 1164 motor
**producteur** 1259 producer
**facteur** 1264 mailman
**travailleur** 1341 worker
**acteur** 1552 actor
**consommateur** 1673 consumer
**conservateur** 1927 conservative
**électeur** 1957 elector
**chercheur** 1961 researcher
**joueur** 2003 player
**gouverneur** 2089 governor
**lecteur** 2100 reader
**docteur** 2176 doctor
**éditeur** 2183 publisher
**ordinateur** 2201 computer
**mineur** 2233 miner

### -ie  (all are F)

**partie** 118 nf part
**économie** 387 nf economy
**industrie** 692 nf industry
**énergie** 720 nf energy
**compagnie** 775 nf company
**série** 836 nf series
**maladie** 973 nf illness

**sortie** 1174 nf exit
**envie** 1237 nf envy
**démocratie** 1279 nf democracy
**stratégie** 1286 nf strategy
**technologie** 1388 nf technology
**catégorie** 1402 nf category
**théorie** 1773 nf theory
**tragédie** 1910 nf tragedy

### -isme (all are M)

**organisme** 1299 organism
**mécanisme** 1573 mechanism
**terrorisme** 2834 terrorism
**tourisme** 2955 tourism
**optimisme** 3250 optimism
**capitalisme** 3568 capitalism
**communisme** 3923 communism
**dynamisme** 3924 dynamism
**racisme** 4044 racism
**scepticisme** 4719 scepticism

### -iste (all are MF)

**journaliste** 1337 journalist
**spécialiste** 1588 specialist
**communiste** 1696 communist
**socialiste** 1768 socialist
**artiste** 1797 artist
**réformiste** 2146 reformist
**terroriste** 2415 terrorist

**réaliste** 2630 realist
**touriste** 2653 tourist
**optimiste** 2751 optimistic
**économiste** 2943 economist
**islamiste** 3542 Islamist
**séparatiste** 4190 separatist
**nationaliste** 4195 nationalist
**progressiste** 4799 progressive

### -ure (all are F)

**heure** 99 hour
**mesure** 262 measure
**nature** 542 nature
**voiture** 881 car
**culture** 913 culture
**structure** 964 structure
**procédure** 993 procedure
**lecture** 1016 reading
**ouverture** 1455 opening
**couverture** 1698 blanket
**figure** 1825 figure
**rupture** 1867 break, rupture
**littérature** 2083 literature
**agriculture** 2088 agriculture
**aventure** 2090 adventure
**signature** 2187 signature
**nourriture** 2285 food
**infrastructure** 2287 infrastructure
**blessure** 2481 injury, wound
**fermeture** 2562 closing

---

**2224 avertir** v  to warn
• pourquoi ne m'avais-tu pas averti? – *why didn't you warn me?*
74 | 594

**2225 rédaction** nf  writing, composition
• j'ai terminé la rédaction de ma thèse – *I finished writing my thesis*
74 | 601

**2226 enceinte** adjf,nf  pregnant; enclosure
• je suis enceinte de six mois – *I am six months pregnant*
78 | 494

**2227 substance** nf  substance
• telle est son essence et sa substance – *such is its essence and its substance*
68 | 779

**2228 soigner** v  to treat, look after, take care over
• toi, va soigner ton chien – *you, go take care of your dog*
79 | 471

**2229 récit** nm  account, narrative
• le soir, j'écoutais les récits de Robert – *that evening, I listened to Robert's stories*
62 | 945

**2230 revendication** *nf* claim, demand
- on parle souvent de revendications historiques – *we often speak of historical claims*
77 | 522

**2231 incroyable** *nadj(f)* incredible, unbelievable
- moi, j'ai passé une nuit incroyable – *me, I had an incredible night*
71 | 693+s

**2232 sondage** *nm* poll
- ce sondage représente la désinformation pure et simple – *this poll represents pure and simple disinformation*
66 | 820-l

**2233 mineur** *nadj* minor; miner
- les mineurs sont devenus fous – *the miners went crazy*
77 | 525

**2234 composition** *nf* composition, essay, dialling
- le roman se développe comme une composition musicale – *the novel unfolds like a musical composition*
80 | 440

**2235 débarrasser** *v* to clear, get rid of
- ils trouveront le moyen de se débarrasser de leur chef – *they'll find a way to get rid of their leader*
78 | 503

**2236 accusation** *nf* accusation, indictment
- il s'agit d'une accusation très grave – *it's a very grave accusation*
67 | 793

**2237 invitation** *nf* invitation
- nous lui enverrons bien sûr une invitation – *of course we will send her an invitation*
83 | 359

**2238 présidentiel** *adj* presidential
- l'administration présidentielle sort sa batterie de combat – *the president's administration brought out its big guns*
55 | 1179-l +n

**2239 concurrent** *nadj* competitor, rival
- c'est un concurrent politique – *he's a political rival*
76 | 537

**2240 prévu** *nadj* planned
- la période actuelle prévue est de 92 ans – *the currently planned period is 92 years*
77 | 528

**2241 suisse** *nadj(f)* Swiss
- l'économie suisse a glissé dans une légère récession – *the Swiss economy slid into a slight recession*
53 | 1271-l +n -s

**2242 franchement** *adv* frankly
- franchement, cela ne m'étonne pas – *frankly that doesn't surprise me*
79 | 474

**2243 paiement** *nm* payment
- la firme me réclame le paiement d'une indemnité – *the firm is demanding that I pay a penalty*
64 | 899

**2244 comparaison** *nf* comparison
- il n'y a pas de comparaison avec l'Afrique – *there's no comparison with Africa*
74 | 584

**2245 musulman** *nadj* Muslim, Moslem
il y a plein de femmes musulmanes qui ont écrit des livres – *many Muslim women have written books*
60 | 1021+n

**2246 déplacement** *nm* movement, displacement, trip, travel
- je consacre toute mon énergie aux déplacements – *I spend all my energy in traveling*
77 | 503

**2247 légal** *adj* legal, lawful
- à l'époque, il était légal de battre sa femme – *at the time, it was legal to beat one's wife*
76 | 541

**2248 dispositif** *nm* device, apparatus
- il y a un dispositif d'urgence – *there's an emergency apparatus*
62 | 931+n

**2249 constitutionnel** *nadj* constitutional
- je suis un praticien du droit constitutionnel – *I practice constitutional law*
62 | 945-l +s

**2250 contrainte** *nf* constraint
- les banques ont été contraintes de fermer leurs guichets – *the banks had to close their teller stations*
71 | 672

**2251 tarder** *v* to delay
- je ne vais pas tarder à y aller – *I'm going there without delay*
80 | 439

**2252 refaire** *v* to redo, make again
- tu sais que ta mère avait refait la salle de bains – *you know that your mother redid the bathroom*
74 | 583

**2253 pleurer** *v* to cry
- promets-moi que tu ne pleureras pas à mon enterrement – *promise me that you won't cry at my funeral*
59 | 1060-n

**2254 débattre** *v* to discuss, debate
- nous ne sommes pas les seuls à débattre de cette question – *we're not the only ones to debate this question*
65 | 841+s

**2255 immigration** *nf* immigration
- son passeport portait un cachet d'immigration – *his passport had an immigration stamp*
65 | 837-l +s

**2256 cancer** *nm* cancer
- l'apparition de certains cancers peut être affectée par le mode de vie – *the onset of certain cancers can be affected by lifestyle*
71 | 669

**2257 lâcher** *v* to let go, release
- je vous ai dit de lâcher ces couteaux – *I told you to let go of those knives*
61 | 979

**2258 cercle** *nm* circle, cycle
- comment sortir de ce cercle vicieux? – *how to escape this vicious cycle?*
75 | 562

**2259 génétique** *nadj(f)* genetic
- l'effet génétique des radiations est cumulatif – *the genetic effect of radiation is cumulative*
54 | 1217-l

**2260 importation** *nf* import
- le Japon envisage de s'ouvrir aux importations de riz – *Japan plans to open itself to rice imports*
63 | 899

**2261 tonne** *nf* ton
- ils mangent des millions de tonnes de poisson – *they eat millions of tons of fish*
66 | 819

**2262 dieu** *intj,nm* god
- aujourd'hui, les vrais dieux sont en colère – *today the real gods are angry*
58 | 1078-n

**2263 référendum** *nm* referendum
- ils se préparent à un référendum – *they're preparing for a referendum*
67 | 789

**2264 perdu** *nadj* lost, stray, wasted
- ça ne sera pas du temps perdu – *it won't be wasted time*
77 | 497

**2265 obligé** *nadj* necessary, required
- vous n'êtes pas obligés de me donner une réponse – *you're not obligated to respond to me*
78 | 482

**2266 visiteur** *nm* visitor
- nous avons des visiteurs. de très grands visiteurs! – *we have visitors. very important visitors!*
84 | 329

**2267 remporter** *v* to take away, win
- l'autorité revenait à celui qui remportait la victoire – *the authority was conferred on the one who won the victory*
57 | 1094+n

**2268 rond** *nadj* round
- il a le visage rond, le nez cassé – *he has a round face, a crooked nose*
72 | 643

**2269 étage** *nm* floor
- elle est tombée du troisième étage en secouant un tapis – *she fell from the third floor while shaking out a rug*
71 | 678

**2270 intense** *adj(f)* intense, severe, dense
- elle me faisait vivre des moments intenses – *she made me experience intense moments*
81 | 402

**2271 bébé** *nadj(f)* baby
- elle va avoir un bébé – *she's going to have a baby*
69 | 732

**2272 amitié** *nf* friendship
- l'amitié a remplacé la peur – *friendship replaced fear*
66 | 805+l

**2273 cinquante** *det,nmi* fifty
- encore cinquante mètres et il tourna—à gauche – *fifty more meters and he turned—to the left*
62 | 933

**2274 zéro** *nm* zero
- froid intense, très en dessous de zéro – *intense cold, far below zero*
59 | 1043

**2275 drame** *nm* drama
- son œuvre est dominée par un drame personnel – *his work is dominated by a personal drama*
77 | 512

**2276 visible** *adj(f)* visible, obvious
- il a toujours des partenaires, visibles ou invisibles – *there are always visible or invisible partners*
76 | 527

**2277 haine** *nf* hatred, hate
- l'amour se change en haine – *love changes to hatred*
75 | 565

**2278 instance** *nf* authority, proceedings, hearing
- j'ai perdu un première instance – *I lost a first hearing*
71 | 670

**2279 cérémonie** *nf* ceremony
- je participai pendant une heure à une cérémonie sacrée – *I attended a sacred ceremony for an hour*
67 | 770

**2280 ambition** *nf* ambition
- je n'avais aucune ambition d'écrire des livres – *I didn't have any ambition to write books*
74 | 581

**2281 recourir** *v* to turn to, run again
- voyons, qui recourrait aux tirs d'artillerie? – *let's see—who resorted to artillery fire?*
71 | 675

**2282 sanction** *nf* sanction
- le Congrès américain vote des sanctions contre l'Afrique du Sud – *the American Congress is voting on sanctions against South Africa*
62 | 925

**2283 géant** *nadj* giant, gigantic
- un écran géant avait été installé face à la tribune – *a giant screen was installed before the gallery*
71 | 649

**2284 jardin** *nm* garden
- la promenade au jardin le calma un peu – *a stroll through the garden calmed him a little*
62 | 928+l

**2285 nourriture** *nf* food
- leur nourriture, c'est l'herbe – *their food is grass*
77 | 493

**2286 engendrer** *v* to father, breed, generate
- la violence engendre la violence – *violence breeds violence*
75 | 566

**2287 infrastructure** *nf* infrastructure
- les infrastructures sont dans une situation bien pire – *the infrastructure is in a much worse condition*
65 | 840-l

**2288 adversaire** *nm,nf* opponent, adversary
- on élimine son adversaire en le touchant – *adversaries can be eliminated by touching them*
74 | 569

**2289 africain** *nadj* African
- il se sent avant tout africain – *he feels most of all African*
60 | 987

**2290 royal** *adj* royal
- préfères-tu une escorte royale? – *would you prefer a royal escort?*
63 | 885

**2291 mobile** *nadj(f)* mobile, portable
- les organisateurs louent des toilettes mobiles – *the organizers rented portable toilets*
78 | 470

**2292 significatif** *adj* significative
- le mystère me paraît plus significatif que le secret – *mysteries seem more significant to me than secrets*
73 | 610

**2293 circulation** *nf* circulation, traffic
- la circulation des trains locaux a été suspendue – *local train service has been suspended*
69 | 710

**2294 cotisation** *nf* subscription
- les cotisations doivent augmenter – *subscriptions must increase*
52 | 1274-l +s

**2295 entente** *nf* understanding, agreement
- je sais quelle entente il y a entre Robert et toi – *I know about the agreement you and Robert have*
56 | 1121-n +s

**2296 cheveu** *nm* hair
- elle avait de longs cheveux bouclés, toujours bien peignés – *she had long curly hair, always well brushed*
58 | 1047+l

**2297 ralentir** *v* to slow down
- je vais pas ralentir. je vais même accélérer – *I'm not gonna slow down. I'm even gonna accelerate*
79 | 441

**2298 cadeau** *nm* present, gift
- je lui ai apporté un cadeau – *I brought her a present*
72 | 625

**2299 affirmation** *nf* assertion, affirmation
- j'ai été étonnée de cette affirmation – *I was stunned by this statement*
81 | 395

**2300 requérir** *v* to require
- cela requiert sans doute un certain effort – *this will undoubtedly require some effort*
70 | 680

**2301 destination** *nf* destination
- quelle est votre destination rêvée? – *what is your dream destination?*
53 | 1233+n -s

**2302 stabilité** *nf* stability
- je veille à la stabilité du continent – *I watch over the stability of the continent*
67 | 757

**2303 louer** *v* to rent, praise
- elle pourrait louer une cabane au bord de la mer – *she could rent a cabin by the seashore*
78 | 461

**2304 gars** *nm(pl)* guy
- t'es un gars sympa – *you're a cool guy*
55 | 1149-n +s

**2305 fleur** *nf* flower
- on t'a apporté tes fleurs préférées – *we've brought you your favorite flowers*
61 | 932

**2306 agriculteur** *nm* farmer
- j'ai moi-même été agriculteur – *I was a farmer myself*
55 | 1159-l +s

**2307 poète** *nm* poet
- j'ai découvert que j'étais poète – *I found out I was a poet*
69 | 718

**2308 fabrication** *nf* manufacture, production
- après ces deux échecs, la fabrication fut abandonnée – *after these failures, production was abandoned*
77 | 496

**2309 vin** *nm* wine
- du vin, s'il vous plaît – *wine, please*
69 | 706

**2310 soudain** *adj,adv* sudden, suddenly
- j'étais soudain libre – *suddenly I was free*
56 | 1090+l -s

**2311 balle** *nf* ball, bullet
- les balles sifflaient au-dessus d'eux – *bullets were whining above them*
62 | 908

**2312 inflation** *nf* inflation
- l'inflation est en train de devenir un problème – *inflation is becoming a problem*
59 | 1001+n

**2313 sec** *adj,adv,nm* dry
- j'ai les yeux secs – *my eyes are dry*
68 | 718

**2314 arrêté** *nadj* decree, order
- cet arrêté prend effet à compter du 1 mai prochain – *this decree will go into effect on May 1*
70 | 668

**2315 enfermer** *v* to shut
- il alla s'enfermer dans sa cabine sans dire un mot – *without a word he went to shut himself inside his cubicle*
73 | 596

**2316 abattre** *v* to pull down, kill, beat
- le jeune homme a été abattu par la police – *the young man was killed by the police*
71 | 656

**2317 paysan** *nadj* farmer, peasant
- je donnerais tout pour être un simple paysan – *I would give anything to be a simple peasant boy*
64 | 839

**2318 transition** *nf* transition
- la transition a démobilisé les forces sociales – *the transition demobilized the social forces*
73 | 605

**2319 humanitaire** *adj(f)* humanitarian
- l'aide humanitaire est, certes, nécessaire – *humanitarian aide is, of course, necessary*
63 | 863-l

**2320 répandre** *v* to spread, spill
- la lumière du couloir se répandait dans la chambre – *light from the hall spilled into the room*
75 | 534

**2321 adoption** *nf* adoption, passing
- je propose l'adoption de cette motion – *I propose to accept this motion*
58 | 1037-l +s

**2322 adorer** *v* to adore, worship
- elle adorait sa grand-mère maternelle – *she adored her maternal grandmother*
62 | 907-n +s

**2323 appartement** *nm* appartment, flat
- j'aimerais bien acheter un appartement – *I would really like to buy an apartment*
73 | 582

**2324 session** *nf* session
- il y a seulement eu une session de débriefing – *there was only one debriefing session*
67 | 755-l

**2325 entamer** *v* to start
- nous entamons notre descente – *we are beginning our descent*
68 | 738

**2326 ménage** *nm* housekeeping, housework
- j'ai un peu de ménage à faire pour l'instant – *I have some housework I need to do now*
74 | 555

**2327 purement** *adv* purely
- ma démarche est purement professionnelle – *my interest is purely professional*
79 | 432

**2328 enjeu** *nm* stake
- c'est un enjeu de taille pour les femmes – *a great deal is at stake for women*
67 | 746

**2329 passager** *nadj* passenger, temporary
- les 287 passagers ont probablement tous péri – *all the 287 passengers likely perished*
71 | 639

**2330 transformation** *nf* transformation, change
- la recherche scientifique est constamment en transformation – *scientific research is constantly changing*
72 | 612

**2331 calculer** *v* to calculate
- j'ai conçu un autre ordinateur pour calculer cela – *I designed another computer to calculate that*
72 | 605

**2332 misère** *nf* poverty, misery
- il y a trop de misère et trop de crimes – *there's too much poverty and too much crime*
74 | 559

**2333 légèrement** *adv* lightly, slightly
- elle baissa légèrement la vitre – *she slightly lowered the window*
69 | 690-s

**2334 écraser** *v* to crush, grind
- nous écraserons toute armée qu'on enverra contre nous – *we will crush any army sent against us*
72 | 604

**2335 enrichir** *v* to expand, enrich, make somebody rich
- ces différences enrichissent notre pays – *these differences enrich our country*
84 | 318

**2336 restaurant** *nm* restaurant
- j'avais pensé l'emmener au restaurant – *I thought about taking her out to the restaurant*
79 | 441

**2337 destin** *nm* fate, destiny
- le destin joue parfois de sales tours – *destiny sometimes plays dirty tricks*
69 | 684

**2338 discrimination** *nf* discrimination
- ils ont toujours été victime de discrimination – *they have always been victims of discrimination*
67 | 746-l +s

**2339 certitude** *nf* certainty
- il est impossible de prévoir avec certitude où nous en arriverons – *it's impossible to foretell with certainty where we'll end up*
77 | 485

**2340 huile** *nf* oil
- faire chauffer l'huile dans une poêle – *heat up the oil in a pan*
84 | 322

**2341 sacré** *nadj* sacred
- je dois vous charger d'une mission sacrée – *I have to confer a sacred mission upon you*
72 | 616

**2342 autonomie** *nf* autonomy
- nous voulons conserver notre autonomie – *we want to keep our autonomy*
73 | 580

**2343 sac** *nm* bag, sack
- tu as besoin de 4 sacs à dos de livres? – *you need 4 backpacks of books?*
62 | 882

**2344 stock** *nm* stock, to supply
- il conserve et protège nos stocks de poisson – *he keeps and protects our stock of fish*
72 | 608

**2345 invoquer** *v* to call upon
- le gouvernement tentera d'invoquer deux excuses – *the government will try to make two excuses*
63 | 866

**2346 compromettre** *v* to compromise
- le premier ministre a compromis le processus de paix – *the prime minister compromised the peace process*
81 | 394

**2347 arracher** *v* to pull up, tear up
- ils lui ont arraché sa caméra – *they yanked his camera away from him*
68 | 700

**2348 sombre** *adj(f)* dark
- la nuit était fort sombre – *the night was very dark*
66 | 757+l

**2349 barre** *nf* bar, rod
- prends la barre! comme ça, tu tomberas pas – *hold onto the bar! that way you won't fall*
79 | 427

**2350 contradiction** *nf* contradiction
- il y a une contradiction entre les deux – *there's a contradiction between the two*
72 | 603

**2351 maîtriser** *v* to control, overcome, master
- il fallait aussi démontrer qu'on maîtrisait deux langues étrangères – *we also had to demonstrate mastery of two foreign languages*
77 | 469

**2352 violer** *v* to rape, infringe
- j'ai pas envie de me faire violer – *I don't want to get raped*
76 | 495

**2353 souveraineté** *nf* sovereignty
- nous avons abandonné la souveraineté sur notre propre monnaie – *we abandoned the sovereignty of our own money*
75 | 539

**2354 épargner** *v* to save, spare
- j'espérais épargner cette infortune à mon fils – *I was hoping to spare my son this misfortune*
80 | 403

**2355 concentration** *nf* concentration
- il perd sa concentration, donc son sens – *he loses his concentration and therefore his reason*
74 | 538

**2356 téléphonique** *adj(f)* telephone
- le service téléphonique est un lien de sécurité – *telephone service is a connection for safety*
51 | 1230-l +n -s

**2357 remise** *nf* presentation, delivery
- c'est la remise en ordre du clan au pouvoir – *it's the overhauling of the clan in power*
69 | 674

**2358 mec** *nm* guy
- vous faites quoi les mecs, ce soir? – *what are you guys doing tonight?*
51 | 1246-n +s

**2359 solidarité** *nf* solidarity
- y a-t-il une solidarité assez forte entre les groupes? – *is there a fairly strong solidarity between groups?*
64 | 820

**2360 restreindre** *v* to restrict, cut down, decrease
- il a restreint les travaux du comité à trois jours – *he restricted the committee's work to three days*
77 | 482

**2361 décennie** *nf* decade
- cet objectif sera atteint en quelques décennies – *this goal will be achieved in a few decades*
70 | 644

**2362 aussitôt** *adv* straight away, immediately
- on décida aussitôt de dîner ensemble – *we immediately decided to have supper together*
62 | 878+l -s

**2363 officiellement** *adv* officially
- je suis officiellement une étudiante en première année – *I am officially a first-year student*
67 | 719

**2364 chasser** *v* to hunt, chase away
- l'ennemi devait être chassé de chez nous – *the enemy had to be chased from our home*
74 | 551

**2365 dîner** *nm,v* dinner; to dine
- le dîner sera bientôt prêt – *supper will be ready soon*
62 | 871

**2366 personnellement** *adv* personally
- j'en ai fait personnellement l'expérience – *I have had that experience myself*
71 | 614+s

**2367 fréquenter** *v* to frequent, go around with
- je fréquente un homme riche – *I'm dating a rich man*
80 | 415

**2368 projeter** *v* to plan, project, throw out
- on va projeter un autre film – *we're going to show another film*
83 | 346

**2369 littéraire** *nadj(f)* literary
- la poésie est beaucoup plus qu'un genre littéraire – *poetry is much more than a literary genre*
57 | 1030

**2370 présider** *v* to preside
- il présidait ses repas – *he presided over her meals*
70 | 646

**2371 fortune** *nf* fortune
- elle ne dépendait ni de la fortune ni du succès – *she depended neither on fortune nor on success*
73 | 571

**2372 malheureux** *nadj(pl)* unhappy, miserable
- tu es l'homme le plus malheureux que je connaisse – *you're the most miserable man I know*
70 | 638

**2373 numérique** *adj(f)* numerical
- il faut faire appel à des simulations numériques – *we need to refer to digital simulations*
46 | 1414-l +n -s

**2374 combattant** *adj,nm* fighter
- vous êtes les combattants les mieux entraînés – *you are the best-trained combattants*
65 | 794

**2375 soupçonner** *v* to suspect
- comme elle le soupçonnait, il souffrait de douleurs – *since she suspected him, he suffered pain*
69 | 668

**2376 merde** *intj,nf* sh\*t, crap
- je vois ton genou dans une merde de chien – *I see your knee's in a pile of dog sh\*t*
46 | 1403-n +s

**2377 entrepreneur** *nm* contractor, entrepreneur
- l'entrepreneur et le marchand détruisent la forêt – *the entrepreneur and the merchant are destroying the forest*
74 | 536

**2378 exposition** *nf* exhibition, show
- ça sera ta meilleure exposition – *this will be your best showing yet*
67 | 720

**2379 marchand** *nadj* merchant
- la marine marchande a été la clé de la victoire – *the merchant marine was the key to victory*
71 | 605

**2380 cri** *nm* shout, cry
- sa déclaration a été saluée par des cris de joie – *his declaration was greeted with shouts of joy*
64 | 813+l

**2381 féminin** *nadj* feminine
- j'adore créer les personnages féminins – *I love creating female characters*
73 | 577

**2382 désert** *adj,nm* desert, wilderness
- ils font fleurir le désert et fonctionner la démocratie – *they're making the desert blossom and democracy flourish*
67 | 710

**2383 vêtement** *nm* garment, item or article of clothing
- ça, c'est un vêtement de marque – *this is a brand-name piece of clothing*
73 | 555

**2384 autrefois** *adv* in the past
- nous nous sommes aimés autrefois – *we loved each other once*
68 | 700+l

**2385 surmonter** *v* to overcome, top, surmount
- nous pouvons surmonter ces obstacles – *we can overcome these obstacles*
80 | 408

**2386 marchandise** *nf* merchandise, commodity
- la marchandise s'est vendue de façon incroyable – *the merchandise was sold out in an incredible manner*
75 | 520

**2387 autochtone** *nadj(f)* native, indigenous peoples
- nous pouvons répondre aux préoccupations des autochtones – *we can respond to the worries of the indigenous peoples*
48 | 1344-l -n +s

**2388 continent** *adj,nm* continent
- le continent africain souffre de tous les maux – *the African continent suffers all the evils*
71 | 603

**2389 définitivement** *adv* definitely, permanently, for good
- je m'étais définitivement métamorphosée en enfant sage – *I was permanently morphed into a well-behaved child*
79 | 421

**2390 heureusement** *adv* fortunately, luckily
- heureusement, nous venons juste d'arriver – *luckily we have just arrived*
73 | 562

**2391 digne** *adj(f)* dignified, worthy
- ce n'est pas digne d'une dame – *that's not something worthy of a woman*
76 | 499

**2392 guide** *nm,nf* guide
- tout seul, sans guide? – *alone, without a guide?*
85 | 297

**2393 tabac** *nm* tobacco
- les odeurs de tabac vous gênent? – *do tobacco smells bother you?*
72 | 596

**2394 rendement** *nm* yield, output
- elles ne donnent pas le même rendement de lait – *they don't produce the same yield of milk*
63 | 816

**2395 ampleur** *nf* extent, scope, range
- une réflexion de grande ampleur s'impose – *wide-ranging thought is needed*
73 | 550

**2396 pleinement** *adv* fully, thoroughly
- je suis pleinement d'accord avec elle – *I fully agree with her*
74 | 527

**2397 désastre** *nm* disaster
- le grand désastre était proche – *a big disaster was looming*
83 | 335

**2398 joli** *adj* pretty, attractive
- les jolies petites secrétaires ne mentent jamais – *pretty little secretaries never tell a lie*
57 | 1023-n

# 14 Relationships

The words in this list describe some kind of status or relationship that holds with people, as individuals or in groups. However, it doesn't include any family relationships or professions, which are listed in previous tables.

**monsieur** 79 M mister
**homme** 136 M man
**jeune** 152 MF young
**étranger** 305 M foreigner
**membre** 390 MF member
**ami** 467 M friend
**riche** 599 MF rich
**pauvre** 699 MF poor
**contact** 894 M contact
**amour** 967 M love
**témoin** 1055 M witness
**étudiant** 1064 M student
**malade** 1066 MF sick
**élève** 1068 MF pupil
**libéral** 1080 M liberal
**maître** 1092 M master
**collègue** 1099 MF colleague
**habitant** 1333 M inhabitant
**fou** 1357 M crazy
**personnage** 1449 M character
**expert** 1557 M expert
**catholique** 1578 MF Catholic
**adulte** 1580 MF adult
**spécialiste** 1588 MF specialist
**prisonnier** 1618 M prisoner
**consommateur** 1673 M consumer
**volontaire** 1675 MF volunteer
**communiste** 1696 MF Communist
**saint** 1702 M saint

**ennemi** 1715 M enemy
**intellectuel** 1794 M intellectual
**chrétien** 1895 M Christian
**conservateur** 1927 M conservative
**personnalité** 1963 F personality
**dame** 1983 F lady
**partisan** 2029 M partisan
**adolescent** 2085 M teenager
**intermédiaire** 2102 MF intermediary
**radical** 2127 M radical
**mineur** 2233 M minor
**concurrent** 2239 M competitor
**musulman** 2245 M Moslem
**visiteur** 2266 M visitor
**adversaire** 2288 MF adversary
**passager** 2329 M passenger
**mec** 2358 M guy
**porteur** 2430 M carrier
**champion** 2443 M champion
**collaborateur** 2459 M collaborator
**sauvage** 2464 MF savage
**invité** 2478 M guest
**militant** 2479 M militant
**participant** 2480 M participant
**utilisateur** 2523 M user
**contemporain** 2557 M contemporary

**suspect** 2571 M suspect
**créateur** 2613 M creator
**voyageur** 2629 M traveler
**réaliste** 2630 MF realist
**sage** 2643 MF wise
**touriste** 2653 MF tourist
**meurtrier** 2681 M murderer
**observateur** 2687 M observer
**accusé** 2706 M defendant
**républicain** 2718 M republican
**détenu** 2741 M prisoner
**optimiste** 2751 MF optimistic
**amateur** 2760 MF amateur
**universitaire** 2782 MF university
**camarade** 2825 MF friend
**sourd** 2854 M deaf
**spectateur** 2877 M spectator
**fondateur** 2899 M founder
**copain** 3020 M friend
**compagnon** 3023 M companion
**nazi** 3053 M Nazi
**interlocuteur** 3085 M speaker
**aveugle** 3095 MF blind
**voleur** 3163 M thief
**survivant** 3302 M survivor
**otage** 3334 M hostage
**savant** 3378 M scholar
**esclave** 3468 MF slave

2399 **promouvoir** v to promote
• il est toujours plus facile de promouvoir la haine que de la combattre – *it's always easier to promote hate than to combat it*
71 | 623

2400 **écho** nm echo
• j'entendis l'écho d'un souvenir détesté – *I heard the echo of a repugnant memory*
63 | 825

2401 **fusion** nf fusion, melting, merging
• ceci renforcera notre fusion organique – *this will reinforce our structural incorporation*
76 | 495

2402 **innovation** nf innovation
• les entreprises maintiennent leurs efforts d'innovation – *companies maintain their innovation efforts*
72 | 589

**2403 sélection** *nf* selection
- notons que la sélection, dans ce contexte, signifie un tri – *note that selection, in this context, implies sorting*
63 | 837+n

**2404 confondre** *v* to mix up, confuse
- je confonds peut-être, avec d'autres bourses – *I might be mixed up, with other stock markets*
69 | 656

**2405 honnête** *adj(f)* honest, decent, fair
- c'est un homme juste et honnête – *he's a just and honest man*
76 | 494

**2406 tournant** *adj,nm* revolving, swivel, encircling, bend, turning point
- c'est en ce moment, le tournant de ta vie – *this moment is the turning point of your life*
82 | 349

**2407 automobile** *nadj(f)* automobile
- l'industrie automobile européenne est parfaitement compétitive – *the European automobile industry is perfectly competitive*
64 | 791

**2408 collectivité** *nf* community, group
- les membres de la collectivité ont uni leurs efforts – *the co-op's members united their efforts*
55 | 1065+s

**2409 record** *nm* record
- il avait atteint un nouveau record historique – *he has set a new historic record*
63 | 816+n

**2410 excessif** *nadj* excessive, inordinate
- votre réaction est un peu excessive – *your reaction is somewhat excessive*
80 | 383

**2411 ridicule** *nadj(f)* ridiculous, silly
- c'est ridicule. n'y pense même plus – *that's ridiculous. don't even think about it any more*
72 | 571-n

**2412 modalité** *nf* mode, method, modality
- il semble donc exister deux modalités de la vision – *there seem to be two ways that seeing works*
79 | 414

**2413 paquet** *nm* packet
- c'était un paquet de cigarettes anglaises – *it was a pack of English cigarettes*
65 | 773

**2414 fondation** *nf* foundation
- les fondations seront conçues après étude du sol – *the foundations will be formed after a soil study*
72 | 579

**2415 terroriste** *nm,nf* terrorist
- le président condamne cet attentat terroriste – *the president condemned that terrorist attack*
56 | 1015+n

**2416 retrait** *nadj* withdrawal
- ces pays ont demandé un retrait volontaire des jouets – *these countries demanded a voluntary recall of the toys*
61 | 879

**2417 organe** *nm* organ
- un peu jeune pour du trafic d'organes, non? – *a little young to be trafficking in organs, hey?*
74 | 535

**2418 protocole** *nm* etiquette, protocol
- ce protocole a permis de découvrir de nouveaux antigènes – *this protocol enabled discovery of new antigens*
58 | 960-l +n

**2419 apparition** *nf* appearance, apparition
- l'araignée a fait une nouvelle apparition – *the spider made a new appearance*
71 | 591-s

**2420 gain** *nm* gain
- c'est un gain net pour lui – *it's a clear gain for him*
67 | 706

**2421 écran** *nm* screen
- ils voulaient installer un écran géant sur la place du village – *they wanted to install a huge screen in the village square*
73 | 546

**2422 sonner** *v* to ring
- une cloche sonna dans le lointain – *bells rang in the distance*
67 | 694

**2423 protester** *v* to protest
- leurs gosses, ils n'osent plus protester – *their kids, they don't dare protest any more*
71 | 602

**2424 curieux** *nadj(pl)* curious
- j'étais trop curieuse – *I was too curious*
71 | 593

**2425 effacer** *v* to erase, clean
- l'homme décide, la femme s'efface – *the man decides, the woman demurs*
73 | 547

**2426 débuter** *v* to start
- la descente a débuté une demi-heure plus tard – *the descent started a half-hour later*
70 | 627

**2427 creuser** *v* to dig
- ils entreprennent de creuser un tunnel – *they undertook the digging of a tunnel*
77 | 444

**2428 allusion** *nf* allusion
- le texte auquel vous faites allusion date de 1989 – *the text you are alluding to is dated 1989*
76 | 487

**2429 lancement** *nm* launch
- le lancement a été retardé par une météo défavorable – *the launch was postponed because of bad weather*
64 | 774+n

**2430 porteur** *nm* carrier, holder
- je suis porteur d'une bonne nouvelle – *I'm the bearer of good news*
57 | 987+n -s

**2431 préalable** *nadj(f)* prior, previous, preliminary, prerequisite
- un inconnu avait au préalable averti le journal – *an anonymous source had previously warned the newspaper*
78 | 422

**2432 programmer** *v* to program, schedule
- ils mêleront sons acoustiques et programmés – *they will mix acoustic and digital sounds*
78 | 422

**2433 traîner** *v* to drag, pull
- elle me traîna à travers le plancher – *she dragged me across the floor*
68 | 680

**2434 domicile** *nm* home, place of residence
- j'ai eu une urgence à domicile – *I had an emergency at home*
69 | 643

**2435 oiseau** *nm* bird
- j'ai vu un oiseau faire son nid – *I saw a bird making its nest*
70 | 626

**2436 quarante** *det,nmi* forty
- j'ai quarante ans, elle en a vingt-cinq! – *I'm forty years old, she's twenty-five!*
62 | 843

**2437 sacrifice** *nm* sacrifice
- la ville a prévu un sacrifice humain – *the city was planning a human sacrifice*
75 | 503

**2438 barrière** *nf* fence, barrier, gate
- il est difficile de franchir la barrière linguistique et de dialoguer – *it's difficult to break the language barrier and to dialogue*
81 | 352

**2439 biais** *nm(pl)* way, device; bias
- nous devons attaquer ce problème par le biais de la législation – *we must attack this problem by way of legislation*
74 | 516

**2440 feuille** *nf* leaf, sheet, slip
- l'arbre porte quelques feuilles – *the tree has some leaves*
65 | 750

**2441 délégation** *nf* delegation
- notre délégation a été accueillie à l'aéroport – *our delegation was welcomed at the airport*
62 | 831

**2442 épuiser** *v* to exhaust, tire out, wear out, use up
- ils ont épuisé leurs ressources et veulent puiser dans les nôtres – *they exhausted their resources and wanted to dip into ours*
79 | 393

**2443 champion** *nadj* champion
- il deviendra un champion en un rien de temps – *he will become a champion in no time*
56 | 987

**2444 librement** *adv* freely
- seuls les piétons peuvent passer librement – *only pedestrians can pass through freely*
83 | 313

**2445 congé** *nm* holiday, time off, day off, notice
- il vous faudra prendre un congé d'un mois, au moins – *you will have to take one month's vacation, at least*
81 | 360

**2446 taxe** *nf* tax
- vous payez pas de taxes. vous payez pas d'impôts – *you don't pay taxes. you don't pay duties.*
59 | 900-l +s

**2447 onze** *det,nmi* eleven
- il était onze heures du soir – *it was eleven o'clock at night*
70 | 613

**2448 téléphoner** *v* to telephone, phone, call
- j'ai essayé de vous téléphoner chez vous – *I tried to telephone you at your place*
76 | 476

**2449 serrer** *v* to tighten, squeeze
- elle serre les mains – *she clenches her fists*
60 | 870+l

**2450 caractériser** *v* to characterize
- une époque ne se caractérise pas seulement par ses idées – *an era is not only characterized by its ideas*
72 | 572

**2451 préparation** *nf* preparation
- un document à ce sujet est en préparation – *a document on this subject is in preparation*
70 | 604

**2452 inverse** *nadj(f)* opposite, reverse
- c'est l'inverse de ce que tu m'as raconté – *it's the exact opposite of what you told me*
74 | 522

**2453 intituler** *v* to entitle, call
- la séquence s'intitulera «Cinq minutes pour survivre» – *the sequence was entitled "Five minutes of survival"*
73 | 535

**2454 possession** *nf* possession, ownership
- il était en possession de matériel d'intérêt – *he had targeted materials in his possession*
78 | 425

**2455 rejet** *nm* rejection
- le Soudan réaffirme son rejet absolu des menaces – *the Sudan reiterates its categorial rejection of threats*
67 | 686

**2456 enseignant** *nadj* teacher
- le métier d'enseignant n'est pas un métier comme les autres – *the teacher's job is like none other*
68 | 659

**2457 avérer** *v* to prove to be, turn out
- cette explication s'avéra la bonne, par la suite – *this explanation turned out the be the right one*
78 | 424

**2458 papa** *nm* dad, daddy
• je t'aime aussi papa – *I love you too daddy*
53 | 1070-n

**2459 collaborateur** *nm* associate, fellow worker, contributor, collaborator
• je remercie donc tous les collaborateurs – *so I thank all of the collaborators*
76 | 465

**2460 gêner** *v* to bother, trouble
• tu vois, tu gênes tout le monde – *you see, you bother everybody*
72 | 566

**2461 technicien** *nm* technician
• il faut des experts, des techniciens – *we need experts, technicians*
81 | 363

**2462 cycle** *nm* cycle
• le cycle de la violence peut être enrayé – *the cycle of violence can be broken*
73 | 537

**2463 accumuler** *v* to accumulate, amass, store, stockpile
• les bombes atomiques s'accumulent – *atomic bombs are being stockpiled*
77 | 438

**2464 sauvage** *nadj(f)* savage, wild
• c'étaient des oiseaux sauvages – *they were wild birds*
74 | 499

**2465 alcool** *nm* alcohol
• limitez votre consommation d'alcool et de sucre – *limit your intake of alcohol and sugar*
81 | 346

**2466 prétexte** *nadj(f),nm* pretext
• je pris prétexte de mon travail pour suspendre ces séances – *I used my job as an excuse to stop these meetings*
74 | 499

**2467 impressionnant** *adj* impressive, upsetting
• la science évolue à une vitesse impressionnante – *science is evolving at an impressive speed*
84 | 294

**2468 scénario** *nm* scenario, script
• j'ai reçu le scénario, je l'ai lu et j'ai adoré – *I received the screenplay, I read it, and I loved it*
70 | 603

**2469 électricité** *nf* electricity
• tu t'y connais en électricité? non – *do you know anything about electricity? no*
69 | 621

**2470 gratuit** *adj* free, gratuitous, unwarranted
• hé, un spectacle gratuit! – *hey, a free show!*
79 | 395

**2471 révolutionnaire** *nadj(f)* revolutionary
• je veux mourir en révolutionnaire – *I want to die as a revolutionary*
71 | 587

**2472 jambe** *nf* leg
• elle s'assit, croisa les jambes, alluma une cigarette – *she sat, crossed her legs, lit a cigarette*
59 | 900+l

**2473 insuffisant** *adj* insufficient, inadequate
• ce que nous avons accompli reste insuffisant – *what we accomplished is still inadequate*
76 | 451

**2474 privilège** *nm* privilege
• nous avons des droits et des privilèges – *we have rights and privileges*
57 | 953+s

**2475 week-end** *nm* weekend
• que fais-tu, ce week-end? – *what are you doing this weekend?*
63 | 789

**2476 équivalent** *nadj* equivalent
• cela n'a pas d'équivalent avec les autres pays – *this has no equivalent in the other countries*
61 | 824+n

**2477 regrouper** *v* to group together, regroup
• le ministre des Finances a regroupé tout ça dans un seul programme – *the finance minister regrouped all of that in a single program*
71 | 586

**2478 invité** *nm* guest
• les invités les plus attendus ne sont pas venus – *the most-anticipated guests didn't show up*
68 | 639

**2479 militant** *nadj* militant
• nous ne sommes militants d'aucune organisation politique – *we are not the militants of any political organization*
60 | 873

**2480 participant** *nadj* participant
• il y avait une cinquantaine de participants – *there were some fifty participants*
70 | 587-l

**2481 blessure** *nf* injury, wound
• ces problèmes sociaux sont des blessures qui ne sont pas encore guéries – *these social problems are wounds that remain unhealed*
74 | 510

**2482 privilégier** *v* to favour
• il refuse de privilégier les insurgés cubains! – *he refuses to legitimize the Cuban insurgents*
70 | 606

**2483 midi** *nm* noon
• mon père rentre pour le repas de midi – *my father's going home for lunch*
68 | 636

**2484 disque** *nm* disc
• nous écoutions des disques en buvant du whisky – *we listened to records while drinking whisky*
68 | 635

**2485 couche** *nf* layer, coat
• la couche d'ozone n'était pas menacée
– *the ozone layer wasn't threatened*
58 | 918+n -s

**2486 dater** *v* to date
• le dernier film concerné date de 1990 – *the last relevant film was made in 1990*
77 | 437

**2487 habituer** *v* to accustom, get used to
• on s'habitue à tout, quand on est obligé – *you can get used to anything when you have to*
76 | 453

**2488 inévitable** *adj(f)* unavoidable, inevitable
• le terrorisme n'est jamais inévitable – *terrorism is never inevitable*
82 | 335

**2489 recommencer** *v* to resume, start again
• recommence depuis le début, s'il te plaît – *start again from the beginning, please*
67 | 672

**2490 race** *nf* breed, race
• elle n'est pas de ta race – *she's not of your race*
79 | 381

**2491 vivement** *adv* sharply, brusquely, lively
• le groupe socialiste soutient vivement tous les amendements – *the socialist group strongly supports all the amendments*
72 | 543

**2492 beauté** *nf* beauty
• je veux leur montrer la beauté de ma langue – *I want to show them the beauty of my language*
61 | 816+l -n

**2493 atmosphère** *nf* atmosphere
• j'aime bien l'atmosphère des pubs – *I really like the atmosphere in pubs*
77 | 436

**2494 épaule** *nf* shoulder
• je déteste regarder par-dessus mon épaule – *I hate looking back over my shoulder*
54 | 1036+l -n -s

**2495 amoureux** *nadj(pl)* in love, amorous
• moi, j'ai toujours été amoureux de toi – *I have always been in love with you*
63 | 766-n

**2496 circonscription** *nf* district, constituency
• je viens d'une circonscription qui repose sur l'industrie de la forêt – *I come from an electoral district that relies on the forest industry*
48 | 1221-l -n +s

**2497 debout** *adv* standing
• je ne peux pas rester debout, sans rien faire – *I can't remain standing, doing nothing*
60 | 843+l -n

**2498 influencer** *v* to influence
• je n'influence pas la politique – *I don't influence politics*
75 | 482

**2499 recul** *nm* backward movement, setback, slip
• sur un an, le recul du chômage atteint 5 % – *in one year, the slip in unemployment reaches 5%*
64 | 734+n

**2500 mortel** *nadj* mortal, deadly, lethal
• nous ne sommes que mortels. nous sommes tous humains – *we're only mortals. we're all humans.*
77 | 437

**2501 flux** *nm(pl)* flow
• les flux mondiaux de migration se sont énormément développés – *worldwide migration flows have developed enormously*
64 | 742-s

**2502 horizon** *nm* horizon, skyline
• mes yeux parcoururent cet horizon désert – *my eyes surveyed this desert horizon*
71 | 556

**2503 délivrer** *v* to set free, rid, relieve
• il était temps de se délivrer de ce poids – *it was time to get rid of that burden*
78 | 398

**2504 subvention** *nf* subsidy
• nous accordons des subventions à l'industrie – *we provide subsidies to industry*
60 | 833-l +s

**2505 formel** *adj* formal, definite
• la morale, quand elle est formelle, dévore – *morality, when it is formal, devours*
78 | 397

**2506 aggraver** *v* to worsen, aggravate
• tous ces facteurs aggravent la situation – *all of these factors aggravate the situation*
78 | 415

**2507 lait** *nm* milk
• va prendre un verre de lait et fais tes devoirs – *go get a glass of milk and do your homework*
76 | 447

**2508 alimenter** *v* to feed, supply
• j'alimentais ma peur en mangeant – *I fed my fears by eating*
78 | 409

**2509 intelligent** *adj* intelligent, clever, bright
• c'est un gars très intelligent – *he's a very intelligent guy*
73 | 504

**2510 équilibrer** *v* to balance
• pour être équilibrées, elles doivent être négociées – *to be balanced, they have to be negotiated*
70 | 586

**2511 bibliothèque** *nf* library
• il y avait une grande bibliothèque – *there was a large library there*
70 | 578

**2512 absurde** *nadj(f)* absurd
• cela semble tout à fait absurde – *this seems completely absurd*
76 | 454

**2513 océan** *nm* ocean
- il repose au fond de l'océan – *it's sitting on the bottom of the ocean*
76 | 438

**2514 quelques-uns** *pro* some, a few
- j'ai retrouvé quelques-uns de ces poèmes – *I recovered some of these poems*
76 | 448

**2515 dicter** *v* to dictate, lay down
- écris ce que je te dicte, mot pour mot – *write down what I dictate to you, word for word*
84 | 274

**2516 tenant** *nadj* tenant; incumbent, holder
- à ma gauche, le tenant du titre – *on my left, the record-holder*
81 | 330

**2517 stable** *adj(f)* stable
- l'univers est stable et l'homme y aura toujours sa place – *the universe is stable and mankind will always have its place*
72 | 534

**2518 capitaine** *nm* captain
- il est mort. le capitaine est mort – *he died. the captain is dead*
63 | 758

**2519 solliciter** *v* to request, solicit, appeal
- elle sollicite un visa pour aller à La Mecque – *she applied for a visa to go to Mecca*
80 | 358

**2520 convoquer** *v* to call, summon
- vous serez convoquée au commissariat – *you will be summoned to the police office*
76 | 452

**2521 prévention** *nf* prevention, custody
- nous faisons de la prévention auprès des jeunes enfants – *we're being preventive with our young children*
70 | 568

**2522 terrestre** *adj(f)* land, earth
- les frontières terrestres et les aéroports sont fermés – *the border crossings and airports are closed*
78 | 407

**2523 utilisateur** *nadj* user
- éditez le dictionnaire utilisateur pour le réduire à 10.000 mots maximum – *edit the user dictionary to reduce it to at most 10,000 words*
47 | 1216-l +n -s

**2524 obligatoire** *adj(f)* mandatory, compulsory
- la quarantaine est obligatoire – *the forty-hour work week is mandatory*
68 | 625

**2525 terminal** *nadj* terminal
- il demande une nouvelle retransmission au terminal sémaphore distant – *it requires a new retransmission to the remote signal terminal*
44 | 1321-l +n -s

**2526 choquer** *v* to shock, offend, shake, disturb
- personnellement, ces mesures ne me choquent pas – *personally, these measures don't shock me*
79 | 375

**2527 primaire** *nadj(f)* primary
- un hôpital et une école primaire ont été détruits – *a hospital and an elementary school were destroyed*
70 | 569

**2528 vital** *adj* vital
- surveille les signes vitaux – *keep an eye on the vital signs*
80 | 355

**2529 destinée** *nf* fate, destiny
- notre destination, c'est aussi notre destinée – *our destination is also our destiny*
83 | 296

**2530 patrimoine** *nm* heritage, assets
- vous voulez protéger une partie de votre patrimoine – *you want to protect a part of your heritage*
67 | 643

**2531 conforme** *adj(f)* conform
- la construction était conforme aux plans produits – *the construction followed the specifications*
62 | 759

**2532 adjoint** *nadj* assistant, deputy
- choisissez un adjoint. deux, si besoin est – *choose an assistant. two if there's a need*
63 | 748-l

**2533 ultime** *adj(f)* ultimate
- cette station est à présent l'ultime puissance de l'univers – *this station is currently the ultimate power of the universe*
80 | 358

**2534 intégration** *nf* integration
- les immigrants ont payé leur intégration au prix fort – *the immigrants payed dearly for their integration*
68 | 619

**2535 rarement** *adv* rarely, seldom
- ma mère me punissait rarement – *my mother rarely punished me*
76 | 431

**2536 couler** *v* to flow, run, sink
- elle regardait silencieusement couler ces larmes – *she watched tears flow silently*
68 | 630

**2537 diversité** *nf* diversity
- la richesse de la France, c'est sa diversité culturelle – *France's richness is its cultural diversity*
65 | 702

**2538 amuser** *v* to amuse
- il faut s'amuser un peu dans la vie – *you have to have a little fun in life*
61 | 806-n

**2539 complémentaire** *adj(f)* complementary, supplementary
- j'ai des informations additionnelles et complémentaires à fournir – *I have additional and complementary information to present*
70 | 572

**2540 satisfaisant** *adj*  satisfactory, satisfying
• je ne trouvais pas d'emploi satisfaisant en région – *I wasn't finding any satisfying work in the area*
70 | 573

**2541 accueil** *nm*  welcome, reception
• l'émission a reçu un très bon accueil – *the broadcast was very well received*
77 | 422

**2542 camion** *nm*  truck
• ils ont trouvé le camion stationné à l'extérieur – *they found the truck parked outside*
71 | 544

**2543 douloureux** *adj(pl)*  painful, grievous, distressing
• les témoignages étaient douloureux à entendre – *the testimony was sometimes painful to listen to*
79 | 365

**2544 glisser** *v*  to slide, slip
• il glisse sa main dans sa poche – *he slips his hand into his pocket*
60 | 814+l -s

**2545 prêtre** *nm*  priest
• le prêtre lève alors les bras au ciel – *then the priest raises his arms to the heavens*
69 | 590

**2546 indication** *nf*  indication
• suis mes indications à la lettre – *follow my instructions precisely*
50 | 1109+n -s

**2547 exagérer** *v*  to exaggerate, overdo
• peut-être a-t-on tout simplement exagéré – *maybe we just exaggerated*
82 | 310

**2548 décès** *nm(pl)*  death
• le suicide est une forme de décès – *suicide is a form of death*
67 | 625

**2549 parisien** *nadj*  Parisian
ils vivent en France, banlieue parisienne – *they live in France, in the Paris suburbs*
62 | 747

**2550 psychologique** *adj(f)*  psychological
• son état était psychologique, pas physique – *his condition was psychological, not physical*
80 | 349

**2551 réviser** *v*  to review, revise, overhaul
• j'ai révisé votre plan de vol – *I revised your flight plan*
81 | 329

**2552 profil** *nm*  profile, outline, contour
• il n'a pas le profil du Père Noël – *he doesn't have the profile of Santa Claus*
81 | 327

**2553 rater** *v*  to miss, misfire
• vous avez raté tout l'opéra – *you missed the whole opera*
73 | 492

**2554 respectif** *adj*  respective
• nous ne parlerons plus de nos amours respectives – *we will no longer speak of our respective loves*
82 | 304

**2555 tranquille** *adj(f)*  quiet
• laisse-le tranquille, reste tranquille – *leave it alone, settle down*
61 | 779-n

**2556 registre** *nm*  log, register, registry
• nous avons réclamé un registre des délinquants sexuels – *we have called for a sexual offenders registry*
78 | 380

**2557 contemporain** *nadj*  contemporary
• ce n'était pas un langage contemporain – *it wasn't a modern language*
62 | 748

**2558 exclusif** *nadj*  exclusive, sole
• je suis son amour exclusif – *I'm his only love*
84 | 270

**2559 performance** *nf*  performance
• la performance d'hier est simplement fa-bu-leu-se – *yesterday's performance was simply fa-bu-lous!*
68 | 601

**2560 angle** *nm*  angle, point of view
• on a fait l'analyse sous deux angles – *the analysis was made from two angles*
76 | 424

**2561 divorce** *nm*  divorce
• 70 % des divorces sont motivés par la toxicomanie du conjoint – *70% of divorces are caused by drug addiction*
82 | 302

**2562 fermeture** *nf*  closing
• c'est l'heure de fermeture. la piscine est fermée – *it's closing time. the pool's closed*
74 | 472

**2563 affaiblir** *v*  to weaken
• il ne mange rien, il s'affaiblit – *he's not eating anything, he's weakening*
77 | 403

**2564 constamment** *adv*  constantly, continuously, consistent
• notre corps bouge constamment – *our body moves constantly*
75 | 448

**2565 horreur** *nf*  horror
• j'ai horreur des silences pesants – *I abhor pregnant silence*
68 | 603

**2566 envahir** *v*  to invade, overrun
• un désespoir sinistre envahissait son esprit – *a dark despair invaded her mind*
77 | 403

**2567 pétrolier** *nadj*  oil; oil tanker
• des dizaines de sites pétroliers sont occupés – *dozens of oil rigs have been occupied*
61 | 768-l +n

# 15 Nouns – differences across registers

This table lists the nouns that occur with a much higher frequency than expected in the three registers: spoken language, literature, and non-fiction. In each case, the words listed are among those in the top 10 percent of words for that register, in terms of relative frequency to the other two registers. Note that the spoken register has several government-related terms due to the presence of oral debates in the corpus; familiar and vulgar words also occur exclusively in this genre.

**Spoken:**

**député** 424 M deputy
**canadien** 611 M Canadian
**sénateur** 684 M senator
**motion** 855 F motion
**merci** 1070 MF thank-you
**collègue** 1099 MF colleague
**amendement** 1438 M amendment
**prestation** 1830 F benefit
**québécois** 1970 M Quebecker
**bonjour** 1972 M hello
**truc** 1991 M thingamajig
**réformiste** 2146 M reformist
**provincial** 2184 M provincial
**mec** 2358 M guy
**merde** 2376 F sh*t
**autochtone** 2387 M native
**circonscription** 2496 F constituency
**contribuable** 2658 MF taxpayer
**putain** 2704 F whore
**entrevue** 2860 F interview
**consentement** 2907 M consent
**pétition** 2920 F petition
**flic** 3559 MF cop
**programmation** 3844 F programming
**bonsoir** 3938 M good evening
**rapporteur** 3996 M reporter
**équité** 4101 F equity
**contrevenant** 4118 M offender
**vérificateur** 4257 M auditor
**bravo** 4564 M bravo
**félicitation** 4589 F congratulation
**hépatite** 4877 F hepatitis
**procès-verbal** 4899 M minutes

**législature** 4954 F legislature

**Literature:**

**silence** 1281 M silence
**visage** 1292 M face
**sourire** 1476 M smile
**ciel** 1538 M sky
**âme** 1647 F soul
**épaule** 2494 F shoulder
**révolte** 2720 F revolt
**gris** 2769 M grey
**uranium** 2844 M uranium
**larme** 2853 F tear
**lèvre** 2927 F lip
**genou** 2967 M knee
**chair** 3260 F flesh
**odeur** 3273 F odor
**infini** 3377 M infinity
**sommeil** 3393 M sleep
**solitude** 3448 F solitude
**charme** 3682 M charm
**escalier** 3705 M staircase
**grand-père** 3748 M grandfather
**bourgeois** 3817 M middle class
**joue** 3932 F cheek
**abbé** 4061 M abbot
**vitre** 4106 F windowpane
**poitrine** 4168 F breast
**gorge** 4194 F throat
**amant** 4284 M lover
**tendresse** 4472 F tenderness
**blond** 4585 M blond
**fatigue** 4595 F fatigue
**comte** 4598 M count
**lampe** 4699 F lamp
**vieillard** 4736 M old man
**charité** 4750 F charity

**Nonfiction**

**signal** 978 M signal
**jeudi** 1112 M Thursday
**mercredi** 1168 M Wednesday
**circuit** 1309 M circuit
**canal** 1919 M channel
**réception** 1926 F reception
**transmission** 1933 F transmission
**connexion** 2154 F connection
**fréquence** 2178 F frequency
**terminal** 2525 M terminal
**indicateur** 2592 M indicator
**paramètre** 2626 M parameter
**trimestre** 2763 M quarter
**gène** 2807 M gene
**abonné** 3003 M subscriber
**usager** 3167 M user
**fichier** 3176 M file
**interface** 3240 F interface
**blocage** 3429 M block
**trame** 3457 F framework
**faisceau** 3490 M bundle
**islamiste** 3542 MF Islamist
**affaiblissement** 3686 M weakening
**acheminement** 3778 M routing
**transit** 3848 M transit
**yen** 4017 M yen
**versant** 4134 M hillside
**distorsion** 4231 F distortion
**boursier** 4384 M scholarship holder
**avalanche** 4426 F avalanche
**mark** 4427 M mark
**maintenance** 4512 F maintenance
**récepteur** 4552 M receiver
**spécification** 4642 F specification

**2568 faculté** *nf* ability, right, option; faculty, university
• sa faculté de travail est énorme – *his capacity for work is enormous*
75 | 445

**2569 brillant** *adj,nm* brilliant
• en plus, c'est une personnalité brillante, intelligente, sympathique – *moreover, he's a brilliant, intelligent, likable person*
74 | 458

**2570 pacte** *nm* pact, treaty
• il y avait un pacte entre nous – *there was a pact between us*
77 | 409

**2571 suspect** *nadj* suspicious, suspect
• les suspects sont armés et très dangereux – *the suspects are armed and very dangerous*
66 | 647

**2572 lent** *adj* slow
• un prêtre s'avance à pas lents – *a priest walked slowly forward*
71 | 533

**2573 assistance** *nf* attendance, assistance
• il a été chaudement applaudi par l'assistance – *he was warmly applauded by the audience*
71 | 537

**2574 négliger** *v* to neglect
• il ne faut négliger absolument aucun détail – *absolutely no detail must be overlooked*
79 | 363

**2575 injuste** *adj(f)* unfair, unjust
• ce qui leur arrive ainsi est injuste – *what happens to them is unjust*
75 | 450

**2576 plaider** *v* to plead
• il vous a envoyé plaider sa cause? – *he sent you to plead his case?*
74 | 459

**2577 récompenser** *v* to reward, recompense
• il récompensait mes efforts d'un compliment – *he rewarded my efforts with a compliment*
84 | 262

**2578 suppression** *nf* deletion, suppression
• Lucent avait annoncé la suppression de 900 emplois – *Lucent announced a reduction of 900 jobs*
66 | 639

**2579 coupure** *nf* cut, cutting
• il y a eu une coupure de courant – *there was a power blackout*
77 | 408

**2580 glace** *nf* ice, ice cream; mirror
• j'aime manger des glaces – *I like eating ice cream cones*
69 | 580

**2581 gare** *intj,nf* station, railway station; beware
• on retrouve le mec à la gare – *the guy was found at the train station*
68 | 590

**2582 drapeau** *nm* flag
• le drapeau est plus qu'un simple bout de tissu – *the flag is more than a simple piece of cloth*
70 | 552

**2583 réparer** *v* to repair, fix, correct, make up
• il est plombier. il répare les conduites d'eau – *he's a plumber—he repairs water pipes*
77 | 398

**2584 sensibilité** *nf* sensitivity, sensibility
• mettons ta sensibilité à l'épreuve – *let's put your good sense to the test*
80 | 350

**2585 jaune** *adv,nadj(f)* yellow
• ils regardent avec confiance les murs jaunes – *they look confidently at the yellow walls*
67 | 614+l -s

**2586 existant** *adj* existing
• cela constitue une atteinte aux traités existants – *this is an attack on existing treaties*
69 | 561

**2587 procureur** *nm* prosecutor
• Michael était procureur adjoint, à l'époque – *Michael was a deputy prosecutor at the time*
61 | 760

**2588 informatique** *nadj(f)* computer science, computing
• je veux faire mon bac en informatique – *I want to get a bachelor's degree in computer science*
69 | 581-l

**2589 restriction** *nf* restriction
• nous sommes aussi en faveur de cette restriction – *we're also in favor of this restriction*
72 | 515

**2590 pacifique** *adj(f)* peaceful, peace-loving
• il est retombé dans l'Océan pacifique – *it sank into the Pacific Ocean*
79 | 367

**2591 bête** *nadj(f)* animal, beast; stupid
• laissez cette petite bête tranquille – *let this little critter alone*
61 | 766-n

**2592 indicateur** *nadj* indicator
• on se réfère aux indicateurs entrée des commandes – *check the data input lights*
50 | 1072+n -s

**2593 racine** *nf* root
• il n'a jamais oublié ses racines – *he never forgot his roots*
75 | 432

**2594 compenser** *v* to compensate for, make up for
• le gouvernement entend-il compenser totalement ces pertes? – *does the government intend to totally compensate for these losses?*
73 | 489

**2595 maritime** *adj(f)* maritime
• je viens d'une ville maritime – *I come from a maritime city*
68 | 590

**2596 gravité** *nf* seriousness, solemnity, graveness, gravity
- la gravité, ce n'est pas vraiment mon style – *seriousness is not really my style*
80 | 331

**2597 pénétrer** *v* to penetrate
- il est très difficile de pénétrer dans le monde des vraies gitanes – *it's very difficult to penetrate the world of real Gypsies*
70 | 552-s

**2598 civilisation** *nf* civilization
- on cherchait des signes de civilisation – *we were looking for signs of civilization*
74 | 466

**2599 rouler** *v* to roll
- il est difficile de réfléchir en roulant – *it's difficult to reflect on things while driving*
63 | 712+l

**2600 technologique** *adj(f)* technological
- il en résultera un influx technologique – *this will result in a technological explosion*
71 | 531

**2601 heurter** *v* to strike, hit, collide
- j'ai heurté la voiture de ma femme – *I collided with my wife's car*
77 | 407

**2602 football** *nm* football, soccer
- j'ai beaucoup joué au football – *I played a lot of soccer*
51 | 1039

**2603 décevant** *adj* disappointing
- je trouvais très décevants les commentaires de nos journaux – *I was very disappointed by the commentary in our newspapers*
88 | 192

**2604 législation** *nf* legislation
- une législation européenne serait libérale par définition – *a European law would be liberal by definition*
63 | 710

**2605 approprier** *v* to adapt, appropriate, take over
- dommage que les touristes anglais se l'approprient – *too bad the English tourists have taken it over*
67 | 623

**2606 tactique** *nadj(f)* tactics, tactical
- les Allemands avaient changé de tactique – *the Germans changed tactics*
84 | 262

**2607 thèse** *nf* thesis, argument
- vous avez publié cette thèse? – *did you publish this thesis?*
70 | 550

**2608 acceptable** *adj(f)* acceptable, satisfactory
- une personne doit avoir un revenu acceptable – *a person must have a decent income*
70 | 536

**2609 surgir** *v* to spring up
- de Transylvanie surgit un chevalier roumain – *from Transylvania a Romanian knight suddenly appeared*
75 | 442

**2610 prince** *nm* prince
- je suis une princesse et je dois épouser un prince – *I'm a princess and I must marry a prince*
66 | 644

**2611 vidéo** *adji,nf* video
- montre-lui tes nouveaux jeux vidéo – *show him your new video games*
69 | 560

**2612 semer** *v* to sow, scatter, spread
- ça sème la confusion dans l'esprit des gens – *it sows confusion in people's minds*
82 | 303

**2613 créateur** *nadj* creator
- il faut que les créateurs d'entreprises deviennent des employeurs – *entrepreneurs must become employers*
69 | 572

**2614 partenariat** *nm* partnership
- nous pouvons renforcer notre partenariat – *we can strenghten our partnership*
65 | 652-l +s

**2615 file** *nf* line, queue
- les fichiers seront placés dans la file d'attente – *the files were placed in the queue*
77 | 398

**2616 chômeur** *nm* unemployed person
- je me suis retrouvé plus ou moins chômeur – *I found myself more or less unemployed*
60 | 775-l

**2617 correct** *adj* correct
- d'accord, ça me paraît correct – *OK, that seems correct to me*
73 | 476

**2618 cuisine** *nf* cooking, kitchen
- je croyais que tu aimais la cuisine chinoise – *I thought you liked Chinese food*
64 | 685

**2619 succéder** *v* to succeed, take over
- il est extrêmement difficile de lui succéder – *it's extremely difficult to take over his position*
72 | 497

**2620 royaume** *nm* kingdom
- au début, son royaume était de taille moyenne – *at first, his kingdom was of average size*
74 | 452

**2621 rebelle** *nadj(f)* rebel, rebellious
- la bande rebelle n'échappera pas à la justice – *the rebel band will not escape justice*
55 | 893+n

**2622 provenance** *nf* origin, strange
- les investissements en provenance de l'extérieur diminuent – *investments from abroad are decreasing*
65 | 657

**2623 fumer** *v* to smoke
- j'ai déjà fumé deux cigarettes – *I had already smoked two cigarettes*
68 | 572

**2624 dessin** *nm* drawing, pattern, design
- vous aimez les dessins animés? – *do you like cartoons?*
68 | 583

**2625 viande** *nf* meat
- depuis, je ne mange plus de viande – *since then, I don't eat any meat*
75 | 425

**2626 paramètre** *nm* parameter
- le commutateur d'origine fixe les paramètres – *the master switch sets the parameters*
45 | 1223-l +n -s

**2627 gré** *nm* liking
- je vous sais gré de votre compréhension – *I am grateful that you have understood*
79 | 359

**2628 dessous** *adv,nm(pl),prep* underneath, below, bottom, underside
- il retira la main de dessous sa chemise – *he pulled his hand out from underneath his shirt*
75 | 424

**2629 voyageur** *nadj* traveler
- c'est un voyageur chevronné – *he's an accomplished traveler*
70 | 539

**2630 réaliste** *nadj(f)* realist, realistic
- la reproduction est absolument réaliste – *the reproduction is absolutely realistic*
77 | 387

**2631 condamnation** *nf* condemnation
- le jury doit prononcer sa condamnation vendredi – *the jury must sentence him on Friday*
68 | 589

**2632 similaire** *adj(f)* similar
- les relevés indiquent une atmosphère similaire à la nôtre – *the statements point to an atmosphere similar to ours*
74 | 454

**2633 employeur** *nm* employer
- l'employeur et les employés ont tous deux contribué – *both the employers and the employees contributed*
59 | 783-l +s

**2634 paysage** *nm* landscape, scenery, countryside
- ma bibliothèque est mon paysage mental – *my library is my mental countryside*
68 | 571

**2635 discret** *adj* discreet, tactful, quiet
- ils voulaient un mariage discret – *they wanted to have a low-key marriage*
80 | 329

**2636 longueur** *nf* length
- la longueur d'un document d'opérateur est arbitraire – *the length of an operator's manual is arbitrary*
63 | 700-s

**2637 lentement** *adv* slowly
- il se mit à rouler lentement le long du trottoir – *he started rolling slowly along the sidewalk*
64 | 665+l

**2638 miracle** *nm* miracle
- les miracles arrivent tous les jours – *miracles happen every day*
73 | 465

**2639 déboucher** *v* to unblock, uncork
- il déboucha la bouteille et nous servit – *he uncorked the bottle and served us*
77 | 390

**2640 illégal** *adj* illegal
- je veux m'assurer que cela devienne illégal – *I want to be sure that this becomes illegal*
71 | 515-l

**2641 expansion** *nf* expansion
- on est dans une ère d'expansion – *we're in an era of expansion*
70 | 527

**2642 mutuel** *adj* mutual
- c'est un accord obtenu par consentement mutuel – *it's an agreement obtained by mutual consent*
83 | 278

**2643 sage** *nadj(f)* wise, good, sound, sensible
- vous avez pris une sage décision – *you have made a wise decision*
71 | 512

**2644 commandement** *nm* command, order, commandment
- vous avez transgressé le premier commandement – *you have broken the first commandment*
69 | 550

**2645 correspondant** *nadj* correspondent
- pas un envoyé spécial mais un correspondant permanent – *not a special envoy but a permanent correspondent*
60 | 763+n -s

**2646 grimper** *v* to climb, go up
- tu peux grimper à la corde? – *can you climb a rope?*
79 | 353

**2647 pause** *nf* break, pause
- nous allons prendre une pause pour le déjeuner – *we're going to take a break for lunch*
76 | 411

**2648 répartition** *nf* distribution, spreading
- je suis pour la répartition des tâches – *I'm for dividing up the tasks*
67 | 604

**2649 sacrifier** *v* to sacrifice, give away
- il sacrifiera sa vie pour sauver la tienne – *he sacrificed his life to save yours*
75 | 417

**2650 chimique** *adj(f)* chemical
- aujourd'hui ce qui est chimique est ressenti comme dangereux – *today what's chemical is felt to be dangerous*
69 | 544

**2651 compétition** *nf* competition
- la compétition est donc très ouverte et féroce – *the competition is thus very open and ferocious*
67 | 593

**2652 combiner** *v* to combine, devise
- vous avez réussi à combiner écologie et rentabilité – *you have succeeded in combining ecology and profitability*
79 | 343

**2653 touriste** *nm,nf* tourist
- suis-moi et joue les touristes – *follow me and pretend to be tourists*
73 | 466

**2654 ravir** *v* to delight, rob
- je suis ravi de vous voir – *I'm thrilled to see you*
71 | 506

**2655 pardon** *nm* forgiveness
- je suis venu pour te demander pardon – *I came to ask your forgiveness*
57 | 837-n +s

**2656 filet** *nm* dribble, trickle, wisp, streak, thread, fillet, net
- le navire a même coupé ses filets – *the boat even cut his nets*
79 | 338

**2657 atomique** *adj(f)* atomic
- comment survivre à une attaque atomique? – *how can one survive an atomic attack?*
56 | 844+l -s

**2658 contribuable** *nm,nf* taxpayer
- ces études sont financées par les contribuables – *these studies are financed by the taxpayers*
49 | 1060-l -n +s

**2659 progressivement** *adv* progressively
- il commença à perdre progressivement la vue – *he gradually began to lose his sight*
75 | 417

**2660 progression** *nf* progression
- ces capacités sont en faible progression – *these capacities are progressing weakly*
59 | 768+n -s

**2661 nez** *nm(pl)* nose
- le sang coulait de son nez sur ses vêtements – *blood flowed from his nose onto his clothing*
62 | 710+l -n

**2662 antérieur** *nadj* previous, earlier, front
- j'ai connu le système judiciaire antérieur – *I knew the previous judiciary system*
76 | 402

**2663 inacceptable** *adj(f)* unacceptabe
- selon nous, c'est totalement inacceptable – *according to us, that's totally unacceptable*
68 | 569

**2664 progressif** *adj* progressive
- nous avons effectivement un système progressif – *we do indeed have a progressive system*
75 | 418

**2665 adhésion** *nf* membership, support
- l'adhésion des États candidats à l'Union européenne – *membership of the candidate states in the European Union*
66 | 607

**2666 portrait** *nm* portrait, photograph
- il nous dit que nous sommes les portraits de Dieu – *he told us we are portraits of God*
72 | 472

**2667 détailler** *v* to detail
- j'ai reçu une lettre détaillée – *I received a detailed letter*
71 | 490

**2668 valable** *adj(f)* valid
- comme toute histoire valable, celle-ci concerne une fille – *like every worthwhile story, this one is about a girl*
72 | 472

**2669 coordination** *nf* coordination
- la coordination est considérée comme un problème de gestion – *coordination is considered a management problem*
73 | 459

**2670 sportif** *nadj* sports, athletic, competitive
- il est jeune et sportif – *he's young and athletic*
65 | 625

**2671 rose** *nadj(f),nf* rose; pink
- j'ai regardé le ciel tout rose derrière les arbres noirs – *I watched the pink sky with black trees in the foreground*
63 | 682+l

**2672 quête** *nf* quest, pursuit, collection
- au lycée, la quête de popularité est une guerre – *in high school, the pursuit of popularity is warfare*
79 | 349

**2673 compromis** *nm(pl)* compromise, agreement
- la vie est un compromis – *life is a compromise*
68 | 556

**2674 investisseur** *nm* investor
- les investisseurs semblaient satisfaits par les résultats – *the investors seemed satisfied by the results*
65 | 630-l +n

**2 675 présumer** *v* to presume, assume
- je présume que vous êtes carnivore – *I assume you're a carnivore*
63 | 673

**2676 abandon** *nm* abandonment, desertion, withdrawal
- c'est ce qu'on appelle un abandon de poste – *that's what you call dereliction of duty*
73 | 449

**2677 identique** *adj(f)* identical
- les circonstances sont identiques – *the circumstances are identical*
72 | 476

**2678 exploser** *v* to explode, blow up
- trois bombes ont successivement explosé mercredi matin – *three bombs exploded successively Wednesday morning*
68 | 559

**2679 mensonge** *nm* lie
- j'en ai marre de vos mensonges – *I'm fed up with your lies*
68 | 568

**2680 défaite** *nf* defeat
- malgré la défaite, la foule a ovationné l'équipe – *in spite of the defeat, the crowd gave the team a standing ovation*
66 | 604-s

**2681 meurtrier** *nadj* murderer, deadly, lethal
• je serai la meurtrière de mon mari – *I will be the murderer of my husband*
75 | 406

**2682 rigoureux** *adj(pl)* rigorous, harsh, strict
• il est méthodique, rigoureux et, pire que tout, patient – *he is methodical, rigorous, and worst of all patient*
78 | 349

**2683 mentir** *v* to lie
• je t'ai menti. je t'ai caché des choses – *I lied to you. I hid things from you*
59 | 762-n

**2684 fréquent** *adj* frequent
• les visites peuvent être plus fréquentes – *the visits can be more frequent*
81 | 299

**2685 œuf** *nm* egg
• n'oublie pas de chercher tes œufs de Pâques – *don't forget to look for your Easter eggs*
76 | 386

**2686 ambassadeur** *nm* ambassador
• le Pakistan renvoie un ambassadeur en Inde – *Pakistan is sending its ambassador back to India*
65 | 623

**2687 observateur** *nadj* observer, observant
• je suis un observateur clinique de la comédie humaine – *I'm a clinical observer of human comedy*
68 | 547

**2688 revêtir** *v* to take on, assume
• on revêt les nouvelles lunettes de soleil – *you put on the new sunglasses*
76 | 385

**2689 accessoire** *nm* accessory
• on ne vend ni ski ni accessoire – *we don't sell skis or accessories*
90 | 143

**2690 acquisition** *nf* acquisition, acquire, purchase
• nous ne souhaitons ni fusion ni acquisition – *we don't want a merger or an acquisition*
77 | 380

**2691 tournée** *nf* tour, round
• c'est la dernière tournée. le bar va fermer – *that's the last round. the bar's going to close*
65 | 622

**2692 tranche** *nf* slice, edge, section, bracket, slot
• il tient une tranche serrée dans sa main – *he's holding a slice tightly in his hand*
79 | 344

**2693 plage** *nf* beach
• il marchait pieds nus sur la plage – *he walked barefoot along the beach*
75 | 417

**2694 inspecteur** *nm* inspector
• tu seras un excellent inspecteur – *you will be an excellent inspector*
64 | 638

**2695 tempête** *nf* storm, gale, turmoil
• la tempête se calme, j'ai l'impression – *the storm is dying down, I think*
78 | 354

**2696 tissu** *nadj* fabric, material, cloth, tissue, woven
• j'ai fait des dessins sur le tissu de vieux rideaux – *I made drawings on the cloth from old curtains*
77 | 381

**2697 souverain** *nadj* sovereign, supreme ruler, monarch
• ce sera le 66e séjour du souverain pontife à l'étranger – *this will be the 66th stay abroad for the sovereign pontiff*
72 | 467

**2698 distinct** *adj* distinct
• Henri et moi nous étions deux êtres distincts – *Henri and I were two separate beings*
70 | 514

**2699 survie** *nf* survival
• je peux calculer vos chances de survie – *I can calculate your chances for survival*
77 | 378

**2700 repousser** *v* to push away, postpone
• elle m'a repoussée, elle s'est jetée sur l'herbe – *she pushed me away, she threw herself on the lawn*
72 | 475

**2701 adaptation** *nf* adaptation
• je fais surtout des adaptations d'auteurs étrangers – *I mostly do adaptations based on foreign authors*
72 | 463

**2702 plante** *nf* plant
• tu es une belle plante. tu es la fleur de ma passion – *you're a beautiful plant—the flower of my passion.*
77 | 367

**2703 nuire** *v* to harm
• ils nuisent à la santé – *they are harmful to one's health*
79 | 337

**2704 putain** *nf* whore, bitch; stupid
• putain mais qu'est-ce que tu fais? – *what're you doin', stupid?*
45 | 1151-n +s

**2705 imagination** *nf* imagination
• mon imagination folle m'a trompée – *my foolish imagination deceived me*
70 | 515

**2706 accusé** *nadj* defendant
• l'accusé devra remettre son passeport – *the accused must surrender his passport*
57 | 804+n -s

**2707 repérer** *v* to spot, pick out, locate, find
• ils ont repéré le tireur, vers le sud – *they located the sniper, towards the south*
75 | 410

**2708 directive** *nf* guideline
• tout est prêt. j'attends vos directives – *everything's ready. I await your orders*
55 | 854+s

**2709 rural** *nadj* rural
• les régions rurales constituent un genre de refuge – *rural regions are a kind of refuge*
60 | 719

**2710 persister** *v*  to persist, keep up, linger
- vous persistez à vouloir faire votre devoir? –
  *do you still want to do your duty?*
  79 | 328

**2711 coalition** *nf*  coalition
- un soldat de la coalition a été blessé dans
  l'opération – *a coalition soldier was injured
  during the operation*
  60 | 733

**2712 diplomatique** *nadj(f)*  diplomatic
- nous préférons une solution diplomatique –
  *we prefer a diplomatic solution*
  58 | 782

**2713 excellence** *nf*  excellence
- celle-ci sera un centre d'excellence – *this
  one will be a center of excellence*
  82 | 274

**2714 apparence** *nf*  appearance
- les apparences sont trompeuses –
  *appearances are deceiving*
  66 | 584+l

**2715 oriental** *nadj*  Oriental
- il portait de somptueux vêtements orientaux
  – *he wore sumptuous Oriental clothing*
  68 | 539

**2716 écriture** *nf*  writing
- l'écriture, c'est un besoin pour moi – *writing
  is a need that I have*
  61 | 701

**2717 parcours** *nm(pl)*  journey, course, route
- je suis en bout de parcours – *I'm at the end
  of a journey*
  67 | 572

**2718 républicain** *nadj*  republican
- vous votez démocrate ou républicain? – *are
  you voting Democrat or Republican?*
  60 | 735+n

**2719 embarquer** *v*  to embark, board, take on
board, load
- les hommes chantaient en embarquant sur
  les navires anglais – *the men sang while
  boarding the English ships*
  80 | 320

**2720 révolte** *nf*  revolt
- ma raison d'écrire naît de la révolte – *my
  reason for writing began in the rebellion*
  59 | 743+l -s

**2721 intéressé** *nadj*  concerned, involved
- je ne m'étais jamais vraiment intéressé à la
  question – *I wasn't ever really interested in
  the question*
  73 | 439

**2722 formidable** *adj(f)*  tremendous, considerable
- j'ai fait quelques rencontres formidables – *I
  had some tremendous meetings*
  71 | 476

**2723 tas** *nm(pl)*  pile, lots of
- ça explique des tas de choses – *that explains
  lots of things*
  64 | 625-n

**2724 déjeuner** *nm,v*  lunch; to have lunch
- nous achevons de déjeuner à la française –
  *we have just finished eating a French lunch*
  64 | 639

**2725 disputer** *v*  to dispute
- nous avons tort de nous disputer ainsi – *it's
  wrong for us to quarrel like this*
  56 | 817+n -s

**2726 élite** *nf*  elite
- l'élite se définissait selon lui par l'intelligence – *according to him, the elite are
  defined by intelligence*
  72 | 456

**2727 malheur** *nm*  misfortune
- je n'aime pas profiter du malheur des autres
  – *I don't like to profit from the misery of
  others*
  60 | 729+l -n

**2728 aube** *nf*  dawn, daybreak
- il était parti avant l'aube, comme un fuyard
  – *he left before dawn, like a runaway*
  74 | 426

**2729 salon** *nm*  lounge, living room
- nous étions assis dans le grand salon – *we
  were sitting in the large living room*
  65 | 613+l

**2730 infliger** *v*  to inflict
- désolée de devoir vous infliger ça maintenant – *sorry to have to inflict this upon you
  now*
  78 | 351

**2731 repos** *nm(pl)*  rest
- ça faisait trois heures de repos – *the rest was
  three hours long*
  66 | 591

**2732 déranger** *v*  to disturb, bother
- ça vous dérange si je m'assieds? – *will it
  bother you if I sit down?*
  66 | 577-n

**2733 inhabituel** *adj*  unusual
- nous nous trouvons dans une situation
  inhabituelle – *we find ourselves in an
  unusual situation*
  89 | 160

**2734 interdiction** *nf*  ban, banning
- cette interdiction s'applique aux télévisions
  – *this ban applies to televisions*
  68 | 538

**2735 consentir** *v*  to consent, agree
- les syndicats ont consenti une réduction des
  salaires – *the unions agreed to a salary
  reduction*
  66 | 573

**2736 variable** *nadj(f)*  variable
- c'est très variable, ça dépend – *it's quite
  variable, it depends*
  67 | 552+n -s

**2737 médecine** *nf*  medicine, medical science
- deux étudiants en médecine suédois
  m'écrivaient – *two Swedish medical students
  wrote me*
  69 | 517

**2738 contradictoire** *adj(f)*  contradictory,
conflicting
- la colonisation française fut un processus
  contradictoire – *French colonization was a
  contradictory process*
  80 | 313

## 16 Colors

| | | |
|---|---|---|
| **clair** 335 clear | **vert** 1060 green | **blond** 4585 blond |
| **argent** 472 silver (also money) | **couleur** 1211 color | **doré** 4833 golden |
| | **bleu** 1216 blue | **brun** 5068 brown |
| **noir** 572 black | **jaune** 2585 yellow | **roux** 6182 auburn |
| **blanc** 708 white (also blank) | **rose** 2671 pink (also rose) | **foncé** 7189 dark |
| | **gris** 2769 grey | **violet** 7643 violet |
| **rouge** 987 red | **orange** 3912 orange | **teint** 8010 colored |

**2739 exclusivement** *adv* exclusively, solely
• ils avaient des ventes exclusivement au Japon – *they had sales exclusively in Japan*
78 | 348

**2740 cible** *nf* target
• les cibles des terroristes représentaient les symboles du capitalisme – *terrorist targets represented the symbols of capitalism*
66 | 575

**2741 détenu** *nadj* prisoner
• le pourcentage de détenus séropositifs est très élevé – *the percentage of HIV-positive detainees is very high*
69 | 527

**2742 volontiers** *adv* with pleasure, willingly, gladly
• je serais volontiers mort dans cette maison – *I would gladly die in this house*
72 | 458

**2743 fauteuil** *nm* armchair, seat
• j'étais assis dans ce fauteuil – *I was sitting in this armchair*
68 | 530-n

**2744 couloir** *nm* corridor, aisle
• j'emprunte le couloir – *I'm taking the hallway*
68 | 533

**2745 enthousiasme** *nm* enthusiasm, enthusiastically
• l'enthousiasme fit place à une méfiance extrême – *enthusiasm gave way to extreme distrust*
76 | 387

**2746 télé** *nf* TV
• on n'avait pas de télé, de CD, de DVD – *we had no TV, no CD player, no DVD player*
56 | 820-n +s

**2747 éthique** *nadj(f)* ethical, ethics
• le clonage représente évidemment plusieurs problèmes éthiques – *cloning obviously poses several ethical problems*
64 | 624

**2748 révision** *nf* review, revision, overhaul
• il y aura une révision périodique du régime – *there will be periodic regime change*
71 | 470

**2749 pointer** *nm,v* to mark off, clock in, clock out, aim
• pourquoi cette femme pointe-t-elle une arme sur toi? – *why is that woman aiming a gun at you?*
81 | 293

**2750 assassiner** *v* to murder, assassinate
• il mourut assassiné – *he was assassinated*
72 | 465

**2751 optimiste** *nadj(f)* optimistic
• êtes-vous optimiste quant à l'avenir des jeunes? – *are you optimistic about the future of the youth?*
74 | 411

**2752 instaurer** *v* to institute, introduce
• notre nouveau directeur a instauré un programme pour travailler en équipe – *our new director started a teamwork program*
74 | 420

**2753 isolé** *nadj* remote, isolated, insolated
• dans quelques semaines, on sera isolés par la glace – *in a few weeks, we will be isolated by the ice*
78 | 336

**2754 revendiquer** *v* to claim
• l'attentat n'a pas été revendiqué – *no responsibility has been claimed for the attack*
66 | 571

**2755 secouer** *v* to shake
• elle secoue mes couvertures dans tous les sens – *she shakes out my bedding in every direction*
68 | 530+l

**2756 bizarre** *nadj(f)* strange, odd
• les effets de la maladie sont bizarres – *the effects of the sickness are bizarre*
64 | 624-n

**2757 abus** *nm(pl)* abuse, misuse, breach
• il y a eu des abus sexuels – *there was sexual abuse*
75 | 398

**2758 procédé** *nm* processus
• c'est un procédé continuel chez moi – *it's an ongoing process with me*
75 | 396

**2759 pêcheur** *nadj* fisherman
- les pêcheurs sont les hommes de la liberté – *fishermen are men of freedom*
64 | 607

**2760 amateur** *nm,nf* amateur
- j'ai eu des parents amateurs de théâtre – *I have parents who love the theater*
79 | 330

**2761 regret** *nm* regret, regretfully
- aux vacances, nous nous séparions sans regret – *on vacation, we separated without regrets*
72 | 455

**2762 accroissement** *nm* increase
- nous sommes tous atterrés par l'accroissement du chômage – *we're all crushed by the growth in unemployment*
67 | 558

**2763 trimestre** *nm* quarter; three months
- les perspectives sont bonnes pour le troisième trimestre – *the outlook is good for the third quarter*
52 | 904-l +n -s

**2764 onde** *nf* wave
- c'est comme une onde de choc – *it's like a shock wave*
54 | 852

**2765 spatial** *adj* spatial, space
- la Station spatiale internationale n'a aucun rôle militaire – *the International Space Station has no military role*
67 | 549

**2766 brut** *adv,nadj* raw, crude
- la surface totale brute de ce bâtiment est de 215.000 m² – *the total unfinished area of this building is 215,000 square meters*
62 | 660+n -s

**2767 éventuellement** *adv* possibly
- des sanctions seront éventuellement prises – *sanctions will eventually be taken*
69 | 513

**2768 vache** *adj(f),nf* cow
- dans d'immenses champs des vaches mâchaient – *cows munched in immense fields*
73 | 421

**2769 gris** *nadj(pl)* grey
- c'était une poule grise – *it was a grey hen*
59 | 735+l -s

**2770 aise** *nadj(f)* comfort, joy, pleasure, ease
- je suis mal à l'aise dehors – *I am uneasy in the outdoors*
75 | 393

**2771 agression** *nf* agression
- les agressions contre les femmes ont augmenté – *aggression against women has increased*
69 | 510

**2772 loisir** *nm* leisure
- je dresse des chevaux dans mes loisirs – *I groom horses in my leisure time*
79 | 316

**2773 chaleur** *nf* heat
- le soleil et la chaleur devenaient en outre excessifs – *the sun and the heat were becoming intense*
62 | 642+l

**2774 ranger** *nm,v* to tidy up, put away
- il range les deux tasses de café dans l'évier – *he places the two coffee mugs into the sink*
69 | 501

**2775 partage** *nm* division, cutting, sharing
- la frontière régie jusqu'au partage de l'ombre et de la lumière – *the border extends to where the shadows and the light divide*
76 | 373

**2776 étoile** *nf* star
- nous couchions à la belle étoile – *we slept under the stars*
71 | 472

**2777 mystère** *nm* mystery
- il y a des mystères que je ne peux résoudre – *there are mysteries that I can't resolve*
66 | 570+l

**2778 quasi** *adv,nm* almost, nearly
- on entretient un lien quasi mystique avec son pays natal – *we maintain an almost mystical connection with our native country*
76 | 378

**2779 description** *nf* description
- nous commençons par une brève description de mon père – *we start with a brief description of my father*
63 | 626

**2780 serbe** *nadj(f)* Serbian
- un vieil homme serbe a été tué par balle – *an old Serbian man was shot dead*
51 | 903-l +n

**2781 biologique** *adj(f)* biological, nature
- les études sur les effets biologiques des radiations sont restées rares – *studies on biological effects of radiation have been rare*
69 | 498

**2782 universitaire** *nadj(f)* university, academic
- j'étais occupée à des travaux de recherches universitaires – *I was busy doing university research work*
67 | 540

**2783 emparer** *v* to seize, grab, snatch
- il n'était pas possible de s'emparer de la clef – *it wasn't possible to grab the key*
75 | 382

**2784 dent** *nf* tooth
- elle repart en grinçant des dents – *she walks away gnashing her teeth*
64 | 602

**2785 neutre** *adj(f)* neutral
- mais mon travail n'est pas neutre et objectif – *but my work isn't neutral and objective*
81 | 278

**2786 aîné** *nadj* oldest
- mon fils aîné a onze ans – *my oldest son is eleven years old*
70 | 476

**2787 trahir** *v* to betray, give away
- personne ne te trahit, personne ne t'humilie – *nobody is betraying you, nobody is humiliating you*
68 | 510

**2788 intelligence** *nf* intelligence
- je n'insulterai pas votre intelligence – *I won't insult your intelligence*
66 | 568

**2789 admirer** *v* to admire
- j'admire ce que vous faites – *I admire what you do*
66 | 562+I

**2790 licence** *nf* licence, permit
- il pourra imposer des conditions de licence particulières – *he can impose individual conditions on licenses*
60 | 696+s

**2791 rigueur** *nf* harshness, severity, rigidness, rigor strictness
- l'optimisme est en revanche de rigueur dans les assurances – *on the other hand optimism is mandatory in insurance dealings*
73 | 430

**2792 maternel** *adj* motherly, maternal
- ils s'écrivaient en yiddish, leur langue maternelle – *they wrote to each other in Yiddish, their first language*
80 | 300

**2793 métal** *nm* metal
- ils ont été équipés de détecteurs de métaux – *they were equipped with metal detectors*
74 | 408

**2794 palais** *nm(pl)* palace, palate
- la Garde du palais n'est guère efficace – *the palace guard is no longer efficient*
63 | 620

**2795 belge** *nadj(f)* Belgian
- nous voudrions féliciter la présidence belge pour l'initiative – *we would like to congratu-late the Belgian presidency for the initiative*
59 | 704

**2796 brutal** *nadj* brutal
- je trouve leur méthode de revendication brutale, injuste – *I find their reclamation method brutal, injust*
76 | 366

**2797 extraire** *v* to extract, mine, quarry, pull out, remove
- l'ingénieur a extrait l'expertise empirique des pilotes – *the engineer extracted empirical expertise from the pilots*
76 | 373

**2798 signification** *nf* significance
- cette appellation a une signification politique très claire – *this trade name has a very clear political significance*
69 | 502

**2799 filer** *v* to spin, run, get out
- terminons le reportage et filons d'ici – *let's stop our reporting and get out of here*
61 | 666

**2800 automatique** *adj(f)* automatic
- la perte de mémoire est presque automatique – *loss of memory is almost automatic*
55 | 814+n -s

**2801 accrocher** *v* to hang up, hang on, put up
- les manifestants ont accroché une pancarte – *the demonstrators put up a poster*
70 | 474

**2802 pain** *nm* bread
- ça grille le pain pendant qu'on le tranche – *it toasts the bread while it's being sliced*
68 | 516

**2803 plateau** *nm* plateau, tray, set, stage
- il repose la bouteille vide sur le plateau – *he sets the empty bottle on the tray*
72 | 436

**2804 répétition** *nf* repetition, rehearsal
- on recommence les répétitions ce soir – *tonight we resume the rehearsals*
69 | 491

**2805 diminution** *nf* reduction, decreasing
- les stocks de poissons sont en diminution, voire en disparition – *fishery resources are declining, even disappearing*
65 | 577

**2806 collection** *nf* collection, series
- j'ai une collection des lettres inédites de Freud – *I have a collection of Freud's unpublished letters*
70 | 477

**2807 gène** *nm* gene
- ils collent des gènes ensemble, je crois – *they splice genes, I think*
44 | 1111-I +n -s

**2808 permanence** *nf* permanence, duty, service
- les deux pieds doivent rester en permanence dans le triangle – *both feet must remain in the triangle*
76 | 369

**2809 reine** *nf* queen
- il a appartenu à une reine ... la reine de Perse – *it belonged to a queen ... the queen of Persia*
67 | 523

**2810 privatisation** *nf* privatization
- la privatisation des entreprises du Kosovo a enfin commencé – *the privatization of companies in Kosovo has finally begun*
61 | 662-I +n

**2811 correspondance** *nf* correspondance, connection
- il avait brûlé un tas de correspondances, de carnets de notes – *he burned a pile of letters, notebooks*
78 | 328

**2812 planter** *v* to plant, pitch
- vous achèterez vos bulbes d'oignons à planter – *you'll buy the onion bulbs to be planted*
68 | 513

**2813 strictement** *adv* strictly
- nous ne sommes pas strictement obligés –
  *we aren't strictly obligated*
  77 | 348

**2814 violation** *nf* violation, transgression
- cela constitue une violation de sa probation
  – *that constitutes a violation of his probation*
  67 | 536-l

**2815 compensation** *nf* compensation, clearing
  nous avons offert une compensation aux
  provinces qui ont perdu de l'argent – *we
  offered compensation to the provinces that
  lost money*
  76 | 357

**2816 lycée** *nm* high school
- il est professeur de philosophie au lycée –
  *he's a high school philosophy teacher*
  71 | 450

**2817 con** *nadj* stupid
- on va le finir, ce con – *we're gonna take out
  that a\*\*hole*
  57 | 740-n +s

**2818 combinaison** *nf* combination
- il était le seul à avoir la combinaison et tu
  l'as tué – *he alone knew the combination,
  and you killed him*
  58 | 718-s

**2819 injustice** *nf* injustice, unfairness
- l'inégalité nourrit l'injustice, le soupçon et
  les préjugés – *inequality feeds injustice,
  suspicion, and prejudice*
  75 | 387

**2820 reportage** *nm* report, reporting
- selon le reportage, son intervention aurait
  été annulée – *according to the report his talk
  was canceled*
  71 | 461

**2821 déception** *nf* disappointment, let-down
- la déception pourrait n'être que temporaire
  – *the disappointment could only be
  temporary*
  80 | 294

**2822 soucier** *v* to care about, show concern for
- tu n'as pas à te soucier de tes manières ici –
  *no need to worry about your manners here*
  79 | 315

**2823 plafond** *nm* ceiling, roof, maximum
- il y a des caméras dans le plafond – *there
  are cameras in the ceiling*
  73 | 415

**2824 opérateur** *nm* operator
- nous ne pouvions même pas appeler une
  opératrice – *we couldn't even call an
  operator*
  59 | 693-l +n

**2825 camarade** *nm,nf* friend, comrade, pal, mate
- je me hâtai de revoir mes camarades – *I
  hurried back to see my comrades*
  71 | 441

**2826 traduction** *nf* translation
- alors, lis la traduction – *so, read the
  translation*
  63 | 599

**2827 compréhension** *nf* understanding,
comprehension
- je vous suis reconnaissant de votre
  compréhension – *I thank you for your
  understanding*
  71 | 446

**2828 réglementation** *nf* regulation
- ces réglementations échappent au contrôle
  des parlementaires – *these regulations will
  escape parliamentary control*
  62 | 631-l +s

**2829 déplorer** *v* to deplore
- il déplore la montée des superstitions – *he
  deplores the upswing in superstition*
  71 | 456

**2830 mobiliser** *v* to mobilize, call up
- il espère mobiliser le peuple – *he hopes to
  mobilize the people*
  67 | 531

**2831 encadrer** *v* to frame, train
- les élèves seront encadrés par environ
  850.000 enseignants – *the students will be
  trained by some 850,000 teachers*
  76 | 363

**2832 gentil** *nadj* nice, kind
- elles sont extrêmement gentilles – *they are
  extremely nice*
  58 | 707-n

**2833 folie** *nf* madness, folly, insanity
- certains jeunes tombent dans la folie –
  *some youth lapse into folly*
  67 | 521

**2834 terrorisme** *nm* terrorism
- les Américains ont déclaré la guerre au
  terrorisme – *the Americans declared war on
  terrorism*
  57 | 751+n

**2835 illusion** *nf* illusion
- ne nous faisons pas d'illusions – *we aren't
  deceiving ourselves*
  70 | 473

**2836 portefeuille** *nm* wallet
- il m'a pris mon portefeuille! – *he took my
  wallet!*
  76 | 352

**2837 séduire** *v* to seduce, charm, captivate, appeal
to
- j'ai été séduite par votre jeunesse – *I was
  seduced by your youth*
  76 | 350

**2838 précipiter** *v* to quicken, hasten, precipitate
- je jetai mon parapluie et me précipitai hors
  de la chambre – *I tossed my umbrella and
  dashed out of the room*
  73 | 416

**2839 clôture** *nf* enclosure; termination, closure
- la clôture est trop haute – *the fence is too
  high*
  68 | 497

**2840 piloter** *v* to fly, pilot, drive
- et qui pilotera l'avion? – *and who will fly the
  airplane?*
  76 | 361

**2841 agréable** *nadj(f)* pleasant, nice, agreeable
- c'est une chambre très agréable – *it's a very comfortable bedroom*
72 | 421

**2842 télécommunication** *nf* telecommunication
- le secteur des télécommunications a connu la plus forte hausse – *the telecommunications sector experienced the greatest growth*
56 | 752-l +n -s

**2843 désaccord** *nm* disagreement, discord, conflict
- ces désaccords constituent une tension bénéfique – *these disagreements create beneficial tension*
78 | 319

**2844 uranium** *nm* uranium
- la séparation du plutonium de l'uranium est relativement facile – *separating plutonium from uranium is relatively easy*
61 | 650+l -s

**2845 aliment** *nm* food
- je cultive des aliments pour nourrir les gens – *I cultivate food to nourish people*
58 | 704+s

**2846 alimentation** *nf* diet, food, groceries, supply
- l'alimentation et la santé sont étroitement reliées – *diet and health are intertwined*
68 | 509

**2847 pomme** *nf* apple
- elle croqua la pomme avec un bruit qu'il détesta – *she crunched into the apple with a noise that he detested*
79 | 304

**2848 ingénieur** *nm,nf* engineer
- son père était un ingénieur des chemins de fer – *her father was an railroad engineer*
71 | 453

**2849 vider** *v* to empty, vacate
- que personne ne bouge! toi, vide ce coffre – *nobody move! you, empty this safe*
68 | 497

**2850 attentif** *adj* attentive, scrupulous, careful
- sois attentif, sois intelligent, sois rationnel – *be attentive, be intelligent, be rational*
77 | 337

**2851 démarrer** *v* to start up
- le feu a démarré dans l'escalier d'un restaurant – *the fire broke out in the stairwell of a restaurant*
69 | 478

**2852 coordonner** *v* to coordinate
- il faut coordonner nos efforts pour le plus grand bien – *we have to coordinate our efforts for the greatest good*
80 | 284

**2853 larme** *nf* tear
- je suis sortie du cinéma en larmes – *I left the movie theater in tears*
58 | 716+l -n

**2854 sourd** *nadj* deaf
- le gouvernement fait la sourde oreille – *the government is turning a deaf ear*
73 | 411

**2855 cigarette** *nf* cigarette
- je fumerai bien une cigarette – *I would sure like to smoke a cigarette*
67 | 511

**2856 vallée** *nf* valley
- je marche dans la vallée de la mort – *I'm walking in the valley of death*
72 | 427

**2857 artificiel** *adj* artificial
- je joue à des simulateurs de vie artificielle – *I play in artificial life simulations*
70 | 469

**2858 différer** *v* to differ, vary
- cette idée diffère sensiblement d'une hypothèse concurrente – *this idea differs noticeably from a current hypothesis*
68 | 493

**2859 honorer** *v* to honour, do credit to
- c'était un soldat de Rome. honorez sa mémoire – *he was a Roman soldier. honor his memory*
79 | 303

**2860 entrevue** *nf* meeting, interview
- j'ai l'impression que cette entrevue commence très mal – *I have the feeling that this interview has started out very poorly*
49 | 921-n +s

**2861 ressort** *nm* spring; resort; spirit
- l'Etat intervient en dernier ressort – *the state intervenes as a last resort*
78 | 317

**2862 fixe** *nadj* fixed
- j'ai l'idée fixe d'un crime étincelant – *I'm fixated on a glittering crime*
67 | 525-s

**2863 opportunité** *nf* opportunity, timeliness
- c'est une merveilleuse opportunité de passer de belles vacances – *it's a wonderful opportunity to take a fine vacation*
76 | 360

**2864 robe** *nf* dress
- ta robe te va très bien, ma chérie – *your dress looks very nice on you, dear*
58 | 714+l -n

**2865 plaque** *nf* plate, tag, plaque
- il subsiste un danger local élevé de plaques de neige – *there are increased local risks of snow accumulations*
55 | 765+n -s

**2866 découler** *v* to ensue, follow
- une conséquence importante en découle – *an important consequence follows from that*
69 | 484

**2867 décisif** *adj* decisive
- nous arrivons à un moment décisif – *we have come upon a decisive moment*
74 | 381

**2868 piège** *nm* trap
- c'est un piège dans lequel je ne veux pas tomber – *it's a trap I don't want to fall into*
79 | 305

**2869 prédire** *v* to predict
- il lui a prédit qu'elle aurait un enfant – *he predicted that she would have a child*
82 | 245

**2870 enterrer** *v* to bury, lay aside
- enterre-moi dans un tombeau sans nom – *bury me in an unmarked grave*
72 | 418

**2871 refuge** *nm* refuge
- j'ai trouvé refuge dans de piètres endroits – *I found refuge in dismal places*
79 | 294

**2872 recouvrir** *v* to cover, hide, conceal
- la Terre est recouverte d'eau – *the Earth is covered with water*
74 | 393

**2873 pente** *nf* slope
- la route gravit maintenant des pentes abruptes – *now the road climbs up steep inclines*
51 | 863+n -s

**2874 album** *nm* album
- j'ai toujours rêvé de faire un album – *I always dreamt of making an album*
52 | 830+s

**2875 mixte** *adj(f)* mixed
- trois enfants issus d'un couple mixte périssent dans un incendie – *three mixed-race children perish in a fire*
65 | 560

**2876 clinique** *nadj(f)* clinic
- je l'ai emmenée à la clinique – *I took her to the clinic*
70 | 458

**2877 spectateur** *nm* member of the audience, spectator, onlooker
- les spectateurs s'enfuient épouvantés – *the onlookers fled, terror-stricken*
71 | 440

**2878 axe** *nm* axis, axle, main line
- désormais, nous nous concentrons sur deux axes – *from now on, we will focus on two dimensions*
72 | 424

**2879 chasseur** *nm* hunter, fighter, page, messenger
- je suis un chasseur qui ne tue pas sans hésiter – *I'm a hunter who doesn't kill without hesitation*
77 | 338

**2880 chéri** *nadj* darling, love, dear
- bonjour, chéri. comment s'est passée ta journée? – *hello, dear. how was your day?*
48 | 951-n +s

**2881 peinture** *nf* painting, paint, picture
- j'ai pensé à détruire ces peintures pas mal de fois – *I thought of destroying these paintings fairly often*
72 | 421

**2882 déchet** *nm* scrap, waste, trash, garbage
- les déchets de l'aire métropolitaine continueront de s'accumuler – *the trash from the metropolitain area will continue to accumulate*
74 | 376

**2883 siéger** *v* to sit
- moi-même et mon gouvernement siégions en Algérie – *I and my government reign in Algeria*
58 | 694+s

**2884 grand-chose** *nmi* not very much
- ça ne veut pas dire grand-chose – *that doesn't mean very much*
77 | 338

**2885 temporaire** *adj(f)* temporary
- la célébrité de tout président est temporaire – *the fame of every president is fleeting*
74 | 383

**2886 affiche** *nf* poster, public notice, bill
- j'ai mon nom sur des affiches – *I have my name on posters*
78 | 312

**2887 massacre** *nm* massacre, slaughter
- ce massacre n'a pas été revendiqué – *nobody has claimed responsibility for this massacre*
69 | 463

**2888 actualité** *nf* current events, news
- le présent, l'actualité ne m'intéressent pas – *the present, current events don't interest me*
58 | 688+s

**2889 redevenir** *v* to become again
- je vais redevenir célibataire – *I'm going to become single again*
76 | 352

**2890 crucial** *adj* crucial, critical
- nous sommes à un moment crucial de notre histoire – *we are at a critical moment of our history*
74 | 377

**2891 marine** *adj,nf* marine, navy
- aujourd'hui, vous êtes des marines – *today you are marines*
66 | 525

**2892 cadavre** *nm* corpse
- son cadavre apparaîtra à la fin du film – *his corpse will appear at the end of the film*
68 | 490

**2893 fleuve** *nm* river
- le fleuve coule toujours dans le même sens – *the river always flows in the same direction*
77 | 336

**2894 toit** *nm* roof
- ils sont sur le toit de mon bus – *they're on the roof of my bus*
67 | 506

**2895 mécanique** *adj(f)* mechanical
- c'était aussi un piano mécanique – *it was also a player piano*
70 | 446

**2896 transparence** *nf* transparency
- nous préférons le dirigisme à la transparence – *we prefer active leadership to transparency*
66 | 516

**2897 amorcer** *v* to bait, prime, begin, initiate
- la réaction en chaîne est amorcée – *the chain reaction has been initiated*
75 | 353

**2898 détester** *v* to hate, detest
- je déteste la viande, je suis végétarien – *I hate meat—I'm a vegetarian*
59 | 661-n

**2899 fondateur** *nm* founder
- il faut rappeler le rôle fondateur qu'a joué – *let me remind you of the founding role that he played*
69 | 470

**2900 charte** *nf* charter
- la charte olympique interdit toute discrimination – *the Olympic charter forbids any discrimination*
61 | 623+s

**2901 productivité** *nf* productivity
- il faut augmenter la productivité du travail – *we have to increase work productivity*
69 | 458

**2902 succession** *nf* succession
- c'est une succession de catastrophes – *it's a succession of catastrophes*
77 | 323

**2903 simplifier** *v* to simplify
- je pourrais peut-être simplifier les choses pour vous – *perhaps I can simplify things for you*
81 | 263

**2904 briller** *v* to shine
- la lune brillait maintenant dans tout son éclat – *the moon shone now in full glory*
63 | 588+l

**2905 ambitieux** *nadj(pl)* ambitious, man with ambition
- les socialistes appuient un plan ambitieux – *the socialists are supporting an ambitious plan*
80 | 275

**2906 sale** *nadj(f)* dirty
- je déteste cette sale ville – *I hate this dirty city*
60 | 650

**2907 consentement** *nm* consent
- il n'y a pas consentement unanime – *there is no unanimous consent*
49 | 901-n +s

**2908 chapeau** *nm* hat
- il se pencha pour ramasser son chapeau et ses sacs – *he leaned over to gather his hat and his bags*
59 | 661+l -n

**2909 calmer** *v* to calm down
- j'ai pas besoin de me calmer – *I don't need to calm myself*
67 | 499

**2910 mythe** *nm* myth
- le mythe grec est le produit d'une tradition orale – *the Greek myth is the result of oral tradition*
69 | 460

**2911 alternative** *nf* alternative, choice
- il y avait une autre alternative à la guerre – *there was another alternative to war*
80 | 283

**2912 soulager** *v* to relieve, soothe, ease
- puis je me réveillais, soulagée d'avoir 23 ans – *then I woke up, relieved to be 23 years old*
79 | 296

**2913 scrutin** *nm* ballot, poll
- nous établirions des dates de scrutin fixes – *we will establish fixed dates for voting*
61 | 618

**2914 culpabilité** *nf* guilt
- la police a rassemblé les preuves établissant leur culpabilité – *the police gathered proof to establish their guilt*
83 | 223

**2915 considérablement** *adv* considerably, significantly, extensively
- nous proposons de réduire considérablement les impôts – *we propose to reduce taxes considerably*
73 | 399

**2916 bouleverser** *v* to upset, distress, disturb, turn upside down
- nous avons toujours le moyen de bouleverser le cours des évènements – *we always have the means to upset the course of events*
76 | 335

**2917 introduction** *nf* introduction
- nous ne pouvons accepter l'introduction d'amendements – *we cannot accept the introduction of new amendments*
65 | 546

**2918 dramatique** *nadj(f)* dramatic, tragic, drama
- ça va être dramatique pour la facture de téléphone – *the telephone bill will be spectacular*
73 | 385

**2919 vaincre** *v* to beat, defeat, overcome, conquer
- nous sommes nés pour vaincre – *we were born to conquer*
69 | 468

**2920 pétition** *nf* petition
- je voudrais déposer cette pétition – *I would like to submit this petition*
53 | 793-n +s

**2921 renseigner** *v* to give information, get information
- renseigne-moi, je veux savoir – *tell me, I want to know*
79 | 292

**2922 ordonnance** *nf* prescription, organisation, edict, ruling
- le policier ignore si l'ordonnance est encore en vigueur – *the policeman doesn't know whether the ruling is still in effect*
79 | 284

**2923 aile** *nf* wing, sail, blade
- l'oiseau battra des ailes jusqu'à sa mort – *the bird will beat its wings until its death*
73 | 397

**2924 température** *nf* temperature
- il faut que j'aille prendre ma température – *I have to go take my temperature*
60 | 629

## 17 Opposites

Comment: Note that in most cases the positive term ranks higher than the negative term.

| WORD 1 | # | # | WORD 2 | DEF 1 | DEF 2 |
|---|---|---|---|---|---|
| plus | 19 | 62 | moins | more | less |
| avant | 40 | 82 | après | before | after |
| bien | 47 | 277 | mal | well | bad |
| nouveau | 52 | 392 | ancien | new | ancient |
| grand | 59 | 138 | petit | large | small |
| non | 75 | 284 | oui | no | yes |
| bon | 94 | 274 | mauvais | good | bad |
| toujours | 103 | 179 | jamais | always | never |
| fort | 107 | 723 | faible | strong | weak |
| fin | 111 | 364 | début | end | beginning |
| jeune | 152 | 671 | vieux | young | old |
| meilleur | 194 | 743 | pire | better | worse |
| devant | 198 | 805 | derrière | ahead | behind |
| long | 202 | 545 | court | long | short |
| simple | 212 | 933 | complexe | simple | complex |
| mieux | 217 | 3579 | pis | better | worse |
| vrai | 292 | 555 | faux | true | false |
| difficile | 296 | 822 | facile | difficult | easy |
| tard | 348 | 513 | tôt | late | early |
| plein | 394 | 1473 | vide | full | empty |
| gros | 419 | 3534 | maigre | stout | thin |
| riche | 599 | 699 | pauvre | rich | poor |
| capable | 610 | 1605 | incapable | capable | incapable |
| vite | 711 | 2572 | lent | fast | slow |
| heureux | 764 | 1843 | triste | happy | sad |
| commun | 780 | 1233 | rare | common | rare |
| supérieur | 876 | 1905 | inférieur | superior | inferior |
| positif | 949 | 1520 | négatif | positive | negative |
| indépendant | 954 | 3308 | dépendant | independent | dependent |
| extraordinaire | 1234 | 1327 | ordinaire | extraordinary | ordinary |
| majeur | 1306 | 2233 | mineur | major | minor |
| froid | 1307 | 1852 | chaud | cold | hot |

**2925 coupe** *nf* bowl, dish, cut
- votre coupe jamais ne sera vide – *your bowl will never be empty*
70 | 439

**2926 rayon** *nm* ray, beam, radius; department, section, shelf
- un rayon de lune traversait la chambre – *a moonbeam shone across the room*
67 | 504

**2927 lèvre** *nf* lip
- je regardai ses lèvres pleines et roses – *I looked at her full, pink lips*
57 | 689+l -s

**2928 promener** *v* to take for a walk, go for a walk
- les amis se promènent dans la rue – *the friends are walking along the street*
61 | 614+l -n

**2929 boulot** *adj,nm* work, job
- il a un boulot très sérieux dans l'informatique – *he has an important job in computer science*
52 | 810-n +s

**2930 correctement** *adv* properly
- faisons les choses correctement – *let's do things correctly*
74 | 372

**2931 colonne** *nf* column
- des colonnes de fumée s'élevaient au-dessus des arbres – *columns of smoke rose above the trees*
63 | 568-s

**2932 arranger** *v* to arrange
- c'est moi qui ai tout arrangé – *I'm the one who arranged everything*
61 | 604-n

**2933 lointain** *nadj* distant, faraway
- on voulait aller dans une terre lointaine – *we wanted to go to a faraway land*
62 | 598+l -s

**2934 danser** *v* to dance
- je danserai avec toi, le soir de nos noces – *I will dance with you, on our wedding night*
62 | 583-n

**2935 charbon** *nm* coal
- la production de charbon est en train de chuter – *coal production is falling off*
73 | 390

**2936 passionner** *v* to fascinate, grip
- je suis passionné de mon travail – *I'm passionate about my work*
68 | 484

**2937 colline** *nf* hill
- arrivée au sommet de la colline, elle s'arrêta – *reaching the top of the hill, she stopped*
73 | 392

**2938 poésie** *nf* poetry
- la poésie est souvent dite de façon ennuyeuse – *poetry is often recited boringly*
59 | 650-n

**2939 généraliser** *v* to generalize
- il faudrait généraliser ce type d'initiatives – *we would need to generalize this type of initiative*
75 | 345

**2940 transaction** *nf* transaction
- le montant de la transaction n'a pas été dévoilé – *the amount of the transaction was not revealed*
59 | 649+n

**2941 extrémité** *nf* end, extremity
- l'un d'eux attachait l'autre extrémité – *one of them grasped the other end*
47 | 921+n -s

**2942 pénal** *adj* penal
- il permet la clôture des procédures pénales – *it allows for termination of criminal proceedings*
60 | 627-l

**2943 économiste** *nm,nf* economist
- je ne connais pas un seul économiste – *I don't know a single economist*
73 | 383

**2944 banlieue** *nf* suburbs, outskirts
- on a toujours habité en banlieue – *we have always lived in the suburbs*
65 | 536

**2945 bancaire** *adj(f)* banking
- l'entreprise offre des services bancaires aux particuliers et aux sociétés – *the firm offers banking services to individuals and to companies*
65 | 534-l +n

**2946 défaire** *v* to undo, dismantle, strip, break up
- mon lacet est défait, comme d'habitude – *my shoelace is undone, as usual*
78 | 297

**2947 calendrier** *nm* calendar
- nous devrions respecter notre calendrier – *we should respect our calendar*
70 | 439

**2948 repas** *nm(pl)* meal
- c'est le repas kasher? oui, kasher – *it's a kosher meal? yes, kosher*
68 | 471

**2949 cul** *nm* bum, arse, ass
- je vais lui botter le cul – *I'm gonna kick his ass*
54 | 746-n +s

**2950 vouer** *v* to devote, dedicate to, vow to
- nous leur vouons un grand respect – *we pay them great respect*
77 | 323

**2951 surprenant** *adj* surprising
- le contraire aurait été moins surprenant – *the opposite would have been less surprising*
81 | 255

**2952 paradis** *nm(pl)* paradise, heaven
- tu aimes notre coin de paradis? – *do you like our corner of paradise?*
72 | 398

**2953 transparent** *nadj* transparent, see-through, evident
- il faut que les choses soient transparentes – *things must be transparent*
75 | 354

**2954 élu** *nadj* elected, elected member
- j'exprime ma déception auprès des élus politiques – *I express my disappointment to the elected officials*
72 | 404

**2955 tourisme** *nm* tourism, sightseeing
- le tourisme culturel est très important – *cultural tourism is very important*
68 | 472

**2956 démonstration** *nf* demonstration
- il a répondu par une démonstration de force – *he responded with a demonstration of force*
78 | 295

**2957 gravement** *adv*  seriously, solemnly, gravely
- deux maisons ont été gravement endommagées – *two houses were seriously damaged*
79 | 286

**2958 infraction** *nf*  offence, infrigement, infraction
- ceux qui commettent des infractions doivent payer – *those who break the law must pay*
60 | 626-l +s

**2959 tir** *nm*  fire, shot, launch
- il y a eu des tirs dans le couloir – *there were shots fired in the hallway*
56 | 715

**2960 envoi** *nm*  sending, dispatching
- il faut empêcher l'envoi de ces signaux – *you must stop sending these signals*
57 | 694+n

**2961 arrangement** *nm*  arrangement, layout, order, agreement
- j'ai conclu un arrangement avec le diable – *I made an agreement with the devil*
81 | 248

**2962 pardonner** *v*  to forgive, excuse
- si tu m'aimes vraiment, pardonne-moi – *if you really love me, forgive me*
58 | 651-n

**2963 collaborer** *v*  to collaborate, contribute
- ce groupe de travail a collaboré avec toutes sortes de spécialistes – *this work group collaborated with all kinds of specialists*
67 | 479+s

**2964 danse** *nf*  dance, dancing
- m'accorderez-vous cette danse? – *may I have this dance?*
73 | 372

**2965 tester** *v*  to test
- opératrice, veuillez tester ce numéro – *operator, please test this number*
72 | 403

**2966 proclamer** *v*  to proclaim, declare
- les résultats officiels seront proclamés samedi – *the official results will be announced Saturday*
71 | 406

**2967 genou** *nm*  knee
- la victime était à genoux devant le chien – *the victim was kneeling in front of the dog*
60 | 616+l

**2968 dominant** *adj*  dominant, prevailing
- dans toute relation il y a un dominant et un dominé – *in every relation there is dominator and a dominee*
63 | 558-s

**2969 péril** *nm*  peril
- aujourd'hui, notre porte-parole est en péril – *today our spokesman is in danger*
78 | 305

**2970 préférence** *nf*  preference, preferably
- ma préférence va toujours et encore à la poésie – *my preference is still and forever poetry*
72 | 391

**2971 vain** *adj*  vain
- j'ai tout essayé ... mais en vain – *I tried everything ... but in vain*
60 | 621+l -s

**2972 rentrée** *nf*  reopening, return, start
- j'attendis la rentrée avec impatience – *I awaited the reopening of school impatiently*
74 | 368

**2973 coller** *v*  to stick, paste
- les timbres étaient bien collés sur ces cartes postales – *the stamps were securely stuck onto these postcards*
64 | 537

**2974 monopole** *nm*  monopoly
- nul n'a le monopole des bonnes idées – *no one has the monopoly on good ideas*
68 | 462

**2975 approfondir** *v*  to deepen, make deeper, go further into
- le sujet mérite donc d'être approfondi – *the subject therefore deserves further study*
70 | 419

**2976 incendie** *nm*  fire, blaze
- les pompiers ont maitrisé tous les incendies – *the firemen brought all of the fires under control*
64 | 531

**2977 proximité** *nf*  proximity, nearness, closeness
- ils restaient à proximité – *they stayed close by*
69 | 437

**2978 hélicoptère** *nm*  helicopter
- des hélicoptères survolaient l'ambassade – *helicopters were flying over the embassy*
57 | 670-l

**2979 bouteille** *nf*  bottle
- j'ai cassé une bouteille de bière – *I broke a beer bottle*
64 | 533

**2980 championnat** *nm*  championship
- elle a participé à 15 championnats canadiens en neuf ans – *she participated in 15 Canadian championships in nine years*
48 | 892-l +n

**2981 hériter** *v*  to inherit
- sa femme héritait des dettes – *his wife inherited debts*
82 | 237

**2982 élémentaire** *adj(f)*  elementary, rudimentary, basic
- il posait des questions élémentaires – *he asked very basic questions*
76 | 324

**2983 entité** *nf*  entity
- ce ne sont pas des entités commerciales – *these are not commercial entities*
60 | 619+n -s

**2984 souffler** *v*  to blow, puff
- vous êtes là où le vent souffle – *you're there where the wind blows*
68 | 454

**2985 dit** *nadj* said, so-called; tale
• l'OTAN s'est transformée en organisation dite « de sécurité » – *NATO transformed into a so-called "security" organization*
79 | 275

**2986 mélange** *nm* mixing, mixture, blend
• il m'écouta avec un mélange de crainte et d'admiration – *he listened to me with a mixture of fear and admiration*
73 | 377

**2987 pourcentage** *nm* percentage, commission, cut
• elles calculent les pourcentages sur leurs profits – *they calculate the percentages on their profits*
71 | 404

**2988 permis** *nm(pl)* license, permit, permitted
• vos papiers? pièce d'identité, permis de conduire – *your papers? identity card, driver's license*
72 | 391+s

**2989 mélanger** *v* to mix, mix up, confuse
• il mélangeait un peu les dates – *he got the dates a little bit mixed up*
80 | 257

**2990 proprement** *adv* cleanly, neatly, properly
• je trouve cela proprement scandaleux – *I find that properly scandalous*
74 | 351

**2991 enfoncer** *v* to ram, drive in, hammer in, sink in
• commencons par enfoncer les portes – *let's start by knocking down the doors*
69 | 444

**2992 clandestin** *nadj* underground, clandestine
• le flux des immigrés clandestins en Espagne n'a cessé de grossir – *the flow of illegal immigrants in Spain grew unchecked*
70 | 430

**2993 super** *adji,nm* great
• si vous pouviez, ce serait super – *if you could, that would be great*
51 | 794-l -n +s

**2994 encontre** *adv* contrary to
• tu ne peux pas aller à l'encontre de sa personnalité – *you can't go contrary to his personality*
65 | 512

**2995 syndical** *adj* (trade-) union
• le mouvement syndical devra lui aussi être aidé – *the union movement will also have to be helped*
62 | 557

**2996 deviner** *v* to guess, solve
• sa tête baissée laissait deviner une calvitie naissante – *his bowed head betrayed the onset of balding*
59 | 627+l -n

**2997 tracer** *v* to draw, write, mark out
• la voie est tracée mais elle est difficile – *the route is marked but it is difficult*
75 | 333

**2998 sagesse** *nf* wisdom, moderation
• j'ai profité énormément de sa sagesse – *I profited enormously from his wisdom*
71 | 402

**2999 baiser** *nm,v* to kiss
• votre amoureux vous a donné un baiser d'adieu – *your lover gave you a goodbye kiss*
52 | 767-n

**3000 user** *v* to wear out, wear away, use up
• use de ton charme pour le convaincre – *use some of your charm to convince him*
69 | 445+l

**3001 enfer** *nm* hell
• l'infatuation est l'enfer de l'esprit – *infatuation is the mind's hell*
64 | 521

**3002 pilote** *nm,nf* pilot, experimental
• y a-t-il encore un pilote dans l'avion? – *is there still a pilot in the airplane?*
67 | 467

**3003 abonné** *nadj* subscribed, subscriber
• le texte du message reçu de l'abonné – *the text of the message received by the subscriber*
42 | 1030-l +n -s

**3004 objection** *nf* objection
• il n'y pas d'objections de votre part – *there are no objections on your behalf*
77 | 308

**3005 correction** *nf* correction
• alors j'ai fait cette correction – *so I made this correction*
68 | 462

**3006 vocation** *nf* vocation, calling
• c'est là qu'il trouva sa vocation – *that's where he found his calling in life*
72 | 391

**3007 facture** *nf* invoice, bill
• les gens ne peuvent payer leurs factures – *people can't pay their bills*
76 | 326

**3008 relancer** *v* to throw back, restart, relaunch
• cela aurait pour effet de relancer l'économie – *this will produce an economic recovery*
68 | 459

**3009 luxe** *nm* luxury
• la colère est un luxe que je ne peux me permettre – *anger is a luxury I can't afford*
72 | 391

**3010 nomination** *nf* appointment, nomination
• j'ai été très heureux d'apprendre votre nomination – *I was very pleased to hear of your nomination*
65 | 499

**3011 poster** *nm,v* poster; to post, mail
• nous y avons posté une vigie – *we set up a stakeout*
86 | 179

**3012 bar** *nm* bar
• nous buvons un café dans le bar voisin – *we're drinking a coffee in the local bar*
65 | 498

**3013 tantôt** *adv* this afternoon, sometimes
- des voix tantôt masculines, tantôt féminines – *voices that were sometimes masculine, sometimes feminine*
60 | 596+l

**3014 publiquement** *adv* publicly
- il ne voulait pas critiquer publiquement ses supérieurs – *he didn't want to publicly criticize his superiors*
75 | 341

**3015 gueule** *nf* mouth, trap
- ferme ta grande gueule! – *shut your big trap!*
58 | 634-n +s

**3016 comparable** *adj(f)* comparable
- le bruit était comparable à une explosion – *the noise was like an explosion*
72 | 384

**3017 sympathie** *nf* liking, warmth, friendship, sympathie
- vous avez ma sympathie – *you have my sympathy*
74 | 352

**3018 structurel** *adj* structural
- il y a des pressions structurelles dans le système de santé – *there are structural pressures in the health system*
52 | 771

**3019 dispenser** *v* to exempt, avoid
- vous pouvez me dispenser de vos commentaires – *you can spare me your commentaries*
80 | 254

**3020 copain** *nm* friend, buddy, mate
- ils deviennent copains, amis, amoureux bientôt – *they soon became buddies, friends, lovers*
63 | 538-n

**3021 aligner** *v* to lign up, align
- il aligna sur le comptoir les trois piécettes d'argent – *he lined up three small silver coins on the counter*
77 | 296

**3022 absorber** *v* to absorb, remove, take up, take over
- j'étais absorbé, obsédé par mes recherches – *I was absorbed, obsessed by my research*
73 | 367

**3023 compagnon** *nm* companion, craftsman, journeyman
- il invitait souvent des compagnons de son âge à venir – *he often invited his same-age companions to come over*
75 | 335

**3024 déroulement** *nm* development, progress
- nous avons examiné le déroulement des événements – *we studied the unfolding of the events*
81 | 247

**3025 dévoiler** *v* to unveil, reveal, disclose
- pouvez-vous nous dévoiler l'évolution de l'intrigue? – *can you reveal to us how the affair unfolded?*
76 | 314

**3026 opérationnel** *adj* operational, operating
- tous les systèmes sont opérationnels – *all systems are operational*
75 | 336-l

**3027 freiner** *v* to brake, slow down
- il se peut que je freine brusquement – *I might brake suddenly*
78 | 289

**3028 rattraper** *v* to recapture, recover, catch up, make up for
- il a fallu plus tard rattraper le temps perdu – *later we had to make up for lost time*
76 | 316

**3029 matinée** *nf* morning
- j'ai passé la matinée à lire – *I spent the morning reading*
64 | 523

**3030 régir** *v* to govern
- nous avons des lois pour régir les activités de la presse – *we have laws to govern the activities of the press*
68 | 445

**3031 poème** *nm* poem
- souviens-toi du poème que je t'ai fait lire – *remember the poem that I had you read*
62 | 561-n

**3032 bassin** *nm* bowl, basin
- une large allée centrale menait à un bassin – *a large central alley led to a reservoir*
75 | 337

**3033 éteindre** *v* to extinguish, put out, turn off
- elle a éteint la lumière – *she turned off the light*
61 | 570+l

**3034 ministériel** *adj* ministerial; minister
- les ministériels devraient voter selon leur conscience – *the ministers should vote according to their conscience*
59 | 611-l +s

**3035 rage** *nf* rage, fury, rabies
- la guerre fait rage dans les ténèbres – *war is raging in the darkness*
74 | 351

**3036 enregistrement** *nm* recording, registration, check-in, logging
- pour moi, les enregistrements falsifient la psychanalyse – *for me, recordings falsify psychoanalysis*
68 | 447-l

**3037 débarquer** *v* to unload, land, disembark
- de nouveaux groupes étrangers ont débarqué en Italie – *new groups of foreigners have landed in Italy*
77 | 297

**3038 systématiquement** *adv* systematically
- ce genre de choses sort systématiquement – *this kind of thing happens systematically*
77 | 307

**3039 énormément** *adv* enormously
- j'ai énormément d'admiration pour lui – *I have a lot of admiration for him*
63 | 540+s

**3040 respirer** *v* to breath
- respirez à fond, calmez-vous – *breathe deeply, calm down*
59 | 615+l -n

**3041 dictature** *nf* dictatorship
- nous voulons éviter une nouvelle dictature – *we want to avoid a new dictatorship*
74 | 344

**3042 acheteur** *nm* buyer, purchaser
- le gouvernement est le plus gros acheteur de biens – *the government is the greatest purchaser of goods*
83 | 212

**3043 équiper** *v* to equip, kit out, fit out, tool up
- quelque 1.800 caméras de surveillance équipent les gares – *the train stations are equipped with some 1,800 surveillance cameras*
69 | 423

**3044 édifice** *nm* building
- un édifice s'élève pierre à pierre – *a building is constructed one stone at a time*
79 | 269

**3045 lot** *nm* share, prize, lot
- la négligence sera le lot de cet enfant du malheur – *negligence will be the lot of this child of misfortune*
83 | 218

**3046 fondement** *nm* foundation
- l'avenir reposait sur ces fondements – *the future rested on this foundation*
71 | 396

**3047 spirituel** *nadj* witty, spiritual, sacred
- c'est une fiction moderne spirituelle et intelligente – *it's a modern work of fiction that's spiritual and intelligent*
67 | 460

**3048 fournisseur** *nm* supplier, provider
- je ne suis que le fournisseur. je ne sais rien – *I'm only the middleman. I don't know anything*
73 | 360

**3049 détriment** *nm* detriment
- la mondialisation se fait au détriment des moins forts – *globalizaton occurs to the detriment of the weak*
76 | 318

**3050 unanime** *adj(f)* unanimous
- elle a reçu l'approbation unanime de l'opinion publique – *she received unanimous approval from public opinion*
53 | 733-n +s

**3051 agiter** *v* to shake, disturb
- le sujet agite beaucoup la presse – *the subject really stirs up the press*
64 | 518+l

**3052 élimination** *nf* elimination
- il avait programmé l'élimination des paysans – *he engineered the elimination of all peasants*
72 | 378

**3053 nazi** *nadj* Nazi
- négocier avec les nazis? jamais – *negotiate with the Nazis? never*
77 | 296

**3054 col** *nm* collar, mountain pass
- tu devrais arranger un peu ton col – *you should adjust your collar*
73 | 363

**3055 impressionner** *v* to impress, upset
- vous avez impressionné nos collègues – *you impressed our colleagues*
80 | 257

**3056 accessible** *adj(f)* accessible, approachable
- je pense être un patron plutôt accessible – *I think I'm a rather approachable boss*
71 | 393

**3057 résidence** *nf* residence, block of flats
- bienvenue dans ma résidence d'été – *welcome to my summer residence*
71 | 396

**3058 dedans** *adv,nm(pl),prep* inside, indoors
- je suis tombé dedans quand j'étais petit – *I fell into it when I was young*
62 | 547-n

**3059 agressif** *nadj* aggressive
- elle est devenue agressive, hostile – *she has become aggressive, hostile*
81 | 236

**3060 loger** *v* to put up, accommodate, stay, find accommodation
- nous savons maintenant où ils se logent – *we know where they live now*
81 | 234

**3061 ouvertement** *adv* openly, overtly
- il a parlé assez ouvertement – *he spoke openly enough*
81 | 240

**3062 patience** *nf* patience
- leur patience avait des limites – *their patience had limits*
77 | 298

**3063 stimuler** *v* to stimulate
- elle ne stimule aucunement l'immunité cellulaire – *it in no way stimulates the cell's immunity*
72 | 369

**3064 classement** *nm* classification, ranking
- tes classements aux courses ont été excellents l'an dernier – *your race results were excellent last year*
49 | 811-l +n -s

**3065 arrestation** *nf* arrest
- vous êtes en état d'arrestation – *you are under arrest*
58 | 617

**3066 longuement** *adv* at length
- elle m'a longuement regardé, sans colère – *she looked at me for a long time, without anger*
71 | 385

**3067 ancêtre** *nm,nf* ancestor, forerunner
- en fait, mes ancêtres viennent d'Inde – *in fact, my ancestors come from India*
82 | 229

**3068 intensité** *nf* intensity
- ils relayent la vérité avec la même intensité que les mensonges – *they convey the truth as intently as they do lies*
79 | 272

**3069 grandeur** *nf* size, greatness
- la grandeur dominait dans ce cercle d'élite – *the grandeur dominated in this circle of the elite*
69 | 415+l

**3070 entraînement** *nm* training, coaching, drive
- bien joué, ton entraînement est terminé – *well done—your training is complete*
72 | 373

**3071 déborder** *v* to overflow, boil over, go out, go over
- je suis débordé au travail – *I'm swamped at work*
78 | 284

**3072 conducteur** *nadj* driver, operator, conductor
- le conducteur a été tué sur le coup – *the driver was killed instantly*
74 | 336

**3073 pollution** *nf* pollution
- il y a des risques importants de pollution – *there's a significant risk of pollution*
69 | 416-l

**3074 islamique** *adj(f)* Islamic
- nous incarnons un mouvement islamique révolutionnaire – *we embody a revolutionary Islamic movement*
54 | 693+n

**3075 attribution** *nf* awarding, allocation, assignment, attribution
- certaines attributions en matière nucléaire relèvent encore des états – *some prerogatives relative to nuclear power still depend on the states*
68 | 442

**3076 caméra** *nf* camera
- ils ont souri devant les caméras – *they smiled in front of the cameras*
66 | 470-l +s

**3077 dissimuler** *v* to conceal, hide
- l'homme semble dissimuler un passé secret – *the man seems to conceal a secret past*
70 | 404

**3078 chronique** *nadj(f)* chronic, column, page, chronicle
- c'est un mal chronique auquel il va falloir s'attaquer – *it's a chronic illness that should be attacked*
73 | 358

**3079 ère** *nf* era
- nous vivons à l'ère de la mondialisation – *we live in an era of globalization*
77 | 291

**3080 rappel** *nm* reminder, summary, recall, return, remember
- je suis un rappel d'un moment douloureux de ta vie – *I'm a reminder of a painful time of your life*
70 | 396

**3081 fabricant** *nm* manufacturer
- rien ne semble effrayer le fabricant français – *nothing seems to scare the French manufacturer*
68 | 438

**3082 utilité** *nf* use, usefulness,
- tu ne m'es d'aucune utilité – *you are of no use to me*
80 | 253

**3083 ethnique** *nadj(f)* ethnic
- les luttes politiques entre divers groupes ethniques – *the political struggle between different ethnic groups*
70 | 399

**3084 annexe** *adj(f),nf* annex, appendix, related issue
- le texte du rapport figure à l'annexe – *the text of the report is located in the appendix*
56 | 663

**3085 interlocuteur** *nm* speaker
- vous aimez voir les yeux de vos interlocuteurs – *you like to see the eyes of the people you talk to*
76 | 314

**3086 spécifier** *v* to specify
- je ne peux pas spécifier l'année – *I can't specify the year*
43 | 952+n -s

**3087 souple** *adj(f)* supple, agile, soft, floppy, flexible
- faut être agile et souple – *you gotta be agile and flexible*
82 | 219

**3088 rémunération** *nf* remuneration, payment, pay
- comment jugez-vous la rémunération des dirigeants français – *what do you think of French leaders' pay?*
70 | 392

**3089 faillite** *nf* bankruptcy, collapse, failure
- beaucoup d'entre eux devront déclarer faillite – *many of them will have to declare bankruptcy*
70 | 396

**3090 touchant** *adj,prep* with regard to, concerning, touching, moving
- c'est un personnage très touchant – *he has a very touching personality*
72 | 366

**3091 hostile** *adj(f)* hostile
- les rues me semblaient hostiles – *the streets seemed hostile to me*
71 | 383

**3092 imprimer** *v* to print, print out
- je demande que ce rapport soit imprimé – *I request that this report be printed*
78 | 274

**3093 abuser** *v* to abuse, mislead, take advantage
- j'ai été injuste, j'ai abusé de ma force – *I was unjust, I abused my authority*
78 | 277

**3094 vérification** *nf* check, verification
- arrêtez-le au coin pour vérification – *stop him at the corner for an identity check*
56 | 643-l

## 18  Nationalities

This table lists the most frequently occurring words describing nationalities, languages, and cultural, ethnic, or religious groups.

| | | |
|---|---|---|
| **français** 251 French | **arabe** 1994 Arabic | **libanais** 3993 Lebanese |
| **américain** 374 American | **grec** 2026 Greek | **yougoslave** 4077 Yugoslavian |
| **européen** 445 European | **japonais** 2097 Japanese | |
| **canadien** 611 Canadian | **suisse** 2241 Swiss | **égyptien** 4137 Egyptian |
| **anglais** 784 English | **africain** 2289 African | **algérien** 4163 Algerian |
| **allemand** 844 German | **parisien** 2549 Parisian | **syrien** 4453 Syrian |
| **britannique** 1296 British | **oriental** 2715 Oriental | **mexicain** 4541 Mexican |
| **russe** 1325 Russian | **serbe** 2780 Serbian | **néerlandais** 4640 Dutch |
| **israélien** 1468 Israeli | **belge** 2795 Belgian | **suédois** 4647 Swedish |
| **italien** 1477 Italian | **turc** 3134 Turkish | **basque** 4658 Basque |
| **juif** 1510 Jewish | **romain** 3144 Roman | **kurde** 4694 Kurd |
| **espagnol** 1666 Spanish | **asiatique** 3277 Asian | **danois** 4809 Danish |
| **soviétique** 1674 Soviet | **iranien** 3405 Iranian | **anglo-saxon** 4854 Anglo-Saxon |
| **indien** 1679 Indian | **marocain** 3469 Moroccan | **albanais** 4912 Albanian |
| **latin** 1844 Latin | **polonais** 3660 Polish | **bosniaque** 4977 Bosnian |
| **irakien** 1913 Iraqi | **portugais** 3684 Portuguese | **brésilien** 5016 Brazilian |
| **chinois** 1914 Chinese | **tchèque** 3793 Czech | **autrichien** 5018 Austrian |
| **québécois** 1970 Quebecker | **irlandais** 3963 Irish | **cubain** 5065 Cuban |

3095 **aveugle** *nadj(f)* blind
 • un jour tu seras aveugle. comme moi
 – *someday you'll be blind. like me*
 64 | 504+l

3096 **jurer** *v* to swear
 • je jure sur la tombe de ma grand-mère
 – *I swear on my grandmother's grave*
 59 | 588

3097 **trésor** *nm* treasure, treasury
 • t'es complètement obsédé par un
 trésor – *you're completely obsessed by
 a treasure*
 72 | 362

3098 **vingtaine** *nf* about twenty
 • une vingtaine de personnes auraient été
 interpellées – *about 20 persons were
 apparently summoned*
 66 | 457

3099 **séquence** *nf* sequence
 • certaines séquences virales protègent les
 cellules – *some viral sequences protect
 cells*
 48 | 829+n -s

3100 **musicien** *nadj* musician
 • ça prend de vrai musiciens pour jouer du
 blues – *it takes true musicians to play the
 blues*
 62 | 531

3101 **routier** *nadj* road, long-distance lorry
 or truck driver
 • nous avons besoin d'un réseau routier
 continental – *we need a continental network
 of roads*
 63 | 524-l

3102 **embrasser** *v* to kiss, embrace
 • je n'embrasse pas des inconnus. moi non
 plus – *I don't kiss strangers. neither do I*
 60 | 577

3103 **échéance** *nf* expiration date, date of payment,
 deadline
 • le contrat arrive à échéance dans quelques
 mois – *the contract expires in a few months*
 72 | 373

3104 **surplus** *nm(pl)* surplus
 • s'il y a des surplus, je les prends – *if there's
 a surplus, I'll take them*
 57 | 628-n +s

3105 **prématuré** *nadj* premature
 • c'est le résultat de la mort prématurée de ta
 mère – *it results from the premature death
 of your mother*
 85 | 172

3106 **décrocher** *v* to take down, take off, pick up,
 lift
 • je me suis enfin décidé à décrocher le
 téléphone – *I finally decided to pick up the
 telephone receiver*
 74 | 328

**3107 rembourser** *v* to reimburse, pay back, pay off, repay
• la compagnie d'assurance me remboursera de toute manière – *anyway, the insurance company will reimburse me*
71 | 380

**3108 adhérer** *v* to stick to, support, join, be a member of
• quoi que vous fassiez, adhérez à l'Union – *whatever you do, join the Union!*
76 | 310

**3109 défenseur** *nm,nf* defender
• mon fusil et moi sommes les défenseurs de ma patrie – *my rifle and I are the defenders of my homeland*
72 | 366

**3110 citation** *nf* quote, quotation, citation
• j'aimerai mentionner quelques citations – *I would like to mention some citations*
73 | 352

**3111 reconstruction** *nf* reconstruction
• après notre victoire, la reconstruction sera très rapide – *after our victory, reconstruction will be very swift*
65 | 485

**3112 retomber** *v* to fall again, fall down again
• il essaie de se lever, retombe – *he tried to stand up, falls down again*
71 | 383+I

**3113 pourvoir** *v* to provide, equip, supply, furnish
• dans quelques années, l'Iran sera pourvu de l'arme nucléaire – *in a few years, Iran will be equipped with the nuclear weapon*
77 | 281

**3114 systématique** *nadj(f)* systematic
• la théologie comporte une partie systématique – *theology includes a systematic component*
75 | 320

**3115 véritablement** *adv* truly, really
• elle me démolit, véritablement. elle vous démolit? – *she destroys me, really. does she destroy you?*
71 | 378

**3116 parallèlement** *adv* in parallel, similarly
• j'ai toujours mené parallèlement le travail poétique et le travail social – *I always kept my poetic work and social work in parallel*
70 | 393

**3117 légume** *nm,nf* vegetable
• je ne mange pas de légumes non plus – *I don't eat vegetables either*
81 | 229

**3118 francophone** *adj(f)* French-speaking, French speaker, francophone
• nous devons parler français avec les francophones – *we should speak French with francophones*
58 | 608-I +s

**3119 émaner** *v* to issue from, emanate from, come from, radiate from
• quelque chose émane de lui, non? – *something radiates from him, doesn't it?*
74 | 328

**3120 souffle** *nm* breath, puff
• je détournais la tête en retenant mon souffle – *I turned away my head and held my breath*
65 | 476+I

**3121 lac** *nm* lake
• je vais vous faire courir autour du lac – *I'm going to make you run around the lake*
73 | 344

**3122 souhait** *nm* wish
• fais un souhait, mon chéri – *make a wish, my dear*
78 | 277

**3123 prévaloir** *v* to prevail
• les Etats-Unis se félicitent d'avoir fait prévaloir leurs vues – *the U.S. is proud of having made its views prevail*
75 | 321

**3124 sixième** *det,nm,nf* sixth
• je crois que c'est la sixième saison de cette émission – *I think it's this program's sixth season*
71 | 371

**3125 enveloppe** *nf* envelope
• elle a fait tomber une enveloppe dans ma chambre – *she dropped an envelope in my room*
75 | 319

**3126 extension** *nf* extension, stretching, expansion
• on craint surtout l'extension de la guerre civile – *our worst fear is an extension of the civil war*
67 | 446

**3127 effondrer** *v* to collapse, cave in, fall down
• notre pays était complètement effondré – *our country had suffered a complete meltdown*
75 | 322

**3128 apprêter** *v* to prepare, get ready, dress
• nous nous apprêtons à adopter un nouveau système – *we're preparing to adopt a new system*
71 | 368

**3129 anonyme** *adj(f)* anonymous
• on parle d'une adresse anonyme sur l'Internet – *people talk about an anonymous Internet address*
76 | 298

**3130 cibler** *v* to target
• elles pourront frapper des groupes ciblés – *they can strike the targeted groups*
73 | 337-I

**3131 additionnel** *adj* additional
• elle n'a pas besoin de fonds additionnels – *she has no need of additional funds*
71 | 367

**3132 excès** *nm(pl)* excess, surplus, abuse
• il y a eu un excès de confiance chez certains – *some of them had an excess of confidence*
72 | 364

**3133 douzaine** *nf* dozen
• il a écrit une douzaine de poèmes courts – *he wrote about a dozen short poems*
83 | 199

**3134 turc** *adj,nm* Turk, Turkish
• les Turcs musulmans se répandirent en
  Europe – *the Moslem Turks spread across
  Europe*
  52 | 720

**3135 incertain** *nadj* uncertain, unsure
• la frontière qui les sépare est incertaine –
  *the border separating them is poorly defined*
  72 | 356

**3136 épouser** *v* to marry, wed
• je veux t'épouser – *I want to marry you*
  60 | 552

**3137 consensus** *nm(pl)* consensus
• il faut obtenir un vaste consensus – *we need
  a vast consensus*
  66 | 452-l

**3138 chat** *nm* cat; chat
• je crois qu'un chat a dormi sur ma tête hier
  – *I think a cat slept on my head yesterday*
  67 | 438

**3139 avertissement** *nm* warning
• tu m'avais déjà donné un avertissement –
  *you had already warned me*
  77 | 284

**3140 excédent** *nm* surplus
• nous savons que l'excédent va cesser
  d'augmenter – *we know that the surplus will
  stop increasing*
  56 | 640-l

**3141 mondialisation** *nf* internationalisation,
globalisation
• je suis pour une mondialisation avec des
  règles éthiques – *I'm all for globalization
  with ethical rules*
  63 | 509

**3142 conventionnel** *nadj* conventional
• ces missiles étaient équipés de têtes
  conventionnelles – *these missiles were
  equipped with conventional warheads*
  79 | 250

**3143 unanimité** *nf* unanimity
• leur décision devra être prise à l'unanimité
  – *their decision will have to be made
  unanimously*
  63 | 496

**3144 romain** *adj* Roman
• elle heurta le soldat romain sur le casque –
  *she slugged the Roman soldier on the helmet*
  74 | 320

**3145 inégalité** *nf* difference, uneveness, inequality
• il protesta avec véhémence contre cette
  inégalité – *he vehemently protested this
  inequality*
  70 | 390

**3146 originaire** *adj(f)* original, first, native to
• je suis originaire d'Europe de l'Est – *I come
  from Eastern Europe*
  72 | 351

**3147 finale** *nm,nf* finale, final event
• c'est la finale du foot, le Super Bowl
  – *it's the football championship, the Super
  Bowl*
  48 | 809-l +n

**3148 mademoiselle** *nf* Miss
• excusez moi, mademoiselle. vous pouvez
  m'aider? – *excuse me, miss. can you help
  me?*
  54 | 670+l -n

**3149 coûteux** *adj(pl)* expensive, costly
• l'équipement individuel est extrêmement
  coûteux – *the standalone equipment is very
  expensive*
  73 | 342

**3150 ventre** *nm* belly, stomach
• il s'approchait, son ventre brillait entre les
  vagues – *he approached, his stomach
  glistening among the waves*
  58 | 583+l

**3151 soixante** *det,nmi* sixty
• il y a plus de soixante ans que j'en ai perdu
  l'habitude – *I dropped the habit over sixty
  years ago*
  64 | 483

**3152 bière** *nf* beer; coffin
• je veux prendre deux bouteilles de bière
  avant de partir – *I want to take two bottles
  of beer before leaving*
  68 | 419

**3153 passif** *nadj* passive, liabilities
• nous ne jouons pas un rôle passif – *we're
  not playing a passive role*
  76 | 291

**3154 interrogation** *nf* question, interviewing,
interrogation, questioning, test
• je laisse toutes ces interrogations à votre
  réflexion – *I leave all these questions to
  your pondering*
  79 | 255

**3155 voile** *nm,nf* veil, sail
• j'ai le vent dans les voiles – *I have the wind
  in my sails*
  74 | 320

**3156 accentuer** *v* to stress, to emphasize, become
more pronounced
• la méfiance entre salariés et employeurs
  s'accentue – *the mistrust between salaried
  workers and employers is growing*
  74 | 324

**3157 rattacher** *v* to attach, join, tie
• a quelle école vous rattachez-vous? – *what
  school do you go to?*
  78 | 260

**3158 manuel** *adj,nm* manual
• il faudra écrire un manuel d'utilisation –
  *we'll need to write a user's manual*
  73 | 337

**3159 contracter** *v* to contract, take out, tense
• elles ont contracté la maladie – *they
  contracted the sickness*
  74 | 321

**3160 territorial** *adj* territorial, land
• le droit à l'intégrité territoriale est inscrit
  dans la loi – *the right to territorial integrity
  is upheld in the law*
  66 | 454

**3161 subsister** *v* to subsist, remain
• le racisme, lui, subsiste encore – *but racism still remains*
64 | 483-s

**3162 carré** *nadj* square, broad, plain
• la salle était petite et carrée – *the room was small and square*
72 | 350

**3163 voleur** *nadj* thief, light-fingered
• je ne suis pas un voleur – *I'm not a thief*
75 | 304

**3164 centrale** *nf* power station, central office
• ce devait être la plus grande centrale électrique au gaz naturel – *it was supposed to be the largest natural gas electrical power station*
71 | 370

**3165 pôle** *nm* pole
• il sera parti au Pôle Nord – *he will have left for the North Pole*
72 | 356

**3166 délit** *nm* crime, offence
• tous avaient été surpris en flagrant délit – *they were all caught in the act*
76 | 286

**3167 usager** *nm* user
• l'usager modifie les paramètres de renvoi d'appel – *the user modifies the call forwarding parameters*
46 | 826-l +n -s

**3168 musical** *adj* musical
• ce genre musical est plus anglophone que francophone – *this style of music is more English than French*
60 | 551

**3169 allumer** *v* to switch on, light up, turn on
• allumons la télé – *let's turn on the TV*
60 | 543+l

**3170 quelquefois** *adv* sometimes
• quelquefois je pense qu'il a raison – *sometimes I think he's right*
56 | 613+l -n -s

**3171 disperser** *v* to scatter, spread, disperse
• l'armée va disperser la foule – *the army's going to disperse the crowd*
77 | 280

**3172 déchirer** *v* to tear up, tear, rip
• le papier était déchiré – *the paper was torn*
69 | 399+l

**3173 mépris** *nm(pl)* contempt, scorn, disdain
• je n'ai plus que du mépris pour elle – *I have nothing but disdain for her*
72 | 344

**3174 échantillon** *nm* sample
• les échantillons sont faciles à transporter – *the samples are easy to transport*
67 | 423

**3175 continuité** *nf* continuity, continuation
• nous sommes conscients de la continuité de cet effort – *we are aware of the ongoing nature of this effort*
59 | 559+n

**3176 fichier** *nm* file
• ouvrez simplement un nouveau fichier – *just open a new file*
46 | 825-l +n -s

**3177 conquête** *nf* conquest
• il rêve de conquêtes militaires – *he dreams of military conquests*
75 | 309

**3178 contourner** *v* to bypass, go round
• avec les chariots, on va contourner les rapides – *with the wagons, we'll bypass the rapids*
82 | 206

**3179 supplément** *nm* supplement, extra
• on pourrait peut-être obtenir en douce un supplément de papier – *maybe they can sneak us an extra quantity of paper*
79 | 246

**3180 sincère** *adj(f)* sincere
• j'offre mes sincères condoléances à sa famille – *I offer my sincere sympathies to his family*
72 | 342

**3181 optique** *nadj(f)* optical, optic, perspective
• j'étais dans une optique de colonie de vacances – *I was in a vacation colony frame of mind*
75 | 302

**3182 maximal** *adj* maximal
• le seuil de pollution maximale avait été atteint – *the maximum pollution level was reached*
62 | 504-l

**3183 permission** *nf* permission, leave
• avec votre permission, je me retire – *with your permission, I shall withdraw*
61 | 516-n +s

**3184 méchant** *nadj* nasty, wicked, mean
• ce vilain méchant ne te fera rien – *this no-good jerk won't do anything to you*
65 | 460-n

**3185 idéologie** *nf* ideology
• je n'approuvais pas son idéologie économique – *I didn't approve of his economic ideology*
69 | 388

**3186 interview** *nf* interview
• ils préfèrent donner des interviews téléphoniques – *he prefers being interviewed on the telephone*
56 | 615

**3187 désespoir** *nm* despair
• votre rire trahit un désespoir hystérique – *your laugh betrays a hysterical despair*
67 | 426+l

**3188 humeur** *nf* mood, temper
• il paraissait de bonne humeur – *he seemed to be in a good mood*
62 | 496+l

**3189 demandeur** *nm* seeker, complainant
• personne n'avait voulu accueillir les demandeurs d'asile – *nobody wanted to welcome the asylum seekers*
52 | 684-l +n -s

**3190 horrible** *adj(f)* horrible, terrible, dreadful, hideous
• la violence est une chose horrible – *violence is a horrible thing*
70 | 373-n

**3191 conquérir** *v* to conquer
• tu dois conquérir la foule ... pour conquérir ta liberté – *you must conquer the crowds ... to conquer your freedom*
74 | 311

**3192 horaire** *nadj(f)* schedule, timetable, hourly
• j'ai un horaire assez chargé – *I have a rather busy schedule*
72 | 339

**3193 encouragement** *nm* encouragement
• je crois qu'il apprécie les encouragements – *I think he appreciated the encouragement*
87 | 147

**3194 motiver** *v* to justify, account for, motivate
• qu'est-ce qui vous a motivé à écrire ce livre? – *what motivated you to write this book?*
72 | 345

**3195 plier** *v* to fold, fold up, fold back, bend
• j'ai un lit pliant – *I have a folding cot*
72 | 343

**3196 homologue** *adj(f)* counterpart, homologue
• j'en discuterai avec mon homologue – *I'll discuss it with my counterpart*
62 | 509-l

**3197 successif** *adj* successive
• les déplacés sont arrivés par vagues successives – *the displaced persons arrived in successive waves*
72 | 351

**3198 manifestement** *adv* manifestly, clearly
• elle a manifestement bénéficié d'un large soutien – *she clearly enjoyed widespread support*
76 | 293

**3199 olympique** *adj(f)* Olympic
• il s'était dopé pour les Jeux olympiques – *he doped himself for the Olympic Games*
51 | 718-l +n

**3200 littéralement** *adv* literally
• les radiations vont littéralement cuire la planète – *radiation will literally cook the planet*
81 | 223

**3201 reproduction** *nf* reproduction
• j'ai une superbe collection de reproductions – *I have a superb collection of reproductions*
73 | 331

**3202 propice** *adj(f)* favorable, auspicious propitious
• la situation n'était pas très propice – *the situation was not ideal*
84 | 175

**3203 chèque** *nm* check
• nous réglerons par chèque en fin de mois de livraison – *we will pay by check at the end of each delivery's month*
70 | 378

**3204 explorer** *v* to explore, investigate, examine
• il faudrait explorer le coin – *the place should be explored*
72 | 342

**3205 matériau** *nm* material
• le granit est un matériau noble, solide, éternel – *granite is a noble, solid, eternal material*
72 | 346

**3206 dépendance** *nf* dependence, dependency
• la cocaïne ne crée pas de dépendance physique – *cocaine doesn't create a physical addiction*
73 | 322

**3207 nu** *nadj* naked, nude
• au fait . . . j'aime dormir nu – *in fact . . . I like to sleep in the nude*
64 | 473+l

**3208 poignée** *nf* handful, fistful, handle
• il saisit la valise par la poignée – *he grasped the suitcase by the handle*
76 | 278

**3209 abaisser** *v* to pull down, lower, reduce
• les prix ne sont pas abaissés proportionnellement aux coûts – *the prices aren't reduced proportionately to costs*
72 | 340

**3210 divergence** *nf* divergence, difference
• les divergences persistent entre les grandes puissances – *differences persist among the superpowers*
74 | 307

**3211 restant** *adj,nm* remaining, the rest, the remainder
• elle sera toujours là, pour le restant de mes jours – *she will always be there, for the rest of my days*
79 | 237

**3212 détention** *nf* detention, possession
• il existe des règles sur la détention de prisonniers – *there are rules for detaining prisoners*
64 | 472

**3213 étouffer** *v* to suffocate, smother, muffle
• elle avait été contrainte de l'étouffer – *she was forced to suffocate him*
72 | 334

**3214 inscription** *nf* registration, enrolment; engraving
• c'est quoi, l'inscription, sur votre casque? – *what does the engraving on your helmet say?*
78 | 250

**3215 montée** *nf* climb, ascent, rise, raising
• la demande interne reste bridée par la montée du chômage – *internal demand remains flat due to the climb in unemployment*
71 | 354

**3216 approvisionnement** *nm* supply, supplies, stock, supplying, stocking
• les approvisionnements ont été réduits de 25 % – *supplies have been reduced by 25%*
68 | 398

**3217 municipalité** *nf* municipality
- dans chaque municipalité on en trouve des écoles françaises – *in every municipality there are French schools*
61 | 506+s

**3218 consécutif** *adj* consecutive
- pour la seconde année consécutive, la croissance sera négative – *for the second consecutive year, growth will be negative*
61 | 505+n

**3219 nuage** *nm* cloud
- quelques petits nuages se roulaient en boule dans le ciel – *a few small clouds somersaulted through the sky*
61 | 515

**3220 institutionnel** *adj* institutional
- là, plus aucun lieu institutionnel ne les protège – *there, no institutional tie protects them*
64 | 469

**3221 confédération** *nf* confederation
- les quatre confédérations ont arrêté leur décision mardi – *the four confederations announced their decision Tuesday*
63 | 479-l

**3222 quiconque** *pro* whoever, anyone who
- je donnerais ma chemise à quiconque en aurait besoin – *I would give my shirt to anyone who needed it*
72 | 342

**3223 vendeur** *nm* salesman, seller
- ça, c'est un vendeur. il a fait une promesse – *now there's a salesman. he's made a promise*
77 | 264

**3224 réplique** *nf* reply, retort; replica
- c'est une réplique de la Grande Pyramide de Giza – *it's a replica of the Great Pyramid of Giza*
78 | 259

**3225 acquitter** *v* to acquit, pay, settle, pay off
- il a été acquitté de l'accusation – *he was acquitted of the charge*
70 | 367

**3226 intervalle** *nm* space, distance, interval
- il passe devant moi à des intervalles sans doute réguliers – *he passes before me in what must be regular intervals*
55 | 621+n -s

**3227 métro** *nm* underground, metro
- toutes les lignes de métro fonctionnaient – *all the subway lines were working*
71 | 347

**3228 coutume** *nf* custom
- la coutume est une seconde nature – *customs are a kind of second nature*
79 | 246

**3229 fatiguer** *v* to tire, get tired
- si j'étais fatigué, je dormais – *if I was tired, I went to sleep*
62 | 490

**3230 panique** *nadj(f)* panic
- ils essaient de créer la panique – *they are trying to cause panic*
78 | 254

**3231 abriter** *v* to shelter, shade
- je sais où ce monstre s'abrite – *I know where this monster is hiding out*
70 | 363

**3232 variété** *nf* variety
- il y a une variété infinie de biocombustibles – *there's an infinite variety of biofuels*
70 | 361

**3233 bulletin** *nm* bulletin, report
- mais vous avez quand même un bulletin de météo – *but you at least have a weather forecast*
64 | 467

**3234 flotte** *nf* fleet
- la flotte japonaise a pris la fuite – *the Japanese fleet escaped*
77 | 267

**3235 décourager** *v* to discourage, dishearten, lose heart
- il ne faut surtout pas se décourager – *whatever you do, don't get discouraged*
77 | 268

**3236 poussière** *nf* dust
- tu es poussière et tu retourneras en poussière – *dust thou art and unto dust shalt thou return*
64 | 456+l

**3237 fierté** *nf* pride
- ils ont la fierté d'être des propriétaires – *they have the pride of ownership*
70 | 370-n

**3238 épisode** *nm* episode
- cette musique ne ressemblait à aucun épisode de son existence – *this music didn't resemble any episode of his existence*
72 | 330

**3239 détacher** *v* to untie, detach, remove
- détachez votre roue de secours – *remove your spare tyre*
69 | 375+l

**3240 interface** *nf* interface
- trois éléments d'interface sont définis pour le flux d'information – *three interfaces are defined for the information flow*
42 | 902-l +n -s

**3241 administrateur** *nm* administrator
- voyez comme on est de très bons administrateurs – *see how we're such good administrators*
70 | 369

**3242 doucement** *adv* gently, softly
- il a refermé la porte tout doucement – *he closed the door very gingerly*
55 | 615+l -n

**3243 quoique** *conj* although, though
- je n'écrirai plus, quoique j'en souffre – *I don't write any more, though I suffer because of it*
67 | 412+l

**3244 projection** *nf* projection, ejection, discharge
• il y avait des projections sur un écran –
  *there were projections on a screen*
  77 | 261

**3245 treize** *det,nmi* thirteen
• onze cafards ... douze cafards ... treize
  cafards – *eleven cockroaches ... twelve
  cockroaches ... thirteen cockroaches*
  63 | 478

**3246 antenne** *nf* antenna
• il y a une antenne sur le toit? – *is there an
  antenna on the roof?*
  61 | 507-I

**3247 tarif** *nm* price, rate, fare, tariff
• le contenu du message dépendra du tarif –
  *the content of the message will depend on
  the rate*
  68 | 398

**3248 remplacement** *nm* replacement, standing in
• il vous en donne une nouvelle en remplacement de votre carte perdue – *he's giving you
  a new replacement for your lost card*
  69 | 380

**3249 devise** *nf* currency, motto, slogan
• le dollar progressait également face aux
  autres devises – *the dollar also gained over
  the other currencies*
  70 | 364-s

**3250 optimisme** *nm* optimism
• selon moi, son optimisme ne se justifie
  pas – *in my opinion, his optimism isn't
  justified*
  78 | 253

**3251 chanteur** *nadj* singer
• elle réalisait son rêve. elle était chanteuse –
  *she fulfilled her dream. she was a singer*
  66 | 420

**3252 décret** *nm* decree
• le président a signé un décret – *the
  president signed a decree*
  68 | 385

**3253 écrit** *nadj* writing
• hélas, tous ses écrits sont perdus! – *alas, all
  of his writings have been lost!*
  64 | 459

**3254 suggestion** *nf* suggestion
• cette suggestion enchanta le directeur – *this
  suggestion charmed the director*
  70 | 354+s

**3255 queue** *nf* tail, handle, stalk, stem, rear
• faites la queue et ne poussez pas – *get in
  line and don't push*
  69 | 375

**3256 durement** *adv* harshly, severely
• nous avons assez durement vécu, en tant
  que nation – *we have lived quite a harsh life,
  as a nation*
  78 | 248

**3257 applaudir** *v* to clap, applaud
• il voudrait que nous applaudissions son
  discours – *he wanted us to applaud his
  talk*
  77 | 265

**3258 sucre** *nm* sugar
• le marché du sucre se présentait comme
  une gourmandise – *the sugar market
  resembled a piece of candy*
  76 | 272

**3259 prioritaire** *nadj(f)* priority, having priority,
having right of way
• je te fais un passe prioritaire – *I'll give you a
  special-entry pass*
  73 | 321

**3260 chair** *nf* flesh
• elle était bien en chair – *she looked
  overweight*
  57 | 562+I -n

**3261 exécutif** *nadj* executive
• la responsabilité du pouvoir exécutif doit
  être entière – *the responsibility of executive
  power must be complete*
  67 | 399

**3262 compétent** *adj* competent
• je ne suis pas compétent pour ce type
  d'opération – *I'm not competent for this type
  of operation*
  68 | 384+s

**3263 sable** *adji,nm* sand
• j'ai dormi dans le sable des dunes – *I slept in
  the sand dunes*
  65 | 436+I

**3264 corruption** *nf* corruption
• la population souffre de la corruption des
  politiciens – *the population suffers from
  politicians' corruption*
  63 | 470

**3265 blé** *nm* wheat
• le blé n'est plus cultivé dans cette région –
  *wheat is not cultivated in this region*
  69 | 377

**3266 chaos** *nm(pl)* chaos
• pour éviter la panique et le chaos, le public
  ne doit rien savoir – *to avoid panic and
  chaos, the public must know nothing*
  77 | 265

**3267 référer** *v* to refer, consult, refer to
• je vous réfère à notre défense – *I refer you
  to our defense*
  68 | 388

**3268 obéir** *v* to obey, comply with, respond to
• il n'obéit à aucune loi – *he doesn't obey any
  law*
  64 | 445

**3269 fusil** *nm* rifle, gun
• sans mon fusil, je ne suis rien – *without my
  rifle, I'm nothing*
  68 | 383

**3270 taper** *v* to beat, slam, bang, type
• tapez Control-U pour vider le champ
  Répertoire – *type Control-U to erase the
  Index field*
  67 | 398

**3271 cohérent** *adj* coherent
• votre récit paraît cohérent et logique – *your
  account seems coherent and logical*
  72 | 325

## 19 Creating nouns – 2

**-sion (all are F)**

**décision** 370 decision

**occasion** 423 chance

**commission** 461 commission

**mission** 627 mission

**impression** 825 impression

**pression** 845 pressure

**discussion** 882 discussion

**expression** 952 expression

**émission** 1074 transmission

**version** 1165 version

**télévision** 1179 television

**conclusion** 1215 conclusion

**division** 1440 division

**vision** 1505 vision

**prévision** 1602 forecast

**dimension** 1717 dimension

**confusion** 1755 confusion

**précision** 1756 precision

**tension** 1799 tension

**pension** 1821 pension

**passion** 1866 passion

**transmission** 1933 transmission

**explosion** 2121 explosion

**diffusion** 2129 diffusion

**profession** 2163 profession

**-tion (all are F)**

**question** 144 question

**situation** 223 situation

**condition** 281 condition

**information** 317 information

**action** 355 action

**relation** 356 relationship

**position** 383 position

**attention** 482 attention

**population** 509 population

**fonction** 516 function

**organisation** 570 organization

**nation** 576 nation

**direction** 582 direction

**solution** 608 solution

**création** 634 creation

**production** 638 production

**intervention** 746 intervention

**opération** 763 operation

**intention** 782 intention

**proposition** 799 proposition

**formation** 831 training

**motion** 855 motion

**élection** 862 election

**institution** 937 institution

**négociation** 941 negotiation

---

3272 **discrétion** nf discretion
- elle était connue pour son absolue discrétion – she was well known for her total discretion
82 | 198

3273 **odeur** nf smell, odor
- il sentait mauvais, l'odeur des vieillards – he smelled bad, the stench of old men
55 | 598+l -n -s

3274 **identification** nf identification
- il n'a pas de papiers d'identification – he doesn't have identity papers
61 | 501+n

3275 **fêter** v to celebrate
- je crois qu'on devrait fêter ça – I think we should celebrate that
75 | 288

3276 **substantiel** adj substantial
- on a fait une progression substantielle – we have made substantial progress
75 | 285

3277 **asiatique** nadj(f) Asian
- la Russie n'est un pays ni asiatique ni européen – Russia is neither an Asian country nor a European one
69 | 376

3278 **aspiration** nf aspiration
- nous devons répondre aux aspirations de ces pays – we must respond to the aspirations of these countries
78 | 253

3279 **photographie** nf photography
- vos photographies m'ont fait passer des heures inoubliables – I have spent several unforgettable hours with your photographs
74 | 297

3280 **exclusion** nf exclusion, expulsion
- la pauvreté et l'exclusion sociale sont en grave augmentation – poverty and social exclusion are increasing seriously
66 | 413

3281 **préconiser** v to recommend, advocate
- je préconise la souplesse plutôt que la ligne dure – I recommend flexibility rather than a hard line
66 | 410

3282 **tribune** nf platform, forum, gallery
- divers orateurs défilèrent à la tribune – various speakers filed up to the speaker's gallery
71 | 342

3283 **bénéficiaire** nadj(f) beneficiary
- nous demeurons les bénéficiaires des sacrifices – we are the beneficiaries of sacrifices
62 | 486

3284 **historien** nm historian
- les historiens en débattront pendant longtemps – historians will debate this for a long time
72 | 331

**3285 seize** *det,nmi* sixteen
- elle y chante depuis l'âge de seize ans – *she has been singing there since she was sixteen years old*
63 | 463

**3286 tentation** *nf* temptation
- des tentations lui revinrent à l'esprit – *temptations came into his mind*
75 | 284

**3287 gloire** *nf* glory, fame
- il ne recherche ni gloire, ni fortune – *he seeks neither glory nor fortune*
65 | 438+l

**3288 vanter** *v* to vaunt, boast, brag
- je suis con et je m'en vante – *I'm an idiot and I'm proud of it*
74 | 297

**3289 coincer** *v* to jam, hinder, get stuck
- nous sommes coincés dans les embouteillages – *we're stuck in traffic jams*
69 | 367

**3290 silencieux** *nadj(pl)* silent, noiseless, silencer
- elle était silencieuse la plupart du temps – *she was silent most of the time*
69 | 377+l

**3291 continu** *nadj* continuous
- vous êtes fier de ce succès continu? – *are you proud of this ongoing success?*
73 | 308

**3292 chantier** *nm* construction site, roadworks
- je vais louer du matériel de chantier – *I will rent construction-site equipment*
67 | 404

**3293 croyance** *nf* belief
- votre salut viendra de votre croyance en la vérité – *your salvation will come from your belief in truth*
77 | 261

**3294 ennui** *nm* boredom, trouble, worry
- je parie que vous mourez d'ennui – *I bet you're dying of boredom*
60 | 507+l

**3295 pompier** *adj,nm* fireman, firefighter
- les pompiers restaient pessimistes – *the firemen remained pessimistic*
65 | 428

**3296 inspection** *nf* inspection
- je dois faire une inspection sur place très minutieuse – *I have to do a very thorough on-site inspection*
72 | 333

**3297 convertir** *v* to convert
- vous vous êtes converti, vous avez changé d'idée – *you have converted, you have new ideas*
71 | 345

**3298 pouce** *nm* thumb, inch
- votre père lève les pouces pour dire bravo – *your father is giving a "well-done" thumbs-up sign*
75 | 281

**3299 clientèle** *nf* customers, clientele
- on a une clientèle d'habitués qui viennent et reviennent – *we have a clientele of regulars who come and go*
69 | 372

**3300 atténuer** *v* to lessen, diminish, dim, subdue, reduce
- nous voulons atténuer la pauvreté – *we want to reduce poverty*
78 | 244

**3301 révélation** *nf* diclosure, revelation
- ce livre a été pour moi une révélation – *this book was a revelation for me*
76 | 273

**3302 survivant** *nadj* survivor, surviving
- on n'a trouvé que 2 survivants pour l'instant – *so far only 2 survivors have been found*
70 | 354

**3303 applicable** *adj(f)* applicable
- plusieurs techniques sont sans doute applicables – *several techniques are undoubtedly applicable*
56 | 581

**3304 équitable** *adj(f)* equitable, fair
- ce n'était ni juste ni équitable – *it was neither just nor fair*
58 | 537+s

**3305 schéma** *nm* diagram, outline
- le tyrannosaure obéit à aucune schéma de groupe – *the tyrannosaurus didn't follow any group scenarios*
67 | 395

**3306 acier** *nm* steel
- l'industrie de l'acier est confrontée à la dure réalité – *the steel industry is confronted with a grim reality*
74 | 301

**3307 vainqueur** *nm,nf* winner
- si vous pensez en vainqueurs, vous le deviendrez – *if you think like winners, that's what you'll become*
57 | 563+n -s

**3308 dépendant** *adj* answerable, responsible, dependent
- en amour, vous serez dépendant, heureux ou malheureux – *in love you'll be dependent, whether happy or unhappy*
81 | 209

**3309 sud-est** *nmi* south-east
- 15 séismes ont affecté le sud-est de la France – *15 earthquakes affected south-eastern France*
59 | 528+n

**3310 brancher** *v* to plug in, connect
- ils n'étaient pas branchés sur le réseau – *they weren't connected to the network*
76 | 269

**3311 concession** *nf* concession
- toute négociation est faite de concessions mutuelles – *every negotiation results from mutual concessions*
70 | 353

**3312 mystérieux** *nadj(pl)* mysterious, secretive
- l'eau pour moi est un élément mystérieux – *water for me is a mysterious substance*
71 | 341+l

**3313 assassinat** *nm* murder, assassination
- quiconque meurt de faim meurt d'un assassinat – *whoever starves to death suffers an assassination*
57 | 554+n

**3314 rive** *nf* shore, bank
- je regagnais la rive gauche, et mon domicile – *I arrived at the left bank, and my home*
74 | 290

**3315 tolérance** *nf* tolerance
- vous apprendrez la tolérance – *you're learning tolerance*
70 | 354

**3316 clarté** *nf* lightness, brightness clearness, clarity
- j'ai toujours été impressionné par la clarté de ses pensées – *I have always been impressed with the clarity of his thoughts*
70 | 349

**3317 conjoint** *nadj* spouse, joint
- je parle le français mais mon conjoint est anglophone – *I speak French but my spouse is English-speaking*
62 | 473+s

**3318 fermement** *adv* firmly
- nous croyons fermement en ce principe – *we firmly believe in this principle*
74 | 301

**3319 redonner** *v* to give back, return, give more
- il faut leur redonner un peu de dignité – *we have to give them back a little dignity*
76 | 268

**3320 assortir** *v* to match, accompany
- j'essaye d'assortir votre visage avec vos cheveux – *I'm trying to match your face with your hair*
81 | 201

**3321 change** *nm* exchange
- sur le marché des changes l'euro est extrêmement ferme – *on the currency market the euro is extremely solid*
59 | 515+n -s

**3322 star** *nf* star
- t'es devenu une grande star de cinéma – *you've become a great movie star*
65 | 424

**3323 grain** *nm* grain, bean, bead; spot, mole
- un seul grain de sel dissout un bloc de glace – *a single grain of salt dissolves a block of ice*
67 | 394

**3324 compliqué** *nadj* complicated, complex
- vous voyez la situation est très compliquée – *you see that the situation is very complicated*
77 | 255

**3325 malaise** *nm* uneasiness, discomfort
- les malaises sont souvent soulagés par le rire – *discomfort is often alleviated by laughter*
74 | 292

**3326 restaurer** *v* to restore, feed
- nous allons d'abord nous restaurer – *we're going to eat first of all*
80 | 212

**3327 ambassade** *nf* embassy
- faites une réclamation à votre ambassade! – *complain to your embassy!*
59 | 522+n

**3328 diplôme** *nm* diploma, certificate
- tous aspiraient à avoir un diplôme de la Sorbonne – *everyone wanted a diploma from the Sorbonne*
77 | 257

**3329 miroir** *nm* mirror
- on avait un miroir mais quelqu'un l'a cassé – *we had a mirror but somebody broke it*
67 | 386

**3330 spectaculaire** *adj(f)* spectacular
- c'est un changement historique et spectaculaire – *it's a historical and spectacular change*
70 | 350

**3331 restructuration** *nf* restructure, restructuring
- parallèlement, une restructuration va être lancée – *in parallel, a restructuring will begin*
63 | 450-l

**3332 proie** *nf* prey
- ils sont régulièrement la proie des nombreuses prostituées – *they regularly fall prey to numerous prostitutes*
75 | 277

**3333 domination** *nf* domination, dominion, rule
- il faut craindre une domination américaine excessive – *we should fear excessive American domination*
64 | 435

**3334 otage** *nm* hostage
- il a pris un flic en otage – *he took a cop hostage*
53 | 628-l +n

**3335 moquer** *v* to mock, make fun of
- il s'est moqué de moi, comme de vous – *he made fun of me, and of you as well*
63 | 451-n

**3336 allier** *v* to ally, match, unite
- le Hezbollah est allié à toutes les forces de résistance – *Hezbollah is allied with all the resistance forces*
71 | 338

**3337 couvert** *nadj* covered, overcast; place, seat, cutlery
- je me sauvai, sous le couvert de la nuit – *I fled under the cover of night*
71 | 333

**3338 demi-heure** *nf* half an hour
- ça fait une demi-heure que je vous attends – *I have been waiting for you for half an hour*
75 | 275

**3339 placement** *nm* investment, placing
- il gère des placements pour l'argent de la drogue – *he launders drug money*
57 | 545

**3340 difficilement** *adv* with difficulty
- leur insatiabilité les rend parfois difficilement supportables – *sometimes their
instability renders them barely tolerable*
74 | 286

**3341 grille** *nf* railings, gate, grid, scale
- il tapait du poing sur la grille – *he pounded
the gate*
67 | 388

**3342 vieillir** *v* to grow old
- en vieillissant, les choix se réduisent –
*getting old, your choices become more
limited*
74 | 289

**3343 abord** *nm* manner; approach, access, environs
- ils vivent aux abords de Madrid dans leurs
caravanes – *they live in the outskirts of
Madrid in their trailers*
78 | 240

**3344 exigeant** *adj* demanding, difficult
- Simone était une femme exigeante –
*Simone was a demanding woman*
82 | 196

**3345 primitif** *nadj* primitive
- nous ne pouvons pas accepter cette forme
primitive de justice – *we can't countenance
this primitive form of justice*
47 | 728+n -s

**3346 lune** *nf* moon
- le soleil se couche, la lune se lève – *the sun
sets, the moon rises*
60 | 492

**3347 mention** *nf* mention, note, comment, notice
- on n'a même pas fait mention du problème
– *nobody even mentioned the problem*
76 | 261

**3348 pertinent** *adj* pertinent, relevant
- je lui posai quelques questions pertinentes
– *I asked him some relevant questions*
61 | 476-l

**3349 brièvement** *adv* briefly
- messieurs, je voudrais intervenir très
brièvement – *sirs, may I interrupt briefly*
72 | 319

**3350 actionnaire** *nm,nf* shareholder
- les actionnaires recevront un dividende –
*the shareholders will receive a dividend*
57 | 536-l +n -s

**3351 emprisonner** *v* to imprison, jail, put in jail,
trap
- vous avez été harcelé et emprisonné pour
vos opinions – *you have been harrassed and
imprisoned for your opinions*
82 | 186

**3352 raisonnement** *nm* reasoning
- le livre explique en détail ce raisonnement
assez simple – *the book details this rather
simple rationale*
72 | 316

**3353 monstre** *nadj(f)* monster
- vous êtes bien le monstre que j'ai créé –
*you are indeed the monster that I created*
66 | 394

**3354 quai** *nm* platform, quay, embankment
- ce quai est interdit d'accès aux civils
– *this quay is off limits to civilians*
68 | 378+l

**3355 légende** *nf* legend, caption, key
- je lisais des contes et légendes
mythologiques – *I read mythological fables
and legends*
76 | 267

**3356 spécialité** *nf* specialty
- la santé n'est pas ma spécialité – *health isn't
my specialty*
81 | 200

**3357 cruel** *adj* cruel, ferocious, bitter
- ce type est aussi intelligent que cruel – *this
guy is as intelligent as he is cruel*
70 | 344

**3358 démission** *nf* resignation
- le conseil de direction veut ta démission
sous 30 jours – *the board of directors
wants your resignation within 30 days*
60 | 496+n

**3359 quatorze** *det,nmi* fourteen
- elle échoue quatorze mois plus tard – *it
failed fourteen months later*
61 | 478

**3360 redouter** *v* to dread, fear
- elle redoutait que sa fille ne devînt une
intellectuelle – *she was afraid her
daughter would become an intellectual*
67 | 380-s

**3361 médaille** *nf* medal
- comme si j'avais gagné une médaille
– *as if I had won a medal*
68 | 374

**3362 célibataire** *nadj(f)* single, unmarried
- au fait, je suis célibataire, sans aucune
attache – *in fact, I'm single, without any
attachments*
80 | 212

**3363 impasse** *nf* dead end, cul-de-sac
- il nous laisse dans l'impasse – *it leaves us at
a stalemate*
75 | 269

**3364 contredire** *v* to contradict
- j'aimerais que vous le contredisiez – *I would
like you to contradict him*
81 | 197

**3365 atelier** *nm* workshop, studio
- j'étais seul dans un petit atelier – *I was
alone in a small studio*
71 | 330

**3366 amical** *adj* friendly
- on avait des rapports très amicaux – *we had
a very friendly relationship*
75 | 275

**3367 empire** *nm* empire
- il laissait à son fils un empire florissant
– *he left to his son a flourishing empire*
63 | 441-s

**3368 redresser** *v* to straighten, set right, redress, turn around
- il se redresse légèrement sur sa chaise – *he straightened up in his chair almost imperceptibly*
66 | 403+l -s

**3369 invisible** *adj(f)* invisible
- vous traversez maintenant une frontière invisible – *you're now crossing an invisible border*
68 | 366

**3370 ramasser** *v* to pick up, collect, gather
- je ramassai mon parapluie – *I gathered up my umbrella*
64 | 434-n

**3371 politicien** *nadj* politician
- tous les politiciens disent : les gens ordinaires sont intelligents – *all politicians say: ordinary people are intelligent*
69 | 355+s

**3372 acheminer** *v* to forward, dispatch, transport
- d'autres produits doivent être acheminés au port – *other products will have to be shipped to the port*
55 | 567+n -s

**3373 comédie** *nf* comedy, playacting
- c'est une comédie et les gens ont besoin de rire – *it's a comedy and people need to laugh*
69 | 350

**3374 propagande** *nf* propaganda
- la propagande nous permettra de conquérir le monde – *propaganda will enable us to conquer the world*
79 | 222

**3375 colonie** *nf* colony
- l'esclavage a été aboli dans les colonies françaises en 1848 – *slavery was abolished in French colonies in 1848*
62 | 459

**3376 désordre** *nm* disorder, confusion
- il y a du désordre dans la cuisine – *the kitchen is relatively messy*
72 | 307

**3377 infini** *nadj* ininfinite, infinity
- il m'a écoutée, avec une infinie patience – *he listened to me with infinite patience*
58 | 518+l -s

**3378 savant** *nadj* scientist, scholar, learned, scholarly, clever, skilfull
- on pouvait être homme sans être savant – *you could be a man without having to be a scholar*
64 | 426

**3379 terreur** *nf* terror, dread
- de terreur, ses cheveux sont devenus blancs – *his hair has become white from terror*
68 | 362

**3380 recruter** *v* to recruit
- nous avons ainsi recruté un linguiste! – *so we have recruited a linguist!*
71 | 324

**3381 conformer** *v* to model, conform
- cet objectif est conforme au mandat – *this goal conforms with the mandate*
72 | 308

**3382 virus** *nm(pl)* virus
- elle porte un virus extraterrestre – *she carries an extraterrestrial virus*
59 | 498-l

**3383 reconnaissant** *adj* grateful
- nous avons de quoi être reconnaissants – *we have something to be thankful for*
77 | 247

**3384 délibérer** *v* to deliberate, debate
- il délibéra longtemps avec lui-même – *for a long time he debated within himself*
81 | 194

**3385 inattendu** *adj* unexpected
- tout cela est bien inattendu – *all of this is quite unexpected*
76 | 259

**3386 tunnel** *nm* tunnel
- ils entreprennent de creuser un tunnel – *they undertake the digging of a tunnel*
71 | 319

**3387 cousin** *nm* cousin
- seule ma cousine Madeleine enfreignait cet interdit – *only my cousin Madeleine violated this proscription*
63 | 433

**3388 puiser** *v* to draw, take
- où puisez-vous tout cet optimisme, cette sérénité? – *whence comes all of this optimism and serenity of yours?*
79 | 227

**3389 géographique** *adj(f)* geographic, geographical
- ils sont découpés en zones géographiques – *they are carved into geographic zones*
72 | 306

**3390 réacteur** *nm* reactor, jet engine
- le conduit mène directement au réacteur – *the pipe leads directly to the reactor*
63 | 438-s

**3391 ajuster** *v* to adjust, alter, aim, aim at
- je vais essayer de m'ajuster – *I'll try to adjust*
80 | 213

**3392 œuvrer** *v* to work
- nous n'avons cessé d'œuvrer pour la promotion des femmes – *we haven't stopped working to promote women*
73 | 299

**3393 sommeil** *nm* sleep, sleepiness
- ton père est mort dans son sommeil – *your father died in his sleep*
59 | 504+l -s

**3394 automatiquement** *adv* automatically
- les résultats seront automatiquement enregistrés – *the results will be automatically stored*
72 | 308

**3395 balance** *nf* scales, balance
• la balance commerciale franco-allemande a été équilibrée en janvier – *the German-French commercial balance was evened out in January*
70 | 336

**3396 dépression** *nf* depression
• il ne se remettra pas de sa dernière dépression – *he won't recover from his last depression*
79 | 227

**3397 pompe** *nf* pump
• les prix de l'essence à la pompe varient – *the price of gas at the pump varies*
77 | 242

**3398 contestation** *nf* questioning, protest
• il n'y a aucune contestation à cet égard – *there is no disputing that*
69 | 354

**3399 inconvénient** *nm* snag, drawback, disadvantage, inconvenience
• c'était là un inconvénient que je ne pouvais éviter – *that was a setback that I couldn't avoid*
79 | 218

**3400 frein** *nm* brake
• vos freins marchent pas? – *your brakes don't work?*
82 | 187

**3401 inspiration** *nf* inspiration
• j'ai eu l'inspiration pour faire cette peinture – *I was inspired to make this painting*
73 | 294

**3402 candidature** *nf* application, candidacy, candidature
• ma candidature ne pouvait pas être considérée – *my candidacy couldn't be considered*
62 | 449

**3403 armement** *nm* arms, weapons, armament
• l'industrie des armements avait une importance – *the arms industry has some importance*
64 | 414

**3404 épargne** *nf* savings, saving
• le portefeuille des fonds d'épargne devrait fortement progresser – *the savings funds portfolio should strengthen considerably*
63 | 436-s

**3405 iranien** *nadj* Iranian
• la puissance iranienne est inquiétante – *Iranian power is worrisome*
51 | 631-l +n -s

**3406 conférer** *v* to confer
• ce statut nous confère des privilèges inaliénables – *this law grants us inalienable rights*
71 | 324

**3407 stupide** *adj(f)* stupid, silly, bemused
• ah que je suis stupide! – *gee, I'm stupid!*
67 | 383

**3408 surpris** *adj(pl)* surprised, amazed
• vous avez l'air surpris de me voir – *you seem surprised to see me*
80 | 209

**3409 interpeller** *v* to call out to, question
• enfin, cinq personnes ont été interpellées – *in all, five people were taken in for questioning*
59 | 504

**3410 fréquemment** *adv* frequently
• les victimes sont fréquemment des femmes – *the victims are often women*
80 | 211

**3411 symbolique** *nadj(f)* symbolic
• c'est un échec au moins symbolique – *it's at least a symbolic failure*
68 | 362

**3412 pavillon** *nm* country house, villa, wing pavilliion, flag
• il m'emmena bavarder dans le pavillon de la piscine – *he took me to chat in the pool's pavilion*
77 | 241

**3413 pape** *nm* pope
• le pape condamne les camps de concentration – *the Pope condemns the concentration camps*
59 | 495+n -s

**3414 préliminaire** *nadj(f)* preliminary, introductory
• les résultats préliminaires nous promettent une longue et difficile nuit – *the preliminary results guarantee us a long and difficult night*
79 | 222

**3415 sensation** *nf* sensation
• il y a une sensation de flottement quand tu cours – *there's a sensation of floating when you run*
68 | 365

**3416 troubler** *v* to disturb, disrupt, cloud
• j'ai cru que cela me troublerait – *I thought that would bother me*
67 | 368+l

**3417 angoisse** *nf* distress, anguish, dread, fear
• je m'étais endormi dans l'angoisse – *I fell asleep amidst anguish*
67 | 379+l

**3418 générosité** *nf* generosity, generously
• je vous remercie beaucoup de votre générosité – *thank you very much for your generosity*
80 | 212

**3419 chaise** *nf* chair
• nous étions assis sur de petites chaises en bois – *we were seated on little wooden chairs*
59 | 486+l

**3420 hautement** *adv* highly
• c'est hautement improbable – *that's highly improbable*
83 | 174

**3421 légitimité** *nf* legitimacy
• il faut reconnaître la légitimité de leur revendication – *we have to recognize the legitimacy of their claim*
71 | 323

**3422 emprunt** *nm* loan
- la durée de l'emprunt sera de sept ans – *the loan period will be seven years*
60 | 485+n

**3423 clause** *nf* clause
- ces clauses devraient respecter les droits de la personne – *these clauses must respect personal rights*
72 | 310

**3424 clef** *nf* key
- j'ai tourné la clef dans la serrure – *I turned the key in the lock*
62 | 446+l

**3425 répression** *nf* repression, suppression, crack-down
- la répression entraîne un surcroît d'activisme – *repression entails excessive activism*
65 | 397

**3426 tombe** *nf* grave, tomb
- je jure ... sur la tombe de ma grand-mère – *I swear ... on my grandmother's grave*
70 | 325

**3427 dériver** *v* to divert, derive
- leurs tissus sont dérivés des cellules de l'embryon – *their tissue is derived from embryonic cells*
76 | 253

**3428 évacuer** *v* to evacuate, clear
- vous avez cinq minutes pour évacuer les lieux – *you have five minutes to evacuate the premises*
59 | 499

**3429 blocage** *nm* block
- il a pour résultat de supprimer le blocage – *as a result it removes the blockage*
51 | 632-l +n -s

**3430 faille** *nf* fault
- c'était un homme avec des failles – *he was a man with faults*
83 | 169

**3431 fouiller** *v* to search, frisk, go through, rummage through
- on a fouillé sa maison, ses entrepôts – *his house, his warehouses were searched*
69 | 340

**3432 respectivement** *adv* respectively
- ces deux types de manoeuvres se déroulent respectivement depuis 1976 et 1973 – *these two types of manoeuvres have taken place respectively since 1976 and 1973*
63 | 430+n -s

**3433 éternel** *nadj* eternal, everlasting
- je ferai de Rome une merveille éternelle – *I will make Rome an eternal wonder*
63 | 435+l

**3434 intime** *nadj(f)* intimate, close, secret, private
- je préfère publier mon journal intime – *I prefer to publish my personal diary*
65 | 393

**3435 cerner** *v* to surround, encircle, delimit
- vous m'aidez à cerner mes problèmes – *you help me put a finger on my problems*
81 | 198

**3436 hostilité** *nf* hostility, hostilities
- je ressens beaucoup d'hostilité de ta part – *I sense much hostility on your part*
71 | 312

**3437 manche** *nm,nf* handle, sleeve
- je l'essuie avec ma manche – *I wipe it with my sleeve*
64 | 420

**3438 mathématique** *nadj(f)* mathematical; mathematics
- les mathématiques vous aident à vous connaître – *math helps you know yourself*
55 | 554

**3439 gamin** *nm* kid
- tu penses que le gamin a menti? – *you think the kid lied?*
61 | 460-n

**3440 induire** *v* to infer, induce, result in , lead to
- je ne veux pas vous induire en erreur – *I don't want to lead you into error*
74 | 280

**3441 temple** *nm* temple
- j'ai trouvé le temple – *I found the temple*
61 | 454+l -s

**3442 maîtrise** *nf* mastery, command, control, master's degree
- la maîtrise de la douleur semblait être l'autre problème – *controlling pain seemed to be the other problem*
63 | 428

**3443 arbitrage** *nm* refereeing, umpiring, arbitration
- l'arbitrage peut être long et coûteux – *the arbitration might be long and costly*
77 | 238

**3444 boucler** *v* to fasten, loop, resolve
- je suis content qu'on ait bouclé cette affaire rapidement – *I'm happy this affair was resolved quickly*
76 | 256

**3445 réparation** *nf* repair, repairing, correction, compensation
- les travaux de réparation ont été arrêtés – *repair work was stopped*
76 | 250

**3446 évêque** *nm* bishop
- je ne suis pas évêque, mon fils – *I'm not a bishop, my son*
69 | 347

**3447 déléguer** *v* to delegate
- elle dit avoir délégué ce pouvoir à sa sous-ministre – *she said she delegated this power to her deputy*
69 | 346

**3448 solitude** *nf* solitude, loneliness
- il vivait dans la solitude – *he lived in solitude*
59 | 481+l -n

**3449 miner** *v* to mine, erode
- ce conflit mine le quatrième pays le plus peuplé du monde – *this conflict is eroding the fourth most populous country in the world*
77 | 239

## 20 Emotions

This table lists the most frequently occurring words that describe emotions, states of mind, or attitudes.

| Positive: | Neutral: | Negative: |
|---|---|---|
| **grand** 59 great | **seul** 101 alone | **mauvais** 274 wrong |
| **bon** 94 good | **jeune** 152 young | **difficile** 296 difficult |
| **fort** 107 strong | **simple** 212 simple | **grave** 443 serious |
| **certain** 110 certain | **public** 285 public | **faux** 555 false |
| **important** 215 important | **social** 301 social | **contraire** 619 contrary |
| **propre** 237 clean | **différent** 350 different | **impossible** 652 impossible |
| **sûr** 270 sure | **particulier** 381 particular | **dangereux** 713 dangerous |
| **juste** 304 fair | **unique** 402 unique | **faible** 723 weak |
| **clair** 335 clear | **prêt** 422 ready | **lourd** 1026 heavy |
| **libre** 344 free | **publique** 554 public | **dur** 1029 hard |
| **beau** 393 handsome | **secret** 796 secret | **violent** 1119 violent |
| **sérieux** 412 serious | **facile** 822 easy | **froid** 1307 cold |
| **responsable** 511 responsible | **normal** 833 normal | **terrible** 1310 dreadful |
| **objectif** 518 objective | **direct** 839 direct | **fou** 1357 crazy |
| **riche** 599 rich | **critique** 909 critical | **inquiet** 1392 worried |
| **capable** 610 capable | **complexe** 933 complex | **criminel** 1411 criminal |
| **précis** 643 precise | **ferme** 1024 firm | **coupable** 1442 guilty |
| **réel** 665 real | **physique** 1146 physical | **inconnu** 1451 unknown |
| **spécial** 726 special | **disponible** 1205 available | **vide** 1473 empty |
| **naturel** 760 natural | **rare** 1233 rare | **incapable** 1605 incapable |
| **heureux** 764 happy | **moderne** 1239 modern | **sévère** 1733 severe |
| **supérieur** 876 superior | **extrême** 1270 extreme | **étroit** 1828 narrow |
| **honorable** 893 honorable | **absolu** 1284 absolute | **triste** 1843 sad |
| **ouvert** 897 open | **permanent** 1322 permanent | **partiel** 1871 partial |
| **civil** 929 civil | **ordinaire** 1327 ordinary | **inférieur** 1905 inferior |

**3450 superbe** *nadj(f)* superb, magnificient, handsome, gorgeous
- votre gazon semble superbe – *your lawn looks magnificent*
69 | 344

**3451 gonfler** *v* to inflate, blow up, swell
- cette pensée lui gonfla le cœur – *this thought swelled his heart*
76 | 256

**3452 missile** *nm* missile
- seize missiles air-sol ont visé cette base – *sixteen surface-to-air missiles were aimed at this base*
56 | 527-l +n

**3453 minuit** *nm* midnight
- elles se sont endormies peu après minuit – *they fell asleep shortly after midnight*
70 | 330

**3454 composante** *nf* component
- certaines composantes de son environnement sont plastiques – *certain components of his environment are plastic*
69 | 336

**3455 veuf** *nadj* surviving spouse
- vous savez, moi-même je suis veuf – *you know, I'm a widower myself*
72 | 307

**3456 comparaître** *v* to appear
- certains témoins ont accepté de comparaître devant nous – *some witnesses agreed to appear before us*
61 | 458

**3457 trame** *nf* weft, framework; tram
- les trames urbaine et péri-urbaine changent plus rapidement – *urban and suburban trams are changing more quickly*
45 | 742+n -s

**3458 bain** *nm* bath, bathing
- un jour, ils sont allés au bain public – *one day, they went to the public baths*
63 | 421

**3459 sûreté** *nf* safety, reliability
- j'ajoute, pour plus de sûreté, ceci – *for more security, I add this*
77 | 237

**3460 hâte** *nf* haste, impatience
- on avait caché en hâte les drapeaux – *they hastily hid the flags*
71 | 307

**3461 instituer** *v* to introduce, impose, establish, institute
- ils ont institué un plan de réduction du déficit – *they adopted a deficit reduction plan*
78 | 227

**3462 format** *nm* format
- j'aime beaucoup le format court – *I really like the short format*
51 | 620+n

**3463 hiérarchie** *nf* hierarchy
- il était vite monté dans la hiérarchie – *he quickly climbed the hierarchy*
73 | 288

**3464 estimation** *nf* appraisal, valuation, assessment, estimate
- c'est une estimation prudente – *it's a safe guess*
64 | 406-l +n

**3465 mutation** *nf* transfer, transformation, mutation
- il peut identifier une mutation chez les patients affectés – *he can identify a mutation in the patients who were affected*
61 | 453

**3466 imminent** *adj* imminent, impending
- j'annonçai mon retrait imminent – *I announced my pending retirement*
83 | 165

**3467 héroïne** *nf* heroine
- l'héroïne avait mon âge, dix-huit ans – *the heroine was my age, eighteen years*
80 | 198

**3468 esclave** *nadj(f)* slave
- l'esclave se révolte contre le maître – *the slave rebels against the master*
63 | 428

**3469 marocain** *nadj* Moroccan
- les chèvres marocaines ont quasiment tout mangé – *the Moroccan goats ate practically everything*
52 | 597

**3470 menu** *adv,nadj* menu, slender, slim, minor
- il y a du poulet au menu – *there's chicken on the menu*
69 | 342

**3471 imaginaire** *nadj(f)* imaginary
- tu as vécu dans un monde imaginaire – *you have lived in an imaginary world*
64 | 407

**3472 administrer** *v* to manage, run, administer; to give
- on leur administre souvent des médicaments – *they are often given medications*
69 | 333

**3473 atteinte** *nf* reach; attack, blow
- notre père voulait se mettre hors d'atteinte – *our father wanted to get out of the line of attack*
71 | 306

**3474 démissionner** *v* to resign
- j'ai donc décidé de démissionner de mon poste de coach – *so I decided to resign my coaching position*
68 | 346

**3475 racheter** *v* to repurchase, buy back, redeem
- j'ai apporté de l'argent pour racheter mon fils – *I brought money to buy back my son*
73 | 287

**3476 théorique** *adj(f)* theoretical
- ma question n'était pas purement théorique – *my question was not exclusively theoretical*
66 | 373

**3477 guise** *nf* wish; like, by way of
- ils ne veulent pas voter à sa guise – *they don't want to vote the way he wants them to*
80 | 203

**3478 scandaleux** *adj(pl)* scandalous, outrageous
- le coût des études est devenu scandaleux – *the cost of an education has become scandalous*
77 | 232

**3479 vulnérable** *adj(f)* vulnerable
- une femme tamoule est une personne vulnérable au Sri Lanka – *a Tamil woman is a vulnerable person in Sri Lanka*
79 | 211

**3480 ennuyer** *v* to bore, worry, bother
- j'espère que je ne vous ennuie pas – *I hope I'm not boring you*
59 | 485+l -n

**3481 élan** *nm* momentum, surge, rush; elk, moose
- il suffisait d'un élan du cœur pour le désarmer – *a mere outpouring of the heart caught him off guard*
69 | 341+l

**3482 nominal** *nadj* nominal
- selon notre enquête, les ventes nominales ont augmenté – *according to our research, small-ticket item sales increased*
50 | 622+n

**3483 manipuler** *v* to handle, manipulate
- le gouvernement espagnol nous manipule depuis longtemps – *the Spanish government has been manipulating us for a long time*
79 | 207

**3484 peiner** *v* to toil, labor, struggle
- les étudiants diplômés peinent à trouver du travail – *the graduates are struggling to find work*
78 | 218

**3485 renouvellement** *nm* replacement, recurrence, repetition
• nous appuyons le renouvellement de la licence de la station – *we support renewal of the station's license*
67 | 362

**3486 noble** *nadj(f)* noble
• l'eau est une matière plus noble, et sans doute plus précieuse – *water is a nobler resource, and undoubtedly more precious*
62 | 430+l -n

**3487 hebdomadaire** *nadj(f)* weekly
• je vais animer une autre émission hebdomadaire – *I'm going to host another weekly broadcast*
63 | 413+n

**3488 approbation** *nf* approval
• elle a reçu l'approbation unanime – *she received unanimous approval*
65 | 385

**3489 protestant** *nadj* Protestant
• j'ai commencé à fréquenter une église protestante – *I have started going to a Protestant church*
75 | 259

**3490 faisceau** *nm* bundle, beam, stack
• elle émettait un faisceau de lumière jaune – *it emitted a beam of yellow light*
42 | 777+n -s

**3491 regagner** *v* to win again, regain, get back, make up
• vous pouvez regagner votre ville – *you can go back to your city*
67 | 355

**3492 dégât** *nm* damage
• ils essaient de nettoyer les dégâts – *they're trying to clean up the damage*
66 | 371

**3493 pilier** *nm* pillar
• elle avait l'air liée au pilier de fer – *she looked like she was tied to an iron pillar*
76 | 250

**3494 animateur** *nadj* animator, host
• vous étiez animateur et pas chanteur – *you were a show host and not a singer*
54 | 563+s

**3495 multinational** *adj* multinational
• on n'est pas une entreprise multinationale – *we aren't a multinational corporation*
67 | 357-l

**3496 méfier** *v* to distrust, mistrust
• il se méfie des étrangers – *he's wary of strangers*
71 | 304

**3497 étroitement** *adv* closely
• on pourrait penser qu'ils sont étroitement liés – *one might think that they are closely connected*
76 | 240

**3498 jouet** *nm* toy
• les boutons ne sont pas des jouets – *buttons are not playthings*
71 | 303

**3499 formé** *nm* formed
• une fois formé, le profit est réglementé – *once it's formulated, profit is regulated*
79 | 213

**3500 complice** *nadj(f)* accomplice
• je restai longtemps leur complice – *for a long time I remained their accomplice*
71 | 302

**3501 homosexuel** *nadj* homosexual
• il n'avait plus honte d'être homosexuel – *he wasn't ashamed to be homosexual*
68 | 348

**3502 toile** *nf* cloth, canvass, web
• j'ai horreur des toiles d'araignée – *I hate spider webs*
69 | 328+l

**3503 laver** *v* to wash, clean
• lavez-vous les mains avant de manger – *wash your hands before eating*
66 | 375

**3504 empreinte** *nf* imprint, print, mark, impression
• la police a retrouvé des empreintes – *the police found fingerprints*
71 | 312

**3505 faillir** *v* to have almost, fail, fail to
• j'ai failli tout perdre – *I almost lost everything*
68 | 347

**3506 curiosité** *nf* curiosity
• ma curiosité reste insatisfaite sur certains points – *my curiosity remains unsatisfied on a few points*
62 | 422+l

**3507 passeport** *nm* passport
• billet et passeport, s'il vous plaît – *ticket and passport, please*
79 | 205

**3508 creux** *nadj(pl)* hollow, empty, hole
• aux heures creuses – durant la nuit, par exemple – *in the off hours—during the night, for example*
67 | 359+l

**3509 livraison** *nf* delivery
• la livraison du navire est prévue en avril – *delivery of the ship is slated for April*
67 | 352

**3510 château** *nm* castle
• je viens prendre possession de son château – *I have come to take over his castle*
71 | 308

**3511 nous-mêmes** *pro* ourselves
• on n'aurait pas fait mieux nous-mêmes – *we wouldn't have done better ourselves*
74 | 268

**3512 forum** *nm* forum, newsgroup
• elle va organiser un forum – *she will organize a forum*
67 | 358-l

**3513 via** *prep* via
• j'ai déjà fait des interviews via Internet – *I have already been interviewed over the Internet*
65 | 384

**3514 coter** *v* to quote, rate
- en septembre, le dollar cotait encore 1.20 euro – *In September, the dollar still stood at 1.20 euros*
66 | 364

**3515 éclat** *nm* splinter, fragment, brightness, burst
- des éclats de rire se firent entendre derrière une porte – *peals of laughter could be heard behind a door*
63 | 409+l -s

**3516 sincèrement** *adv* sincerely
- je pense sincèrement qu'il est un type bien – *I sincerely think he's a decent fellow*
72 | 294-n +s

**3517 thé** *nm* tea
- je vous ai aussi apporté du thé – *I have also brought you some tea*
64 | 400

**3518 préférable** *adj(f)* preferable
- madame, je crois préférable que nous discutions en privé – *ma'am, I belive it would be preferable for us to discuss this in private*
77 | 233

**3519 attachement** *nm* attachment, affection
- il éprouva une sorte d'attachement pour ce vieillard – *he felt some kind of affection for this old-timer*
82 | 177

**3520 liquide** *nadj(f)* liquid
- il a avalé du liquide vaisselle – *he swallowed some liquid dishwashing detergent*
71 | 309

**3521 gamme** *nf* range, scale
- nous avons déjà une bonne gamme de programmes – *we already have a good range of programs*
59 | 467+n

**3522 motivation** *nf* motivation, application
- cet assassinat n'aurait pas de motivations politiques – *this assassination presumably lacks political motives*
74 | 272

**3523 protestation** *nf* protest, protestation
- j'ai reçu des lettres de protestation – *I received letters of protest*
69 | 332

**3524 demeure** *nf* residence, home
- ils retrouvent leurs demeures pillées, brûlées, leurs champs dévastés – *they find their homes looted, burned, their fields devastated*
72 | 288

**3525 adéquat** *adj* appropriate, suitable, adequate
- la protection sociale n'est pas adéquate – *the social safety net is not adequate*
63 | 416-l

**3526 geler** *v* to freeze, ice over, suspend
- vous allez geler avec ce petit manteau – *you're going to freeze with this light coat*
77 | 233

**3527 défiler** *v* to unthread, parade
- les manifestants ont défilé silencieusement dans la rue – *the protesters paraded silently in the street*
71 | 308

**3528 peintre** *nm* painter
- je suis le seul peintre valable des Etats-Unis – *I'm the only worthwhile painter in the U.S.*
71 | 301

**3529 volontairement** *adv* voluntarily, willingly
- volontairement, je fermai les yeux – *willingly, I closed my eyes*
82 | 169

**3530 magique** *adj(f)* magic; magical
- je n'ai pas de pouvoir magique moi – *me, I don't have any magic powers*
72 | 285

**3531 bien-être** *nmi* well being
- tous ces services dépendent au bien-être économique de notre pays – *all of these services depend on the economic well-being of our country*
68 | 347

**3532 cap** *nm* cape
- mettez le cap sur la rive gauche, commanda-t-il – *set course for the left bank, he ordered*
75 | 255

**3533 raide** *adj(f)* stiff, straight
- elle se tient immobile, raide, les regardant – *she remained immobile and stiff while looking at them*
51 | 599+n -s

**3534 maigre** *nadj(f)* thin, skinny, slim, lean
- c'était un homme maigre et chauve – *he was a thin, bald man*
71 | 303

**3535 artistique** *adj(f)* artistic
- ils ont une vraie vision artistique – *they have truly artistic vision*
66 | 363

**3536 aspirer** *v* to breathe in, inhale, aspire to
- Paule aspira la fumée de sa cigarette – *Paule breathed in the smoke of his cigarette*
77 | 234

**3537 habituellement** *adv* usually, generally
- les groupes sont habituellement composés de huit élèves – *the groups are usually made up of eight students*
72 | 284

**3538 quasiment** *adv* almost, early
- il a quasiment tout gagné – *he almost won everything*
68 | 340

**3539 allure** *nf* speed, pace, walk, look, appearance
- les voitures filaient à vive allure – *the cars sped away*
71 | 297

**3540 deuil** *nm* mourning, grief
- il laisse dans le deuil son épouse – *he leaves behind a grieving wife*
72 | 289

**3541 énoncer** *v* to state, set out, express
- ce qui se conçoit bien s'énonce clairement
  – *that which is conceived well is expressed clearly*
  66 | 368

**3542 islamiste** *nm,nf* Islamist
- je pense que la piste islamiste progresse plus que les autres – *I think the Islamic way is progressing more than the others*
  50 | 609-l +n -s

**3543 prénom** *nm* first name
- il appelle les journalistes par leur prénom – *the calls journalists by their first name*
  69 | 320

**3544 réussi** *adj* successful
- sa vie est beaucoup plus réussie que la nôtre – *his life is much more successful than ours*
  84 | 151

**3545 bilatéral** *adj* bilateral
- les relations bilatérales ont enregistré récemment des changements positifs – *bilateral relations recently involved positive changes*
  66 | 365

**3546 rétablissement** *nm* restoring, re-establishment, recovery
- nous leur souhaitons un prompt rétablissement – *we wish them a swift recovery*
  70 | 318

**3547 cynique** *nadj(f)* cynical, cynic
- leur cinéma est terriblement cynique – *their cinema is terribly cynical*
  83 | 165

**3548 environnemental** *adj* environmental
- les questions environnementales transcendent les frontières – *environmental issues transcend borders*
  57 | 495-l +s

**3549 constructeur** *nadj* builder, manufacturer
- VW est devenu le premier constructeur européen – *VW has become the largest European manufacturer*
  58 | 475+n -s

**3550 colonel** *nm* colonel
- le colonel voudrait vous voir immédiatement – *the colonel wishes to see you immediately*
  65 | 384

**3551 nœud** *nm* knot
- fais un double nœud, mais doucement – *make a double knot, but do it carefully*
  52 | 573+n -s

**3552 peindre** *v* to paint, depict, portray
- le mur était peint d'une couleur ocre – *the wall was painted ochre*
  63 | 411+l

**3553 bâton** *nm* tick, club, baton
- elles sont armées de bâtons – *they're armed with clubs*
  70 | 309

**3554 démocrate** *nadj(f)* democrat, democratic
- pour certains responsables démocrates la réponse est claire – *for certain democratic leaders the answer is clear*
  57 | 493+n

**3555 précédemment** *adv* previously
- j'ai développé tout ceci précédemment – *I had already developed this*
  71 | 294

**3556 idiot** *nadj* idiot, fool, stupid
- bouge-toi, espèce d'idiot – *move, you idiot*
  58 | 482-n

**3557 querelle** *nf* quarrel
- les querelles politiciennes n'intéressent pas le peuple – *political squabbles don't interest the populace*
  76 | 240

**3558 explosif** *nadj* explosive
- il y a assez d'explosif pour raser tout un quartier – *there are enough explosives to level a whole neighborhood*
  63 | 399-s

**3559 flic** *nm,nf* cop
- si tu vois des flics, appelle-moi – *call me if you see any cops*
  48 | 642-n +s

**3560 solitaire** *nadj(f)* solitary, lone, lonely
- vous avez une vie plutôt solitaire – *you lead a rather solitary existence*
  67 | 346

**3561 déceler** *v* to discover, detect
- l'erreur administrative a été décelée puis corrigée – *the administrative error was found and corrected*
  77 | 232

**3562 herbe** *nf* grass, herb
- l'herbe est plus verte ailleurs – *the grass is greener elsewhere*
  62 | 420+l

**3563 élevé** *adj* high, heavy, tall
- c'est un pourcentage assez élevé – *that's quite a high percentage*
  64 | 387

**3564 acharner** *v* to go at fiercely and unrelentingly
- c'est une lutte acharnée pour la vie – *it's a fierce fight to the death*
  76 | 242

**3565 bombardement** *nm* bombing, shelling
- jamais le nombre des victimes des bombardements n'a été publié – *the number of bombing victims was never published*
  59 | 467

**3566 bagage** *nm* luggage, baggage
- je voyageais sans bagages – *I travelled without luggage*
  76 | 243

**3567 singulier** *nadj* unique, singular
- il n'arrive pas de choses singulières – *unusual things don't happen*
  61 | 424+l

**3568 capitalisme** *nm* capitalism
- tout le capitalisme est fondé sur la notion de rareté – *capitalism is completely founded on the notion of scarcity*
  60 | 438

**3569 suspension** *nf* hanging, suspending, breaking off, postponement, suspension
• Pyongyang confirme publiquement la suspension des tirs de missiles – *Pyongyang publicly confirms a suspension of missile launches*
67 | 350

**3570 mince** *adj(f),intj* thin, slim, slender
• elle est mince et jolie et elle ment – *she is thin and beautiful and she lies*
68 | 335

**3571 assimiler** *v* to assimilate, take in
• les gens ne peuvent pas tout assimiler – *people can't take it all in*
74 | 260

**3572 plume** *nm,nf* feather
• cet oiseau a beaucoup plus de plumes blanches – *this bird has many white feathers*
65 | 374+l

**3573 publicitaire** *nadj(f)* advertising, promotional
• nous n'avons pratiquement pas de budget publicitaire – *we have almost no advertising budget*
68 | 332

**3574 incarner** *v* to embody, incarnate
• en cela, il incarne la quintessence de l'esprit poétique – *herein he embodies the essence of the poetic spirit*
71 | 292

**3575 opter** *v* to opt, decide
• j'ai donc opté pour une coiffure simple – *so I chose a simple haircut*
80 | 195

**3576 habiller** *v* to dress, get dressed
• il s'habille comme un vampire – *he's dressed like a vampire*
65 | 379

**3577 trajet** *nm* journey, route
• durant le trajet, nous avons été peu bavards – *during the trip, we did very little talking*
52 | 576+n -s

**3578 sinistre** *nadj(f)* disaster, sinister
• leurs rires résonnaient de façon sinistre – *their laughter echoed ominously*
76 | 238

**3579 pis** *adv,nm(pl)* worse
• les choses vont de mal en pis – *things are going from bad to worse*
68 | 335

**3580 reconstruire** *v* to rebuild, reconstruct
• on a donc reconstruit la planète – *so we rebuilt the planet*
78 | 210

**3581 tueur** *nm* killer, hit man
• oh vous savez, un tueur est rarement drôle – *oh, you know, a killer is rarely funny*
66 | 363

**3582 tournoi** *nm* tournament
• j'ai gagné ce tournoi – *I won the tournament*
48 | 640-l +n

**3583 cimetière** *nm* cemetery, graveyard
• dans un cimetière, la mort est supportable – *in a cemetery, death is bearable*
67 | 342

**3584 douane** *nf* customs, duty
• nos agents de douane ne sont pas équipés – *our customs agents are not equipped*
65 | 379

**3585 domestique** *nadj(f)* servant, domestic
• c'est au foyer domestique qu'elles avaient pris leurs leçons – *home is where they learned their lessons*
65 | 369+l

**3586 soucieux** *adj(pl)* concerned, worried
• j'en suis soucieux mais non surpris – *I'm worried about it but not surprised*
77 | 229

**3587 premièrement** *adv* first
• pour nous, jouer, performer est premièrement une passion! – *for us playing, performing is first of all a passion*
57 | 482-n +s

**3588 complicité** *nf* complicity
• il y a une complicité d'instinct entre elle et moi – *there's an instinctive collusion between her and me*
72 | 288

**3589 décréter** *v* to declare, decree
• le gouvernement a décrété un deuil de sept jours – *the government declared a week-long period of mourning*
71 | 300

**3590 flamme** *nf* flame, fire, fervor, brilliance
• ils ont dû voir les flammes – *they must have seen the flames*
66 | 355

**3591 approprié** *adj* appropriate
• il faudra prendre des mesures appropriées – *appropriate measures must be taken*
58 | 472

**3592 dix-huit** *det,nmi* eighteen
• j'ai une fille de dix-huit ans – *I have an eighteen-year-old daughter*
62 | 417

**3593 nouveauté** *nf* novelty, new release
• l'émission a perdu son parfum de nouveauté – *the broadcast lost its new feel*
68 | 331

**3594 brusquement** *adv* abruptly, suddenly
• je me retournai brusquement, surpris de son silence – *I turned around suddenly, surprised by her silence*
53 | 551+l -s

**3595 coïncider** *v* to coincide, correspond
• avec Caïn, la première révolte coïncide avec le premier crime – *with Cain, the first rebellion coincided with the first crime*
75 | 243

**3596 déterminé** *nadj* determined, resolute, specific
• nous avons passé un contrat à durée déterminée avec Unilever – *we concluded a fixed-period contract with Unilever*
70 | 305-s

**3597 ménager** *nadj,v* to handle, arrange;
domestic
- cela permettait aussi de ménager la surprise
  – *it also enabled arranging the surprise*
74 | 253

**3598 millénaire** *nadj(f)* millennium, thousand-year-
old
- le tournant du millénaire approche à grands
  pas – *the millennial changeover is nearing
  quickly*
58 | 475+s

**3599 alerte** *adj(f),nf* agile, alert, warning
- l'armée de terre est en alerte – *the ground
  forces are on alert*
62 | 409

**3600 renforcement** *nm* reinforcement,
strengthening
- on peut se féliciter du renforcement des
  mesures pour la formation – *we can be
  proud of strengthening the measures for
  training*
64 | 377-l

**3601 ange** *nm* angel
- est-ce qu'on peut faire un ange d'un
  démon? – *can you turn a devil into an
  angel?*
59 | 452-n

**3602 guérir** *v* to cure, heal, get better
- le rire guérit tout – *laughter heals everything*
68 | 331

**3603 immobilier** *nadj* property, real estate,
property business, real estate business
- une autre société immobilière a été créée –
  *another real estate company was formed*
60 | 435+n

**3604 certificat** *nm* certificate
- elle avait raté de justesse son certificat
  d'études supérieures – *she barely failed her
  higher-education certificate*
83 | 162

**3605 contaminer** *v* to contaminate, infect
- j'ai l'impression d'être contaminé. c'est
  répugnant – *I feel like I'm contaminated. it's
  disgusting*
66 | 352

**3606 pénurie** *nf* shortage
- il n'y a pas de pénurie d'uranium au niveau
  mondial – *there's no world shortage of
  uranium*
76 | 237

**3607 tirage** *nm* drawing, circulation, run
- vous finirez par présenter le tirage du loto –
  *you will end by presenting the lottery drawing*
74 | 261

**3608 perception** *nf* perception, collection
- ça ne correspond pas à ma perception de la
  ville – *that doesn't fit my impression of the
  city*
65 | 370

**3609 philosophe** *nadj(f)* philosopher
- il est plus homme que philosophe – *he is
  more a man than a philosopher*
62 | 407

**3610 planche** *nf* plank, board
- il a cloué la planche sur la porte – *he nailed
  the plank onto the door*
72 | 280

**3611 crédibilité** *nf* credibility
- la crédibilité de tous les états financiers est
  compromisé – *the credibility of our financial
  state is compromised*
70 | 305-l

**3612 fiction** *nf* fiction
- ce livre est bien une fiction – *this book is
  truly a piece of fiction*
54 | 522+s

**3613 handicapé** *nadj* disabled, handicapped
- il y a aussi les handicapés physiques – *there
  are also the physically handicapped*
68 | 325-l +s

**3614 boisson** *nf* drink, beverage
- le thé représente la deuxième boisson
  consommée dans le monde – *tea is
  the second-most consumed drink in the
  world*
77 | 222

**3615 élaboration** *nf* working-out, development
- vous allez demander l'élaboration d'un
  dossier – *you're going to ask that a file be
  put together*
65 | 369

**3616 habitation** *nf* residence, home, dwelling,
housing
- environ 200 habitations ont été détruites
  – *about 200 dwellings were destroyed*
67 | 346

**3617 représentatif** *adj* representative
- le Danemark a des syndicats puissants, très
  représentatifs – *Denmark has powerful
  unions, very representative*
74 | 251

**3618 débrouiller** *v* to untangle, sort out, manage,
get by
- tu te débrouilles très bien – *you're
  managing very well*
73 | 269

**3619 imposition** *nf* taxation
- il veut un taux d'imposition uniforme – *he
  wants a uniform tax rate*
56 | 496-l +s

**3620 générer** *v* to generate
- les aérosols génèrent des pluies acides
  – *aerosols produce acid rain*
66 | 358-l

**3621 ajustement** *nm* adjustment
- l'ajustement reste aussi insuffisant – *the
  adjustment is still inadequate*
68 | 328

**3622 princesse** *nf* princess
- une princesse ne peut pas embrasser un
  crapaud? – *a princess can't kiss a toad?*
65 | 365

**3623 virer** *v* to turn, change, transfer, kick out
- il vire encore une fois à droite – *he turns
  right one more time*
62 | 410+s

# 21  Adjectives – differences across registers

This table lists the adjectives that occur with a much higher frequency than expected in the three registers: spoken language, literature, and non-fiction. In each case, the words listed are among those in the top 10 percent of words for that register, in terms of relative frequency to the other two registers.

**Spoken:**

**honorable** 893 honorable

**excellent** 1225 excellent

**intéressant** 1244 interesting

**permanent** 1322 permanent

**fier** 1331 proud

**évident** 1488 obvious

**fiscal** 1637 fiscal

**juridique** 1665 legal

**communautaire** 1811 communal

**royal** 2290 royal

**inacceptable** 2663 unacceptabe

**boulot** 2929 job

**super** 2993 great

**structurel** 3018 structural

**ministériel** 3034 ministerial

**unanime** 3050 unanimous

**francophone** 3118 French-speaking

**compétent** 3262 competent

**équitable** 3304 equitable

**environnemental** 3548 environmental

**génial** 3872 brilliant

**constructif** 4039 constructive

**écologique** 4206 ecological

**confidentiel** 4210 confidential

**opportun** 4485 timely

**intergouvernemental** 4539 intergovernmental

**saisonnier** 4543 seasonal

**Literature:**

**soudain** 2310 sudden

**sombre** 2348 dark

**désert** 2382 desert

**tranquille** 2555 quiet

**atomique** 2657 atomic

**dominant** 2968 dominant

**vain** 2971 vain

**cruel** 3357 cruel

**invisible** 3369 invisible

**pénible** 3691 tiresome

**confus** 3761 confused

**divin** 3787 divine

**épais** 3789 thick

**obscur** 3819 dark

**charmant** 4030 charming

**grossier** 4054 unrefined

**gai** 4243 gay

**pâle** 4433 pale

**immobile** 4463 motionless

**innombrable** 4588 innumerable

**amer** 4599 bitter

**mou** 4655 soft

**aimable** 4668 pleasant

**humble** 4680 humble

**élégant** 4747 elegant

**humide** 4841 moist

**perpétuel** 4889 perpetual

**Nonfiction:**

**franc** 942 frank

**nord** 1090 north

**sud** 1242 south

**monétaire** 1739 monetary

**initial** 2137 initial

**présidentiel** 2238 presidential

**suisse** 2241 Swiss

**téléphonique** 2356 telephone

**numérique** 2373 numerical

**spatial** 2765 spatial

**serbe** 2780 Serbian

**automatique** 2800 automatic

**bancaire** 2945 banking

**syndical** 2995 union

**islamique** 3074 Islamic

**turc** 3134 Turkish

**maximal** 3182 maximal

**olympique** 3199 Olympic

**consécutif** 3218 consecutive

**raide** 3533 stiff

**alerte** 3599 alert

**ultérieur** 3862 subsequent

**fonctionnel** 3966 functional

**filial** 4126 filial

**vocal** 4316 vocal

**préventif** 4666 preventive

**inchangé** 4701 unchanged

---

3624 **facilité** *nf* easiness, ease, aptitude
- il lit avec facilité – *he reads easily*
72 | 273

3625 **postal** *adj* postal, mail
- ils lui écrivaient une carte postale – *they wrote her a postcard*
77 | 221

3626 **perturber** *v* to disrupt, disturb
- je suis perturbée par une enquête que je mène – *I'm disturbed by an investigation that I'm leading*
67 | 341

3627 **répercussion** *nf* repercussion
- le transport a des répercussions sur tous les aspects de notre vie – *transportation impacts on all aspects of life*
57 | 469+s

3628 **oncle** *nm* uncle
- je vis avec mon oncle et ma tante – *I live with my uncle and my aunt*
59 | 451-n

3629 **viol** *nm* rape
- je vais crier au viol – *I'm going to cry rape*
74 | 248

**3630 culte** *nm* worship, cult
• le culte des anciens dieux a été réinstauré
  – *the worship of ancient gods was reinstated*
  71 | 284

**3631 gosse** *nm,nf* kid
• nous, on était gosses, on savait pas – *we were just kids, we didn't know*
  60 | 432-n +s

**3632 équipage** *nm* crew, gear
• les membres d'équipage ont retiré la femme de l'eau – *the crew members pulled the woman from the water*
  67 | 339

**3633 carburant** *nadj* fuel
• les prix élevés des carburants ont frappé tous les secteurs de l'économie – *high gas prices have affected all sectors of the economy*
  68 | 324

**3634 canon** *nm* gun, cannon
• ils nous ont attaqués au canon à eau et au gaz lacrymogène – *they attacked us with water cannons and tear gas*
  70 | 296

**3635 prometteur** *nadj* promising
• l'avenir n'est pas prometteur – *the future is not promising*
  82 | 160

**3636 apprentissage** *nm* learning, apprenticeship
• chaque poste possède un plan d'apprentissage – *each job has a training plan*
  61 | 416

**3637 soi-disant** *adji* so-called, supposedly
• il m'a donné un bijou soi-disant précieux – *he gave me a supposedly precious jewel*
  78 | 204-n

**3638 chaussure** *nf* shoe, sneaker
• il faut enlever vos chaussures – *you must remove your shoes*
  65 | 357

**3639 salarial** *adj* salary
• le problème de l'équité salariale existe – *there's a problem with equitable salaries*
  61 | 414-l

**3640 abolir** *v* to abolish, do away with
• l'esclavage n'a jamais vraiment été aboli – *slavery never really was abolished*
  72 | 277

**3641 pâte** *nf* paste, dough, pasta
• ils mangent du riz et des pâtes tous les jours – *they eat rice and noodles every day*
  83 | 157

**3642 cohésion** *nf* cohesion
• tant que cette situation durera, la cohésion ne sera jamais atteinte – *as long as this situation lasts, unity will never be achieved*
  52 | 555+s

**3643 ruine** *nf* ruin, ruins
• la maison était en ruine – *the house was in ruins*
  64 | 375+l -s

**3644 percer** *v* to pierce, drill, break into
• le couteau avait percé la chair avec précision – *the knife pierced the flesh with exactness*
  72 | 273

**3645 rassemblement** *nm* gathering, collecting, assembling
• rassemblement au gymnase pour une annonce spêciale – *there's an assembly in the gymnasium for a special annoucement*
  67 | 335

**3646 malentendu** *nm* misunderstanding
• ce n'est qu'un malentendu ridicule – *it's nothing but a ridiculous misunderstanding*
  64 | 369+l

**3647 soigneusement** *adv* tidily, neatly, carefully
• j'ai soigneusement examiné le document – *I examined the document carefully*
  76 | 225

**3648 pot** *nm* jar, pot
• j'ai arrêté de vendre du pot puis de la coke – *I stopped selling pot, then coke*
  67 | 337

**3649 règne** *nm* reign
• en France, c'est le règne du politiquement correct – *in France, it's the reign of political correctness*
  75 | 243

**3650 impulsion** *nf* impulse, pulse
• il y avait une impulsion qui nous poussait – *there was an impulse that pushed us*
  60 | 426+n -s

**3651 physiquement** *adv* physically
• il était physiquement plus fort que moi – *he was physically stronger than me*
  81 | 171

**3652 minimal** *adj* minimal, minimum
• une peine minimale de quatre ans est juste et équitable – *a minimum sentence of four years is just and equitable*
  62 | 404-l

**3653 fossé** *nm* ditch
• la forêt se terminait par un fossé – *the forest ended at a ditch*
  78 | 200

**3654 dépens** *nmpl* expense
• la Russie a affirmé ses ambitions aux dépens de l'Italie – *Russia affirmed its ambitions at Italy's expense*
  83 | 157

**3655 implanter** *v* to implant, set up, establish
• il est nécessaire d'implanter un nouveau système – *it's necessary to set up a new system*
  71 | 286

**3656 descendant** *nadj* downward, descending, descendant
• les descendants parleront de leurs ancêtres disparus – *the descendants will speak of their ancestors who have disappeared*
  76 | 228

3657 **politiquement** *adv* politically, diplomatically
• il est politiquement correct d'être
anti-américain – *it's politically correct to be
anti-American*
72 | 273

3658 **crever** *v* to burst, puncture
• quel pneu est crevé? c'est pas de ton côté
– *which tire is flat. it's not on your side*
57 | 474-n

3659 **interruption** *nf* interruption, break
• elle parlait sans interruption, d'un air
raisonnable – *she spoke uninterrupted, quite
reasonably*
60 | 428+n

3660 **polonais** *nadj(pl)* Polish
• vous dites avoir des racines polonaises
– *you say you have Polish roots*
69 | 301

3661 **patrie** *nf* homeland, home country
• ils ont parlé de protection de la patrie
– *they talked about protecting the homeland*
67 | 333+l

3662 **prélèvement** *nm* imposition, levying,
withdrawal, removal, deduction
• un prélèvement est, en réalité, une taxe
– *a deduction is, in fact, a tax*
64 | 369

3663 **ex** *nmfi* ex
• mon ex serait ravie que je vous parle
– *my ex will be thrilled that I'm speaking
to you*
51 | 565+n -s

3664 **studio** *nm* studio, studio apartment
• mon bureau était en face du studio – *my
office is across from the studio*
64 | 366

3665 **intégrité** *nf* integrity
• lui au moins a gardé son intégrité – *at least
he kept his integrity*
68 | 313

3666 **prescrire** *v* to order, command, prescribe,
stipulate
• ils prescrivent ces médicaments – *they
prescribe these medicines*
72 | 273

3667 **exhorter** *v* to exhort, urge
• je l'exhorte à retirer sa motion – *I exhort her
to repeal her motion*
57 | 468

3668 **tribu** *nf* tribe
• nous sommes une tribu, une communauté
– *we're a tribe, a community*
76 | 222

3669 **globe** *nm* globe
• ils viennent de toutes les régions du globe
– *they come from all parts of the globe*
83 | 155

3670 **apaiser** *v* to calm, appease, calm down
• officiellement, les tensions s'apaisent
– *officially, tensions are cooling*
75 | 235

3671 **sélectionner** *v* to select
• il faut avant tout sélectionner les rôles qui
nous plaisent – *above all we have to select
the roles that we enjoy*
58 | 457+n

3672 **familier** *nadj* familiar, informal
• apparemment, cette voix t'est familière –
*apparently this voice is familiar to you*
66 | 346+l

3673 **quinzaine** *nf* about fifteen, two weeks
• dans moins d'une quinzaine, vous serez un
homme libre – *in less than two weeks, you'll
be a free man*
69 | 304

3674 **paralyser** *v* to paralyze
• la mine est paralysée par la grève – *the mine
is paralyzed by the strike*
76 | 229

3675 **impatience** *nf* impatience
• nous vous attendons avec impatience –
*we're waiting impatiently for you*
70 | 298+l

3676 **logiciel** *nm* software, program, application
• il vous faudra peut-être réinstaller votre
logiciel – *you might have to reinstall your
software*
59 | 440-l

3677 **visiblement** *adv* obviously, clearly, visibly
• il se tait, se domine visiblement – *he shuts
up, visibly controlling himself*
72 | 271

3678 **suicider** *v* to commit suicide
• quatre suspects se sont suicidés samedi –
*four suspects committed suicide Saturday*
70 | 297

3679 **préjugé** *nm* prejudice, bias
• il est moins facile de désintégrer un préjugé
qu'un atome – *it's harder to smash a
prejudice than an atom*
77 | 216

3680 **impératif** *nadj* need, necessity, urgent,
imperative
• c'est impératif, c'est nécessaire – *it's
imperative, it's necessary*
72 | 265

3681 **renvoi** *nm* dismissal, expulsion, suspension,
cross-reference
• il allait demander ton renvoi de la police –
*he was going to seek your suspension from
the police force*
58 | 455-l

3682 **charme** *nm* charm
• la liberté est une espèce de charme – *liberty
is a kind of charm*
59 | 438+l

3683 **atout** *nm* trump, asset
• l'Oscar est un atout commercial de calibre
mondial – *the Oscar is a worldwide
commercial asset*
75 | 240

3684 **portugais** *nadj(pl)* Portuguese
• admettons que je sois portugais – *let's
assume I'm Portuguese*
64 | 367

**3685 nord-ouest** *nmi* north-west
- un tremblement de terre secoue le nord-ouest de la Turquie – *an earthquake shakes northwestern Turkey*
59 | 439+n

**3686 affaiblissement** *nm* weakening
- l'euro a profité de l'affaiblissement du dollar – *the euro has profited from the weakened dollar*
43 | 702-l +n -s

**3687 balayer** *v* to sweep up, sweep out
- une fois qu'on aura balayé, ce sera à nouveau impeccable – *once we've swept it, it will be impeccable again*
75 | 239

**3688 peupler** *v* to populate, inhabit
- l'enfer est peuplé d'anges – *hell is populated by angels*
76 | 222

**3689 cauchemar** *nm* nightmare, bad dream
- toute cette affaire est un vrai cauchemar – *this whole affair is a real nightmare*
69 | 301

**3690 pénible** *adj(f)* hard, difficult, painful, tiresome
- ton incompétence devient extrêmement pénible – *your incompetence is becoming extremely bothersome*
69 | 302+l

**3691 venue** *nf* coming
- une grande nouveauté récente est la venue des nouveaux dépanneurs – *a big recent trend is the arrival of new convenience stores*
78 | 205

**3692 ballon** *nm* ball
- l'usage de tout autre ballon est strictement interdit – *use of any other ball is strictly forbidden*
67 | 326

**3693 abstenir** *v* to abstain, refrain
- vous feriez mieux de vous abstenir – *you would do better to abstain*
74 | 244

**3694 affrontement** *nm* clash, confrontation
- il y a eu des affrontements dans les rues – *there were confrontations in the streets*
55 | 493+n

**3695 expulser** *v* to expel, evict, deport, throw out
- les policiers l'expulseront légalement de la propriété – *the police will evict her legally from the property*
70 | 295

**3696 resserrer** *v* to tighten up, strengthen
- nous devrions nous voir plus souvent, resserrer nos relations – *we should see each other more often, strengthen our relations*
83 | 146

**3697 activement** *adv* actively
- les évadés sont activement recherchés – *the fugitives are being actively sought*
75 | 239

**3698 décor** *nm* scenery, décor, set
- on a déjà changé le décor en milieu d'année – *we already changed the decor mid-year*
66 | 341

**3699 compassion** *nf* compassion
- nous avons toujours réagi avec compassion – *we have always reacted with compassion*
67 | 325-n +s

**3700 couronne** *nf* crown, wreath
- aucune couronne ne tient sur aucune tête – *crowns don't stay on anybody's head*
67 | 326-s

**3701 descente** *nf* descent, raid, downward slope
- le PCF poursuit sa descente aux enfers – *the French Communist Party continues its descent into hell*
65 | 356+n -s

**3702 plancher** *nm,v* floor
- il entendit la clef tomber sur le plancher – *he heard the key fall onto the floor*
69 | 307

**3703 trentaine** *nf* about thirty
- je suis contente d'arriver à la trentaine – *I'm happy to have reached thirty years old*
68 | 317

**3704 détresse** *nf* distress
- nous répondons à votre signal de détresse – *we are responding to your distress signal*
80 | 180

**3705 escalier** *nm* stairs, staircase
- il montait et descendait l'escalier – *he climbed up and down the stairs*
57 | 462+l -n -s

**3706 barrage** *nm* barrier, obstruction, dam, roadblock
- de nombreux barrages ont été érigés par la police – *many barricades were erected by the police*
64 | 360

**3707 néant** *nm* nothingness
- vous réduisez ma vie à néant – *you're reducing my life to oblivion*
75 | 237

**3708 support** *nm* support, stand
- reste là. c'est un support moral – *stay there. it's a moral support*
55 | 489+n -s

**3709 effondrement** *nm* collapse, caving-in, falling-in, breaking-down
- on va assister à l'effondrement de l'histoire de la finance – *we'll witness a collapse of financial history*
68 | 309

**3710 encaisser** *v* to receive, collect, cash
- j'encaisserai son chèque dans la matinée – *I will cash her check in the morning*
82 | 163

**3711 déduire** *v* to deduct, deduce, infer, figure out
- j'en ai déduit de façon certaine que je l'avais perdue – *I figured out for sure that I had lost it*
76 | 225

**3712 baptiser** *v* to name, christen, baptize
- j'ai baptisé presque tous les habitants de la ville – *I baptized almost everyone living in the city*
73 | 251

**3713 incompatible** *adj(f)* incompatible
- les deux choses sont tout à fait incompatibles – *the two things are completely incompatible*
82 | 160

**3714 bienvenu** *nadj* welcome
- j'aimerais vous souhaiter à tous la bienvenue – *I would like to welcome you all*
60 | 414+s

**3715 espérance** *nf* hope
- je pars donc dans l'espérance de vous revoir – *so I'm leaving in the hopes of seeing you again*
71 | 282

**3716 synthèse** *nf* summary, synthesis
- il s'agit d'une synthèse fondée sur les connaissances – *it's a synthesis based on knowledge*
61 | 402+n -s

**3717 conjoncture** *nf* situation, climate
- la conjoncture économique n'est plus la même – *the economic climate is not the same*
54 | 496+n -s

**3718 défier** *v* to challenge, defy, distrust
- il aimait à défier le destin par fierté – *he liked to defy destiny with pride*
77 | 209

**3719 baie** *nf* bay; berry
- la baie immense de Naples s'éployait sans fin – *the immense bay of Naples extended endlessly*
81 | 165

**3720 récompense** *nf* reward, award
- ton courage mérite récompense – *your courage should be rewarded*
74 | 248

**3721 étendue** *nf* area, expanse, duration, extent, range
- il fut surpris de l'étendue de son savoir – *he was surprised at the extent of her knowledge*
70 | 284

**3722 tiens** *nadjpl,intj* ah, well
- tiens, je te rends tes 5 livres – *here, I'm returning your 5 books*
50 | 567-n +s

**3723 carnet** *nm* notebook, notepad
- j'inscrivais les rendez-vous sur mon carnet – *I wrote the meetings in my notebook*
75 | 235

**3724 banc** *nm* bench, workbench, pew
- il alla s'asseoir sur le banc – *he went to sit on the bench*
63 | 368+l

**3725 réformer** *v* to re-form, reform, discharge
- il était nécessaire de réformer l'ancien système d'assurance-chômage – *it was necessary to reform the old unemployment insurance system*
73 | 257

**3726 assise** *nf* basis, foundation
- l'équité est l'une des assises fondamentales – *equity is one of the fundamental bases*
71 | 277

**3727 énergétique** *nadj(f)* energic, vigorous
- c'est l'industrie des services énergétiques – *it's the energy services industry*
62 | 388-l

**3728 reléguer** *v* to relegate
- ils sont relégués aux banquettes arrières – *they have been relegated to the back bench*
86 | 123

**3729 architecte** *nm,nf* architect
- c'est un architecte merveilleux – *he's a marvelous architect*
82 | 155

**3730 deuxièmement** *adv* secondly
- deuxièmement, ce n'est pas ma faute – *second, it's not my fault*
55 | 483-l -n +s

**3731 vedette** *nf* star, patrol boat
- des tas de vedettes viennent ici, vous savez – *lots of movie stars come here, you know*
65 | 341

**3732 intervenant** *nadj* contributor, intervener
- j'ai été un intervenant de notre système de justice – *I was an intervener in our justice system*
59 | 424-l +s

**3733 séminaire** *nm* seminar, seminary
- je vais vous dire. ces séminaires m'excitent à mort – *I'll tell you. these seminars bore me to death*
70 | 288

**3734 contrer** *v* to counter
- heureusement, je sais comment contrer ça – *happily, I know how to counter this*
80 | 177

**3735 nerveux** *nadj(pl)* nervous, irritable
- les tests me rendent nerveux – *tests make me nervous*
69 | 301

**3736 assaut** *nm* assault, attack, bout
- vous mènerez la 1ère vague d'assaut – *you will lead the first wave of attack*
70 | 290

**3737 couteau** *nm* knife
- pourquoi t'achètes des couteaux? – *why are you buying knives?*
65 | 340

**3738 arbitraire** *nadj(f)* arbitrary
- la police se livre à des activités arbitraires – *the police are prone to arbitrary activities*
72 | 267

**3739 vraisemblablement** *adv* most probably
- les prix resteront vraisemblablement stables – *the prices will likely remain stable*
75 | 233

**3740 propagation** *nf* propagation, spreading
- vous vous acheminez vers une propagation de votre théorie? – *you're making progress towards spreading your theory?*
54 | 497+n -s

**3741 masculin** *nadj* male, masculine
- je n'entendis que des voix masculines – *all I heard was masculine voices*
72 | 257

**3742 imiter** *v* to imitate
- j'imitais les gestes de mes voisins – *I imitated the gestures of my neghbors*
72 | 263

**3743 embaucher** *v* to hire
- en onze mois, il a embauché sept personnes – *in eleven months he hired seven people*
72 | 267

**3744 primordial** *adj* primordial, basic, vital, primary
- la citoyenneté revêt une importance primordiale – *citizenship assumes primary importance*
76 | 220

**3745 arbitre** *nm,nf* referee, arbitrer, arbitrator
- c'est un bon arbitre. il arbitre bien – *he's a good arbitrator. he judges well*
74 | 238

**3746 manteau** *nm* coat, overcoat
- j'aurais dû enlever mon manteau et le jeter par la fenêtre – *I should have removed my coat and thrown it out the window*
58 | 434+l -s

**3747 implication** *nf* implication
- ceci peut avoir d'énormes implications – *this could have enormous implications*
67 | 325

**3748 grand-père** *nm* grandfather
- c'est grand-père qui me l'a fait comprendre – *Grandfather's the one who helped me understand that*
61 | 396+l -n

**3749 reflet** *nm* reflection, glint, highlight
- mes livres sont le reflet de mes propres expériences – *my books reflect my own experiences*
64 | 361

**3750 requête** *nf* request, petition
- la requête iranienne bloque les négociations – *the Iranian request has stalled negotiations*
77 | 209

**3751 décliner** *v* to decline, refuse, turn down
- vous avez décliné notre offre – *you have declined our offer*
79 | 188

**3752 rideau** *nm* curtain
- «ferme les rideaux», dis-je – *"close the curtains", I said*
61 | 398+l

**3753 fermé** *adj* shut, closed, locked
- je pourrais dessiner les yeux fermés – *I could draw with my eyes closed*
72 | 258

**3754 manipulation** *nf* handling, manipulation
- la manipulation génétique n'est pas une bonne chose – *genetic manipulation isn't a good thing*
71 | 267

**3755 piquer** *v* to sting, bite, prick, be hot; to steal
- ne me piquez pas mon taxi ... passez votre chemin – *don't you take my taxi ... scram*
64 | 354

**3756 assiette** *nf* plate, dish, bowl
- je prendrai l'assiette de crudités – *I will take the veggie plate*
73 | 249

**3757 gigantesque** *nadj(f)* gigantic, immense
- il s'agit là d'un problème gigantesque – *that's a huge problem*
76 | 213

**3758 rival** *nadj* rival
- ils ne peuvent pas tuer leur rival – *they can't kill their rival*
62 | 380-s

**3759 refermer** *v* to close again, shut again, close up
- j'entends la porte se refermer derrière moi – *I hear the door close behind me*
60 | 407+l -s

**3760 écu** *nm* ecu
- plus de 100 millions d'écus seront gaspillés – *over 100 million ecus will be wasted*
48 | 585

**3761 confus** *adj(pl)* confused, embarrassed
- je suis très confus, je ne sais pas pourquoi – *I'm very confused – I don't know why*
72 | 263

**3762 expédition** *nf* dispatch, shipping, shipment, expedition
- je n'ai jamais regretté une seule expédition – *I never regretted a single expedition*
81 | 164

**3763 reconstituer** *v* to reconstitute, restore, reconstruct
- je dois donc reconstituer des réserves – *I therefore have to rebuild some reserves*
76 | 212

**3764 protégé** *nadj* protected, protégé
- elle était sa protégée et devait normalement lui succéder – *she was his protégée and should normally have replaced him*
84 | 137

**3765 chant** *nm* song
- nous allons prendre des cours de chant à domicile – *we're going to take singing lessons at home*
66 | 328

**3766 diplomatie** *nf* diplomacy
- il y faut toute une diplomatie et une patience infinie – *there we need true diplomacy and infinite patience*
56 | 455

**3767 lieutenant** *nm* lieutenant
- la guerre est finie, mon lieutenant – *the war is over, Lieutenant*
62 | 372

**3768 réputé** *adj* famous, renowned
- son personnel est réputé pour son service hors pair – *its staff has a reputation for unequalled service*
68 | 304

**3769 indirect** *adj* indirect
- est-ce une référence indirecte à la religion? – *is that an indirect reference to religion?*
78 | 190

**3770 apte** *adj(f)* capable
- la France est parfaitement apte à s'adapter
  – *France is perfectly able to adapt*
  85 | 124

**3771 dépêcher** *v* to dispatch, send, hurry
- j'ai bloqué l'ascenseur, dépêchez vous, vite
  – *I'm holding the elevator—hurry up, quick*
  64 | 346

**3772 démentir** *v* to deny, refute, contradict
- la Maison Blanche a démenti cette nouvelle version – *the White House contradicted this new version*
  61 | 384+n -s

**3773 sud-ouest** *nmi* south-west
- quelque chose approche en provenance du sud-ouest – *something is coming from the south-west*
  60 | 397

**3774 envergure** *nf* wingspan, breadth, scope
- quel projet d'envergure se fait instantané-ment? – *what large-scale project happens in an instant?*
  79 | 188

**3775 touche** *nf* button, key, touch, touchline
- elle appuie sur une touche. allo? – *she pushes a button. hello?*
  75 | 221

**3776 déterminant** *nadj* determining, deciding, crucial
- il a joué un rôle déterminant lors du coup d'Etat – *he played a crucial role during the insurrection*
  73 | 246

**3777 sous-marin** *nadj* submarine, underwater
- la marine chinoise dispose de 69 sous-marins – *the Chinese navy has 69 submarines*
  78 | 192

**3778 acheminement** *nm* routing, shipment
- il aurait organisé l'acheminement des explosifs – *he allegedly organized the shipment of explosives*
  41 | 694-l +n -s

**3779 externe** *nadj(f)* external, outer
- les problèmes externes se révèlent aussi importants – *the external problems prove as important*
  69 | 295

**3780 hôte** *nm* host, guest
- je sais accueillir mes hôtes – *I know how to welcome my guests*
  75 | 224

**3781 assassin** *nadj* murderer, assassin
- l'assassin cache peut-être ses victimes – *the assassin might be hiding his victims*
  68 | 300

**3782 confirmation** *nf* confirmation
- les syndicats veulent une confirmation écrite – *the unions want written confirmation*
  64 | 348+n

**3783 tapis** *nm(pl)* carpet, mat, covering
- il faut les accueillir avec le tapis rouge – *they should be given a red-carpet welcome*
  74 | 236

**3784 corde** *nf* rope, chord, string
- je l'ai étranglé. avec une corde – *I strangled him. with a rope*
  66 | 326

**3785 notable** *nadj(f)* notable, noteworthy
- il y a des disparités notables entre pays – *there are noteworthy disparities among countries*
  72 | 251

**3786 rationnel** *nadj* rational
- il y a une explication rationnelle à tout cela – *there's a rational explanation for all that*
  70 | 274

**3787 divin** *adj,nm* divine, heavenly
- vous êtes divine, adorable – *you're divine, adorable*
  61 | 391+l

**3788 endormir** *v* to put to sleep, fall asleep
- je ne voulais surtout pas m'endormir au volant – *I certainly didn't want to fall asleep at the wheel*
  57 | 437+l -n

**3789 épais** *adj(pl),adv* thick, pitch dark, thickly
- c'était des lunettes très épaisses – *they were very thick eyeglasses*
  63 | 355+l -s

**3790 exposé** *nadj* account, statement, talk
- j'en ai parlé dans mon exposé – *I spoke of it in my statement*
  70 | 276+s

**3791 boutique** *nf* shop
- les émeutiers pillèrent les boutiques, les maisons, les ateliers – *the rioters looted shops, houses, workshops*
  71 | 261

**3792 récolter** *v* to harvest, gather
- je récolte en permanence les histoires des gens – *I gather for posterity people's stories*
  83 | 146

**3793 tchèque** *nadj(f)* Czech
- la République tchèque est l'une des grandes démocraties – *the Czech Republic is one of the great democracies*
  58 | 429+n

**3794 autoroute** *nf* motorway, highway, freeway
- de nombreuses autoroutes ont dû être fermées – *many highways had to be closed*
  66 | 325

**3795 maternité** *nf* maternity, motherhood
- j'ai pris un congé maternité – *I took maternity leave*
  84 | 129

**3796 là-dedans** *adv* inside, in it
- maintenant rentre là-dedans et fais-moi du thé – *now go back inside and make me some tea*
  61 | 384-n +s

**3797 différend** *nm* disagreement, controversy
- nous venons de régler le différend qui nous opposait – *we have just resolved the disagreement that separated us*
  65 | 338

## 22   Verbs of movement

| | | |
|---|---|---|
| **prendre** 43 to take | **poursuivre** 463 to pursue | **visiter** 1378 to visit |
| **aller** 53 to go | **conduire** 487 to drive | **courir** 1447 to run |
| **venir** 88 to come | **quitter** 507 to leave | **franchir** 1487 to get over |
| **passer** 90 to pass | **tomber** 547 to fall | **écarter** 1492 to separate |
| **suivre** 120 to follow | **amener** 655 to bring | **marcher** 1532 to walk |
| **partir** 163 to leave | **tourner** 669 to turn | **éloigner** 1541 to move away |
| **arriver** 174 to arrive | **déplacer** 714 to move | **approcher** 1576 to approach |
| **sortir** 309 to go out | **accompagner** 727 | **descendre** 1705 to go down |
| **mener** 316 to lead |    to accompany | **circuler** 1721 to drive |
| **chercher** 336 to look for | **échapper** 940 to escape | **progresser** 1856 to progress |
| **entrer** 337 to enter | **retourner** 999 to return | **bouger** 1893 to move |
| **apporter** 339 to bring | **ramener** 1097 to bring back | **reculer** 1922 to move back |
| **atteindre** 346 to reach | **emporter** 1128 to take | **transporter** 1929 |
| **importer** 354 to import | **étendre** 1173 to spread out |    to transport |
| **tirer** 391 to pull | **jeter** 1202 to throw | **parcourir** 2065 to cover |
| **arrêter** 420 to stop | **rapprocher** 1329 to bring | **accélérer** 2082 to accelerate |
| **avancer** 449 to advance |    closer | **emmener** 2098 to take |
| **élever** 459 to lift | **asseoir** 1360 to sit | **transférer** 2128 to transfer |

---

**3798 explicite** *adj(f)* explicitly
- c'étaient des impératifs assez explicites
– *they were rather explicit requirements*
79 | 184

**3799 comté** *nm* county, earldom
- c'est un des plus beaux comtés au Canada
– *it's one of the most beautiful counties in Canada*
62 | 373+s

**3800 par-dessus** *adv* over
- elle voulait un enfant par-dessus tout – *she wanted a child more than anything*
62 | 375+l -n

**3801 quota** *nm* quota
- il ne peut justifier une hausse des quotas de phoques – *he can't justify raising the seal quota*
65 | 334-l

**3802 tailler** *v* to cut, carve, engrave, sharpen, trim
- le résultat fut une cote mal taillée – *the result was a badly tailored quote*
72 | 253

**3803 apparent** *adj* apparent, obvious
- je me surprenais à pleurer sans cause apparente – *I surprised myself by weeping without any apparent cause*
76 | 213

**3804 enfuir** *v* to run away, flee
- je voudrais m'enfuir, mais je suis comme paralysée – *I wanted to escape but it's like I'm paralyzed*
67 | 315

**3805 assistant** *nm* assistant
- j'ai demandé à être assistant stagiaire
– *I asked to be an intern*
75 | 221

**3806 portion** *nf* portion, share
- les pannes ont frappé de larges portions du sud de Moscou – *blackouts hit large portions of southern Moscow*
83 | 141

**3807 allocation** *nf* allocation, granting, allotment, allowance
- il dirigeait l'allocation des ressources – *he directed the allocation of resources*
70 | 275

**3808 spéculation** *nf* speculation
- la fièvre de la spéculation a produit les mariages d'argent – *speculation madness led to money marriages*
72 | 251

**3809 décéder** *v* to die, pass away, pass on
- une vieille dame est décédée pendant qu'elle dormait – *an elderly woman died in her sleep*
61 | 379

**3810 serré** *adj,adv* tight, packed, crowded
- le budget est serré cette année – *the budget is tight this year*
76 | 214

**3811 enquêter** *v* to investigate, hold inquiry, conduct a survey
- tu veux vraiment enquêter sur lui? – *you really want to investigate him?*
73 | 241

**3812 dix-sept** *det,nmi* seventeen
- la ville brûla pendant dix-sept jours – *the city burned for seventeen days*
59 | 408

**3813 allonger** *v* to lengthen, extend, stretch out
- je m'allongeai sur mon lit – *I stretched out on my bed*
66 | 324

**3814 chauffeur** *nm* driver, chauffeur
- le chauffeur du véhicule n'a pas été identifié – *the driver of the vehicle has not been identified*
68 | 294

**3815 prospérité** *nf* prosperity
- la société japonaise a connu une grande prospérité – *Japanese society enjoyed great prosperity*
72 | 252

**3816 ambiguïté** *nf* ambiguity
- cette affirmation cache encore bien des ambiguïtés – *this assertion still hides several ambiguities*
77 | 198

**3817 bourgeois** *nadj(pl)* middle class
- ses parents vivaient comme des bourgeois – *her parents lived like middle-class people*
60 | 396+l

**3818 touristique** *adj(f)* holiday, tourist
- elle évite les lieux touristiques – *she avoids tourist traps*
76 | 210

**3819 obscur** *adj* dark, vague, obscure
- c'est le combat entre les forces obscures et les forces de la lumière – *it's the struggle between the dark forces and the forces of light*
64 | 347+l

**3820 cou** *nm* neck
- elle nouait ses bras à mon cou – *she wrapped her arms around my neck*
58 | 420+l

**3821 invention** *nf* invention
- le calendrier est une invention humaine – *the calendar is a human invention*
71 | 265

**3822 boucle** *nf* loop, buckle, curl
- ils sont si mignons avec leurs boucles blondes – *they are so cute with their blond curls*
64 | 338

**3823 flou** *adj* blurred, fuzzy, vague
- tout dans la pièce lui sembla flou, déformé – *everything in the room seemed blurred to him*
74 | 226

**3824 redire** *v* to say again, repeat
- je te l'ai dit et redit – *I told you once, and then again*
79 | 179

**3825 consultatif** *adj* advisory
- ils seront réduits à un rôle consultatif – *they will be relegated to an advisory role*
65 | 325

**3826 torturer** *v* to torture
- elle m'a torturée mentalement toute l'année – *she tortured me mentally all year long*
73 | 235

**3827 carton** *nm* cardboard, card, score
- il y a une petite boîte de carton où vous trouverez un carnet de timbres – *there is a little cardboard box where you will find a book of stamps*
69 | 288

**3828 effrayer** *v* to frighten, scare
- le futur m'attirait et m'effrayait à la fois – *the future both attracted me and scared me*
66 | 314

**3829 pitié** *nf* pity, mercy
- enfin le ciel eut pitié de cette mère malheureuse – *finally heaven had pity on this unhappy mother*
56 | 445+l -n

**3830 complexité** *nf* complexity
- le livre explore la complexité de la société de l'information – *the book explores the complexity of the information society*
69 | 282

**3831 favori** *nadj* favorite
- le favori a gagné. nous le félicitons – *the faorite won. we congratulated him*
68 | 291

**3832 noyau** *nm* core, nucleus, pit
- il recracha le noyau d'une olive – *he spat out an olive pit*
67 | 305

**3833 brandir** *v* to brandish, wield, wave
- il brandit longuement les poings sous l'ovation – *he pumped his fists as the crowd cheered*
77 | 201

**3834 repenser** *v* to rethink
- il faut complètement repenser le tourisme – *tourism must be completely rethought*
80 | 169

**3835 timide** *nadj(f)* timid, shy, bashful
- sois pas timide, petit minou – *don't be timid, little buddy*
73 | 242

**3836 audition** *nf* hearing, examination, audition
- on a assisté aux auditions – *we attended the hearings*
72 | 250

**3837 comptabilité** *nf* accountancy, accounting, book-keeping
- il a fait beaucoup de travail en comptabilité – *he worked extensively in accounting*
77 | 195

**3838 précaire** *adj(f)* precarious, makeshift
- le futur de leurs fils devient précaire – *their son's future was becoming precarious*
77 | 199

**3839 trône** *nm* throne
- nous sommes des auxiliaires du trône pontifical – *we are assistants to the pontifical throne*
64 | 343

**3840 insulter** *v* to insult
- jamais je ne vous aurais insulté de propos délibérés – *I never would have insulted you deliberately*
- 78 | 185

**3841 saut** *nm* jump, leap
- il a fait le grand saut – *he made the big leap*
- 75 | 216

**3842 amende** *nf* fine
- il devra payer l'amende – *he'll have to pay the fine*
- 67 | 307

**3843 différemment** *adv* differently
- les femmes ont voté différemment de leurs maris – *the women voted differently from their husbands*
- 72 | 243+s

**3844 programmation** *nf* programming
- c'est trois heures de programmation par jour en direct – *it's three hours of live daily programming*
- 50 | 522-l +s

**3845 crédible** *adj(f)* credible
- notre système est crédible, reconnu mondialement – *our system is credible, recognized worldwide*
- 76 | 204

**3846 justification** *nf* justification, proof
- on ne saurait trouver de justification au terrorisme – *there's no justification for terrorism*
- 76 | 210

**3847 conservation** *nf* preservation, preserving, retention
- quelles mesures de conservation peuvent être prises – *what conservation measures can be taken*
- 65 | 324+s

**3848 transit** *nm* transit
- le fric est en transit. bouge pas – *the loot is on its way. don't move*
- 45 | 602-l +n -s

**3849 organisateur** *nadj* organiser, organising
- il a été l'un des principaux organisateurs – *he was one of the principal organizers*
- 64 | 332

**3850 galerie** *nf* gallery
- il y a toute une galerie de personnages – *there's a whole range of personalities*
- 74 | 228

**3851 aménagement** *nm* development, planning, fitting, adjustment
- alors, on a fait des aménagements – *so, we made some adjustments*
- 70 | 267

**3852 manifestant** *nm* protester, demonstrator
- les manifestants ont fait monter la pression – *the protesters increased the pressure*
- 51 | 507-l +n -s

**3853 char** *nm* tank
- j'entends vaguement les chars qui s'approchent – *I barely hear the tanks as they approach*
- 66 | 307

**3854 criminalité** *nf* crime
- la prévention de la criminalité devrait être notre objectif final – *crime prevention should be our ultimate goal*
- 57 | 418-l +s

**3855 masquer** *v* to mask, conceal, put on a mask
- le brouillard descendit des montagnes, masquant le coucher de soleil – *the fog rolled down the mountains, masking the sunset*
- 73 | 238

**3856 masque** *nm* mask
- je voudrais voir le visage derrière ce masque – *I would like to see the face behind that mask*
- 71 | 257

**3857 dorénavant** *adv* from now on, henceforth
- j'écrirai dorénavant sur les deux côtés de la page – *from now on I will write on both sides of the page*
- 80 | 162

**3858 festival** *nm* festival
- j'étais dans un festival de musique – *I was in a music festival*
- 57 | 417+s

**3859 prôner** *v* to laud, extol, advocate, commend
- l'évangile prône la pauvreté – *the gospel preaches poverty*
- 72 | 245

**3860 radicalement** *adv* radically
- aujourd'hui, la situation est radicalement différente – *today, the situation is radically different*
- 77 | 191

**3861 franchise** *nf* frankness, exemption, duty-free, franchise, deductible
- vous parlez avec une grande franchise – *you speak very frankly*
- 77 | 192

**3862 ultérieur** *adj* later, subsequent
- sauvegardez-la pour un traitement ultérieur – *save it for subsequent processing*
- 56 | 429

**3863 expédier** *v* to send, dispatch
- nous l'expédions dans des pays comme le Japon – *we send him to countries like Japan*
- 77 | 194

**3864 axer** *v* to center
- sa morale privée était axée sur le culte de la famille – *her private morals centered on family worship*
- 69 | 273

**3865 propager** *v* to propagate, spread
- vous propagez le malheur des gens au monde entier – *you're spreading people's misery throughout the world*
- 74 | 219

**3866 rectifier** *v* to rectify, correct
- nul n'osa l'interrompre pour rectifier – *nobody dared interrupt her to correct her*
- 83 | 138

**3867 tennis** *nmi* tennis
- la télévision retransmettait un match de tennis – *the television rebroadcast a tennis match*
54 | 465

**3868 avenue** *nf* avenue
- ils empruntèrent d'abord une grande avenue – *first they took a broad street*
73 | 236

**3869 vengeance** *nf* revenge
- le désir de vengeance est bon pour la santé – *the desire for revenge is healthy*
76 | 199

**3870 émouvoir** *v* to move, touch
- j'ai été profondément ému par la cérémonie – *I was deeply moved by the ceremony*
67 | 303+l

**3871 hé** *intj* hey
- hé, les gars, regardez par ici – *hey, guys, look over here*
46 | 585-n +s

**3872 génial** *adj* inspired, great, brilliant
- j'ai une idée géniale – *I have a brilliant idea*
53 | 471-n +s

**3873 réduit** *nm* reduced, scaled-down, cut-down, tiny room, hideout
- nous avions une équipe très réduite – *we had a team that had been greatly reduced*
80 | 169

**3874 alléger** *v* to lighten, alleviate,
- il est temps d'alléger les impôts – *it's time to reduce taxes*
73 | 238

**3875 vierge** *nadj(f)* virgin
- la Vierge est célébrée deux fois l'an – *the Virgin is celebrated twice a year*
65 | 324+l

**3876 meuble** *nadj(f)* piece of furniture
- on me cache derrière un meuble – *they hid me behind a piece of furniture*
65 | 321

**3877 rapprochement** *nm* bringing together, coming closer, parallel
- nous cherchons un rapprochement entre les deux extrêmes – *we're seeking a consensus between the two extremes*
67 | 298

**3878 confession** *nf* confession
- la confession de mes fautes me permet de recommencer – *confessing my faults allows me to start afresh*
75 | 212

**3879 suspens** *nm(pl)* suspension, abeyance
- trop de questions vont rester en suspens – *too many questions will remain unresolved*
82 | 143

**3880 dégradation** *nf* degrading, damaging, erosion; demotion
- il vient de subir une nouvelle dégradation – *he has just been demoted again*
62 | 356+n

**3881 vingtième** *det,nm,nf* twentieth
- la chambre obscure, au vingtième étage, cuit à gros feu – *the dark room, on the twentieth floor, is burning intensely*
69 | 276

**3882 agenda** *nm* diary, planner
- j'écris mes poèmes dans un agenda – *I write my poems in a day planner*
82 | 145

**3883 grand-mère** *nf* grandmother
- elle est allée chez sa grand-mère – *she went to her grandmother's place*
65 | 321

**3884 phare** *nm* lighthouse, headlight
- éteignez les phares! restez où vous êtes! – *turn off the lights! stay where you are!*
68 | 287

**3885 virtuel** *adj* virtual, potential
- c'est pire que l'espace virtuel, le cyberespace – *cyberspace is worse than virtual space*
73 | 228

**3886 gagnant** *nadj* winner, winning
- j'en sortirai gagnant, finalement – *I will finally end up being the winner*
71 | 255

**3887 nettoyer** *v* to clean
- elle nettoyait la chambre – *she cleaned the room*
68 | 282

**3888 diagnostic** *nm* diagnosis
- comment confirme-t-on le diagnostic de l'Alzheimer? – *how does one confirm a diagnosis of Alzheimer's?*
71 | 250

**3889 poing** *nm* fist, punch
- je vais t'envoyer mon poing dans la figure! – *I'm gonna give you a fist in the mug!*
65 | 321+l

**3890 étiquette** *nf* label, ticket, etiquette, sticker, tag
- l'étiquette distingue un élément d'information d'un autre – *the tag distinguishes one data item from another*
60 | 377+n

**3891 tante** *nf* aunt
- j'avais été élevé par ma tante – *I was raised by my aunt*
57 | 416+l -n

**3892 chemise** *nf* shirt, folder
- le col de sa chemise était largement ouvert – *the collar of her shirt was mostly open*
59 | 390+l

**3893 pile** *nf* pile, stack, battery, tails
- j'ai retiré les piles du détecteur d'oxyde de carbone – *I removed the batteries from the carbon monoxide detector*
63 | 339+l

**3894 kilo** *nm* kilo
- j'ai perdu 7 kilos en un an – *I lost 7 kilos in one year*
68 | 288

**3895 citoyenneté** *nf* citizenship
- la citoyenneté nous donne un sens de la communauté – *citizenship gives us a sense of belonging*
56 | 433-l +s

**3896 douceur** *nf* softness, smoothness, mildness, gentleness, sweetness
- nous venons de goûter la douceur de la victoire – *we have just tasted the sweetness of victory*
62 | 351+l

**3897 attester** *v* to attest, confirm
- comme l'attesteront les amis qui me connaissent bien – *as those friends who know me well will attest*
82 | 145

**3898 attraper** *v* to catch, get, pick up
- attention quand même : vous allez attraper un rhume – *now be careful—you're going to catch a cold*
58 | 402-n

**3899 prestigieux** *adj(pl)* prestigious
- le jeune homme cumule trois diplômes prestigieux – *the young man is earning three prestigious degrees*
73 | 228

**3900 ruiner** *v* to ruin, bankrupt oneself
- maintenant je suis ruiné. je suis divorcé – *I'm ruined now. I'm divorced*
71 | 249

**3901 croix** *nf(pl)* cross
- fais alors un signe de croix – *then make the sign of the cross*
60 | 376+l

**3902 nullement** *adv* not in the least
- il n'est nullement indispensable – *he's by no means indispensable*
69 | 275

**3903 incorporer** *v* to incorporate, insert, merge
- ce texte a été incorporé éventuellement dans le chapitre – *this text was eventually merged into the chapter*
75 | 206

**3904 débloquer** *v* to free, unfreeze, unjam, release, unblock
- le premier ministre cherchait sans doute à débloquer le projet – *the prime minister clearly sought to unblock the project*
75 | 208

**3905 ficher** *v* to file; to make fun of, not care, not give a damn
- je me fiche pas mal de ce que tu fais! – *I really don't give a damn what you do*
60 | 381+s

**3906 censure** *nf* censorship
- j'ai toujours eu des problèmes de censure – *I always had problems with censorship*
71 | 250

**3907 linguistique** *nadj(f)* linguistic, linguistics
- il est difficile de franchir la barrière linguistique – *it's difficult to overcome the language barrier*
59 | 387-l

**3908 accompli** *adj* accomplished
- mission accomplie, hein? c'est fini – *mission accomplished, eh? it's over*
82 | 141

**3909 terriblement** *adv* terribly, awfully
- je suis terriblement navré – *I'm terribly embarrassed*
81 | 157

**3910 main-d'œuvre** *nf* manpower, labor, workforce
- une main-d'œuvre hautement qualifiée existe dans le Sud-Est asiatique – *highly qualified manpower exists in south-east Asia*
60 | 379

**3911 invasion** *nf* invasion
- personne ne sait exactement combien l'invasion de l'Irak va coûter – *nobody knows exactly how much the invasion of Iraq will cost*
68 | 278

**3912 orange** *adji,nf* orange
- ils cultivent des oranges – *they grow oranges*
76 | 203

**3913 jury** *nm* jury, board of examiners
- c'est un jury exclusivement blanc – *it's an all-white jury*
68 | 278

**3914 bœuf** *nm* ox, steer, beef
- il est bien possible que ce bœuf ait été engraissé aux hormones – *this cow may have been fattened with hormones*
77 | 193

**3915 rallier** *v* to rally, win over, join
- on veut faire de l'argent, on veut rallier les gens, faire le party – *we want to make money, we want to gather people, to party*
74 | 219

**3916 roue** *nf* wheel
- avance doucement, dis-je. les roues se mirent à tourner – *inch slowly forward, I said. the wheels began turning*
72 | 243

**3917 barrer** *v* to close, block, bar, cross
- les deux autres me barraient la sortie – *the two others blocked my way*
68 | 284

**3918 réaffirmer** *v* to reaffirm, reassert
- il faut réaffirmer ce droit fondamental – *we must reaffirm this fundamental right*
59 | 382-l

**3919 assigner** *v* to assign, allocate, attach, attribute
- deux grandes tâches lui sont assignées – *two great tasks are assigned to her*
74 | 222

**3920 souhaitable** *adj(f)* desirable
- une dictature militaire n'est pas souhaitable dans ce pays – *a military dictatorship isn't desirable in this country*
68 | 276

**3921 soupçon** *nm* suspicion
- elle l'examina avec soupçon – *she examined it with suspicion*
72 | 234

**3922 constat** *nm* report, statement
- ces associations en sont arrivées à ce constat
  – *these associations arrived at this agreement*
  65 | 319

**3923 communisme** *nm* communism
- nous avons hérité du communisme une destruction massive de l'environnement – *we inherited from communism massive destruction of the environment*
  71 | 244

**3924 dynamisme** *nm* dynamism
- quel est le secret de votre dynamisme? – *what's the secret of your vitality?*
  77 | 189

**3925 flagrant** *adj* blatant, glaring
- c'est une contradiction flagrante – *it's a blatant contradiction*
  77 | 192

**3926 paire** *nf* pair
- une paire de gants nous suffisait – *a pair of gloves was sufficient for us*
  66 | 296

**3927 loup** *nm* wolf
- ce n'était pas un loup, ce n'en était que l'ombre – *it wasn't a wolf, just the shadow of one*
  74 | 219

**3928 concerter** *v* to devise, consult
- l'occasion de nous concerter avec nos groupes – *the chance to consult together in our groups*
  80 | 159

**3929 désespérer** *v* to despair
- il faut désespérer de ce peuple et le subjuguer – *you must lose hope in this people and take them captive*
  68 | 280

**3930 subit** *adj* sudden
- une chaleur subite l'envahissait – *a sudden heat overcame him*
  76 | 201

**3931 diplomate** *nadj(f),nm* diplomat, diplomatic
- ils sont accompagnés par un diplomate russe – *they're accompanied by a Russian diplomat*
  57 | 404+n -s

**3932 joue** *nf* cheek
- des larmes coulaient sur mes joues, sans arrêt – *tears rolled down my cheeks continually*
  55 | 430+l -n -s

**3933 essuyer** *v* to wipe, dry, mop, dust
- essuie tes larmes – *wipe away your tears*
  69 | 271

**3934 exporter** *v* to export
- le Canada exporte un certain nombre de produits alimentaires – *Canada exports some food products*
  69 | 272

**3935 étaler** *v* to spread, display, apply
- j'ai étalé mon manteau sur votre lit – *I spread out my coat on your bed*
  69 | 264

**3936 reconduire** *v* to renew, drive back
- je te reconduis à l'aéroport – *I'll drive you back to the airport*
  79 | 172

**3937 handicap** *nm* handicap
- mon handicap est très sérieux – *my handicap is very serious*
  74 | 212

**3938 bonsoir** *intj,nm* good evening
- bonsoir cher ami. quel plaisir de vous voir – *good evening, dear friend. how nice to see you*
  49 | 519-n +s

**3939 casque** *nm* helmet
- je suis la seule à porter un casque au travail – *I was the only one to wear a helmet at work*
  70 | 261

**3940 autrui** *pro* others
- vous ne pouvez pas les louer à autrui – *you're not allowed to rent them to others*
  71 | 242

**3941 bousculer** *v* to knock over, knock into
- je voulais bousculer les habitudes des gens – *I wanted to shake up people's habits*
  74 | 215

**3942 ériger** *v* to erect, set up
- Hitler avait érigé un vieux symbole hindou – *Hitler had erected an ancient Hindu symbol*
  78 | 177

**3943 conversion** *nf* conversion
- pouvez-vous expliquer votre notion de conversion psychique? – *can you explain your notion of psychic conversion?*
  58 | 398

**3944 patte** *nf* paw, foot, leg
- elles marchaient de côté avec des pattes de crabe – *they walked sideways crab-style*
  64 | 318

**3945 planifier** *v* to plan
- plus nous planifions longtemps d'avance, mieux c'est – *the longer ahead we plan, the better*
  72 | 231

**3946 transitoire** *adj(f)* transient, interim, provisional
- il y a installé l'administration transitoire – *there he set up the transitional administration*
  67 | 285

**3947 tardif** *adj* late
- je vous prie d'excuser mon arrivée tardive – *I beg you to excuse my late arrival*
  79 | 172

**3948 prédécesseur** *nm* predecessor
- il est substantiellement semblable à son prédécesseur – *he's largely similar to his predecessor*
  69 | 267

**3949 natal** *adj* native, home
- il voulait quitter sa ville natale – *he wanted to leave his hometown*
  74 | 212

**3950 humour** *nm* humour
- sans humour, tu ne survis pas – *without humor, you don't survive*
67 | 288

**3951 défaillance** *nf* fault, failure, breakdown, blackout, weakness
- je connaissais mes défaillances et je les regrettais – *I knew my shortcomings and I regretted them*
54 | 447+n -s

**3952 hélas** *intj* alas
- hélas, je ne pourrai pas – *alas, I won't be able to*
71 | 248

**3953 cabine** *nf* hut, cubicle, booth, box, room
- elle dort dans une cabine – *she's sleeping in a cabin*
62 | 348

**3954 fardeau** *nm* burden
- le gouvernement doit alléger le fardeau des entreprises – *the government must lighten the load of companies*
62 | 343+s

**3955 héritier** *nm* heir
- il n'a pas d'héritiers directs – *he has no direct heirs*
69 | 263

**3956 apport** *nm* supply, contribution
- cite-moi un seul apport positif de la technologie – *name me one positive contribution from technology*
70 | 252

**3957 remboursement** *nm* reimbursement
- s'ils veulent un remboursement, je le prendrais sur ta paye – *if they want reimbursement, I'll take it from your paycheck*
67 | 283

**3958 échelon** *nm* rung, step, grade, echelon
- j'ai tenté de grimper encore un échelon, pour lui échapper – *I tried to crawl up one more rung to escape him*
75 | 205

**3959 fondre** *v* to melt, merge
- quel pudding exquis, il fond dans la bouche – *what exquisite pudding—it melts in the mouth*
73 | 228

**3960 occurrence** *nf* instance, case, occurrence
- nous pourrions compter sur les doigts de la main les occurrences du mot – *we could count on the fingers of one hand the occurrences of the word*
67 | 281

**3961 authentique** *adj(f)* genuine, authentic
- mon objectif premier : rester authentique – *my main objective: to remain authentic*
78 | 172

**3962 attentivement** *adv* attentively, carefully, closely
- écoute-moi attentivement – *listen to me carefully*
65 | 307+s

**3963 irlandais** *nadj(pl)* Irish
- ma femme est d'origine irlandaise – *my wife is of Irish background*
59 | 372

**3964 confortable** *adj(f)* comfortable
- ce canapé n'est pas très confortable – *this sofa is not very comfortable*
78 | 175

**3965 au-dessous** *adv* underneath
- la température descend au-dessous de -40 – *the temperature is falling below –40*
57 | 396-s

**3966 fonctionnel** *adj* functional
- vous savez, tout est fonctionnel – *you know, everything works*
46 | 561+n -s

**3967 panne** *nf* breakdown, failure
- ton téléphone est en panne – *your telephone doesn't work*
68 | 274

**3968 adieu** *intj,nm* goodbye, farewell, adieu
- je ne t'aime plus. adieu – *I don't love you any more. farewell*
60 | 367-n

**3969 entre-temps** *adv,nm(pl)* meanwhile, in the meantime
- entre-temps, la population vieillit et augmente – *in the meantime the population is aging and increasing*
76 | 198

**3970 insérer** *v* to insert
- j'insère ma carte dans la machine – *I insert my card into the machine*
62 | 342

**3971 confrère** *nm* colleague
- mes confrères de classe ont bénéficié de ces bourses – *my classmates benefited from those scholarships*
74 | 217

**3972 litre** *nm,nf* litre
- il vient de boire deux litres de bière d'un coup – *he just drank two litres of beer in one sitting*
79 | 164

**3973 suivi** *nadj* follow-up; consistent, continuous
- il n'y a pas assez de suivi psychiatrique et sanitaire en prison – *there isn't enough psychiatric and sanitary follow-up in prison*
69 | 260

**3974 variation** *nf* variation, change
- les variations peuvent être compensées – *the variations can be compensated*
56 | 413+n -s

**3975 productif** *adj* productive
- j'essaie de rendre le gens les moins productifs que possible – *I try to make people the least productive possible*
69 | 267

**3976 groupement** *nm* grouping, group, categorization
- j'étais dans toutes sortes de groupements – *I was in all kinds of groups*
74 | 210

## 23  Verbs of communication

| | | |
|---|---|---|
| **dire** 37 to say | **annoncer** 521 to announce | **révéler** 810 to reveal |
| **demander** 80 to ask for | **interdire** 533 to forbid | **souligner** 816 to stress |
| **parler** 106 to speak | **noter** 541 to note | **promettre** 854 to promise |
| **entendre** 149 to hear | **convaincre** 575 to convince | **remarquer** 874 to remark |
| **appeler** 157 to call | **signifier** 586 to mean | **condamner** 878 to condemn |
| **répondre** 200 to answer | **indiquer** 590 to indicate | **justifier** 884 to justify |
| **poser** 218 to pose, ask | **nommer** 601 to call | **raconter** 890 to tell |
| **offrir** 224 to offer | **inviter** 624 to invite | **insister** 899 to insist |
| **expliquer** 252 to explain | **répéter** 630 to repeat | **définir** 916 to define |
| **refuser** 271 to efuse | **prouver** 635 to prove | **commander** 959 to command |
| **lire** 278 to read | **admettre** 680 to admit | **manifester** 968 to display |
| **représenter** 293 to represent | **affirmer** 686 to affirm | **autoriser** 989 to authorize |
| **assurer** 302 to assure | **prononcer** 706 to pronounce | **inscrire** 1004 to register, write down |
| **proposer** 338 to propose | **exiger** 733 to require | **confirmer** 1014 to confirm |
| **ajouter** 359 to add | **intervenir** 734 to intervene | **citer** 1082 to quote |
| **écrire** 382 to write | **discuter** 737 to discuss | **interroger** 1093 to question, interrogate |
| **défendre** 385 to forbid | **adresser** 744 to address | **impliquer** 1113 to imply, implicate |
| **souhaiter** 403 to wish | **préciser** 745 to clarify | **traduire** 1125 to translate |
| **écouter** 429 to isten to | **publier** 768 to publish | |
| **exprimer** 466 to express | **désigner** 790 to designate | |
| **déclarer** 503 to declare | **signer** 809 to sign | |

**3977 modernisation** *nf* modernization
- il va nous amener à poursuivre notre modernisation – *he's going to push us to pursue our modernization*
68 | 274

**3978 déploiement** *nm* deployment, spreading, unfurling, display
- il s'agirait du premier déploiement de missiles sol-air – *it would be the first deployment of surface-to-air missiles*
70 | 248

**3979 impuissant** *nadj* powerless, helpless
- la justice est complètement impuissante – *justice is completely powerless*
76 | 190

**3980 restauration** *nf* restoration; catering
- la restauration emploie beaucoup de jeunes – *catering employs many young people*
76 | 189

**3981 haïr** *v* to detest, hate, abhor
- j'ai toujours haï la campagne – *I always hated the countryside*
57 | 398-n

**3982 marée** *nf* tide
- c'est à marée haute qu'il faut venir – *you must come at high tide*
72 | 233

**3983 souscrire** *v* to subscribe
- elle ne souscrit pas complètement à nos principes – *she doesn't altogether subscribe to our principles*
63 | 329

**3984 diable** *intj,nm* devil
- vous croyez que je suis le diable? – *you think I'm the devil?*
62 | 335

**3985 suffrage** *nm* vote
- le suffrage est le court moment du souverain – *the popular vote is the beginning of the end for a monarch*
67 | 283

**3986 spontané** *adj* spontaneous
- sois spontanée pour une fois dans ta vie – *be spontaneous for once in your life*
69 | 264

**3987 joyeux** *nadj(pl)* merry, joyful, happy
- je ne regrette pas cette époque très joyeuse de ma vie – *I don't regret this very joyful time in my life*
62 | 337-n

**3988 concilier** *v* to reconcile
- j'arriverai à concilier plaisir et nécessité – *I managed to reconcile pleasure and duty*
76 | 194

**3989 tristesse** *nf* sadness, gloominess, dreariness
• je n'ai jamais pris leur tristesse au sérieux –
*I never took their sadness seriously*
62 | 333+l

**3990 asile** *nm* shelter, asylum, hospital
• ils veulent m'enfermer à l'asile! – *they want
to commit me to an asylum!*
70 | 247

**3991 sombrer** *v* to darken; to sink, lapse
• je sombrai dans le chaos – *I sank into
chaos*
75 | 199

**3992 photographe** *nm,nf* photographer
• je suis en quelque sorte son photographe
non officiel – *I'm somewhat of his unofficial
photographer*
68 | 269

**3993 libanais** *nadj(pl)* Lebanese
• mais nous, les Libanais, nous reviendrons –
*but we Lebanese, we will return*
55 | 428-l +n

**3994 archives** *nfpl* archives, records
• je suis allée aux archives – *I went to the
archives*
75 | 202

**3995 honteux** *adj(pl)* ashamed, shameful
• je trouve cela absolument honteux – *I find
that absolutely shameful*
71 | 241

**3996 rapporteur** *nadj* telltale, rapporteur
• je vous en informe comme rapporteur – *I'm
telling you this as a reporter*
41 | 628-l -n +s

**3997 dix-neuvième** *det,nm,nf* nineteenth
• la ville paraît sortie du dix-neuvième siècle
– *the city seemed to come straight out of the
nineteenth century*
67 | 282

**3998 indemnisation** *nf* indemnification,
compensation
• jamais une période d'indemnisation n'a été
aussi longue – *no period of compensation
has ever been this long*
55 | 416-l +s

**3999 harceler** *v* to harass, plague
• la police des mœurs harcèle encore les
jeunes – *the vice squad is still harassing the
youth*
87 | 97

**4000 leadership** *nm* leadership
• nous devons faire preuve de leadership
– *we must show leadership*
58 | 386+s

**4001 cahier** *nm* notebook
• d'accord, fermez les cahiers. commençons
cet examen – *OK, close your workbooks.
let's begin this exam*
65 | 300

**4002 portable** *adj(f),nm* portable, wearable;
cell phone
• j'achèterai un portable et je t'appellerai – *I'll
buy a cell phone and I'll call you*
70 | 244

**4003 précoce** *adj(f)* early, precocious
• nous favorisons la détection précoce et la
prévention – *we support early detection
and prevention*
81 | 149

**4004 qualification** *nf* qualification
• on n'a pas passé les qualifications – *we
didn't pass the qualifying exam*
61 | 344

**4005 insulte** *nf* insult
• je m'enfuis, poursuivie par ses insultes
– *I took off, pursued by her insults*
78 | 171

**4006 planer** *v* to glide, soar
• un grand oiseau planait – *a large bird was
soaring*
78 | 175

**4007 stage** *nm* internship, training course
• j'ai découvert la secte lors d'un stage d'été
en Slovénie – *I found the sect during a
summer internship in Slovenia*
70 | 247

**4008 dédier** *v* to dedicate
• ce livre est dédié à ma sœur qui est décédée
– *this book is dedicated to my sister who
passed away*
75 | 199

**4009 carrément** *adv* completely, directly, straight
out
• ici, on passe carrément par-dessus la tête
des syndicats – *here, frankly, we go over the
heads of the unions*
71 | 235+s

**4010 exil** *nm* exile
• elle mourut dans l'exil, dans la pauvreté –
*she died in exile, in poverty*
67 | 278

**4011 artisan** *nm* craftsman, self-employed
• nous sommes les artisans de notre propre
destin – *we are the captains of our own
destiny*
73 | 219

**4012 rassurant** *adj* reassuring, comforting
• c'est rassurant des bruits de cuisine
– *kitchen sounds are reassuring*
78 | 169

**4013 remède** *nm* cure, remedy
• leur herbier fournit des remèdes, des
tisanes – *the herbalist provides remedies,
herbal teas*
71 | 238

**4014 composant** *nadj* component, constituent
• c'est une organisation politique avec un
forte composante terroriste – *it's a political
organization with a strong terrorist component*
50 | 480+n -s

**4015 économiquement** *adv* economically
• ce sont des régions qui actuellement
explosent économiquement – *these are
regions that are currently exploding with
economic activity*
73 | 217

**4016 hurler** *v* to scream, yell
- tout le monde la cherchait, hurlait son prénom – *everyone was looking for her, yelling her name*
63 | 321

**4017 yen** *nm* yen
- par ailleurs, le yen doit être soutenu – *elsewhere, the yen must be shored up*
50 | 486-l +n -s

**4018 gras** *adj(pl),nm(pl)* fatty, fat, greasy
- il y a 20 % de matières grasses dedans – *it has a 20% fat content*
72 | 228

**4019 médiatique** *adj(f)* media
- c'est un coup médiatique incroyable pour cette compagnie-là – *it's an incredible public relations coup for that company*
59 | 373

**4020 statue** *nf* statue
- elevons une statue de moi – *let's erect a statue of me*
67 | 278+l

**4021 frappe** *nf* strike, striking, stamp, impression, punch
- les frappes aériennes ne vont résoudre aucun problème – *air strikes won't resolve any problems*
57 | 396

**4022 industrialiser** *v* to industrialize
- la France vend surtout aux principaux pays industrialisés – *France sells mostly to the principal industrialized countries*
67 | 278+n

**4023 efficacement** *adv* efficiently, effectively
- nous avons toujours travaillé efficacement ensemble – *we have always worked effectively together*
70 | 250

**4024 golfe** *nm* gulf
- les gens du Golfe sont très fiers – *the people of the Gulf are very proud*
61 | 341

**4025 ambiance** *nf* atmosphere, mood
- il y a une ambiance sympa dans cette ville – *there's a great atmosphere in this city*
68 | 264

**4026 coopérer** *v* to cooperate
- je pense qu'il va falloir coopérer – *I think we will have to cooperate*
70 | 249

**4027 bus** *nm(pl)* bus
- à Rome, nous avons pris le bus. un bus rouge – *in Rome, we took the bus. a red bus*
61 | 340

**4028 septième** *det,nm,nf* seventh
- le septième enfant est mort – *the seventh child died*
72 | 227

**4029 façade** *nf* front, façade
- la façade est formée par le massif – *the facade is formed by the massif*
63 | 321+l -s

**4030 charmant** *adj* charming
- c'était une femme tout à fait charmante – *she was an absolutely charming woman*
57 | 394-n

**4031 marginal** *nadj* marginal
- j'ai jamais pensé que j'étais marginal – *I never thought of myself as marginal*
73 | 217

**4032 comptable** *nadj(f)* accountant, accountable
- le fruit d'une froide évaluation comptable – *the fruit of passionless accounting evaluation*
68 | 270

**4033 isolement** *nm* loneliness, isolation, insulation
- vous avez été maintenu quatorze ans en isolement – *you were kept fourteen years in isolation*
73 | 221-s

**4034 modérer** *v* to restrain, moderate, reduce
- malheureusement la prudence ne modérait pas toujours les élans de son coeur – *sadly, prudence didn't always restrain the outbursts of her heart*
58 | 380+n -s

**4035 volant** *adj,nm* steering wheel
- vas-y, prends le volant – *go ahead, take hold of the steering wheel*
71 | 232

**4036 porc** *nm* pig, pork
- on a été manger des côtes de porc dans un bistro – *we went to eat pork ribs in a bistro*
75 | 194

**4037 appartenance** *nf* membership, belonging
- le sentiment d'appartenance doit être entretenu – *the sense of belonging must be maintained*
75 | 197

**4038 émeute** *nf* riot, rioting
- c'était le point zéro des émeutes de Los Angeles – *it was ground zero for the Los Angeles riots*
74 | 205

**4039 constructif** *adj* constructive
- trouvez une facon constructive de vous améliorer – *find a constructive way to improve yourself*
65 | 302+s

**4040 minime** *nadj(f)* minor, minimal
- beaucoup de ces différences sont minimes – *many of these differences are minimal*
84 | 118

**4041 ralentissement** *nm* slowing down
- l'économie japonaise est en net ralentissement – *the Japanese economy is clearly slowing down*
59 | 365+n -s

**4042 mobilisation** *nf* mobilization
- rapidement la mobilisation se construit dans la communauté éducative – *rapidly mobilization was established in the educational community*
60 | 352

**4043 tâcher** v to endeavor
- tâchez donc à faire plus simple – *so try to simplify*
  72 | 224

**4044 racisme** nm racism
- cette fausse image contribue au racisme – *this false image feeds racism*
  67 | 273

**4045 mairie** nf town hall, city hall
- ils se marièrent à la mairie – *they got married at the city hall*
  67 | 281

**4046 aptitude** nf ability
- ses aptitudes en mathématiques me désespèrent – *his aptitude for mathematics left me in despair*
  75 | 200

**4047 fumée** nf smoke
- on a senti des odeurs de fumée – *we smelled smoke*
  67 | 281-s

**4048 sauvetage** nm rescue, salvaging
- nos équipes de recherche et de sauvetage sont sur place – *our search and rescue teams are in place*
  70 | 241

**4049 récession** nf recession
- si on parle de récession, les gens n'achètent plus – *if there's talk of a recession, people will stop buying*
  54 | 421-l +n

**4050 convaincant** adj convincing
- tu as été convaincant à la télé aujourd'hui – *you were convincing on TV today*
  81 | 145

**4051 sou** nm penny
- ils étaient des réfugiés sans le sou – *they were refugees without a single penny*
  73 | 213

**4052 analyste** nm,nf analyst
- quand ces personnes sont elles-mêmes devenues analystes? – *when did these people become analysts too?*
  60 | 350+n

**4053 prétendu** nadj so-called, alleged
- il est impossible d'accepter cette prétendue réponse – *it's impossible to accept this so-called response*
  75 | 199

**4054 grossier** adj unrefined, crude, coarse, rude, rough
- excusez-moi. j'ai été grossier – *excuse me. I was rude*
  71 | 237

**4055 ignorance** nf ignorance
- tu m'as aimé par ignorance! – *you loved me out of ignorance!*
  68 | 262+l

**4056 pervers** nadj(pl) pervert, perverse, perverted
- vous aimez les trucs pervers, hein? – *you like perverted stuff, hey?*
  76 | 191

**4057 sensiblement** adv approximately, more or less, noticeably
- le gouvernement fédéral a réduit sensiblement sa contribution – *the federal government reduced its contribution sizably*
  63 | 321+n

**4058 léguer** v to bequeath, hand down, pass on
- il aurait dû me léguer la maison tout entière – *he should have bequeathed me the whole house*
  87 | 95

**4059 prélever** v to impose, levy, withdraw, remove
- l'argent est prélevé sur les chèques toutes les semaines – *money is debited against the checks every week*
  70 | 241

**4060 noyer** nm,v walnut; to drown, flood, blur, water down
- tous trois ont péri noyés, prisonniers du véhicule – *all three of them drowned, trapped in the vehicle*
  68 | 268

**4061 abbé** nm abbot, priest
- je vous présente M. l'abbé – *may I introduce the abbey*
  55 | 407+l -s

**4062 détecter** v to detect
- les fuites sont difficiles à détecter – *leaks are difficult to detect*
  56 | 403-l +n -s

**4063 capter** v to pick up, capture, tap
- puis ses yeux captèrent un mouvement – *then her eyes caught a motion*
  77 | 179

**4064 sceptique** nadj(f) sceptical, sceptic
- le monde scientifique reste en majorité sceptique – *the scientific world for the most part remains sceptical*
  81 | 146

**4065 vôtre** nadj(f) yours
- ça fera deux cafés, le vôtre et celui du monsieur – *that will be two coffees, yours and the gentleman's*
  68 | 261-n +s

**4066 problématique** nadj(f) problematic; problem
- quelle est la problématique environnementale principale? – *what is the principal environmental issue?*
  61 | 333+s

**4067 voiler** v to veil
- les femmes doivent se voiler – *women must wear a veil*
  69 | 251

**4068 nationalité** nf nationality
- il avait la possibilité de choisir la nationalité française – *he had the chance to choose French nationality*
  61 | 333

**4069 serment** nm oath, vow
- tu ne peux pas rompre un serment, c'est sacré – *you can't break an oath – it's sacred*
  72 | 225

**4070 envoler** *v* to fly away, fly off, take off
- son âme s'envolait, portée par les anges
  – *his soul flew away, carried by the angels*
  69 | 252

**4071 pasteur** *nm* minister, clergyman, pastor
- elle aime mieux le pasteur que le Jésuite
  – *she prefers the pastor to the Jesuit*
  73 | 216

**4072 activer** *v* to activate, speed up, stoke, get moving
- il faut activer votre réseau – *you have to activate your network*
  63 | 313

**4073 chimie** *nf* chemistry
- je ferais mieux d'étudier ma chimie – *I would do better to study my chemistry*
  65 | 292+n

**4074 erroné** *adj* erroneous
- cette idée est complètement erronée
  – *this idea is completely false*
  66 | 285

**4075 fantôme** *nm* ghost, phantom
- j'ai encore vu un fantôme dans ma maison
  – *I saw a ghost in my house again*
  63 | 311

**4076 naviguer** *v* to navigate, sail
- il naviguait sur Internet en quête de sujets scientifiques – *he surfed the Internet looking for science topics*
  84 | 114

**4077 yougoslave** *nadj(f)* Yugoslav, Yugoslavian
- la crise yougoslave gêne surtout leurs grands rivaux – *the Yugoslavian crisis bothers their major rivals the most*
  55 | 402-l +n

**4078 explicitement** *adv* explicitly
- se séparer explicitement de l'amour
  – *to separate oneself explicitly from love*
  76 | 186

**4079 alerter** *v* to alert, inform, warn
- il ne faudrait pas alerter la population
  – *we shouldn't alert the population*
  75 | 191

**4080 vigilance** *nf* vigilance, watchfulness
- le pinot demande une vigilance constante
  – *pinot demands constant vigilance*
  76 | 188

**4081 rock** *nm* rock music
- j'avais souhaité parler du rock de mon adolescence – *I wanted to talk about the rock of my teenage years*
  61 | 338+s

**4082 réconciliation** *nf* reconciliation
- une Europe unie a besoin de cette réconciliation – *a unified Europe needs this reconciliation*
  68 | 263

**4083 revers** *nm(pl)* back, reverse, setback
- il y a le revers de la médaille – *there is the other side of the coin*
  76 | 185

**4084 aviation** *nf* aviation
- l'aviation israélienne avait mené une série de raids – *the Israeli air force carried out a series of raids*
  67 | 275

**4085 souplesse** *nf* suppleness, flexibility
- je préfère la souplesse d'âme à la souplesse de peau – *I prefer a gentle soul to soft skin*
  68 | 264

**4086 respectueux** *adj(pl)* respectful
- il est extrêmement respectueux avec les gens – *he is extremely respectful of people*
  77 | 172

**4087 trahison** *nf* betrayal, treachery, treason
- c'était rien, juste une petite trahison – *it was nothing, just a little bit of treason*
  75 | 197

**4088 débit** *nm* debit, turnover, delivery, rate
- le débit était aussi rapide qu'avant – *turnover was as rapid as it was previously*
  54 | 422+n -s

**4089 sursis** *nm(pl)* reprieve, deferment
- une peine d'emprisonnement avec sursis ne suffirait pas – *jail time with remission of sentence would not be enough*
  57 | 383

**4090 simultanément** *adv* simultaneously
- je répondrai donc aux deux questions simultanément – *so I will answer both questions at the same time*
  66 | 278

**4091 techniquement** *adv* technically
- je ne te connais pas ... techniquement
  – *I don't know you ... technically*
  82 | 129

**4092 os** *nm(pl)* bone
- je jette un os à un chien – *I toss a bone to a dog*
  59 | 361+l

**4093 cote** *nf* rating, share index, quoted value
- l'or a dépassé la cote des $ 380 – *gold rose above a quoted value of $380*
  75 | 190

**4094 dictionnaire** *nm* dictionary
- nous avons développé un dictionnaire assez élaboré – *we have developed quite an elaborate dictionary*
  66 | 277

**4095 symptôme** *nm* symptom
- les symptômes se sont nettement aggravés
  – *the symptoms got much worse*
  74 | 198

**4096 délibérément** *adv* deliberately
- il marcha délibérément vers la porte – *he strode deliberately towards the door*
  80 | 153

**4097 écoute** *nf* listening
- il faut se tenir à l'écoute de tout ce qui se passe – *you have to keep informed about everything that happens*
  63 | 310

**4098 contingent** *nadj* contingent, draft, quota
• c'est le plus fort contingent d'étudiants étrangers – *that's the strongest contingent of foreign students*
73 | 208

**4099 émerger** *v* to emerge, rise up, come out
• cette façon de penser émerge presque partout – *this kind of thinking is emerging almost everywhere*
66 | 277

**4100 instruire** *v* to teach, educate, inform
• ils sauront l'instruire sur leurs anciennes pratiques – *they know how to teach him their ancient practices*
68 | 264

**4101 équité** *nf* equity, fairly
• il faudra renforcer l'équité en matière d'emploi – *it will be necessary to strengthen equity in the workplace*
49 | 483-n +s

**4102 inconscient** *nadj* unconscious, thoughtless
• après cela, je suis resté inconscient pendant 24 heures – *afterwards, I was unconscious for 24 hours*
69 | 248

**4103 chaleureux** *adj(pl)* warm
• c'était quand même un accueil très chaleureux – *yet it was a very warm welcome*
82 | 133

**4104 déguiser** *v* to disguise
• je me déguise en quelqu'un d'autre – *I'm disguised as somebody else*
75 | 191

**4105 fièvre** *nf* fever
• vous êtes brûlante de fièvre – *you're burning up with fever*
64 | 304+l -s

**4106 vitre** *nf* pane, window
• derrière la vitre, il l'observait, il la jugeait – *from behind the windowpane he watched her, he judged her*
60 | 345+l -s

**4107 fantastique** *nadj(f)* fantastic, terrific, great, weird, eerie
• ils ont fait un travail fantastique – *they did a fantastic job*
65 | 288+s

**4108 courbe** *nadj(f)* curve, curved
• la courbe qu'il spécifie est une spirale – *the curve that it describes is a spiral*
59 | 357-s

**4109 soustraire** *v* to substract, remove, shield, escape from
• nul homme ne peut se soustraire au terme de sa vie – *no man can escape from the endpoint of his life*
73 | 206

**4110 instable** *adj(f)* unstable
• je regardai avec effroi ces êtres instables – *I watched with fear these unstable beings*
75 | 188

**4111 vapeur** *nm,nf* vapor, steam, steamship
• j'aperçus au loin une vapeur bleuâtre – *I noticed a blueish vapor in the distance*
74 | 199

**4112 beurre** *nm* butter
• j'aurais appris à faire du beurre, du fromage – *I would have learned to make butter and cheese*
75 | 191

**4113 monument** *nm* monument
• ce devait être un monument aux morts – *it must have been a monument to the dead*
70 | 237

**4114 oral** *nadj* oral
• ces histoires constituent le folklore oral moderne – *these stories comprise modern oral folklore*
61 | 327+s

**4115 téléviser** *v* to televise
• la concurrence des journaux télévisés est indéniable – *competition among TV newscasts is undeniable*
68 | 256

**4116 consolider** *v* to strengthen, reinforce
• la société consolide sa position en matière de propriété intellectuelle – *the company is solidifying its position on intellectual property*
62 | 318

**4117 muet** *nadj* mute, silent, dumb
• j'ai un fils aussi muet qu'une carpe – *I have a son as mute as a carp*
65 | 290+l

**4118 contrevenant** *nadj* offender, offending
• cela évite au contrevenant d'aller en prison – *this prevents the offender from having to go to prison*
44 | 553-l -n +s

**4119 offensive** *nf* offensive, offence
• la seule défense est une bonne offensive – *the only defence is a good offence*
57 | 380+n -s

**4120 routine** *nf* routine
• les routines, très vite, reprirent leurs droits – *routines quickly gained the upper hand*
78 | 161

**4121 coder** *v* to code, encode
• chaque langue code une culture déterminée – *each language encodes a particular culture*
49 | 483-l +n -s

**4122 gel** *nm* frost, freezing, gel
• ils ont besoin d'un gel des frais de scolarité – *they need a freeze in tuition*
72 | 220

**4123 rénovation** *nf* renovation, restoration
• les travaux de transformation et de rénovation iront également bon train – *transformation and renovation work will proceed together at a good pace*
80 | 145

**4124 controverse** *nf* controversy
• il y a beaucoup de controverses au sujet des châtiments corporels – *there are many controversies about corporal punishment*
71 | 230

**4125 médiocre** *nadj(f)* mediocre, second-rate
• pire encore, il est médiocre et inefficace –
*even worse, he is mediocre and inefficient*
73 | 204

**4126 filial** *adj* filial; branch office
• il fallait créer une entreprise filiale – *it was
necessary to create a subsidiary company*
57 | 370+n -s

**4127 relais** *nm(pl)* shift, relay
• les paroles avaient pris le relais de ses larmes
– *words took over from his tears*
61 | 326+n -s

**4128 opposant** *nadj* opponent, opposing
• mais les opposants sont sceptiques – *but
the opponents are sceptical*
57 | 376-l

**4129 aval** *nm* downstream, downhill
• on parle des avantages en aval – *we're
talking about downstream benefits*
70 | 232

**4130 rubrique** *nf* column, heading, rubric
• l'émission propose également de
nombreuses rubriques – *the broadcast
also offers several categories*
69 | 246

**4131 préfet** *nm* prefect
• le préfet ne fera rien pour nous – *the police
commissioner will do nothing for us*
64 | 294

**4132 provocation** *nf* provocation
• c'est de la provocation indue, non
souhaitable et injustifiée – *it's undeserved,
undesirable and unjustified provocation*
78 | 161

**4133 sommaire** *nadj(f)* summary, brief, cursory
• l'examen est certes assez sommaire – *the
examination is certainly rather cursory*
73 | 211

**4134 versant** *nm* hillside, mountainside
• voilà succinctement résumé un versant de
sa nature – *there, briefly put, is one side of
his nature*
45 | 535+n -s

**4135 réticence** *nf* reluctance, hesitation
• je ne ressens pas de réticence de la part
des auteurs français – *I don't sense any
reluctance on behalf of French authors*
77 | 169

**4136 grossesse** *nf* pregnancy
• elle m'avait annoncé sa grossesse – *she told
me she was pregnant*
76 | 177

**4137 égyptien** *nadj* Egyptian
• nous avons mangé de la cuisine égyptienne
– *we ate Egyptian food*
54 | 403+n

**4138 timbre** *nm* to stamp
• je regarde un peu mes timbres – *I'm just
looking over my stamps*
74 | 197

**4139 découper** *v* to carve, cut,
• je ne découpe pas les articles – *I don't cut
out articles*
74 | 194

**4140 distributeur** *nadj* distributor, machine
• les distributeurs quittaient la salle en
courant – *the distributors ran out of the
room*
72 | 218

**4141 élargissement** *nm* widening, letting-out,
stretching, broadening
• il n'y aura pas d'élargissement de la
Communauté – *there will be no expansion
of the Community*
57 | 372

**4142 dégrader** *v* to degrade, debase, damage,
erode
• la situation se dégrade depuis 1984
– *the situation has been worsening since
1984*
73 | 203

**4143 colonial** *nadj* colonial
• la Suisse n'a pas de passé colonial –
*Switzerland has no colonial history*
69 | 247

**4144 pourparler** *nm* talk, discussion, negotiation
• on va bientôt participer à ces pourparlers
– *we'll soon participate in these
discussions*
60 | 336+n -s

**4145 incidence** *nf* effect, incidence
• les catastrophes ont des incidences
économiques importantes – *catastrophes
cause important economic consequences*
58 | 357

**4146 béton** *nm* concrete
• les murs étaient en béton – *the walls were of
cement*
82 | 128

**4147 fiable** *adj(f)* reliable, trustworthy
• elle est très fiable, croyez-moi – *she's very
trustworthy, believe me*
74 | 197

**4148 génocide** *nm* genocide
• il est également accusé de génocide – *he is
also accused of genocide*
61 | 330-l

**4149 vingt-quatre** *det,nmi* twenty four
• Air France propose toujours vingt-quatre
vols quotidiens – *Air France still offers
24 daily flights*
55 | 393

**4150 épouvantable** *adj(f)* terrible, appalling,
dreadful
• c'est un épouvantable malentendu – *it's a
horrible misunderstanding*
78 | 158

**4151 indifférent** *nadj* indifferent, unconcerned,
unimportant
• apparemment, je lui suis complètement
indifférente – *apparently, I'm completely
unimportant to him*
65 | 280+l

**4152 audacieux** *nadj(pl)* daring, audacious, bold
• il est temps de prendre des décisions
audacieuses – *it's time to make bold
decisions*
80 | 144

## 24  Use of the pronoun "se"

The third person pronoun "se" in French has several different functions: reflexives (*il se voit dans le miroir* "he sees himself in the mirror"), reciprocals (*ils se battent* "they fight each other"), subjectives or expletives (*elle se moque de lui* "she makes fun of him"), and passives or middles (*le fromage se mange* "cheese is eaten").

The following list illustrates how some verbs interact with "se" and its variant "s'". It shows how frequently verbs from the top 5,000 words of this dictionary pattern with this pronoun. The number after each verb shows that verb's ranking in the dictionary, and the number before the verb shows what percentage of that verb's occurrences involve the pronoun. Because some verb instances involve other persons besides the third person, the total percentage of occurrences for all persons for these verbs is likely around 20% higher than the number shown here.

| | | | |
|---|---|---|---|
| 0.99 **ensuivre** 4958 **to result** | | 0.65 **empresser** 4943 **to hasten** | |
| 0.92 **emparer** 2788 **to snatch away** | | 0.64 **borner** 4586 **to limit** | |
| 0.88 **dérouler** 1438 **to unwind** | | 0.64 **épanouir** 4735 **to blossom** | |
| 0.88 **écrier** 4880 **to cry out** | | 0.62 **replier** 4267 **to fold up** | |
| 0.86 **apprêter** 3135 **to prepare** | | 0.61 **moquer** 3344 **to make fun of** | |
| 0.83 **avérer** 2462 **to prove to be** | | 0.61 **pencher** 1798 **to lean** | |
| 0.81 **effondrer** 3134 **to collapse** | | 0.59 **propager** 3876 **to propagate** | |
| 0.8 **envoler** 4081 **to fly away** | | 0.58 **plaindre** 1372 **to complain** | |
| 0.75 **efforcer** 2044 **to strive** | | 0.56 **heurter** 2606 **to collide** | |
| 0.73 **conformer** 3391 **to conform** | | 0.55 **redresser** 3378 **to straighten** | |
| 0.72 **contenter** 1079 **to be content** | | 0.54 **référer** 3276 **to refer** | |
| 0.72 **enfuir** 3813 **to flee** | | 0.52 **débrouiller** 3628 **to get by** | |
| 0.71 **soucier** 2828 **to worry** | | 0.52 **incliner** 4380 **to tilt** | |
| 0.70 **agir** 212 **to pertain** | | 0.51 **dégrader** 4152 **to degrade** | |
| 0.68 **abstenir** 3703 **to abstain** | | 0.49 **acquitter** 3233 **to discharge** | |

**4153 poudre** *nf* powder
• ta copine a besoin de sa poudre magique – *your girlfriend needs her magic powder*
75 | 184

**4154 teneur** *nf* content
• il n'a révélé la teneur exacte de sa conversation – *he didn't reveal the exact content of his conversation*
75 | 185

**4155 inverser** *v* to reverse, invert
• l'infirmière s'est trompée. elle a tout inversé – *the nurse was wrong. she got everything backwards*
74 | 196

**4156 naval** *adj* naval
• les chantiers navals fonctionnaient à plein rendement – *the naval shipyards were operating at full capacity*
66 | 274

**4157 dérive** *nf* drift
• j'imagine mal cependant des dérives extrémistes – *I have a hard time imagining extremist tendencies*
73 | 206

**4158 mécontent** *nadj* discontented, dissatisfied, displeased
• je regrette que vous soyez mécontent mais je ne puis rien y faire – *I'm sorry you're displeased but I can no longer do anything about it*
79 | 150

**4159 vocabulaire** *nm* vocabulary
• ce n'est pas dans mon vocabulaire – *it's not in my vocabulary*
71 | 219

**4160 stabiliser** *v* to stabilize
• stabilisez vos déflecteurs arrière – *tighten your rear deflectors*
72 | 212

**4161 délégué** *nadj* delegate
• les délégués de 190 pays se sont retrouvés samedi – *delegates from 190 countries met Saturday*
63 | 301

**4162 centrer** *v* to center
• je centrerai mon intervention sur quatre points précis – *I will center my talk on four specific points*
74 | 198

**4163 algérien** *nadj* Algerian
- je ne suis ni français ni algérien – *I'm neither French nor Algerian*
56 | 376

**4164 sympathique** *nadj(f)* likeable, nice, pleasant
- je vous trouve incroyablement sympathiques – *I find you incredibly likable*
72 | 214

**4165 alentour** *adv* around, round about
- il n'y avait personne aux alentours immédiats – *there was nobody in the immediate vicinity*
73 | 200

**4166 corrompre** *v* to corrupt, bribe
- le régime actuel me semble absolument corrompu – *the current regime seems absolutely corrupt to me*
77 | 169

**4167 commerçant** *nadj* shopkeeper, merchant, commercial
- c'était plein de petits commerçants, d'artisans – *it was full of shopkeepers, artisans*
71 | 227

**4168 poitrine** *nf* chest, breast, breasts, bosom
- ils avaient mal dans la poitrine, aux oreilles et à la tête – *they had sore chests, ears, and heads*
55 | 396+l -n -s

**4169 couronner** *v* to crown, award
- ces rencontres ont vraiment été couronnées de succès – *these meetings were crowned with success*
76 | 174

**4170 relire** *v* to reread, proofread
- il relisait, corrigeait et reprenait le travail du jour – *he reread, corrected, and reviewed the day's work*
63 | 303-n

**4171 perpétuer** *v* to perpetuate, carry on
- ces traditions se perpétuent au Moyen Âge – *these traditions continue through in the Middle Ages*
76 | 176

**4172 doctrine** *nf* doctrine
- il a enseigné des doctrines trompeuses et répugnantes – *he taught deceitful and loathsome doctrine*
62 | 306-s

**4173 compétitif** *adj* competitive
- l'industrie automobile européenne peut être compétitive – *the European auto industry can be competitive*
69 | 241

**4174 majesté** *nf* majesty
- sa majesté le roi a été salué à son départ – *his majesty the king was saluted on his departure*
56 | 377-n +s

**4175 mouton** *nadj* sheep
- les moutons commençaient à se désin-téresser de moi – *the sheep stopped showing interest in me*
67 | 262

**4176 indifférence** *nf* indifference
- je dois subir avec indifférence les conséquences – *I must suffer the consequences unflinchingly*
63 | 299+l -s

**4177 omettre** *v* to leave out, miss out, omit
- je n'y omettrai rien – *I won't leave anything out*
80 | 147

**4178 typique** *nadj(f),nf* typical
- c'est typique. cela ne m'étonne pas – *it's typical. that doesn't surprise me*
69 | 242

**4179 concurrentiel** *adj* competitive
- divers éléments nous procurent cet avantage concurrentiel – *many factors bring us this competitive advantage*
70 | 228

**4180 désarmement** *nm* disarmament, disarming
- j'ai besoin des codes de désarmement – *I need the deactivation codes*
60 | 335

**4181 quotidiennement** *adv* daily, every day
- les gangs font la manchette presque quotidiennement – *gangs make the headlines almost every day*
74 | 198

**4182 architecture** *nf* architecture
- l'architecture doit beaucoup aux Arabes – *architecture owes much to the Arabs*
68 | 249

**4183 éventualité** *nf* eventuality, possibility
- je suis prêt à toute éventualité – *I'm ready for any eventuality*
77 | 167

**4184 massacrer** *v* to slaughter, massacre
- ils massacraient des indigènes – *they massacred some natives*
73 | 203

**4185 réciproque** *nadj(f)* mutual, reciprocal, the opposite
- j'ai proposé des retraits réciproques dans tous les arrondissements – *I proposed a mutual withdrawal in all of the neighborhoods*
76 | 173

**4186 état-major** *nm* staff, staff headquarters
- l'état-major entendait écraser la résistance tchétchène – *headquarters intended to crush the Chechen resistance*
64 | 291

**4187 attarder** *v* to linger
- je m'attardais longtemps à ma fenêtre – *I lingered a long while at my window*
73 | 201

**4188 englober** *v* to include, encompass, incorporate
- mon goût englobe les escargots et les huîtres – *my tastes incorporate escargots and oysters*
76 | 179

**4189 grossir** *v* to get larger
• son ventre grossissait – *her stomach got larger*
82 | 130

**4190 séparatiste** *nadj(f)* separatist
• cette démarche pourrait désamorcer les visées séparatistes – *this approach could defuse separatist aims*
53 | 408-l

**4191 surcroît** *nm* extra, additional
• la motivation financière venait de surcroît – *financial motivation appeared excessive*
68 | 252

**4192 sortant** *nadj* outgoing
• l'administration américaine sortante se révélant incapable de négocier – *the outgoing American administration proved incapable of negotiation*
55 | 389+n -s

**4193 plomb** *nm* lead
• le plomb ordinaire serait trop lourd pour le véhicule – *ordinary lead would be too heavy for the vehicle*
73 | 201

**4194 gorge** *nf* throat
• elle porte la main à sa gorge – *she brings her hand to her throat*
57 | 363+l -n

**4195 nationaliste** *nadj(f)* nationalist
• qu'est-ce qu'on veut comme nationalistes? – *what do we nationalists want?*
57 | 362+n

**4196 exportateur** *nadj* exportateur, exporting
• tous les pays exportateurs profitent de la situation – *all exporting countries are benefiting from the situation*
65 | 274

**4197 montre** *nf* watch
• c'est une vraie course contre la montre – *is a real race against time*
68 | 252

**4198 ratifier** *v* to ratify
• le texte doit désormais être ratifié – *the text must henceforth be ratified*
64 | 283

**4199 exploit** *nm* exploit
• peu de grands exploits s'accomplissent seuls – *few great exploits are accomplished by oneself*
78 | 156

**4200 encourageant** *adj* encouraging
• la situation ne semble guère encourageante – *the situation seems hardly encouraging*
77 | 170

**4201 climatique** *adj(f)* climatic
• les gens parlent du changement climatique, du réchauffement de la planète – *people talk of climate change, of global warming*
68 | 252-l

**4 202 aviser** *v* to notice, advise
• tu aurais dû nous en aviser – *you should have told us about it*
72 | 207

**4203 épidémie** *nf* epidemic
• l'épidémie de SIDA en Afrique est au pire – *the AIDS epidemic in Africa is the worst*
62 | 304

**4204 alarme** *nf* alarm
• que se passe-t-il? l'alarme s'est déclenchée – *what's happening? the alarm just went off*
60 | 325

**4205 parier** *v* to bet
• j'espère que tu n'as pas parié beaucoup – *I hope you didn't bet a lot*
58 | 351+s

**4206 écologique** *adj(f)* ecological
• je crois en la conscience écologique des Français – *I believe in the ecological conscience of the French*
63 | 301-l

**4207 lunette** *nf* telescope, glasses
• portez-vous des lunettes ou verres de contact? – *do you wear glasses or contact lenses?*
60 | 333+l

**4208 entourage** *nm* circle, entourage
• mon entourage m'encourage à profiter de la vie – *my circle of friends encourages me to take advantage of life*
67 | 253

**4209 sphère** *nf* sphere
• on quittait les sphères du sacré pour entrer dans la politique – *we left more sacred spheres to go into politics*
69 | 241

**4210 confidentiel** *adj* confidential
• soyez attentif, ce message est confidentiel – *be careful, this message is confidential*
73 | 198+s

**4211 sanctionner** *v* to sanction, punish, approve
• la décision a été sanctionnée par le secrétaire général des Nations Unies – *the decision was endorsed by the Secretary General of the United Nations*
70 | 225

**4212 recrutement** *nm* recruiting, recruitment
• j'ai déclaré un gel du recrutement – *I declared a hiring freeze*
64 | 282

**4213 détendre** *v* to release, slacken, loosen, relax
• entrez, détendez-vous. prenez un verre de champagne – *come in, relax. have a glass of champagne*
65 | 280

**4214 aisé** *adj* easy, well off, well-to-do
• beaucoup venaient de familles aisées – *many came from well-to-do families*
77 | 167

**4215 toilette** *nf* washing, toilet, lavatory, bathroom, restroom
• excusez-moi, je cherchais les toilettes – *excuse me, I was looking for the restrooms*
58 | 345

**4216 autobus** *nm(pl)*  bus
- je préférais l'autobus au métro – *I preferred the bus to the subway*
74 | 190

**4217 défavoriser** *v*  to put at a disadvantage
- il avait à cœur le sort des défavorisés – *he dwelled on the lot of the underprivileged*
73 | 204

**4218 résistant** *nadj*  robust, sturdy, resistance fighter
- les bactéries résistantes disparaissent en quelques jours – *resistant bacteria will disappear in a few days*
73 | 200

**4219 admiration** *nf*  admiration
- j'ai de l'admiration pour cet homme – *I have admiration for this man*
68 | 246+l

**4220 acide** *nadj(f)*  acid
- j'ai dissous le sang à l'acide – *I dissolved the blood with acid*
76 | 177

**4221 banal** *adj*  banal, trite, commonplace, ordinary
- la situation est devenue presque banale – *the situation has almost become commonplace*
69 | 240

**4222 poulet** *nm*  chicken
- il y a du poulet dans le frigo – *there's some chicken in the fridge*
68 | 245

**4223 pêcher** *nm,v*  to fish, go fishing; peach tree
- on pêchera des tonnes de crevettes! – *we'll go fishing and catch tons of shrimps!*
74 | 193

**4224 brigade** *nf*  team, squad, brigade
- une brigade de policiers a réussi à rattraper les chiens – *the squad of policemen succeeded in catching the dogs*
63 | 298

**4225 trembler** *v*  to shiver, tremble, shake, flicker
- il sourit toujours, ses joues tremblent – *he always smiles, cheeks trembling*
56 | 373+l -n -s

**4226 reçu** *nm*  receipt, accepted
- il ne voulait pas me faire un reçu – *he didn't want to give me a receipt*
63 | 292

**4227 civiliser** *v*  to civilze
- ce sont des nations civilisées – *these are civilized nations*
80 | 139

**4228 relance** *nf*  boost, reminder, recovery
- la relance économique commence à se faire sentir – *the economic recovery is starting to be felt*
62 | 307-l

**4229 dose** *nf*  dose, amount
- vous avez mal calculé la dose – *you miscalculated the dose*
70 | 227

**4230 loyer** *nm*  rent
- je n'ai pas payé le loyer du mois prochain – *I haven't paid next month's rent*
61 | 312+n

**4231 distorsion** *nf*  distortion
- la distorsion peut réduire la durée de cet intervalle – *the distortion can reduce the duration of that interval*
45 | 506+n -s

**4232 octroyer** *v*  to grant, bestow
- on continue à octroyer des brevets pour des séquences – *we continue to grant patents for sequences*
67 | 254

**4233 arrivant** *nm*  arrival, comer
- il y a un nouvel arrivant dans le jeu – *there's a newcomer in the game*
86 | 94

**4234 standard** *adji,nm*  standard, switchboard
- vos cartes sont de type standard? – *your cards are the standard type?*
67 | 256

**4235 taxi** *nm*  taxi
- je vais rentrer en taxi – *I'm going to take a taxi home*
62 | 304

**4236 limitation** *nf*  limitation, restriction, limit
- il y a des limitations d'âge – *there are age limitations*
65 | 274

**4237 irréversible** *adj(f)*  irreversible
- beaucoup de processus sont probablement déjà irréversibles – *many processes are probably already irreversible*
76 | 175

**4238 fatal** *adj*  fatal, deadly, fateful
- une maladie du foie fatale – *a fatal liver disease*
72 | 204

**4239 furieux** *nadj(pl)*  furious, raging, violent
- il est furieux contre moi – *he's furious with me*
65 | 274

**4240 verbal** *adj*  verbal
- on ne parle que de beauté verbale – *we only speak of verbal beauty*
68 | 244

**4241 contacter** *v*  to contact, get in touch with
- comment puis-je vous contacter? – *how can I contact you?*
63 | 292

**4242 commissariat** *nm*  police station
- le commissariat local a été chargé de l'enquête – *the local police station was given charge of the investigation*
67 | 253

**4243 gai** *adj*  cheerful, merry, gay
- nous étions si beaux, si gais – *we were so beautiful, so cheerful*
60 | 327+l -n

**4244 confrontation** *nf* confrontation
- comprendre n'est possible qu'après la confrontation – *understanding is only possible after confrontation*
68 | 245

**4245 chier** *v* to sh\*t, piss off, get pissed off
- elle pissait et chiait partout – *she pissed and crapped everywhere*
56 | 363-n +s

**4246 atlantique** *nadj(f)* Atlantic
- j'habite dans le Canada atlantique – *I live in Atlantic Canada*
59 | 333

**4247 rude** *nadj(f)* rough, harsh, hard, tough
- l'hiver fut rude. il fut malade deux fois – *the winter was severe. he was sick twice*
72 | 210

**4248 panneau** *nm* sign, notice, panel
- ils ont fini d'installer les gigantesques panneaux solaires – *they finished installing giant solar panels*
73 | 200

**4249 appréciation** *nf* appreciation, assessment, appraisal
- les courses à ski exigent une appréciation réfléchie du terrain – *ski races require thoughtful assessment of the terrain*
68 | 246

**4250 réflexe** *nadj(f)* reflex
- j'ai gardé des réflexes comme me laver à l'eau froide – *I kept old habits like washing in cold water*
77 | 160

**4251 complément** *nm* complement
- c'était un complément qui lui permettait de vivre – *it was supplementary information that allowed her to live*
56 | 368+n -s

**4252 initialement** *adv* initially
- initialement, cette opération devait être amicale – *at first, this operation was supposed to be friendly*
66 | 265+n

**4253 comédien** *nadj* comedian, comedy
- j'ai pensé au métier de comédien – *I thought about the comedian's craft*
60 | 322

**4254 successeur** *nm* successor
- mon successeur sera comme un lion furieux – *my successor will be like a ferocious lion*
68 | 242

**4255 méfiance** *nf* distrust, mistrust, suspicion
- il refusait les médicaments toujours par méfiance – *he always refused the medication because of distrust*
72 | 204

**4256 replier** *v* to fold, roll up, fold up, withdraw
- je repliai la lettre – *I folded up the letter*
73 | 196

**4257 vérificateur** *nadj* checker, inspector, auditor
- le vérificateur général a lui-même porté ce jugement – *the auditor general himself made this evaluation*
46 | 492-l -n +s

**4258 dictateur** *nm* dictator
- comment négocier avec un dictateur pareil? – *how can you negotiate with a dictator like that?*
63 | 288

**4259 prétention** *nf* claim
- toute prétention contraire n'est absolument pas fondée – *all claims to the contrary are absolutely unfounded*
72 | 210

**4260 rédacteur** *nm* editor, writer, drafter, compiler
- j'ai d'abord été journaliste rédacteur pour la presse – *first I was an editorial journalist for the press*
73 | 197

**4261 avaler** *v* to swallow
- il a avalé un peu trop d'eau – *he swallowed a little too much water*
62 | 302

**4262 extraction** *nf* extraction
- ce projet d'extraction minière constitue une agréable occasion de développement – *this mineral extraction project constitutes a nice development opportunity*
80 | 142

**4263 banquier** *nm* banker
- tu feras confiance à un banquier des Bahamas? – *you would trust a banker from the Bahamas?*
75 | 178

**4264 titulaire** *nadj(f)* holder, with tenure, occupant
- oui, vous êtes le titulaire – *yes, you're the incumbent*
66 | 256

**4265 stabilisation** *nf* stabilisation
- la stabilisation du fonds est primordiale – *stabilizing the funds is all-important*
71 | 218

**4266 mutuellement** *adv* mutually, one another
- ils se sont traités mutuellement de criminels de guerre – *they treated each other like wartime criminals*
83 | 112

**4267 légion** *nf* legion
- la légion remplit vaillamment sa mission – *the legion valiantly fulfilled its mission*
77 | 166

**4268 lacune** *nf* gap, deficiency
- il y a une lacune énorme dans la formation – *there's a huge gap in training*
63 | 288+s

**4269 engin** *nm* machine, tool, vehicle, device
- l'engin était dissimulé dans une poubelle et a explosé – *the device was concealed in a trash can and exploded*
67 | 248

**4270 mépriser** *v* to scorn, look down, spurn, disdain
- il méprise l'art et les musées – *he disdains art and museums*
60 | 315+l

**4271 minoritaire** *nadj(f)* minority
- ces gens appartiennent à un groupe minoritaire – *these people belong to a minority group*
67 | 253

**4272 idéologique** *adj(f)* ideological
- il faut cesser ce discours idéologique – *this ideological discussion must cease*
61 | 313

**4273 cloche** *nf* bell
- on ententit sonner la cloche de l'église – *we heard the church bells chiming*
70 | 218

**4274 compatriote** *nm,nf* compatriot
- comme beaucoup de mes compatriotes, j'ai eu l'occasion de voyager – *like many of my compatriots, I had the chance to travel*
63 | 291

**4275 affection** *nf* affection, ailment
- l'affection grandit par l'épreuve – *affection grows through difficulties*
65 | 265+l -s

**4276 sel** *nm* salt
- il devait faire un régime sans sel – *he had to go on a no-salt diet*
70 | 220

**4277 majoritaire** *adj(f)* majority
- la France utilise le système majoritaire dans ses élections nationales – *France uses the majority system in national elections*
66 | 258-l

**4278 redressement** *nm* straightening up, upturn, righting
- le redressement d'Air France est un impératif – *straightening out Air France is an urgent necessity*
65 | 269+n -s

**4279 paradoxe** *nm* paradox
- nous sommes toujours en présence du paradoxe de la transgression divine – *we're all a part of the paradox of divine transgression*
65 | 271

**4280 chiffrer** *v* to put a figure to, assess, quantify, number
- tout ça est chiffré à chaque fois par les ministères – *all of this is quantified each time by the ministers*
75 | 178

**4281 catastrophique** *adj(f)* catastrophic, disastrous
- on a hérité d'une situation catastrophique – *we inherited a catastrophic situation*
73 | 197

**4282 magistrat** *nm* magistrate, judge
- son père était un magistrat de la cour d'assises – *his father was a judge in the assize court*
61 | 311-s

**4283 extrait** *nm* extract, excerpt
- ce qui suit est un extrait du rapport – *what follows is an excerpt from the report*
71 | 213

**4284 amant** *nm* lover
- elle était folle de son amant – *she was crazy about her lover*
58 | 344+l -n

**4285 farce** *nf* joke, prank, hoax, farce
- c'est une vraie farce et c'est honteux – *it's a real hoax and it's shameful*
84 | 106

**4286 compétitivité** *nf* competitiveness
- nous avons décidé d'accroître la compétitivité et l'efficacité de nos industries – *we decided to increase the competitiveness and the efficiency of our industries*
58 | 337-l

**4287 enthousiaste** *adj(f)* enthusiastic
- ils m'ont accordé un appui enthousiaste – *they gave me enthusiastic support*
79 | 143

**4288 quarantaine** *nf* about forty
- une quarantaine de filles nous attendaient à la sortie – *some forty girls were waiting for us at the exit*
69 | 231

**4289 sous-sol** *nm* basement, lower ground floor, subsoil, underground
- il utilisait les parkings en sous-sol – *he used underground parking lots*
79 | 147

**4290 rat** *adj(f),nm* rat
- il y a un rat dans la cuisine – *there's a rat in the kitchen*
61 | 302

**4291 flot** *nm* floodtide, stream of, flood of
- un flot ininterrompu de mots et de larmes – *an uninterrupted flow of words and tears*
71 | 214-s

**4292 mordre** *v* to bite, overlap into
- on allait le tuer pour avoir mordu un garde – *it was going to be killed for having bitten a guard*
60 | 316-n

**4293 partiellement** *adv* partly
- le ciel était partiellement dégagé – *the skies were partly cloudy*
62 | 292

**4294 radioactif** *adj* radioactive
- les particules radioactives tombent avec les gouttes de pluie – *radioactive particles fall with raindrops*
65 | 268

**4295 passe** *nm,nf* pass, channel
- puis-je utiliser mon passe? – *can I use my pass?*
73 | 190

**4296 indépendamment** *adv* independently, irrespective of, regardless of
- chaque paquet est traité indépendamment – *each package is processed individually*
69 | 226

**4297 location** *nf* renting
- c'est un meublé mis en location pour quelques mois – *it's a furnished apartment being rented out for a few months*
83 | 113

**4298 naïf** *nadj* naïve, innocent
• elle reste extrêmement naïve sur le sujet
– *she remains extremely naïve on the topic*
69 | 228

**4299 retraité** *nadj* retired
• les retraités ne peuvent dépenser l'argent
– *retired people can't spend money*
61 | 306

**4300 innocence** *nf* innocence
• vous êtes d'une innocence extrême – *you're extremely innocent*
65 | 265+l

**4301 bijou** *nm* jewel
• j'aime bien les bijoux anciens – *I like old jewelry*
69 | 230

**4302 messe** *nf* mass
• les dimanches, j'allais à la messe – *on Sundays I used to go to mass*
63 | 288

**4303 coïncidence** *nf* coincidence
• est-ce là une coïncidence? – *is that a coincidence?*
76 | 165

**4304 torture** *nf* torture
• j'ai raconté les tortures, les coups, les viols – *I told them about the torture, the blows, the rapes*
70 | 216

**4305 protecteur** *nadj* protective, protector, guardian
• sa mère était sa protectrice morale, physique et même matérielle – *his mother was his moral, physical, and even material protector*
77 | 159

**4306 rayonnement** *nm* radiance
• le danger des rayonnements pour l' homme est réel – *radiation danger for humans is real*
67 | 250

**4307 récolte** *nf* harvest, crop
• les récoltes de certains agriculteurs sont gelées – *some farmers' crops are frozen*
74 | 186

**4308 valise** *nf* suitcase
• dépêche-toi de faire les valises – *hurry up and pack your suitcases*
57 | 347+l -n

**4309 danseur** *nm* dancer
• quand elle était jeune, elle était danseuse – *when she was young, she was a dancer*
70 | 219

**4310 expertise** *nf* expertise
• il y a également beaucoup d'expertise – *there is also much expertise*
69 | 232-l

**4311 minier** *adj* mining
• les dépenses de prospection minière ont augmenté – *costs for mining exploration have risen*
71 | 206

**4312 vitrine** *nf* window, display cabinet
• la marchandise est en vitrine – *the goods are in the display window*
73 | 190

**4313 ébranler** *v* to shake, rattle
• le train s'ébranla de nouveau – *the train shook once more*
72 | 203

**4314 crâne** *adj(f),nm* skull
• son crâne est à moitié couvert par ce bonnet noir – *his skull is half covered by this black bonnet*
58 | 337+l

**4315 anéantir** *v* to annihilate, wipe out, ruin, vanish
• vous êtes venus ici pour m'anéantir – *you came here to annihilate me*
73 | 196

**4316 vocal** *adj* vocal
• empreinte vocale inconnue – *unknown voiceprint*
48 | 446+n -s

**4317 unilatéral** *adj* unilateral
• c'est un plan de désengagement unilatéral – *it's a plan for unilateral withdrawal*
70 | 219

**4318 combustible** *nadj(f)* fuel, combustible
• les importations de carburants et de combustibles liquides ont reculé – *imports of gas and liquid fuels retreated*
72 | 197

**4319 économiser** *v* to save, save on, conserve
• cela permettrait d'économiser beaucoup d'argent – *that would help save lots of money*
71 | 212

**4320 tisser** *v* to weave
• elle tisse des sacs en soie – *she weaves silk pouches*
80 | 136

**4321 poule** *nf* hen, chick
• je ne suis pas ta poule, ok! – *I'm not your chick, OK!*
67 | 242

**4322 punition** *nf* punishment
• la mort ne doit pas être une punition – *death should not be a punishment*
84 | 108

**4323 hésitation** *nf* hesitation
• je n'ai aucune hésitation à lui parler – *I don't have any qualms about talking to him*
72 | 199

**4324 rentable** *adj(f)* profitable
• cette activité a été rapidement rentable – *this activity quickly became profitable*
68 | 231-l

**4325 loyal** *adj* loyal, faithful
• tu as toujours été un ami loyal – *you were always a loyal friend*
79 | 144

**4326 renfort** *nm* help, back-up, support
• encore quelques minutes. les renforts arrivent – *a few more minutes. the reinforcements are arriving*
66 | 252

**4327 cohérence** *nf* coherence, consistency
• il faut assurer une cohérence entre les objectifs et les actions – *there must be consistency between the goals and the actions*
69 | 227

**4328 souris** *nf(pl)* mouse
• le chat mange la souris – *the cat eats the mouse*
62 | 290

**4329 bombarder** *v* to bomb
• l'aviation gouvernementale bombarde deux villes contrôlées par les rebelles – *the government air forces are bombing two cities controlled by the rebels*
69 | 228

**4330 éveiller** *v* to arouse, stimulate, awaken
• la nuit, je restais éveillée dans mon lit – *during the night I remained awake in my bed*
63 | 278+l

**4331 semestre** *nm* semester, six-month period
• ils faisaient un semestre d'intégration – *they did six months on-the-job training*
58 | 332+n -s

**4332 croyant** *nadj* believer
• que le croyant vive sa foi – *may the believer live his faith*
73 | 188

**4333 réalisateur** *nadj* director
• quand le réalisateur dit «écoutez», vous écoutez – *when the director says "listen", you listen*
59 | 326

**4334 brutalement** *adv* brutally
• elle referma brutalement la porte – *she slammed the door shut*
74 | 184

**4335 lourdement** *adv* heavily
• il m'examina lourdement de la tête aux pieds – *he gave me a thorough inspection from head to foot*
76 | 165

**4336 tente** *nf* tent
• Fabrice et moi partagions la même tente – *Fabrice and I were sharing the same tent*
75 | 172

**4337 goutte** *nf* drop
• tu transpirais à grosses gouttes – *you were sweating great drops*
66 | 253+l

**4338 poussée** *nf* push, rise, upsurge
• une petite poussée dans n'importe quelle direction suffira – *a little push in any direction will be enough*
74 | 183

**4339 moine** *nm* monk, friar
• il vit modestement, comme un moine – *he lives modestly, like a monk*
66 | 254

**4340 modéré** *nadj* moderate, restrained, reasonable
• j'espère que vous êtes modéré dans vos habitudes – *I hope you are steady in your habits*
63 | 280+n -s

**4341 négligeable** *adj(f)* negligible, trivial
• ça donne une force de frappe non négligeable – *it gives a strike force to be reckoned with*
70 | 212

**4342 vice** *nm* fault, defect, vice
• ce vice mineur me reste, la familiarité – *I still have one minor vice: being too familiar*
71 | 202

**4343 symboliser** *v* to symbolize
• le papillon symbolisait l'âme – *the butterfly was symbolic of the soul*
78 | 147

**4344 substituer** *v* to substitute
• les insultes ne sauraient se substituer – *the insults can't be smoothed over*
69 | 220

**4345 subtil** *adj* subtle, nice
• il faut les coincer de façon subtile – *wedge them together carefully*
71 | 202

**4346 commandant** *nadj* commander
• il s'est autoproclamé commandant en chef de l'organisation – *he named himself chief of the organization*
65 | 261

**4347 chuter** *v* to fall
• la tempête m'a fait chuter – *the storm made me fall*
65 | 263+n

**4348 fidélité** *nf* loyalty, faithfulness, accuracy, reliability
• je tiens absolument à la fidélité – *I absolutely value loyalty*
70 | 217

**4349 basculer** *v* to topple, fall over, knock off
• je crus que la terre avait basculé sous mes pieds – *I thought the earth moved under my feet*
75 | 169

**4350 gestionnaire** *adj(f),nm,nf* administrator, administrative
• je serai le gestionnaire assigné au dossier – *I will be the administrator assigned to the case*
65 | 258-l

**4351 redoutable** *adj(f)* fearsome, formidable
• tu as été notre plus redoutable ennemi – *you were our most formidable enemy*
69 | 225

**4352 immigrant** *nadj* immigrant
• nous avons aidé de nouveaux immigrants à s'établir – *we helped new immigrants to get settled*
64 | 264-l +s

## 25 Verbs – differences across registers

This table lists the verbs that occur with a much higher frequency than expected in the three registers: spoken language, literature, and non-fiction. In each case, the words listed are among those in the top 10 percent of words for that register, in terms of relative frequency to the other two registers.

**Spoken:**

**travailler** 290 to work
**aider** 413 to help
**adopter** 676 to adopt
**remercier** 1218 to thank
**voter** 1248 to vote
**aborder** 1535 to approach
**féliciter** 1749 to congratulate
**mentionner** 1805 to mention
**préoccuper** 1979 to preoccupy
**excuser** 1987 to excuse
**dépenser** 2051 to spend
**désoler** 2081 to be sorry
**débattre** 2254 to discuss
**adorer** 2322 to adore
**siéger** 2883 to sit
**collaborer** 2963 to collaborate
**virer** 3623 to turn
**ficher** 3905 to not give a damn
**parier** 4205 to bet
**chier** 4245 to sh*t
**filmer** 4393 to film
**remédier** 4519 to remedy
**bosser** 4532 to work hard
**déménager** 4611 to move
**incomber** 4617 to be incumbent upon
**emmerder** 4676 to bother
**clarifier** 4894 to clarify
**réglementer** 4929 to regulate

**Literature:**

**jeter** 1202 to throw
**sourire** 1476 to smile
**apercevoir** 1891 to notice
**crier** 1950 to shout
**serrer** 2449 to tighten
**glisser** 2544 to slide
**briller** 2904 to shine
**promener** 2928 to go for a walk
**éteindre** 3033 to extinguish
**refermer** 3759 to close again
**endormir** 3788 to fall asleep
**trembler** 4225 to tremble
**mépriser** 4270 to scorn
**éveiller** 4330 to arouse
**pendre** 4360 to hang down
**incliner** 4368 to tilt
**révolter** 4370 to revolt
**ôter** 4405 to remove
**flotter** 4520 to float
**envelopper** 4604 to wrap
**brouiller** 4682 to mix-up
**figer** 4708 to congeal
**murmurer** 4730 to murmur
**vêtir** 4734 to clothe
**hâter** 4754 to quicken
**guetter** 4852 to watch over
**caresser** 4861 to caress
**écrier** 4865 to exclaim

**Nonfiction:**

**annoncer** 521 to announce
**indiquer** 590 to indicate
**affirmer** 686 to affirm
**préciser** 745 to state
**provoquer** 1095 to provoke
**émettre** 1787 to emit
**progresser** 1856 to progress
**détenir** 2056 to detain
**déclencher** 2152 to trigger
**remporter** 2267 to win
**disputer** 2725 to dispute
**équiper** 3043 to equip
**spécifier** 3086 to specify
**acheminer** 3372 to dispatch
**interpeller** 3409 to question
**sélectionner** 3671 to select
**démentir** 3772 to deny
**décéder** 3809 to die
**réaffirmer** 3918 to reaffirm
**industrialiser** 4022 to industrialize
**modérer** 4034 to moderate
**détecter** 4062 to detect
**activer** 4072 to activate
**consolider** 4116 to consolidate
**coder** 4121 to encode
**chuter** 4347 to fall
**piéger** 4358 to trap
**inculper** 4638 to charge

4353 **polémique** *nadj(f)* controversial, controversy
• c'est vrai que j'aime la polémique, le débat d'idées – *it's true that I like controversy, debating ideas*
62 | 286

4354 **alourdir** *v* to weigh down, make heavy
• je sens mes doigts s'alourdir – *I feel my fingers getting heavier*
76 | 161

4355 **avancée** *nf* advanced, overhung
• reculez. vous empêchez notre avancée – *step back. you're blocking our way*
63 | 272

4356 **sévir** *v* to act ruthlessly, be rife
• la violence qui sévit dans ce pays nous inquiète aussi beaucoup – *the violence that is tearing this country apart also troubles us greatly*
77 | 156

**4357 jumeau** *nadj* twin
- les jumeaux ont besoin l'un de l'autre – *the twins need each other*
53 | 376-s

**4358 piéger** *v* to trap, booby-trap
- il a été hyper facile à piéger – *it was super-easy to trap him*
59 | 314

**4359 confiant** *adj* trusting, confident
- vous êtes malgré tout confiant? – *you're confident in spite of it all?*
77 | 158

**4360 pendre** *v* to hang down
- ses immenses cheveux blonds pendaient jusqu' à terre – *her extremely thick blond hair hung right down to the ground*
59 | 318+l

**4361 intact** *adj* intact
- elle le retrouvait intact dans cet hiver nocturne – *she found it intact in this dark winter*
71 | 208

**4362 rapidité** *nf* speed, quickness
- je ne travaille pas avec la rapidité d'autrefois – *I don't work as quickly as I used to*
61 | 300+n -s

**4363 localité** *nf* town, village
- ce sont toutes des petites localités – *they are all small localities*
56 | 347-l

**4364 récupération** *nf* recovery, retrieval, salvage
- vous aurez besoin d'une récupération lente et salutaire – *you will need a slow and wholesome recovery*
71 | 207

**4365 vigoureux** *adj(pl)* vigorous
- ces territoires suscitent une vigoureuse contrebande – *these territories support a vibrant black market*
78 | 150

**4366 rentabilité** *nf* profitability
- la rentabilité n'a cessé de décroître – *profitability didn't stop decreasing*
65 | 256

**4367 delà** *adv* beyond, above, over
- mais je n'irai pas au delà – *but I won't go any farther than that*
63 | 276+l

**4368 incliner** *v* to tilt, tend towards
- incline-toi devant moi – *bow before me*
63 | 277+l -s

**4369 affreux** *nadj(pl)* dreadful, awful, horrible
- j'ai fait un cauchemar affreux – *I had a horrible nightmare*
55 | 356+l -n

**4370 révolter** *v* to revolt, rebel, outrage
- ils se révolteront avec colère, une colère implacable – *they will rebel with anger, an implacable anger*
58 | 321+l -s

**4371 conte** *nm* tale
- je vis un rêve, un conte de fées, un miracle – *I lived a dream, a fairy tale, a miracle*
66 | 247

**4372 évasion** *nf* escape, evasion
- il lui parla longuement de l'évasion – *he spoke to her at length about the escape*
77 | 158

**4373 repère** *nm* reference, benchmark, landmark
- les chrétiens ont besoin de repères, sinon ils sont perdus – *Christians need reference points, otherwise they're lost*
73 | 188

**4374 philosophique** *adj(f)* philosophical
- son travail philosophique porte sur la responsabilité – *his philosophical work focuses on responsability*
62 | 286

**4375 arrivé** *adj* arrived
- des tas de choses étaient arrivées – *many things happened*
77 | 151

**4376 ironie** *nf* irony
- son ironie me fit souffrir mille morts – *the irony of it killed me a thousand times over*
72 | 197

**4377 serveur** *nm* waiter, server
- je ne suis pas une serveuse de bar – *I'm not a barmaid*
70 | 212

**4378 bannir** *v* to banish, ban
- la religion est bannie de chez nous – *religion is banished from our house*
84 | 103

**4379 insuffisance** *nf* inadequacy, insufficiency
- nous voulons corriger les insuffisances actuelles – *we want to correct current inadequacies*
76 | 163

**4380 librairie** *nf* bookstore, bookshop
- les prix, dans cette librairie, sont très compétitifs – *the prices in this bookstore are very competitive*
64 | 264

**4381 parenthèse** *nf* parenthesis, bracket, aside
- je dirais en parenthèses que l'histoire présente est opaque – *I would add parenthetically that this story is opaque*
64 | 268

**4382 miser** *v* to bet, stake
- si vous allez miser pour moi...alors on sera quittes – *if you're going to bet for me...then we'll be even*
76 | 158

**4383 stupéfiant** *nadj* drug, narcotic; stunning, astounding
- on servit un repas stupéfiant – *we served a stunning meal*
73 | 187

**4384 boursier** *nadj* grant-holder, scholarship holder; stock
- en un an, sa valeur boursière a été divisée par 350 – *in one year, its stock value sunk to 1/350 of its value*
55 | 357+n -s

**4385 levée** *nf* raising, levying, levee
- la Commission européenne a voté la levée de cet embargo – *the European Commission voted to lift this embargo*
60 | 299

**4386 déformer** *v* to bend, distort, deform
- ils ont déformé les faits – *they have distorted the facts*
76 | 158

**4387 menaçant** *adj* threatening, menacing
- elle le chasse en le menaçant avec un couteau – *she chased him brandishing a knife*
76 | 164

**4388 nord-est** *nmi* north-east
- le nord-est des Etats-Unis frappé par les pluies verglaçantes – *northeastern U.S. hit by freezing rains*
54 | 363+n -s

**4389 substitution** *nf* substitution, mix-up
- il y a la substitution du dialogue homme/machine au dialogue homme/femme – *there is a substitution of man/machine dialog for man/woman dialogue*
57 | 335+s

**4390 parer** *v* to adorn, put on; to ward off, parry
- parez les équipements de sauvetage – *put on the lifesaving equipment*
68 | 228

**4391 avantageux** *nadj(pl)* profitable, worthwhile, advantageous, attractive
- les prix étaient plus avantageux – *the prices were more attractive*
71 | 204

**4392 handicaper** *v* to handicap
- la croissance mondiale risque d'handicaper leurs exportations – *worldwide growth threatens to handicap their exports*
74 | 174

**4393 filmer** *v* to film, shoot
- c'était filmé pour la télé – *it was filmed for TV*
60 | 297+s

**4394 délinquant** *nadj* delinquent, offender
- nous avons réclamé un registre des délinquants sexuels – *we have called for a sexual offenders registry*
57 | 329-l +s

**4395 perdant** *nadj* losing, loser
- je suis le plus grand perdant – *I'm the greatest loser*
80 | 128

**4396 altitude** *nf* altitude, height
- il a plu à basse altitude – *it was raining at lower altitudes*
56 | 345+n -s

**4397 imputer** *v* to impute to, attribute to
- il est facile d'imputer aux autres sa propre mauvaise volonté – *it's easy to blame others for one's own ill will*
78 | 143

**4398 plaisanter** *v* to joke
- du calme, je plaisante – *take it easy, I'm joking*
60 | 299

**4399 poétique** *nadj(f)* poetic, poetical, poetics
- le français est un langage poétique – *French is a poetic language*
56 | 342-n

**4400 desservir** *v* to clear, go against, harm, serve
- nous ne desservons pas adéquatement les auditeurs – *we don't adequately serve our listening audience*
65 | 257

**4401 mensuel** *nadj* monthly
- il touchait un salaire mensuel de 70.000 francs – *he earned a monthly salary of 70,000 francs*
66 | 248+n

**4402 connerie** *nf* crap, bullsh*t, stupidity
- oui, mec. arrête tes conneries – *yeah, man. stop your bullsh*t*
51 | 394-n +s

**4403 sanglant** *adj* bloody, cruel, covered in blood
- il avait un trou sanglant – *he had a bloody hole*
70 | 211

**4404 coude** *nm* elbow
- j'ai mal au coude – *I have a sore elbow*
70 | 212

**4405 ôter** *v* to remove, take away, take off, take out
- j'ôtai donc ma veste et mes chaussures – *so I removed my jacket and my shoes*
58 | 316+l

**4406 report** *nm* postponement, deferment
- nous sommes contre le report des élections – *we're against postponing the elections*
60 | 297-l

**4407 créature** *nf* creature
- tu es la plus belle créature que j'aie jamais vue – *you are the most beautiful creature I have ever seen*
57 | 326+l -n

**4408 aucunement** *adv* in no way, not in the least, not at all
- je ne me sens aucunement coupable – *I don't feel at all guilty*
73 | 182

**4409 globalement** *adv* globally
- globalement, la réponse humanitaire a été positive – *the worldwide humanitarian response was positive*
62 | 284-l

**4410 convenable** *adj(f)* suitable, appropriate, correct, proper, acceptable
- ils ont droit à une retraite convenable – *they have the right to a reasonable retirement*
72 | 192

**4411 itinéraire** *nadj(f)* itinerary, route
- leur itinéraire n'est pas encore fixé – *their itinerary is not yet set*
73 | 180

**4412 purger** *v* to purge, bleed, drain
- ça va purger son système en une nuit – *this will purge his system in one night*
66 | 239

**4413 fâcher** *v* to anger, make angry, get angry
- il est sûrement fâché contre moi – *he's surely upset with me*
64 | 262-n

**4414 repasser** *v* to cross again, retake, show again, iron
- si je te dérange je peux repasser – *if I'm disturbing you I can come back another time*
69 | 218

**4415 alternatif** *adj* alternate, alternating
- le rock alternatif francophone est en train de mourir – *French alternative rock is dying out*
63 | 271

**4416 palier** *nm* landing, level, flat
- j'allai sur le palier et frappai à sa porte – *I went onto the porch and knocked at her door*
70 | 211

**4417 prochainement** *adv* shortly, soon
- prévoyez-vous d'autres séries de concert prochainement? – *are you planning other concert series soon?*
65 | 251

**4418 réglementaire** *adj(f)* regulation, control, statutory
- il démantèle la structure réglementaire de la loi actuellement en vigueur – *it dismantles the regulatory structure of the current law*
72 | 189

**4419 costume** *nm* suit, costume, dress
- voici un très beau costume, en pure laine – *here's a very beautiful suit, made of pure wool*
61 | 292

**4420 thérapie** *nf* therapy
- mon jardin c'est une thérapie – *my garden is a therapy*
61 | 288-l

**4421 reproche** *nm* reproach
- ce sont surtout là les reproches des communistes – *that is mostly communist innuendo*
65 | 253-l

**4422 curé** *nm* parish priest
- je me confesserai au curé – *I will confess to my parish priest*
60 | 302+l -n

**4423 contrôleur** *nm* inspector, controller
- les contrôleurs en grève ont obtenu jeudi soir satisfaction – *the striking controllers reached agreement Thursday night*
67 | 236

**4424 soulagement** *nm* relief
- j'ai besoin du soulagement – *I need relief*
71 | 197

**4425 dissoudre** *v* to dissolve, disband, break up
- je fis dissoudre dans le lait une poudre somnifère – *I dissolved some sleeping powder in the milk*
76 | 161

**4426 avalanche** *nf* avalanche
- le danger d'avalanches est encore faible – *avalanche danger is still low*
45 | 461+n -s

**4427 mark** *nm* mark
- sa monnaie de référence est le mark allemand – *its reference currency is the German mark*
48 | 423-l +n -s

**4428 brèche** *nf* breach, gap
- c'était une brèche, dans la clôture, une large brèche – *it was a gap in the fence—a large gap*
79 | 136

**4429 incitation** *nf* incitement, incentive
- il y a eu de l'incitation au piratage – *there was an incentive to engage in piracy*
71 | 200

**4430 entraîneur** *nm* coach, trainer
- maintenant je travaille avec quelques entraîneurs – *now I work with some trainers*
58 | 315-l

**4431 éditorial** *nadj* editorial
- pourriez-vous nous parler de vos choix éditoriaux? – *could you talk about your editorial choices?*
63 | 267

**4432 conjugal** *adj* conjugal, married
- ils vivent dans une relation conjugale – *they live in a conjugal relationship*
61 | 287-n

**4433 pâle** *adj(f)* pale
- monsieur, vous êtes pâle, vous avez l'air fatigué – *sir, your're pale, you look tired*
52 | 377+l -n -s

**4434 relâcher** *v* to loosen, release, let go
- le plus âgé a depuis été relâché – *the oldest one has since been let go*
68 | 222

**4435 visa** *nm* visa, stamp
- il s'est avéré que le visa était faux – *it turned out that the visa was false*
62 | 280-l

**4436 vingt-cinq** *det,nmi* twenty five
- ils nous envoyaient quinze, vingt, vingt-cinq films de plus – *they sent us fifteen, twenty, twenty-five more films*
65 | 250

**4437 péché** *nm* sin
- pardonnez-moi mon père car j'ai péché – *forgive me Father, for I have sinned*
59 | 304+l

**4438 gendarme** *nm,nf* policeman
- les gendarmes poursuivent leurs investigations – *the policemen are pursuing their investigations*
60 | 294

**4439 sécheresse** *nf* dryness, drought
- après dix années de sécheresse, il pleut au Sahel – *after ten years, of drought, it's raining in the Sahel*
72 | 186

**4440 score** *nm* score
- c'est vrai que les bons scores me font plaisir – *it's true that I enjoy good scores*
58 | 320-l

**4441 goûter** *nm,v* to taste, snack
- je goûtai à la confiture – *I tasted the jam*
60 | 294-n

**4442 renier** *v* to disown, repudiate, go back on
- tu renies ton passé, notre amour, TA fille – *you're disowning your past, our love, YOUR daughter*
73 | 184

**4443 juridiction** *nf* jurisdiction, court of law
- la haute juridiction a mis sa décision en délibéré – *the upper jurisdiction put its decision to debate*
63 | 269-l

**4444 prostitution** *nf* prostitution
- on légalise la prostitution – *we're legalizing prostitution*
63 | 263+s

**4445 fiche** *nf* card, sheet, slip, form
- mais je dois remplir cette fiche – *but I have to fill out this form*
75 | 168

**4446 déséquilibre** *nm* imbalance
- mon budget personnel est en déséquilibre – *my personal budget is out of balance*
68 | 219

**4447 probabilité** *nf* probability, likelihood
- t'es-tu intéressé à la théorie des probabilités? – *are you interested in probability theory?*
62 | 279

**4448 entraver** *v* to hinder, hamper, get in the way of
- son pantalon entravait la liberté de ses mouvements – *his trousers hampered his freedom of movement*
72 | 187

**4449 sous-estimer** *v* to underestimate
- ne sous-estimez pas votre charme – *don't underestimate your charm*
75 | 165

**4450 embargo** *nm* embargo
- l'OTAN se préparent à décréter un embargo pétrolier – *NATO is preparing to announce an oil embargo*
53 | 368-l +n

**4451 interdit** *nadj* prohibited, banned
- l'entrée était strictement interdite – *entry was strictly forbidden*
70 | 205

**4452 brouillard** *nm* fog, mist, haze
- peu à peu le brouillard se fait moins épais – *the fog gradually lifted*
61 | 280

**4453 syrien** *nadj* Syrian
- le président syrien avait confirmé cet entretien – *the Syrian president confirmed this interview*
53 | 365+n

**4454 jet** *nm* jet, throw, spray, nozzle
- il traversait cet etat dans un jet privé – *he crossed this state in a private jet*
67 | 230

**4455 trêve** *nf* truce
- nous rejetons toute idée de trêve ou de négociation politique – *we reject any idea of a truce or political negotiation*
54 | 353

**4456 occupant** *nadj* occupant, occupier, occupying
- le parlement négocie avec les occupants – *the parliament is negotiating with the occupants*
69 | 213

**4457 ponctuel** *adj* punctual
- c'est à vous dégoûter d'être toujours ponctuel – *I'm always on time in order to annoy you*
76 | 154

**4458 défini** *nadj* definite
- vous n'avez aucun rôle défini dans ce partenariat – *you have no definite role in this partnership*
75 | 161

**4459 détachement** *nm* detachment
- elle parle de tout avec un détachement singulier – *she talks about everything with remarkable indifference*
72 | 186

**4460 manuscrit** *adj* manuscript, handwritten
- je jetterai au feu tous mes manuscrits – *I will toss all my manuscripts into the fire*
61 | 286

**4461 panier** *nm* basket
- par terre s'empilaient encore des paniers et des caisses – *still more baskets and boxes were piling up on the ground*
69 | 215

**4462 bouton** *nm* button, knob, spot
- elle pressa le bouton qui commande l'ouverture de la porte – *she pushed the button that opened the door*
62 | 274

**4463 immobile** *adj(f)* still, motionless
- je restais là, immobile – *I stayed there, motionless*
50 | 404+l -n -s

**4464 fermeté** *nf* firmness, solidity, steadiness
- la patience, la tolérance et la fermeté sont nécessaires – *patience, tolerance, and firmness are necessary*
70 | 204

**4465 véhiculer** *v* to transport, convey
- je peux véhiculer ça sans aucun problème – *I can deliver this by vehicle, no problem*
70 | 207

**4466 répliquer** *v* to reply
- l'orateur répliqua que c'était presque fait – *the speaker responded that it was almost done*
75 | 167

**4467 passionnant** *adj*  fascinating, exciting
• j'aimais tant étudier que je trouvais
passionnant d'enseigner – *I loved studying
so much that I found teaching exciting*
71 | 197

**4468 théologie** *nf*  theology
• en théologie, on m'enseignait des choses
intelligentes – *in theology I was taught
intelligent things*
54 | 358-n +s

**4469 advenir** *v*  to happen that, happen to
• on ignore ce qu'il est advenu de lui – *we
have no idea what has become of him*
72 | 188

**4470 immigrer** *v*  to immigrate
• mes grands-parents ont immigré au Canada
– *my grandparents immigrated to Canada*
62 | 274

**4471 tache** *nf*  stain, spot, mark
• c'est une tache d'humidité, dis-je – *it's a
humidity stain, I said*
61 | 281+l

**4472 tendresse** *nf*  tenderness, fondness
• la femme a plus de tendresse que l'homme
– *women have more tenderness than men*
54 | 351+l -n -s

**4473 privilégié** *nadj*  privileged
• j'ai eu une vie protégée et privilégiée – *I had
a protected and privileged life*
72 | 186

**4474 slogan** *nm*  slogan
• quand je l'écoute, un slogan me vient en
tête – *while listening to her, I thought of a
motto*
68 | 217

**4475 fromage** *nm*  cheese
• je n'ai jamais vraiment aimé les fromages
– *I have never really liked cheese*
67 | 231

**4476 toxique** *nadj(f)*  toxic, toxin
• attention aux produits de jardinage toxiques
– *be careful of toxic gardening products*
60 | 292

**4477 incapacité** *nf*  incompetence, incapability
• tout démontre notre incapacité à prendre
des décisions collectives – *everything
demonstrates our inability to make collective
decisions*
75 | 165

**4478 pharmaceutique** *nadj(f)*  pharmaceutical
• les compagnies pharmaceutiques sont très,
très, très riches – *pharmaceutical
companies are very, very, very rich*
61 | 278-l +n

**4479 parfum** *nm*  perfume, scent, fragrance
• divers sont les parfums des fleurs – *flowers'
scents vary widely*
61 | 278+l

**4480 antique** *nadj(f)*  antique, ancient
• le château me semblait immense et
antique – *the castle seemed immense and
ancient to me*
68 | 217+l

**4481 controversé** *adj*  much debated, controversial
• des problèmes difficiles et controversés,
mais tout aussi urgents – *difficult and
controversial problems that are nonetheless
urgent*
69 | 213-l

**4482 instinct** *nm*  instinct
• tu as tous les mauvais instincts – *you have
all the wrong instincts*
60 | 287+l -n

**4483 barreau** *nm*  bar
• je me suis trouvé derrière les barreaux
– *I found myself behind bars*
70 | 202

**4484 insupportable** *adj(f)*  intolerable
• l'horreur de cette agonie était insupportable
– *the horror of this agony was unbearable*
68 | 221

**4485 opportun** *adj*  timely,
• je n'ai pas trouvé le moment opportun
– *I didn't find the right moment*
63 | 263+s

**4486 parquet** *nm*  parquet floor, hardwood floor,
prosecutor's office
• une autopsie a été ordonnée par le parquet
– *the prosecutor ordered an autopsy*
55 | 342+n

**4487 navigation** *nf*  navigation
• la navigation sur le Danube est bloquée
depuis 18 mois – *navigation on the
Danube has been blocked for 18 months*
80 | 128

**4488 contrarier** *v*  to annoy, bother, thwart
• je les soupçonnais de vouloir me contrarier
– *I suspected them of wanting to hassle
me*
69 | 212

**4489 nouer** *v*  to knot, tie
• l'estomac noué, j'oubliais la compétition
– *my stomach in knots, I forgot the
competition*
66 | 235

**4490 frustration** *nf*  frustration
• cela ne va pas sans frustration chez moi –
*it's not without frustration on my part*
72 | 182

**4491 cinquantaine** *nf*  about fifty
• certains d'entre eux emploient une
cinquantaine de salariés – *some of them
have about fifty employees*
66 | 234

**4492 improviser** *v*  to improvise
• je suis doué pour improviser – *I'm gifted at
improvisation*
74 | 171

**4493 désespéré** *nadj*  desperate, hopeless
• j'envoyai un regard désespéré à mon père –
*I looked desperately at my father*
77 | 150

**4494 auto** *nm,nf*  car
• des amis venaient nous chercher en
auto – *friends came by car to pick us up*
62 | 268+l -n

**4495 troupeau** *nm* herd, flock
- tu fais partie de mon troupeau, à présent. bienvenue – *you're part of my flock, now. welcome*
70 | 205

**4496 gendarmerie** *nf* police force, police station
- ils ont aussitôt alerté la gendarmerie – *they immediately warned police headquarters*
59 | 298

**4497 génétiquement** *adv* genetically
- nous consommons des aliments génétiquement modifiés – *we consume genetically modified foods*
55 | 340-l +s

**4498 analogue** *nadj(f)* similar, analogous
- la situation est analogue sur le plan mondial – *the situation is similar on a worldwide scale*
62 | 271

**4499 venu** *nadj* come
le moment venu, on allumera le phare de la liberté – *when the time comes, we will light the flame of liberty*
71 | 189

**4500 ironique** *adj(f)* ironic
- il a un sourire ironique et satisfait – *he has an ironic and satisfied smile*
73 | 176

**4501 sanitaire** *nadj(f)* health, sanitary, medical
- il n'a pas respecté les règles sanitaires – *he didn't obey the sanitation rules*
60 | 285

**4502 sonore** *nadj(f)* sound, resonant, sonorous, voiced
- il éclata d'un rire sonore – *he broke into a hearty laugh*
65 | 239

**4503 initier** *v* to initiate, introduce
- j'ai commencé à m'initier à la Bible – *I started to become familiar with the Bible*
73 | 180

**4504 mœurs** *nfpl* morals, customs, habits, manners, ways
- il avait des mœurs un peu bizarres – *his morals were somewhat bizarre*
66 | 235+l

**4505 cessez-le-feu** *nmi* ceasefire
- ces nouvelles violences menacent le fragile cessez-le-feu – *this new violence is threatening the fragile ceasefire*
51 | 385-l

**4506 bénévole** *nadj(f)* volunteer, voluntary, unpaid
- je félicite le personnel et les bénévoles de l'UNICEF – *I congratulate the UNICEF employees and volunteers*
64 | 249+s

**4507 boue** *nf* mud
- le trottoir était couvert d'une boue glacée – *the sidewalk was covered with frozen mud*
68 | 217

**4508 empereur** *nm* emperor
- ton empereur te demande ta loyauté – *your emperor demands your loyalty*
72 | 186

**4509 dissiper** *v* to dispel, disperse, clear away
- le soleil avait dissipé les nuages – *the sun dispersed the clouds*
66 | 235+l

**4510 déclin** *nm* decline, deterioration
- leur nombre est en déclin, mais ils sont encore assez nombreux – *their number is declining, but they are still numerous enough*
69 | 206

**4511 liquider** *v* to liquidate, sell off, clear
- sommes-nous en train de dissiper nos actifs les plus précieux? – *are we liquidating our most precious assets?*
73 | 180

**4512 maintenance** *nf* maintenance, servicing
- la maintenance des bateaux est moins bien assurée – *upkeep of the boats is less certain*
43 | 474-l +n -s

**4513 prévisible** *adj(f)* predictable, forseeable
- le déni est la plus prévisible des réponses humaines – *denial is the most predictable of human responses*
77 | 146

**4514 pneu** *nm* tire
- je changerai le pneu – *I'll change the tire*
76 | 153

**4515 fraude** *nf* fraud
- tu es coupable de fraude – *you're guilty of fraud*
65 | 243

**4516 coton** *nm* cotton
- l'industrie du coton y est une source majeure de pollution – *the cotton industry is a major source of pollution*
72 | 181

**4517 entrevoir** *v* to make out, catch a glimpse of, foresee
- pour l'avenir, elle entrevoit des débouchés intéressants – *for the future, she anticipates interesting opportunities*
67 | 226+l

**4518 stipuler** *v* to state, stipulate, specify
- les voeux ne stipulent pas le bébé – *the vows don't stipulate the baby*
69 | 211-l

**4519 remédier** *v* to cure, remedy, put right
- pour remédier à cette affaire, il faut du courage – *to resolve this matter, courage will be necessary*
63 | 260+s

**4520 flotter** *v* to float, hang, stream
- j'étais équipée pour flotter par-dessus les nuages – *I was outfitted to float above the clouds*
64 | 251+l

**4521 fraction** *nf* fraction
- tu fais une fraction de ce que tu suis – *you do a fraction of what you follow*
65 | 241

**4522 impossibilité** *nf* impossibility
- c'est une impossibilité physiologique – *it's a physiological impossibility*
68 | 219

**4523 conditionnel** *nadj* conditional
- le meurtrier pourra demander une libération conditionnelle – *the murderer will be able to request parole*
59 | 296+s

**4524 nuance** *nf* shade, hue, nuance
- vous ne pensez pas que c'est une belle nuance de bleu? – *don't you think it's a pretty shade of blue?*
68 | 218+l

**4525 improbable** *adj(f)* unlikely, improbable
- l'unanimité était assez improbable – *unanimity was rather improbable*
78 | 135

**4526 enquêteur** *nm* investigator, pollster
- les enquêteurs ont nié vendredi avoir torturé le suspect – *on Friday the interrogators denied having tortured the suspect*
54 | 345+n

**4527 conjointement** *adv* jointly
- nous devons conjointement exercer une pression – *we must exert pressure together*
73 | 175

**4528 éclaircir** *v* to brighten up, clear up
- le temps éclaircira ce mystère – *time will clear up this mystery*
77 | 143

**4529 bordel** *nm* brothel, mess, chaos
- un jour, la patronne du bordel m'envoya chez un autre libertin – *one day, the madame of the brothel sent me to another libertine's place*
50 | 384-n +s

**4530 impatient** *nadj* impatient
- je suis impatiente de relever ces défis – *I'm eager to take up these challenges*
72 | 180

**4531 versement** *nm* payment
- les versements aux hôpitaux publics progressent de 0,7 % – *payments to public hospitals increased by 0.7%*
67 | 224-l

**4532 bosser** *v* to work, bash on
- j'avais bossé dessus toute la nuit – *I had been working on it all night*
52 | 369-n +s

**4533 articuler** *v* to articulate
- il parlait lentement et articulait avec soin – *he spoke slowly and articulated carefully*
72 | 179

**4534 successivement** *adv* successively
- mes recherches ont successivement porté sur deux domaines – *my research focused sequentially on two areas*
75 | 158

**4535 assurément** *adv* most certainly
- la thèse se discute, assurément – *the argument is most assuredly being discussed*
74 | 167

**4536 provision** *nf* stock, supply
- tu as acheté les provisions pour le repas de midi? – *did you buy supplies for lunch?*
67 | 219

**4537 amplifier** *v* to amplify, magnify, expand
- amplifiez le son – *amplify the sound*
73 | 174

**4538 ceinture** *nf* belt, waist
- veuillez attacher votre ceinture – *please attach your seatbelt*
67 | 224

**4539 intergouvernemental** *adj* intergovernmental
- l'esprit des accords intergouvernementaux conclus avec les provinces – *the spirit of intergovernmental agreements involving the provinces*
53 | 358-l +s

**4540 délibération** *nf* deliberation, debate, consideration
- lisez la transcription des délibérations – *read the transcript of the debate*
56 | 322+s

**4541 mexicain** *nadj* Mexican
- j'étais couchée sur la couverture mexicaine – *I was lying down on the Mexican blanket*
67 | 222

**4542 seigneur** *nm* lord
- le Seigneur est mon berger – *the Lord is my shepherd*
60 | 280

**4543 saisonnier** *adj* seasonal
- le tourisme est une industrie saisonnière – *tourism is a seasonal industry*
53 | 354-l +s

**4544 souterrain** *nadj* underground, underground passage
- ils découvraient un corridor souterrain – *they discovered an underground corridor*
73 | 174

**4545 merveille** *nf* marvel, wonder
- je suis une merveille de la nature – *I'm a wonder of nature*
69 | 207

**4546 restituer** *v* to return, restore, refund
- en cas de rupture, il ne restituera rien – *in case of breach of contract, he will not refund anything*
79 | 129

**4547 démon** *nm* demon, fiend
- les démons aussi ont la foi – *devils have faith too*
67 | 218

**4548 balancer** *v* to swing, sway
- cela plie terriblement et se balance à la moindre brise – *this folds terribly and sways with the slightest breeze*
58 | 297-n

**4549 disponibilité** *nf* availability
- les objectifs de disponibilité sont des facteurs importants – *goals for availability are important factors*
60 | 284

**4550 infiniment** *adv* infinitely
- votre idée me fait infiniment plaisir – *your idea pleases me infinitely*
67 | 220+l

# 26 Adverbs – differences across registers

This table lists the adverbs that occur with a much higher frequency than expected in the three registers: spoken language, literature, and non-fiction. In each case, the words listed are among those in the top 10 percent of words for that register, in terms of relative frequency to the other two registers.

**Spoken:**

**beaucoup** 150 much

**maintenant** 192 now

**pourquoi** 193 why

**comment** 234 how

**oui** 284 yes

**juste** 304 only just

**vraiment** 361 really

**simplement** 615 simply

**combien** 800 how much

**exactement** 857 exactly

**tellement** 869 so much

**absolument** 1009 absolutely

**complètement** 1013 completely

**certainement** 1071 certainly

**clairement** 1319 clearly

**justement** 1332 exactly

**évidemment** 1340 obviously

**malheureusement** 1543 unfortunately

**extrêmement** 1545 extremely

**effectivement** 1550 effectively

**là-bas** 1777 over there

**ben** 2010 well

**là-dessus** 2208 on top

**personnellement** 2366 personally

**énormément** 3039 enormously

**brièvement** 3349 briefly

**Literature:**

**loin** 341 far

**presque** 481 almost

**derrière** 805 behind

**guère** 1591 hardly

**naturellement** 2036 naturally

**soudain** 2310 suddenly

**aussitôt** 2362 immediately

**autrefois** 2384 in the past

**vivement** 2491 sharply

**debout** 2497 standing

**lentement** 2637 slowly

**volontiers** 2742 with pleasure

**proprement** 2990 cleanly

**tantôt** 3013 sometimes

**dedans** 3058 inside

**longuement** 3066 at length

**quelquefois** 3170 sometimes

**doucement** 3242 gently

**brusquement** 3594 abruptly

**par-dessus** 3800 over

**nullement** 3902 not in the least

**économiquement** 4015 economically

**delà** 4367 beyond

**assurément** 4535 most certainly

**infiniment** 4550 infinitely

**jadis** 4795 formerly

**Nonfiction:**

**lors** 411 at the time of

**notamment** 439 notably

**environ** 678 about

**désormais** 1025 henceforth

**largement** 1382 widely

**arrière** 1504 back

**voire** 1547 indeed

**généralement** 1710 generally

**fortement** 1769 strongly

**principalement** 1965 principally

**normalement** 2018 normally

**nettement** 2055 clearly

**légèrement** 2333 slightly

**officiellement** 2363 officially

**progressivement** 2659 progressively

**éventuellement** 2767 possibly

**parallèlement** 3116 in parallel

**automatiquement** 3394 automatically

**respectivement** 3432 respectively

**quasiment** 3538 almost

**précédemment** 3555 previously

**vraisemblablement** 3739 most probably

**au-dessous** 3965 underneath

**sensiblement** 4057 more or less

**simultanément** 4090 simultaneously

**initialement** 4252 initially

**4551 acquis** *nadj(pl)* acquired, experience
- comptez-vous consolider vos acquis en France? – *do you plan to consolidate your acquisitions in France?*
67 | 217

**4552 récepteur** *nm* receiver, receiving
- il avait négligé de décrocher le récepteur – *he had forgotten to lift up the receiver*
45 | 442+n -s

**4553 glissement** *nm* sliding, slipping, skidding
- des glissements de neige humide pourraient se produire – *wet snowslides could occur*
54 | 341+n -s

**4554 auditeur** *nm* auditor, listener
- mais le choix appartient aux auditeurs – *but the choice belongs to the listener*
58 | 303+s

**4555 indigène** *nadj(f)* native, local
- il reste à convaincre les indigènes de vendre leurs terres – *the natives still have to be convinced to sell their lands*
68 | 215

**4556 chocolat** *adji,nm* chocolate
- je t'ai apporté des chocolats – *I brought you some chocolates*
74 | 166

**4557 indirectement** *adv* indirectly
- j'étais impliqué aussi bien directement qu'indirectement – *I was implicated as directly as I was indirectly*
75 | 159

**4558 obtention** *nf* obtaining, achievement
- l'obtention d'un diplôme est une occasion spéciale – *obtaining a diploma is a special occasion*
78 | 132

**4559 grandissant** *adj* growing, increasing
- l'insatisfaction grandissante exige une action rapide – *growing dissatisfaction requires a rapid response*
82 | 106

**4560 chagrin** *adj,nm* grief, sorrow,
- j'en ai eu des moments de chagrin dans ma vie – *I have had moments of sorrow in my life*
60 | 277+l

**4561 prostitué** *nadj* prostitute
- toutes deux étaient filles de prostituée – *both were daughters of a prostitute*
76 | 153

**4562 lumineux** *adj(pl)* luminous, illuminated; light
- la salle est bruyante, très lumineuse – *the room is noisy, very bright*
69 | 207

**4563 soupe** *nf* soup
- mange ta soupe, dis-je – *eat your soup, I said*
68 | 209

**4564 bravo** *intj,nm* bravo, well done
- j'ai de bonnes nouvelles. bravo. vos appels ont porté leurs fruits – *I have good news. congratulations. your appeals worked*
53 | 347-n +s

**4565 appréhender** *v* to dread, apprehend
- 15.000 clandestins ont été appréhendés – *15,000 illegal immigrants were apprehended*
77 | 139

**4566 concitoyen** *nm* fellow citizen
- mes chers concitoyens, je sais que vous êtes fatigués – *my dear fellow citizens, I know you're exhausted*
65 | 237+s

**4567 flèche** *nf* arrow
- cette flèche indique l'ordre de traitement – *this arrow shows the order of processing*
73 | 175

**4568 libéralisation** *nf* liberalization
- la libéralisation économique est désormais quasiment achevée – *economic freedom is henceforth largely achieved*
60 | 284-l

**4569 complot** *nm* plot, conspiracy
- je n'aime pas les complots, les mystères – *I don't like conspiracies or mysteries*
77 | 145

**4570 signataire** *nm,nf* signatory
- je crois qu'il faut 30 signataires – *I think we need 30 signatures*
68 | 213

**4571 ski** *nm* ski, skiing
- je fais du ski – *I ski*
57 | 306-l +n -s

**4572 douanier** *nadj* customs officer
- il n'y avait pas de contrôle douanier – *there was no customs check*
62 | 260

**4573 syndrome** *nm* syndrome
- je souffre ... du syndrome du manque d'amour – *I suffer from lack-of-love syndrome*
71 | 185

**4574 météo** *nf* weather forecast
- on nous annonçait la météo du lendemain – *the next day's weather forecast was given to us*
57 | 310-l +s

**4575 borner** *v* to limit, confine
- nous nous bornons à faire notre travail – *we confine ourselves to doing our work*
68 | 208-s

**4576 triompher** *v* to triumph, beat
- la démocratie finit toujours par triompher – *democracy always triumphs*
65 | 233+l -s

**4577 concrétiser** *v* to materialise
- j'espère vraiment concrétiser ce rêve un jour! – *I really hope to realize this dream one day!*
71 | 183

**4578 soumission** *nf* submission
- le foulard symbolise la soumission à Dieu – *the head scarf symbolizes submission to God*
75 | 159

**4579 continuellement** *adv* continually, continuously
- je dors continuellement, et j'ai de la fièvre – *I sleep constantly, and I have a fever*
78 | 134

**4580 dérober** *v* to steal, hide
- on leur déroba leurs valises – *their luggage was stolen*
71 | 184

**4581 romancier** *nm* novelist
- un romancier raconte toujours une histoire, son histoire – *a novelist always tells a story, his story*
60 | 281

**4582 sorcier** *nm* sorcerer, witch
- les sorcières aussi tombent malades? – *witches get sick too?*
71 | 188

**4583 consigne** *nf* deposit, orders, detention
- il rappelle quelques consignes générales – *he recalls some general orders*
74 | 164

**4584 harmonie** *nf* harmony
- nous devons travailler ensemble en parfaite harmonie – *we must work together in perfect harmony*
70 | 192

**4585 blond** *nadj* blond, fair-haired
- elle avait de jolis cheveux blonds – *she had pretty blonde hair*
57 | 308+l -n

**4586 pleuvoir** *v* to rain
- il trouve qu'il pleut tous les jours – *he finds that it rains every day*
67 | 216

**4587 déplaire** *v* to displease, be unhappy
- tout ce qui est superflu déplaît à Dieu et à la nature – *anything superfluous displeases God and nature*
70 | 190

**4588 innombrable** *adj(f)* innumerable, countless
- son existence résulte d'innombrables morts – *its existence stems from an untold number of deaths*
67 | 216+l

**4589 félicitation** *nf* congratulation
- nous recevons de nombreuses lettres de félicitations – *we receive many letters of congratulation*
61 | 268-n +s

**4590 inédit** *nadj* unpublished; original, new
- dix-sept films inédits seront en compétition – *seventeen unedited films will be competing*
68 | 207

**4591 lance** *nf* lance
- ils forgeront des charrues, des lances – *they will make chariots, lances*
80 | 117

**4592 désireux** *adj(pl)* avid for, anxious to, desirous of
- beaucoup seraient désireux de vous rencontrer – *many people would be happy to meet you*
77 | 138

**4593 diversifier** *v* to vary, diversify
- on a un pays très diversifié – *we have a very diversified country*
67 | 219

**4594 vélo** *nm* bike, bicycle
- elles se sont amenées hier en vélo – *they arrived here yesterday by bicycle*
73 | 166

**4595 fatigue** *nf* tiredness, fatigue
- les gens sont peut-être fatigués – *the people are perhaps tired*
60 | 276+l -s

**4596 instabilité** *nf* instability
- l'instabilité politique demeure – *political instability remains*
66 | 222

**4597 pénaliser** *v* to penalize, punish
- on est en train de pénaliser nos travailleurs – *we're punishing our workers*
64 | 238-l

**4598 comte** *nm* count
- le mari était comte. l'amant était marquis – *the husband was a count. the lover was a marquis*
56 | 316+l -s

**4599 amer** *adj,nm* bitter
- une surprise amère l'attend – *a bitter surprise awaits her*
65 | 231+l

**4600 orchestre** *nm* orchestra
- les orchestres ne veulent pas de ma musique – *orchestras don't want my music*
71 | 184

**4601 foncier** *adj* land-related, land, fundamental
- le code foncier va permettre cela – *the land-use laws will allow that*
61 | 267

**4602 dixième** *det,nm,nf* tenth
- on ne comprend pas le dixième de ce que vous dites – *we don't understand a tenth of what you're saying*
76 | 146

**4603 est** *nmi* east
- toutes les églises sont tournées vers l'est – *all of the churches have turned their attention eastwards*
75 | 152

**4604 envelopper** *v* to wrap, surround, veil
- donne-moi quelque chose pour envelopper le petit – *give me something to wrap the infant in*
63 | 252+l -s

**4605 troublant** *adj* disturbing
- c'est là quelque chose de très troublant – *something's very wrong here*
78 | 133

**4606 irrégulier** *adj* irregular, uneven
- leurs revenus sont incertains et irréguliers – *their income is uncertain and irregular*
77 | 136

**4607 fouet** *nm* whip
- il marchait sous le fouet du maître – *he walked under the whip of the master*
74 | 162

**4608 baigner** *v* to bathe, wash, get a bath, go for a swim
- je me baignai avec Anne, elle nageait doucement – *I swam with Anne; she was gently swimming*
67 | 214

**4609 fixation** *nf* fixation, fixing
- le peintre procède alors à une fixation – *the painter then becomes fixated*
79 | 122

**4610 encadrement** *nm* training, framing, supervision
- le personnel d'encadrement des ateliers est réduit – *supervisory staff in the workshops is reduced*
74 | 157

**4611 déménager** *v* to move
- on a déménagé dans un petit local – *we moved into a little nook*
74 | 157

**4612 esthétique** *nadj(f)* aesthetics, attractiveness; attractive
- je ressens une passion esthétique – *I feel an aesthetic passion*
62 | 259

**4613 photographier** *v* to photograph
- allons nous faire photographier aux îles – *let's go get photographed in the islands*
77 | 141

**4614 insensé** *nadj* insane
- t'as un comportement insensé – *your behavior is crazy*
72 | 173

**4615 moderniser** *v* to modernize
- nous devons simplement moderniser ce système – *we must simply modernize the system*
70 | 194

**4616 expérimental** *adj* experimental
- du point de vue expérimental, il est bon de vérifier – *from an experimental standpoint, it's good to double-check*
65 | 232

**4617 incomber** *v* to be incumbent upon
- ce rôle leur incombe maintenant – *this role falls to them now*
62 | 254+s

**4618 retombée** *nf* fallout, consequences, effects
- je n'ai pas eu de mauvaises retombées – *I haven't had any bad effects*
75 | 153

**4619 équivaloir** *v* to be equivalent, amount to
- cela équivaut à une taxe sur les malades – *this amounts to a tax on sick people*
67 | 211

**4620 différencier** *v* to differentiate
- je sais différencier un compliment d'une flatterie – *I know the difference between a compliment and flattery*
72 | 175

**4621 éventail** *nm* fan, range
- le gouvernement finance un éventail d'initiatives de recherche – *the government is financing a range of research initiatives*
73 | 166

**4622 solde** *nm,nf* balance; pay; sale
- tout est en solde dans Paris – *everything's on sale in Paris*
64 | 240

**4623 gâcher** *v* to waste, spoil
- je ne voulais pas gâcher votre fête – *I didn't want to ruin your party*
67 | 210

**4624 régiment** *nm* regiment
- c'est le meilleur soldat du régiment – *he's the best soldier in the regiment*
75 | 150

**4625 chiite** *nadj(f)* Shiite
- la conférence devait réunir des leaders chiites, sunnites et kurdes – *the conference was meant to bring together Shiite, Sunni, and Kurdish leaders*
49 | 380-I +n

**4626 bouleversement** *nm* upheaval
- le bouleversement est profond autour de nous – *profound upheaval is all around us*
75 | 155

**4627 relater** *v* to relate, recount
- ils m'ont relaté des histoires cauchemardesques – *they recounted nightmarish stories*
78 | 130

**4628 décent** *adj* decent, proper
- en surface, elle paraissait décente, prude et tout – *outwards, she appeared proper, prudish, and so on*
81 | 112

**4629 éminent** *adj* eminent, distinguished
- je souscris volontiers au verdict d'un éminent psychanalyste – *I gladly concur with the verdict of a distinguished psychoanalyst*
77 | 140

**4630 instituteur** *nm* school teacher
- l'instituteur feuilletait un manuel de sociologie – *the teacher paged through a sociology manual*
72 | 173

**4631 rayer** *v* to scratch, streak, stripe; to erase, strike out
- tu portes une chemise rayée et une cravate rayée – *you're wearing a striped shirt and a striped necktie*
77 | 136

**4632 concrètement** *adv* in concrete terms
- je vous demande concrètement si vous allez prendre des mesures sérieuses – *I ask you concretely if you are going to take serious measures*
68 | 206

**4633 coulisse** *nf* backstage, wings, behind the scenes
- car, en coulisse, on négocia – *for, behind the scenes, there were negotiations*
77 | 141

**4634 enchaîner** *v* to chain up, connect, string together
- tout semble s'enchaîner dans cette sinistre marche des événements – *everything seemed to link together in this sinister sequence of events*
72 | 174

**4635 ratification** *nf* ratification
- le processus de ratification n'est pas mort – *the ratification process is not dead*
66 | 223

**4636 emplacement** *nm* site, location
- les emplacements de camping sont séparés – *the camping sites are separated*
69 | 196

**4637 copier** *v* to copy, reproduce
- j'ai copié l'article – *I copied the article*
75 | 154

**4638 inculper** *v* to charge
- les preuves étaient insuffisantes pour l'inculper – *the evidence was insufficient to charge him*
58 | 292+n

**4639 renouveau** *nm* renewal
- ce renouveau doit, naturellement, commencer par en haut – *this renewal of course has to come top-down*
78 | 132

**4640 néerlandais** *nadj(pl)* Dutch
- la multinationale néerlandaise a annoncé de nouvelles pertes – *the Dutch multinational announced new losses*
54 | 323-l +n

**4641 intégral** *adj* complete, unabridged
- ils constituent un élément intégral de notre histoire – *they constitute an integral part of our history*
75 | 152

**4642 spécification** *nf* specification
- il convient alors de respecter les spécifications supplémentaires – *then it would be appropriate to honour the supplementary specifications*
40 | 482-l +n -s

**4643 documentation** *nf* documentation, literature
- j'écris aussi des documentations en français – *I also write documentation in French*
72 | 172

**4644 logiquement** *adv* logically
- logiquement, il fallait que cette vie se termine – *logically, this life had to end*
78 | 129

**4645 spectre** *nm* spectrum, ghost
- le spectre d'un conflit nucléaire généralisé s'écarte – *the threat of a widespread nuclear conflict is lessening*
57 | 302+n -s

**4646 harmoniser** *v* to harmonize, harmonize with
- il harmonise les règles – *he reconciled the rules*
72 | 173

**4647 suédois** *nadj(pl)* Swedish, Swede
- nous avons même un correspondant suédois – *we even have a Swedish correspondent*
58 | 284+n

**4648 rouvrir** *v* to reopen
- quant aux écoles militaires, elles étaient rouvertes sans délai – *the military schools were reopened without delay*
68 | 206

**4649 débouché** *nm* prospect, opportunity, opening
- il existe de nombreux débouchés dans plusieurs branches – *there are several openings in many branches*
68 | 202

**4650 croisé** *nadj* twill; alternate; crusader; crossed
- nos chemins se sont croisés de façon intéressante – *our paths crossed in an interesting manner*
78 | 127

**4651 fléau** *nm* scourge, plague
- la pauvreté est un fléau – *poverty is a plague*
78 | 130

**4652 traversée** *nf* crossing
- la traversée avait duré juste trois heures – *it only took three hours to make the crossing*
77 | 140

**4653 solaire** *adj(f)* solar
- nous pensons que le système solaire est issu d'une étoile – *we think the solar system emerged from a star*
73 | 164

**4654 secrétariat** *nm* secretaryship, secretariat, secretarial offices, secretary's office
- les clés seront au secrétariat – *the keys are at the secretary's office*
73 | 163

**4655 mou** *adj,nm* soft
- je devenais froide et molle comme un vieux cadavre – *I became cold and soft like an old cadaver*
65 | 230+l

**4656 venger** *v* to avenge, take revenge
- tu t'es vengé. réjouis-toi avant d'oublier – *you got your revenge. enjoy it before you forget*
65 | 230

**4657 détenteur** *nadj* holder, possessor, bearer
- cette carte plastifiée devrait permettre à son détenteur de voter – *this plastic card should allow the bearer to vote*
76 | 146

**4658 basque** *nadj(f)* Basque
- il y avait un couple de jeunes basques aussi qui était venu au Sénégal – *there was also a couple of Basque youths who came to Senegal*
55 | 313

**4659 soif** *nf* thirst
- si tu as soif, tu bois – *if you're thirsty, you drink*
65 | 229

**4660 accumulation** *nf* accumulation, amassing, storage, stockpiling, build-up
- il y a de dangereuses accumulations de neige – *there are dangerous accumulations of snow*
62 | 252+n -s

**4661 autoritaire** *adj(f)* authoritarian
- c'est un régime extraordinairement autoritaire – *its an extraordinarily authoritative regime*
73 | 163

**4662 essor** *nm* expansion, development, flight
- cette ville a pris un nouvel essor économique et touristique – *this city has made new strides in the economy and tourism*
72 | 174

**4663 obséder** *v* to obsess, haunt
- je ne suis pas obsédée du tout par la réussite – *I'm not at all obsessed by success*
73 | 167

**4664 intolérable** *adj(f)* intolerable
- leurs conditions de vie deviennent intolérables – *their living conditions are becoming intolerable*
80 | 118

**4665 rébellion** *nf* rebellion
- la rébellion va éclater, des gouvernments vont tomber! – *rebellion will break out, governments will fall!*
58 | 282+n

**4666 préventif** *adj* preventive
- les antibiotiques sont utilisés de façon préventive – *the antibiotics are used for prevention*
66 | 219

**4667 désignation** *nf* designation
- une désignation rapide et positive est nécessaire – *a swift and positive designation is necessary*
73 | 167

**4668 aimable** *adj(f)* pleasant, kind, nice
- je voulais juste être aimable – *I just wanted to be likable*
62 | 254+l -n

**4669 conformité** *nf* conformity
- on a un problème de conformité au niveau des registres – *we have a consistency problem with the books*
66 | 219

**4670 pantalon** *nm* trousers, pants
- ôtez votre pantalon et entrez, je vais vous examiner – *take off your pants and come in, I'm going to examine you*
57 | 298+l -n

**4671 anormal** *nadj* abnormal
- c'est tout à fait anormal – *it's completely abnormal*
60 | 264+n -s

**4672 inhérent** *adj* inherent
- nous reconnaissons le droit inhérent des autochtones – *we recognize the inherent rights of natives*
71 | 179

**4673 réconcilier** *v* to reconcile
- la mère et le fils se réconcilient – *mother and son reconciled*
75 | 150

**4674 réservoir** *nm* tank, reservoir
- le réservoir ainsi formé est un immense lac – *the reservoir thus formed is an immense lake*
77 | 135

**4675 aveu** *nm* confession
- je considère votre silence comme un aveu – *I take your silence to be a confession*
70 | 182

**4676 emmerder** *v* to bug, bother
- je serais bien emmerdé si tu attrapais une pneumonie – *I would be pissed off if you catch a cold*
52 | 341-n +s

**4677 inondation** *nf* flood, deluge
- l'école est fermée pour inondation – *the school is closed due to flooding*
63 | 237

**4678 câble** *nm* cable, wire
- le câble est bloqué – *the cable is blocked*
62 | 247

**4679 poumon** *nm* lung
- ils respiraient à pleins poumons – *they breathed very deeply*
72 | 169

**4680 humble** *adj(f)* humble, lowly
- veuillez accepter mes humbles excuses – *please accept my humble apologies*
68 | 199+l -n

**4681 perturbation** *nf* disruption, disturbance
- la circulation n'a pas connu d'importantes perturbations – *traffic hasn't been greatly affected*
64 | 236+n

**4682 brouiller** *v* to mix-up, confuse, scramble
- le récit des confessions brouille tout – *the written confession muddles up everything*
66 | 216+l

**4683 illustration** *nf* illustration
- les illustrations sont originales – *the illustrations are original*
69 | 192

**4684 appliqué** *adj* assiduous, industrious, careful
- oui, j'étais une élève appliquée – *yes, I was a diligent student*
75 | 148

**4685 fermier** *nadj* farmer
- les fermiers ont des journées très remplies – *farmers have very busy days*
72 | 170

**4686 hanter** *v* to haunt
- tu hantes mes rêves – *you haunt my dreams*
74 | 153

**4687 cordon** *nm* cord, string, lead
- elle a sectionné le cordon avec ses dents – *she cut the cord with her teeth*
74 | 156

**4688 néfaste** *adj(f)* harmful, ill-fated
- ces polluants sont néfastes pour tous – *these pollutants are harmful to everyone*
72 | 168

**4689 lasser** *v* to tire, weary, grow weary
- je ne veux pas lasser le public – *I don't want to make the public weary*
67 | 209+l

**4690 influer** *v* to influence, have an influence on
- chaque vie, influe sur les autres – *each life influences others*
74 | 154

**4691 présentement** *adv* at present, presently
- nous étudions ce besoin présentement – *we're currently studying this need*
52 | 338-n +s

**4692 plate-forme** *nf* platform
- ils restèrent debout sur la plate-forme – *they remained standing on the platform*
76 | 139

**4693 stopper** *v* to stop, halt
- vous pourriez me stopper avec un seul mot – *you could stop me with one single word*
72 | 169

**4694 kurde** *nadj(f)* Kurd, Kurdish
- la langue kurde est interdite à l'école – *the Kurdish language is forbidden at school*
53 | 328-l

**4695 amusant** *nadj* funny, amusing, entertaining
- j'avais trouvé une phrase amusante – *I had found a funny phrase*
65 | 222-n

**4696 tremblement** *nm* shiver, trembling, shaking
- il y avait dans sa voix un tremblement – *there was trembling in her voice*
66 | 217

**4697 rail** *nm* rail, track
- j'ai suivi les rails pour arriver ici – *I followed the tracks to get here*
74 | 154

**4698 fondamentalement** *adv* basically, fundamentally, inherently
- telle est fondamentalement notre position – *fundamentally that is our position*
67 | 210+s

**4699 lampe** *nf* lamp, light
- la scène est éclairée par une lampe à pétrole – *the scene was lit by a kerosene lamp*
56 | 301+l -n -s

**4700 triple** *nadj(f)* triple
- t'as vu mon triple saut? je peux le refaire – *did you see my triple jump? I can do it again*
76 | 140

**4701 inchangé** *adj* unchanged
- l'état de la route demeure inchangé – *road conditions remain unchanged*
61 | 255+n -s

**4702 supplier** *v* to beg, implore
- je t'en supplie, ne pars pas – *I beg you, don't leave*
60 | 268-n

**4703 multiplication** *nf* multiplication
- j'avais prédit une multiplication de travail pour l'automne – *I predicted an increase in workload for the fall*
67 | 205

**4704 camoufler** *v* to cover up, conceal, camouflage
- certaines araignées changent leurs couleurs pour se camoufler – *some spiders change colours as camouflage*
84 | 89

**4705 cliché** *nm* cliché; negative
- cette théorie est devenue un vieux cliché freudien – *this theory has become an old Freudian cliché*
73 | 165

**4706 diamant** *nm* diamond
- c'est le plus beau diamant du monde – *it's the most beautiful diamond in the world*
71 | 180

**4707 guerrier** *nadj* warrior; warlike
- t'as une âme de guerrier – *you have a warrior's soul*
68 | 198

**4708 figer** *v* to clot, coagulate, congeal, set
- le pauvre animal resta figé sur place – *the poor animal remained frozen in its tracks*
62 | 249+l

**4709 comique** *nadj(f)* comical; comic, comedian
- le malentendu serait plutôt comique – *the misunderstanding would be rather comical*
73 | 162

**4710 planification** *nf* planning
- ils doivent payer pour la mauvaise planification – *they have to pay for bad planning*
63 | 240

**4711 éloge** *nm* praise
- je ferai votre éloge – *I will sing your praises*
76 | 143

**4712 regroupement** *nm* regrouping, reassembly
- ils inventent les regroupements de populations – *they create population regroupings*
72 | 171

**4713 odieux** *adj(pl)* hateful, odious
- ces façons de parler sont odieuses – *these are heinous manners of speaking*
74 | 155

**4714 désastreux** *adj(pl)* disastrous
- ce sera un mariage désastreux – *that will be a disastrous marriage*
72 | 172

**4715 nocturne** *nadj(f)* nocturnal, nocturne
- ils ajustèrent leurs lunettes à vision nocturne – *they adjusted their night vision goggles*
69 | 193+l -s

**4716 configuration** *nf* configuration, layout
- la configuration institutionnelle rendrait une partition très difficile – *the institutional configuration would render a partition very difficult*
52 | 342+n

**4717 escompter** *v* to discount; to expect
- cela n'a pas eu les résultats escomptés – *that didn't have the expected results*
58 | 281+n

**4718 intensif** *nadj* intensive
- une telle traduction représente un travail intensif – *a translation like this involves intense work*
76 | 143

**4719 scepticisme** *nm* scepticism
- je vous concède que le scepticisme n'est pas très sexy – *I admit that scepticism isn't very sexy*
80 | 111

**4720 croisière** *nf* cruise
- on a décidé de faire cette croisière en Mer Rouge – *we decided to take a Red Sea cruise*
76 | 142

**4721 plénier** *adj* plenary, full
- l'assemblée plénière est tombée d'accord – *the plenary assembly came to agreement*
57 | 285+s

**4722 athlète** *nm,nf* athlete
- les athlètes doivent être de bons leaders – *athletes must be good leaders*
63 | 234

**4723 poil** *nm* hair, bristle
- il est allergique au poil de chat – *he's allergic to cat hair*
59 | 273-n

**4724 épanouir** *v* to bloom, blossom
- elle est très vivante et s'épanouit de plus en plus – *she's very lively and is blossoming more and more*
75 | 149

**4725 minimiser** *v* to minimize, play down
- il tend donc à minimiser le problème – *so he tends to minimize the problem*
73 | 160

**4726 inévitablement** *adv* inevitably
- le chômage augmenterait inévitablement – *unemployment would inevitably increase*
77 | 131

**4727 informé** *nadj* informed
- la population doit être mieux informée au sujet – *the population must be better informed on the subject*
76 | 140

**4728 islam** *nm* Islam
- l'Islam est aujourd'hui la deuxième religion de France – *Islam is the second largest religion in France today*
57 | 287+n

**4729 échéant** *adj* if need be
- c'est moi qui le cas échéant prendrai la décision – *I'm the one who will make the decision if necessary*
62 | 241

**4730 murmurer** *v* to murmur
- elle a murmuré dans mon oreille – *she mumbled into my ear*
50 | 355+l -n -s

**4731 implantation** *nf* implanting, setting up, establishment, implantation, installation
- quelle est votre stratégie d'implantation? – *what is your installation strategy?*
70 | 185

**4732 décerner** *v* to award, give, issue
- en science, on ne décerne pas de distinction pour les redécouvertes – *in science nobody receives a prize for rediscovering something*
71 | 173

**4733 replacer** *v* to replace, put back
- il replaça le paquet dans sa poche – *he returned the package to his pocket*
81 | 106

**4734 vêtir** *v* to clothe, dress, put on
- c'était un vieil homme, vêtu bourgeoisement – *he was an old man, dressed simply*
59 | 270+l -s

**4735 trottoir** *nm* pavement
- mets-moi sur le trottoir, je me débrouillerai – *put me on the sidewalk, I'll manage*
60 | 257+l

**4736 vieillard** *nm* old man
- le vieillard haussa les épaules – *the old man shrugged his shoulders*
57 | 285+l -s

**4737 fillette** *nf* little girl, girl
- certes la fillette semblait précoce – *the little girl certainly seemed precocious*
66 | 211

**4738 enchanter** *v* to delight, enchant, rejoice
- mais il est enchanté de me voir, hein? – *he's sure delighted to see me, eh?*
57 | 286-n

**4739 singe** *nm* monkey
- ils imitent le cri des singes – *they're imitating the monkeys' scream*
66 | 209

**4740 superficiel** *adj* superficial, shallow
- t'es un mec superficiel, un vrai nul – *you're a shallow guy, a real nobody*
72 | 170

**4741 rigide** *adj(f)* rigid, stiff
- il y a de rigides paramètres en place – *there are fixed parameters in place*
76 | 138

**4742 démographique** *adj(f)* demographic
- nous vivons en une époque d'évolution démographique – *we live in an era of demographic evolution*
68 | 197

**4743 fourniture** *nf* supply, provision
- l'accord prévoit la fourniture de 3 millions de tonnes de pétrole – *the agreement anticipates a supply of 3 million tonnes of oil*
71 | 172

**4744 taxer** *v* to tax
- il est injuste de le taxer de caprice – *it's injust to tax indiscriminately*
71 | 171

**4745 milice** *nf* militia
- les milices sont responsables de crimes contre l'humanité – *the militias are responsible for crimes against humanity*
55 | 301+n -s

**4746 foire** *nf* fair
• hier, j'étais à la foire aux livres – *yesterday I was at the book fair*
76 | 136

**4747 élégant** *adj* elegant, stylish
• les pauvres sont désormais plus élégants que les riches – *the poor are henceforth more elegant than the rich*
67 | 206+l

**4748 crème** *adji,nf* cream
• son père lui appliqua une crème désinfectante et lui banda la main – *his father applied some disinfectant cream and bandaged his hand*
72 | 166

**4749 mentalité** *nf* mentality
• il faut instaurer une mentalité de gagnant et de bosseur – *we need to establish a winning and hard-working mentality*
67 | 203

**4750 charité** *nf* charity
• beaucoup de laïcs ont plus de charité qu'eux – *many lay clergy have more charity than they do*
61 | 252+l -s

**4751 borne** *nf* milestone, boundary stone
• je vous ai affirmé notre admiration sans bornes – *I have asserted to you our unqualified admiration*
66 | 213

**4752 organique** *adj(f)* organic
• une forme de vie organique vient à ma rescousse – *an organic life form came to my rescue*
70 | 179

**4753 dévouer** *v* to devote, sacrifice oneself
• elle se dévoua à la gloire de son ami – *she devoted herself to the glory of her friend*
69 | 190

**4754 hâter** *v* to quicken, hasten
• hâte-toi de revenir – *hurry back*
65 | 215+l

**4755 mobilité** *nf* mobility
• la mobilité de la population a changé – *the mobility of the population has changed*
72 | 169

**4756 exclu** *nm,adj* outcast
• je ne me suis jamais senti exclu – *I never felt excluded*
74 | 149

**4757 boucher** *nm,v* butcher; to fill in, get clogged up
• il faudra sans doute boucher des trous – *it will of course be necessary to plug the holes*
67 | 206

**4758 bénéfique** *adj(f)* beneficial
• les faits prouvent que le mariage est bénéfique pour les enfants – *the facts prove that marriage is beneficial for children*
73 | 161

**4759 commencement** *nm* beginning, start
• ce n'est que le commencement et non la fin – *it's only the beginning and not the end*
58 | 272+l -s

**4760 licenciement** *nm* dismissal, sacking
• on va vous notifier votre licenciement, par courrier – *we will notify you of your dismissal by mail*
54 | 313-l +n

**4761 chancelier** *nm* chancellor
• le chancelier doit rencontrer le président du parlement – *the chancellor must meet the speaker of the parliament*
54 | 315+n -s

**4762 retenue** *nf* deduction; restraint, self-control
• je me suis racontée sans aucune retenue – *I talked about myself without any restraint*
72 | 168

**4763 visée** *nf* aim, design, sighting
• nous n'avons aucune visée sur l'Indochine – *we have no designs for Indochina*
81 | 103

**4764 dénonciation** *nf* denunciation
• la dénonciation ne doit pas être acide ou sarcastique – *the denunciation need not be acerbic or sarcastic*
77 | 129

**4765 plaie** *nf* wound
• il lavera et séchera nos plaies – *he will wash and dry our wounds*
75 | 141

**4766 exiler** *v* to exile
• il se lamentait d'être exilé – *he rued at being exiled*
71 | 171

**4767 rocher** *nm* rock, boulder
• il a disparu derrière les rochers – *he disappeared behind the rocks*
62 | 237+l

**4768 mortalité** *nf* mortality, death rate
• la mortalité par cancer continue à décroître aux Etats-Unis – *cancer deaths continue to decrease in the U.S.*
78 | 122

**4769 cruauté** *nf* cruelty
• c'est tout simplement un acte de cruauté – *it's simply an act of cruelty*
75 | 146

**4770 regrettable** *adj(f)* unfortunate, regrettable
• la perte d'une vie est toujours regrettable – *the loss of a life is always regrettable*
71 | 168

**4771 droguer** *v* to drug, take drugs
• je me suis déjà drogué – *I was already high on drugs*
80 | 111

**4772 connecter** *v* to connect, go on-line
• tous les pays sont connectés à Internet – *all countries are connected to the Internet*
50 | 352-l +n -s

**4773 confort** *nm* comfort
• tout le monde vit dans le confort – *everyone lives in comfort*
74 | 152

# 27 Word length

A commonly observed property in language is that the most frequently occurring words often happen to be the shortest. Conversely, the longer a word is, the less frequently it tends to occur. This table shows results from the French corpus used for this dictionary. Over 9 million of the 23 million words in the corpus are one or two characters long. There are about 1.2 million three-letter words, and only about 84,000 fourteen-letter words. The table also lists the number of distinct word forms ("word types") and the most commonly occurring words for each word length.

| Number of letters | Unique word forms (types) | Total number of occurrences (tokens) | Most common words |
|---|---|---|---|
| 1 | 123 | 3670733 | à, a, y |
| 2 | 844 | 5521284 | de, la, le |
| 3 | 4500 | 3075735 | les, des, que |
| 4 | 9436 | 2372122 | dans, pour, plus |
| 5 | 16872 | 1829016 | cette, comme, était |
| 6 | 24982 | 1625657 | autres, encore, depuis |
| 7 | 28977 | 1476231 | premier, comment, quelque |
| 8 | 29522 | 1211544 | ministre, monsieur, toujours |
| 9 | 26599 | 957645 | président, politique, peut-être |
| 10 | 21942 | 634806 | maintenant, commission, économique |
| 11 | 16337 | 368912 | aujourd'hui, entreprises, information |
| 12 | 11700 | 261149 | gouvernement, c'est-à-dire, actuellement |
| 13 | 7947 | 139793 | développement, international, environnement |
| 14 | 5362 | 84020 | internationale, recommandation, responsabilité |
| 15+ | 9657 | 81339 | investissements, malheureusement, recommandations |

**4774 compréhensible** *adj(f)* comprehensible, understandable
- il est compréhensible que le public soit inquiet – *it's understandable that the public is disturbed*
79 | 119

**4775 tube** *nm* tube
- deux fois déjà le tube a été retiré puis remis – *twice already the tube was pulled out, then reinserted*
66 | 210

**4776 coffre** *nm* trunk, boot, chest
- les bagages sont dans le coffre – *the suitcases are in the trunk*
64 | 226+s

**4777 intimider** *v* to intimidate
- il essayait de m'intimider – *he tried to intimidate me*
72 | 162

**4778 huitième** *det,nm,nf* eighth
- il a terminé la course huitième – *he finished the race in eighth place*
64 | 223

**4779 forger** *v* to forge, contrive, make up
- il nous faut forger des concepts inconcevables – *we need to invent inconceivable concepts*
73 | 157

**4780 périr** *v* to perish
- je périrais sans toi – *I would perish without you*
70 | 179

**4781 notoire** *adj(f)* notorious, well-known
- nous détenons en ce moment un meurtrier notoire – *at the moment we have a notorious murderer in custody*
89 | 54

**4782 graphique** *nadj(f)* graph, graphic
- j'aimerais avoir un graphique ici – *I would like to have a graph here*
56 | 288+n

**4783 annulation** *nf* cancellation, annulment
- l'annulation est due à la défection de certains partenaires – *the annulment results from the defection of some partners*
65 | 213-l

**4784 acceptation** *nf* acceptance
- la foi suppose l'acceptation du mystère – *faith requires acceptance of the mystery*
72 | 164

**4785 textile** *nadj(f)* textile
- mère, enfants travaillent dans le textile – *mother and children are working in the textile industry*
56 | 292+n

**4786 hormis** *prep* save, but
- hormis vous, personne n'a vu ce gamin – *except for you, nobody saw this kid*
76 | 136

**4787 chirurgien** *nm* surgeon
- les chirurgiens disent qu'il n'a pas souffert – *the surgeons say he didn't suffer*
71 | 168

**4788 orage** *nm* storm, thunderstorm
- au loin un orage grondait – *in the distance a storm thundered*
64 | 221

**4789 boule** *nf* ball
- je lui ai offert une boule à neige – *I offered her a snowball*
61 | 248

**4790 médiation** *nf* mediation, arbitration
- les tentatives américaines de médiation ont continué – *American attempts at negotiation continued*
73 | 155

**4791 réprimer** *v* to suppress, repress
- vous réprimez ce que vous ressentez – *you're repressing what you feel*
74 | 150

**4792 hall** *nm* foyer, lobby
- je l'ai rencontré dans le hall d'un immeuble – *I met him in the foyer of the building*
74 | 150

**4793 visuel** *adj* visual
- mais garde le contact visuel – *but keep visual contact*
54 | 309

**4794 semblant** *nm* semblance, pretence
- faites semblant d'être désespérée – *pretend to be desperate*
68 | 194

**4795 jadis** *adv* formerly, long ago
- jadis, nous étions des esclaves – *long ago, we were slaves*
62 | 239+l -s

**4796 rémunérer** *v* to remunerate, pay
- il était rémunéré par une excellente nourriture – *he was paid with excellent food*
68 | 192

**4797 fasciner** *v* to fascinate
- c'est un sujet qui me fascine – *it's a subject that fascinates me*
64 | 225

**4798 dilemme** *nm* dilemma
- c'est l'éternel dilemme de la carotte et du bâton – *it's the eternal dilemma of the carrot and the stick*
78 | 123

**4799 progressiste** *nm,nf* progressive
- on a un système scolaire progressiste – *we have a progressive school system*
62 | 239

**4800 ours** *adji,nm(pl)* bear
- cet ours polaire doit aller dormir – *this polar bear needs to go to sleep*
76 | 137

**4801 décharger** *v* to unload
- aidez Grégoire à décharger le van – *help Grégoire unload the van*
75 | 139

**4802 excéder** *v* to exceed
- le total ne peut excéder 55 000 francs – *the total cannot exceed 55,000 francs*
73 | 156

**4803 blâmer** *v* to blame, reprimand
- il cherche quelqu'un d'autre à blâmer – *he's looking for someone else to blame*
68 | 189-n

**4804 duc** *nm* duke
- un mari outragé, un duc, vient se plaindre – *an outraged husband, a duke, comes to complain*
58 | 268+l -s

**4805 raciste** *nadj(f)* racist
- je ne tolère aucun comportement raciste à bord – *I don't tolerate any racist behavior on board*
68 | 186

**4806 stress** *nm(pl)* stress
- le stress, ça rend un peu dingue – *stress makes you a little bit crazy*
65 | 212

**4807 inexistant** *adj* non-existent
- la coopération entre pays voisins était quasiment inexistante – *cooperation between neighboring countries was practically non-existent*
76 | 135

**4808 théoriquement** *adv* theoretically
- l'accès en resterait théoriquement interdit aux femmes seules – *access would theoretically remain forbidden to unaccompanied women*
76 | 136

**4809 danois** *nadj(pl)* Danish, Dane
- le compromis danois aura un statut équivalent – *the Danish compromise will have an equivalent status*
58 | 272

**4810 concéder** *v* to grant, concede
- le dollar a concédé une partie du terrain gagné – *the dollar lost some of the ground it had gained*
70 | 172

**4811 retrancher** *v* to deduct, remove; to entrench
- son air passif la retranchait du monde – *his passive attitude removed him from the rest of the world*
72 | 160

**4812 renfermer** *v* to contain, shut, lock, enclose
- c'est un homme renfermé et primitif, mais profondément loyal – *he's an uncommunicative, primitive man but deeply loyal*
62 | 234

**4813 vieillesse** *nf* old age
- ce que jeunesse désire, vieillesse l'a en abondance – *what youth wants, old age has abundantly*
66 | 207

**4814 navette** *nf* shuttle
- les navettes pour l'aéroport? elles sont là – *the airport shuttles? they're here*
58 | 269+n -s

**4815 traditionnellement** *adv* traditionally
- traditionnellement, le cadre est un manager – *traditionally, the executive is a manager*
68 | 192

**4816 batterie** *nf* battery; drum set
- ces batteries devraient avoir une longue durée de vie – *these batteries should have a long life*
70 | 173

**4817 foie** *nm* liver
- souffrir de problèmes graves au foie – *to suffer from serious liver problems*
80 | 108

**4818 gratuitement** *adv* free, gratuitously
- il nous a tout donné gratuitement – *he gave us everything for free*
77 | 129

**4819 incompréhensible** *adj(f)* incomprehensible
- je trouve cela incompréhensible et ignoble – *I find that unbelievable and disgraceful*
76 | 135

**4820 détour** *nm* bend, curve, detour
- j'ai fait un détour pour sortir sans passer devant lui – *I went out of my way to avoid passing in front of him*
66 | 204+l

**4821 boulevard** *nm* boulevard
- nous nous promenions sur les boulevards – *we were walking along the boulevards*
64 | 217+l -s

**4822 blague** *nf* joke
- je ne raconte plus de blagues – *I don't tell jokes any more*
57 | 271-n +s

**4823 mécontentement** *nm* displeasure, dissatisfaction
- les exemples de mécontentement sont nombreux et variés – *examples of dissatisfaction were numerous and wide-ranging*
76 | 135

**4824 inaugurer** *v* to unveil, open
- il inaugura les fêtes célébrant le centenaire de la Révolution – *he opened the Revolution Centennial celebrations*
70 | 175

**4825 repli** *nm* bend, twist, wrinkle, fold, fallback
- c'est plutôt la saison d'un repli frileux – *it was instead the time for a chilly retreat*
68 | 187-s

**4826 contrepartie** *nf* counterpart, opposite, alternative
- la solitude n'est pas la seule contrepartie de l'amitié – *loneliness isn't the only alternative to friendship*
69 | 181

**4827 proportionnel** *adj* proportional
- dans le système proportionnel, chaque vote a la même valeur – *in the proportional system, each vote has the same value*
64 | 214

**4828 aboutissement** *nm* outcome, result
- je suis l'aboutissement de tous ces instincts – *I'm the outcome of all of these instincts*
78 | 117

**4829 triomphe** *nm* triumph
- tout mariage marque le triomphe de l'espoir sur l'expérience – *every marriage marks a triumph of hope over experience*
65 | 207+l -s

**4830 libre-échange** *nm* free trade
- la concurrence et le libre-échange sont liés – *competition and free trade are connected*
58 | 263-l

**4831 sincérité** *nf* sincerity
- je parle vraiment en toute sincérité – *I'm really talking with complete sincerity*
69 | 178

**4832 serre** *nf* greenhouse
- l'effet de serre est un phénomène naturel – *the greenhouse effect is a natural phenomenon*
72 | 159

**4833 doré** *adj* golden
- la jeunesse étudiante est encore une jeunesse dorée – *student youthfulness is still golden youthfulness*
62 | 236+l -s

**4834 convoi** *nm* convoy, train
- de quel hangar part le convoi? – *the convoy is leaving from which hangar?*
59 | 253

**4835 terrien** *nadj* earthling; landowner, countryman
- le Terrien est sur le point de vomir – *the Earthling is about to vomit*
42 | 425-l +n -s

**4836 psychologie** *nf* psychology
- il se spécialise en psychologie – *he specialized in psychology*
66 | 199

**4837 maltraiter** *v* to manhandle, ill-treat, misuse, slight
- vous me forcez vraiment à vous maltraiter – *you're really forcing me to mistreat you*
84 | 82

**4838 puits** *nm(pl)* well, shaft, pit
- je suis tombé dans un puits abandonné – *I fell into an abandoned pit*
74 | 146

**4839 intimité** *nf* privacy, intimacy
- il est gêné par l'intimité masculine – *he's troubled by masculine intimacy*
68 | 187

**4840 équation** *nf* equation
• cette quantité se précise dans une équation
– *this amount is figured out in an equation*
72 | 158

**4841 humide** *adj(f)* moist, damp, humid, wet
• il faisait froid et humide dans la cabine
– *it was cold and humid in the cabin*
61 | 237+l -s

**4842 bétail** *nm* livestock, cattle
• vos chevaux sont là-bas, avec votre bétail
– *your horses are there, with your cattle*
79 | 111

**4843 prophète** *nm* prophet
• demandons aux prophètes comment on
devrait appeler ça – *let's ask the prophets
what we should call this*
73 | 152

**4844 micro** *nm* mike, micro, microphone
• venez donc parler dans le micro – *come and
speak into the mike*
62 | 230+s

**4845 gâteau** *nadj* cake
• qui mange du gâteau d'anniversaire? – *who
wants to eat some birthday cake?*
68 | 186

**4846 continental** *adj* continental
• nous avons besoin d'un réseau routier
continental – *we need a continental road
network*
76 | 132

**4847 réitérer** *v* to reiterate, repeat
• il a réitéré sa demande aujourd'hui – *he
reiterated his request today*
67 | 195

**4848 énumérer** *v* to enumerate
• il est bien inutile d'énumérer les obstacles
– *it's totally useless to enumerate the
obstacles*
66 | 198

**4849 embauche** *nf* job vacancy, hiring
• les embauches ont repris au troisième
trimestre – *hiring stepped up in the third
quarter*
69 | 179-l

**4850 verdict** *nm* verdict
• les jurés, avez-vous rendu votre verdict?
– *members of the jury, have you arrived at
a verdict?*
65 | 204

**4851 dix-neuf** *det,nmi* nineteen
• je suis entré chez les Jésuites à dix-neuf
ans – *I became a Jesuit at the age of
nineteen*
58 | 265

**4852 guetter** *v* to watch over, watch out for
• tu vas guetter les flics – *you're going to be
on the lookout for the cops*
61 | 241+l

**4853 frustrer** *v* to frustrate
• j'ai cependant été frustré par un nouvel
échec – *I was nonetheless frustrated by a
new failure*
80 | 107

**4854 anglo-saxon** *nadj* Anglo-Saxon
• c'est un humour plus anglo-saxon que
français – *that humor is more Anglo-Saxon
than French*
65 | 204

**4855 détente** *nf* release, relaxation, détente,
loosening
• ce n'est pas un week-end de détente – *it's
not a relaxing weekend*
68 | 182

**4856 questionner** *v* to question
• elle me questionnait sans cesse – *they
questioned me continually*
73 | 151

**4857 injecter** *v* to inject
• nous avons injecté de l'argent dans le
programme – *we injected money into the
program*
71 | 166

**4858 préjudice** *nm* loss, harm, damage
• avez-vous déjà subi des préjudices? – *have
you already suffered any losses?*
64 | 211

**4859 couramment** *adv* fluently, commonly
• elle parlait couramment deux autres langues
aussi – *she also spoke two other languages
fluently*
77 | 126

**4860 exploration** *nf* exploration, investigation,
examination
• rien ne vaut l'exploration du terrain –
*nothing is worth the exploration of the land*
71 | 166

**4861 caresser** *v* to fondle, caress
• embrassez-moi et caressez-moi, mon cher
époux – *kiss me and hug me, my dear
husband*
56 | 280+l -n

**4862 hymne** *nm,nf* hymn, anthem
• j'ai chanté l'hymne national – *I sang the
national anthem*
79 | 110

**4863 sécuritaire** *adj(f)* safe
• le niveau de décontamination sera
totalement sécuritaire – *the contamination
level will be perfectly safe*
65 | 203-l

**4864 famine** *nf* famine
• une grande famine venait de dévaster la
Chine – *a great famine devastated China*
73 | 149

**4865 écrier** *v* to exclaim, cry out
• venez, venez tous, s'écria-t-elle – *come here,
everybody, she yelled*
47 | 365+l -n -s

**4866 précipitation** *nf* haste, precipitation
• la précipitation est rarement une bonne
conseillère – *haste is rarely a wise counselor*
66 | 201+n -s

**4867 caution** *nf* deposit, guarantee, bail
• le prévenu doit également régler une
caution de 80.000 euros – *the accused must
also post a bail of 80,000 euros*
75 | 139

**4868 affectation** *nf* appointment, allocation; show, pretence
• il bâilla avec affectation – *he made a show of yawning*
71 | 167

**4869 salaud** *nadj* bastard
• les hommes sont des salauds – *men are pigs*
53 | 308-n

**4870 cave** *adj(f),nm,nf* cellar, basement
• il faut descendre dans la cave – *we had to go down into the cellar*
65 | 205

**4871 bond** *nm* leap, rebound
• la richesse du pays a fait un bond – *the wealth of the country rebounded*
68 | 184-s

**4872 enclin** *adj* enclined, prone
• je suis enclin à les laisser pourrir – *I'm inclined to let them rot*
85 | 76

**4873 nettoyage** *nm* cleaning, cleansing
• j'ai un job spécial de nettoyage : tout le local à bateaux – *I have a special cleaning job: all of the boat docks*
71 | 166

**4874 foudre** *nf* lightning
• vous avez été frappé par la foudre – *you were struck by lightning*
74 | 142

**4875 justesse** *nf* accuracy, precision
• la question de la justesse se pose – *the question of correctness is relevant here*
78 | 120

**4876 rente** *nf* annuity, pension
• l'accumulation des rentes est funeste pour le monde occidental – *the accumulation of income is deadly for the West*
69 | 176

**4877 hépatite** *nf* hepatitis
• l'hépatite C est très différente du VIH – *hepatitis C is very different from HIV*
44 | 391-l -n +s

**4878 blindé** *adj* armoured
• la majorité de nos véhicules blindés sont des blindés légers – *most of our armored vehicles are light tanks*
67 | 193

**4879 clan** *nm* clan
• j'ai besoin de savoir à quel clan la personne appartient – *I need to know what clan the person belonged to*
72 | 155

**4880 accélération** *nf* acceleration
• l'accélération de la mondialisation économique – *the acceleration of economic globalization*
73 | 151

**4881 garage** *nm* garage
• allez au garage chercher des voitures – *go to the garage to get some cars*
74 | 141

**4882 résolument** *adv* resolutely
• il faut se tourner résolument vers l'avenir – *you need to be forward-looking*
77 | 124

**4883 négociateur** *nadj* negotiator
• les négociateurs restent pratiquement muets – *the negotiators are practically keeping mum*
62 | 224

**4884 romantique** *nadj(f)* romantic
• les romantiques, justement, désiraient toujours au-delà – *exactly: romanticists always wanted more*
65 | 202

**4885 obscurité** *nf* darkness
• elle commença dans l'obscurité à monter l'escalier – *she started to climb the stairs in the dark*
56 | 278+l -s

**4886 vulgaire** *nadj(f)* vulgar, common, popular
• tu es vulgaire – *you're vulgar*
65 | 205-n

**4887 soixante-dix** *det,nmi* seventy
• quand tu auras soixante-dix ans, tu seras toujours toi – *when you're seventy years old, you'll still be yourself*
63 | 222

**4888 féroce** *adj(f)* ferocious, fierce
• son regard était noir et féroce – *his glare was dark and ferocious*
75 | 133

**4889 perpétuel** *adj* perpetual, everlasting, never-ending
• elle est une tension perpétuelle – *she is highly strung*
67 | 189

**4890 militer** *v* to militate
• nous avons toujours milité contre l'exploitation – *we have always mobilized against exploitation*
66 | 196

**4891 jungle** *nf* jungle
• les rebelles ont opéré depuis la jungle – *the rebels were operating from the jungle*
77 | 126

**4892 case** *nf* box, hut, field
• je vous laisse choisir la case qui me convient le mieux – *I'll let you choose the box that will fit me the best*
60 | 243

**4893 craquer** *v* to creak, squeak, crackle, give in, strike
• les livres neufs craquaient entre les doigts – *the new books were crisp between his fingers*
66 | 200

**4894 clarifier** *v* to clarify
• il faut clarifier ces questions maintenant – *these questions must be clarified now*
66 | 200-l +s

**4895 crête** *nf* crest, top, ridge
• un grand nuage noir emmitoufle la crête des montagnes – *a large black cloud hugged the crest of the mountains*
51 | 321+n -s

**4896 traite** *nf* trade, draft, stretch, milking
- je l'ai lue d'une traite – *I read it in one sitting*
80 | 105

**4897 démarrage** *nm* start, moving off
- généralement le démarrage d'un livre se passe très bien – *generally, starting a book goes very well*
78 | 116

**4898 oubli** *nm* forgetting, leaving behind, missing
- mais certaines choses méritent l'oubli – *some things deserve to be forgotten*
72 | 154

**4899 procès-verbal** *nm* minutes, statement
- cette intervention ne figure pas dans le procès-verbal – *this speech isn't included in the transcript*
46 | 373-n +s

**4900 formalité** *nf* formality
- oubliez ces formalités, mon enfant – *forget these formalities, my child*
80 | 106

**4901 insensible** *adj(f)* insensitive
- vous êtes insensible à la raison – *you're unmoved by reason*
76 | 130

**4902 distant** *adj* far-off, distant, faraway
- il me fit un salut distant – *he waved at me from afar*
50 | 332+n -s

**4903 émetteur** *nm* transmitter, issuer
- on va s'acheter un émetteur et on va se promener dans une van – *we're going to buy a transmitter and drive around in a van*
56 | 271+n -s

**4904 montage** *nm* assembly, setting, pitching, putting, editing
- tout le montage du film s'est fait en digital – *all of the editing of the film was done digitally*
60 | 244

**4905 énergique** *adj(f)* energetic
- je suis très énergique et passionnée – *I'm very energetic and passionate*
79 | 110

**4906 claquer** *v* to flap, bang, slam, snap
- j'avais envie de claquer violemment la porte derrière lui – *I wanted to slam the door violently behind him*
64 | 208+l

**4907 simplicité** *nf* simplicity, straightforwardness
- la simplicité de ces adieux le toucha – *the simplicity of this farewell touched him*
66 | 197+l

**4908 buter** *v* to stumble, trip, run into, prop up, score
- elle s'est butée à toutes sortes de délais – *she stumbled into all kinds of delays*
60 | 241

**4909 bulle** *nf* bubble
- ce gouvernement est dans une bulle qui lui cache la réalité – *this government is in a bubble that hides it from reality*
73 | 150

**4910 défavorable** *adj(f)* unfavorable
- le climat était trop défavorable – *the climate was too unfavorable*
62 | 225+n

**4911 promoteur** *nm* promoter, instigator, developer
- les promoteurs croient que les salles seront remplies – *the promoters think the shows will be sold out*
69 | 174

**4912 albanais** *nadj(pl)* Albanian
- des snipers albanais avaient ouvert le feu – *the Albanian snipers had opened fire*
53 | 299-l +n

**4913 obsession** *nf* obsession
- je suis devenue son obsession – *I became his obsession*
71 | 159

**4914 exciter** *v* to arouse, waken, excite, turn on
- je suis très excitée d'aller voter – *I'm very excited to go and vote*
62 | 223

**4915 voisinage** *nm* neighborhood
- tout le voisinage en parle – *the whole neighborhood is talking about it*
68 | 180

**4916 savoir-faire** *nmi* know-how
- mon papa est le roi du savoir-faire! – *my daddy knows how to do everything!*
69 | 172

**4917 sévèrement** *adv* severely, harshly
- mon père m'aurait sévèrement corrigé – *my father would have severely disciplined me*
75 | 137

**4918 écrasant** *adj* crushing, overwhelming
- ce sont des pertes écrasantes pour n'importe quel pays – *those would be crushing losses for any country*
77 | 121

**4919 vendu** *nadj* sold, bribed
- 122.000 billets ont été vendus – *122,000 tickets were sold*
81 | 95

**4920 munition** *nf* ammunition, supplies
- j'ai acheté toutes les munitions que je voulais – *I bought all the ammunition that I wanted*
71 | 161

**4921 capturer** *v* to capture, catch
- il faut capturer ce type à tout prix – *this guy must be caught at any price*
66 | 193

**4922 compliment** *nm* compliment
- merci pour le compliment – *thanks for the compliment*
69 | 175-n

**4923 allouer** *v* to allocate
- cinq minutes sont allouées pour deux questions – *five minutes are allocated for two questions*
69 | 175

**4924 scandaliser** *v* to shock, scandalize
- chaque Américain devrait aussi être scandalisé – *every American should also be scandalized*
75 | 135

**4925 cassette** *nf* cassette
- la cassette vidéo a été retrouvée – *the video cassette was found*
67 | 185

**4926 résident** *nm* foreign national, foreign resident
- j'ai rencontré presque tous les résidents – *I met almost all the residents*
66 | 195

**4927 empresser** *v* to bustle about, hasten to do
- ils se sont empressés d'obéir – *they hastened to obey*
72 | 153

**4928 inonder** *v* to flood
- il faut inonder les jeunes de messages préventifs – *youth must be flooded with preventive messages*
74 | 141

**4929 réglementer** *v* to regulate, control
- une drogue est plus ou moins réglementée – *a drug is more or less controlled*
59 | 247+s

**4930 sonder** *v* to probe, poll, sound out
- je viens sonder, pour une sondation – *I'm here to take a poll, for a poll*
77 | 119

**4931 vigilant** *adj* vigilant, watchful
- nous devons rester vigilants et critiques – *we must remain vigilant and critical*
80 | 103

**4932 rhétorique** *nadj(f)* rhetorical, rhetoric
- la rhétorique des moralistes latins refleurissait – *the rhetoric of the Latin moralists blossomed anew*
74 | 141

**4933 cage** *nf* cage
- on devrait les mettre en cage et faire payer l'entrée – *we should put them in a cage and make them pay the entrance fee*
64 | 209

**4934 réglé** *adj* regular, steady, well-ordered, ruled
- si tout est réglé, on peut y aller – *if everything's set up, we can go*
84 | 80

**4935 téléspectateur** *nm* TV viewer
- il y avait des millions de téléspectateurs – *there were millions of TV viewers*
56 | 267-l +s

**4936 golf** *nm* golf, golf course
- ils jouent au golf ensemble – *they play golf together*
70 | 166

**4937 forestier** *nadj* forest, forester
- l'industrie forestière est très importante – *the forest industry is very important*
69 | 174

**4938 hum** *intj* um, uh
- hum, je suis nerveux, seulement – *uh, I'm just nervous*
42 | 411-l -n +s

**4939 ravager** *v* to ravage, devastate
- la peste ravage Londres, mais Paris est épargnée – *the plague ravages London, but Paris is spared*
70 | 168

**4940 réveil** *nm* waking up, awakening, alarm clock
- sur ma table de nuit, le réveil indiquait cinq heures – *on my night table, the alarm clock indicated five o'clock*
65 | 197

**4941 racial** *adj* racial
- la préférence raciale joue depuis longtemps dans le recrutement – *racial preference has long figured in recruitment*
71 | 156

**4942 ensuivre** *v* to follow, result, ensue
- il dit qu'il va s'ensuivre une augmentation du tourisme – *he says that an increase in tourism is going to follow*
72 | 155

**4943 relevé** *nadj* statement, list; relieved; put in relief; rolled up
- navré, mais vous êtes relevé de vos fonctions – *so sorry, but you're relieved of your functions*
75 | 136

**4944 ajourner** *v* to adjourn, defer, postpone
- je suis prête à ajourner le débat – *I'm ready to adjourn the debate*
50 | 325-n +s

**4945 détérioration** *nf* deterioration
- la poste vous dédommagera de la détérioration des colis – *the post office will reimburse you for damaged packages*
68 | 182

**4946 viable** *adj(f)* viable, workable
- la négociation est le seul moyen viable de résoudre le conflit – *negotiation is the only viable means to resolve this conflict*
68 | 180

**4947 cochon** *nadj* pig
- on mange comme des cochons – *we're eating like pigs*
64 | 208-n

**4948 barbare** *nadj(f)* barbaric; barbarian
- je viens de voir les barbares détruire un continent – *I have just seen barbarians destroying a continent*
75 | 134

**4949 atroce** *adj(f)* atrocious
- tu as couché avec cet atroce barbu? – *you had sex with that atrocious bearded loser?*
72 | 153

**4950 civique** *adj(f)* civil; civics
- les droits civiques sont accordés aux 336.000 Arabes israéliens – *civil rights are granted to the 336,000 Israeli Arabs*
72 | 152

**4951 ancrer** *v* to anchor
- ces valeurs sont fermement ancrées dans notre héritage – *these values are firmly anchored in our heritage*
73 | 145

**4952 raccrocher** *v* to hang up
- j'ai décidé de raccrocher ma toge – *I decided to hang up my toga*
62 | 219

**4953 cirque** *nm* circus; cirque
- nous allâmes en excursion au cirque – *we went on an outing to the circus*
68 | 176

**4954 législature** *nf* legislature
- cette nouvelle législature a une occasion unique dans l'histoire – *this new legislature has a unique occasion in history*
50 | 321-l +s

**4955 audiovisuel** *nadj* audio-visual
- depuis cette date, le paysage audiovisuel français a changé – *since that date, the French audiovisual landscape has changed*
63 | 213-l

**4956 confiner** *v* to confine
- le plasma reste confiné à la surface du solide – *the plasma remains confined to the surface of the solid*
78 | 113

**4957 agrandir** *v* to enlarge, extend
- cliquez sur l'image pour agrandir la carte – *click on the picture to enlarge the map*
74 | 141

**4958 occasionner** *v* to cause, give rise to
- le conflit occasionne des pertes énormes – *the conflict is causing enormous losses*
75 | 130

**4959 allégement** *nm* lightening, unweighting, reduction
- il a effectué un allégement général des impôts – *he implemented overall tax relief*
50 | 318-l +s

**4960 malin** *nadj* smart, shrewd, cunning
- enfin, il faut être malin, très malin – *well, you have to be shrewd, very shrewd*
59 | 240-n

**4961 performant** *adj* productive, efficient
- je veux rester performant et ne pas avoir une fin de carrière – *I want to stay productive and not have my career end*
67 | 182-l

**4962 sérénité** *nf* serenity, peacefulness
- le temps était d'une sérénité désespérante – *time had a desperate clarity*
73 | 142

**4963 cuire** *v* to cook, bake, roast
- on dit que le spaghetti est cuit s'il reste collé – *they say that spaghetti is cooked if it sticks together*
65 | 197

**4964 raser** *v* to shave, raze
- ils avaient tous le crâne rasé – *they all had shaved heads*
64 | 203

**4965 ha** *intj* oh
- ha. ha. très drôle – *ha. ha. very funny*
60 | 232-n

**4966 revivre** *v* to live again, come back life, revive
- il lui faut un souvenir pour revivre l'événement – *he needs a souvenir to relive the event*
67 | 185+l

**4967 piano** *adv,nm* piano
- elle retournait au piano et recommençait à jouer – *she returned to the piano and resumed playing*
61 | 225-n

**4968 concertation** *nf* meeting, consultation
- il faut travailler ensemble plus, en concertation – *we must work together more, in consultation*
63 | 215-l

**4969 vaisseau** *nm* ship, vessel
- faites un diagnostic complet du vaisseau – *perform a complete check of the ship*
53 | 294+s

**4970 interaction** *nf* interaction
- on est en interaction avec les membres de l'équipe des émissions – *we're interacting with the members of the broadcast team*
54 | 285

**4971 pessimiste** *nadj(f)* pessimistic; pessimist
- je ne suis pas aussi pessimiste que lui – *I'm not as pessimistic as he is*
70 | 161

**4972 sillage** *nm* wake, slipstream
- j'étais dans le sillage de Nicolas Sarkozy – *I was in the wake of Nicolas Sarkozy*
77 | 121

**4973 synonyme** *nadj(f)* synonymous; synonym
- la Communauté européenne n'est plus synonyme de l'Europe – *the European Union is no longer synonymous with Europe*
78 | 115

**4974 hisser** *v* to hoist, raise up
- nous voulons maintenant hisser la barre encore plus haut – *now we want to raise the bar even higher*
72 | 150

**4975 agréer** *v* to accept, approve of
- veuillez agréer, monsieur, mes salutations distinguées – *sincerely yours*
69 | 168

**4976 comble** *nadj(f)* despair; summit, overmeasure; roof
- comble du malheur, COOL-FM a changé d'orientation – *depths of unhappiness: COOL-FM has changed its orientation*
67 | 182+l

**4977 bosniaque** *nadj(f)* Bosnian
- le gouvernement bosniaque a accepté le plan de paix – *the Bosnian government accepted the peace plan*
49 | 325-l +n -s

**4978 insignifiant** *adj* insignificant, unimportant
- nous parlions de choses insignifiantes, avec gaieté – *we were merrily talking of insignificant things*
74 | 139

**4979 décoller** *v* to take off; to loosen, unstick
- s'ils décollent, les otages sont morts – *if they take off, the hostages are dead*
  68 | 179

**4980 solidaire** *adj(f)* interdependent, jointly dependent
- on cesse de se sentir responsable et solidaire d'autrui – *we're ceasing to feel responsible for others and interdependent with them*
  66 | 187

**4981 ferroviaire** *adj(f)* railway, rail
- le trafic ferroviaire régional a été interrompu – *regional railway traffic has been interrupted*
  59 | 241-l

**4982 dépouiller** *v* to skin, strip away, deprive, analyze
- il faut savoir se dépouiller de très belles choses – *you have to know how to rid yourself of very pretty things*
  72 | 150

**4983 céréale** *nf* cereal
- les céréales sont le premier solde excédentaire de la France – *cereals are the leading surplus commodity of France*
  65 | 197-l

**4984 aménager** *v* to develop, plan, fit, adjust
- l'avion aménagé en hôpital volant était attendu mercredi – *the airplane outfitted as a flying hospital was expected Wednesday*
  77 | 117

**4985 agitation** *nf* agitation, excitement
- il semble indifférent à l'agitation dont il est cause – *he seems unaffected by the agitation he has caused*
  68 | 172-s

**4986 exode** *nm* exodus
- je contemple l'énorme exode des campagnards – *I'm pondering the enormous exodus of country-dwellers*
  72 | 151

**4987 aire** *nf* surface, area
- les déchets de l'aire métropolitaine continueront de s'accumuler – *the trash from the metropolitain area will continue to accumulate*
  71 | 158

**4988 orgueil** *nm* pride
- ça flatte ton orgueil de mâle, ça, hein? – *that strokes your male ego, eh?*
  54 | 280+l -n -s

**4989 socialisme** *nm* socialism
- c'est le grand défi du socialisme du XXIe siècle – *it's the grand challenge for socialism in the 21st century*
  65 | 195

**4990 harmonisation** *nf* harmonization
- il y aura aussi un régime d'harmonisation des lois environnementales – *there will also be a system for harmonizing environmental laws*
  64 | 206+s

**4991 provisoirement** *adv* temporarily, provisionally
- je décidai provisoirement de m'en contenter – *I decided to be happy with it for the time being*
  72 | 148-s

**4992 cocktail** *nm* cocktail, cocktail party
- tu es capable de faire des cocktails assez élaborés? – *are you able to make fairly fancy cocktails?*
  75 | 129

**4993 moyenne** *nf* average
- les chercheurs font en moyenne une carrière beaucoup plus courte – *researchers on average have a much shorter career*
  69 | 168

**4994 rigoler** *v* to laugh,
- ça rigole pas au labo! – *no laughing in the lab!*
  60 | 231-n

**4995 compression** *nf* compression; cutback, reduction
- toutes les compressions ont eu un prix très élevé – *all of the cutbacks have exacted a very heavy price*
  54 | 283+s

**4996 réfléchi** *adj* thoughtful, well thought out
- nous devrions agir de façon réfléchie et responsable – *we should act in a thoughtful and responsible manner*
  79 | 105

**4997 expérimenter** *v* to experiment
- les skieurs peu expérimentés devraient renoncer aux courses – *inexperienced skiers should forego racing*
  76 | 124

**4998 détériorer** *v* to deteriorate
- il a laissé nos routes se détériorer et se désintégrer – *he has let our roads deteriorate and disintegrate*
  69 | 170

**4999 exprès** *adj(pl),adv* deliberately, on purpose, intentionally
- je ne le fais pas exprès ou plutôt ce n'est pas conscient – *I don't do it on purpose, or rather it's not conscious*
  59 | 242

**5000 écrouler** *v* to collapse, tumble
- on le trouva mort, écroulé dans les W.C. – *they found him dead, collapsed in the restroom*
  72 | 148

# Alphabetical index

## Aa

**à** *prep* to, at, in 4

**abaisser** *v* to pull down, lower, reduce 3209

**abandon** *nm* abandonment, desertion, withdrawal 2676

**abandonner** *v* to give up, abandon 740

**abattre** *v* to pull down, kill, beat 2316

**abbé** *nm* abbot, priest 4061

**abolir** *v* to abolish, do away with 3640

**abonné** *nadj* subscribed, subscriber 3003

**abord** *nm* manner; approach, access, environs 3343

**aborder** *v* to reach, approach 1535

**aboutir** *v* to succeed, end up at 1377

**aboutissement** *nm* outcome, result 4828

**abri** *nm* shelter 1708

**abriter** *v* to shelter, shade 3231

**absence** *nf* absence 802

**absent** *nadj* absent 2016

**absolu** *nadj* absolute 1284

**absolument** *adv* absolutely 1009

**absorber** *v* to absorb, remove, take up, take over 3022

**abstenir** *v* to abstain, refrain 3693

**absurde** *nadj(f)* absurd 2512

**abus** *nm(pl)* abuse, misuse, breach 2757

**abuser** *v* to abuse, mislead, take advantage 3093

**accéder** *v* to access, reach, attain 1781

**accélération** *nf* acceleration 4880

**accélérer** *v* to speed up, accelerate 2082

**accent** *nm* accent 1694

**accentuer** *v* to stress, emphasize, become more pronounced 3156

**acceptable** *adj(f)* acceptable, satisfactory 2608

**acceptation** *nf* acceptance 4784

**accepter** *v* to accept 210

**accès** *nm(pl)* access 846

**accessible** *adj(f)* accessible, approachable 3056

**accessoire** *nm* accessory 2689

**accident** *nm* accident 1227

**accompagner** *v* to accompany 727

**accompli** *adj* accomplished 3908

**accomplir** *v* to accomplish 1301

**accord** *nm* agreement 496

**accorder** *v* to grant 668

**accrocher** *v* to hang up, hang on, put up 2801

**accroissement** *nm* increase 2762

**accroître** *v* to increase 1523

**accueil** *nm* welcome, reception 2541

**accueillir** *v* to welcome, greet, accommodate 1189

**accumulation** *nf* accumulation, amassing, storage, stockpiling, build-up 4660

**accumuler** *v* to accumulate, amass, store, stockpile 2463

**accusation** *nf* accusation, indictment 2236

**accusé** *nadj* defendant 2706

**accuser** *v* to accuse 1147

**acharner** *v* to go at fiercely and unrelentingly 3564

**achat** *nm* purchase 1804

**acheminement** *nm* routing, shipment 3778

**acheminer** *v* to forward, dispatch, transport 3372

**acheter** *v* to buy 636

**acheteur** *nm* buyer, purchaser 3042

**achever** *v* to complete, finish, end 1630

**acide** *nadj(f)* acid 4220

**acier** *nm* steel 3306

**acquérir** *v* to acquire 1104

**acquis** *nadj(pl)* acquired, experience 4551

**acquisition** *nf* acquisition, acquire, purchase 2690

**acquitter** *v* to acquit, pay, settle, pay off 3225

**acte** *nm* act 492

**acteur** *nm* actor 1552

**actif** *nadj* active 1219

**action** *nf* action 355

**actionnaire** *nm,nf* shareholder 3350

**activement** *adv* actively 3697

**activer** *v* to activate, speed up, stroke, get moving 4072

**activité** *nf* activity 452

**actualité** *nf* current events, news 2888

**actuel** *adj* current, present 584

**actuellement** *adv* at present, at the moment 728

**adaptation** *nf* adaptation 2701

**adapter** *v* to adapt 1553

**additionnel** *adj* additional 3131

**adéquat** *adj* appropriate, suitable, adequate 3525

**adhérer** *v* to stick to, support, join, be a member of 3108

**adhésion** *nf* membership, support 2665

**adieu** *intj,nm* goodbye, farewell, adieu 3968

**adjoint** *nadj* assistant, deputy 2532

**admettre** *v* to admit 680

**administrateur** *nm* administrator 3241

**administratif** *nadj* administrative 1809

**administration** *nf* administration 1057

**administrer** *v* to manage, run, administer; to give 3472

**admiration** *nf* admiration 4219

**admirer** *v* to admire 2789

**adolescent** *nm* teenager, adolescent 2085

**adopter** *v* to adopt 676

**adoption** *nf* adoption, passing 2321

**adorer** *v* to adore, worship 2322

**adresse** *nf* address 1925

**adresser** *v* to address 744

**adulte** *nadj(f)* adult 1580

**advenir** *v* to happen that, happen to 4469

**adversaire** *nm,nf* opponent, adversary 2288

**aérien** *adj* aerial 1765

**aéroport** *nm* airport 2113

**affaiblir** *v* to weaken 2563

**affaiblissement** *nm* weakening 3686

**affaire** *nf* business, matter 170

**affectation** *nf* appointment, allocation; show, pretence 4868

**affecter** *v* to affect 1396

**affection** *nf* affection, ailment 4275

**affiche** *nf* poster, public notice, bill 2886

**afficher** *v* to display 2106

**affirmation** *nf* assertion, affirmation 2299

**affirmer** *v* to affirm, maintain, declare, allege 686

**affreux** *nadj(pl)* dreadful, awful, horrible 4369

**affrontement** *nm* clash, confrontation 3694

**affronter** *v* to confront, face 1941

**afin** *in* order to, so that 404

**africain** *nadj* African 2289

**âge** *nm* age 502

**âgé** *adj* old 1597

**agence** *nf* agency 1481

**agenda** *nm* diary, planner 3882

**agent** *nm,nf* agent 885

**aggraver** *v* to worsen, aggravate 2506

**agir** *v* to act 211

**agitation** *nf* agitation, excitement 4985

**agiter** *v* to shake, disturb 3051

**agrandir** *v* to enlarge, extend 4957

**agréable** *nadj(f)* pleasant, nice, agreeable 2841

**agréer** *v* to accept, approve of 4975

**agressif** *nadj* aggressive 3059

**agression** *nf* aggression 2771

**agricole** *adj(f)* agricultural, farming 1793

**agriculteur** *nm* farmer 2306

**agriculture** *nf* agriculture 2088

**ah** *intj* ah, oh 1405

**aide** *nm,nf* help, assistance 457

**aider** *v* to help, assist 413

**aile** *nf* wing, sail, blade 2923

**ailleurs** *adv* elsewhere, somewhere else 360

**aimable** *adj(f)* pleasant, kind, nice 4668

**aimer** *v* to like, love 242

**aîné** *nadj* oldest, eldest 2786

**ainsi** *adv* thus 98

**air** *nm* air, appearance 761

**aire** *nf* surface, area 4987

**aise** *nadj(f)* comfort, joy, pleasure, ease 2770

**aisé** *adj* easy, well off, well-to-do 4214

**ajourner** *v* to adjourn, defer, postpone 4944

**ajouter** *v* to add 359

**ajustement** *nm* adjustment 3621

**ajuster** *v* to adjust, alter, aim, aim at 3391

**alarme** *nf* alarm 4204

**albanais** *nadj(pl)* Albanian 4912

**album** *nm* album 2874

**alcool** *nm* alcohol 2465

**alentour** *adv* around, round about 4165

**alerte** *adj(f),nf* agile, alert, warning 3599

**alerter** *v* to alert, inform, warn 4079

**algérien** *nadj* Algerian 4163

**aligner** *v* to lign up, align 3021

**aliment** *nm* food 2845

**alimentaire** *adj(f)* food 2099

**alimentation** *nf* diet, food, groceries, supply 2846

**alimenter** *v* to feed, supply 2508

**allégement** *nm* lightening, unweighting, reduction 4959

**alléger** *v* to lighten, alleviate 3874

**allemand** *nadj* German 844

**aller** *nm,v* to go 53

**alliance** *nf* alliance 1846

**allié** *nadj* allied; ally 1992

**allier** *v* to ally, match, unite 3336

**allocation** *nf* allocation, granting, allotment, allowance 3807

**allonger** *v* to lengthen, extend, stretch out 3813

**allouer** *v* to allocate 4923

**allumer** v  to switch on, light up, turn on 3169

**allure** nf  speed, pace, walk, look, appearance 3539

**allusion** nf  allusion 2428

**alors** adv  then, so 81

**alourdir** v  to weigh down, make heavy 4354

**alternatif** adj  alternate, alternating 4415

**alternative** nf  alternative, choice 2911

**altitude** nf  altitude, height 4396

**amant** nm  lover 4284

**amateur** nm,nf  amateur 2760

**ambassade** nf  embassy 3327

**ambassadeur** nm  ambassador 2686

**ambiance** nf  atmosphere, mood 4025

**ambiguïté** nf  ambiguity 3816

**ambitieux** nadj(pl)  ambitious, man with ambition 2905

**ambition** nf  ambition 2280

**âme** nf  soul 1647

**amélioration** nf  improvement 2012

**améliorer** v  to improve 1056

**aménagement** nm  development, planning, fitting, adjustment 3851

**aménager** v  to develop, plan, fit, adjust 4984

**amende** nf  fine 3842

**amendement** nm  amendment 1438

**amener** v  to bring 655

**amer** adj,nm  bitter 4599

**américain** nadj  American 374

**ami** nadj  friend 467

**amical** adj  friendly 3366

**amitié** nf  friendship 2272

**amorcer** v  to bait, prime, begin, initiate 2897

**amour** nm  love 967

**amoureux** nadj(pl)  in love, amorous 2495

**ampleur** nf  extent, scope, range 2395

**amplifier** v  to amplify, magnify, expand 4537

**amusant** nadj  funny, amusing, entertaining 4695

**amuser** v  to amuse 2538

**an** nm  year 76

**analogue** nadj(f)  similar, analogous 4498

**analyse** nf  analysis 1204

**analyser** v  to analyse 1209

**analyste** nm,nf  analyst 4052

**ancêtre** nm,nf  ancestor, forerunner 3067

**ancien** adj,nm  ancient; former 392

**ancrer** v  to anchor 4951

**anéantir** v  to annihilate, wipe out, ruin, vanish 4315

**ange** nm  angel 3601

**anglais** nadj(pl)  English 784

**angle** nm  angle, point of view 2560

**anglo-saxon** nadj  Anglo-Saxon 4854

**angoisse** nf  distress, anguish, dread, fear 3417

**animal** nadj  animal 1002

**animateur** nadj  animator, host 3494

**animer** v  to lead, conduct, animate 1900

**année** nf  year 102

**annexe** adj(f),nf  annex, appendix, related issue 3084

**anniversaire** nadj(f)  anniversary, birthday 2043

**annonce** nf  announcement 1887

**annoncer** v  to announce 521

**annuel** adj  annual 1684

**annulation** nf  cancellation, annulment 4783

**annuler** v  to cancel 2002

**anonyme** adj(f)  anonymous 3129

**anormal** nadj  abnormal 4671

**antenne** nf  antenna 3246

**antérieur** nadj  previous, earlier, front 2662

**anticiper** v  to anticipate, foresee, look or think ahead 2219

**antique** nadj(f)  antique, ancient 4480

**août** nm  August 1445

**apaiser** v  to calm, appease, calm down 3670

**apercevoir** v  to see, notice 1891

**apparaître** v  to appear 693

**appareil** nm  apparatus, device 1420

**apparemment** adv  apparently 1734

**apparence** nf  appearance 2714

**apparent** adj  apparent, obvious 3803

**apparition** nf  appearance, apparition 2419

**appartement** nm  apartment, flat 2323

**appartenance** nf  membership, belonging 4037

**appartenir** v  to belong 319

**appel** nm  call 567

**appeler** v  to call 157

**applaudir** v  to clap, applaud 3257

**applicable** adj(f)  applicable 3303

**application** nf  application 1030

**appliqué** adj  assiduous, industrious, careful 4684

**appliquer** v  to apply 753

**apport** nm  supply, contribution 3956

**apporter** v  to bring 339

**appréciation** nf  appreciation, assessment, appraisal 4249

**apprécier** v  to appreciate 1061

**appréhender** v  to dread, apprehend 4565

**apprendre** v  to learn 327

**apprentissage** nm  learning, apprenticeship 3636

**apprêter** v  to prepare, get ready, dress 3128

**approbation** *nf* approval 3488

**approche** *nf* approach 1521

**approcher** *v* to approach 1576

**approfondir** *v* to deepen, make deeper, go further into 2975

**approprié** *adj* appropriate 3591

**approprier** *v* to adapt, appropriate, take over 2605

**approuver** *v* to approve 1663

**approvisionnement** *nm* supply, supplies, stock, supplying, stocking 3216

**appui** *nm* support 1700

**appuyer** *v* to lean, support 923

**après** *adv,prep* after 82

**après-midi** *nmi* afternoon 1324

**apte** *adj(f)* capable 3770

**aptitude** *nf* ability 4046

**arabe** *nadj(f)* Arabic, Arab 1994

**arbitrage** *nm* refereeing, umpiring, arbitration 3443

**arbitraire** *nadj(f)* arbitrary 3738

**arbitre** *nm,nf* referee, arbitrer, arbitrator 3745

**arbre** *nm* tree 2111

**architecte** *nm,nf* architect 3729

**architecture** *nf* architecture 4182

**archives** *nfpl* archives, records 3994

**argent** *nm* money, silver 472

**argument** *nm* argument 1874

**armé** *adj* armed 1625

**arme** *nf* weapon 648

**armée** *nf* army 1011

**armement** *nm* arms, weapons, armament 3403

**armer** *v* to arm 2091

**arracher** *v* to pull up, tear up 2347

**arrangement** *nm* arrangement, layout, order, agreement 2961

**arranger** *v* to arrange 2932

**arrestation** *nf* arrest 3065

**arrêt** *nm* stop 1374

**arrêté** *nadj* decree, order 2314

**arrêter** *v* to stop, arrest 420

**arrière** *adji,adv,nm* back, rear 1504

**arrivant** *nm* arrival, comer 4233

**arrivé** *adj* arrived 4375

**arrivée** *nf* arrival 1075

**arriver** *v* to arrive, happen 174

**art** *nm* art 1181

**article** *nm* article 604

**articuler** *v* to articulate 4533

**artificiel** *adj* artificial 2857

**artisan** *nm* craftsman, self-employed 4011

**artiste** *nadj(f)* artist 1797

**artistique** *adj(f)* artistic 3535

**asiatique** *nadj(f)* Asian 3277

**asile** *nm* shelter, asylum, hospital 3990

**aspect** *nm* aspect 998

**aspiration** *nf* aspiration 3278

**aspirer** *v* to breathe in, inhale, aspire to 3536

**assassin** *nadj* murderer, assassin 3781

**assassinat** *nm* murder, assassination 3313

**assassiner** *v* to murder, assassinate 2750

**assaut** *nm* assault, attack, bout 3736

**assemblée** *nf* assembly, meeting 1073

**asseoir** *v* to sit 1360

**assez** *adv* enough 321

**assiette** *nf* plate, dish, bowl 3756

**assigner** *v* to assign, allocate, attach, attribute 3919

**assimiler** *v* to assimilate, take in 3571

**assise** *nf* basis, foundation 3726

**assistance** *nf* attendance, assistance 2573

**assistant** *nm* assistant 3805

**assister** *v* to attend; assist, help 683

**association** *nf* association 956

**associer** *v* to associate 1422

**assortir** *v* to match, accompany 3320

**assumer** *v* to assume 1870

**assurance** *nf* insurance, confidence 1656

**assurément** *adv* most certainly 4535

**assurer** *v* to assure, insure 302

**atelier** *nm* workshop, studio 3365

**athlète** *nm,nf* athlete 4722

**atlantique** *nadj(f)* Atlantic 4246

**atmosphère** *nf* atmosphere 2493

**atomique** *adj(f)* atomic 2657

**atout** *nm* trump, asset 3683

**atroce** *adj(f)* atrocious 4949

**attachement** *nm* attachment, affection 3519

**attacher** *v* to attach 1358

**attaque** *nf* attack 1655

**attaquer** *v* to attack 1018

**attarder** *v* to linger 4187

**atteindre** *v* to reach 346

**atteinte** *nf* reach; attack, blow 3473

**attendre** *v* to wait 155

**attentat** *nm* attack, assassination attempt 1878

**attente** *nf* wait 936

**attentif** *adj* attentive, scrupulous, careful 2850

**attention** *nf* attention 482

**attentivement** *adv* attentively, carefully, closely 3962

**atténuer** *v* to lessen, diminish, dim, subdue, reduce 3300

**attester** *v* to attest, confirm 3897

**attirer** *v* to attract 747

**attitude** *nf* attitude 834

**attraper** *v* to catch, get, pick up 3898

**attribuer** *v* to award, grant, attribute 1446

**attribution** *nf* awarding, allocation, assignment, attribution 3075

**aube** *nf* dawn, daybreak 2728

**aucun** *det,adj,pro* none, either, neither, not any 63

**aucunement** *adv* in no way, not in the least, not at all 4408

**audacieux** *nadj(pl)* daring, audacious, bold 4152

**au-delà** *adv,nmi* beyond 1172

**au-dessous** *adv* underneath 3965

**au-dessus** *adv* above 1480

**audience** *nf* audience, hearing 2071

**audiovisuel** *nadj* audio-visual 4955

**auditeur** *nm* auditor, listener 4554

**audition** *nf* hearing, examination, audition 3836

**augmentation** *nf* increase, rise 1263

**augmenter** *v* to increase, raise 823

**aujourd'hui** *adv* today 233

**auparavant** *adv* beforehand 1001

**auprès** *adv* nearby, close to 614

**aussi** *adv,conj* too, also, as 44

**aussitôt** *adv* straight away, immediately 2362

**autant** *adv* as much, as many 377

**auteur** *nm,nf* author 762

**authentique** *adj(f)* genuine, authentic 3961

**auto** *nm,nf* car 4494

**autobus** *nm(pl)* bus 4216

**autochtone** *nadj(f)* native, indigenous peoples 2387

**automatique** *adj(f)* automatic 2800

**automatiquement** *adv* automatically 3394

**automne** *nm* fall, autumn 1503

**automobile** *nadj(f)* automobile 2407

**autonome** *nadj(f)* autonomous, independent 2192

**autonomie** *nf* autonomy 2342

**autorisation** *nf* authorization, permission, permit 1649

**autoriser** *v* to authorize 989

**autoritaire** *adj(f)* authoritarian 4661

**autorité** *nf* authority 783

**autoroute** *nf* motorway, highway, freeway 3794

**autour** *adv,nm* around 594

**autre** *det,nadj(f),pro* other 28

**autrefois** *adv* in the past 2384

**autrement** *adv* differently, something else, otherwise 1023

**autrui** *pro* others 3940

**aval** *nm* downstream, downhill 4129

**avalanche** *nf* avalanche 4426

**avaler** *v* to swallow 4261

**avance** *nf* advance 1087

**avancée** *nf* advanced, overhung 4355

**avancer** *v* to advance, move forward 449

**avant** *adji,adv,nm,prep* before 40

**avantage** *nm* advantage 900

**avantageux** *nadj(pl)* profitable, worthwhile, advantageous, attractive 4391

**avec** *prep* with 23

**avenir** *nm* future 471

**aventure** *nf* adventure 2090

**avenue** *nf* avenue 3868

**avérer** *v* to prove to be, turn out 2457

**avertir** *v* to warn 2224

**avertissement** *nm* warning 3139

**aveu** *nm* confession 4675

**aveugle** *nadj(f)* blind 3095

**aviation** *nf* aviation 4084

**avion** *nm* plane 1409

**avis** *nm(pl)* opinion, mind 741

**aviser** *v* to notice, advise 4202

**avocat** *nm* lawyer 1188

**avoir** *nm,v* to have 8

**avouer** *v* to admit 1619

**avril** *nm* April 1022

**axe** *nm* axis, axle, main line 2878

**axer** *v* to center 3864

# Bb

**bagage** *nm* luggage, baggage 3566

**baie** *nf* bay; berry 3719

**baigner** *v* to bathe, wash, get a bath, go for a swim 4608

**bain** *nm* bath, bathing 3458

**baiser** *nm,v* to kiss 2999

**baisse** *nf* fall, drop 1466

**baisser** *v* to lower, turn down, bend down 911

**balance** *nf* scales, balance 3395

**balancer** *v* to swing, sway 4548

**balayer** *v* to sweep up, sweep out 3687

**balle** *nf* ball, bullet 2311

**ballon** *nm* ball 3692

**banal** *adj* banal, trite, commonplace, ordinary 4221

**banc** *nm* bench, workbench, pew 3724

**bancaire** *adj(f)* banking 2945

**bande** *nf* band, strip 977

**banlieue** *nf* suburbs, outskirts 2944

**bannir** *v* to banish, ban 4378

**banque** *nf* bank 774

**banquier** *nm* banker 4263

**baptiser** *v* to name, christen, baptize 3712

**bar** *nm* bar 3012

**barbare** *nadj(f)* barbaric; barbarian 4948

**barrage** *nm* barrier, obstruction, dam, roadblock 3706

**barre** *nf* bar, rod 2349

**barreau** *nm* bar 4483

**barrer** *v* to close, block, bar, cross 3917

**barrière** *nf* fence, barrier, gate 2438

**bas** *adv,nadj(pl),nm(pl)* low; stockings 468

**basculer** *v* to topple, fall over, knock off 4349

**base** *nf* base 416

**baser** *v* to base 1712

**basque** *nadj(f)* Basque 4658

**bassin** *nm* bowl, basin 3032

**bataille** *nf* battle 1303

**bateau** *nm* boat, ship 1287

**bâtiment** *nm* building 1952

**bâtir** *v* to build 2093

**bâton** *nm* tick, club, baton 3553

**batterie** *nf* battery; drum set 4816

**battre** *v* to beat, hit 742

**beau** *adj,nm* handsome, fine, right 393

**beaucoup** *adv* much, a lot of, many 150

**beauté** *nf* beauty 2492

**bébé** *nadj(f)* baby 2271

**belge** *nadj(f)* Belgian 2795

**ben** *adv* well 2010

**bénéfice** *nm* benefit, profit 1915

**bénéficiaire** *nadj(f)* beneficiary 3283

**bénéficier** *nm,v* to benefit 1272

**bénéfique** *adj(f)* beneficial 4758

**bénévole** *nadj(f)* volunteer, voluntary, unpaid 4506

**besoin** *nm* need 183

**bétail** *nm* livestock, cattle 4842

**bête** *nadj(f)* animal, beast; stupid 2591

**béton** *nm* concrete 4146

**beurre** *nm* butter 4112

**biais** *nm(pl)* way, device; bias 2439

**bibliothèque** *nf* library 2511

**bien** *adji,adv,nm* well 47

**bien-être** *nmi* well being 3531

**bientôt** *adv* soon 1208

**bienvenu** *nadj* welcome 3714

**bière** *nf* beer, coffin 3152

**bijou** *nm* jewel 4301

**bilan** *nm* balance sheet, outcome 1758

**bilatéral** *adj* bilateral 3545

**billet** *nm* ticket 1916

**biologique** *adj(f)* biological, nature 2781

**bizarre** *nadj(f)* strange, odd 2756

**blague** *nf* joke 4822

**blâmer** *v* to blame, reprimand 4803

**blanc** *adj,nm* white 708

**blé** *nm* wheat 3265

**blessé** *nadj* injured 2203

**blesser** *v* to hurt 2024

**blessure** *nf* injury, wound 2481

**bleu** *adj,nm* blue 1216

**blindé** *adj* armored 4878

**bloc** *nm* block 2066

**blocage** *nm* block 3429

**blond** *nadj* blond, fair-haired 4585

**bloquer** *v* to block 2004

**bœuf** *nm* ox, steer, beef 3914

**boire** *nm,v* to drink 1879

**bois** *nm(pl)* wood 1425

**boisson** *nf* drink, beverage 3614

**boîte** *nf* box 1771

**bombardement** *nm* bombing, shelling 3565

**bombarder** *v* to bomb 4329

**bombe** *nf* bomb 1751

**bon** *adj,adv,intj,nm* good 94

**bond** *nm* leap, rebound 4871

**bonheur** *nm* happiness 1948

**bonjour** *nm* hello 1972

**bonsoir** *nm* good evening 3938

**bord** *nm* edge, side 991

**bordel** *nm* brothel, mess, chaos 4529

**borne** *nf* milestone, boundary stone 4751

**borner** *v* to limit, confine 4575

**bosniaque** *nadj(f)* Bosnian 4977

**bosser** *v* to work, bash on 4532

**bouche** *nf* mouth 1838

**boucher** *nm,v* butcher; to fill in, get clogged up 4757

**boucle** *nf* loop, buckle, curl 3822

**boucler** *v* to fasten, loop, resolve 3444

**boue** *nf* mud 4507

**bouger** *v* to move, shift, budge 1893

**boule** *nf* ball 4789

**boulevard** *nm* boulevard 4821

**bouleversement** *nm* upheaval 4626

**bouleverser** *v* to upset, distress, disturb, turn upside down 2916

**boulot** *adj,nm* work, job 2929

**bourgeois** *nadj(pl)* middle class 3817

**bourse** *nf* purse, scholarship 1716

**boursier** *nadj* grant-holder, scholarship holder; stock 4384

**bousculer** *v* to knock over, knock over, knock into 3941

**bout** *nm* bit, tip, end 508

**bouteille** *nf* bottle 2979

**boutique** *nf* shop 3791

**bouton** *nm* button, knob, spot 4462

**branche** *nf* branch 2140

**brancher** *v* to plug in, connect 3310

**brandir** *v* to brandish, wield, wave 3833

**bras** *nm(pl)* arm 1253

**bravo** *intj,nm* bravo, well done 4564

**brèche** *nf* breach, gap 4428

**bref** *adj,adv,nm* brief 600

**brièvement** *adv* briefly 3349

**brigade** *nf* team, squad, brigade 4224

**brillant** *adj,nm* brilliant 2569

**briller** *v* to shine 2904

**briser** *v* to break 1920

**britannique** *nadj(f)* British 1296

**brouillard** *nm* fog, mist, haze 4452

**brouiller** *v* to mix-up, confuse, scramble 4682

**bruit** *nm* noise 1524

**brûler** *v* to burn 1930

**brusquement** *adv* abruptly, suddenly 3594

**brut** *adv,nadj* raw, crude 2766

**brutal** *nadj* brutal 2796

**brutalement** *adv* brutally 4334

**budget** *nm* budget 962

**budgétaire** *adj(f)* budgetary 1996

**bulle** *nf* bubble 4909

**bulletin** *nm* bulletin, report 3233

**bureau** *nm* office, desk 273

**bus** *nm(pl)* bus 4027

**but** *nm* goal, aim, objective, purpose 441

**buter** *v* to stumble, trip, run into, prop up, score 4908

## Cc

**cabine** *nf* hut, cubicle, booth, box, room 3953

**cabinet** *nm* cabinet, agency, office 1742

**câble** *nm* cable, wire 4678

**cacher** *v* to hide 914

**cadavre** *nm* corpse 2892

**cadeau** *nm* present, gift 2298

**cadre** *nm* frame, executive 483

**café** *nm* coffee, café 1886

**cage** *nf* cage 4933

**cahier** *nm* notebook 4001

**caisse** *nf* till, cash desk 1881

**calcul** *nm* calculation 1624

**calculer** *v* to calculate 2331

**calendrier** *nm* calendar 2947

**calme** *nadj(f)* calm 1731

**calmer** *v* to calm down 2909

**camarade** *nm,nf* friend, comrade, pal, mate 2825

**caméra** *nf* camera 3076

**camion** *nm* truck 2542

**camoufler** *v* to cover up, conceal, camouflage 4704

**camp** *nm* camp 1084

**campagne** *nf* countryside 666

**canadien** *nadj* Canadian 611

**canal** *nm* canal, channel 1919

**cancer** *nm* cancer 2256

**candidat** *nm* candidate 1328

**candidature** *nf* application, candidacy, candidature 3402

**canon** *nm* gun, cannon 3634

**cap** *nm* cape 3532

**capable** *adj(f)* able, capable 610

**capacité** *nf* capacity, ability 789

**capitaine** *nm* captain 2518

**capital** *nadj* major, chief, principal; capital, assets 879

**capitale** *nf* capital 1818

**capitalisme** *nm* capitalism 3568

**capter** *v* to pick up, capture, tap 4063

**capturer** *v* to capture, catch 4921

**car** *conj,nm* because 176

**caractère** *nm* nature, character 927

**caractériser** *v* to characterize 2450

**caractéristique** *nadj(f)* characteristic 2050

**carburant** *nadj* fuel 3633

**caresser** *v* to fondle, caress 4861

**carnet** *nm* notebook, notepad 3723

**carré** *nadj* square, broad, plain 3162

**carrément** *adv* completely, directly, straight out 4009

**carrière** *nf* career 1247

**carte** *nf* card 955

**carton** *nm* cardboard, card, score 3827

**cas** *nm(pl)* case 137

**case** *nf* box, hut, field 4892

**casque** *nm* helmet 3939

**casser** *v* to break 2185

**cassette** *nf* cassette 4925

**catastrophe** *nf* catastrophe, disaster 1832

**catastrophique** *adj(f)* catastrophic, disastrous 4281

**catégorie** *nf* category 1402

**catholique** *nadj(f)* catholic **1578**

**cauchemar** *nm* nightmare, bad dream **3689**

**cause** *nf* cause **127**

**causer** *v* to cause; to chat **1089**

**caution** *nf* deposit, guarantee, bail **4867**

**cave** *adj(f),nm,nf* cellar, basement **4870**

**ce** *det,pro* this, that **12**

**ceci** *pro* this **732**

**céder** *v* to give up, give way **1565**

**ceinture** *nf* belt, waist **4538**

**cela** *pro* that, it **54**

**célèbre** *adj(f)* famous **1689**

**célébrer** *v* to celebrate **2170**

**célibataire** *nadj(f)* single, unmarried **3362**

**cellule** *nf* cell **2151**

**celui** *pro* that, the one, he, him **45**

**censé** *adj* supposed **2052**

**censure** *nf* censorship **3906**

**cent** *det,nm* one hundred, cent **704**

**centaine** *nf* hundred **1417**

**central** *nadj* central **992**

**centrale** *nf* power station, central office **3164**

**centre** *nm* center **491**

**centrer** *v* to center **4162**

**cependant** *adv,conj* however **352**

**cercle** *nm* circle, cycle **2258**

**céréale** *nf* cereal **4983**

**cérémonie** *nf* ceremony **2279**

**cerner** *v* to surround, encircle, delimit **3435**

**certain** *adj,det,nm,pro* certain, sure **110**

**certainement** *adv* certainly **1071**

**certes** *adv* indeed, certainly, of course **1021**

**certificat** *nm* certificate **3604**

**certitude** *nf* certainty **2339**

**cerveau** *nm* brain **1990**

**cesser** *v* to cease, stop **462**

**cessez-le-feu** *nmi* ceasefire **4505**

**c'est-à-dire** *adv* in other words **560**

**chacun** *pro* each **323**

**chagrin** *adj,nm* grief, sorrow **4560**

**chaîne** *nf* chain, channel **1159**

**chair** *nf* flesh **3260**

**chaise** *nf* chair **3419**

**chaleur** *nf* heat **2773**

**chaleureux** *adj(pl)* warm **4103**

**chambre** *nf* bedroom, chamber **633**

**champ** *nm* field, realm **847**

**champion** *nadj* champion **2443**

**championnat** *nm* championship **2980**

**chance** *nf* luck; chance **438**

**chancelier** *nm* chancellor **4761**

**change** *nm* exchange **3321**

**changement** *nm* change **530**

**changer** *v* to change **283**

**chanson** *nf* song **2142**

**chant** *nm* song **3765**

**chanter** *v* to sing **1820**

**chanteur** *nadj* singer **3251**

**chantier** *nm* construction site, roadworks **3292**

**chaos** *nm(pl)* chaos **3266**

**chapeau** *nm* hat **2908**

**chapitre** *nm* chapter **1317**

**chaque** *det,adj* each **151**

**char** *nm* tank **3853**

**charbon** *nm* coal **2935**

**charge** *nf* to charge, load **849**

**charger** *v* to load, charge **544**

**charité** *nf* charity **4750**

**charmant** *adj* charming **4030**

**charme** *nm* charm **3682**

**charte** *nf* charter **2900**

**chasse** *nf* chase, hunt, hunting **2115**

**chasser** *v* to hunt, chase away **2364**

**chasseur** *nm* hunter, fighter, page, messenger **2879**

**chat** *nm* cat; chat **3138**

**château** *nm* castle **3510**

**chaud** *adv,nadj* warm, hot **1852**

**chauffeur** *nm* driver, chauffeur **3814**

**chaussure** *nf* shoe, sneakers **3638**

**chef** *nm* head, leader, chief **386**

**chemin** *nm* path, way **859**

**chemise** *nf* shirt, folder **3892**

**chèque** *nm* check **3203**

**cher** *adj,adv* expensive **803**

**chercher** *v* to look for **336**

**chercheur** *nadj* researcher **1961**

**chéri** *nadj* darling, love, dear **2880**

**cheval** *nm* horse **2220**

**cheveu** *nm* hair **2296**

**chez** *prep* at, with **206**

**chien** *nm* dog **1744**

**chier** *v* to sh\*t, piss off, get pissed off **4245**

**chiffre** *nm* figure, number **749**

**chiffrer** *v* to put a figure to, assess, quantify, number **4280**

**chiite** *nadj(f)* Shiite **4625**

**chimie** *nf* chemistry **4073**

**chimique** *adj(f)* chemical **2650**

**chinois** *nadj(pl)* Chinese 1914

**chirurgien** *nm* surgeon 4787

**choc** *nm* shock, clash 1917

**chocolat** *adji,nm* chocolate 4556

**choisir** *v* to choose 226

**choix** *nm(pl)* choice 436

**chômage** *nm* unemployment 1430

**chômeur** *nm* unemployed person 2616

**choquer** *v* to shock, offend, shake, disturb 2526

**chose** *adj(f),nf* thing 125

**chrétien** *nadj* christian 1895

**chronique** *nadj(f)* chronic, column, page, chronicle 3078

**chute** *nf* fall 1761

**chuter** *v* to fall 4347

**ci** *adv,pro* this one, here 247

**cible** *nf* target 2740

**cibler** *v* to target 3130

**ciel** *nm* sky 1538

**cigarette** *nf* cigarette 2855

**cimetière** *nm* cemetary, graveyard 3583

**cinéma** *nm* cinema 1623

**cinq** *det,nm(pl)* five 288

**cinquantaine** *nf* about fifty 4491

**cinquante** *det,nmi* fifty 2273

**cinquième** *det,nm,nf* fifth 2030

**circonscription** *nf* district, constituency 2496

**circonstance** *nf* circumstance 1054

**circuit** *nm* circuit 1309

**circulation** *nf* circulation, traffic 2293

**circuler** *v* to drive, circulate 1721

**cirque** *nm* circus; cirque 4953

**citation** *nf* quote, quotation, citation 3110

**cité** *nf* city 1246

**citer** *v* to quote 1082

**citoyen** *nadj* citizen 1081

**citoyenneté** *nf* citizenship 3895

**civil** *nadj* civil; civilian 929

**civilisation** *nf* civilization 2598

**civiliser** *v* to civilize 4227

**civique** *adj(f)* civil; civics 4950

**clair** *adv,nadj* clear 335

**clairement** *adv* clearly 1319

**clan** *nm* clan 4879

**clandestin** *nadj* underground, clandestine 2992

**claquer** *v* to flap, bang, slam, snap 4906

**clarifier** *v* to clarify 4894

**clarté** *nf* lightness, brightness clearness, clarity 3316

**classe** *nf* class 778

**classement** *nm* classification, ranking 3064

**classer** *v* to classify, file, grade, rate 2070

**classique** *nadj(f)* classic 1845

**clause** *nf* clause 3423

**clé** *nf* key 1200

**clef** *nf* key 3424

**cliché** *nm* cliché; negative 4705

**client** *nm* client 917

**clientèle** *nf* customers, clientele 3299

**climat** *nm* climate 2006

**climatique** *adj(f)* climatic 4201

**clinique** *nadj(f)* clinic 2876

**cloche** *nf* bell 4273

**clore** *v* to close 1823

**clôture** *nf* enclosure; termination, closure 2839

**club** *nm* club 1860

**coalition** *nf* coalition 2711

**cochon** *nadj* pig 4947

**cocktail** *nm* cocktail, cocktail party 4992

**code** *nm* code 1228

**coder** *v* to code, encode 4121

**cœur** *nm* heart 568

**coffre** *nm* trunk, boot, chest 4776

**cohérence** *nf* coherence, consistency 4327

**cohérent** *adj* coherent 3271

**cohésion** *nf* cohesion 3642

**coin** *nm* corner 1798

**coincer** *v* to jam, hinder, get stuck 3289

**coïncidence** *nf* coincidence 4303

**coïncider** *v* to coincide, correspond 3595

**col** *nm* collar, mountain pass 3054

**colère** *nf* anger 1568

**collaborateur** *nm* associate, fellow worker, contributor, collaborator 2459

**collaboration** *nf* collaboration 2037

**collaborer** *v* to collaborate, contribute 2963

**collectif** *nadj* collective 1224

**collection** *nf* collection, series 2806

**collectivité** *nf* community, group 2408

**collège** *nm* secondary school, college 2116

**collègue** *nm,nf* colleague 1099

**coller** *v* to stick, paste 2973

**colline** *nf* hill 2937

**colonel** *nm* colonel 3550

**colonial** *nadj* colonial 4143

**colonie** *nf* colony 3375

**colonne** *nf* column 2931

**combat** *nm* fight, combat 1062

**combattant** *adj,nm* fighter 2374

**combattre** *v* to fight 1118

**combien** *adv,conj* how much, how many 800

**combinaison** *nf* combination 2818

**combiner** *v* to combine, devise 2652

**comble** *nadj(f)* despair; summit, overmeasure; roof 4976

**combler** *v* to fill, fill in, fulfil 2000

**combustible** *nadj(f)* fuel, combustible 4318

**comédie** *nf* comedy, playacting 3373

**comédien** *nadj* comedian, comedy 4253

**comique** *nadj(f)* comical; comic, comedian 4709

**comité** *nm* committee 651

**commandant** *nadj* commander 4346

**commande** *nf* order, control 2123

**commandement** *nm* command, order, commandment 2644

**commander** *v* to order, command 959

**comme** *adv,conj* like, as 32

**commencement** *nm* beginning, start 4759

**commencer** *v* to begin, start 139

**comment** *adv,conj,intj,nmi* how 234

**commentaire** *nm* comment, remark 1685

**commenter** *v* to comment 2211

**commerçant** *nadj* shopkeeper, merchant, commercial 4167

**commerce** *nm* trade, commerce 934

**commercial** *nadj* commercial 908

**commettre** *v* to commit 1196

**commissaire** *nm,nf* superintendent, commissioner 1737

**commissariat** *nm* police station 4242

**commission** *nf* commission 461

**commun** *nadj* common 780

**communautaire** *adj(f)* community, communal 1811

**communauté** *nf* community 558

**commune** *nf* locality; common, joint 851

**communication** *nf* communication 1036

**communiqué** *nm* communiqué, release, statement 2221

**communiquer** *v* to communicate 1514

**communisme** *nm* communism 3923

**communiste** *nadj(f)* communist 1696

**compagnie** *nf* company 775

**compagnon** *nm* companion, craftsman, journeyman 3023

**comparable** *adj(f)* comparable 3016

**comparaison** *nf* comparison 2244

**comparaître** *v* to appear 3456

**comparer** *v* to compare 1560

**compassion** *nf* compassion 3699

**compatriote** *nm,nf* compatriot 4274

**compensation** *nf* compensation, clearing 2815

**compenser** *v* to compensate for, make up for 2594

**compétence** *nf* competence 1757

**compétent** *adj* competent 3262

**compétitif** *adj* competitive 4173

**compétition** *nf* competition 2651

**compétitivité** *nf* competitiveness 4286

**complément** *nm* complement 4251

**complémentaire** *adj(f)* complementary, supplementary 2539

**complet** *adj,nm* full, complete 965

**complètement** *adv,nm* completely 1013

**compléter** *v* to complete 2034

**complexe** *nadj(f)* complex 933

**complexité** *nf* complexity 3830

**complice** *nadj(f)* accomplice 3500

**complicité** *nf* complicity 3588

**compliment** *nm* compliment 4922

**compliqué** *nadj* complicated, complex 3324

**compliquer** *v* to complicate 1869

**complot** *nm* plot, conspiracy 4569

**comportement** *nm* behavior 1489

**comporter** *v* to comprise, include; to behave 1120

**composant** *nadj* component, constituent 4014

**composante** *nf* component 3454

**composer** *v* to compose, dial 858

**composition** *nf* composition, essay, dialling 2234

**compréhensible** *adj(f)* comprehensible, understandable 4774

**compréhension** *nf* understanding, comprehension 2827

**comprendre** *v* to understand 95

**compression** *nf* compression; cutback, reduction 4995

**compromettre** *v* to compromise 2346

**compromis** *nm(pl)* compromise, agreement 2673

**comptabilité** *nf* accountancy, accounting, book-keeping 3837

**comptable** *nadj(f)* accountant, accountable 4032

**compte** *nm* account, count 254

**compter** *v* to count 140

**comte** *nm* count 4598

**comté** *nm* county, earldom 3799

**con** *nadj* stupid 2817

**concéder** *v* to grant, concede 4810

**concentration** *nf* concentration 2355

**concentrer** *v* to concentrate 856

**concept** *nm* concept 1989

**conception** *nf* conception 2105

**concerner** *v* to concern 324

**concert** *nm* concert 1697

**concertation** *nf* meeting, consultation 4968

**concerter** *v* to devise, consult 3928

**concession** *nf* concession 3311

**concevoir** *v* to conceive 1100

**concilier** *v* to reconcile 3988

**concitoyen** *nm* fellow citizen 4566

**conclure** *v* to conclude 895

**conclusion** *nf* conclusion 1215

**concours** *nm(pl)* entrance exam, competition 1375

**concret** *nadj* concrete 1660

**concrètement** *adv* in concrete terms 4632

**concrétiser** *v* to materialize 4577

**concurrence** *nf* competition 1005

**concurrent** *nadj* competitor, rival 2239

**concurrentiel** *adj* competitive 4179

**condamnation** *nf* condemnation 2631

**condamner** *v* to condemn 878

**condition** *nf* condition 281

**conditionnel** *nadj* conditional 4523

**conducteur** *nadj* driver, operator, conductor 3072

**conduire** *v* to lead, drive 487

**conduite** *nf* behavior, driving 1512

**confédération** *nf* confederation 3221

**conférence** *nf* conference 1094

**conférer** *v* to confer 3406

**confession** *nf* confession 3878

**confiance** *nf* confidence, trust 435

**confiant** *adj* trusting, confident 4359

**confidentiel** *adj* confidential 4210

**confier** *v* to entrust 873

**configuration** *nf* configuration, layout 4716

**confiner** *v* to confine 4956

**confirmation** *nf* confirmation 3782

**confirmer** *v* to confirm 1014

**conflit** *nm* conflict 864

**confondre** *v* to mix up, confuse 2404

**conforme** *adj(f)* conform 2531

**conformément** *adv* in accordance 2189

**conformer** *v* to model, conform 3381

**conformité** *nf* conformity 4669

**confort** *nm* comfort 4773

**confortable** *adj(f)* comfortable 3964

**confrère** *nm* colleague 3971

**confrontation** *nf* confrontation 4244

**confronter** *v* to confront 1858

**confus** *adj(pl)* confused, embarrassed 3761

**confusion** *nf* confusion, mix-up 1755

**congé** *nm* holiday, time off, day off, notice 2445

**congrès** *nm(pl)* congress, conference 1977

**conjoint** *nadj* spouse, joint 3317

**conjointement** *adv* jointly 4527

**conjoncture** *nf* situation, climate 3717

**conjugal** *adj* conjugal, married 4432

**connaissance** *nf* knowledge 806

**connaître** *v* to know 133

**connecter** *v* to connect, go on-line 4772

**connerie** *nf* crap, bullsh*t, stupidity 4402

**connexion** *nf* connection 2154

**conquérir** *v* to conquer 3191

**conquête** *nf* conquest 3177

**consacrer** *v* to devote, consecrate 750

**conscience** *nf* conscience, consciousness 1124

**conscient** *adj* conscious, aware 1564

**consécutif** *adj* consecutive 3218

**conseil** *nm* advice, counsel, council 577

**conseiller** *nm,v* adviser, to advise 970

**consensus** *nm(pl)* consensus 3137

**consentement** *nm* consent 2907

**consentir** *v* to consent, agree 2735

**conséquence** *nf* consequence 617

**conséquent** *nadj* logical, rational, consistent 1703

**conservateur** *nadj* conservative 1927

**conservation** *nf* preservation, preserving, retention 3847

**conserver** *v* to keep, preserve 664

**considérable** *adj(f)* considerable, significant 1511

**considérablement** *adv* considerably, significantly, extensively 2915

**considération** *nf* consideration 1981

**considérer** *v* to consider 255

**consigne** *nf* deposit, orders, detention 4583

**consister** *v* to consist 1051

**consolider** *v* to strengthen, reinforce 4116

**consommateur** *nm* consumer, customer 1673

**consommation** *nf* consumption 1428

**consommer** *v* to eat, consume, drink, use, consummate 2048

**constamment** *adv* constantly, continuously, consistent 2564

**constant** *adj* constant 1762

**constat** *nm* report, statement 3922

**constater** *v* to note, notice; to establish, certify 705

**constituer** *v* to constitute 495

**constitution** *nf* constitution 1350

**constitutionnel** *nadj* constitutional 2249

**constructeur** *nadj* builder, manufacturer 3549

**constructif** *adj* constructive 4039

**construction** *nf* construction, building 976

**construire** *v* to build, construct **793**

**consultatif** *adj* advisory **3825**

**consultation** *nf* consultation **1969**

**consulter** *v* to consult **1595**

**contact** *nm* contact **894**

**contacter** *v* to contact, get in touch with **4241**

**contaminer** *v* to contaminate, infect **3605**

**conte** *nm* tale **4371**

**contemporain** *nadj* contemporary **2557**

**contenir** *v* to contain **1033**

**content** *adj* glad, pleased, happy **1841**

**contenter** *v* to satisfy, please **1078**

**contenu** *nadj* contents **1501**

**contestation** *nf* questioning, protest **3398**

**contester** *v* to contest, question **1974**

**contexte** *nm* context **1441**

**continent** *adj,nm* continent **2388**

**continental** *adj* continental **4846**

**contingent** *nadj* contingent, draft, quota **4098**

**continu** *nadj* continuous **3291**

**continuellement** *adv* continually, continuously **4579**

**continuer** *v* to continue **113**

**continuité** *nf* continuity, continuation **3175**

**contourner** *v* to bypass, go round **3178**

**contracter** *v* to contract, take out, tense **3159**

**contradiction** *nf* contradiction **2350**

**contradictoire** *adj(f)* contradictory, conflicting **2738**

**contraindre** *v* to compel, force **2144**

**contrainte** *nf* constraint **2250**

**contraire** *nadj(f)* opposite, contrary **619**

**contrairement** *adv* contrary **1766**

**contrarier** *v* to annoy, bother, thwart **4488**

**contrat** *nm* contract **832**

**contre** *adv,nm,prep* against **121**

**contredire** *v* to contradict **3364**

**contrepartie** *nf* counterpart, opposite, alternative **4826**

**contrer** *v* to counter **3734**

**contrevenant** *nadj* offender, offending **4118**

**contribuable** *nm,nf* taxpayer **2658**

**contribuer** *v* to contribute **1017**

**contribution** *nf* contribution **1785**

**contrôle** *nm* control **662**

**contrôler** *v* to control, check, inspect, monitor **1069**

**contrôleur** *nm* inspector, controller **4423**

**controversé** *adj* much debated, controversial **4481**

**controverse** *nf* controversy **4124**

**convaincant** *adj* convincing **4050**

**convaincre** *v* to convince **575**

**convenable** *adj(f)* suitable, appropriate, correct, proper, acceptable **4410**

**convenir** *v* to agree, be suitable **1106**

**convention** *nf* agreement, convention **1513**

**conventionnel** *nadj* conventional **3142**

**conversation** *nf* conversation **1747**

**conversion** *nf* conversion **3943**

**convertir** *v* to convert **3297**

**conviction** *nf* conviction, belief **2054**

**convoi** *nm* convoy, train **4834**

**convoquer** *v* to call, summon **2520**

**coopération** *nf* cooperation **1496**

**coopérer** *v* to cooperate **4026**

**coordination** *nf* coordination **2669**

**coordonner** *v* to coordinate **2852**

**copain** *nm* friend, buddy, mate **3020**

**copie** *nf* copy, replica, paper **2133**

**copier** *v* to copy, reproduce **4637**

**corde** *nf* rope, cord, string **3784**

**cordon** *nm* cord, string, lead **4687**

**corps** *nm(pl)* body **561**

**correct** *adj* correct **2617**

**correctement** *adv* properly **2930**

**correction** *nf* correction **3005**

**correspondance** *nf* correspondance, connection **2811**

**correspondant** *nadj* correspondent **2645**

**correspondre** *v* to correspond **1415**

**corriger** *v* to correct **1639**

**corrompre** *v* to corrupt, bribe **4166**

**corruption** *nf* corruption **3264**

**costume** *nm* suit, costume, dress **4419**

**côte** *nf* coast **1385**

**cote** *nf* rating, share index, quoted value **4093**

**côté** *nm* side **123**

**coter** *v* to quote, rate **3514**

**cotisation** *nf* subscription **2294**

**coton** *nm* cotton **4516**

**cou** *nm* neck **3820**

**couche** *nf* layer, coat **2485**

**coucher** *nm,v* lie down, sleep **2160**

**coude** *nm* elbow **4404**

**couler** *v* to flow, run, sink **2536**

**couleur** *nf* color **1211**

**coulisse** *nf* backstage, wings, behind the scenes **4633**

**couloir** *nm* corridor, aisle **2744**

**coup** *nm* coup, blow, knock, stroke **299**

**coupable** *nadj(f)* guilty **1442**

**coupe** *nf* bowl, dish; cut **2925**

**couper** *v* to cut **811**

**couple** *nm,nf* couple 1167

**coupure** *nf* cut, cutting 2579

**cour** *nf* yard, court 1554

**courage** *nm* courage 1431

**courageux** *nadj(pl)* courageous 2198

**couramment** *adv* fluently, commonly 4859

**courant** *adj,nm* current 314

**courbe** *nadj(f)* curve, curved 4108

**courir** *v* to run 1447

**couronne** *nf* crown, wreath 3700

**couronner** *v* to crown, award 4169

**courrier** *nm* mail, post 1935

**cours** *nfpl,nm(pl)* course 169

**course** *nf* race, shopping 1289

**court** *adj,adv,nm* short 545

**cousin** *nm* cousin 3387

**coût** *nm* cost 830

**couteau** *nm* knife 3737

**coûter** *v* to cost 984

**coûteux** *adj(pl)* expensive, costly 3149

**coutume** *nf* custom 3228

**couvert** *nadj* covered, overcast; place, seat, cutlery 3337

**couverture** *nf* blanket 1698

**couvrir** *v* to cover 682

**craindre** *v* to fear, be afraid of 500

**crainte** *nf* fear 1195

**crâne** *adj(f),nm* skull 4314

**craquer** *v* to creak, squeak, crackle, give in, strike 4893

**créateur** *nadj* creator 2613

**création** *nf* creation 634

**créature** *nf* creature 4407

**crédibilité** *nf* credibility 3611

**crédible** *adj(f)* credible 3845

**crédit** *nm* credit 1157

**créer** *v* to create 332

**crème** *adji,nf* cream 4748

**crête** *nf* crest, top, ridge 4895

**creuser** *v* to dig 2427

**creux** *nadj(pl)* hollow, empty, hole 3508

**crever** *v* to burst, puncture 3658

**cri** *nm* shout, cry 2380

**crier** *v* to shout, scream, cry out 1950

**crime** *nm* crime 819

**criminalité** *nf* crime 3854

**criminel** *nadj* criminal 1411

**crise** *nf* crisis 765

**critère** *nm* criterion, criteria 1923

**critique** *nadj(f)* criticism, critic, critical 909

**critiquer** *v* to criticize 1654

**croire** *v* to believe 135

**croisé** *nadj* twill; alternate; crusader; crossed 4650

**croiser** *v* to cross 2190

**croisière** *nf* cruise 4720

**croissance** *nf* growth 646

**croissant** *nadj* growing, crescent, crescent-shape 2069

**croître** *v* to grow, increase 2131

**croix** *nf(pl)* cross 3901

**croyance** *nf* belief 3293

**croyant** *nadj* believer 4332

**cruauté** *nf* cruelty 4769

**crucial** *adj* crucial, critical 2890

**cruel** *adj* cruel, ferocious, bitter 3357

**cuire** *v* to cook, bake, roast 4963

**cuisine** *nf* cooking, kitchen 2618

**cul** *nm* bum, arse, ass 2949

**culpabilité** *nf* guilt 2914

**culte** *nm* worship, cult 3630

**cultiver** *v* to cultivate, grow 2061

**culture** *nf* culture 913

**culturel** *adj* cultural 1495

**curé** *nm* parish priest 4422

**curieux** *nadj(pl)* curious 2424

**curiosité** *nf* curiosity 3506

**cycle** *nm* cycle 2462

**cynique** *nadj(f)* cynical, cynic 3547

# Dd

**d'abord** *adv* first of all 326

**d'accord** *intj* okay, alright 736

**d'ailleurs** *adv* moreover, besides, for that matter 588

**dame** *intj,nf* lady 1983

**danger** *nm* danger 932

**dangereux** *adj(pl)* dangerous 713

**danois** *nadj(pl)* Danish, Dane 4809

**dans** *prep* in, into, from 11

**danse** *nf* dance, dancing 2964

**danser** *v* to dance 2934

**danseur** *nm* dancer 4309

**d'après** according to 596

**date** *nf* date 660

**dater** *v* to date 2486

**d'autant** since 1498

**davantage** *adv* more 718

**de** *det,prep* of, from, some, any 2

**débarquer** *v* to unload, land, disembark 3037

**débarrasser** *v* to clear, get rid of 2235

**débat** *nm* debate 628

**débattre** *v* to discuss, debate 2254

**débit** *nm* debit, turnover, delivery, rate 4088

**débloquer** *v* to free, unfreeze, unjam, release, unblock 3904

**déborder** *v* to overflow, boil over, go out, go over 3071

**débouché** *nm* prospect, opportunity, opening 4649

**déboucher** *v* to unblock, uncork 2639

**debout** *adv* standing 2497

**débrouiller** *v* to untangle, sort out, manage, get by 3618

**début** *nm* beginning 364

**débuter** *v* to start 2426

**décéder** *v* to die, pass away, pass on 3809

**déceler** *v* to discover, detect 3561

**décembre** *nm* December 891

**décennie** *nf* decade 2361

**décent** *adj* decent, proper 4628

**déception** *nf* disappointment, let-down 2821

**décerner** *v* to award, give, issue 4732

**décès** *nm(pl)* death 2548

**décevant** *adj* disappointing 2603

**décevoir** *v* to disappoint 1302

**décharger** *v* to unload 4801

**déchet** *nm* scrap, waste, trash, garbage 2882

**déchirer** *v* to tear up, tear, rip 3172

**décider** *v* to decide 165

**décisif** *adj* decisive 2867

**décision** *nf* decision 370

**déclaration** *nf* declaration 1006

**déclarer** *v* to declare 503

**déclencher** *v* to trigger, release, unleash 2152

**déclin** *nm* decline, deterioration 4510

**décliner** *v* to decline, refuse, turn down 3751

**décoller** *v* to take off; to loosen, unstick 4979

**décor** *nm* scenery, décor, set 3698

**découler** *v* to ensue, follow 2866

**découper** *v* to carve, cut 4139

**décourager** *v* to discourage, dishearten, lose heart 3235

**découverte** *nf* discovery 1791

**découvrir** *v* to discover 681

**décret** *nm* decree 3252

**décréter** *v* to declare, decree 3589

**décrire** *v* to describe 1176

**décrocher** *v* to take down, take off, pick up, lift 3106

**dedans** *adv,nm(pl),prep* inside, indoors 3058

**dédier** *v* to dedicate 4008

**déduire** *v* to deduct, deduce, infer, figure out 3711

**défaillance** *nf* fault, failure, breakdown, blackout, weakness 3951

**défaire** *v* to undo, dismantle, strip, break up 2946

**défaite** *nf* defeat 2680

**défaut** *nm* fault, flaw, shortcoming 1276

**défavorable** *adj(f)* unfavorable 4910

**défavoriser** *v* to put at a disadvantage 4217

**défendre** *v* to defend, forbid 385

**défense** *nf* defence 938

**défenseur** *nm,nf* defender 3109

**défi** *nm* challenge 1728

**déficit** *nm* deficit 1657

**défier** *v* to challenge, defy, distrust 3718

**défiler** *v* to unthread, parade 3527

**défini** *nadj* definite 4458

**définir** *v* to define 916

**définitif** *nadj* definitive, final 1681

**définition** *nf* definition 1587

**définitivement** *adv* definitely, permanently, for good 2389

**déformer** *v* to bend, distort, deform 4386

**dégager** *v* to free, clear 1285

**dégât** *nm* damage 3492

**dégradation** *nf* degrading, damaging, erosion; demotion 3880

**dégrader** *v* to degrade, debase, damage, erode 4142

**degré** *nm* degree 1311

**déguiser** *v* to disguise 4104

**dehors** *adv,nm(pl),prep* outside 1217

**déjà** *adv* already 58

**déjeuner** *nm,v* lunch, to have lunch 2724

**delà** *adv* beyond, above, over 4367

**délai** *nm* delay 1522

**délégation** *nf* delegation 2441

**délégué** *nadj* delegate 4161

**déléguer** *v* to delegate 3447

**délibération** *nf* deliberation, debate, consideration 4540

**délibérément** *adv* deliberately 4096

**délibérer** *v* to deliberate, debate 3384

**délicat** *nadj* delicate, fine, gentle 1877

**délinquant** *nadj* delinquent, offender 4394

**délit** *nm* crime, offence 3166

**délivrer** *v* to set free, rid, relieve 2503

**demain** *adv,nm* tomorrow 871

**demande** *nf* request, demand 490

**demander** *v* to ask for 80

**demandeur** *nm* seeker, complainant 3189

**démarche** *nf* walk, process 1638

**démarrage** *nm* start, moving off 4897

**démarrer** *v* to start up 2851

**déménager** *v* to move 4611

**démentir** *v* to deny, refute, contradict 3772

**demeure** *nf* residence, home 3524

**demeurer** *v* to remain, live 748

**demi** *adji,adv,nm* half 1117

**demi-heure** *nf* half an hour 3338

**démission** *nf* resignation 3358

**démissionner** *v* to resign 3474

**démocrate** *nadj(f)* democrat, democratic 3554

**démocratie** *nf* democracy 1279

**démocratique** *adj(f)* democratic 1380

**démographique** *adj(f)* demographic 4742

**démon** *nm* demon, fiend 4547

**démonstration** *nf* demonstration 2956

**démontrer** *v* to demonstrate 1519

**dénoncer** *v* to denounce 1450

**dénonciation** *nf* denunciation 4764

**dent** *nf* tooth 2784

**départ** *nm* departure 548

**département** *nm* department 2161

**dépasser** *v* to pass, go beyond 685

**dépêcher** *v* to dispatch, send, hurry 3771

**dépendance** *nf* dependence, dependency 3206

**dépendant** *adj* answerable, responsible, dependent 3308

**dépendre** *v* to depend 791

**dépens** *nmpl* expense 3654

**dépense** *nf* expense, expenditure 1555

**dépenser** *v* to spend 2051

**dépit** *nm* spite, heartache 1390

**déplacement** *nm* movement, displacement, trip, travel 2246

**déplacer** *v* to move, displace 714

**déplaire** *v* to displease, be unhappy 4587

**déploiement** *nm* deployment, spreading, unfurling, display 3978

**déplorer** *v* to deplore 2829

**déployer** *v* to deploy, open 1718

**déposer** *v* to deposit, put down 1034

**dépôt** *nm* deposit, depot 1980

**dépouiller** *v* to skin, strip away, deprive; to analyze 4982

**dépression** *nf* depression 3396

**depuis** *adv,prep* since, for 96

**député** *nm* deputy, parlementary delegate 424

**déranger** *v* to disturb, bother 2732

**dérive** *nf* drift 4157

**dériver** *v* to divert, derive 3427

**dernier** *nadj* last 87

**dérober** *v* to steal, hide 4580

**déroulement** *nm* development, progress 3024

**dérouler** *v* to unwind, enroll 1436

**derrière** *adv,nm,prep* last; behind 805

**dès** *prep* from, as soon 185

**désaccord** *nm* disagreement, discord, conflict 2843

**désarmement** *nm* disarmament, disarming 4180

**désastre** *nm* disaster 2397

**désastreux** *adj(pl)* disastrous 4714

**descendant** *nadj* downward, descending, descendant 3656

**descendre** *v* to go down, come down 1705

**descente** *nf* descent, raid, downward slope 3701

**description** *nf* description 2779

**déséquilibre** *nm* imbalance 4446

**désert** *adj,nm* desert, wilderness 2382

**désespéré** *nadj* desperate, hopeless 4493

**désespérer** *v* to despair 3929

**désespoir** *nm* despair 3187

**désignation** *nf* designation 4667

**désigner** *v* to designate 790

**désir** *nm* desire 1642

**désirer** *v* to desire 1384

**désireux** *adj(pl)* avid for, anxious to, desirous of 4592

**désoler** *v* to upset, sadden 2081

**désordre** *nm* disorder, confusion 3376

**désormais** *adv* from now on, henceforth 1025

**desservir** *v* to clear, go against, harm, serve 4400

**dessin** *nm* drawing, pattern, design 2624

**dessiner** *v* to draw, design 2086

**dessous** *adv,nm(pl),prep* underneath, below, bottom, underside 2628

**dessus** *adv,nm(pl),prep* above, on top 1629

**destin** *nm* fate, destiny 2337

**destination** *nf* destination 2301

**destinée** *nf* fate, destiny 2529

**destiner** *v* to intend, be used 1088

**destruction** *nf* destruction 1921

**détachement** *nm* detachment 4459

**détacher** *v* to untie, detach, remove 3239

**détail** *nm* detail 318

**détailler** *v* to detail 2667

**détecter** *v* to detect 4062

**détendre** *v* to release, slacken, loosen, relax 4213

**détenir** *v* to hold, detain 2056

**détente** *nf* release, relaxation, détente, loosening 4855

**détenteur** *nadj* holder, possessor, bearer 4657

**détention** *nf* detention, possession 3212

**détenu** *nadj* prisoner 2741

**détérioration** *nf* deterioration 4945

**détériorer** *v* to deteriorate 4998

**déterminant** *nadj* determining, deciding, crucial **3776**

**détermination** *nf* determination, resolution **1976**

**déterminé** *nadj* determined, resolute, specific **3596**

**déterminer** *v* to determine, find out, specify **961**

**détester** *v* to hate, detest **2898**

**détour** *nm* bend, curve, detour **4820**

**détourner** *v* to redirect **2020**

**détresse** *nf* distress **3704**

**détriment** *nm* detriment **3049**

**détruire** *v* to destroy **928**

**dette** *nf* debt **1817**

**deuil** *nm* mourning, grief **3540**

**deux** *det,nmi* two **41**

**deuxième** *det,nm,nf* second **427**

**deuxièmement** *adv* secondly **3730**

**devant** *adv,nm,prep* in front, ahead **198**

**développement** *nm* development **384**

**développer** *v* to develop **892**

**devenir** *nm,v* to become **162**

**deviner** *v* to guess, solve **2996**

**devise** *nf* currency, motto, slogan **3249**

**dévoiler** *v* to unveil, reveal, disclose **3025**

**devoir** *nm,v* to have to, owe; duty **39**

**dévouer** *v* to devote, sacrifice oneself **4753**

**diable** *intj,nm* devil **3984**

**diagnostic** *nm* diagnosis **3888**

**dialogue** *nm* dialogue **1719**

**diamant** *nm* diamond **4706**

**dictateur** *nm* dictator **4258**

**dictature** *nf* dictatorship **3041**

**dicter** *v* to dictate, lay down **2515**

**dictionnaire** *nm* dictionary **4094**

**dieu** *intj,nm* god **2262**

**différemment** *adv* differently **3843**

**différence** *nf* difference **738**

**différencier** *v* to differentiate **4620**

**différend** *nm* disagreement, controversy **3797**

**différent** *adj* different **350**

**différer** *v* to differ, vary **2858**

**difficile** *nadj(f)* difficult **296**

**difficilement** *adv* with difficulty **3340**

**difficulté** *nf* difficulty **564**

**diffuser** *v* to diffuse, broadcast **1995**

**diffusion** *nf* diffusion, spreading, circulation **2129**

**digne** *adj(f)* dignified, worthy **2391**

**dignité** *nf* dignity **2171**

**dilemme** *nm* dilemma **4798**

**dimanche** *nm* Sunday **1235**

**dimension** *nf* dimension **1717**

**diminuer** *v* to diminish, decrease **1507**

**diminution** *nf* reduction, decreasing **2805**

**dîner** *nm,v* dinner; to dine **2365**

**diplomate** *nadj(f),nm* diplomat, diplomatic **3931**

**diplomatie** *nf* diplomacy **3766**

**diplomatique** *nadj(f)* diplomatic **2712**

**diplôme** *nm* diploma, certificate **3328**

**dire** *nm,v* to say **37**

**direct** *nadj* direct **839**

**directement** *adv* directly **888**

**directeur** *nadj* director **640**

**direction** *nf* direction, management **582**

**directive** *nf* guideline **2708**

**dirigeant** *nadj* leader **1343**

**diriger** *v* to lead, direct **540**

**discipline** *nf* discipline **2120**

**discours** *nm(pl)* speech, talk, discourse **773**

**discret** *adj* discreet, tactful, quiet **2635**

**discrétion** *nf* discretion **3272**

**discrimination** *nf* discrimination **2338**

**discussion** *nf* discussion **882**

**discuter** *v* to discuss, debate; to question **737**

**disparaître** *v* to disappear, vanish **493**

**disparition** *nf* disappearance **2077**

**dispenser** *v* to exempt, avoid **3019**

**disperser** *v* to scatter, spread, disperse **3171**

**disponibilité** *nf* availability **4549**

**disponible** *adj(f)* available **1205**

**disposer** *v* to arrange, set **551**

**dispositif** *nm* device, apparatus **2248**

**disposition** *nf* arrangement, disposition **948**

**disputer** *v* to dispute **2725**

**disque** *nm* disc **2484**

**dissimuler** *v* to conceal, hide **3077**

**dissiper** *v* to dispel, disperse, clear away **4509**

**dissoudre** *v* to dissolve, disband, break up **4425**

**distance** *nf* distance **1502**

**distant** *adj* far-off, distant, faraway **4902**

**distinct** *adj* distinct **2698**

**distinction** *nf* distinction **2031**

**distinguer** *v* to distinguish **1807**

**distorsion** *nf* distortion **4231**

**distribuer** *v* to distribute, give out **1152**

**distributeur** *nadj* distributor, machine **4140**

**distribution** *nf* distribution **1911**

**dit** *nadj* said, so-called; tale **2985**

**divergence** *nf* divergence, difference **3210**

**divers** *adj(pl),det* diverse, various **752**

**diversifier** *v* to vary, diversify **4593**

**diversité** *nf* diversity 2537

**divin** *adj,nm* divine, heavenly 3787

**diviser** *v* to divide 1567

**division** *nf* division 1440

**divorce** *nm* divorce 2561

**dix** *det,nmi* ten 372

**dix-huit** *det,nmi* eighteen 3592

**dixième** *det,nm,nf* tenth 4602

**dix-neuf** *det,nmi* nineteen 4851

**dix-neuvième** *det,nm,nf* nineteenth 3997

**dix-sept** *det,nmi* seventeen 3812

**dizaine** *nf* approximately ten 1628

**docteur** *nm* doctor 2176

**doctrine** *nf* doctrine 4172

**document** *nm* document 997

**documentation** *nf* documentation, literature 4643

**doigt** *nm* finger 1938

**dollar** *nm* dollar 432

**domaine** *nm* domain, field 539

**domestique** *nadj(f)* servant, domestic 3585

**domicile** *nm* home, place of residence 2434

**dominant** *adj* dominant, prevailing 2968

**domination** *nf* domination, dominion, rule 3333

**dominer** *v* to dominate 1648

**dommage** *nm* damage, harm; too bad 1156

**don** *nm* gift 1800

**donc** *conj* so, then, therefore, thus 145

**donnée** *nf* fact, datum 1116

**donner** *v* to give 46

**dont** *pro* whose, of which 74

**doré** *adj* golden 4833

**dorénavant** *adv* from now on, henceforth 3857

**dormir** *v* to sleep 1836

**dos** *nm(pl)* back 1672

**dose** *nf* dose, amount 4229

**dossier** *nm* file, record; case 798

**doter** *v* to endow, provide 1784

**douane** *nf* customs, duty 3584

**douanier** *nadj* customs officer 4572

**double** *nadj(f)* double 574

**doubler** *v* to double, pass; to dub 1135

**doucement** *adv* gently, softly 3242

**douceur** *nf* softness, smoothness, mildness, gentleness, sweetness 3896

**douleur** *nf* pain 2013

**douloureux** *adj(pl)* painful, grievous, distressing 2543

**doute** *nm* doubt 362

**douter** *v* to doubt 1592

**doux** *adv,nadj(pl)* soft, sweet 2062

**douzaine** *nf* dozen 3133

**douze** *det,nmi* twelve 1664

**dramatique** *nadj(f)* dramatic, tragic, drama 2918

**drame** *nm* drama 2275

**drapeau** *nm* flag 2582

**dresser** *v* to draw up, put up, raise 2104

**drogue** *nf* drug 1659

**droguer** *v* to drug, take drugs 4771

**droit** *adj,adv,nm* right 143

**droite** *nf* right 1293

**drôle** *adj(f),nm* funny, strange 2166

**duc** *nm* duke 4804

**dur** *adv,nadj* hard 1029

**durable** *adj(f)* durable, long-lasting 1985

**durant** *prep* during, for 795

**durée** *nf* length, duration 1464

**durement** *adv* harshly, severely 3256

**durer** *v* to last 605

**dynamique** *nadj(f)* dynamic 2078

**dynamisme** *nm* dynamism 3924

# Ee

**eau** *nf* water 475

**ébranler** *v* to shake, rattle 4313

**écart** *nm* space, gap 1743

**écarter** *v* to separate, move apart, keep away 1492

**échange** *nm* exchange 785

**échanger** *v* to exchange 1452

**échantillon** *nm* sample 3174

**échapper** *v* to escape 940

**échéance** *nf* expiration date, date of payment, deadline 3103

**échéant** *adj* if need be 4729

**échec** *adji,nm* failure 1039

**échelle** *nf* ladder, scale 1266

**échelon** *nm* rung, step, grade, echelon 3958

**écho** *nm* echo 2400

**échouer** *v* to fail 1383

**éclaircir** *v* to brighten up, clear up 4528

**éclairer** *v* to light up 2047

**éclat** *nm* splinter, fragment, brightness, burst 3515

**éclater** *v* to burst, explode 1942

**école** *nf* school 477

**écologique** *adj(f)* ecological 4206

**économie** *nf* economy 387

**économique** *nadj(f)* economic, economical 261

**économiquement** *adv* economically 4015

**économiser** *v* to save, save on, conserve 4319

**économiste** *nm,nf* economist 2943

**écouler** *v* to sell, run off, flow out 2155

**écoute** *nf* listening 4097

**écouter** *v* to listen to 429

**écran** *nm* screen 2421

**écrasant** *adj* crushing, overwhelming 4918

**écraser** *v* to crush, grind 2334

**écrier** *v* to exclaim, cry out 4865

**écrire** *v* to write 382

**écrit** *nadj* writing 3253

**écriture** *nf* writing 2716

**écrivain** *nm* writer 1738

**écrouler** *v* to collapse, tumble 5000

**écu** *nm* ecu 3760

**édifice** *nm* building 3044

**éditeur** *nm* publisher, editor 2183

**édition** *nf* publishing, editing, edition 1298

**éditorial** *nadj* editorial 4431

**éducation** *nf* education 995

**effacer** *v* to erase, clean 2425

**effectif** *nadj* effective; size, workforce 1810

**effectivement** *adv* effectively 1550

**effectuer** *v* to carry out, undergo 990

**effet** *nm* effect 173

**efficace** *adj(f)* efficient, effective 1243

**efficacement** *adv* efficiently, effectively 4023

**efficacité** *nf* efficiency, effectiveness 1752

**effondrement** *nm* collapse, caving-in, falling-in, breaking-down 3709

**effondrer** *v* to collapse, cave in, fall down 3127

**efforcer** *v* to endeavor 2041

**effort** *nm* effort 388

**effrayer** *v* to frighten, scare 3828

**égal** *nadj* equal 1183

**également** *adv* also, too, as well, equally 246

**égalité** *nf* equality 1898

**égard** *nm* consideration, respect, regard 875

**église** *nf* church 1782

**égyptien** *nadj* Egyptian 4137

**eh** *intj* hey, uh 1692

**élaboration** *nf* working-out, development 3615

**élaborer** *v* to work out, develop 1937

**élan** *nm* momentum, surge, rush; elk, moose 3481

**élargir** *v* to widen, expand 1956

**élargissement** *nm* widening, letting-out, stretching, broadening 4141

**électeur** *nm* elector, voter 1957

**élection** *nf* election 862

**électoral** *adj* electoral 1714

**électricité** *nf* electricity 2469

**électrique** *adj(f)* electric 2067

**électronique** *nadj(f)* electronic 2195

**élégant** *adj* elegant, stylish 4747

**élément** *nm* element 621

**élémentaire** *adj(f)* elementary, rudimentary, basic 2982

**élevé** *adj* high, heavy, tall 3563

**élève** *nm,nf* pupil, student 1068

**élever** *v* to grow, lift, raise 459

**élimination** *nf* elimination 3052

**éliminer** *v* to eliminate 1454

**élire** *v* to elect 1465

**élite** *nf* elite 2726

**elle** *pro* she, her 38

**elle-même** *pro* herself, itself 1379

**éloge** *nm* praise 4711

**éloigner** *v* to move away, take away, distance 1541

**élu** *nadj* elected, elected member 2954

**émaner** *v* to issue from, emanate from, come from, radiate from 3119

**embargo** *nm* embargo 4450

**embarquer** *v* to embark, board, take on board, load 2719

**embauche** *nf* job vacancy, hiring 4849

**embaucher** *v* to hire 3743

**embrasser** *v* to kiss, embrace 3102

**émerger** *v* to emerge, rise up, come out 4099

**émetteur** *nm* transmitter, issuer 4903

**émettre** *v* to emit, issue 1787

**émeute** *nf* riot, rioting 4038

**éminent** *adj* eminent, distinguished 4629

**émission** *nf* transmision, broadcasting, programme 1074

**emmener** *v* to take 2098

**emmerder** *v* to bug, bother 4676

**émotion** *nf* emotion, feeling 1854

**émouvoir** *v* to move, touch 3870

**emparer** *v* to seize, grab, snatch 2783

**empêcher** *v* to prevent 306

**empereur** *nm* emperor 4508

**empire** *nm* empire 3367

**emplacement** *nm* site, location 4636

**emploi** *nm* employment, work, use 517

**employé** *nm* employee 1485

**employer** *v* to use, employ 724

**employeur** *nm* employer 2633

**emporter** *v* to take, remove 1128

**empreinte** *nf* imprint, print, mark, impression 3504

**empresser** *v* to bustle about, hasten to do 4927

**emprisonner** *v* to imprison, jail, put in jail, trap 3351

**emprunt** *nm* loan 3422

**emprunter** *v* to borrow 1123

**en** *adv,prep,pro* in, by 7

**encadrement** *nm* training, framing, supervision 4610

**encadrer** *v* to frame, train 2831

**encaisser** *v* to receive, collect, cash 3710

**enceinte** *adjf,nf* pregnant; enclosure 2226

**enchaîner** *v* to chain up, connect, string together 4634

**enchanter** *v* to delight, enchant, rejoice 4738

**enclin** *adj* enclined, prone 4872

**encontre** *n* contrary to 2994

**encore** *adv* again, yet 51

**encourageant** *adj* encouraging 4200

**encouragement** *nm* encouragement 3193

**encourager** *v* to encourage 1434

**endormir** *v* to put to sleep, fall asleep 3788

**endroit** *nm* place, spot 650

**énergétique** *nadj(f)* energetic, vigorous 3727

**énergie** *nf* energy 720

**énergique** *adj(f)* energetic 4905

**enfance** *nf* childhood 2207

**enfant** *nm,nf,adj(f)* child 126

**enfer** *nm* hell 3001

**enfermer** *v* to shut 2315

**enfin** *adv* at last, finally 349

**enfoncer** *v* to ram, drive in, hammer in, sink in 2991

**enfuir** *v* to run away, flee 3804

**engagement** *nm* agreement, commitment 1042

**engager** *v* to hire, involve 408

**engendrer** *v* to father, breed, generate 2286

**engin** *nm* machine, tool, vehicle, device 4269

**englober** *v* to include, encompass, incorporate 4188

**enjeu** *nm* stake 2328

**enlever** *v* to remove 1201

**ennemi** *nadj* enemy 1715

**ennui** *nm* boredom, trouble, worry 3294

**ennuyer** *v* to bore, worry, bother 3480

**énoncer** *v* to state, set out, express 3541

**énorme** *adj(f)* enormous 663

**énormément** *adv* enormously 3039

**enquête** *nf* inquiry, enquiry, investigation 866

**enquêter** *v* to investigate, hold inquiry, conduct a survey 3811

**enquêteur** *nm* investigator, pollster 4526

**enregistrement** *nm* recording, registration, check-in, logging 3036

**enregistrer** *v* to record, check in 1238

**enrichir** *v* to expand, enrich, make somebody rich 2335

**enseignant** *nadj* teacher 2456

**enseignement** *nm* education, teaching 1626

**enseigner** *v* to teach 2134

**ensemble** *adv,nm* together 124

**ensuite** *adv* next 265

**ensuivre** *v* to follow, result, ensue 4942

**entamer** *v* to start 2325

**entendre** *v* to hear 149

**entente** *nf* understanding, agreement 2295

**enterrer** *v* to bury, lay aside 2870

**enthousiasme** *nm* enthusiasm, enthusiastically 2745

**enthousiaste** *adj(f)* enthusiastic 4287

**entier** *nadj* whole, full 455

**entièrement** *adv* entirely, completely 1316

**entité** *nf* entity 2983

**entourage** *nm* circle, entourage 4208

**entourer** *v* to surround 1509

**entraînement** *nm* training, coaching, drive 3070

**entraîner** *v* to carry along, train 550

**entraîneur** *nm* coach, trainer 4430

**entraver** *v* to hinder, hamper, get in the way of 4448

**entre** *prep* between 55

**entrée** *nf* entrance 808

**entreprendre** *v* to begin, start, undertake 1171

**entrepreneur** *nm* contractor, entrepreneur 2377

**entreprise** *nf* enterprise, business 298

**entrer** *v* to enter, go in, come in 337

**entre-temps** *adv,nm(pl)* meanwhile, in the meantime 3969

**entretenir** *v* to maintain 1185

**entretien** *nm* interview, discussion, maintenance 1433

**entrevoir** *v* to make out, catch a glimpse of, foresee 4517

**entrevue** *nf* meeting, interview 2860

**énumérer** *v* to enumerate 4848

**envahir** *v* to invade, overrun 2566

**enveloppe** *nf* envelope 3125

**envelopper** *v* to wrap, surround, veil 4604

**envergure** *nf* wingspan, breadth, scope 3774

**envers** *nm(pl),prep* towards 1151

**envie** *nf* envy 1237

**environ** *adv,prep,nm* about, thereabouts, or so 678

**environnement** *nm* environment 945

**environnemental** *adj* environmental 3548

**envisager** *v* to view, contemplate 850

**envoi** *nm* sending, dispatching 2960

**envoler** *v* to fly away, fly off, take off 4070

**envoyer** *v* to send 526

**épais** *adj(pl),adv* thick, pitch dark, thickly 3789

**épanouir** *v* to bloom, blossom 4724

**épargne** *nf* savings, saving **3404**

**épargner** *v* to save, spare **2354**

**épaule** *nf* shoulder **2494**

**épidémie** *nf* epidemic **4203**

**épisode** *nm* episode **3238**

**époque** *nf* era, period **465**

**épouser** *v* to marry, wed **3136**

**épouvantable** *adj(f)* terrible, appalling, dreadful **4150**

**époux** *nm(pl)* husband, spouse **1953**

**épreuve** *nf* test, ordeal, trial **1668**

**éprouver** *v* to feel, experience **1872**

**épuiser** *v* to exhaust, tire out, wear out, use up **2442**

**équation** *nf* equation **4840**

**équilibre** *nm* balance, equilibrium **1391**

**équilibrer** *v* to balance **2510**

**équipage** *nm* crew, gear **3632**

**équipe** *nf* team **814**

**équipement** *nm* equipment **1704**

**équiper** *v* to equip, kit out, fit out, tool up **3043**

**équitable** *adj(f)* equitable, fair **3304**

**équité** *nf* equity, fairly **4101**

**équivalent** *nadj* equivalent **2476**

**équivaloir** *v* to be equivalent, amount to **4619**

**ère** *nf* era **3079**

**ériger** *v* to erect, set up **3942**

**erreur** *nf* mistake, error **612**

**erroné** *adj* erroneous **4074**

**escalier** *nm* stairs, staircase **3705**

**esclave** *nadj(f)* slave **3468**

**escompter** *v* to discount; to expect **4717**

**espace** *nm,nf* space **870**

**espagnol** *nadj* Spanish **1666**

**espèce** *nf* species **1049**

**espérance** *nf* hope **3715**

**espérer** *v* to hope **417**

**espoir** *nm* hope **717**

**esprit** *nm* mind, spirit **538**

**essai** *nm* attempt, try, test **1475**

**essayer** *v* to try **303**

**essence** *nf* gas, petrol **1795**

**essentiel** *nadj* essential **675**

**essentiellement** *adv* essentially **1518**

**essor** *nm* expansion, development, flight **4662**

**essuyer** *v* to wipe, dry, mop, dust **3933**

**est** *nmi* east **4603**

**esthétique** *nadj(f)* aesthetics, attractiveness; attractive **4612**

**estimation** *nf* appraisal, valuation, assessment, estimate **3464**

**estimer** *v* to estimate; to consider, deem **649**

**et** *conj* and **6**

**établir** *v* to establish **529**

**établissement** *nm* establishment, organization **1085**

**étage** *nm* floor **2269**

**étaler** *v* to spread, display, apply **3935**

**étape** *nf* stage, step **1145**

**état** *nm* state **333**

**état-major** *nm* staff, staff headquarters **4186**

**etc** etc., et cetera **1177**

**été** *nm* summer **623**

**éteindre** *v* to extinguish, put out, turn off **3033**

**étendre** *v* to spread out, stretch out **1173**

**étendue** *nf* area, expanse, duration, extent, range **3721**

**éternel** *nadj* eternal, everlasting **3433**

**éthique** *nadj(f)* ethical, ethics **2747**

**ethnique** *nadj(f)* ethnic **3083**

**étiquette** *nf* label, ticket, etiquette, sticker, tag **3890**

**étoile** *nf* star **2776**

**étonnant** *nadj* surprising, amazing, incredible **1627**

**étonner** *v* to astonish, amaze **1778**

**étouffer** *v* to suffocate, smother, muffle **3213**

**étrange** *nadj(f)* strange, odd **2159**

**étranger** *nadj* foreigner; foreign **305**

**être** *nm,v* to be; being **5**

**étroit** *adj* narrow, tight **1828**

**étroitement** *adv* closely **3497**

**étude** *nf* study **446**

**étudiant** *nadj* student **1064**

**étudier** *v* to study **960**

**euh** *intj* er, um, uh **889**

**euro** *nm* euro **1753**

**européen** *nadj* European **445**

**eux** *pro* them **161**

**évacuer** *v* to evacuate, clear **3428**

**évaluation** *nf* evaluation **2057**

**évaluer** *v* to evaluate **1544**

**évasion** *nf* escape, evasion **4372**

**éveiller** *v* to arouse, stimulate, awaken **4330**

**événement** *nm* event **573**

**éventail** *nm* fan, range **4621**

**éventualité** *nf* eventuality, possibility **4183**

**éventuel** *nadj* possible **2023**

**éventuellement** *adv* possibly **2767**

**évêque** *nm* bishop **3446**

**évidemment** *adv* obviously **1340**

**évidence** *nf* evidence **1517**

**évident** *adj* obvious **1488**

**éviter** *v* to avoid **396**

**évoluer** *v*  to evolve **1658**

**évolution** *nf*  evolution **1352**

**évoquer** *v*  to recall, evoke **1143**

**ex** *nmfi*  ex **3663**

**exact** *adj*  exact, correct **1133**

**exactement** *adv*  exactly **857**

**exagérer** *v*  to exaggerate, overdo **2547**

**examen** *nm*  exam **1448**

**examiner** *v*  to examine **1108**

**excédent** *nm*  surplus **3140**

**excéder** *v*  to exceed **4802**

**excellence** *nf*  excellence **2713**

**excellent** *adj*  excellent **1225**

**exception** *nf*  exception **1134**

**exceptionnel** *nadj*  exceptional **1255**

**excès** *nm(pl)*  excess, surplus, abuse **3132**

**excessif** *nadj*  excessive, inordinate **2410**

**exciter** *v*  to arouse, waken, excite, turn on **4914**

**exclu** *nm,adj*  outcast **4756**

**exclure** *v*  to exclude **1457**

**exclusif** *nadj*  exclusive, sole **2558**

**exclusion** *nf*  exclusion, expulsion **3280**

**exclusivement** *adv*  exclusively, solely **2739**

**excuse** *nf*  excuse, apology **1839**

**excuser** *v*  to excuse **1987**

**exécuter** *v*  to execute, carry out **1909**

**exécutif** *nadj*  executive **3261**

**exécution** *nf*  execution, accomplishment **1806**

**exemplaire** *nadj(f)*  exemplary; copy **1459**

**exemple** *nm*  example **259**

**exercer** *v*  to exercise, exert, practice, carry out **966**

**exercice** *nm*  exercise, **1290**

**exhorter** *v*  to exhort, urge **3667**

**exigeant** *adj*  demanding, difficult **3344**

**exigence** *nf*  demand, strictness **1312**

**exiger** *v*  to require, demand **733**

**exil** *nm*  exile **4010**

**exiler** *v*  to exile **4766**

**existant** *adj*  existing **2586**

**existence** *nf*  existence **1153**

**exister** *v*  to exist **269**

**exode** *nm*  exodus **4986**

**expansion** *nf*  expansion **2641**

**expédier** *v*  to send, dispatch **3863**

**expédition** *nf*  dispatch, shipping, shipment, expedition **3762**

**expérience** *nf*  experience **679**

**expérimental** *adj*  experimental **4616**

**expérimenter** *v*  to experiment **4997**

**expert** *nadj*  expert **1557**

**expertise** *nf*  expertise **4310**

**explication** *nf*  explanation **1418**

**explicite** *adj(f)*  explicitly **3798**

**explicitement** *adv*  explicitly **4078**

**expliquer** *v*  to explain **252**

**exploit** *nm*  exploit **4199**

**exploitation** *nf*  operation, exploitation **1834**

**exploiter** *v*  to exploit **1808**

**exploration** *nf*  exploration, investigation, examination **4860**

**explorer** *v*  to explore, investigate, examine **3204**

**exploser** *v*  to explode, blow up **2678**

**explosif** *nadj*  explosive **3558**

**explosion** *nf*  explosion **2121**

**exportateur** *nadj*  exporter, exporting **4196**

**exportation** *nf*  export **1644**

**exporter** *v*  to export **3934**

**exposé** *nadj*  account, statement, talk **3790**

**exposer** *v*  to display, exhibit, expose **918**

**exposition** *nf*  exhibition, show **2378**

**exprès** *adj(pl),adv*  deliberately, on purpose, intentionally **4999**

**expression** *nf*  expression **952**

**exprimer** *v*  to express **466**

**expulser** *v*  to expel, evict, deport, throw out **3695**

**extension** *nf*  extension, stretching, expansion **3126**

**extérieur** *nadj*  exterior **625**

**externe** *nadj(f)*  external, outer **3779**

**extraction** *nf*  extraction **4262**

**extraire** *v*  to extract, mine, quarry, pull out, remove **2797**

**extrait** *nm*  extract, excerpt **4283**

**extraordinaire** *adj(f)*  extraordinary **1234**

**extrême** *nadj(f)*  extreme **1270**

**extrêmement** *adv*  extremely **1545**

**extrémité** *nf*  end, extremity **2941**

# Ff

**fabricant** *nm*  manufacturer **3081**

**fabrication** *nf*  manufacture, production **2308**

**fabriquer** *v*  to manufacture, invent, make **1231**

**façade** *nf*  front, façade **4029**

**face** *nf*  front, side, face **205**

**fâcher** *v*  to anger, make angry, get angry **4413**

**facile** *adj(f)*  easy **822**

**facilement** *adv*  easily **1194**

**facilité** *nf*  easiness, ease, aptitude **3624**

**faciliter** *v*  to make easier, facilitate **1813**

**façon** *nf*  way, manner **248**

**facteur** *nm* postman, mailman; factor 1264

**facture** *nf* invoice, bill 3007

**faculté** *nf* ability, right, option; faculty, university 2568

**faible** *nadj(f)* weak 723

**faiblesse** *nf* weakness 1944

**faille** *nf* fault 3430

**faillir** *v* to have almost, fail, fail to 3505

**faillite** *nf* bankruptcy, collapse, failure 3089

**faim** *nf* hungry 1986

**faire** *nm,v* to do, make 25

**faisceau** *nm* bundle, beam, stack 3490

**fait** *adj,nm* done, fact 141

**falloir** *v* to take, require, need 68

**fameux** *adj(pl)* famous 2060

**familial** *adj* family 1622

**familier** *nadj* familiar, informal 3672

**famille** *nf* family 172

**famine** *nf* famine 4864

**fantastique** *nadj(f)* fantastic, terrific, great, weird, eerie 4107

**fantôme** *nm* ghost, phantom 4075

**farce** *nf* joke, prank, hoax, farce 4285

**fardeau** *nm* burden 3954

**fasciner** *v* to fascinate 4797

**fatal** *adj* fatal, deadly, fateful 4238

**fatigue** *nf* tiredness, fatigue tired 4595

**fatiguer** *v* to tire, get 3229

**faute** *nf* mistake, error, fault 835

**fauteuil** *nm* armchair, seat 2743

**faux** *adv,adj(pl),nm(pl),nf(pl)* false; scythe 555

**faveur** *nf* favor 994

**favorable** *adj(f)* favorable 1443

**favori** *nadj* favourite, favorite 3831

**favoriser** *v* to favor 1407

**fédéral** *nadj* federal 828

**fédération** *nf* federation 1945

**félicitation** *nf* congratulation 4589

**féliciter** *v* to congratulate 1749

**féminin** *nadj* feminine 2381

**femme** *nf* woman, wife 154

**fenêtre** *nf* window 1604

**fer** *nm* iron 1621

**fermé** *adj* shut, closed, locked 3753

**ferme** *adj(f),adv,nf* farm; firm 1024

**fermement** *adv* firmly 3318

**fermer** *v* to close, shut 757

**fermeté** *nf* firmness, solidity, steadiness 4464

**fermeture** *nf* closing 2562

**fermier** *nadj* farmer 4685

**féroce** *adj(f)* ferocious, fierce 4888

**ferroviaire** *adj(f)* railway, rail 4981

**festival** *nm* festival 3858

**fête** *nf* holiday, celebration 1490

**fêter** *v* to celebrate 3275

**feu** *adj(f),nm* fire 786

**feuille** *nf* leaf, sheet, slip 2440

**février** *nm* February 1136

**fiable** *adj(f)* reliable, trustworthy 4147

**fiche** *nf* card, sheet, slip, form 4445

**ficher** *v* to file; to make fun of, not care, not give a damn 3905

**fichier** *nm* file 3176

**fiction** *nf* fiction 3612

**fidèle** *nadj(f)* faithful 1802

**fidélité** *nf* loyalty, faithfulness, accuracy, reliability 4348

**fier** *adj,v* to rely on; proud 1331

**fierté** *nf* pride 3237

**fièvre** *nf* fever 4105

**figer** *v* to clot, coagulate, congeal, set 4708

**figure** *nf* face; figure 1825

**figurer** *v* to represent, appear 841

**fil** *nm* thread, wire 1223

**file** *nf* line, queue 2615

**filer** *v* to spin, run, get out 2799

**filet** *nm* dribble, trickle, wisp, streak, thread, fillet, net 2656

**filial** *adj* filial; branch office 4126

**fille** *nf* girl, daughter 629

**fillette** *nf* little girl, girl 4737

**film** *nm* film 848

**filmer** *v* to film, shoot 4393

**fils** *nm(pl)* son 735

**fin** *adj,adv,nf,nm* end; gist, clever person 111

**final** *nadj* final 1461

**finale** *nm,nf* finale, final event 3147

**finalement** *adv* finally, eventually 843

**finance** *nf* finance 1677

**financement** *nm* financing 1671

**financer** *v* to finance 1772

**financier** *nadj* financial, financier 688

**finir** *v* to finish 534

**firme** *nf* firm 1955

**fiscal** *adj* fiscal 1637

**fixation** *nf* fixation, fixing 4609

**fixe** *nadj* fixed 2862

**fixer** *v* to fix, arrange, set 644

**flagrant** *adj* blatant, glaring 3925

**flamme** *nf* flame, fire, fervor, brilliance 3590

**fléau** *nm*  scourge, plague 4651

**flèche** *nf*  arrow 4567

**fleur** *nf*  flower 2305

**fleuve** *nm*  river 2893

**flic** *nm,nf*  cop 3559

**flot** *nm*  floodtide, stream of, flood of 4291

**flotte** *nf*  fleet 3234

**flotter** *v*  to float, hang, stream 4520

**flou** *adj*  blurred, fuzzy, vague 3823

**flux** *nm(pl)*  flow 2501

**foi** *nf*  faith 1368

**foie** *nm*  liver 4817

**foire** *nf*  fair 4746

**fois** *nf(pl)*  time, times 49

**folie** *nf*  madness, folly, insanity 2833

**foncier** *adj*  land-related, land, fundamental 4601

**fonction** *nf*  function 516

**fonctionnaire** *nm,nf*  state employee, public servant 1631

**fonctionnel** *adj*  functional 3966

**fonctionnement** *nm*  operation, functioning 1598

**fonctionner** *v*  to function, work 1144

**fond** *nm*  bottom 553

**fondamental** *adj*  fundamental 1291

**fondamentalement** *adv*  basically, fundamentally, inherently 4698

**fondateur** *nm*  founder 2899

**fondation** *nf*  foundation 2414

**fondé** *adj,nm,nf*  founded, justified; agent, clerk 2202

**fondement** *nm*  foundation 3046

**fonder** *v*  to found, set 963

**fondre** *v*  to melt, merge 3959

**fonds** *nm(pl)*  funds 983

**football** *nm*  football, soccer 2602

**force** *adv,nf*  force 222

**forcément** *adv*  without question, inevitably 2188

**forcer** *v*  to force 758

**forestier** *nadj*  forest, forester 4937

**forêt** *nf*  forest 1724

**forger** *v*  to forge, contrive, make up 4779

**formalité** *nf*  formality 4900

**format** *nm*  format 3462

**formation** *nf*  training 831

**forme** *nf*  form 369

**formé** *nm*  formed 3499

**formel** *adj*  formal, definite 2505

**former** *v*  to form 486

**formidable** *adj(f)*  tremendous, considerable 2722

**formule** *nf*  formula, expression 1334

**formuler** *v*  to formulate 1949

**fort** *adv,adj,nm*  strong 107

**fortement** *adv*  strongly 1769

**fortune** *nf*  fortune 2371

**forum** *nm*  forum, newsgroup 3512

**fossé** *nm*  ditch 3653

**fou** *adj,nm*  mad, crazy 1357

**foudre** *nf*  lightning 4874

**fouet** *nm*  whip 4607

**fouiller** *v*  to search, frisk, go through, rummage through 3431

**foule** *nf*  crowd 1894

**fournir** *v*  to provide, supply 731

**fournisseur** *nm*  supplier, provider 3048

**fourniture** *nf*  supply, provision 4743

**foutre** *v,nm*  to f*ck, shove off 1890

**foyer** *nm*  home, hearth 1579

**fraction** *nf*  fraction 4521

**fragile** *adj(f)*  fragile, delicate, frail 2107

**frais** *adj(pl),adv,nm(pl)*  cool, fresh; fee, expense 691

**franc** *adj,adv,adj,nm*  frank; franc 942

**français** *nadj(pl)*  French 251

**franchement** *adv*  frankly 2242

**franchir** *v*  to get over 1487

**franchise** *nf*  frankness, exemption, duty-free, franchise, deductible 3861

**francophone** *adj(f)*  French-speaking, French speaker, francophone 3118

**frappe** *nf*  strike, striking, stamp, impression, punch 4021

**frapper** *v*  to hit, strike, knock 754

**fraude** *nf*  fraud 4515

**frein** *nm*  brake 3400

**freiner** *v*  to brake, slow down 3027

**fréquemment** *adv*  frequently 3410

**fréquence** *nf*  frequency 2178

**fréquent** *adj*  frequent 2684

**fréquenter** *v*  to frequent, go around with 2367

**frère** *nm*  brother 1043

**froid** *nadj*  cold 1307

**fromage** *nm*  cheese 4475

**front** *nm*  front, forehead 1729

**frontière** *nf*  border 1182

**fruit** *nm*  fruit 896

**frustration** *nf*  frustration 4490

**frustrer** *v*  to frustrate 4853

**fuir** *v*  to flee 1960

**fuite** *nf*  escape 2053

**fumée** *nf*  smoke 4047

**fumer** *v*  to smoke 2623

**furieux** *nadj(pl)* furious, raging, violent 4239

**fusil** *nm* rifle, gun 3269

**fusion** *nf* fusion, melting, merging 2401

**futur** *nadj* future 484

# Gg

**gâcher** *v* to waste, spoil 4623

**gagnant** *nadj* winner, winning 3886

**gagner** *v* to win, earn 258

**gai** *adj* cheerful, merry, gay 4243

**gain** *nm* gain 2420

**galerie** *nf* gallery 3850

**gamin** *nm* kid 3439

**gamme** *nf* range, scale 3521

**garage** *nm* garage 4881

**garantie** *nf* guarantee 2117

**garantir** *v* to guarantee 1260

**garçon** *nm* boy 1599

**garde** *nm,nf* guard 901

**garder** *v* to keep 531

**gardien** *nadj* guardian, keeper 1924

**gare** *intj,nf* station, railway station; beware 2581

**gars** *nm(pl)* guy 2304

**gâteau** *nadj* cake 4845

**gauche** *nadj(f)* left 607

**gaz** *nm(pl)* gas 1551

**géant** *nadj* giant, gigantic 2283

**gel** *nm* frost, freezing, gel 4122

**geler** *v* to freeze, ice over, suspend 3526

**gendarme** *nm,nf* policeman 4438

**gendarmerie** *nf* police force, police station 4496

**gène** *nm* gene 2807

**gêner** *v* to bother, trouble 2460

**général** *nadj* general 147

**généralement** *adv* generally 1710

**généraliser** *v* to generalize 2939

**génération** *nf* generation 1386

**générer** *v* to generate 3620

**généreux** *adj(pl)* generous 2015

**générosité** *nf* generosity, generously 3418

**génétique** *nadj(f)* genetic 2259

**génétiquement** *adv* genetically 4497

**génial** *adj* inspired, great, brilliant 3872

**génie** *nm* genius 2162

**génocide** *nm* genocide 4148

**genou** *nm* knee 2967

**genre** *nm* type, kind, sort 556

**gens** *nmpl* people 236

**gentil** *nadj* nice, kind 2832

**géographique** *adj(f)* geographic, geographical 3389

**gérer** *v* to manage 1354

**geste** *nm* gesture 1261

**gestion** *nf* management 1140

**gestionnaire** *adj(f),nm,nf* administrator, administrative 4350

**gigantesque** *nadj(f)* gigantic, immense 3757

**glace** *nf* ice, ice cream; mirror 2580

**glissement** *nm* sliding, slipping, skidding 4553

**glisser** *v* to slide, slip 2544

**global** *adj* global 1155

**globalement** *adv* globally 4409

**globe** *nm* globe 3669

**gloire** *nf* glory, fame 3287

**golf** *nm* golf, golf course 4936

**golfe** *nm* gulf 4024

**gonfler** *v* to inflate, blow up, swell 3451

**gorge** *nf* throat 4194

**gosse** *nm,nf* kid 3631

**goût** *nm* taste 1829

**goûter** *nm,v* to taste, snack 4441

**goutte** *nf* drop 4337

**gouvernement** *nm* government 160

**gouvernemental** *adj* governmental 1908

**gouverner** *v* to govern, rule, steer, helm 2063

**gouverneur** *nm,nf* governor 2089

**grâce** *nf* thanks, grace, favor 238

**grain** *nm* grain, bean, bead; spot, mole 3323

**grand** *adv,nadj* great, big, tall 59

**grand-chose** *nmi* not very much 2884

**grandeur** *nf* size, greatness 3069

**grandir** *v* to grow, increase, expand 1936

**grandissant** *adj* growing, increasing 4559

**grand-mère** *nf* grandmother 3883

**grand-père** *nm* grandfather 3748

**graphique** *nadj(f)* graph, graphic 4782

**gras** *adj(pl),adv,nm(pl)* fatty, fat, greasy 4018

**gratuit** *adj* free, gratuitous, unwarranted 2470

**gratuitement** *adv* free, gratuitously 4818

**grave** *adv,nadj(f),nm* serious, grave 443

**gravement** *adv* seriously, solemnly, gravely 2957

**gravité** *nf* seriousness, solemnity, gravity 2596

**gré** *nm* liking 2627

**grec** *nadj* Greek 2026

**grève** *nf* strike 1803

**grille** *nf* railings, gate, grid, scale 3341

**grimper** *v* to climb, go up 2646

**gris** *nadj(pl)* grey 2769

**gros** *adv,nadj(pl)* big 419

**grossesse** *nf* pregnancy 4136

**grossier** *adj* unrefined, crude, coarse, rude, rough 4054

**grossir** *v* to get larger 4189

**groupe** *nm* group 187

**groupement** *nm* grouping, group, categorization 3976

**guère** *adv* hardly 1591

**guérir** *v* to cure, heal, get better 3602

**guerre** *nf* war 266

**guerrier** *nadj* warrior; warlike 4707

**guetter** *v* to watch over, watch out for 4852

**gueule** *nf* mouth, trap 3015

**guide** *nm,nf* guide 2392

**guider** *v* to guide 2008

**guise** *nf* wish; like, by way of 3477

# Hh

**ha** *intj* oh 4965

**habiller** *v* to dress, get dressed 3576

**habitant** *nm* inhabitant 1333

**habitation** *nf* residence, home, dwelling, housing 3616

**habiter** *v* to live 1186

**habitude** *nf* habit 1221

**habituel** *adj* customary, habitual 1347

**habituellement** *adv* usually, generally 3537

**habituer** *v* to accustom, get used to 2487

**haine** *nf* hatred, hate 2277

**haïr** *v* to detest, hate, abhor 3981

**hall** *nm* foyer, lobby 4792

**handicap** *nm* handicap 3937

**handicapé** *nadj* disabled, handicapped 3613

**handicaper** *v* to handicap 4392

**hanter** *v* to haunt 4686

**harceler** *v* to harass, plague 3999

**harmonie** *nf* harmony, 4584

**harmonisation** *nf* harmonization 4990

**harmoniser** *v* to harmonize, harmonize with 4646

**hasard** *nm* chance, luck 1882

**hâte** *nf* haste, impatience 3460

**hâter** *v* to quicken, hasten 4754

**hausse** *nf* rise, raise, increase 1572

**hausser** *v* to raise 2177

**haut** *adv,nadj* top, high 264

**hautement** *adv* highly 3420

**hauteur** *nf* height 1653

**hé** *intj* hey 3871

**hebdomadaire** *nadj(f)* weekly 3487

**hein** *intj* eh, huh 2076

**hélas** *intj* alas 3952

**hélicoptère** *nm* helicopter 2978

**hépatite** *nf* hepatitis 4877

**herbe** *nf* grass, herb 3562

**héritage** *nm* heritage 2193

**hériter** *v* to inherit 2981

**héritier** *nm* heir 3955

**héroïne** *nf* heroine 3467

**héros** *nm(pl)* hero 1883

**hésitation** *nf* hesitation 4323

**hésiter** *v* to hesitate 1606

**heure** *nf* hour 99

**heureusement** *adv* fortunately, luckily 2390

**heureux** *nadj(pl)* happy, lucky, fortunate 764

**heurter** *v* to strike, hit, collide 2601

**hier** *adv* yesterday 872

**hiérarchie** *nf* hierarchy 3463

**hisser** *v* to hoist, raise up 4974

**histoire** *nf* history, story 263

**historien** *nm* historian 3284

**historique** *nadj(f)* historical 902

**hiver** *nm* winter 1586

**hommage** *nm* homage, tribute 1904

**homme** *nm* man 136

**homologue** *adj(f)* counterpart, homologue 3196

**homosexuel** *nadj* homosexual 3501

**honnête** *adj(f)* honest, decent, fair 2405

**honneur** *nm* honor 1141

**honorable** *adj(f)* honorable, worthy 893

**honorer** *v* to honor, do credit to 2859

**honte** *nf* shame 1943

**honteux** *adj(pl)* ashamed, shameful 3995

**hôpital** *nm* hospital 1308

**horaire** *nadj(f)* schedule, timetable, hourly 3192

**horizon** *nm* horizon, skyline 2502

**hormis** *prep* save, but 4786

**horreur** *nf* horror 2565

**horrible** *adj(f)* horrible, terrible, dreadful, hideous 3190

**hors** *adv,prep* except, outside 865

**hostile** *adj(f)* hostile 3091

**hostilité** *nf* hostility, hostilities 3436

**hôte** *nm* host, guest 3780

**hôtel** *nm* hotel 1774

**huile** *nf* oil 2340

**huit** *det,nmi* eight 877

**huitième** *det,nm,nf* eighth 4778

**hum** *intj* um, uh 4938

**humain** *nadj* human 286

**humanitaire** *adj(f)* humanitarian 2319

**humanité** *nf* humanity 1525

**humble** *adj(f)* humble, lowly 4680

**humeur** *nf* mood, temper 3188

**humide** *adj(f)* moist, damp, humid, wet 4841

**humour** *nm* humor 3950

**hurler** *v* to scream, yell 4016

**hymne** *nm,nf* hymn, anthem 4862

**hypothèse** *nf* hypothesis 1669

# Ii

**ici** *adv* here 167

**idéal** *nadj* ideal 1429

**idée** *nf* idea 239

**identification** *nf* identification 3274

**identifier** *v* to identify 1426

**identique** *adj(f)* identical 2677

**identité** *nf* identity 1437

**idéologie** *nf* ideology 3185

**idéologique** *adj(f)* ideological 4272

**idiot** *nadj* idiot, fool, stupid 3556

**ignorance** *nf* ignorance 4055

**ignorer** *v* to ignore 639

**il** *pro* he, it 13

**île** *nf* island 1245

**illégal** *adj* illegal 2640

**illusion** *nf* illusion 2835

**illustration** *nf* illustration 4683

**illustrer** *v* to illustrate 1939

**image** *nf* picture, image 659

**imaginaire** *nadj(f)* imaginary 3471

**imagination** *nf* imagination 2705

**imaginer** *v* to imagine 840

**imiter** *v* to imitate 3742

**immédiat** *nadj* immediate 1254

**immédiatement** *adv* immediately 807

**immense** *adj(f)* immense 1759

**immeuble** *nadj(f)* building 1865

**immigrant** *nadj* immigrant 4352

**immigration** *nf* immigration 2255

**immigrer** *v* to immigrate 4470

**imminent** *adj* imminent, impending 3466

**immobile** *adj(f)* still, motionless 4463

**immobilier** *nadj* property, real estate, property business, real estate business 3603

**impact** *nm* impact 2032

**impasse** *nf* dead end, cul-de-sac 3363

**impatience** *nf* impatience 3675

**impatient** *nadj* impatient 4530

**impératif** *nadj* need, necessity, urgent, imperative 3680

**implantation** *nf* implanting, setting up, establishment, implantation, installation 4731

**implanter** *v* to implant, set up, establish 3655

**implication** *nf* implication 3747

**impliquer** *v* to imply, implicate 1113

**importance** *nf* importance 715

**important** *nadj* important 215

**importation** *nf* import 2260

**importer** *v* to import; to be important 354

**imposer** *v* to impose 469

**imposition** *nf* taxation 3619

**impossibilité** *nf* impossibility 4522

**impossible** *nadj(f)* impossible 652

**impôt** *nm* tax 1241

**impression** *nf* impression 825

**impressionnant** *adj* impressive, upsetting 2467

**impressionner** *v* to impress, upset 3055

**imprimer** *v* to print, print out 3092

**improbable** *adj(f)* unlikely, improbable 4525

**improviser** *v* to improvise 4492

**impuissant** *nadj* powerless, helpless 3979

**impulsion** *nf* impulse, pulse 3650

**imputer** *v* to impute to, attribute to 4397

**inacceptable** *adj(f)* unacceptable 2663

**inattendu** *adj* unexpected 3385

**inaugurer** *v* to unveil, open 4824

**incapable** *nadj(f)* incapable, incompetent 1605

**incapacité** *nf* incompetence, incapability 4477

**incarner** *v* to embody, incarnate 3574

**incendie** *nm* fire, blaze 2976

**incertain** *nadj* uncertain, unsure 3135

**incertitude** *nf* uncertainty 2169

**inchangé** *adj* unchanged 4701

**incidence** *nf* effect, incidence 4145

**incident** *adj,nm* incident 1885

**incitation** *nf* incitement, incentive 4429

**inciter** *v* to incite, encourage 2212

**incliner** *v* to tilt, tend towards 4368

**inclure** *v* to include 1998

**incomber** *v* to be incumbent upon 4617

**incompatible** *adj(f)* incompatible 3713

**incompréhensible** *adj(f)* incomprehensible 4819

**inconnu** *nadj* unknown 1451

**inconscient** *nadj* unconscious, thoughtless 4102

**inconvénient** *nm* snag, drawback, disadvantage, inconvenience 3399

**incorporer** *v* to incorporate, insert, merge 3903

**incroyable** *nadj(f)* incredible, unbelievable 2231

**inculper** *v* to charge 4638

**indemnisation** *nf* indemnification, compensation 3998

**indépendamment** *adv* independently, irrespective of, regardless of **4296**

**indépendance** *nf* independence **1651**

**indépendant** *nadj* independent **954**

**indicateur** *nadj* indicator **2592**

**indication** *nf* indication **2546**

**indice** *nm* indication, sign, clue **2138**

**indien** *nadj* Indian **1679**

**indifférence** *nf* indifference **4176**

**indifférent** *nadj* indifferent, unconcerned, unimportant **4151**

**indigène** *nadj(f)* native, local **4555**

**indiquer** *v* to indicate, signal **590**

**indirect** *adj* indirect **3769**

**indirectement** *adv* indirectly **4557**

**indispensable** *adj(f)* essential **1746**

**individu** *nm* individual **1115**

**individuel** *adj* individual **1812**

**induire** *v* to infer, induce, result in, lead to **3440**

**industrialiser** *v* to industrialize **4022**

**industrie** *nf* industry **692**

**industriel** *nadj* industrial **1131**

**inédit** *nadj* unpublished; original, new **4590**

**inégalité** *nf* difference, unevenness, inequality **3145**

**inévitable** *adj(f)* unavoidable, inevitable **2488**

**inévitablement** *adv* inevitably **4726**

**inexistant** *adj* non-existent **4807**

**inférieur** *nadj* inferior **1905**

**infini** *nadj* inifinite, infinity **3377**

**infiniment** *adv* infinitely **4550**

**infirmier** *nadj* nurse **2049**

**inflation** *nf* inflation **2312**

**infliger** *v* to inflict **2730**

**influence** *nf* influence **1083**

**influencer** *v* to influence **2498**

**influer** *v* to influence, have an influence on **4690**

**information** *nf* information **317**

**informatique** *nadj(f)* computer science, computing **2588**

**informé** *nadj* informed **4727**

**informer** *v* to inform **1356**

**infraction** *nf* offence, infrigement, infraction **2958**

**infrastructure** *nf* infrastructure **2287**

**ingénieur** *nm,nf* engineer **2848**

**inhabituel** *adj* unusual **2733**

**inhérent** *adj* inherent **4672**

**initial** *adj* initial **2137**

**initialement** *adv* initially **4252**

**initiative** *nf* initiative **1129**

**initier** *v* to initiate, introduce **4503**

**injecter** *v* to inject **4857**

**injuste** *adj(f)* unfair, unjust **2575**

**injustice** *nf* injustice, unfairness **2819**

**innocence** *nf* innocence **4300**

**innocent** *nadj* innocent **2059**

**innombrable** *adj(f)* innumerable, countless **4588**

**innovation** *nf* innovation **2402**

**inondation** *nf* flood, deluge **4677**

**inonder** *v* to flood **4928**

**inquiet** *nadj* worried, anxious **1392**

**inquiétant** *adj* worrying, disturbing **1997**

**inquiéter** *v* to worry, disturb **1389**

**inquiétude** *nf* worry, anxiety **1467**

**inscription** *nf* registration, enrolment; engraving **3214**

**inscrire** *v* to register, write down **1004**

**insensé** *nadj* insane **4614**

**insensible** *adj(f)* insensitive **4901**

**insérer** *v* to insert **3970**

**insignifiant** *adj* insignificant, unimportant **4978**

**insister** *v* to insist **899**

**inspecteur** *nm* inspector **2694**

**inspection** *nf* inspection **3296**

**inspiration** *nf* inspiration **3401**

**inspirer** *v* to inspire **1314**

**instabilité** *nf* instability **4596**

**instable** *adj(f)* unstable **4110**

**installation** *nf* installation, setup **2058**

**installer** *v* to install **821**

**instance** *nf* authority, proceedings, hearing **2278**

**instant** *adj,nm* instant, moment **769**

**instaurer** *v* to institute, introduce **2752**

**instinct** *nm* instinct **4482**

**instituer** *v* to introduce, impose, establish, institute **3461**

**institut** *nm* institute **1372**

**instituteur** *nm* school teacher **4630**

**institution** *nf* institution **937**

**institutionnel** *adj* institutional **3220**

**instruction** *nf* instruction, direction **1632**

**instruire** *v* to teach, educate, inform **4100**

**instrument** *nm* instrument **1650**

**insuffisance** *nf* inadequacy, insufficiency **4379**

**insuffisant** *adj* insufficient, inadequate **2473**

**insulte** *nf* insult **4005**

**insulter** *v* to insult **3840**

**insupportable** *adj(f)* intolerable **4484**

**intact** *adj* intact **4361**

**intégral** *adj* complete, unabridged **4641**

**intégration** *nf* integration **2534**

**intégrer** *v* to integrate 1764

**intégrité** *nf* integrity 3665

**intellectuel** *nadj* intellectual 1794

**intelligence** *nf* intelligence 2788

**intelligent** *adj* intelligent, clever, bright 2509

**intense** *adj(f)* intense, severe, dense 2270

**intensif** *nadj* intensive 4718

**intensité** *nf* intensity 3068

**intention** *nf* intention 782

**interaction** *nf* interaction 4970

**interdiction** *nf* ban, banning 2734

**interdire** *v* to forbid, prohibit, ban 533

**interdit** *nadj* prohibited, banned 4451

**intéressant** *adj* interesting 1244

**intéressé** *nadj* concerned, involved 2721

**intéresser** *v* to interest, involve 559

**intérêt** *nm* interest 315

**interface** *nf* interface 3240

**intergouvernemental** *adj* intergovernmental 4539

**intérieur** *nadj* interior, inside 433

**interlocuteur** *nm* speaker 3085

**intermédiaire** *nadj(f)* intermediate, intermediary 2102

**international** *nadj* international 282

**interne** *nadj(f)* internal, interior, intern 1546

**interpeller** *v* to call out to, question 3409

**interprétation** *nf* interpretation 2005

**interpréter** *v* to interpret 1683

**interrogation** *nf* question, interviewing, interrogation, questioning, test 3154

**interroger** *v* to question, interrogate 1093

**interrompre** *v* to interrupt 1479

**interruption** *nf* interruption, break 3659

**intervalle** *nm* space, distance, interval 3226

**intervenant** *nadj* contributor, intervener 3732

**intervenir** *v* to intervene 734

**intervention** *nf* intervention; talk 746

**interview** *nf* interview 3186

**intime** *nadj(f)* intimate, close, secret, private 3434

**intimider** *v* to intimidate 4777

**intimité** *nf* privacy, intimacy 4839

**intituler** *v* to entitle, call 2453

**intolérable** *adj(f)* intolerable 4664

**introduction** *nf* introduction 2917

**introduire** *v* to introduce 1695

**inutile** *nadj(f)* useless 1614

**invasion** *nf* invasion 3911

**inventer** *v* to invent 1964

**invention** *nf* invention 3821

**inverse** *nadj(f)* opposite, reverse 2452

**inverser** *v* to reverse, invert 4155

**investir** *v* to invest 1506

**investissement** *nm* investment 898

**investisseur** *nm* investor 2674

**invisible** *adj(f)* invisible 3369

**invitation** *nf* invitation 2237

**invité** *nm* guest 2478

**inviter** *v* to invite 624

**invoquer** *v* to call upon 2345

**irakien** *nadj* Iraqi 1913

**iranien** *nadj* Iranian 3405

**irlandais** *nadj(pl)* Irish 3963

**ironie** *nf* irony 4376

**ironique** *adj(f)* ironic 4500

**irrégulier** *adj* irregular, uneven 4606

**irréversible** *adj(f)* irreversible 4237

**islam** *nm* Islam 4728

**islamique** *adj(f)* Islamic 3074

**islamiste** *nm,nf* Islamist 3542

**isolé** *nadj* remote, isolated, insulated 2753

**isolement** *nm* loneliness, isolation, insulation 4033

**isoler** *v* to isolate, insulate 1896

**israélien** *nadj* Israeli 1468

**issu** *adj* descended from 2044

**issue** *nf* exit, outcome 2014

**italien** *nadj* Italian 1477

**itinéraire** *nadj(f)* itinerary, route 4411

# Jj

**jadis** *adv* formerly, long ago 4795

**jamais** *adv* never 179

**jambe** *nf* leg 2472

**janvier** *nm* January 939

**japonais** *nadj(pl)* Japanese 2097

**jardin** *nm* garden 2284

**jaune** *adv,nadj(f)* yellow 2585

**je** *pro* I 22

**jet** *nm* jet, throw, spray, nozzle 4454

**jeter** *v* to throw 1202

**jeu** *nm* game 291

**jeudi** *nm* Thursday 1112

**jeune** *nadj(f)* young 152

**jeunesse** *nf* youth 1609

**joie** *nf* joy 1984

**joindre** *v* to join 1320

**joli** *adj* pretty, attractive 2398

**joue** *nf* cheek 3932

**jouer** *v* to play 219

**jouet** *nm* toy 3498

**joueur** *nadj* player 2003

**jouir** *v* to enjoy 2064

**jour** *nm* day 78

**journal** *nm* newspaper, paper 520

**journaliste** *nm,nf* journalist 1337

**journée** *nf* day 587

**joyeux** *nadj(pl)* merry, joyful, happy 3987

**judiciaire** *adj(f)* judiciary 1855

**juge** *nm,nf* judge 1323

**jugement** *nm* judgement 1037

**juger** *v* to judge 395

**juif** *nadj* Jew, Jewish 1510

**juillet** *nm* July 1326

**juin** *nm* June 931

**jumeau** *nadj* twin 4357

**jungle** *nf* jungle 4891

**jurer** *v* to swear 3096

**juridiction** *nf* jurisdiction, court of law 4443

**juridique** *adj(f)* legal, judicial 1665

**jury** *nm* jury, board of examiners 3913

**jusque** *adv,prep* to, up to, until 134

**juste** *adv,nadj(f)* just, only; fair 304

**justement** *adv* exactly, rightly, precisely 1332

**justesse** *nf* accuracy, precision 4875

**justice** *nf* justice 637

**justification** *nf* justification, proof 3846

**justifier** *v* to justify 884

## Kk

**kilo** *nm* kilo 3894

**kilomètre** *nm* kilometer 1435

**kurde** *nadj(f)* Kurd, Kurdish 4694

## Ll

**là** *adv,intj* there, here 109

**là-bas** *adv* over there, out there 1777

**laboratoire** *nm* laboratory 2158

**lac** *nm* lake 3121

**lâcher** *v* to let go, release 2257

**lacune** *nf* gap, deficiency 4268

**là-dedans** *adv* inside, in it 3796

**là-dessus** *adv* on top, about it 2208

**laisser** *v* to leave 196

**lait** *nm* milk 2507

**lampe** *nf* lamp, light 4699

**lance** *nf* lance 4591

**lancement** *nm* launch 2429

**lancer** *nm,v* to throw, launch 514

**langage** *nm* language 1850

**langue** *nf* language, tongue 712

**large** *adj(f),adv,nm* wide, width 618

**largement** *adv* widely 1382

**larme** *nf* tear 2853

**lasser** *v* to tire, weary, grow weary 4689

**latin** *nadj* Latin 1844

**laver** *v* to wash, clean 3503

**le** *det,pro* the; him, her, it, them 1

**leader** *nm,nf* leader 1499

**leadership** *nm* leadership 4000

**leçon** *nf* lesson 1300

**lecteur** *nm* reader 2100

**lecture** *nf* reading 1016

**légal** *adj* legal, lawful 2247

**légende** *nf* legend, caption, key 3355

**léger** *adj* light 1321

**légèrement** *adv* lightly, slightly 2333

**légion** *nf* legion 4267

**législatif** *nadj* legislative 1404

**législation** *nf* legislation 2604

**législature** *nf* legislature 4954

**légitime** *nadj(f)* legitimate 2172

**légitimité** *nf* legitimacy 3421

**léguer** *v* to bequeath, hand down, pass on 4058

**légume** *nm,nf* vegetable 3117

**lendemain** *nm* next day 1258

**lent** *adj* slow 2572

**lentement** *adv* slowly 2637

**lequel** *pro* who, whom, which 92

**lettre** *nf* letter 480

**leur** *det,adj(f),pro* them, their, theirs 35

**levée** *nf* raising, levying, levee 4385

**lever** *v* to lift, raise 837

**lèvre** *nf* lip 2927

**liaison** *nf* liaison, connection 1968

**libanais** *nadj(pl)* Lebanese 3993

**libéral** *nadj* liberal 1080

**libéralisation** *nf* liberalization 4568

**libération** *nf* liberation 1250

**libérer** *v* to free, liberate, release 1190

**liberté** *nf* liberty, freedom 320

**librairie** *nf* bookstore, bookshop 4380

**libre** *adj(f)* free 344

**libre-échange** *nm* free trade 4830

**librement** *adv* freely 2444

**licence** *nf* licence, permit 2790

**licenciement** *nm* dismissal, sacking 4760

**lien** *nm* link, bond 880

**lier** *v* to link, join 498

**lieu** *nm*  place 117

**lieutenant** *nm*  lieutenant 3767

**ligne** *nf*  line 342

**limitation** *nf*  limitation, restriction, limit 4236

**limite** *nf*  limit 515

**limiter** *v*  to limit 883

**linguistique** *nadj(f)*  linguistic, linguistics 3907

**liquide** *nadj(f)*  liquid 3520

**liquider** *v*  to liquidate, sell off, clear 4511

**lire** *nf,v*  to read; lira 278

**liste** *nf*  list 924

**lit** *nm*  bed 1837

**litre** *nm,nf*  litre 3972

**littéraire** *nadj(f)*  literary 2369

**littéralement** *adv*  literally 3200

**littérature** *nf*  literature 2083

**livraison** *nf*  delivery 3509

**livre** *nm,nf*  book; pound 358

**livrer** *v*  to deliver 613

**local** *nadj*  local 622

**localité** *nf*  town, village 4363

**location** *nf*  renting 4297

**logement** *nm*  accommodation 1849

**loger** *v*  to put up, accommodate, stay, find accommodation 3060

**logiciel** *nm*  software, program, application 3676

**logique** *nadj(f)*  logic, logical 1107

**logiquement** *adv*  logically 4644

**loi** *nf*  law 267

**loin** *adv,nm*  far 341

**lointain** *nadj*  distant, faraway 2933

**loisir** *nm*  leisure 2772

**long** *adv,nadj*  long, lengthy 202

**longtemps** *adv*  a long time, a long while 312

**longuement** *adv*  at length 3066

**longueur** *nf*  length 2636

**lors** *adv*  at the time of 411

**lorsque** *conj*  when 256

**lot** *nm*  share, prize, lot 3045

**louer** *v*  to rent, praise 2303

**loup** *nm*  wolf 3927

**lourd** *adj*  heavy 1026

**lourdement** *adv*  heavily 4335

**loyal** *adj*  loyal, faithful 4325

**loyer** *nm*  rent 4230

**lui** *pro*  him, her 64

**lui-même** *pro*  himself 522

**lumière** *nf*  light 1059

**lumineux** *adj(pl)*  luminous, illuminated; light 4562

**lundi** *nm*  Monday 1091

**lune** *nf*  moon 3346

**lunette** *nf*  telescope, glasses 4207

**lutte** *nf*  struggle, fight, conflict 759

**lutter** *v*  to struggle, fight 1031

**luxe** *nm*  luxury 3009

**lycée** *nm*  high school 2816

## Mm

**machine** *nf*  machine 1294

**madame** *nf*  madam, lady 294

**mademoiselle** *nf*  Miss 3148

**magasin** *nm*  store 1736

**magazine** *nm*  magazine 2033

**magique** *adj(f)*  magic; magical 3530

**magistrat** *nm*  magistrate, judge 4282

**magnifique** *adj(f)*  magnificent 2136

**mai** *nm*  May 943

**maigre** *nadj(f)*  thin, skinny, slim, lean 3534

**main** *nf*  hand 418

**main-d'œuvre** *nf*  manpower, labor, work force 3910

**maintenance** *nf*  maintenance, servicing 4512

**maintenant** *adv*  now 192

**maintenir** *v*  to maintain 464

**maintien** *nm*  holding, maintaining 1819

**maire** *nm*  mayor 1876

**mairie** *nf*  town hall, city hall 4045

**mais** *adv,conj,intj*  but 30

**maison** *nf*  house 325

**maître** *nm*  master 1092

**maîtrise** *nf*  mastery, command, control, master's degree 3442

**maîtriser** *v*  to control, overcome, master 2351

**majesté** *nf*  majesty 4174

**majeur** *nadj*  major 1306

**majoritaire** *adj(f)*  majority 4277

**majorité** *nf*  majority 988

**mal** *adji,adv,nm*  bad 277

**malade** *nadj(f)*  ill, sick 1066

**maladie** *nf*  illness, disease 973

**malaise** *nm*  uneasiness, discomfort 3325

**malentendu** *nm*  misunderstanding 3646

**malgré** *prep*  despite, in spite of 406

**malheur** *nm*  misfortune 2727

**malheureusement** *adv*  unfortunately 1543

**malheureux** *nadj(pl)*  unhappy, miserable 2372

**malin** *nadj*  smart, shrewd, cunning 4960

**maltraiter** *v*  to manhandle, ill-treat, misuse, slight 4837

**maman** *nf* mom 2168

**manche** *nm,nf* handle, sleeve 3437

**mandat** *nm* term, mandate 1471

**manger** *nm,v* to eat 1338

**manière** *nf* manner, way 308

**manifestant** *nm* protester, demonstrator 3852

**manifestation** *nf* demonstration, event 1835

**manifestement** *adv* manifestly, clearly 3198

**manifester** *v* to show, demonstrate, display 968

**manipulation** *nf* handling, manipulation 3754

**manipuler** *v* to handle, manipulate 3483

**manœuvre** *nm,nf* manoeuvre, laborer 1931

**manque** *nm* lack 1038

**manquer** *v* to miss 583

**manteau** *nm* coat, overcoat 3746

**manuel** *adj,nm* manual 3158

**manuscrit** *adj* manuscript, handwritten 4460

**marchand** *nadj* merchant 2379

**marchandise** *nf* merchandise, commodity 2386

**marche** *nf* walk, step, march 906

**marché** *nm* market 280

**marcher** *v* to walk 1532

**mardi** *nm* Tuesday 1044

**marée** *nf* tide 3982

**marge** *nf* margin 1707

**marginal** *nadj* marginal 4031

**mari** *nm* husband 1589

**mariage** *nm* marriage 1210

**marier** *v* to marry 1686

**marin** *nadj* sea, marine, sailor 2101

**marine** *adj,nf* marine, navy 2891

**maritime** *adj(f)* maritime 2595

**mark** *nm* mark 4427

**marocain** *nadj* Moroccan 3469

**marque** *nf* brand, mark 1344

**marquer** *v* to mark 454

**mars** *nm(pl)* March; Mars 868

**masculin** *nadj* male, masculine 3741

**masque** *nm* mask 3856

**masquer** *v* to mask, conceal, put on a mask 3855

**massacre** *nm* massacre, slaughter 2887

**massacrer** *v* to slaughter, massacre 4184

**masse** *nf* mass 1826

**massif** *nadj* massive 1760

**match** *nm* match, game 1906

**matériau** *nm* material 3205

**matériel** *nadj* material, equipment 703

**maternel** *adj* motherly, maternal 2792

**maternité** *nf* maternity, motherhood 3795

**mathématique** *nadj(f)* mathematical; mathematics 3438

**matière** *nf* matter, subject, material 562

**matin** *nm* morning 442

**matinée** *nf* morning 3029

**mauvais** *adv,nadj(pl)* bad, wrong 274

**maximal** *adj* maximal 3182

**maximum** *nadj* maximum 1163

**me** *pro* me, to me, myself 61

**mec** *nm* guy 2358

**mécanique** *adj(f)* mechanical 2895

**mécanisme** *nm* mechanism 1573

**méchant** *nadj* nasty, wicked, mean 3184

**mécontent** *nadj* discontented, dissatisfied, displeased 4158

**mécontentement** *nm* displeasure, dissatisfaction 4823

**médaille** *nf* medal 3361

**médecin** *nm* physician, doctor 827

**médecine** *nf* medecine, medical science 2737

**médias** *nmpl* media 1585

**médiation** *nf* mediation, arbitration 4790

**médiatique** *adj(f)* media 4019

**médical** *adj* medical 1566

**médicament** *nm* medicine, drug, medication 1954

**médiocre** *nadj(f)* mediocre, second-rate 4125

**méfiance** *nf* distrust, mistrust, suspicion 4255

**méfier** *v* to distrust, mistrust 3496

**meilleur** *nadj* better, best 194

**mélange** *nm* mixing, mixture, blend 2986

**mélanger** *v* to mix, mix up, confuse 2989

**mêler** *v* to mingle, mix 1947

**membre** *nm* member 390

**même** *adj(f),adv,pro* same, even, self 42

**mémoire** *nm,nf* memory 926

**menaçant** *adj* threatening, menacing 4387

**menace** *nf* threat 1607

**menacer** *v* to threaten 969

**ménage** *nm* housekeeping, housework 2326

**ménager** *nadj,v* to handle, arrange; domestic 3597

**mener** *v* to lead 316

**mensonge** *nm* lie 2679

**mensuel** *nadj* monthly 4401

**mental** *nadj* mental 2182

**mentalité** *nf* mentality 4749

**mention** *nf* mention, note, comment, notice 3347

**mentionner** *v* to mention 1805

**mentir** *v* to lie 2683

**menu** *adv,nadj* menu, slender, slim, minor 3470

**mépris** *nm(pl)* contempt, scorn, disdain 3173

**mépriser** *v* to scorn, look down, spurn, disdain **4270**

**mer** *nf* sea **921**

**merci** *intj,nm,nf* thank you; favor **1070**

**mercredi** *nm* Wednesday **1168**

**merde** *intj,nf* sh*t, crap **2376**

**mère** *adj,nf* mother **645**

**mérite** *nm* merit **2035**

**mériter** *v* to deserve, merit **1122**

**merveille** *nf* marvel, wonder **4545**

**merveilleux** *adj(pl)* marvellous, wonderful **2209**

**message** *nm* message **792**

**messe** *nf* mass **4302**

**messieurs** *nmpl* gentlemen **1549**

**mesure** *nf* measure **262**

**mesurer** *v* to measure **1110**

**métal** *nm* metal **2793**

**météo** *nf* weather forecast **4574**

**méthode** *nf* method, procedure **1149**

**métier** *nm* job, occupation, trade **1582**

**mètre** *nm* meter **1534**

**métro** *nm* underground, metro **3227**

**mettre** *v* to put, place **27**

**meuble** *nadj(f)* piece of furniture **3876**

**meurtre** *nm* murder **1458**

**meurtrier** *nadj* murderer, deadly, lethal **2681**

**mexicain** *nadj* Mexican **4541**

**micro** *nm* mike, micro, microphone **4844**

**midi** *nm* noon **2483**

**mien** *nadj,pro* mine **2165**

**mieux** *adji(pl),adv,nm* better **217**

**milice** *nf* militia **4745**

**milieu** *nm* middle **479**

**militaire** *nadj(f)* military **690**

**militant** *nadj* militant **2479**

**militer** *v* to militate **4890**

**mille** *det,nm,nmi* a thousand **1008**

**millénaire** *nadj(f)* millennium, thousand-year-old **3598**

**milliard** *nm* billion, thousand million **497**

**millier** *nm* thousand **1127**

**million** *nm* million **307**

**mince** *adj(f),intj* thin, slim, slender **3570**

**mine** *nf* mein; appearance, look, mien **1403**

**miner** *v* to mine, erode **3449**

**mineur** *nadj* minor; miner **2233**

**minier** *adj* mining **4311**

**minimal** *adj* minimal, minimum **3652**

**minime** *nadj(f)* minor, minimal **4040**

**minimiser** *v* to minimize, play down **4725**

**minimum** *nadj* minimum **1410**

**ministère** *nm* ministry **910**

**ministériel** *adj* ministerial; minister **3034**

**ministre** *nm,nf* minister **204**

**minoritaire** *nadj(f)* minority **4271**

**minorité** *nf* minority **2073**

**minuit** *nm* midnight **3453**

**minute** *nf* minute **375**

**miracle** *nm* miracle **2638**

**miroir** *nm* mirror **3329**

**mise** *nf* putting, placing **473**

**miser** *v* to bet, stake **4382**

**misère** *nf* poverty, misery **2332**

**missile** *nm* missile **3452**

**mission** *nf* mission **627**

**mixte** *adj(f)* mixed **2875**

**mobile** *nadj(f)* mobile, portable **2291**

**mobilisation** *nf* mobilization **4042**

**mobiliser** *v* to mobilize, call up **2830**

**mobilité** *nf* mobility **4755**

**modalité** *nf* mode, method, modality **2412**

**mode** *nm,nf* mode, way, fashion **1137**

**modèle** *nm* model **958**

**modéré** *nadj* moderate, restrained, reasonable **4340**

**modérer** *v* to restrain, moderate, reduce **4034**

**moderne** *nadj(f)* modern **1239**

**modernisation** *nf* modernization **3977**

**moderniser** *v* to modernize **4615**

**modeste** *adj(f)* modest **1540**

**modification** *nf* modification **1583**

**modifier** *v* to modify, adjust **1035**

**mœurs** *nfpl* morals, customs, habits, manners, ways **4504**

**moi** *nm,pro* me **131**

**moi-même** *pro* myself **1527**

**moindre** *adj(f)* lesser, least, slightest **1105**

**moine** *nm* monk, friar **4339**

**moins** *adji(pl),adv,nm(pl),prep* less **62**

**mois** *nm(pl)* month **178**

**moitié** *nf* half **470**

**moment** *nm* moment **148**

**mon** *det* my **60**

**monde** *nm* world, people **77**

**mondial** *adj* world, global **549**

**mondialisation** *nf* internationalization, globalization **3141**

**monétaire** *adj(f)* monetary **1739**

**monnaie** *nf* currency, coin, change **1932**

**monopole** *nm* monopoly **2974**

**monsieur** *nm* mister, sir, gentleman **79**

**monstre** *nadj(f)* monster 3353

**montage** *nm* assembly, setting, pitching, putting, editing 4904

**montagne** *nf* mountain 1732

**montant** *nadj* upright, upwards, sum, total 1453

**montée** *nf* climb, ascent, rise, raising 3215

**monter** *v* to go up, rise, assemble 853

**montre** *nf* watch 4197

**montrer** *v* to show 108

**monument** *nm* monument 4113

**moquer** *v* to mock, make fun of 3335

**moral** *nadj* moral, morale 1226

**morale** *nf* ethics; moral 1973

**morceau** *nm* piece, bit 2118

**mordre** *v* to bite, overlap into 4292

**mort** *adj,nf* dead; death 276

**mortalité** *nf* mortality, death rate 4768

**mortel** *nadj* mortal, deadly, lethal 2500

**mot** *nm* word 220

**moteur** *nadj* motor 1164

**motif** *nm* motive, purpose 1369

**motion** *nf* motion 855

**motivation** *nf* motivation, application 3522

**motiver** *v* to justify, account for, motivate 3194

**mou** *adj,nm* soft 4655

**mourir** *v* to die 722

**mouton** *nadj* sheep 4175

**mouvement** *nm* movement 485

**moyen** *adj,nm* means, way; medium 186

**moyenne** *nf* average 4993

**muet** *nadj* mute, silent, dumb 4117

**multinational** *adj* multinational 3495

**multiple** *nadj(f)* multiple 2072

**multiplication** *nf* multiplication 4703

**multiplier** *v* to multiply 1982

**municipal** *adj* municipal 2204

**municipalité** *nf* municipality 3217

**munition** *nf* ammunition, supplies 4920

**mur** *nm* wall 1335

**murmurer** *v* to murmur 4730

**musée** *nm* museum 2216

**musical** *adj* musical 3168

**musicien** *nadj* musician 3100

**musique** *nf* music 1139

**musulman** *nadj* Muslim, Moslem 2245

**mutation** *nf* transfer, transformation, mutation 3465

**mutuel** *adj* mutual 2642

**mutuellement** *adv* mutually, one another 4266

**mystère** *nm* mystery 2777

**mystérieux** *nadj(pl)* mysterious, secretive 3312

**mythe** *nm* myth 2910

# Nn

**naïf** *nadj* naïve, innocent 4298

**naissance** *nf* birth 1305

**naître** *v* to be born 667

**natal** *adj* native, home 3949

**nation** *nf* nation 576

**national** *nadj* national 227

**nationaliste** *nadj(f)* nationalist 4195

**nationalité** *nf* nationality 4068

**nature** *nf* nature 542

**naturel** *nadj* natural 760

**naturellement** *adv* naturally 2036

**naval** *adj* naval 4156

**navette** *nf* shuttle 4814

**navigation** *nf* navigation 4487

**naviguer** *v* to navigate, sail 4076

**navire** *nm* ship 1416

**nazi** *nadj* Nazi 3053

**ne** *adv* not 15

**néanmoins** *adv,conj* nevertheless 1271

**néant** *nm* nothingness 3707

**nécessaire** *nadj(f)* necessary, required 451

**nécessairement** *adv* necessarily 1975

**nécessité** *nf* necessity, need 930

**nécessiter** *v* to require, necessitate 2214

**néerlandais** *nadj(pl)* Dutch 4640

**néfaste** *adj(f)* harmful, ill-fated 4688

**négatif** *nadj* negative 1520

**négligeable** *adj(f)* negligible, trivial 4341

**négliger** *v* to neglect 2574

**négociateur** *nadj* negotiator 4883

**négociation** *nf* negotiation 941

**négocier** *v* to negotiate 1676

**neige** *nf* snow 1824

**nerveux** *nadj(pl)* nervous, irritable 3735

**net** *adj,nm* clear; Internet 1367

**nettement** *adv* clearly, distinctly 2055

**nettoyage** *nm* cleaning, cleansing 4873

**nettoyer** *v* to clean 3887

**neuf** *det,adj,nmi* nine; new 787

**neutre** *adj(f)* neutral 2785

**nez** *nm(pl)* nose 2661

**ni** *conj* nor 229

**nier** *v* to deny 1775

**niveau** *nm* level 328

**noble** *nadj(f)* noble 3486

**nocturne** *nadj(f)* nocturnal, nocturne 4715

**nœud** *nm* knot 3551

**noir** *nadj* black 572

**nom** *nm* name 171

**nombre** *nm* number 249

**nombreux** *adj(pl)* numerous 366

**nominal** *nadj* nominal 3482

**nomination** *nf* appointment, nomination 3010

**nommer** *v* to call, name, appoint 601

**non** *adv,nmi* no, not 75

**nord** *adji,nm* north 1090

**nord-est** *nmi* north-east 4388

**nord-ouest** *nmi* north-west 3685

**normal** *adj* normal 833

**normalement** *adv* normally 2018

**norme** *nf* norm, standard 1897

**notable** *nadj(f)* notable, noteworthy 3785

**notamment** *adv* notably 439

**note** *nf* note, grade 1161

**noter** *v* to note, notice 541

**notion** *nf* notion 1570

**notoire** *adj(f)* notorious, well-known 4781

**notre** *det* our 73

**nôtre** *nadj(f)* ours, our own 2046

**nouer** *v* to knot, tie 4489

**nourrir** *v* to feed, nourish 1251

**nourriture** *nf* food 2285

**nous** *pro* we, us 31

**nous-mêmes** *pro* ourselves 3511

**nouveau** *adj,nm* new 52

**nouveauté** *nf* novelty, new release 3593

**novembre** *nm* November 982

**noyau** *nm* core, nucleus, pit 3832

**noyer** *nm,v* walnut; to drown, flood, blur, water down 4060

**nu** *nadj* naked, nude 3207

**nuage** *nm* cloud 3219

**nuance** *nf* shade, hue, nuance 4524

**nucléaire** *adj(f)* nuclear 1130

**nuire** *v* to harm 2703

**nuit** *nf* night 580

**nul** *adj,det,pro* nil, null 801

**nullement** *adv* not in the least 3902

**numérique** *adj(f)* numerical 2373

**numéro** *nm* number 766

# Oo

**obéir** *v* to obey, comply with, respond to 3268

**objectif** *adj,nm* objective, aim, goal; lens 518

**objection** *nf* objection 3004

**objet** *nm* objective; object 401

**obligation** *nf* obligation, bond 1444

**obligatoire** *adj(f)* mandatory, compulsory 2524

**obligé** *nadj* necessary, required 2265

**obliger** *v* to require, force, oblige 499

**obscur** *adj* dark, vague, obscure 3819

**obscurité** *nf* darkness 4885

**obséder** *v* to obsess, haunt 4663

**observateur** *nadj* observer, observant 2687

**observation** *nf* observation 1863

**observer** *v* to observe, watch 788

**obsession** *nf* obsession 4913

**obstacle** *nm* obstacle 1393

**obtenir** *v* to get, obtain 334

**obtention** *nf* obtaining, achievement 4558

**occasion** *nf* chance, opportunity 423

**occasionner** *v* to cause, give rise to 4958

**occidental** *nadj* western 1536

**occupant** *nadj* occupant, occupier, occupying 4456

**occupation** *nf* occupation, pastime 2096

**occuper** *v* to occupy 159

**occurrence** *nf* instance, case, occurrence 3960

**océan** *nm* ocean 2513

**octobre** *nm* October 826

**octroyer** *v* to grant, bestow 4232

**odeur** *nf* smell, odor 3273

**odieux** *adj(pl)* hateful, odious 4713

**œil** *nm* eye 474

**œuf** *nm* egg 2685

**œuvre** *nf* work, task 331

**œuvrer** *v* to work 3392

**offensive** *nf* offensive, offence 4119

**office** *nm* office, bureau 1868

**officiel** *nadj* official 996

**officiellement** *adv* officially 2363

**officier** *nm,nf,v* officer; officiate 2039

**offre** *nf* offer 1346

**offrir** *v* to offer 224

**oh** *intj* oh 1361

**oiseau** *nm* bird 2435

**olympique** *adj(f)* Olympic 3199

**ombre** *nm,nf* shade, shadow 2001

**omettre** *v* to leave out, miss out, omit 4177

**on** *pro* one, we 29

**oncle** *nm* uncle 3628

**onde** *nf* wave 2764

**onze** *det,nmi* eleven 2447

**opérateur** *nm* operator 2824

**opération** *nf* operation 763

**opérationnel** *adj* operational, operating 3026

**opérer** *v* to operate, carry out 1315

**opinion** *nf* opinion 777

**opportun** *adj* timely, 4485

**opportunité** *nf* opportunity, timeliness 2863

**opposant** *nadj* opponent, opposing 4128

**opposer** *v* to oppose 585

**opposition** *nf* opposition 972

**opter** *v* to opt, decide 3575

**optimisme** *nm* optimism 3250

**optimiste** *nadj(f)* optimistic 2751

**option** *nf* option 2156

**optique** *nadj(f)* optical, optic, perspective 3181

**or** *conj,nm* gold; hence, thus 300

**orage** *nm* storm, thunderstorm 4788

**oral** *nadj* oral 4114

**orange** *adji,nf* orange 3912

**orchestre** *nm* orchestra 4600

**ordinaire** *adv,nadj(f)* ordinary 1327

**ordinateur** *nadj* computer 2201

**ordonnance** *nf* prescription, organization, edict, ruling 2922

**ordonner** *v* to ordain, organize, order 1971

**ordre** *nm* order 197

**oreille** *nf* ear 1884

**organe** *nm* organ 2417

**organique** *adj(f)* organic 4752

**organisateur** *nadj* organizer, organizing 3849

**organisation** *nf* organization 570

**organiser** *v* to organize 701

**organisme** *nm* organism 1299

**orgueil** *nm* pride 4988

**oriental** *nadj* Oriental 2715

**orientation** *nf* orientation, trend 2025

**orienter** *v* to position, give advice, direct, orientate 2124

**originaire** *adj(f)* original, first, native to 3146

**original** *nadj* original 1814

**origine** *nf* origin, source 709

**os** *nm(pl)* bone 4092

**oser** *v* to dare 1634

**otage** *nm* hostage 3334

**ôter** *v* to remove, take away, take off, take out 4405

**où** *adv,pro* where 48

**ou** *conj* or 33

**ouais** *intj* yeah 1928

**oubli** *nm* forgetting, leaving behind, missing 4898

**oublier** *v* to forget 504

**ouest** *adji,nm* west 1690

**oui** *adv,nmi* yes 284

**ours** *adji,nm(pl)* bear 4800

**outil** *nm* tool 1725

**outre** *adv,nf,prep* besides 974

**ouvert** *adj* open 897

**ouvertement** *adv* openly, overtly 3061

**ouverture** *nf* opening 1455

**ouvrage** *nm* work 1740

**ouvrier** *nadj* worker 1861

**ouvrir** *v* to open 257

# Pp

**pacifique** *adj(f)* peaceful, peace-loving 2590

**pacte** *nm* pact, treaty 2570

**page** *nm,nf* page 434

**paiement** *nm* payment 2243

**pain** *nm* bread 2802

**pair** *adj,nm* peer, pair, even 2143

**paire** *nf* pair 3926

**paix** *nf(pl)* peace 579

**palais** *nm(pl)* palace, palate 2794

**pâle** *adj(f)* pale 4433

**palestinien** *nm* Palestinian 1257

**palier** *nm* landing, level, flat 4416

**panier** *nm* basket 4461

**panique** *nadj(f)* panic 3230

**panne** *nf* breakdown, failure 3967

**panneau** *nm* sign, notice, panel 4248

**pantalon** *nm* trousers, pants 4670

**papa** *nm* dad, daddy 2458

**pape** *nm* pope 3413

**papier** *nm* paper 951

**paquet** *nm* packet 2413

**par** *prep* by 21

**paradis** *nm(pl)* paradise, heaven 2952

**paradoxe** *nm* paradox 4279

**paragraphe** *nm* paragraph 2126

**paraître** *v* to appear 519

**parallèle** *nadj(f)* parallel, similar 2196

**parallèlement** *adv* in parallel, similarly 3116

**paralyser** *v* to paralyze 3674

**paramètre** *nm* parameter 2626

**parc** *nm* park 1240

**parcourir** *v* to cover, travel 2065

**parcours** *nm(pl)* journey, course, route 2717

**par-dessus** *adv* over 3800

**pardon** *nm* forgiveness 2655

**pardonner** *v* to forgive, excuse 2962

**pareil** *nadj* similar, likewise; peer, equal **1470**

**parent** *nadj* parent **546**

**parenthèse** *nf* parenthesis, bracket, aside **4381**

**parer** *v* to adorn, put on; to ward off, parry **4390**

**parfait** *nadj* perfect **1600**

**parfaitement** *adv* perfectly **1148**

**parfois** *adv* sometimes **410**

**parfum** *nm* perfume, scent, fragrance **4479**

**pari** *nm* bet **1688**

**parier** *v* to bet **4205**

**parisien** *nadj* Parisian **2549**

**parlement** *nm* parliament **756**

**parlementaire** *nadj(f)* parliamentary; member of parliament **1214**

**parler** *nm,v* to speak **106**

**parmi** *prep* among **389**

**parole** *nf* word **552**

**parquet** *nm* parquet floor, hardwood floor, prosecutor's office **4486**

**part** *nf* share **86**

**partage** *nm* division, cutting, sharing **2775**

**partager** *v* to share **527**

**partenaire** *nm,nf* partner **1077**

**partenariat** *nm* partnership **2614**

**parti** *nadj* party **400**

**participant** *nadj* participant **2480**

**participation** *nf* participation **1351**

**participer** *v* to participate **670**

**particulier** *nadj* particular, peculiar; person **381**

**particulièrement** *adv* particularly **779**

**partie** *nf* part **118**

**partiel** *nadj* partial **1871**

**partiellement** *adv* partly **4293**

**partir** *v* to leave **163**

**partisan** *nadj* partisan, supporter **2029**

**partout** *adv* everywhere **581**

**parvenir** *v* to reach, achieve **565**

**pas** *adv,nm(pl)* not, n't; footstep **18**

**passage** *nm* passage, way **674**

**passager** *nadj* passenger, temporary **2329**

**passé** *nadj,prep* past **501**

**passe** *nm,nf* pass, channel **4295**

**passeport** *nm* passport **3507**

**passer** *v* to pass **90**

**passif** *nadj* passive, liabilities **3153**

**passion** *nf* passion **1866**

**passionnant** *adj* fascinating, exciting **4467**

**passionner** *v* to fascinate, grip **2936**

**pasteur** *nm* minister, clergyman, pastor **4071**

**pâte** *nf* paste, dough, pasta **3641**

**patience** *nf* patience **3062**

**patient** *nadj* patient **1569**

**patrie** *nf* homeland, home country **3661**

**patrimoine** *nm* heritage, assets **2530**

**patron** *nm* boss **1706**

**patte** *nf* paw, foot, leg **3944**

**pause** *nf* break, pause **2647**

**pauvre** *nadj(f)* poor **699**

**pauvreté** *nf* poverty **1951**

**pavillon** *nm* country house, villa, wing, pavilion; flag **3412**

**payer** *v* to pay **537**

**pays** *nm(pl)* country **114**

**paysage** *nm* landscape, scenery, countryside **2634**

**paysan** *nadj* farmer, peasant **2317**

**peau** *nf* skin **2122**

**pêche** *nf* fishing; peach **1790**

**péché** *nm* sin **4437**

**pêcher** *nm,v* to fish, go fishing; peach tree **4223**

**pêcheur** *nadj* fisherman **2759**

**peindre** *v* to paint, depict, portray **3552**

**peine** *nf* effort, trouble **405**

**peiner** *v* to toil, labor, struggle **3484**

**peintre** *nm* painter **3528**

**peinture** *nf* painting, paint, picture **2881**

**pénal** *adj* penal **2942**

**pénaliser** *v* to penalize, punish **4597**

**pencher** *v* to lean, tilt **1796**

**pendant** *adj,prep,nm* during; pendant **89**

**pendre** *v* to hang down **4360**

**pénétrer** *v* to penetrate **2597**

**pénible** *adj(f)* hard, difficult, painful, tiresome **3690**

**pensée** *nf* thought **1269**

**penser** *nm,v* to think **116**

**pension** *nf* pension; room and board, boarding school **1821**

**pente** *nf* slope **2873**

**pénurie** *nf* shortage **3606**

**perception** *nf* perception, collection **3608**

**percer** *v* to pierce, drill, break into **3644**

**percevoir** *v* to perceive **1661**

**perdant** *nadj* losing, loser **4395**

**perdre** *v* to lose **250**

**perdu** *nadj* lost, stray, wasted **2264**

**père** *nm* father **569**

**performance** *nf* performance **2559**

**performant** *adj* productive, efficient **4961**

**péril** *nm* peril **2969**

**période** *nm,nf* period 407

**périr** *v* to perish 4780

**permanence** *nf* permanence, duty, service 2808

**permanent** *adj* permanent 1322

**permettre** *v* to allow 158

**permis** *nm(pl)* license, permit, permitted 2988

**permission** *nf* permission, leave 3183

**perpétuel** *adj* perpetual, everlasting, never-ending 4889

**perpétuer** *v* to perpetuate, carry on 4171

**persister** *v* to persist, keep up, linger 2710

**personnage** *nm* character, individual 1449

**personnalité** *nf* personality 1963

**personne** *nf,pro* person, people, anybody, anyone, nobody 84

**personnel** *nadj* personnel, personal 398

**personnellement** *adv* personally 2366

**perspective** *nf* perspective, viewpoint 1275

**persuader** *v* to convince, persuade 1682

**perte** *nf* loss 1079

**pertinent** *adj* pertinent, relevant 3348

**perturbation** *nf* disruption, disturbance 4681

**perturber** *v* to disrupt, disturb 3626

**pervers** *nadj(pl)* pervert, perverse, perverted 4056

**peser** *v* to weigh 1584

**pessimiste** *nadj(f)* pessimistic; pessimist 4971

**petit** *adv,nadj* small, little 138

**pétition** *nf* petition 2920

**pétrole** *nm* crude oil, petroleum 2157

**pétrolier** *nadj* oil; oil tanker 2567

**peu** *adv* little 91

**peuple** *nm* people 378

**peupler** *v* to populate, inhabit 3688

**peur** *nf* fear 755

**peut-être** *adv* perhaps, maybe 190

**phare** *nm* lighthouse, headlight 3884

**pharmaceutique** *nadj(f)* pharmaceutical 4478

**phase** *nf* phase 1754

**phénomène** *nm* phenomenon 1776

**philosophe** *nadj(f)* philosopher 3609

**philosophie** *nf* philosophy 2173

**philosophique** *adj(f)* philosophical 4374

**photo** *nf* photo 1412

**photographe** *nm,nf* photographer 3992

**photographie** *nf* photography 3279

**photographier** *v* to photograph 4613

**phrase** *nf* sentence, phrase 2074

**physique** *nadj(f)* physical, physics 1146

**physiquement** *adv* physically 3651

**piano** *adv,nm* piano 4967

**pièce** *nf* piece, part, component; room 813

**pied** *nm* foot 626

**piège** *nm* trap 2868

**piéger** *v* to trap, booby-trap 4358

**pierre** *nf* stone 1767

**pile** *nf* pile, stack, battery, tails 3893

**pilier** *nm* pillar 3493

**pilote** *nm,nf* pilot, experimental 3002

**piloter** *v* to fly, pilot, drive 2840

**piquer** *v* to sting, bite, prick, be hot; to steal 3755

**pire** *nadj(f)* worse, worst 743

**pis** *adv,nm(pl)* worse 3579

**piste** *nf* track, trail 1902

**pitié** *nf* pity, mercy 3829

**place** *nf* room, space, square, place 129

**placement** *nm* investment, placing 3339

**placer** *v* to place 535

**plafond** *nm* ceiling, roof, maximum 2823

**plage** *nf* beach 2693

**plaider** *v* to plead 2576

**plaie** *nf* wound 4765

**plaindre** *v* to pity, feel sorry for, complain 1370

**plainte** *nf* moan, groan, complaint 1851

**plaire** *v* to please 804

**plaisanter** *v* to joke 4398

**plaisir** *nm* pleasure 797

**plan** *adj,nm* plan 164

**planche** *nf* plank, board 3610

**plancher** *nm,v* floor 3702

**planer** *v* to glide, soar 4006

**planète** *nf* planet 1875

**planification** *nf* planning 4710

**planifier** *v* to plan 3945

**plante** *nf* plant 2702

**planter** *v* to plant, pitch 2812

**plaque** *nf* plate, tag, plaque 2865

**plastique** *nadj(f)* plastic 2191

**plat** *adj,nm* dish, flat 2167

**plateau** *nm* plateau, tray, set, stage 2803

**plate-forme** *nf* platform 4692

**plein** *adv,nadj,prep* full 394

**pleinement** *adv* fully, thoroughly 2396

**plénier** *adj* plenary, full 4721

**pleurer** *v* to cry 2253

**pleuvoir** *v* to rain 4586

**plier** *v* to fold, fold up, fold back, bend 3195

**plomb** *nm* lead 4193

**plonger** *v* to dive 1958

**pluie** *nf* rain 2217

**plume** *nm,nf* feather 3572

**plupart** most, the majority more 426

**plus** *adv* more, no 19

**plusieurs** *det,adj,pro* several 213

**plutôt** *adv* rather 272

**pneu** *nm* tire 4514

**poche** *nf* pocket 1940

**poème** *nm* poem 3031

**poésie** *nf* poetry 2938

**poète** *nm* poet 2307

**poétique** *nadj(f)* poetic, poetical, poetics 4399

**poids** *nm(pl)* weight 1102

**poignée** *nf* handful, fistful, handle 3208

**poil** *nm* hair, bristle 4723

**poing** *nm* fist, punch 3889

**point** *adv,nm* point 97

**pointe** *nf* point, tip 1907

**pointer** *nm,v* to mark off, clock in, clock out, aim 2749

**poisson** *nm* fish 1616

**poitrine** *nf* chest, breast, breasts, bosom 4168

**pôle** *nm* pole 3165

**polémique** *nadj(f)* controversial, controversy 4353

**police** *nf* police 829

**policier** *nadj* policeman 1265

**politicien** *nadj* politician 3371

**politique** *nadj(f)* politics; political 128

**politiquement** *adv* politically, diplomatically 3657

**pollution** *nf* pollution 3073

**polonais** *nadj(pl)* Polish 3660

**pomme** *nf* apple 2847

**pompe** *nf* pump 3397

**pompier** *adj,nm* fireman, firefighter 3295

**ponctuel** *adj* punctual 4457

**pont** *nm* bridge 1889

**populaire** *nadj(f)* popular 1349

**population** *nf* population 509

**porc** *nm* pig, pork 4036

**port** *nm* harbor, port 1304

**portable** *adj(f),nm* portable, wearable; cell phone 4002

**porte** *nf* door 696

**portée** *nf* range, reach, scope 1067

**portefeuille** *nm* wallet 2836

**porte-parole** *nmi* spokesperson, spokesman, spokeswoman 1722

**porter** *nm,v* to wear, carry 105

**porteur** *nm* carrier, holder 2430

**portion** *nf* portion, share 3806

**portrait** *nm* portrait, photograph 2666

**portugais** *nadj(pl)* Portuguese 3684

**poser** *v* to put, pose, ask 218

**positif** *nadj* positive 949

**position** *nf* position 383

**posséder** *v* to possess, own, have 702

**possession** *nf* possession, ownership 2454

**possibilité** *nf* possibility 725

**possible** *adj(f)* possible 175

**postal** *adj* postal, mail 3625

**poste** *nm,nf* post, position; post office 489

**poster** *nm,v* poster; to post, mail 3011

**pot** *nm* jar, pot 3648

**potentiel** *nadj* potential 1792

**pouce** *nm* thumb, inch 3298

**poudre** *nf* powder 4153

**poule** *nf* hen, chick 4321

**poulet** *nm* chicken 4222

**poumon** *nm* lung 4679

**pour** *prep* for, in order to 10

**pourcentage** *nm* percentage, commission, cut 2987

**pourparler** *nm* talk, discussion, negotiation 4144

**pourquoi** *adv,conj,nmi* why 193

**poursuite** *nf* chase, pursuit 2045

**poursuivre** *v* to pursue 463

**pourtant** *adv* yet, nonetheless, nevertheless 460

**pourvoir** *v* to provide, equip, supply, furnish 3113

**poussée** *nf* push, rise, upsurge 4338

**pousser** *v* to push 771

**poussière** *nf* dust 3236

**pouvoir** *nm,v* can, to be able to 20

**pratique** *nadj(f)* practice, practical 842

**pratiquement** *adv* practically 1633

**pratiquer** *v* to practice 1268

**préalable** *nadj(f)* prior, previous, preliminary, prerequisite 2431

**précaire** *adj(f)* precarious, makeshift 3838

**précaution** *nf* precaution 2218

**précédemment** *adv* previously 3555

**précédent** *nadj* precedent; previous 820

**précéder** *v* to precede 1413

**précieux** *nadj(pl)* precious 1277

**précipitation** *nf* haste, precipitation 4866

**précipiter** *v* to quicken, hasten, precipitate 2838

**précis** *nadj(pl)* precise 643

**précisément** *adv* precisely 1197

**préciser** *v* to state, specify, clarify 745

**précision** *nf* precision 1756

**précoce** *adj(f)* early, precocious 4003

**préconiser** *v* to recommend, advocate 3281

**prédécesseur** *nm* predecessor 3948

**prédire** *v* to predict 2869

**préférable** *adj(f)* preferable 3518

**préférence** *nf* preference, preferably 2970

**préférer** *v* to prefer 597

**préfet** *nm* prefect 4131

**préjudice** *nm* loss, harm, damage 4858

**préjugé** *nm* prejudice, bias 3679

**prélèvement** *nm* imposition, levying, withdrawal, removal, deduction 3662

**prélever** *v* to impose, levy, withdraw, remove 4059

**préliminaire** *nadj(f)* preliminary, introductory 3414

**prématuré** *nadj* premature 3105

**premier** *det,nadj* first 56

**premièrement** *adv* first 3587

**prendre** *v* to take 43

**prénom** *nm* first name 3543

**préoccupation** *nf* worry, concern 1847

**préoccuper** *v* to worry, preoccupy 1979

**préparation** *nf* preparation 2451

**préparer** *v* to prepare 368

**près** *adv,prep* near, nearby, close by 225

**prescrire** *v* to order, command, prescribe, stipulate 3666

**présence** *nf* presence 365

**présent** *nadj* present 216

**présentation** *nf* presentation 1723

**présentement** *adv* at present, presently 4691

**présenter** *v* to present 209

**préserver** *v* to preserve 1903

**présidence** *nf* presidency 1735

**président** *nm* president 268

**présidentiel** *adj* presidential 2238

**présider** *v* to preside 2370

**presque** *adv* almost 481

**presse** *nf* press 986

**presser** *v* to squeeze, press 1946

**pression** *nf* pressure 845

**prestation** *nf* benefit 1830

**prestigieux** *adj(pl)* prestigious 3899

**présumer** *v* to presume, assume 2675

**prêt** *adj,nm* ready 422

**prétendre** *v* to pretend 1154

**prétendu** *nadj* so-called, alleged 4053

**prétention** *nf* claim 4259

**prêter** *v* to lend 915

**prétexte** *nadj(f),nm* pretext 2466

**prêtre** *nm* priest 2545

**preuve** *nf* proof 653

**prévaloir** *v* to prevail 3123

**prévenir** *v* to prevent, warn; to notify 1207

**préventif** *adj* preventive 4666

**prévention** *nf* prevention, custody 2521

**prévisible** *adj(f)* predictable, forseeable 4513

**prévision** *nf* forecast, prediction, expectation 1602

**prévoir** *v* to foresee, anticipate 437

**prévu** *nadj* planned 2240

**prier** *v* to pray 1645

**prière** *nf* prayer 2213

**primaire** *nadj(f)* primary 2527

**prime** *nadj(f),nf* free gift, premium, bonus 2094

**primitif** *nadj* primitive 3345

**primordial** *adj* primordial, basic, vital, primary 3744

**prince** *nm* prince 2610

**princesse** *nf* princess 3622

**principal** *nadj* principal 458

**principalement** *adv* principally, mainly, primarily 1965

**principe** *nm* principle 447

**printemps** *nm(pl)* spring 1288

**prioritaire** *nadj(f)* priority, having priority, having right of way 3259

**priorité** *nf* priority 1408

**prise** *nf* grip, hold, seizure, catch 444

**prison** *nf* prison 1010

**prisonnier** *nadj* prisoner, captive 1618

**privatisation** *nf* privatization 2810

**privé** *nadj* private 1401

**priver** *v* to deprive 494

**privilège** *nm* privilege 2474

**privilégié** *nadj* privileged 4473

**privilégier** *v* to favor 2482

**prix** *nm(pl)* price; prize 310

**probabilité** *nf* probability, likelihood 4447

**probable** *adj(f)* probable, likely 2186

**probablement** *adv* probably 903

**problématique** *nadj(f)* problematic; problem 4066

**problème** *nm* problem 188

**procédé** *nm* processus 2758

**procéder** *v* to proceed 1101

**procédure** *nf* procedure 993

**procès** *nm(pl)* trial, proceedings 1561

**processus** *nm(pl)* process 689

**procès-verbal** *nm* minutes, statement 4899

**prochain** *nadj* next 380

**prochainement** *adv* shortly, soon 4417

**proche** *adv,nadj(f),prep* nearby, close 838

**proclamer** *v* to proclaim, declare 2966

**procurer** *v* to get, bring 2038

**procureur** *nm* prosecutor 2587

**producteur** *nadj* producer 1259

**productif** *adj* productive 3975

**production** *nf* production 638

**productivité** *nf* productivity 2901

**produire** *v* to product 367

**produit** *nm* product 373

**professeur** *nm,nf* professor, teacher 1150

**profession** *nf* profession 2163

**professionnel** *nadj* professional 1000

**profil** *nm* profile, outline, contour 2552

**profit** *nm* profit, benefit 1032

**profiter** *v* to take advantage, profit 632

**profond** *adv,nadj* deep 1175

**profondément** *adv* profoundly, deeply 1612

**profondeur** *nf* depth 1786

**programmation** *nf* programming 3844

**programme** *nm* program 340

**programmer** *v* to program, schedule 2432

**progrès** *nm(pl)* progress 919

**progresser** *v* to progress 1856

**progressif** *adj* progressive 2664

**progression** *nf* progression 2660

**progressiste** *nm,nf* progressive 4799

**progressivement** *adv* progressively 2659

**proie** *nf* prey 3332

**projection** *nf* projection, ejection, discharge 3244

**projet** *nm* project 228

**projeter** *v* to plan, project, throw out 2368

**prolonger** *v* to prolong, extend 1515

**promener** *v* to take for a walk, go for a walk 2928

**promesse** *nf* promise 1184

**prometteur** *nadj* promising 3635

**promettre** *v* to promise 854

**promoteur** *nm* promoter, instigator, developer 4911

**promotion** *nf* promotion, advertising 2139

**promouvoir** *v* to promote 2399

**prôner** *v* to laud, extol, advocate, commend 3859

**prononcer** *v* to pronounce 706

**propagande** *nf* propaganda 3374

**propagation** *nf* propagation, spreading 3740

**propager** *v* to propagate, spread 3865

**prophète** *nm* prophet 4843

**propice** *adj(f)* favorable, auspicious, propitious 3202

**proportion** *nf* proportion 1918

**proportionnel** *adj* proportional 4827

**propos** *nm(pl)* remark 505

**proposer** *v* to propose 338

**proposition** *nf* proposition, proposal 799

**propre** *nadj(f)* clean, proper 237

**proprement** *adv* cleanly, neatly, properly 2990

**propriétaire** *nm,nf* owner 1406

**propriété** *nf* property 1460

**prospérité** *nf* prosperity 3815

**prostitué** *nadj* prostitute 4561

**prostitution** *nf* prostitution 4444

**protecteur** *nadj* protective, protector, guardian 4305

**protection** *nf* protection 953

**protégé** *nadj* protected, protégé 3764

**protéger** *v* to protect 739

**protestant** *nadj* Protestant 3489

**protestation** *nf* protest, protestation 3523

**protester** *v* to protest 2423

**protocole** *nm* etiquette, protocol 2418

**prouver** *v* to prove 635

**provenance** *nf* origin 2622

**provenir** *v* to be from, come from 1562

**province** *nf* province 861

**provincial** *nadj* provincial 2184

**provision** *nf* stock, supply 4536

**provisoire** *adj(f)* temporary, provisional 2075

**provisoirement** *adv* temporarily, provisionally 4991

**provocation** *nf* provocation 4132

**provoquer** *v* to provoke 1095

**proximité** *nf* proximity, nearness, closeness 2977

**prudence** *nf* prudence, care, caution 1966

**prudent** *adj* prudent, careful, cautious 1529

**psychologie** *nf* psychology 4836

**psychologique** *adj(f)* psychological 2550

**public** *nadj* public, audience 285

**publication** *nf* publication 1421

**publicitaire** *nadj(f)* advertising, promotional 3573

**publicité** *nf* advertising, advertisement, publicity 2110

**publier** *v* to publish 768

**publique** *adj,nf* public 554

**publiquement** *adv* publicly 3014

**puis** *adv* then, so 230

**puiser** *v* to draw, take 3388

**puisque** *conj* since 528

**puissance** *nf* power 1076

**puissant** *nadj* powerful 1229

**puits** *nm(pl)* well, shaft, pit 4838

**punir** *v* to punish 2149

**punition** *nf* punishment 4322

**pur** *nadj* pure 1643

**purement** *adv* purely 2327

**purger** *v* to purge, bleed, drain 4412

**putain** *nf* whore, bitch; stupid 2704

# Qq

**quai** *nm* platform, quay, embankment **3354**

**qualification** *nf* qualification **4004**

**qualifier** *v* to qualify **1283**

**qualité** *nf* quality **606**

**quand** *adv,conj* when **119**

**quant** *adv* as for **275**

**quantité** *nf* quantity **1680**

**quarantaine** *nf* about forty **4288**

**quarante** *det,nmi* forty **2436**

**quart** *nadj* quarter **1575**

**quartier** *nm* district, quarter **1187**

**quasi** *adv,nm* almost, nearly **2778**

**quasiment** *adv* almost, early **3538**

**quatorze** *det,nmi* fourteen **3359**

**quatre** *det,nmi* four **253**

**quatrième** *det,nm,nf* fourth **1603**

**que** *adv,conj,pro* that, which, who, whom **9**

**québécois** *nadj(pl)* Quebecker, Quebecer, Québécois **1970**

**quel** *det,adj,pro* which, what **146**

**quelconque** *adj(f)* any, some **1934**

**quelque** *adv,adj,det* some **70**

**quelquefois** *adv* sometimes **3170**

**quelques-uns** *pro* some, a few **2514**

**quelqu'un** *pro* somebody, someone **772**

**querelle** *nf* quarrel **3557**

**question** *nf* question **144**

**questionner** *v* to question **4856**

**quête** *nf* quest, pursuit, collection **2672**

**queue** *nf* tail, handle, stalk, stem, rear **3255**

**qui** *pro* who, whom **14**

**quiconque** *pro* whoever, anyone who **3222**

**quinzaine** *nf* about fifteen, two weeks **3673**

**quinze** *det,nmi* fifteen **1472**

**quitter** *v* to leave **507**

**quoi** *pro* what **297**

**quoique** *conj* although, though **3243**

**quota** *nm* quota **3801**

**quotidien** *nadj* daily **1318**

**quotidiennement** *adv* daily, every day **4181**

# Rr

**raccrocher** *v* to hang up **4952**

**race** *nf* breed, race **2490**

**racheter** *v* to repurchase, buy back, redeem **3475**

**racial** *adj* racial **4941**

**racine** *nf* root **2593**

**racisme** *nm* racism **4044**

**raciste** *nadj(f)* racist **4805**

**raconter** *v* to tell **890**

**radical** *nadj* radical **2127**

**radicalement** *adv* radically **3860**

**radio** *adji,nm,nf* radio **1526**

**radioactif** *adj* radioactive **4294**

**rage** *nf* rage, fury, rabies **3035**

**raide** *adj(f)* stiff, straight **3533**

**rail** *nm* rail, track **4697**

**raison** *nf* reason **72**

**raisonnable** *adj(f)* reasonable, fair **2021**

**raisonnement** *nm* reasoning **3352**

**ralentir** *v* to slow down **2297**

**ralentissement** *nm* slowing down **4041**

**rallier** *v* to rally, win over, join **3915**

**ramasser** *v* to pick up, collect, gather **3370**

**ramener** *v* to bring back, return, take back **1097**

**rang** *nm* rank, row **1484**

**ranger** *nm,v* to tidy up, put away **2774**

**rapide** *nadj(f),nm* fast, quick **672**

**rapidement** *adv* quickly, rapidly **593**

**rapidité** *nf* speed, quickness **4362**

**rappel** *nm* reminder, summary, recall, return, remember **3080**

**rappeler** *v* to recall, call back **208**

**rapport** *nm* relationship, report **189**

**rapporter** *v* to bring back, report **922**

**rapporteur** *nadj* telltale, rapporteur **3996**

**rapprochement** *nm* bringing together, coming closer, parallel **3877**

**rapprocher** *v* to bring closer, get closer **1329**

**rare** *adj(f)* rare **1233**

**rarement** *adv* rarely, seldom **2535**

**raser** *v* to shave, raze **4964**

**rassemblement** *nm* gathering, collecting, assembling **3645**

**rassembler** *v* to gather together **1635**

**rassurant** *adj* reassuring, comforting **4012**

**rassurer** *v* to reassure, calm down **1842**

**rat** *adj(f),nm* rat **4290**

**rater** *v* to miss, misfire **2553**

**ratification** *nf* ratification **4635**

**ratifier** *v* to ratify **4198**

**rationnel** *nadj* rational **3786**

**rattacher** *v* to attach, join, tie **3157**

**rattraper** *v* to recapture, recover, catch up, make up for **3028**

**ravager** *v* to ravage, devastate **4939**

**ravir** *v* to delight, rob **2654**

**rayer** *v* to scratch, streak, stripe; to erase, strike out 4631

**rayon** *nm* ray, beam, radius; department, section, shelf 2926

**rayonnement** *nm* radiance 4306

**réacteur** *nm* reactor, jet engine 3390

**réaction** *nf* reaction 947

**réaffirmer** *v* to reaffirm, reassert 3918

**réagir** *v* to react 1052

**réalisateur** *nadj* director 4333

**réalisation** *nf* realization, achievement 1636

**réaliser** *v* to realize, achieve 409

**réaliste** *nadj(f)* realist, realistic 2630

**réalité** *nf* reality 532

**rebelle** *nadj(f)* rebel, rebellious 2621

**rébellion** *nf* rebellion 4665

**récemment** *adv* recently 1222

**récent** *adj* recent 1178

**récepteur** *nm* receiver, receiving 4552

**réception** *nf* reception 1926

**récession** *nf* recession 4049

**recette** *nf* recipe 1709

**recevoir** *v* to receive 199

**recherche** *nf* research, search 357

**rechercher** *v* to search for 1256

**réciproque** *nadj(f)* mutual, reciprocal, the opposite 4185

**récit** *nm* account, narrative 2229

**réclamer** *v* to ask for, call for; to claim 1220

**récolte** *nf* harvest, crop 4307

**récolter** *v* to harvest, gather 3792

**recommandation** *nf* recommendation 1050

**recommander** *v* to recommend 1988

**recommencer** *v* to resume, start again 2489

**récompense** *nf* reward, award 3720

**récompenser** *v* to reward, recompense 2577

**réconciliation** *nf* reconciliation 4082

**réconcilier** *v* to reconcile 4673

**reconduire** *v* to renew, drive back 3936

**reconnaissance** *nf* recognition, gratitude 1432

**reconnaissant** *adj* grateful 3383

**reconnaître** *v* to recognize 221

**reconstituer** *v* to reconstitute, restore, reconstruct 3763

**reconstruction** *nf* reconstruction 3111

**reconstruire** *v* to rebuild, reconstruct 3580

**record** *nm* record 2409

**recourir** *v* to turn to, run again 2281

**recours** *nm(pl)* resort, recourse 1693

**recouvrir** *v* to cover, hide, conceal 2872

**recrutement** *nm* recruiting, recruitment 4212

**recruter** *v* to recruit 3380

**rectifier** *v* to rectify, correct 3866

**reçu** *nm* receipt, accepted 4226

**recueillir** *v* to collect, gather 1230

**recul** *nm* backward movement, setback, slip 2499

**reculer** *v* to move back, back up 1922

**récupération** *nf* recovery, retrieval, salvage 4364

**récupérer** *v* to get back, recover, recuperate 1783

**rédacteur** *nm* editor, writer, drafter, compiler 4260

**rédaction** *nf* writing, composition 2225

**redevenir** *v* to become again 2889

**rédiger** *v* to write, draw up 2135

**redire** *v* to say again, repeat 3824

**redonner** *v* to give back, return, give more 3319

**redoutable** *adj(f)* fearsome, formidable 4351

**redouter** *v* to dread, fear 3360

**redressement** *nm* straightening up, upturn, righting 4278

**redresser** *v* to straighten, set right, redress, turn around 3368

**réduction** *nf* reduction 1494

**réduire** *v* to reduce 595

**réduit** *nm* reduced, scaled-down, cut-down, tiny room, hideout 3873

**réel** *nadj* real 665

**réellement** *adv* really 1563

**refaire** *v* to redo, make again 2252

**référence** *nf* reference 1424

**référendum** *nm* referendum 2263

**référer** *v* to refer, consult, refer to 3267

**refermer** *v* to close again, shut again, close up 3759

**réfléchi** *adj* thoughtful, well thought-out 4996

**réfléchir** *v* to reflect 1058

**reflet** *nm* reflection, glint, highlight 3749

**refléter** *v* to reflect 1892

**réflexe** *nadj(f)* reflex 4250

**réflexion** *nf* reflection 1394

**réforme** *nf* reform 980

**réformer** *v* to re-form, reform, discharge 3725

**réformiste** *nadj(f)* reformist 2146

**refuge** *nm* refuge 2871

**réfugier** *v* to take refuge 1508

**refus** *nm(pl)* refusal 1615

**refuser** *v* to refuse 271

**regagner** *v* to win again, regain, get back, make up 3491

**regard** *nm* look, glance 1206

**regarder** *v* to look, watch 425

**régime** *nm* regime 543

**régiment** *nm* regiment 4624

**région** *nf* region 241

**régional** *nadj* regional 1169

**régir** *v* to govern 3030

**registre** *nm* log, register, registry 2556

**réglé** *adj* regular, steady, well-ordered, ruled 4934

**règle** *nf* rule 488

**règlement** *nm* rule, regulation 1166

**réglementaire** *adj(f)* regulation, control, statutory 4418

**réglementation** *nf* regulation 2828

**réglementer** *v* to regulate, control 4929

**régler** *v* to pay, adjust, settle 957

**règne** *nm* reign 3649

**régner** *v* to reign 1831

**regret** *nm* regret, regretfully 2761

**regrettable** *adj(f)* unfortunate, regrettable 4770

**regretter** *v* to regret 1048

**regroupement** *nm* regrouping, reassembly 4712

**regrouper** *v* to group together, regroup 2477

**régulier** *adj* regular 1770

**régulièrement** *adv* regularly 1888

**reine** *nf* queen 2809

**réitérer** *v* to reiterate, repeat 4847

**rejet** *nm* rejection 2455

**rejeter** *v* to reject 981

**rejoindre** *v* to rejoin, reunite 1007

**réjouir** *v* to delight, rejoice 2148

**relâcher** *v* to loosen, release, let go 4434

**relais** *nm(pl)* shift, relay 4127

**relance** *nf* boost, reminder, recovery 4228

**relancer** *v* to throw back, restart, relaunch 3008

**relater** *v* to relate, recount 4627

**relatif** *nadj* relative 1160

**relation** *nf* relationship 356

**relativement** *adv* relatively 1559

**reléguer** *v* to relegate 3728

**relevé** *nadj* statement, list; relieved; put in relief; rolled up 4943

**relever** *v* to raise 376

**relier** *v* to connect 1670

**religieux** *nadj(pl)* religious 1203

**religion** *nf* religion 1699

**relire** *v* to reread, proofread 4170

**remarquable** *adj(f)* remarkable, outstanding 2040

**remarque** *nf* remark 2019

**remarquer** *v* to remark; to notice, point out 874

**remboursement** *nm* reimbursement 3957

**rembourser** *v* to reimburse, pay back, pay off, repay 3107

**remède** *nm* cure, remedy 4013

**remédier** *v* to cure, remedy, put right 4519

**remercier** *v* to thank 1218

**remettre** *v* to deliver, replace, set, put 156

**remise** *nf* presentation, delivery 2357

**remonter** *v* to go back up 1020

**remplacement** *nm* replacement, standing in 3248

**remplacer** *v* to replace 448

**remplir** *v* to fill, fulfill 751

**remporter** *v* to take away, win 2267

**rémunération** *nf* remuneration, payment, pay 3088

**rémunérer** *v* to remunerate, pay 4796

**rencontre** *nm* meeting 1045

**rencontrer** *v* to meet 329

**rendement** *nm* yield, output 2394

**rendez-vous** *nm(pl)* appointment 1873

**rendre** *v* to render, return, yield, give up 85

**renfermer** *v* to contain, shut, lock, enclose 4812

**renforcement** *nm* reinforcement, strengthening 3600

**renforcer** *v* to reinforce, strengthen 1280

**renfort** *nm* help, back-up, support 4326

**renier** *v* to disown, repudiate, go back on 4442

**renoncer** *v* to give up, renounce 1363

**renouveau** *nm* renewal 4639

**renouveler** *v* to renew 1359

**renouvellement** *nm* replacement, recurrence, repetition 3485

**rénovation** *nf* renovation, restoration 4123

**renseignement** *nm* information 1596

**renseigner** *v* to give information, get information 2921

**rentabilité** *nf* profitability 4366

**rentable** *adj(f)* profitable 4324

**rente** *nf* annuity, pension 4876

**rentrée** *nf* reopening, return, start 2972

**rentrer** *v* to go in, come in, come back, return 925

**renverser** *v* to knock down, turn over, overturn 2079

**renvoi** *nm* dismissal, expulsion, suspension, cross-reference 3681

**renvoyer** *v* to send back, dismiss 1047

**répandre** *v* to spread, spill 2320

**réparation** *nf* repair, repairing, correction, compensation 3445

**réparer** *v* to repair, fix, correct, make up 2583

**répartir** *v* to distribute, spread out, share out, divide up 2197

**repartir** *v* to set off again, start up again 2150

**répartition** *nf* distribution, spreading 2648

**repas** *nm(pl)* meal 2948

**repasser** *v*  to cross again, retake, show again, iron 4414

**repenser** *v*  to rethink 3834

**répercussion** *nf*  repercussion 3627

**repère** *nm*  reference, benchmark, landmark 4373

**repérer** *v*  to spot, pick out, locate, find 2707

**répéter** *v*  to repeat 630

**répétition** *nf*  repetition, rehearsal 2804

**replacer** *v*  to replace, put back 4733

**repli** *nm*  bend, twist, wrinkle, fold, fallback 4825

**replier** *v*  to fold, roll up, fold up, withdraw 4256

**réplique** *nf*  reply, retort; replica 3224

**répliquer** *v*  to reply 4466

**répondre** *v*  to answer 200

**réponse** *nf*  answer, response 456

**report** *nm*  postponement, deferment 4406

**reportage** *nm*  report, reporting 2820

**reporter** *nm,nf,v*  to report; to postpone 2028

**repos** *nm(pl)*  rest 2731

**reposer** *v*  to rest 776

**repousser** *v*  to push away, postpone 2700

**reprendre** *v*  to resume, recover, start again, take back 313

**représentant** *nm*  representative 1232

**représentatif** *adj*  representative 3617

**représentation** *nf*  representation 1469

**représenter** *v*  to represent 293

**répression** *nf*  repression, suppression, crack-down 3425

**réprimer** *v*  to suppress, repress 4791

**reprise** *nf*  resumption, renewal; time 985

**reproche** *nm*  reproach 4421

**reprocher** *v*  to blame, reproach 1581

**reproduction** *nf*  reproduction 3201

**reproduire** *v*  to reproduce, repeat 2125

**républicain** *nadj*  republican 2718

**république** *nf*  republic 1028

**réputation** *nf*  reputation 1741

**réputé** *adj*  famous, renowned 3768

**requérir** *v*  to require 2300

**requête** *nf*  request, petition 3750

**réseau** *nm*  network 721

**réserve** *nf*  reserve 1162

**réserver** *v*  to reserve, keep 695

**réservoir** *nm*  tank, reservoir 4674

**résidence** *nf*  residence, block of flats 3057

**résident** *nm*  foreign national, foreign resident 4926

**résider** *v*  to reside 2084

**résistance** *nf*  resistance 1330

**résistant** *nadj*  robust, sturdy, resistance fighter 4218

**résister** *v*  to resist 1611

**résolument** *adv*  resolutely 4882

**résolution** *nf*  resolution 1342

**résoudre** *v*  to solve, resolve 767

**respect** *nm*  respect 818

**respecter** *v*  to respect 673

**respectif** *adj*  respective 2554

**respectivement** *adv*  respectively 3432

**respectueux** *adj(pl)*  respectful 4086

**respirer** *v*  to breath 3040

**responsabilité** *nf*  responsibility 694

**responsable** *nadj(f)*  responsible 511

**ressembler** *v*  to look like, resemble 1398

**ressentir** *v*  to feel 1593

**resserrer** *v*  to tighten up, strengthen 3696

**ressort** *nm*  spring; resort; spirit 2861

**ressortir** *v*  to go out again, come out again, take out again 1833

**ressource** *nf*  resource 852

**restant** *adj,nm*  remaining, the rest, the remainder 3211

**restaurant** *nm*  restaurant 2336

**restauration** *nf*  restoration; catering 3980

**restaurer** *v*  to restore, feed 3326

**reste** *nm*  rest 363

**rester** *v*  to stay 100

**restituer** *v*  to return, restore, refund 4546

**restreindre** *v*  to restrict, cut down, decrease 2360

**restriction** *nf*  restriction 2589

**restructuration** *nf*  restructure, restructuring 3331

**résultat** *nm*  result, follow-up 428

**résulter** *v*  to result 2095

**résumer** *v*  to summarize, sum up 1601

**rétablir** *v*  to restore, re-establish 1864

**rétablissement** *nm*  restoring, re-establishment, recovery 3546

**retard** *nm*  delay 1278

**retarder** *v*  to delay, hold up 2147

**retenir** *v*  to retain, hold back, remember 557

**retenue** *nf*  deduction; restraint, self-control 4762

**réticence** *nf*  reluctance, hesitation 4135

**retirer** *v*  to remove, withdraw 657

**retombée** *nf*  fallout, consequences, effects 4618

**retomber** *v*  to fall again, fall down again 3112

**retour** *nm*  return 421

**retourner** *v*  to return, go back 999

**retrait** *nadj*  withdrawal 2416

**retraité** *nadj*  retired 4299

**retraite** *nf*  retirement, pension 1180

**retrancher** *v*  to deduct, remove; to entrench 4811

**retrouver** *v* to find, recall **244**

**réunion** *nf* meeting **971**

**réunir** *v* to gather, reunite, raise **824**

**réussi** *adj* successful **3544**

**réussir** *v* to succeed **279**

**réussite** *nf* success **1641**

**revanche** *nf* revenge; return **1397**

**rêve** *nm* dream **1313**

**réveil** *nm* waking up, awakening, alarm clock **4940**

**réveiller** *v* to wake up **2199**

**révélation** *nf* diclosure, revelation **3301**

**révéler** *v* to reveal **810**

**revendication** *nf* claim, demand **2230**

**revendiquer** *v* to claim **2754**

**revenir** *v* to come back **184**

**revenu** *nm* income **1012**

**rêver** *v* to dream **1678**

**revers** *nm(pl)* back, reverse, setback **4083**

**revêtir** *v* to take on, assume **2688**

**réviser** *v* to review, revise, overhaul **2551**

**révision** *nf* review, revision, overhaul **2748**

**revivre** *v* to live again, come back life, revive **4966**

**revoir** *v* to see again, revise **1274**

**révolte** *nf* revolt **2720**

**révolter** *v* to revolt, rebel, outrage **4370**

**révolution** *nf* revolution **1617**

**révolutionnaire** *nadj(f)* revolutionary **2471**

**revue** *nf* review, magazine, journal **1822**

**rhétorique** *nadj(f)* rhetorical, rhetoric **4932**

**riche** *nadj(f)* rich **599**

**richesse** *nf* wealth, richness **1880**

**rideau** *nm* curtain **3752**

**ridicule** *nadj(f)* ridiculous, silly **2411**

**rien** *adv,nm,pro* nothing **168**

**rigide** *adj(f)* rigid, stiff **4741**

**rigoler** *v* to laugh, **4994**

**rigoureux** *adj(pl)* rigorous, harsh, strict **2682**

**rigueur** *nf* harshness, severity, rigidness, rigor, strictness **2791**

**rire** *nm,v* to laugh **1193**

**risque** *nm* risk **647**

**risquer** *v* to risk **322**

**rival** *nadj* rival **3758**

**rive** *nf* shore, bank **3314**

**rivière** *nf* river **2223**

**robe** *nf* dress **2864**

**rocher** *nm* rock, boulder **4767**

**rock** *nm* rock music **4081**

**roi** *nm* king **1364**

**rôle** *nm* role **371**

**romain** *adj* Roman **3144**

**roman** *adj,nm* novel **1262**

**romancier** *nm* novelist **4581**

**romantique** *nadj(f)* romantic **4884**

**rompre** *v* to break **2087**

**rond** *adv,nadj* round **2268**

**rose** *nadj(f),nf* rose; pink **2671**

**roue** *nf* wheel **3916**

**rouge** *nadj(f)* red **987**

**rouler** *v* to roll **2599**

**route** *nf* road **512**

**routier** *nadj* road, long-distance lorry or truck driver **3101**

**routine** *nf* routine **4120**

**rouvrir** *v* to reopen **4648**

**royal** *adj* royal **2290**

**royaume** *nm* kingdom **2620**

**rubrique** *nf* column, heading, rubric **4130**

**rude** *nadj(f)* rough, harsh, hard, tough **4247**

**rue** *nf* street **598**

**ruine** *nf* ruin, ruins **3643**

**ruiner** *v* to ruin, bankrupt oneself **3900**

**rumeur** *nf* rumor **2164**

**rupture** *nf* break, rupture **1867**

**rural** *nadj* rural **2709**

**russe** *nadj(f)* Russian **1325**

**rythme** *nm* rhythm, rate **1662**

# Ss

**sable** *adji,nm* sand **3263**

**sac** *nm* bag, sack **2343**

**sacré** *nadj* sacred **2341**

**sacrifice** *nm* sacrifice **2437**

**sacrifier** *v* to sacrifice, give away **2649**

**sage** *nadj(f)* wise, good, sound, sensible **2643**

**sagesse** *nf* wisdom, moderation **2998**

**sain** *adj* healthy, sane **1763**

**saint** *nadj* saint, holy **1702**

**saisir** *v* to take hold of, grab **719**

**saison** *nf* season **1667**

**saisonnier** *adj* seasonal **4543**

**salaire** *nm* salary, wage **1015**

**salarial** *adj* salary **3639**

**salarié** *nadj* wage-earning, employee **2119**

**salaud** *nadj* bastard **4869**

**sale** *nadj(f)* dirty **2906**

**salle** *nf* room **812**

**salon** *nm* lounge, living room **2729**

**saluer** *v* to greet, salute 1620

**salut** *intj,nm* salute, hi, bye 2205

**samedi** *nm* Saturday 1355

**sanction** *nf* sanction 2282

**sanctionner** *v* to sanction, punish, approve 4211

**sang** *nm* blood 1126

**sanglant** *adj* bloody, cruel, covered in blood 4403

**sanitaire** *nadj(f)* health, sanitary, medical 4501

**sans** *prep* without 71

**santé** *nf* health 641

**satellite** *nm* satellite 2200

**satisfaction** *nf* satisfaction 2108

**satisfaire** *v* to satisfy 781

**satisfaisant** *adj* satisfactory, satisfying 2540

**sauf** *adj,prep* except 476

**saut** *nm* jump, leap 3841

**sauter** *v* to jump 2114

**sauvage** *nadj(f)* savage, wild 2464

**sauver** *v* to rescue, save 1213

**sauvetage** *nm* rescue, salvaging 4048

**savant** *nadj* scientist, scholar; learned, scholarly, clever, skilful 3378

**savoir** *nm,v* to know 67

**savoir-faire** *nmi* know-how 4916

**scandale** *nm* scandal, uproar 1912

**scandaleux** *adj(pl)* scandalous, outrageous 3478

**scandaliser** *v* to shock, scandalize 4924

**scénario** *nm* scenario, script 2468

**scène** *nf* scene 794

**scepticisme** *nm* scepticism 4719

**sceptique** *nadj(f)* sceptical, sceptic 4064

**schéma** *nm* diagram, outline 3305

**science** *nf* science 1114

**scientifique** *nadj(f)* scientific 950

**scolaire** *adj(f)* school, educational, academic 1993

**score** *nm* score 4440

**scrutin** *nm* ballot, poll 2913

**se** *pro* oneself, himself, herself, itself, themselves 17

**séance** *nf* session, meeting 1463

**sec** *adj,adv,nm* dry 2313

**sécheresse** *nf* dryness, drought 4439

**second** *adj,det,nm* second 379

**secondaire** *nadj(f)* secondary 2027

**seconde** *det,nf* second 1542

**secouer** *v* to shake 2755

**secours** *nm(pl)* help, aid, assistance 1857

**secret** *nadj* secret 796

**secrétaire** *nm,nf* secretary 920

**secrétariat** *nm* secretaryship, secretariat, secretarial offices, secretary's office 4654

**secteur** *nm* sector 566

**section** *nf* section 2141

**sécuritaire** *adj(f)* safe 4863

**sécurité** *nf* security, safety 478

**séduire** *v* to seduce, charm, captivate, appeal to 2837

**seigneur** *nm* lord 4542

**sein** *nm* breast, bosom 563

**seize** *det,nmi* sixteen 3285

**séjour** *nm* stay 2007

**sel** *nm* salt 4276

**sélection** *nf* selection 2403

**sélectionner** *v* to select 3671

**selon** *prep* according to 240

**semaine** *nf* week 245

**semblable** *nadj(f)* similar 1978

**semblant** *nm* semblance, pretence 4794

**sembler** *v* to seem 180

**semer** *v* to sow, scatter, spread 2612

**semestre** *nm* semester, six-month period 4331

**séminaire** *nm* seminar, seminary 3733

**sénateur** *nm* senator 684

**sens** *nm(pl)* sense, meaning 243

**sensation** *nf* sensation 3415

**sensibilité** *nf* sensitivity, sensibility 2584

**sensible** *nadj(f)* sensitive 1063

**sensiblement** *adv* approximately, more or less, noticeably 4057

**sentiment** *nm* feeling 886

**sentir** *v* to feel, smell 536

**séparation** *nf* separation 1613

**séparatiste** *nadj(f)* separatist 4190

**séparer** *v* to separate 946

**sept** *det,nmi* seven 905

**septembre** *nm* September 944

**septième** *det,nm,nf* seventh 4028

**séquence** *nf* sequence 3099

**serbe** *adj(f)* Serbian 2780

**sérénité** *nf* serenity, peacefulness 4962

**série** *nf* series 836

**sérieusement** *adv* seriously 1252

**sérieux** *nadj(pl)* serious 412

**serment** *nm* oath, vow 4069

**serré** *adj,adv* tight, packed, crowded 3810

**serre** *nf* greenhouse 4832

**serrer** *v* to tighten, squeeze 2449

**serveur** *nm* waiter, server 4377

**service** *nm* service 203

**servir** *v*  to serve 177

**session** *nf*  session 2324

**seuil** *nm*  doorstep, threshold 2068

**seul** *adj*  alone, only 101

**seulement** *adv*  only 130

**sévère** *adj(f)*  severe 1733

**sévèrement** *adv*  severely, harshly 4917

**sévir** *v*  to act ruthlessly, be rife 4356

**sexe** *nm*  sex 1691

**sexuel** *adj*  sexual 1594

**si** *adv,conj,nmi*  if, whether 34

**siècle** *nm*  century 603

**siège** *nm*  seat, bench 1571

**siéger** *v*  to sit 2883

**sien** *nadj*  his, hers 2210

**signal** *nm*  signal 978

**signaler** *v*  to indicate, signal 1439

**signataire** *nm,nf*  signatory 4570

**signature** *nf*  signature 2187

**signe** *nm*  sign 707

**signer** *v*  to sign 809

**significatif** *adj*  significative 2292

**signification** *nf*  significance 2798

**signifier** *v*  to mean 586

**silence** *nm*  silence 1281

**silencieux** *nadj(pl)*  silent, noiseless, silencer 3290

**sillage** *nm*  wake, slipstream 4972

**similaire** *adj(f)*  similar 2632

**simple** *nadj(f)*  simple 212

**simplement** *adv*  simply 615

**simplicité** *nf*  simplicity, straightforwardness 4907

**simplifier** *v*  to simplify 2903

**simultanément** *adv*  simultaneously 4090

**sincère** *adj(f)*  sincere 3180

**sincèrement** *adv*  sincerely 3516

**sincérité** *nf*  sincerity 4831

**singe** *nm*  monkey 4739

**singulier** *nadj*  unique, singular 3567

**sinistre** *nadj(f)*  disaster, sinister 3578

**sinon** *conj*  otherwise, or else 1170

**site** *nm*  site 1462

**situation** *nf*  situation 223

**situer** *v*  to situate, locate 815

**six** *det,nmi*  six 450

**sixième** *det,nm,nf*  sixth 3124

**ski** *nm*  ski, skiing 4571

**slogan** *nm*  slogan 4474

**social** *nadj*  social 301

**socialisme** *nm*  socialism 4989

**socialiste** *nadj(f)*  socialist 1768

**société** *nf*  society 295

**sœur** *nf*  sister 1558

**soi** *nmi,pro*  one, oneself, self 1365

**soi-disant** *adji*  so-called, supposedly 3637

**soif** *nf*  thirst 4659

**soigner** *v*  to treat, look after, take care over 2228

**soigneusement** *adv*  tidily, neatly, carefully 3647

**soin** *nm*  care 1109

**soir** *nm*  evening 397

**soirée** *nf*  evening 1530

**soit** *adv,conj*  either...or 166

**soixante** *det,nmi*  sixty 3151

**soixante-dix** *det,nmi*  seventy 4887

**sol** *nm*  floor, ground 1491

**solaire** *adj(f)*  solar 4653

**soldat** *nm*  soldier 1098

**solde** *nm,nf*  balance; pay; sale 4622

**soleil** *nm*  sun 1713

**solidaire** *adj(f)*  interdependent, jointly dependent 4980

**solidarité** *nf*  solidarity 2359

**solide** *nadj(f)*  solid 1414

**solitaire** *nadj(f)*  solitary, lone, lonely 3560

**solitude** *nf*  solitude, loneliness 3448

**solliciter** *v*  to request, solicit, appeal 2519

**solution** *nf*  solution 608

**sombre** *adj(f)*  dark 2348

**sombrer** *v*  to darken; to sink, lapse 3991

**sommaire** *nadj(f)*  summary, brief, cursory 4133

**somme** *nm,nf*  amount, sum; nap 912

**sommeil** *nm*  sleep, sleepiness 3393

**sommet** *nm*  summit 1486

**son** *det,nm*  his, her, its; sound; bran 26

**sondage** *nm*  poll 2232

**sonder** *v*  to probe, poll, sound out 4930

**songer** *v*  to dream 2206

**sonner** *v*  to ring 2422

**sonore** *nadj(f)*  sound, resonant, sonorous, voiced 4502

**sorcier** *nm*  sorcerer, witch 4582

**sort** *nm*  fate, curse 1780

**sortant** *nadj*  outgoing 4192

**sorte** *nf*  sort, kind 351

**sortie** *nf*  exit 1174

**sortir** *v*  to go out, leave 309

**sou** *nm*  penny 4051

**souci** *nm*  worry, concern 1556

**soucier** *v*  to care about, show concern for 2822

**soucieux** *adj(pl)*  concerned, worried 3586

**soudain** *adj,adv* sudden, suddenly **2310**

**souffle** *nm* breath, puff **3120**

**souffler** *v* to blow, puff **2984**

**souffrance** *nf* suffering **1862**

**souffrir** *v* to suffer **642**

**souhait** *nm* wish **3122**

**souhaitable** *adj(f)* desirable **3920**

**souhaiter** *v* to wish **403**

**soulagement** *nm* relief **4424**

**soulager** *v* to relieve, soothe, ease **2912**

**soulever** *v* to lift up **1339**

**souligner** *v* to underline, stress **816**

**soumettre** *v* to submit **687**

**soumission** *nf* submission **4578**

**soupçon** *nm* suspicion **3921**

**soupçonner** *v* to suspect **2375**

**soupe** *nf* soup **4563**

**souple** *adj(f)* supple, agile, soft, floppy, flexible **3087**

**souplesse** *nf* suppleness, flexibility **4085**

**source** *nf* source, spring **817**

**sourd** *nadj* deaf **2854**

**sourire** *nm,v* smile; to smile **1476**

**souris** *nf(pl)* mouse **4328**

**sous** *prep* under **122**

**souscrire** *v* to subscribe **3983**

**sous-estimer** *v* to underestimate **4449**

**sous-marin** *nadj* submarine, underwater **3777**

**sous-sol** *nm* basement, lower ground floor, subsoil, underground **4289**

**soustraire** *v* to substract, remove, shield, escape from **4109**

**soutenir** *v* to sustain, support **578**

**souterrain** *nadj* underground, underground passage **4544**

**soutien** *nm* support **1198**

**souvenir** *nm,v* memory; to remember **616**

**souvent** *adv* often **287**

**souverain** *nadj* sovereign, supreme ruler, monarch **2697**

**souveraineté** *nf* sovereignty **2353**

**soviétique** *nadj(f)* Soviet **1674**

**spatial** *adj* spatial, space **2765**

**spécial** *adj* special **726**

**spécialement** *adv* especially, particularly **2130**

**spécialiser** *v* to specialize **2009**

**spécialiste** *nadj(f)* specialist **1588**

**spécialité** *nf* specialty **3356**

**spécification** *nf* specification **4642**

**spécifier** *v* to specify **3086**

**spécifique** *adj(f)* specific **2175**

**spectacle** *nm* sight, show **1687**

**spectaculaire** *adj(f)* spectacular **3330**

**spectateur** *nm* member of the audience, spectator, onlooker **2877**

**spectre** *nm* spectrum, ghost **4645**

**spéculation** *nf* speculation **3808**

**sphère** *nf* sphere **4209**

**spirituel** *nadj* witty, spiritual, sacred **3047**

**spontané** *adj* spontaneous **3986**

**sport** *adji,nm* sport **2011**

**sportif** *nadj* sports, athletic, competitive **2670**

**stabilisation** *nf* stabilization **4265**

**stabiliser** *v* to stabilize **4160**

**stabilité** *nf* stability **2302**

**stable** *adj(f)* stable **2517**

**stade** *nm* stadium, stage **1967**

**stage** *nm* internship, training course **4007**

**standard** *adji,nm* standard, switchboard **4234**

**star** *nf* star **3322**

**station** *nf* station **1399**

**statistique** *nf* statistics, statistical **1901**

**statue** *nf* statue **4020**

**statut** *nm* status **1474**

**stimuler** *v* to stimulate **3063**

**stipuler** *v* to state, stipulate, specify **4518**

**stock** *nm* stock, to supply **2344**

**stopper** *v* to stop, halt **4693**

**stratégie** *nf* strategy **1286**

**stratégique** *adj(f)* strategic **2181**

**stress** *nm(pl)* stress **4806**

**strict** *adj* strict, absolute **1859**

**strictement** *adv* strictly **2813**

**structure** *nf* structure **964**

**structurel** *adj* structural **3018**

**studio** *nm* studio, studio apartment **3664**

**stupéfiant** *nadj* drug, narcotic; stunning, astounding **4383**

**stupide** *adj(f)* stupid, silly, bemused **3407**

**style** *nm* style **1999**

**subir** *v* to undergo, be subjected to, suffer **677**

**subit** *adj* sudden **3930**

**subsister** *v* to subsist, remain **3161**

**substance** *nf* substance **2227**

**substantiel** *adj* substantial **3276**

**substituer** *v* to substitute **4344**

**substitution** *nf* substitution, mix-up **4389**

**subtil** *adj* subtle, nice **4345**

**subvention** *nf* subsidy **2504**

**succéder** *v* to succeed, take over **2619**

**succès** *nm(pl)* success 620

**successeur** *nm* successor 4254

**successif** *adj* successive 3197

**succession** *nf* succession 2902

**successivement** *adv* successively 4534

**sucre** *nm* sugar 3258

**sud** *adji,nm* south 1242

**sud-est** *nmi* south-east 3309

**sud-ouest** *nmi* south-west 3773

**suédois** *nadj(pl)* Swedish, Swede 4647

**suffire** *v* to be sufficient, suffice 716

**suffisamment** *adv* sufficiently 1727

**suffisant** *adj* sufficient 1537

**suffrage** *nm* vote 3985

**suggérer** *v* to suggest 1478

**suggestion** *nf* suggestion 3254

**suicide** *nm* suicide 2222

**suicider** *v* to commit suicide 3678

**suisse** *adj(f)* Swiss 2241

**suite** *nf* result, follow-up, rest 93

**suivant** *nadj,prep* following 1121

**suivi** *nadj* follow-up; consistent, continuous 3973

**suivre** *v* to follow 120

**sujet** *nm* subject, topic 353

**super** *adji,nm* great 2993

**superbe** *nadj(f)* superb, magnificent, handsome, gorgeous 3450

**superficiel** *adj* superficial, shallow 4740

**supérieur** *nadj* superior 876

**supplément** *nm* supplement, extra 3179

**supplémentaire** *adj(f)* additional 1267

**supplier** *v* to beg, implore 4702

**support** *nm* support, stand 3708

**supporter** *nm,v* to support, endure 1400

**supposer** *v* to suppose, assume 730

**suppression** *nf* deletion, suppression 2578

**supprimer** *v* to remove, withdraw 1590

**suprême** *nadj(f)* supreme 2022

**sur** *adj,prep* on, upon 16

**sûr** *adj* sure 270

**surcroît** *nm* extra, additional 4191

**sûrement** *adv* surely 1750

**sûreté** *nf* safety, reliability 3459

**surface** *nf* surface 1748

**surgir** *v* to spring up 2609

**surmonter** *v* to overcome, top, surmount 2385

**surplus** *nm(pl)* surplus 3104

**surprenant** *adj* surprising 2951

**surprendre** *v* to surprise 1053

**surpris** *adj(pl)* surprised, amazed 3408

**surprise** *nf* surprise 1815

**sursis** *nm(pl)* reprieve, deferment 4089

**surtout** *adv,nm* especially, above all 235

**surveillance** *nf* surveillance, monitoring 1745

**surveiller** *v* to watch 1297

**survenir** *v* to occur, take place, appear 2109

**survie** *nf* survival 2699

**survivant** *nadj* survivor, surviving 3302

**survivre** *v* to survive 1348

**susceptible** *adj(f)* sensitive, touchy 1827

**susciter** *v* to arouse, provoke 1027

**suspect** *nadj* suspicious, suspect 2571

**suspendre** *v* to suspend, postpone 1730

**suspens** *nm(pl)* suspension, abeyance 3879

**suspension** *nf* hanging, suspending, breaking off, postponement, suspension 3569

**symbole** *nm* symbol 1427

**symbolique** *nadj(f)* symbolic 3411

**symboliser** *v* to symbolize 4343

**sympathie** *nf* liking, warmth, friendship, sympathie 3017

**sympathique** *nadj(f)* likeable, nice, pleasant 4164

**symptôme** *nm* symptom 4095

**syndical** *adj* (trade-) union 2995

**syndicat** *nm* union 1528

**syndrome** *nm* syndrome 4573

**synonyme** *nadj(f)* synonymous; synonym 4973

**synthèse** *nf* summary, synthesis 3716

**syrien** *nadj* Syrian 4453

**systématique** *nadj(f)* systematic 3114

**systématiquement** *adv* systematically 3038

**système** *nm* system 289

# Tt

**tabac** *nm* tobacco 2393

**table** *nf* table 1019

**tableau** *nm* frame, picture, painting, panel 1456

**tache** *nf* stain, spot, mark 4471

**tâche** *nf* task 887

**tâcher** *v* to endeavor 4043

**tactique** *nadj(f)* tactics, tactical 2606

**taille** *nf* size, height 1500

**tailler** *v* to cut, carve, engrave, sharpen, trim 3802

**taire** *v* to keep quiet 1853

**talent** *nm* talent 2017

**tandis** while 975

**tant** *adv* so much, so many 181

**tante** *nf* aunt 3891

**tantôt** *adv* this afternoon, sometimes 3013

**taper** *v* to beat, slam, bang, type 3270

**tapis** *nm(pl)* carpet, mat, covering 3783

**tard** *adv* late 348

**tarder** *v* to delay 2251

**tardif** *adj* late 3947

**tarif** *nm* price, rate, fare, tariff 3247

**tas** *nm(pl)* pile, lots of 2723

**taux** *nm(pl)* rate 700

**taxe** *nf* tax 2446

**taxer** *v* to tax 4744

**taxi** *nm* taxi 4235

**tchèque** *nadj(f)* Czech 3793

**te** *pro* you, to you, from you 207

**technicien** *nm* technician 2461

**technique** *nadj(f)* technique, technics, technical 592

**techniquement** *adv* technically 4091

**technologie** *nf* technology 1388

**technologique** *adj(f)* technological 2600

**tel** *adj,det,pro* such 142

**télé** *nf* TV 2746

**télécommunication** *nf* telecommunication 2842

**téléphone** *nm* telephone 1366

**téléphoner** *v* to telephone, phone, call 2448

**téléphonique** *adj(f)* telephone 2356

**téléspectateur** *nm* TV viewer 4935

**téléviser** *v* to televise 4115

**télévision** *nf* television 1179

**tellement** *adv* so much 869

**témoignage** *nm* testimony 1548

**témoigner** *v* to testify 1212

**témoin** *nm* witness 1055

**température** *nf* temperature 2924

**tempête** *nf* storm, gale, turmoil 2695

**temple** *nm* temple 3441

**temporaire** *adj(f)* temporary 2885

**temps** *nm(pl)* time 65

**tenant** *nadj* tenant; incumbent, holder 2516

**tendance** *nf* tendency, trend 1158

**tendre** *nadj(f),v* to tighten; to extend, stretch, tender 1138

**tendresse** *nf* tenderness, fondness 4472

**teneur** *nf* content 4154

**tenir** *v* to hold 104

**tennis** *nmi* tennis 3867

**tension** *nf* tension 1799

**tentation** *nf* temptation 3286

**tentative** *nf* attempt 1381

**tente** *nf* tent 4336

**tenter** *v* to tempt, try 347

**tenue** *nf* dress, outfit 1899

**terme** *nm* term, deadline 311

**terminal** *nadj* terminal 2525

**terminer** *v* to finish, end, 415

**terrain** *nm* ground, terrain 867

**terre** *nf* earth, world, soil, land 430

**terrestre** *adj(f)* land, earth 2522

**terreur** *nf* terror, dread 3379

**terrible** *adj(f)* terrible, dreadful 1310

**terriblement** *adv* terribly, awfully 3909

**terrien** *nadj* earthling; landowner, countryman 4835

**territoire** *nm* territory 698

**territorial** *adj* territorial, land 3160

**terrorisme** *nm* terrorism 2834

**terroriste** *nm,nf* terrorist 2415

**test** *nm* test 1788

**tester** *v* to test 2965

**tête** *nf* head 343

**texte** *nm* text 631

**textile** *nadj(f)* textile 4785

**thé** *nm* tea 3517

**théâtre** *nm* theater 1701

**thème** *nm* theme, topic 1720

**théologie** *nf* theology 4468

**théorie** *nf* theory 1773

**théorique** *adj(f)* theoretical 3476

**théoriquement** *adv* theoretically 4808

**thérapie** *nf* therapy 4420

**thèse** *nf* thesis, argument 2607

**tiens** *nadjpl,intj* ah, well 3722

**tiers** *nadj(pl)* third 1533

**timbre** *nm* to stamp 4138

**timide** *nadj(f)* timid, shy, bashful 3835

**tir** *nm* fire, shot, launch 2959

**tirage** *nm* drawing, circulation, run 3607

**tirer** *v* to pull, fire 391

**tisser** *v* to weave 4320

**tissu** *nadj* fabric, material, cloth, tissue, woven 2696

**titre** *nm* title 399

**titulaire** *nadj(f)* holder, with tenure, occupant 4264

**toi** *nm,pro* you, yourself 510

**toile** *nf* cloth, canvas, web 3502

**toilette** *nf* washing, toilet, lavatory, bathroom, restroom 4215

**toit** *nm* roof 2894

**tolérance** *nf* tolerance 3315

**tolérer** *v* to tolerate, access, put up, bear, endure 2132

**tombe** *nf* grave, tomb 3426

**tomber** *v* to fall 547

**ton** *det,nm* your; tone 330

**tonne** *nf* ton 2261

**tort** *nm* wrong 1652

**torture** *nf* torture 4304

**torturer** *v* to torture 3826

**tôt** *adji,adv* early 513

**total** *nadj* total 658

**totalement** *adv* totally 1353

**totalité** *nf* totality, entirety 1779

**touchant** *adj,prep* with regard to, concerning, touching, moving 3090

**touche** *nf* button, key, touch, touchline 3775

**toucher** *nm,v* to touch 231

**toujours** *adv* always 103

**tour** *nm,nf* tower; turn; tour 523

**tourisme** *nm* tourism, sightseeing 2955

**touriste** *nm,nf* tourist 2653

**touristique** *adj(f)* holiday, tourist 3818

**tournant** *adj,nm* revolving, swivel, encircling, bend, turning point 2406

**tournée** *nf* tour, round 2691

**tourner** *v* to turn 669

**tournoi** *nm* tournament 3582

**tout** *adv,det,nadj,pro* all, very 24

**toutefois** *adv,conj* however 770

**toxique** *nadj(f)* toxic, toxin 4476

**trace** *nf* trace, mark, track 1848

**tracer** *v* to draw, write, mark out 2997

**tradition** *nf* tradition 1371

**traditionnel** *adj* traditional 1574

**traditionnellement** *adv* traditionally 4815

**traduction** *nf* translation 2826

**traduire** *v* to translate 1125

**trafic** *nm* traffic, circulation 1577

**tragédie** *nf* tragedy 1910

**tragique** *nadj(f)* tragic 2042

**trahir** *v* to betray, give away 2787

**trahison** *nf* betrayal, treachery, treason 4087

**train** *nm* train 232

**traîner** *v* to drag, pull 2433

**trait** *nm* line, feature 1423

**traite** *nf* trade, draft, stretch, milking 4896

**traité** *nm* treaty 1249

**traitement** *nm* treatment, salary, wage 1111

**traiter** *v* to treat, handle, deal with 589

**trajet** *nm* journey, route 3577

**trame** *nf* weft, framework; tram 3457

**tranche** *nf* slice, edge, section, bracket, slot 2692

**trancher** *v* to cut, sever, settle, decide 2145

**tranquille** *adj(f)* quiet 2555

**transaction** *nf* transaction 2940

**transférer** *v* to transfer 2128

**transfert** *nm* transfer 1362

**transformation** *nf* transformation, change 2330

**transformer** *v* to transform 1041

**transit** *nm* transit 3848

**transition** *nf* transition 2318

**transitoire** *adj(f)* transient, interim, provisional 3946

**transmettre** *v* to forward, transmit 1419

**transmission** *nf* transmission 1933

**transparence** *nf* transparency 2896

**transparent** *nadj* transparent, see-through, evident 2953

**transport** *nm* transportation 935

**transporter** *v* to transport, carry 1929

**travail** *nm* work 153

**travailler** *v* to work 290

**travailleur** *nadj* worker 1341

**travers** *nm(pl)* breadth, across; fault, amiss 661

**traversée** *nf* crossing 4652

**traverser** *v* to cross, traverse 1040

**treize** *det,nmi* thirteen 3245

**tremblement** *nm* shiver, trembling, shaking 4696

**trembler** *v* to shiver, tremble, shake, flicker 4225

**trentaine** *nf* about thirty 3703

**trente** *det,nmi* thirty 1646

**très** *adv* very 66

**trésor** *nm* treasure, treasury 3097

**trêve** *nf* truce 4455

**tribu** *nf* tribe 3668

**tribunal** *nm* court 1336

**tribune** *nf* platform, forum, gallery 3282

**trimestre** *nm* quarter, three months 2763

**triomphe** *nm* triumph 4829

**triompher** *v* to triumph, beat 4576

**triple** *nadj(f)* triple 4700

**triste** *adj(f)* sad 1843

**tristesse** *nf* sadness, gloominess, dreariness 3989

**trois** *det,nmi* three 115

**troisième** *det,nm,nf* third 506

**tromper** *v* to deceive 1539

**trône** *nm* throne 3839

**trop** *adv* too much, too many 195

**trottoir** *nm* pavement 4735

**trou** *nm* hole 2180

**troublant** *adj* disturbing **4605**

**trouble** *adj(f),nm* turmoil, agitation, blurred, cloudy, trouble **2080**

**troubler** *v* to disturb, disrupt, cloud **3416**

**troupe** *nf* troup **1282**

**troupeau** *nm* herd, flock **4495**

**trouver** *v* to find **83**

**truc** *nm* trick; thingamajig **1991**

**tu** *pro* you **112**

**tube** *nm* tube **4775**

**tuer** *v* to kill **591**

**tueur** *nm* killer, hit man **3581**

**tunnel** *nm* tunnel **3386**

**turc** *adj,nm* Turk, Turkish **3134**

**type** *nm* type; guy **440**

**typique** *nadj(f),nf* typical **4178**

# Uu

**ultérieur** *adj* later, subsequent **3862**

**ultime** *adj(f)* ultimate **2533**

**un** *adj,det,nm,pro* a, an, one **3**

**unanime** *adj(f)* unanimous **3050**

**unanimité** *nf* unanimity **3143**

**uni** *nadj* united **2153**

**uniforme** *adj(f),nm* uniform, steady, regular **1801**

**unilatéral** *adj* unilateral **4317**

**union** *nf* union **729**

**unique** *adj(f)* unique **402**

**uniquement** *adv* only **1395**

**unir** *v* to unite **1483**

**unité** *nf* unity; unit **571**

**univers** *nm(pl)* universe **2112**

**universel** *nadj* universal **1608**

**universitaire** *nadj(f)* university, academic **2782**

**université** *nf* university **1192**

**uranium** *nm* uranium **2844**

**urbain** *adj* urban **2215**

**urgence** *nf* emergency **1199**

**urgent** *adj* urgent **2179**

**usage** *nm* use, usage **863**

**usager** *nm* user **3167**

**user** *v* to wear out, wear away, use up **3000**

**usine** *nf* factory **1482**

**utile** *adj(f)* useful **1003**

**utilisateur** *nadj* user **2523**

**utilisation** *nf* use **1345**

**utiliser** *v* to use **345**

**utilité** *nf* use, usefulness **3082**

# Vv

**vacance** *nf* vacancy; vacation **1726**

**vache** *adj(f),nf* cow **2768**

**vague** *nadj(f),nf* vague; wave **1493**

**vain** *adj* vain **2971**

**vaincre** *v* to beat, defeat, overcome, conquer **2919**

**vainqueur** *nm,nf* winner **3307**

**vaisseau** *nm* ship, vessel **4969**

**valable** *adj(f)* valid **2668**

**valeur** *nf* value, worth **453**

**valise** *nf* suitcase **4308**

**vallée** *nf* valley **2856**

**valoir** *v* to be worth **431**

**vanter** *v* to vaunt, boast, brag **3288**

**vapeur** *nm,nf* vapor, steam, steamer, steamship **4111**

**variable** *nadj(f)* variable **2736**

**variation** *nf* variation, change **3974**

**varier** *v* to vary, change **1962**

**variété** *nf* variety **3232**

**vaste** *adj(f)* vast, immense **1142**

**vedette** *nf* star, patrol boat **3731**

**véhicule** *nm* vehicle **1959**

**véhiculer** *v* to transport, convey **4465**

**veille** *nf* the day before, the eve of, night watch **1840**

**veiller** *v* to look after, stay up **1816**

**vélo** *nm* bike, bicycle **4594**

**vendeur** *nm* salesman, seller **3223**

**vendre** *v* to sell **710**

**vendredi** *nm* Friday **1086**

**vendu** *nadj* sold, bribed **4919**

**vengeance** *nf* revenge **3869**

**venger** *v* to avenge, take revenge **4656**

**venir** *v* to come **88**

**vent** *nm* wind **1387**

**vente** *nf* sale **1096**

**ventre** *nm* belly, stomach **3150**

**venu** *nadj* come **4499**

**venue** *nf* coming **3691**

**verbal** *adj* verbal **4240**

**verdict** *nm* verdict **4850**

**vérificateur** *nadj* checker, inspector, auditor **4257**

**vérification** *nf* check, verification **3094**

**vérifier** *v* to check, verify **1236**

**véritable** *adj(f)* real, true **654**

**véritablement** *adv* truly, really **3115**

**vérité** *nf* truth **907**

**verre** *nm* glass **2174**

**vers** *nm(pl),prep* toward; verse **182**

**versant** *nm* hillside, mountainside **4134**

**versement** *nm*  payment 4531

**verser** *v*  to pour, deposit, shed 1516

**version** *nf*  version 1165

**vert** *nadj*  green 1060

**vertu** *nf*  virtue 1497

**vêtement** *nm*  garment, item or article of clothing 2383

**vêtir** *v*  to clothe, dress, put on 4734

**veuf** *nadj*  surviving spouse 3455

**via** *prep*  via 3513

**viable** *adj(f)*  viable, workable 4946

**viande** *nf*  meat 2625

**vice** *nm*  fault, defect, vice 4342

**vice-président** *nm*  vice-president 1789

**victime** *nf*  victim 697

**victoire** *nf*  victory 1373

**vide** *nadj(f)*  empty 1473

**vidéo** *adji,nf*  video 2611

**vider** *v*  to empty, vacate 2849

**vie** *nf*  life 132

**vieillard** *nm*  old man 4736

**vieillesse** *nf*  old age 4813

**vieillir** *v*  to grow old 3342

**vierge** *nadj(f)*  virgin 3875

**vieux** *adj(pl),nm(pl)*  old 671

**vif** *nadj*  lively 1132

**vigilance** *nf*  vigilance, watchfulness 4080

**vigilant** *adj*  vigilant, watchful 4931

**vigoureux** *adj(pl)*  vigorous 4365

**vigueur** *nf*  vigor 1711

**village** *nm*  village 1295

**ville** *nf*  city 260

**vin** *nm*  wine 2309

**vingt** *det,nmi*  twenty 1273

**vingtaine** *nf*  about twenty 3098

**vingt-cinq** *det,nmi*  twenty five 4436

**vingtième** *det,nm,nf*  twentieth 3881

**vingt-quatre** *det,nmi*  twenty four 4436

**viol** *nm*  rape 3629

**violation** *nf*  violation, transgession 2814

**violence** *nf*  violence 602

**violent** *nadj*  violent 1119

**violer** *v*  to rape, infringe 2352

**virer** *v*  to turn, change, transfer, kick out 3623

**virtuel** *adj*  virtual, potential 3885

**virus** *nm(pl)*  virus 3382

**visa** *nm*  visa, stamp 4435

**visage** *nm*  face 1292

**vis-à-vis** *nmpl,prep*  face to face, regarding 1376

**visée** *nf*  aim, design, sighting 4763

**viser** *v*  to aim 656

**visible** *adj(f)*  visible, obvious 2276

**visiblement** *adv*  obviously, clearly, visibly 3677

**vision** *nf*  vision, view 1505

**visite** *nf*  visit 1072

**visiter** *v*  to visit 1378

**visiteur** *nm*  visitor 2266

**visuel** *adj*  visual 4793

**vital** *adj*  vital 2528

**vite** *adv*  fast, quickly 711

**vitesse** *nf*  speed 1065

**vitre** *nf*  pane, window 4106

**vitrine** *nf*  window, display cabinet 4312

**vivant** *nadj*  alive, living 1191

**vivement** *adv*  sharply, brusquely, lively 2491

**vivre** *nm,v*  to live 201

**vocabulaire** *nm*  vocabulary 4159

**vocal** *adj*  vocal 4316

**vocation** *nf*  vocation, calling 3006

**vœu** *nm*  vow, wish, will 2103

**voici** *prep*  here is, here are, this is, these are 1103

**voie** *nf*  road, lane, route, track, way 609

**voilà** *prep*  right, there, here 524

**voile** *nm,nf*  veil, sail 3155

**voiler** *v*  to veil 4067

**voir** *v*  to see 69

**voire** *adv*  even, indeed 1547

**voisin** *nadj*  neighbor 979

**voisinage** *nm*  neighborhood 4915

**voiture** *nf*  car 881

**voix** *nf(pl)*  voice 414

**vol** *nm*  flight, theft 1531

**volant** *adj,nm*  steering wheel 4035

**voler** *v*  to steal, rob 1610

**volet** *nm*  shutter 2092

**voleur** *nadj*  thief, light-fingered 3163

**volontaire** *nadj(f)*  volunteer; voluntary 1675

**volontairement** *adv*  voluntarily, willingly 3529

**volonté** *nf*  will 525

**volontiers** *adv*  with pleasure, willingly, gladly 2742

**volume** *nm*  volume 1640

**vote** *nm*  vote 1046

**voter** *v*  to vote 1248

**votre** *det*  your 214

**vôtre** *nadj(f)*  yours 4065

**vouer** *v*  to devote, dedicate to, vow to 2950

**vouloir** *nm,v*  to want 57

**vous** *pro*  you 50

**voyage** *nm*  trip, journey 904

**voyager** *v* to travel **2194**
**voyageur** *nadj* traveler **2629**
**vrai** *adv,nadj* true **292**
**vraiment** *adv* truly, really, very **361**
**vraisemblablement** *adv* most probably **3739**
**vue** *nf* view **191**
**vulgaire** *nadj(f)* vulgar, common, popular **4886**
**vulnérable** *adj(f)* vulnerable **3479**

## Ww
**week-end** *nm* weekend **2475**

## Yy
**y** *adv,nmi,pro* there **36**
**yen** *nm* yen **4017**
**yougoslave** *nadj(f)* Yugoslav, Yugoslavian **4077**

## Zz
**zéro** *nm* zero **2274**
**zone** *nf* zone, area **860**

# Part of speech index

## Function words

### Conjunctions

6 **et** and
9 **que** that, which, who, whom
30 **mais** but
32 **comme** like, as
33 **ou** or
34 **si** if, whether
44 **aussi** too, also, as
119 **quand** when
145 **donc** so, then, therefore, thus
166 **soit** either...or
176 **car** because
193 **pourquoi** why
229 **ni** nor
234 **comment** how
256 **lorsque** when
300 **or** now
352 **cependant** however
528 **puisque** since
770 **toutefois** however
800 **combien** how much, how many
1170 **sinon** otherwise, or else
1271 **néanmoins** nevertheless
3243 **quoique** although, though

### Determiners

1 **le** the
2 **de** some, any
3 **un** a, an, one
12 **ce** this, that
24 **tout** all, very
26 **son** his, her, its
28 **autre** other
35 **leur** them, their, theirs
41 **deux** two
56 **premier** first
60 **mon** my
63 **aucun** none, either, neither, not any
70 **quelque** some
73 **notre** our
110 **certain** certain
115 **trois** three
142 **tel** such
146 **quel** which, what
151 **chaque** each
213 **plusieurs** several
214 **votre** your
253 **quatre** four
288 **cinq** five
330 **ton** your
372 **dix** ten
379 **second** second
427 **deuxième** second
450 **six** six
506 **troisième** third
704 **cent** one hundred
752 **divers** diverse, various
787 **neuf** nine
801 **nul** nil, null
877 **huit** eight
905 **sept** seven
1008 **mille** a thousand
1273 **vingt** twenty
1472 **quinze** fifteen
1542 **seconde** second
1603 **quatrième** fourth
1646 **trente** thirty
1664 **douze** twelve
2030 **cinquième** fifth
2273 **cinquante** fifty
2436 **quarante** forty
2447 **onze** eleven
3124 **sixième** sixth
3151 **soixante** sixty
3245 **treize** thirteen
3285 **seize** sixteen
3359 **quatorze** fourteen
3592 **dix-huit** eighteen
3812 **dix-sept** seventeen
3881 **vingtième** twentieth
3997 **dix-neuvième** nineteenth
4028 **septième** seventh
4149 **vingt-quatre** twenty four
4436 **vingt-cinq** twenty five
4602 **dixième** tenth
4778 **huitième** eighth
4851 **dix-neuf** nineteen
4887 **soixante-dix** seventy

### Interjections

30 **mais** but
75 **non** no
94 **bon** good
109 **là** there, here
234 **comment** how
284 **oui** yes
736 **d'accord** okay, alright
889 **euh** er, um, uh
1070 **merci** thank you
1361 **oh** oh
1405 **ah** ah, oh
1692 **eh** hey, uh
1928 **ouais** yeah
1979 **bonjour** hello
2076 **hein** eh, huh
2205 **salut** hi, bye
2262 **dieu** god
2376 **merde** sh*t, crap
2581 **gare** look out!
3570 **mince** rats!
3722 **tiens** ah, well
3871 **hé** hey
3952 **hélas** alas
3968 **adieu** goodbye, farewell, adieu
3984 **diable** devil
4564 **bravo** bravo, well done
4938 **hum** um, uh
4965 **ha** oh

## Prepositions

2 **de** of, from, some, any

4 **à** to, at, in

7 **en** in, by

10 **pour** for, in order to

11 **dans** in, into, from

16 **sur** on, upon

21 **par** by

23 **avec** with

40 **avant** before

55 **entre** between

62 **moins** less

71 **sans** without

82 **après** after

89 **pendant** during

96 **depuis** since, for

121 **contre** against

122 **sous** under

134 **jusque** to, up to, until

182 **vers** toward

185 **dès** from, as soon

198 **devant** in front, ahead

206 **chez** at, with

225 **près** near, nearby, close by

240 **selon** according to

389 **parmi** among

394 **plein** full

406 **malgré** despite, in spite of

476 **sauf** except

501 **passé** past

524 **voilà** right, there, here

678 **environ** about, thereabouts, or so

795 **durant** during, for

805 **derrière** behind

838 **proche** nearby, close

865 **hors** except, outside

974 **outre** besides

1103 **voici** here is, here are, this is, these are

1121 **suivant** following

1151 **envers** towards

1217 **dehors** outside

1376 **vis-à-vis** face to face, regarding

1629 **dessus** above, on top

2628 **dessous** underneath, below, bottom, underside

3058 **dedans** inside, indoors

3090 **touchant** with regard to, concerning, touching, moving

3513 **via** via

4786 **hormis** save, but

## Pronouns

1 **le** him, her, it, them

3 **un** a, an, one

7 **en** in, by

9 **que** that, which, who, whom

12 **ce** this, that

13 **il** he, it

14 **qui** who, whom

17 **se** oneself, himself, herself, itself, themselves

22 **je** I

24 **tout** all

28 **autre** other

29 **on** one, we

31 **nous** we, us

35 **leur** them, their, theirs

36 **y** there

38 **elle** she, her

42 **même** same, even, self

45 **celui** that, the one, he, him

48 **où** where

50 **vous** you

54 **cela** that, it

61 **me** me, to me, myself

63 **aucun** none, either, neither, not any

64 **lui** him, her

74 **dont** whose, of which

84 **personne** person, people, anybody, anyone, nobody

92 **lequel** who, whom, which

110 **certain** certain, sure

112 **tu** you

131 **moi** me

142 **tel** such

146 **quel** which, what

161 **eux** them

168 **rien** nothing

207 **te** you, to you, from you

213 **plusieurs** several

247 **ci** this one, here

297 **quoi** what

323 **chacun** each

510 **toi** you, yourself

522 **lui-même** himself

732 **ceci** this

772 **quelqu'un** somebody, someone

801 **nul** nil, null

1365 **soi** one, oneself, self

1379 **elle-même** herself, itself

1527 **moi-même** myself

2165 **mien** mine

2514 **quelques-uns** some, a few

3222 **quiconque** whoever, anyone who

3511 **nous-mêmes** ourselves

3940 **autrui** others

## Adjectives

3 **un** a, an, one

16 **sur** on, upon

35 **leur** them, their, theirs

40 **avant** before

42 **même** same, even, self

47 **bien** well

52 **nouveau** new

62 **moins** less

63 **aucun** none, either, neither, not any

70 **quelque** some

89 **pendant** during

94 **bon** good

101 **seul** alone, only

107 **fort** strong

110 **certain** certain, sure

111 **fin** fine

126 **enfant** child

141 **fait** done, fact

142 **tel** such

143 **droit** right

146 **quel** which, what

151 **chaque** each

175 **possible** possible

186 **moyen** medium

213 **plusieurs** several

217 **mieux** better

270 **sûr** sure

276 **mort** dead

277 **mal** bad

314 **courant** current

344 **libre** free

| | | | | | |
|---|---|---|---|---|---|
| 350 | **différent** different | 1155 | **global** global | 1759 | **immense** immense |
| 366 | **nombreux** numerous | 1178 | **récent** recent | 1762 | **constant** constant |
| 379 | **second** second | 1205 | **disponible** available | 1763 | **sain** healthy, sane |
| 392 | **ancien** ancient; former | 1216 | **bleu** blue | 1765 | **aérien** aerial |
| 393 | **beau** handsome, fine, right | 1225 | **excellent** excellent | 1770 | **régulier** regular |
| 402 | **unique** unique | 1233 | **rare** rare | 1793 | **agricole** agricultural, |
| 422 | **prêt** ready | 1234 | **extraordinaire** | | farming |
| 476 | **sauf** safe | | extraordinary | 1801 | **uniforme** uniform, steady, |
| 513 | **tôt** early | 1242 | **sud** south | | regular |
| 518 | **objectif** objective | 1243 | **efficace** efficient, effective | 1811 | **communautaire** |
| 545 | **court** short | 1244 | **intéressant** interesting | | community, communal |
| 549 | **mondial** world, global | 1267 | **supplémentaire** additional | 1812 | **individuel** individual |
| 554 | **publique** public | 1291 | **fondamental** fundamental | 1827 | **susceptible** sensitive, |
| 555 | **faux** false | 1310 | **terrible** terrible, dreadful | | touchy |
| 584 | **actuel** current, present | 1321 | **léger** light | 1828 | **étroit** narrow, tight |
| 600 | **bref** brief | 1322 | **permanent** permanent | 1841 | **content** glad, pleased, happy |
| 610 | **capable** able, capable | 1331 | **fier** proud | 1843 | **triste** sad |
| 618 | **large** wide, width | 1347 | **habituel** customary, | 1855 | **judiciaire** judiciary |
| 654 | **véritable** real, true | | habitual | 1859 | **strict** strict, absolute |
| 663 | **énorme** enormous | 1357 | **fou** mad, crazy | 1885 | **incident** incident |
| 671 | **vieux** old | 1367 | **net** clear | 1908 | **gouvernemental** |
| 691 | **frais** cool, fresh | 1380 | **démocratique** democratic | | governmental |
| 708 | **blanc** white | 1443 | **favorable** favorable | 1934 | **quelconque** any, some |
| 713 | **dangereux** dangerous | 1488 | **évident** obvious | 1985 | **durable** durable, long- |
| 726 | **spécial** special | 1495 | **culturel** cultural | | lasting |
| 752 | **divers** diverse, various | 1504 | **arrière** back, rear | 1993 | **scolaire** school, educational, |
| 769 | **instant** instant, moment | 1511 | **considérable** considerable, | | academic |
| 786 | **feu** fire | | significant | 1996 | **budgétaire** budgetary |
| 787 | **neuf** new | 1526 | **radio** radio | 1997 | **inquiétant** worrying, |
| 801 | **nul** nil, null | 1529 | **prudent** prudent, careful, | | disturbing |
| 803 | **cher** expensive | | cautious | 2011 | **sport** sport |
| 822 | **facile** easy | 1537 | **suffisant** sufficient | 2015 | **généreux** generous |
| 833 | **normal** normal | 1540 | **modeste** modest | 2021 | **raisonnable** reasonable, fair |
| 893 | **honorable** honorable, | 1564 | **conscient** conscious, aware | 2040 | **remarquable** remarkable, |
| | worthy | 1566 | **médical** medical | | outstanding |
| 897 | **ouvert** open | 1574 | **traditionnel** traditional | 2044 | **issu** descended from |
| 942 | **franc** frank | 1594 | **sexuel** sexual | 2052 | **censé** supposed |
| 965 | **complet** full, complete | 1597 | **âgé** old | 2060 | **fameux** famous |
| 1003 | **utile** useful | 1622 | **familial** family | 2067 | **électrique** electric |
| 1024 | **ferme** firm | 1625 | **armé** armed | 2075 | **provisoire** temporary, |
| 1026 | **lourd** heavy | 1637 | **fiscal** fiscal | | provisional |
| 1039 | **échec** failure | 1665 | **juridique** legal, judicial | 2099 | **alimentaire** food |
| 1090 | **nord** north | 1684 | **annuel** annual | 2107 | **fragile** fragile, delicate, frail |
| 1105 | **moindre** lesser, least, | 1689 | **célèbre** famous | 2136 | **magnifique** magnificent |
| | slightest | 1690 | **ouest** west | 2137 | **initial** initial |
| 1117 | **demi** half | 1714 | **électoral** electoral | 2143 | **pair** peer, pair, even |
| 1130 | **nucléaire** nuclear | 1733 | **sévère** severe | 2166 | **drôle** funny, strange |
| 1133 | **exact** exact, correct | 1739 | **monétaire** monetary | 2167 | **plat** dish, flat |
| 1142 | **vaste** vast, immense | 1746 | **indispensable** essential | 2175 | **spécifique** specific |

3134  **turc** Turk, Turkish
3144  **romain** Roman
3146  **originaire** original, first, native to
3149  **coûteux** expensive, costly
3158  **manuel** manual
3160  **territorial** territorial, land
3168  **musical** musical
3180  **sincère** sincere
3182  **maximal** maximal
3190  **horrible** horrible, terrible, dreadful, hideous
3196  **homologue** counterpart, homologue
3197  **successif** successive
3199  **olympique** Olympic
3202  **propice** favorable, auspicious, propitious
3211  **restant** remaining, the rest, the remainder
3218  **consécutif** consecutive
3220  **institutionnel** institutional
3262  **compétent** competent
3263  **sable** sand
3271  **cohérent** coherent
3276  **substantiel** substantial
3303  **applicable** applicable
3304  **équitable** equitable, fair
3308  **dépendant** answerable, responsible, dependent
3330  **spectaculaire** spectacular
3344  **exigeant** demanding, difficult
3348  **pertinent** pertinent, relevant
3357  **cruel** cruel, ferocious, bitter
3366  **amical** friendly
3369  **invisible** invisible
3383  **reconnaissant** grateful
3385  **inattendu** unexpected
3389  **géographique** geographic, geographical
3407  **stupide** stupid, silly, bemused
3408  **surpris** surprised, amazed
3466  **imminent** imminent, impending
3476  **théorique** theoretical

3478  **scandaleux** scandalous, outrageous
3479  **vulnérable** vulnerable
3495  **multinational** multinational
3518  **préférable** preferable
3525  **adéquat** appropriate, suitable, adequate
3530  **magique** magical
3533  **raide** stiff, straight
3535  **artistique** artistic
3544  **réussi** successful
3545  **bilatéral** bilateral
3548  **environnemental** environmental
3563  **élevé** high, heavy, tall
3570  **mince** thin, slim, slender
3586  **soucieux** concerned, worried
3591  **approprié** appropriate
3599  **alerte** agile, alert, warning
3617  **représentatif** representative
3625  **postal** postal, mail
3637  **soi-disant** so-called, supposedly
3639  **salarial** salary
3652  **minimal** minimal, minimum
3690  **pénible** hard, difficult, painful, tiresome
3713  **incompatible** incompatible
3744  **primordial** primordial, basic, vital, primary
3753  **fermé** shut, closed, locked
3761  **confus** confused, embarrassed
3768  **réputé** famous, renowned
3769  **indirect** indirect
3770  **apte** capable
3787  **divin** divine, heavenly
3789  **épais** thick, pitch dark, thickly
3798  **explicite** explicitly
3803  **apparent** apparent, obvious
3810  **serré** tight, packed, crowded
3818  **touristique** holiday, tourist
3819  **obscur** dark, vague, obscure
3823  **flou** blurred, fuzzy, vague
3825  **consultatif** advisory

3838  **précaire** precarious, makeshift
3845  **crédible** credible
3862  **ultérieur** later, subsequent
3872  **génial** inspired, great, brilliant
3885  **virtuel** virtual, potential
3899  **prestigieux** prestigious
3908  **accompli** accomplished
3912  **orange** orange
3920  **souhaitable** desirable
3925  **flagrant** blatant, glaring
3930  **subit** sudden
3946  **transitoire** transient, interim, provisional
3947  **tardif** late
3949  **natal** native, home
3961  **authentique** genuine, authentic
3964  **confortable** comfortable
3966  **fonctionnel** functional
3975  **productif** productive
3986  **spontané** spontaneous
3995  **honteux** ashamed, shameful
4002  **portable** portable, wearable
4003  **précoce** early, precocious
4012  **rassurant** reassuring, comforting
4018  **gras** fatty, fat, greasy
4019  **médiatique** media
4030  **charmant** charming
4039  **constructif** constructive
4050  **convaincant** convincing
4054  **grossier** unrefined, crude, coarse, rude, rough
4074  **erroné** erroneous
4086  **respectueux** respectful
4103  **chaleureux** warm
4110  **instable** unstable
4126  **filial** filial
4147  **fiable** reliable, trustworthy
4150  **épouvantable** terrible, appalling, dreadful
4156  **naval** naval
4173  **compétitif** competitive
4179  **concurrentiel** competitive
4200  **encourageant** encouraging
4201  **climatique** climatic

4961 **performant** productive, efficient

4978 **insignifiant** insignificant, unimportant

4980 **solidaire** interdependent, jointly dependent

4981 **ferroviaire** railway, rail

4996 **réfléchi** thoughtful, well thought-out

4999 **exprès** deliberately, on purpose, intentionally

## Adverbs

15 **ne** not

18 **pas** not, n't

19 **plus** more, no more

24 **tout** all, very

30 **mais** but

32 **comme** like, as

34 **si** if, whether

36 **y** there

40 **avant** before

42 **même** same, even, self

44 **aussi** too, also, as

47 **bien** well

48 **où** where

51 **encore** again, yet

58 **déjà** already

59 **grand** great, big, tall

62 **moins** less

66 **très** very

70 **quelque** some

75 **non** no, not

81 **alors** then, so

82 **après** after

91 **peu** little

94 **bon** good

96 **depuis** since, for

97 **point** point

98 **ainsi** thus

103 **toujours** always

107 **fort** strong

109 **là** there, here

119 **quand** when

121 **contre** against

124 **ensemble** together

130 **seulement** only

134 **jusque** to, up to, until

143 **droit** right

150 **beaucoup** much, a lot of, many

166 **soit** either...or

167 **ici** here

168 **rien** nothing

179 **jamais** never

181 **tant** so much, so many

190 **peut-être** perhaps, maybe

192 **maintenant** now

193 **pourquoi** why

195 **trop** too much, too many

198 **devant** in front, ahead

202 **long** long, lengthy

217 **mieux** better

225 **près** near, nearby, close by

230 **puis** then, so

233 **aujourd'hui** today

234 **comment** how

235 **surtout** especially, above all

246 **également** also, too, as well, equally

247 **ci** this one, here

264 **haut** top, high

265 **ensuite** next

272 **plutôt** rather

274 **mauvais** bad, wrong

277 **mal** bad

284 **oui** yes

287 **souvent** often

292 **vrai** true

304 **juste** just, only; fair

312 **longtemps** a long time, a long while

321 **assez** enough

326 **d'abord** first of all

335 **clair** clear

341 **loin** far

348 **tard** late

349 **enfin** at last, finally

352 **cependant** however

360 **ailleurs** elsewhere, somewhere else

361 **vraiment** truly, really, very

377 **autant** as much, as many

394 **plein** full

410 **parfois** sometimes

411 **lors** at the time of

419 **gros** big

439 **notamment** notably

443 **grave** serious, grave

460 **pourtant** yet, nonetheless, nevertheless

468 **bas** low

481 **presque** almost

513 **tôt** early

545 **court** short

555 **faux** false

560 **c'est-à-dire** in other words

581 **partout** everywhere

588 **d'ailleurs** moreover, besides, for that matter

593 **rapidement** quickly, rapidly

594 **autour** around

600 **bref** brief

614 **auprès** nearby, close to

615 **simplement** simply

618 **large** wide, width

678 **environ** about, thereabouts, or so

711 **vite** fast, quickly

718 **davantage** more

728 **actuellement** at present, at the moment

770 **toutefois** however

779 **particulièrement** particularly

800 **combien** how much, how many

803 **cher** expensive

805 **derrière** last

807 **immédiatement** immediately

838 **proche** nearby, close

843 **finalement** finally, eventually

857 **exactement** exactly

865 **hors** except, outside

869 **tellement** so much

871 **demain** tomorrow

872 **hier** yesterday

888 **directement** directly

903 **probablement** probably

942 **franc** frank

974 **outre** besides

1001 **auparavant** beforehand

1009 **absolument** absolutely

1013 **complètement** completely

3537 **habituellement** usually, generally

3538 **quasiment** almost, early

3555 **précédemment** previously

3579 **pis** worse

3587 **premièrement** first

3594 **brusquement** abruptly, suddenly

3647 **soigneusement** tidily, neatly, carefully

3651 **physiquement** physically

3657 **politiquement** politically, diplomatically

3677 **visiblement** obviously, clearly, visibly

3697 **activement** actively

3730 **deuxièmement** secondly

3739 **vraisemblablement** most probably

3789 **épais** thick, pitch dark, thickly

3796 **là-dedans** inside, in it

3800 **par-dessus** over

3810 **serré** tight, packed, crowded

3843 **différemment** differently

3857 **dorénavant** from now on, henceforth

3860 **radicalement** radically

3902 **nullement** not in the least

3909 **terriblement** terribly, awfully

3962 **attentivement** attentively, carefully, closely

3965 **au-dessous** underneath

3969 **entre-temps** meanwhile, in the meantime

4009 **carrément** completely, directly, straight out

4015 **économiquement** economically

4023 **efficacement** efficiently, effectively

4057 **sensiblement** approximately, more or less, noticeably

4078 **explicitement** explicitly

4090 **simultanément** simultaneously

4091 **techniquement** technically

4096 **délibérément** deliberately

4165 **alentour** around, round about

4181 **quotidiennement** daily, every day

4252 **initialement** initially

4266 **mutuellement** mutually, one another

4293 **partiellement** partly

4296 **indépendamment** independently, irrespective of, regardless of

4334 **brutalement** brutally

4335 **lourdement** heavily

4367 **delà** beyond, above, over

4408 **aucunement** in no way, not in the least, not at all

4409 **globalement** globally

4417 **prochainement** shortly, soon

4497 **génétiquement** genetically

4527 **conjointement** jointly

4534 **successivement** successively

4535 **assurément** most certainly

4550 **infiniment** infinitely

4557 **indirectement** indirectly

4579 **continuellement** continually, continuously

4632 **concrètement** in concrete terms

4644 **logiquement** logically

4691 **présentement** at present, presently

4698 **fondamentalement** basically, fundamentally, inherently

4726 **inévitablement** inevitably

4795 **jadis** formerly, long ago

4808 **théoriquement** theoretically

4815 **traditionnellement** traditionally

4818 **gratuitement** free, gratuitously

4859 **couramment** fluently, commonly

4882 **résolument** resolutely

4917 **sévèrement** severely, harshly

4967 **piano** piano

4991 **provisoirement** temporarily, provisionally

4999 **exprès** deliberately, on purpose, intentionally

## Nouns

5 **être** being

8 **avoir** possession

18 **pas** footstep

20 **pouvoir** power

26 **son** sound; bran

37 **dire** saying

39 **devoir** duty

40 **avant** before

41 **deux** two

47 **bien** well

49 **fois** time, times

52 **nouveau** new

57 **vouloir** desire

62 **moins** less

65 **temps** time

67 **savoir** knowledge

72 **raison** reason

75 **non** no, not

76 **an** year

77 **monde** world, people

78 **jour** day

79 **monsieur** mister, sir, gentleman

84 **personne** person, people, anybody, anyone, nobody

86 **part** share

89 **pendant** pendant

93 **suite** result, follow-up, rest

94 **bon** good

97 **point** point

99 **heure** hour

102 **année** year

106 **parler** language

107 **fort** strong

110 **certain** certain, sure

111 **fin** end; gist, clever person

114 **pays** country

424 **député** deputy, parlementary delegate

427 **deuxième** second

428 **résultat** result, follow-up

430 **terre** earth, world, soil, land

432 **dollar** dollar

434 **page** page

435 **confiance** confidence, trust

436 **choix** choice

438 **chance** luck; chance

440 **type** type; guy

441 **but** goal, aim, objective, purpose

442 **matin** morning

443 **grave** serious, grave

444 **prise** grip, hold, seizure, catch

446 **étude** study

447 **principe** principle

450 **six** six

452 **activité** activity

453 **valeur** value, worth

456 **réponse** answer, response

457 **aide** help, assistance

461 **commission** commission

465 **époque** era, period

468 **bas** low; stocking

470 **moitié** half

471 **avenir** future

472 **argent** money

473 **mise** putting, placing

474 **œil** eye

475 **eau** water

477 **école** school

478 **sécurité** security, safety

479 **milieu** middle

480 **lettre** letter

482 **attention** attention

483 **cadre** frame, executive

485 **mouvement** movement

488 **règle** rule

489 **poste** post, position; post office

490 **demande** request, demand

491 **centre** center

492 **acte** act

496 **accord** agreement

497 **milliard** billion, thousand million

502 **âge** age

505 **propos** remark

506 **troisième** third

508 **bout** bit, tip, end

509 **population** population

512 **route** road

514 **lancer** release

515 **limite** limit

516 **fonction** function

517 **emploi** employment, work, use

518 **objectif** objective, aim, goal; lens

519 **paraître** appear

520 **journal** newspaper, paper

523 **tour** tower; turn; tour

525 **volonté** will

530 **changement** change

532 **réalité** reality

538 **esprit** mind, spirit

539 **domaine** domain, field

542 **nature** nature

543 **régime** regime

548 **départ** departure

552 **parole** word

553 **fond** bottom

554 **publique** public

555 **faux** scythe

556 **genre** type, kind, sort

558 **communauté** community

561 **corps** body

562 **matière** matter, subject, material

563 **sein** breast, bosom

564 **difficulté** difficulty

566 **secteur** sector

567 **appel** call

568 **cœur** heart

569 **père** father

570 **organisation** organization

571 **unité** unity; unit

573 **événement** event

576 **nation** nation

577 **conseil** advice, counsel, council

579 **paix** peace

580 **nuit** night

582 **direction** direction, management

587 **journée** day

594 **autour** around

598 **rue** street

600 **bref** brief

602 **violence** violence

603 **siècle** century

604 **article** article

606 **qualité** quality

608 **solution** solution

609 **voie** road, lane, route, track, way

612 **erreur** mistake, error

616 **souvenir** memory

617 **conséquence** consequence

618 **large** wide, width

620 **succès** success

621 **élément** element

623 **été** summer

626 **pied** foot

627 **mission** mission

628 **débat** debate

629 **fille** girl, daughter

631 **texte** text

633 **chambre** bedroom, chamber

634 **création** creation

637 **justice** justice

638 **production** production

641 **santé** health

645 **mère** mother

646 **croissance** growth

647 **risque** risk

648 **arme** weapon

650 **endroit** place, spot

651 **comité** committee

653 **preuve** proof

659 **image** picture, image

660 **date** date

661 **travers** breadth, across; fault, amiss

662 **contrôle** control

666 **campagne** countryside

671 **vieux** old

674 **passage** passage, way

678 **environ** about, thereabouts, or so

679 **expérience** experience

684 **sénateur** senator

689 **processus** process

691 **frais** fee, expense

692 **industrie** industry

694 **responsabilité** responsibility

696 **porte** door

697 **victime** victim

698 **territoire** territory

700 **taux** rate

704 **cent** one hundred, cent

707 **signe** sign

708 **blanc** white

709 **origine** origin, source

712 **langue** language, tongue

715 **importance** importance

717 **espoir** hope

720 **énergie** energy

721 **réseau** network

725 **possibilité** possibility

729 **union** union

735 **fils** son

738 **différence** difference

741 **avis** opinion, mind

746 **intervention** intervention; talk

749 **chiffre** figure, number

755 **peur** fear

756 **parlement** parliament

759 **lutte** struggle, fight, conflict

761 **air** air, appearance

762 **auteur** author

763 **opération** operation

765 **crise** crisis

766 **numéro** number

769 **instant** instant, moment

773 **discours** speech, talk, discourse

774 **banque** bank

775 **compagnie** company

777 **opinion** opinion

778 **classe** class

782 **intention** intention

783 **autorité** authority

785 **échange** exchange

786 **feu** fire

787 **neuf** nine; new

789 **capacité** capacity, ability

792 **message** message

794 **scène** scene

797 **plaisir** pleasure

798 **dossier** file, record; case

799 **proposition** proposition, proposal

802 **absence** absence

805 **derrière** last; behind

806 **connaissance** knowledge

808 **entrée** entrance

812 **salle** room

813 **pièce** piece, part, component; room

814 **équipe** team

817 **source** source, spring

818 **respect** respect

819 **crime** crime

825 **impression** impression

826 **octobre** October

827 **médecin** physician, doctor

829 **police** police

830 **coût** cost

831 **formation** training

832 **contrat** contract

834 **attitude** attitude

835 **faute** mistake, error, fault

836 **série** series

845 **pression** pressure

846 **accès** access

847 **champ** field, realm

848 **film** film

849 **charge** charge, load

851 **commune** locality

852 **ressource** resource

855 **motion** motion

859 **chemin** path, way

860 **zone** zone, area

861 **province** province

862 **élection** election

863 **usage** use, usage

864 **conflit** conflict

866 **enquête** inquiry, enquiry, investigation

867 **terrain** ground, terrain

868 **mars** March

870 **espace** space

871 **demain** tomorrow

875 **égard** consideration, respect, regard

877 **huit** eight

880 **lien** link, bond

881 **voiture** car

882 **discussion** discussion

885 **agent** agent

886 **sentiment** feeling

887 **tâche** task

891 **décembre** December

894 **contact** contact

896 **fruit** fruit

898 **investissement** investment

900 **avantage** advantage

901 **garde** guard

904 **voyage** trip, journey

905 **sept** seven

906 **marche** walk, step, march

907 **vérité** truth

910 **ministère** ministry

912 **somme** amount, sum; nap

913 **culture** culture

917 **client** client

919 **progrès** progress

920 **secrétaire** secretary

921 **mer** sea

924 **liste** list

926 **mémoire** memory

927 **caractère** nature, character

930 **nécessité** necessity, need

931 **juin** June

932 **danger** danger

934 **commerce** trade, commerce

935 **transport** transportation

936 **attente** wait

937 **institution** institution

938 **défense** defense

939 **janvier** January

941 **négociation** negotiation

942 **franc** frank; franc

943 **mai** May

944 **septembre** September

945 **environnement** environment

947 **réaction** reaction

948 **disposition** arrangement, disposition

951 **papier** paper

952 **expression** expression

953 **protection** protection

955 **carte** card

956 **association** association

958 **modèle** model

962 **budget** budget

964 **structure** structure

965 **complet** suit

967 **amour** love

970 **conseiller** adviser

971 **réunion** meeting

972 **opposition** opposition

973 **maladie** illness, disease

976 **construction** construction, building

977 **bande** band, strip

978 **signal** signal

980 **réforme** reform

982 **novembre** November

983 **fonds** funds

985 **reprise** resumption, renewal; time

986 **presse** press

988 **majorité** majority

991 **bord** edge, side

993 **procédure** procedure

994 **faveur** favor

995 **éducation** education

997 **document** document

998 **aspect** aspect

1005 **concurrence** competition

1006 **déclaration** declaration

1008 **mille** a thousand

1010 **prison** prison

1011 **armée** army

1012 **revenu** income

1013 **complètement** completely

1015 **salaire** salary, wage

1016 **lecture** reading

1019 **table** table

1022 **avril** April

1024 **ferme** farm

1028 **république** republic

1030 **application** application

1032 **profit** profit, benefit

1036 **communication** communication

1037 **jugement** judgement

1038 **manque** lack

1039 **échec** failure

1042 **engagement** agreement, commitment

1043 **frère** brother

1044 **mardi** Tuesday

1045 **rencontre** meeting

1046 **vote** vote

1049 **espèce** species

1050 **recommandation** recommendation

1054 **circonstance** circumstance

1055 **témoin** witness

1057 **administration** administration

1059 **lumière** light

1062 **combat** fight, combat

1065 **vitesse** speed

1067 **portée** range, reach, scope

1068 **élève** pupil, student

1070 **merci** thank you; favor

1072 **visite** visit

1073 **assemblée** assembly, meeting

1074 **émission** transmision, broadcasting, programme

1075 **arrivée** arrival

1076 **puissance** power

1077 **partenaire** partner

1079 **perte** loss

1083 **influence** influence

1084 **camp** camp

1085 **établissement** establishment, organization

1086 **vendredi** Friday

1087 **avance** advance

1090 **nord** north

1091 **lundi** Monday

1092 **maître** master

1094 **conférence** conference

1096 **vente** sale

1098 **soldat** soldier

1099 **collègue** colleague

1102 **poids** weight

1109 **soin** care

1111 **traitement** treatment, salary, wage

1112 **jeudi** Thursday

1114 **science** science

1115 **individu** individual

1116 **donnée** fact, datum

1117 **demi** half

1124 **conscience** conscience, consciousness

1126 **sang** blood

1127 **millier** thousand

1129 **initiative** initiative

1134 **exception** exception

1136 **février** February

1137 **mode** mode, way, fashion

1139 **musique** music

1140 **gestion** management

1141 **honneur** honor

1145 **étape** stage, step

1149 **méthode** method, procedure

1150 **professeur** professor, teacher

1151 **envers** towards

1153 **existence** existence

1156 **dommage** damage, harm; too bad

1157 **crédit** credit

1158 **tendance** tendency, trend

1159 **chaîne** chain, channel

1161 **note** note, grade

1162 **réserve** reserve

1165 **version** version

1166 **règlement** rule, regulation

1167 **couple** couple

1168 **mercredi** Wednesday

1172 **au-delà** beyond

1174 **sortie** exit

1179 **télévision** television

1180 **retraite** retirement, pension

1181 **art** art

1182 **frontière** border

1184 **promesse** promise

1187 **quartier** district, quarter

1188 **avocat** lawyer

1192 **université** university

1193 **rire** laughing

1195 **crainte** fear

1198 **soutien** support

1199 **urgence** emergency

1200 **clé** key

1204 **analyse** analysis

1206 **regard** look, glance

1210 **mariage** marriage

1211 **couleur** color

1215 **conclusion** conclusion

1216 **bleu** blue

1217 **dehors** outside

1221 **habitude** habit

1466  **baisse** fall, drop

1467  **inquiétude** worry, anxiety

1469  **représentation** representation

1471  **mandat** term, mandate

1472  **quinze** fifteen

1474  **statut** status

1475  **essai** attempt, try, test

1476  **sourire** smile

1481  **agence** agency

1482  **usine** factory

1484  **rang** rank, row

1485  **employé** employee

1486  **sommet** summit

1489  **comportement** behavior

1490  **fête** holiday, celebration

1491  **sol** floor, ground

1493  **vague** vague; wave

1494  **réduction** reduction

1496  **coopération** cooperation

1497  **vertu** virtue

1499  **leader** leader

1500  **taille** size, height

1502  **distance** distance

1503  **automne** fall, autumn

1504  **arrière** back, rear

1505  **vision** vision, view

1512  **conduite** behavior, driving

1513  **convention** agreement, convention

1517  **évidence** evidence

1521  **approche** approach

1522  **délai** delay

1524  **bruit** noise

1525  **humanité** humanity

1526  **radio** radio

1528  **syndicat** union

1530  **soirée** evening

1531  **vol** flight, theft

1534  **mètre** meter

1538  **ciel** sky

1542  **seconde** second

1548  **témoignage** testimony

1549  **messieurs** gentlemen

1551  **gaz** gas

1552  **acteur** actor

1554  **cour** yard, court

1555  **dépense** expense, expenditure

1556  **souci** worry, concern

1558  **sœur** sister

1561  **procès** trial, proceedings

1568  **colère** anger

1570  **notion** notion

1571  **siège** seat, bench

1572  **hausse** rise, raise, increase

1573  **mécanisme** mechanism

1577  **trafic** traffic, circulation

1579  **foyer** home, hearth

1582  **métier** job, occupation, trade

1583  **modification** modification

1585  **médias** media

1586  **hiver** winter

1587  **définition** definition

1589  **mari** husband

1596  **renseignement** information

1598  **fonctionnement** operation, functioning

1599  **garçon** boy

1602  **prévision** forecast, prediction, expectation

1603  **quatrième** fourth

1604  **fenêtre** window

1607  **menace** threat

1609  **jeunesse** youth

1613  **séparation** separation

1615  **refus** refusal

1616  **poisson** fish

1617  **révolution** revolution

1621  **fer** iron

1623  **cinéma** cinema

1624  **calcul** calculation

1626  **enseignement** education, teaching

1628  **dizaine** approximately ten

1629  **dessus** top

1631  **fonctionnaire** state employee, public servant

1632  **instruction** instruction, direction

1636  **réalisation** realization, achievement

1638  **démarche** walk, process

1640  **volume** volume

1641  **réussite** success

1642  **désir** desire

1644  **exportation** export

1646  **trente** thirty

1647  **âme** soul

1649  **autorisation** authorization, permission, permit

1650  **instrument** instrument

1651  **indépendance** independence

1652  **tort** wrong

1653  **hauteur** height

1655  **attaque** attack

1656  **assurance** insurance, confidence

1657  **déficit** deficit

1659  **drogue** drug

1662  **rythme** rhythm, rate

1664  **douze** twelve

1667  **saison** season

1668  **épreuve** test, ordeal, trial

1669  **hypothèse** hypothesis

1671  **financement** financing

1672  **dos** back

1673  **consommateur** consumer, customer

1677  **finance** finance

1680  **quantité** quantity

1685  **commentaire** comment, remark

1687  **spectacle** sight, show

1688  **pari** bet

1690  **ouest** west

1691  **sexe** sex

1693  **recours** resort, recourse

1694  **accent** accent

1697  **concert** concert

1698  **couverture** blanket

1699  **religion** religion

1700  **appui** support

1701  **théâtre** theater

1704  **équipement** equipment

1706  **patron** boss

1707  **marge** margin

1708  **abri** shelter

1709  **recette** recipe

1711  **vigueur** vigor

1713  **soleil** sun

1716  **bourse** purse, scholarship

1717  **dimension** dimension

1719  **dialogue** dialogue

1720  **thème** theme, topic

1933 **transmission** transmission
1935 **courrier** mail, post
1938 **doigt** finger
1940 **poche** pocket
1943 **honte** shame
1944 **faiblesse** weakness
1945 **fédération** federation
1948 **bonheur** happiness
1951 **pauvreté** poverty
1952 **bâtiment** building
1953 **époux** husband, spouse
1954 **médicament** medicine, drug, medication
1955 **firme** firm
1957 **électeur** elector, voter
1959 **véhicule** vehicle
1963 **personnalité** personality
1966 **prudence** prudence, care, caution
1967 **stade** stadium, stage
1968 **liaison** liaison, connection
1969 **consultation** consultation
1972 **bonjour** hello
1973 **morale** ethics; moral
1976 **détermination** determination, resolution
1977 **congrès** congress, conference
1980 **dépôt** deposit, depot
1981 **considération** consideration
1983 **dame** lady
1984 **joie** joy
1986 **faim** hungry
1989 **concept** concept
1990 **cerveau** brain
1991 **truc** trick; thingamajig
1999 **style** style
2001 **ombre** shade, shadow
2005 **interprétation** interpretation
2006 **climat** climate
2007 **séjour** stay
2011 **sport** sport
2012 **amélioration** improvement
2013 **douleur** pain
2014 **issue** exit, outcome
2017 **talent** talent
2019 **remarque** remark

2025 **orientation** orientation, trend
2028 **reporter** reporter
2030 **cinquième** fifth
2031 **distinction** distinction
2032 **impact** impact
2033 **magazine** magazine
2035 **mérite** merit
2037 **collaboration** collaboration
2039 **officier** officer
2045 **poursuite** chase, pursuit
2053 **fuite** escape
2054 **conviction** conviction, belief
2057 **évaluation** evaluation
2058 **installation** installation, setup
2066 **bloc** block
2068 **seuil** doorstep, threshold
2071 **audience** audience, hearing
2073 **minorité** minority
2074 **phrase** sentence, phrase
2077 **disparition** disappearance
2080 **trouble** turmoil, agitation, blurred, cloudy, trouble
2083 **littérature** literature
2085 **adolescent** teenager, adolescent
2088 **agriculture** agriculture
2089 **gouverneur** governor
2090 **aventure** adventure
2092 **volet** shutter
2094 **prime** free gift, premium, bonus
2096 **occupation** occupation, pastime
2100 **lecteur** reader
2103 **vœu** vow, wish, will
2105 **conception** conception
2108 **satisfaction** satisfaction
2110 **publicité** advertising, advertisement, publicity
2111 **arbre** tree
2112 **univers** universe
2113 **aéroport** airport
2115 **chasse** chase, hunt, hunting
2116 **collège** secondary school, college
2117 **garantie** guarantee
2118 **morceau** piece, bit

2120 **discipline** discipline
2121 **explosion** explosion
2122 **peau** skin
2123 **commande** order, control
2126 **paragraphe** paragraph
2129 **diffusion** diffusion, spreading, circulation
2133 **copie** copy, replica, paper
2138 **indice** indication, sign, clue
2139 **promotion** promotion, advertising
2140 **branche** branch
2141 **section** section
2142 **chanson** song
2143 **pair** peer
2151 **cellule** cell
2154 **connexion** connection
2156 **option** option
2157 **pétrole** crude oil, petroleum
2158 **laboratoire** laboratory
2160 **coucher** sleep
2161 **département** department
2162 **génie** genius
2163 **profession** profession
2164 **rumeur** rumor
2167 **plat** dish, flat
2168 **maman** mom
2169 **incertitude** uncertainty
2171 **dignité** dignity
2173 **philosophie** philosophy
2174 **verre** glass
2176 **docteur** doctor
2178 **fréquence** frequency
2180 **trou** hole
2183 **éditeur** publisher, editor
2187 **signature** signature
2193 **héritage** heritage
2200 **satellite** satellite
2202 **fondé** founded, justified; agent, clerk
2205 **salut** salute, hi, bye
2207 **enfance** childhood
2213 **prière** prayer
2216 **musée** museum
2217 **pluie** rain
2218 **précaution** precaution
2220 **cheval** horse
2221 **communiqué** communiqué, release, statement

2222 **suicide** suicide

2223 **rivière** river

2225 **rédaction** writing, composition

2226 **enceinte** enclosure

2227 **substance** substance

2229 **récit** account, narrative

2230 **revendication** claim, demand

2232 **sondage** poll

2234 **composition** composition, essay, dialling

2236 **accusation** accusation, indictment

2237 **invitation** invitation

2243 **paiement** payment

2244 **comparaison** comparison

2246 **déplacement** movement, displacement, trip, travel

2248 **dispositif** device, apparatus

2250 **contrainte** constraint

2255 **immigration** immigration

2256 **cancer** cancer

2258 **cercle** circle, cycle

2260 **importation** import

2261 **tonne** ton

2262 **dieu** god

2263 **référendum** referendum

2266 **visiteur** visitor

2269 **étage** floor

2272 **amitié** friendship

2273 **cinquante** fifty

2274 **zéro** zero

2275 **drame** drama

2277 **haine** hatred, hate

2278 **instance** authority, proceedings, hearing

2279 **cérémonie** ceremony

2280 **ambition** ambition

2282 **sanction** sanction

2284 **jardin** garden

2285 **nourriture** food

2287 **infrastructure** infrastructure

2288 **adversaire** opponent, adversary

2293 **circulation** circulation, traffic

2294 **cotisation** subscription

2295 **entente** understanding, agreement

2296 **cheveu** hair

2298 **cadeau** present, gift

2299 **affirmation** assertion, affirmation

2301 **destination** destination

2302 **stabilité** stability

2304 **gars** guy

2305 **fleur** flower

2306 **agriculteur** farmer

2307 **poète** poet

2308 **fabrication** manufacture, production

2309 **vin** wine

2311 **balle** ball, bullet

2312 **inflation** inflation

2313 **sec** dry

2318 **transition** transition

2321 **adoption** adoption, passing

2323 **appartement** apartment, flat

2324 **session** session

2326 **ménage** housekeeping, housework

2328 **enjeu** stake

2330 **transformation** transformation, change

2332 **misère** poverty, misery

2336 **restaurant** restaurant

2337 **destin** fate, destiny

2338 **discrimination** discrimination

2339 **certitude** certainty

2340 **huile** oil

2342 **autonomie** autonomy

2343 **sac** bag, sack

2344 **stock** stock

2349 **barre** bar, rod

2350 **contradiction** contradiction

2353 **souveraineté** sovereignty

2355 **concentration** concentration

2357 **remise** presentation, delivery

2358 **mec** guy

2359 **solidarité** solidarity

2361 **décennie** decade

2365 **dîner** dinner

2371 **fortune** fortune

2374 **combattant** fighter

2376 **merde** sh*t, crap

2377 **entrepreneur** contractor, entrepreneur

2378 **exposition** exhibition, show

2380 **cri** shout, cry

2382 **désert** desert, wilderness

2383 **vêtement** garment, item or article of clothing

2386 **marchandise** merchandise, commodity

2388 **continent** continent

2392 **guide** guide

2393 **tabac** tabacco

2394 **rendement** yield, output

2395 **ampleur** extent, scope, range

2397 **désastre** disaster

2400 **écho** echo

2401 **fusion** fusion, melting, merging

2402 **innovation** innovation

2403 **sélection** selection

2406 **tournant** revolving, swivel, encircling, bend, turning point

2408 **collectivité** community, group

2409 **record** record

2412 **modalité** mode, method, modality

2413 **paquet** packet

2414 **fondation** foundation

2415 **terroriste** terrorist

2417 **organe** organ

2418 **protocole** etiquette, protocol

2419 **apparition** appearance, apparition

2420 **gain** gain

2421 **écran** screen

2428 **allusion** allusion

2429 **lancement** launch

2430 **porteur** carrier, holder

2434 **domicile** home, place of residence

2435 **oiseau** bird

2436  **quarante** forty

2437  **sacrifice** sacrifice

2438  **barrière** fence, barrier, gate

2439  **biais** way, device; bias

2440  **feuille** leaf, sheet, slip

2441  **délégation** delegation

2445  **congé** holiday, time off, day off, notice

2446  **taxe** tax

2447  **onze** eleven

2451  **préparation** preparation

2454  **possession** possession, ownership

2455  **rejet** rejection

2458  **papa** dad, daddy

2459  **collaborateur** associate, fellow worker, contributor, collaborator

2461  **technicien** technician

2462  **cycle** cycle

2465  **alcool** alcohol

2466  **prétexte** pretext

2468  **scénario** scenario, script

2469  **électricité** electricity

2472  **jambe** leg

2474  **privilège** privilege

2475  **week-end** weekend

2478  **invité** guest

2481  **blessure** injury, wound

2483  **midi** noon

2484  **disque** disc

2485  **couche** layer, coat

2490  **race** breed, race

2492  **beauté** beauty

2493  **atmosphère** atmosphere

2494  **épaule** shoulder

2496  **circonscription** district, constituency

2499  **recul** backward movement, setback, slip

2501  **flux** flow

2502  **horizon** horizon, skyline

2504  **subvention** subsidy

2507  **lait** milk

2511  **bibliothèque** library

2513  **océan** ocean

2518  **capitaine** captain

2521  **prévention** prevention, custody

2529  **destinée** fate, destiny

2530  **patrimoine** heritage, assets

2534  **intégration** integration

2537  **diversité** diversity

2541  **accueil** welcome, reception

2542  **camion** truck

2545  **prêtre** priest

2546  **indication** indication

2548  **décès** death

2552  **profil** profile, outline, contour

2556  **registre** log, register, registry

2559  **performance** performance

2560  **angle** angle, point of view

2561  **divorce** divorce

2562  **fermeture** closing

2565  **horreur** horror

2568  **faculté** ability, right, option, faculty, university

2569  **brillant** brilliant

2570  **pacte** pact, treaty

2573  **assistance** attendance, assistance

2578  **suppression** deletion, suppression

2579  **coupure** cut, cutting

2580  **glace** ice, ice cream; mirror

2581  **gare** station, railway station

2582  **drapeau** flag

2584  **sensibilité** sensitivity, sensibility

2587  **procureur** prosecutor

2589  **restriction** restriction

2593  **racine** root

2596  **gravité** seriousness, solemnity, graveness, gravity

2598  **civilisation** civilization

2602  **football** football, soccer

2604  **législation** legislation

2607  **thèse** thesis, argument

2610  **prince** prince

2611  **vidéo** video

2614  **partenariat** partnership

2615  **file** line, queue

2616  **chômeur** unemployed person

2618  **cuisine** cooking, kitchen

2620  **royaume** kingdom

2622  **provenance** origin, strange

2624  **dessin** drawing, pattern, design

2625  **viande** meat

2626  **paramètre** parameter

2627  **gré** liking

2628  **dessous** underneath, below, bottom, underside

2631  **condamnation** condemnation

2633  **employeur** employer

2634  **paysage** landscape, scenery, countryside

2636  **longueur** length

2638  **miracle** miracle

2641  **expansion** expansion

2644  **commandement** command, order, commandment

2647  **pause** break, pause

2648  **répartition** distribution, spreading

2651  **compétition** competition

2653  **touriste** tourist

2655  **pardon** forgiveness

2656  **filet** dribble, trickle, wisp, streak, thread, fillet, net

2658  **contribuable** taxpayer

2660  **progression** progression

2661  **nez** nose

2665  **adhésion** membership, support

2666  **portrait** portrait, photograph

2669  **coordination** coordination

2671  **rose** rose; pink

2672  **quête** quest, pursuit, collection

2673  **compromis** compromise, agreement

2674  **investisseur** investor

2676  **abandon** abandonment, desertion, withdrawal

2679  **mensonge** lie

2680  **défaite** defeat

2685  **œuf** egg

2686  **ambassadeur** ambassador

2689  **accessoire** accessory

2690 **acquisition** acquisition, acquire, purchase

2691 **tournée** tour, round

2692 **tranche** slice, edge, section, bracket, slot

2693 **plage** beach

2694 **inspecteur** inspector

2695 **tempête** storm, gale, turmoil

2699 **survie** survival

2701 **adaptation** adaptation

2702 **plante** plant

2704 **putain** whore, bitch

2705 **imagination** imagination

2708 **directive** guideline

2711 **coalition** coalition

2713 **excellence** excellence

2714 **apparence** appearance

2716 **écriture** writing

2717 **parcours** journey, course, route

2720 **révolte** revolt

2723 **tas** pile, lots of

2724 **déjeuner** lunch

2726 **élite** elite

2727 **malheur** misfortune

2728 **aube** dawn, daybreak

2729 **salon** lounge, living room

2731 **repos** rest

2734 **interdiction** ban, banning

2737 **médecine** medecine, medical science

2740 **cible** target

2743 **fauteuil** armchair, seat

2744 **couloir** corridor, aisle

2745 **enthousiasme** enthusiasm, enthusiastically

2746 **télé** TV

2748 **révision** review, revision, overhaul

2757 **abus** abuse, misuse, breach

2758 **procédé** processus

2760 **amateur** amateur

2761 **regret** regret, regretfully

2762 **accroissement** increase

2763 **trimestre** quarter

2764 **onde** wave

2768 **vache** cow

2771 **agression** agression

2772 **loisir** leisure

2773 **chaleur** heat

2775 **partage** division, cutting, sharing

2776 **étoile** star

2777 **mystère** mystery

2779 **description** description

2784 **dent** tooth

2788 **intelligence** intelligence

2790 **licence** licence, permit

2791 **rigueur** harshness, severity, rigidness, rigor, strictness

2793 **métal** metal

2794 **palais** palace, palate

2798 **signification** significance

2802 **pain** bread

2803 **plateau** plateau, tray, set, stage

2804 **répétition** repetition, rehearsal

2805 **diminution** reduction, decreasing

2806 **collection** collection, series

2807 **gène** gene

2808 **permanence** permanence, duty, service

2809 **reine** queen

2810 **privatisation** privatization

2811 **correspondance** correspondance, connection

2814 **violation** violation, transgression

2815 **compensation** compsensation, clearing

2816 **lycée** high school

2818 **combinaison** combination

2819 **injustice** injustice, unfairness

2820 **reportage** report, reporting

2821 **déception** disappointment, let-down

2823 **plafond** ceiling, roof, maximum

2824 **opérateur** operator

2825 **camarade** friend, comrade, pal, mate

2826 **traduction** translation

2827 **compréhension** understanding, comprehension

2828 **réglementation** regulation

2833 **folie** madness, folly, insanity

2834 **terrorisme** terrorism

2835 **illusion** illusion

2836 **portefeuille** wallet

2839 **clôture** enclosure; termination, closure

2842 **télécommunication** telecommunication

2843 **désaccord** disagreement, discord, conflict

2844 **uranium** uranium

2845 **aliment** food

2846 **alimentation** diet, food, groceries, supply

2847 **pomme** apple

2848 **ingénieur** engineer

2853 **larme** tear

2855 **cigarette** cigarette

2856 **vallée** valley

2860 **entrevue** meeting, interview

2861 **ressort** spring; resort; spirit

2863 **opportunité** opportunity, timeliness

2864 **robe** dress

2865 **plaque** plate, tag, plaque

2868 **piège** trap

2871 **refuge** refuge

2873 **pente** slope

2874 **album** album

2877 **spectateur** member of the audience, spectator, onlooker

2878 **axe** axis, axle, main line

2879 **chasseur** hunter, fighter, page, messenger

2881 **peinture** painting, paint, picture

2882 **déchet** scrap, waste, trash, garbage

2884 **grand-chose** not very much

2886 **affiche** poster, public notice, bill

2887 **massacre** massacre, slaughter

2888 **actualité** current events, news

2891 **marine** marine, navy

2892 **cadavre** corpse

2893 **fleuve** river

2894 **toit** roof

2896 **transparence** transparency

2899 **fondateur** founder

2900 **charte** charter

2901 **productivité** productivity

2902 **succession** succession

2907 **consentement** consent

2908 **chapeau** hat

2910 **mythe** myth

2911 **alternative** alternative, choice

2913 **scrutin** ballot, poll

2914 **culpabilité** guilt

2917 **introduction** introduction

2920 **pétition** petition

2922 **ordonnance** prescription, organization, edict, ruling

2923 **aile** wing, sail, blade

2924 **température** temperature

2925 **coupe** bowl, dish, cut

2926 **rayon** ray, beam, radius; department, section, shelf

2927 **lèvre** lip

2929 **boulot** work, job

2931 **colonne** column

2935 **charbon** coal

2937 **colline** hill

2938 **poésie** poetry

2940 **transaction** transaction

2941 **extrémité** end, extremity

2943 **économiste** economist

2944 **banlieue** suburbs, outskirts

2947 **calendrier** calendar

2948 **repas** meal

2949 **cul** bum, arse, ass

2952 **paradis** paradise, heaven

2955 **tourisme** tourism, sightseeing

2956 **démonstration** demonstration

2958 **infraction** offence, infringement, infraction

2959 **tir** fire, shot, launch

2960 **envoi** sending, dispatching

2961 **arrangement** arrangement, layout, order, agreement

2964 **danse** dance, dancing

2967 **genou** knee

2969 **péril** peril

2970 **préférence** preference, preferably

2972 **rentrée** reopening, return, start

2974 **monopole** monopoly

2976 **incendie** fire, blaze

2977 **proximité** proximity, nearness, closeness

2978 **hélicoptère** helicopter

2979 **bouteille** bottle

2980 **championnat** championship

2983 **entité** entity

2986 **mélange** mixing, mixture, blend

2987 **pourcentage** percentage, commission, cut

2988 **permis** license, permit, permitted

2993 **super** great

2998 **sagesse** wisdom, moderation

2999 **baiser** kiss

3001 **enfer** hell

3002 **pilote** pilot, experimental

3004 **objection** objection

3005 **correction** correction

3006 **vocation** vocation, calling

3007 **facture** invoice, bill

3009 **luxe** luxury

3010 **nomination** appointment, nomination

3011 **poster** poster

3012 **bar** bar

3015 **gueule** mouth, trap

3017 **sympathie** liking, warmth, friendship, sympathy

3020 **copain** friend, buddy, mate

3023 **compagnon** companion, craftsman, journeyman

3024 **déroulement** development, progress

3029 **matinée** morning

3031 **poème** poem

3032 **bassin** bowl, basin

3035 **rage** rage, fury, rabies

3036 **enregistrement** recording, registration, check-in, logging

3041 **dictature** dictatorship

3042 **acheteur** buyer, purchaser

3044 **édifice** building

3045 **lot** share, prize, lot

3046 **fondement** foundation

3048 **fournisseur** supplier, provider

3049 **détriment** detriment

3052 **élimination** elimination

3054 **col** collar, mountain pass

3057 **résidence** residence, block of flats

3058 **dedans** inside, indoors

3062 **patience** patience

3064 **classement** classification, ranking

3065 **arrestation** arrest

3067 **ancêtre** ancestor, forerunner

3068 **intensité** intensity

3069 **grandeur** size, greatness

3070 **entraînement** training, coaching, drive

3073 **pollution** pollution

3075 **attribution** awarding, allocation, assignment, attribution

3076 **caméra** camera

3079 **ère** era

3080 **rappel** reminder, summary, recall, return, remember

3081 **fabricant** manufacturer

3082 **utilité** use, usefulness,

3084 **annexe** annex, appendix, related issue

3085 **interlocuteur** speaker

3088 **rémunération** remuneration, payment, pay

3089 **faillite** bankruptcy, collapse, failure

3094 **vérification** check, verification

3097 **trésor** treasure, treasury

3295 **pompier** fireman, firefighter

3296 **inspection** inspection

3298 **pouce** thumb, inch

3299 **clientèle** customers, clientele

3301 **révélation** diclosure, revelation

3305 **schéma** diagram, outline

3306 **acier** steel

3307 **vainqueur** winner

3309 **sud-est** south-east

3311 **concession** concession

3313 **assassinat** murder, assassination

3314 **rive** shore, bank

3315 **tolérance** tolerance

3316 **clarté** lightness, brightness clearness, clarity

3321 **change** exchange

3322 **star** star

3323 **grain** grain, bean, bead; spot, mole

3325 **malaise** uneasiness, discomfort

3327 **ambassade** embassy

3328 **diplôme** diploma, certificate

3329 **miroir** mirror

3331 **restructuration** restructure, restructuring

3332 **proie** prey

3333 **domination** domination, dominion, rule

3334 **otage** hostage

3338 **demi-heure** half an hour

3339 **placement** investment, placing

3341 **grille** railings, gate, grid, scale

3343 **abord** manner; approach, access, environs

3346 **lune** moon

3347 **mention** mention, note, comment, notice

3350 **actionnaire** shareholder

3352 **raisonnement** reasoning

3354 **quai** platform, quay, embankment

3355 **légende** legend, caption, key

3356 **spécialité** speciality

3358 **démission** resignation

3359 **quatorze** fourteen

3361 **médaille** medal

3363 **impasse** dead end, cul-de-sac

3365 **atelier** workshop, studio

3367 **empire** empire

3373 **comédie** comedy, playacting

3374 **propagande** propaganda

3375 **colonie** colony

3376 **désordre** disorder, confusion

3379 **terreur** terror, dread

3382 **virus** virus

3386 **tunnel** tunnel

3387 **cousin** cousin

3390 **réacteur** reactor, jet engine

3393 **sommeil** sleep, sleepiness

3395 **balance** scales, balance

3396 **dépression** depression

3397 **pompe** pump

3398 **contestation** questioning, protest

3399 **inconvénient** snag, drawback, disadvantage, inconvenience

3400 **frein** brake

3401 **inspiration** inspiration

3402 **candidature** application, candidacy, candidature

3403 **armement** arms, weapons, armament

3404 **épargne** savings, saving

3412 **pavillon** country house, villa, wing, pavilion; flag

3413 **pape** pope

3415 **sensation** sensation

3417 **angoisse** distress, anguish, dread, fear

3418 **générosité** generosity, generously

3419 **chaise** chair

3421 **légitimité** legitimacy

3422 **emprunt** loan

3423 **clause** clause

3424 **clef** key

3425 **répression** repression, suppression, crack-down

3426 **tombe** grave, tomb

3429 **blocage** block

3430 **faille** fault

3436 **hostilité** hostility, hostilities

3437 **manche** handle, sleeve

3439 **gamin** kid

3441 **temple** temple

3442 **maîtrise** mastery, command, control, master's degree

3443 **arbitrage** refereeing, umpiring, arbitration

3445 **réparation** repair, repairing, correction, compensation

3446 **évêque** bishop

3448 **solitude** solitude, loneliness

3452 **missile** missile

3453 **minuit** midnight

3454 **composante** component

3457 **trame** weft, framework; tram

3458 **bain** bath, bathing

3459 **sûreté** safety, reliability

3460 **hâte** haste, impatience

3462 **format** format

3463 **hiérarchie** hierarchy

3464 **estimation** appraisal, valuation, assessment, estimate

3465 **mutation** transfer, transformation, mutation

3467 **héroïne** heroine

3473 **atteinte** reach; attack, blow

3477 **guise** wish; like, by way of

3481 **élan** momentum, surge, rush; elk, moose

3485 **renouvellement** replacement, recurrence, repetition

3488 **approbation** approval

3490 **faisceau** bundle, beam, stack

3492 **dégât** damage

3493 **pilier** pillar

3498 **jouet** toy

3499 **formé** formed

3502 **toile** cloth, canvas, web

3504 **empreinte** imprint, print, mark, impression

3506 **curiosité** curiosity

3715 **espérance** hope
3716 **synthèse** summary, synthesis
3717 **conjoncture** situation, climate
3719 **baie** bay; berry
3720 **récompense** reward, award
3721 **étendue** area, expanse, duration, extent, range
3723 **carnet** notebook, notepad
3724 **banc** bench, workbench, pew
3726 **assise** basis, foundation
3729 **architecte** architect
3731 **vedette** star, patrol boat
3733 **séminaire** seminar, seminary
3736 **assaut** assault, attack, bout
3737 **couteau** knife
3740 **propagation** propagation, spreading
3745 **arbitre** referee, arbiter, arbitrator
3746 **manteau** coat, overcoat
3747 **implication** implication
3748 **grand-père** grandfather
3749 **reflet** reflection, glint, highlight
3750 **requête** request, petition
3752 **rideau** curtain
3754 **manipulation** handling, manipulation
3756 **assiette** plate, dish, bowl
3760 **écu** ecu
3762 **expédition** dispatch, shipping, shipment, expedition
3765 **chant** song
3766 **diplomatie** diplomacy
3767 **lieutenant** lieutenant
3773 **sud-ouest** south-west
3774 **envergure** wingspan, breadth, scope
3775 **touche** button, key, touch, touchline
3778 **acheminement** routing, shipment
3780 **hôte** host, guest

3782 **confirmation** confirmation
3783 **tapis** carpet, mat, covering
3784 **corde** rope, chord, string
3787 **divin** divine, heavenly
3791 **boutique** shop
3794 **autoroute** motorway, highway, freeway
3795 **maternité** maternity, motherhood
3797 **différend** disagreement, controversy
3799 **comté** county, earldom
3801 **quota** quota
3805 **assistant** assistant
3806 **portion** portion, share
3807 **allocation** allocation, granting, allotment, allowance
3808 **spéculation** speculation
3812 **dix-sept** seventeen
3814 **chauffeur** driver, chauffeur
3815 **prospérité** prosperity
3816 **ambiguïté** ambiguity
3820 **cou** neck
3821 **invention** invention
3822 **boucle** loop, buckle, curl
3827 **carton** cardboard, card, score
3829 **pitié** pity, mercy
3830 **complexité** complexity
3832 **noyau** core, nucleus, pit
3836 **audition** hearing, examination, audition
3837 **comptabilité** accountancy, accounting, book-keeping
3839 **trône** throne
3841 **saut** jump, leap
3842 **amende** fine
3844 **programmation** programming
3846 **justification** justification, proof
3847 **conservation** preservation, preserving, retention
3848 **transit** transit
3850 **galerie** gallery
3851 **aménagement** development, planning, fitting, adjustment

3852 **manifestant** protester, demonstrator
3853 **char** tank
3854 **criminalité** crime
3856 **masque** mask
3858 **festival** festival
3861 **franchise** frankness, exemption, duty-free, franchise, deductible
3867 **tennis** tennis
3868 **avenue** avenue
3869 **vengeance** revenge
3873 **réduit** reduced, scaled-down, cut-down, tiny room, hideout
3877 **rapprochement** bringing together, coming closer, parallel
3878 **confession** confession
3879 **suspens** suspension, abeyance
3880 **dégradation** degrading, damaging, erosion; demotion
3881 **vingtième** twentieth
3882 **agenda** diary, planner
3883 **grand-mère** grandmother
3884 **phare** lighthouse, headlight
3888 **diagnostic** diagnosis
3889 **poing** fist, punch
3890 **étiquette** label, ticket, etiquette, sticker, tag
3891 **tante** aunt
3892 **chemise** shirt, folder
3893 **pile** pile, stack, battery, tails
3894 **kilo** kilo
3895 **citoyenneté** citizenship
3896 **douceur** softness, smoothness, mildness, gentleness, sweetness
3901 **croix** cross
3906 **censure** censorship
3910 **main-d'œuvre** manpower, labor, work force
3911 **invasion** invasion
3912 **orange** orange
3913 **jury** jury, board of examiners
3914 **bœuf** ox, steer, beef
3916 **roue** wheel

4132  **provocation** provocation

4134  **versant** hillside, mountainside

4135  **réticence** reluctance, hesitation

4136  **grossesse** pregnancy

4138  **timbre** stamp

4141  **élargissement** widening, letting-out, stretching, broadening

4145  **incidence** effect, incidence

4146  **béton** concrete

4148  **génocide** genocide

4149  **vingt-quatre** twenty four

4153  **poudre** powder

4154  **teneur** content

4157  **dérive** drift

4159  **vocabulaire** vocabulary

4168  **poitrine** chest, breast, breasts, bosom

4172  **doctrine** doctrine

4174  **majesté** majesty

4176  **indifférence** indifference

4178  **typique** typical

4180  **désarmement** disarmament, disarming

4182  **architecture** architecture

4183  **éventualité** eventuality, possibility

4186  **état-major** staff, staff headquarters

4191  **surcroît** increase

4193  **plomb** lead

4194  **gorge** throat

4197  **montre** watch

4199  **exploit** exploit

4203  **épidémie** epidemic

4204  **alarme** alarm

4207  **lunette** telescope, glasses

4208  **entourage** circle, entourage

4209  **sphère** sphere

4212  **recrutement** recruiting, recruitment

4215  **toilette** washing, toilet, lavatory, bathroom, restroom

4216  **autobus** bus

4219  **admiration** admiration

4222  **poulet** chicken

4223  **pêcher** peach tree

4224  **brigade** team, squad, brigade

4226  **reçu** receipt, accepted

4228  **relance** boost, reminder, recovery

4229  **dose** dose, amount

4230  **loyer** rent

4231  **distorsion** distortion

4233  **arrivant** arrival, comer

4234  **standard** standard, switchboard

4235  **taxi** taxi

4236  **limitation** limitation, restriction, limit

4242  **commissariat** police station

4244  **confrontation** confrontation

4248  **panneau** sign, notice, panel

4249  **appréciation** appreciation, assessment, appraisal

4251  **complément** complement

4254  **successeur** successor

4255  **méfiance** distrust, mistrust, suspicion

4258  **dictateur** dictator

4259  **prétention** claim

4260  **rédacteur** editor, writer, drafter, compiler

4262  **extraction** extraction

4263  **banquier** banker

4265  **stabilisation** stabilization

4267  **légion** legion

4268  **lacune** gap, deficiency

4269  **engin** machine, tool, vehicle, device

4273  **cloche** bell

4274  **compatriote** compatriot

4275  **affection** affection, ailment

4276  **sel** salt

4278  **redressement** straightening up, upturn, righting

4279  **paradoxe** paradox

4282  **magistrat** magistrate, judge

4283  **extrait** extract, excerpt

4284  **amant** lover

4285  **farce** joke, prank, hoax, farce

4286  **compétitivité** competitiveness

4288  **quarantaine** about forty

4289  **sous-sol** basement, lower ground floor, subsoil, underground

4290  **rat** rat

4291  **flot** floodtide, stream of, flood of

4295  **passe** pass, channel

4297  **location** renting

4300  **innocence** innocence

4301  **bijou** jewel

4302  **messe** mass

4303  **coïncidence** coincidence

4304  **torture** torture

4306  **rayonnement** radiance

4307  **récolte** harvest, crop

4308  **valise** suitcase

4309  **danseur** dancer

4310  **expertise** expertise

4312  **vitrine** window, display cabinet

4314  **crâne** skull

4321  **poule** hen, chick

4322  **punition** punishment

4323  **hésitation** hesitation

4326  **renfort** help, back-up, support

4327  **cohérence** coherence, consistency

4328  **souris** mouse

4331  **semestre** semester, six-month period

4336  **tente** tent

4337  **goutte** drop

4338  **poussée** push, rise, upsurge

4339  **moine** monk, friar

4342  **vice** fault, defect, vice

4348  **fidélité** loyalty, faithfulness, accuracy, reliability

4350  **gestionnaire** administrator, administrative

4355  **avancée** advance, overhang

4362  **rapidité** speed, quickness

4363  **localité** town, village

4364  **récupération** recovery, retrieval, salvage

4366  **rentabilité** profitability

4371  **conte** tale

4372  **évasion** escape, evasion

4373  **repère** reference, benchmark, landmark

4376  **ironie** irony

4377  **serveur** waiter, server

4379  **insuffisance** inadequacy, insufficiency

4380  **librairie** bookstore, bookshop

4381  **parenthèse** parenthesis, bracket, aside

4385  **levée** raising, levying, levee

4388  **nord-est** north-east

4389  **substitution** substitution, mix-up

4396  **altitude** altitude, height

4402  **connerie** crap, bullsh*t, stupidity

4404  **coude** elbow

4406  **report** postponement, deferment

4407  **créature** creature

4416  **palier** landing, level, flat

4419  **costume** suit, costume, dress

4420  **thérapie** therapy

4421  **reproche** reproach

4422  **curé** parish priest

4423  **contrôleur** inspector, controller

4424  **soulagement** relief

4426  **avalanche** avalanche

4427  **mark** mark

4428  **brèche** breach, gap

4429  **incitation** incitement, incentive

4430  **entraîneur** coach, trainer

4435  **visa** visa, stamp

4436  **vingt-cinq** twenty five

4437  **péché** sin

4438  **gendarme** policeman

4439  **sécheresse** dryness, drought

4440  **score** score

4441  **goûter** snack

4443  **juridiction** jurisdiction, court of law

4444  **prostitution** prostitution

4445  **fiche** card, sheet, slip, form

4446  **déséquilibre** imbalance

4447  **probabilité** probability, likelihood

4450  **embargo** embargo

4452  **brouillard** fog, mist, haze

4454  **jet** jet, throw, spray, nozzle

4455  **trêve** truce

4459  **détachement** detachment

4461  **panier** basket

4462  **bouton** button, knob, spot

4464  **fermeté** firmness, solidness, steadiness

4468  **théologie** theology

4471  **tache** stain, spot, mark

4472  **tendresse** tenderness, fondness

4474  **slogan** slogan

4475  **fromage** cheese

4477  **incapacité** incompetence, incapability

4479  **parfum** perfume, scent, fragrance

4482  **instinct** instinct

4483  **barreau** bar

4486  **parquet** parquet floor, hardwood floor, prosecutor's office

4487  **navigation** navigation

4490  **frustration** frustration

4491  **cinquantaine** about fifty

4494  **auto** car

4495  **troupeau** herd, flock

4496  **gendarmerie** police force, police station

4504  **mœurs** morals, customs, habits, manners, ways

4505  **cessez-le-feu** ceasefire

4507  **boue** mud

4508  **empereur** emperor

4510  **déclin** decline, deterioration

4512  **maintenance** maintenance, servicing

4514  **pneu** tire

4515  **fraude** fraud

4516  **coton** cotton

4521  **fraction** fraction

4522  **impossibilité** impossibility

4524  **nuance** shade, hue, nuance

4526  **enquêteur** investigator, pollster

4529  **bordel** brothel, mess, chaos

4531  **versement** payment

4536  **provision** stock, supply

4538  **ceinture** belt, waist

4540  **délibération** deliberation, debate, consideration

4542  **seigneur** lord

4545  **merveille** marvel, wonder

4547  **démon** demon, fiend

4549  **disponibilité** availability

4552  **récepteur** receiver, receiving

4553  **glissement** sliding, slipping, skidding

4554  **auditeur** auditor, listener

4556  **chocolat** chocolate

4558  **obtention** obtaining, achievement

4560  **chagrin** grief, sorrow,

4563  **soupe** soup

4564  **bravo** bravo, well done

4566  **concitoyen** fellow citizen

4567  **flèche** arrow

4568  **libéralisation** liberalization

4569  **complot** plot, conspiracy

4570  **signataire** signatory

4571  **ski** ski, skiing

4573  **syndrome** syndrome

4574  **météo** weather forecast

4578  **soumission** submission

4581  **romancier** novelist

4582  **sorcier** sorcerer, witch

4583  **consigne** deposit, orders, detention

4584  **harmonie** harmony

4589  **félicitation** congratulation

4591  **lance** lance

4594  **vélo** bike, bicycle

4595  **fatigue** tiredness, fatigue

4596  **instabilité** instability

4598  **comte** count

4600  **orchestre** orchestra

4602  **dixième** tenth

4603  **est** east

4607  **fouet** whip

4609  **fixation** fixation, fixing

4610 **encadrement** training, framing, supervision

4618 **retombée** fallout, consequences, effects

4621 **éventail** fan, range

4622 **solde** balance; pay; sale

4624 **régiment** regiment

4626 **bouleversement** upheaval

4630 **instituteur** school teacher

4633 **coulisse** backstage, wings, behind the scenes

4635 **ratification** ratification

4636 **emplacement** site, location

4639 **renouveau** renewal

4642 **spécification** specification

4643 **documentation** documentation, literature

4645 **spectre** spectrum, ghost

4649 **débouché** prospect, opportunity, opening

4651 **fléau** scourge, plague

4652 **traversée** crossing

4654 **secrétariat** secretaryship, secretariat, secretarial offices, secretary's office

4659 **soif** thirst

4660 **accumulation** accumulation, amassing, storage, stockpiling, build-up

4662 **essor** expansion, development, flight

4665 **rébellion** rebellion

4667 **désignation** designation

4669 **conformité** conformity

4670 **pantalon** trousers, pants

4674 **réservoir** tank, reservoir

4675 **aveu** confession

4677 **inondation** flood, deluge

4678 **câble** cable, wire

4679 **poumon** lung

4681 **perturbation** disruption, disturbance

4683 **illustration** illustration

4687 **cordon** cord, string, lead

4692 **plate-forme** platform

4696 **tremblement** shiver, trembling, shaking

4697 **rail** rail, track

4699 **lampe** lamp, light

4703 **multiplication** multiplication

4705 **cliché** cliché; negative

4706 **diamant** diamond

4710 **planification** planning

4711 **éloge** praise

4712 **regroupement** regrouping, reassembly

4716 **configuration** configuration, layout

4719 **scepticisme** scepticism

4720 **croisière** cruise

4722 **athlète** athlete

4723 **poil** hair, bristle

4728 **islam** Islam

4731 **implantation** implanting, setting up, establishment, implantation, installation

4735 **trottoir** pavement

4736 **vieillard** old man

4737 **fillette** little girl, girl

4739 **singe** monkey

4743 **fourniture** supply, provision

4745 **milice** militia

4746 **foire** fair

4748 **crème** cream

4749 **mentalité** mentality

4750 **charité** charity

4751 **borne** milestone, boundary stone

4755 **mobilité** mobility

4756 **exclu** outcast

4757 **boucher** butcher

4759 **commencement** beginning, start

4760 **licenciement** dismissal, sacking

4761 **chancelier** chancellor

4762 **retenue** deduction; restraint, self-control

4763 **visée** aim, design, sighting

4764 **dénonciation** denunciation

4765 **plaie** wound

4767 **rocher** rock, boulder

4768 **mortalité** mortality, death rate

4769 **cruauté** cruelty

4773 **confort** comfort

4775 **tube** tube

4776 **coffre** trunk, boot, chest

4778 **huitième** eighth

4783 **annulation** cancellation, annulment

4784 **acceptation** acceptance

4787 **chirurgien** surgeon

4788 **orage** storm, thunderstorm

4789 **boule** ball

4790 **médiation** mediation, arbitration

4792 **hall** foyer, lobby

4794 **semblant** semblance, pretence

4798 **dilemme** dilemma

4799 **progressiste** progressive

4800 **ours** bear

4804 **duc** duke

4806 **stress** stress

4813 **vieillesse** old age

4814 **navette** shuttle

4816 **batterie** battery; drum set

4817 **foie** liver

4820 **détour** bend, curve, detour

4821 **boulevard** boulevard

4822 **blague** joke

4823 **mécontentement** displeasure, dissatisfaction

4825 **repli** bend, twist, wrinkle, fold, fallback

4826 **contrepartie** counterpart, opposite, alternative

4828 **aboutissement** outcome, result

4829 **triomphe** triumph

4830 **libre-échange** free trade

4831 **sincérité** sincerity

4832 **serre** greenhouse

4834 **convoi** convoy, train

4836 **psychologie** psychology

4838 **puits** well, shaft, pit

4839 **intimité** privacy, intimacy

4840 **équation** equation

4842 **bétail** livestock, cattle

4843 **prophète** prophet

4844 **micro** mike, micro, microphone

4849 **embauche** job vacancy, hiring

4850 **verdict** verdict
4851 **dix-neuf** nineteen
4855 **détente** release, relaxation, détente, loosening
4858 **préjudice** loss, harm, damage
4860 **exploration** exploration, investigation, examination
4862 **hymne** hymn, anthem
4864 **famine** famine
4866 **précipitation** haste, precipitation
4867 **caution** deposit, guarantee, bail
4868 **affectation** appointment, allocation; show, pretence
4870 **cave** cellar, basement
4871 **bond** leap, rebound
4873 **nettoyage** cleaning, cleansing
4874 **foudre** lightning
4875 **justesse** accuracy, precision
4876 **rente** annuity, pension
4877 **hépatite** hepatitis
4879 **clan** clan
4880 **accélération** acceleration
4881 **garage** garage
4885 **obscurité** darkness
4887 **soixante-dix** seventy
4891 **jungle** jungle
4892 **case** box, hut, field
4895 **crête** crest, top, ridge
4896 **traite** trade, draft, stretch, milking
4897 **démarrage** start, moving off
4898 **oubli** forgetting, leaving behind, missing
4899 **procès-verbal** minutes, statement
4900 **formalité** formality
4903 **émetteur** transmitter, issuer
4904 **montage** assembly, setting, pitching, putting, editing
4907 **simplicité** simplicity, straightforwardness
4909 **bulle** bubble
4911 **promoteur** promoter, instigator, developer

4913 **obsession** obsession
4915 **voisinage** neighborhood
4916 **savoir-faire** know-how
4920 **munition** ammunition, supplies
4922 **compliment** compliment
4925 **cassette** cassette
4926 **résident** foreign national, foreign resident
4933 **cage** cage
4935 **téléspectateur** TV viewer
4936 **golf** golf, golf course
4940 **réveil** waking up, awakening, alarm clock
4945 **détérioration** deterioration
4953 **cirque** circus; cirque
4954 **législature** legislature
4959 **allégement** lightening, unweighting, reduction
4962 **sérénité** serenity, peacefulness
4967 **piano** piano
4968 **concertation** meeting, consultation
4969 **vaisseau** ship, vessel
4970 **interaction** interaction
4972 **sillage** wake, slipstream
4983 **céréale** cereal
4985 **agitation** agitation, excitement
4986 **exode** exodus
4987 **aire** surface, area
4988 **orgueil** pride
4989 **socialisme** socialism
4990 **harmonisation** harmonization
4992 **cocktail** cocktail, cocktail party
4993 **moyenne** average
4995 **compression** compression; cutback, reduction

## Nouns/adjectives
24 **tout** all
28 **autre** other
56 **premier** first
59 **grand** great, big, tall
87 **dernier** last
128 **politique** politics; political

138 **petit** small, little
147 **général** general
152 **jeune** young
194 **meilleur** better, best
202 **long** long, lengthy
212 **simple** simple
215 **important** important
216 **présent** present
227 **national** national
237 **propre** clean, proper
251 **français** French
261 **économique** economic, economical
264 **haut** top, high
274 **mauvais** bad, wrong
282 **international** international
285 **public** public, audience
286 **humain** human
292 **vrai** true
296 **difficile** difficult
301 **social** social
304 **juste** just, only; fair
305 **étranger** foreigner; foreign
335 **clair** clear
374 **américain** American
380 **prochain** next
381 **particulier** particular, peculiar; person
394 **plein** full
398 **personnel** personnel, personal
400 **parti** party
412 **sérieux** serious
419 **gros** big
433 **intérieur** interior, inside
443 **grave** serious, grave
445 **européen** European
451 **nécessaire** necessary, required
455 **entier** whole, full
458 **principal** principal
467 **ami** friend
468 **bas** low
484 **futur** future
501 **passé** past
511 **responsable** responsible
546 **parent** parent
572 **noir** black
574 **double** double

592 **technique** technique, technics, technical
599 **riche** rich
607 **gauche** left
611 **canadien** Canadian
619 **contraire** opposite, contrary
622 **local** local
625 **extérieur** exterior
640 **directeur** director
643 **précis** precise
652 **impossible** impossible
658 **total** total
665 **réel** real
672 **rapide** fast, quick
675 **essentiel** essential
688 **financier** financial, financier
690 **militaire** military
699 **pauvre** poor
703 **matériel** material, equipment
723 **faible** weak
743 **pire** worse, worst
760 **naturel** natural
764 **heureux** happy, lucky, fortunate
780 **commun** common
784 **anglais** English
796 **secret** secret
820 **précédent** precedent; previous
828 **fédéral** federal
838 **proche** nearby, close
839 **direct** direct
842 **pratique** practice, pratical
844 **allemand** German
876 **supérieur** superior
879 **capital** major, chief, principal; capital, assets
902 **historique** historical
908 **commercial** commercial
909 **critique** criticism, critic, critical
929 **civil** civil; civilian
933 **complexe** complex
949 **positif** positive
950 **scientifique** scientific
954 **indépendant** independent
979 **voisin** neighbor
987 **rouge** red

992 **central** central
996 **officiel** official
1000 **professionnel** professional
1002 **animal** animal
1029 **dur** hard
1060 **vert** green
1063 **sensible** sensitive
1064 **étudiant** student
1066 **malade** ill, sick
1080 **libéral** liberal
1081 **citoyen** citizen
1107 **logique** logic, logical
1119 **violent** violent
1121 **suivant** following
1131 **industriel** industrial
1132 **vif** lively
1138 **tendre** tender
1146 **physique** physical, physics
1160 **relatif** relative
1163 **maximum** maximum
1164 **moteur** motor
1169 **régional** regional
1175 **profond** deep
1183 **égal** equal
1191 **vivant** alive, living
1203 **religieux** religious
1214 **parlementaire** parliamentary; member of parliament
1219 **actif** active
1224 **collectif** collective
1226 **moral** moral, morale
1229 **puissant** powerful
1239 **moderne** modern
1254 **immédiat** immediate
1255 **exceptionnel** exceptional
1259 **producteur** producer
1265 **policier** policeman
1270 **extrême** extreme
1277 **précieux** precious
1284 **absolu** absolute
1296 **britannique** British
1306 **majeur** major
1307 **froid** cold
1318 **quotidien** daily
1325 **russe** Russian
1327 **ordinaire** ordinary
1341 **travailleur** worker
1343 **dirigeant** leader

1349 **populaire** popular
1392 **inquiet** worried, anxious
1401 **privé** private
1404 **législatif** legislative
1410 **minimum** minimum
1411 **criminel** criminal
1414 **solide** solid
1429 **idéal** ideal
1442 **coupable** guilty
1451 **inconnu** unknown
1453 **montant** upright, upwards, sum, total
1459 **exemplaire** exemplary; copy
1461 **final** final
1468 **israélien** Israeli
1470 **pareil** similar, likewise; peer, equal
1473 **vide** empty
1477 **italien** Italian
1493 **vague** vague; wave
1501 **contenu** contents
1510 **juif** Jew, Jewish
1520 **négatif** negative
1533 **tiers** third
1536 **occidental** western
1546 **interne** internal, interior, intern
1557 **expert** expert
1569 **patient** patient
1575 **quart** quarter
1578 **catholique** Catholic
1580 **adulte** adult
1588 **spécialiste** specialist
1600 **parfait** perfect
1605 **incapable** incapable, incompetent
1608 **universel** universal
1614 **inutile** useless
1618 **prisonnier** prisoner, captive
1627 **étonnant** surprising, amazing, incredible
1643 **pur** pure
1660 **concret** concrete
1666 **espagnol** Spanish
1674 **soviétique** Soviet
1675 **volontaire** volunteer; voluntary
1679 **indien** Indian
1681 **définitif** definitive, final

2592 **indicateur** indicator

2606 **tactique** tactics, tactical

2613 **créateur** creator

2621 **rebelle** rebel, rebellious

2629 **voyageur** traveler

2630 **réaliste** realist, realistic

2643 **sage** wise, good, sound, sensible

2645 **correspondant** correspondent

2662 **antérieur** previous, earlier, front

2670 **sportif** sports, athletic, competitive

2671 **rose** rose; pink

2681 **meurtrier** murderer, deadly, lethal

2687 **observateur** observer, observant

2696 **tissu** fabric, material, cloth, tissue, woven

2697 **souverain** sovereign, supreme ruler, monarch

2706 **accusé** defendant

2709 **rural** rural

2712 **diplomatique** diplomatic

2715 **oriental** Oriental

2718 **républicain** republican

2721 **intéressé** concerned, involved

2736 **variable** variable

2741 **détenu** prisoner

2747 **éthique** ethical, ethics

2751 **optimiste** optimistic

2753 **isolé** remote, isolated, insolated

2756 **bizarre** strange, odd

2759 **pêcheur** fisherman

2766 **brut** raw, crude

2769 **gris** grey

2770 **aise** comfort, joy, pleasure, ease

2782 **universitaire** university, academic

2786 **aîné** oldest, eldest

2795 **belge** Belgian

2796 **brutal** brutal

2817 **con** stupid

2832 **gentil** nice, kind

2841 **agréable** pleasant, nice, agreeable

2854 **sourd** deaf

2862 **fixe** fixed

2876 **clinique** clinic

2880 **chéri** darling, love, dear

2905 **ambitieux** ambitious, man with ambition

2906 **sale** dirty

2918 **dramatique** dramatic, tragic, drama

2933 **lointain** distant, faraway

2953 **transparent** transparent, see-through, evident

2954 **élu** elected, elected member

2985 **dit** said, so-called; tale

2992 **clandestin** underground, clandestine

3003 **abonné** subscribed, subscriber

3047 **spirituel** witty, spiritual, sacred

3053 **nazi** Nazi

3059 **agressif** aggressive

3072 **conducteur** driver, operator, conductor

3078 **chronique** chronic, column, page, chronicle

3083 **ethnique** ethnic

3095 **aveugle** blind

3100 **musicien** musician

3101 **routier** road, long-distance lorry or truck driver

3105 **prématuré** premature

3114 **systématique** systematic

3135 **incertain** uncertain, unsure

3142 **conventionnel** conventional

3153 **passif** passive, liabilities

3162 **carré** square, broad, plain

3163 **voleur** thief, light-fingered

3181 **optique** optical, optic, perspective

3184 **méchant** nasty, wicked, mean

3192 **horaire** schedule, timetable, hourly

3207 **nu** naked, nude

3230 **panique** panic

3251 **chanteur** singer

3253 **écrit** writing

3259 **prioritaire** priority, having priority, having right of way

3261 **exécutif** executive

3277 **asiatique** Asian

3283 **bénéficiaire** beneficiary

3290 **silencieux** silent, noiseless, silencer

3291 **continu** continuous

3302 **survivant** survivor, surviving

3312 **mystérieux** mysterious, secretive

3317 **conjoint** spouse, joint

3324 **compliqué** complicated, complex

3337 **couvert** covered, overcast; place, seat, cutlery

3345 **primitif** primitive

3353 **monstre** monster

3362 **célibataire** single, unmarried

3371 **politicien** politician

3377 **infini** ininfinite, infinity

3378 **savant** scientist, scholar; learned, scholarly, clever, skilful

3405 **iranien** Iranian

3411 **symbolique** symbolic

3414 **préliminaire** preliminary, introductory

3433 **éternel** eternal, everlasting

3434 **intime** intimate, close, secret, private

3438 **mathématique** mathematical; mathematics

3450 **superbe** superb, magnificient, handsome, gorgeous

3455 **veuf** surviving spouse

3468 **esclave** slave

3469 **marocain** Moroccan

3470 **menu** menu, slender, slim, minor

3471 **imaginaire** imaginary

3482 **nominal** nominal

3486 **noble** noble

3487 **hebdomadaire** weekly

3489 **protestant** Protestant

3494 **animateur** animator, host

3500 **complice** accomplice

3501 **homosexuel** homosexual

3508 **creux** hollow, empty, hole

3520 **liquide** liquid

3534 **maigre** thin, skinny, slim, lean

3547 **cynique** cynical, cynic

3549 **constructeur** builder, manufacturer

3554 **démocrate** democrat, democratic

3556 **idiot** idiot, fool, stupid

3558 **explosif** explosive

3560 **solitaire** solitary, lone, lonely

3567 **singulier** unique, singular

3573 **publicitaire** advertising, promotional

3578 **sinistre** disaster, sinister

3585 **domestique** servant, domestic

3596 **déterminé** determined, resolute, specific

3597 **ménager** to handle, arrange, domestic

3598 **millénaire** millennium, thousand-year-old

3603 **immobilier** property, real estate, property business, real estate business

3609 **philosophe** philosopher

3613 **handicapé** disabled, handicapped

3633 **carburant** fuel

3635 **prometteur** promising

3656 **descendant** downward, descending, descendant

3660 **polonais** Polish

3672 **familier** familiar, informal

3680 **impératif** need, necessity, urgent, imperative

3684 **portugais** Portuguese

3714 **bienvenu** welcome

3722 **tiens** ah, well

3727 **énergétique** energetic, vigorous

3732 **intervenant** contributor, intervener

3735 **nerveux** nervous, irritable

3738 **arbitraire** arbitrary

3741 **masculin** male, masculine

3757 **gigantesque** gigantic, immense

3758 **rival** rival

3764 **protégé** protected, protégé

3776 **déterminant** determining, deciding, crucial

3777 **sous-marin** submarine, underwater

3779 **externe** external, outer

3781 **assassin** murderer, assassin

3785 **notable** notable, noteworthy

3786 **rationnel** rational

3790 **exposé** account, statement, talk

3793 **tchèque** Czech

3817 **bourgeois** middle class

3831 **favori** favourite, favorite

3835 **timide** timid, shy, bashful

3849 **organisateur** organizer, organizing

3875 **vierge** virgin

3876 **meuble** piece of furniture

3886 **gagnant** winner, winning

3907 **linguistique** linguistic, linguistics

3931 **diplomate** diplomat, diplomatic

3963 **irlandais** Irish

3973 **suivi** follow-up; consistent, continuous

3979 **impuissant** powerless, helpless

3987 **joyeux** merry, joyful, happy

3993 **libanais** Lebanese

3996 **rapporteur** telltale, rapporteur

4014 **composant** component, constituent

4031 **marginal** marginal

4032 **comptable** accountant, accountable

4040 **minime** minor, minimal

4053 **prétendu** so-called, alleged

4056 **pervers** pervert, perverse, perverted

4064 **sceptique** sceptical, sceptic

4065 **vôtre** yours

4066 **problématique** problematic; problem

4077 **yougoslave** Yugoslav, Yugoslavian

4098 **contingent** contingent, draft, quota

4102 **inconscient** unconscious, thoughtless

4107 **fantastique** fantastic, terrific, great, weird, eerie

4108 **courbe** curve, curved

4114 **oral** oral

4117 **muet** mute, silent, dumb

4118 **contrevenant** offender, offending

4125 **médiocre** mediocre, second-rate

4128 **opposant** opponent, opposing

4133 **sommaire** summary, brief, cursory

4137 **égyptien** Egyptian

4140 **distributeur** distributor, machine

4143 **colonial** colonial

4151 **indifférent** indifferent, unconcerned, unimportant

4152 **audacieux** daring, audacious, bold

4158 **mécontent** discontented, dissatisfied, displeased

4161 **délégué** delegate

4163 **algérien** Algerian

4164 **sympathique** likeable, nice, pleasant

4167 **commerçant** shopkeeper, merchant, commercial

4175 **mouton** sheep

4178 **typique** typical

4185 **réciproque** mutual, reciprocal, the opposite

4190 **séparatiste** separatist

4192 **sortant** outgoing

4195 **nationaliste** nationalist

4196 **exportateur** exporter, exporting

4218 **résistant** robust, sturdy, resistance fighter

4220 **acide** acid

4239 **furieux** furious, raging, violent

4246 **atlantique** Atlantic

4247 **rude** rough, harsh, hard, tough

4250 **réflexe** reflex

4253 **comédien** comedian, comedy

4257 **vérificateur** checker, inspector, auditor

4264 **titulaire** holder, with tenure, occupant

4271 **minoritaire** minority

4298 **naïf** naïve, innocent

4299 **retraité** retired

4305 **protecteur** protective, protector, guardian

4318 **combustible** fuel, combustible

4332 **croyant** believer

4333 **réalisateur** director

4340 **modéré** moderate, restrained, reasonable

4346 **commandant** commander

4352 **immigrant** immigrant

4353 **polémique** controversial, controversy

4357 **jumeau** twin

4369 **affreux** dreadful, awful, horrible

4383 **stupéfiant** drug, narcotic; stunning, astounding

4384 **boursier** grant-holder, scholarship holder; stock

4391 **avantageux** profitable, worthwhile, advantageous, attractive

4394 **délinquant** delinquent, offender

4395 **perdant** losing, loser

4399 **poétique** poetic, poetical, poetics

4401 **mensuel** monthly

4411 **itinéraire** itinerary, route

4431 **éditorial** editorial

4451 **interdit** prohibited, banned

4453 **syrien** Syrian

4456 **occupant** occupant, occupier, occupying

4458 **défini** definite

4473 **privilégié** privileged

4476 **toxique** toxic, toxin

4478 **pharmaceutique** phamarceutical

4480 **antique** antique, ancient

4493 **désespéré** desperate, hopeless

4498 **analogue** similar, analogous

4501 **sanitaire** health, sanitary, medical

4502 **sonore** sound, resonant, sonorous, voiced

4506 **bénévole** volunteer, voluntary, unpaid

4523 **conditionnel** conditional

4530 **impatient** impatient

4541 **mexicain** Mexican

4544 **souterrain** underground, underground passage

4551 **acquis** acquired, experience

4555 **indigène** native, local

4561 **prostitué** prostitute

4572 **douanier** customs officer

4585 **blond** blond, fair-haired

4590 **inédit** unpublished; original, new

4612 **esthétique** aesthetics, attractiveness; attractive

4614 **insensé** insane

4625 **chiite** Shiite

4640 **néerlandais** Dutch

4647 **suédois** Swedish, Swede

4650 **croisé** twill; alternate; crusader; crossed

4657 **détenteur** holder, possessor, bearer

4658 **basque** Basque

4671 **anormal** abnormal

4685 **fermier** farmer

4694 **kurde** Kurd, Kurdish

4695 **amusant** funny, amusing, entertaining

4700 **triple** triple

4707 **guerrier** warrior; warlike

4709 **comique** comical; comic, comedian

4715 **nocturne** nocturnal, nocturne

4718 **intensif** intensive

4727 **informé** informed

4782 **graphique** graph, graphic

4785 **textile** textile

4805 **raciste** racist

4809 **danois** Danish, Dane

4835 **terrien** earthling; landowner, countryman

4845 **gâteau** cake

4854 **anglo-saxon** Anglo-Saxon

4869 **salaud** bastard

4883 **négociateur** negotiator

4884 **romantique** romantic

4886 **vulgaire** vulgar, common, popular

4912 **albanais** Albanian

4919 **vendu** sold, bribed

4932 **rhétorique** rhetorical, rhetoric

4937 **forestier** forest, forester

4943 **relevé** statement, list; relieved; put in relief; rolled up

4947 **cochon** pig

4948 **barbare** barbaric; barbarian

4955 **audiovisuel** audio-visual

4960 **malin** smart, shrewd, cunning

4971 **pessimiste** pessimistic; pessimist

4973 **synonyme** synonymous; synonym

4976 **comble** despair; summit, overmeasure; roof

4977 **bosniaque** Bosnian

## Verbs

5 **être** to be, being

8 **avoir** to have

20 **pouvoir** can, to be able to

25 **faire** to do, make

533 **interdire** to forbid, prohibit, ban

534 **finir** to finish

535 **placer** to place

536 **sentir** to feel, smell

537 **payer** to pay

540 **diriger** to lead, direct

541 **noter** to note, notice

544 **charger** to load, charge

547 **tomber** to fall

550 **entraîner** to carry along, train

551 **disposer** to arrange, set

557 **retenir** to retain, hold back, remember

559 **intéresser** to interest, involve

565 **parvenir** to reach, achieve

575 **convaincre** to convince

578 **soutenir** to sustain, support

583 **manquer** to miss

585 **opposer** to oppose

586 **signifier** to mean

589 **traiter** to treat, handle, deal with

590 **indiquer** to indicate, signal

591 **tuer** to kill

595 **réduire** to reduce

597 **préférer** to prefer

601 **nommer** to call, name, appoint

605 **durer** to last

613 **livrer** to deliver

616 **souvenir** to remember

624 **inviter** to invite

630 **répéter** to repeat

632 **profiter** to take advantage, profit

635 **prouver** to prove

636 **acheter** to buy

639 **ignorer** to ignore

642 **souffrir** to suffer

644 **fixer** to fix, arrange, set

649 **estimer** to estimate; to consider, deem

655 **amener** to bring

656 **viser** to aim

657 **retirer** to remove, withdraw

664 **conserver** to keep, preserve

667 **naître** to be born

668 **accorder** to grant

669 **tourner** to turn

670 **participer** to participate

673 **respecter** to respect

676 **adopter** to adopt

677 **subir** to undergo, be subjected to, suffer

680 **admettre** to admit

681 **découvrir** to discover

682 **couvrir** to cover

683 **assister** to attend; assist, help

685 **dépasser** to pass, go beyond

686 **affirmer** to affirm, maintain, declare, allege

687 **soumettre** to submit

693 **apparaître** to appear

695 **réserver** to reserve, keep

701 **organiser** to organize

702 **posséder** to possess, own, have

705 **constater** to note, notice; to establish, certify

706 **prononcer** to pronounce

710 **vendre** to sell

714 **déplacer** to move, displace

716 **suffire** to be sufficient, suffice

719 **saisir** to take hold of, grab

722 **mourir** to die

724 **employer** to use, employ

727 **accompagner** to accompany

730 **supposer** to suppose, assume

731 **fournir** to provide, supply

733 **exiger** to require, demand

734 **intervenir** to intervene

737 **discuter** to discuss, debate; to question

739 **protéger** to protect

740 **abandonner** to give up, abandon

742 **battre** to beat, hit

744 **adresser** to address

745 **préciser** to state, specify, clarify

747 **attirer** to attract

748 **demeurer** to remain, live

750 **consacrer** to devote, consecrate

751 **remplir** to fill, fulfill

753 **appliquer** to apply

754 **frapper** to hit, strike, knock

757 **fermer** to close, shut

758 **forcer** to force

767 **résoudre** to solve, resolve

768 **publier** to publish

771 **pousser** to push

776 **reposer** to rest

781 **satisfaire** to satisfy

788 **observer** to observe, watch

790 **désigner** to designate

791 **dépendre** to depend

793 **construire** to build, construct

804 **plaire** to please

809 **signer** to sign

810 **révéler** to reveal

811 **couper** to cut

815 **situer** to situate, locate

816 **souligner** to underline, stress

821 **installer** to install

823 **augmenter** to increase, raise

824 **réunir** to gather, reunite, raise

837 **lever** to lift, raise

840 **imaginer** to imagine

841 **figurer** to represent, appear

850 **envisager** to view, contemplate

853 **monter** to go up, rise, assemble

854 **promettre** to promise

856 **concentrer** to concentrate

858 **composer** to compose, dial

873 **confier** to entrust

874 **remarquer** to remark; to notice, point out

878 **condamner** to condemn

883 **limiter** to limit

884 **justifier** to justify

890 **raconter** to tell

892 **développer** to develop

895 **conclure** to conclude

899 **insister** to insist

911 **baisser** to lower, turn down, bend down

914 **cacher** to hide

915 **prêter** to lend

916 **définir** to define

918 **exposer** to display, exhibit, expose

922 **rapporter** to bring back, report

923 **appuyer** to lean, support

925 **rentrer** to go in, come in, come back, return

928 **détruire** to destroy

940 **échapper** to escape

946 **séparer** to separate

957 **régler** to pay, adjust, settle

959 **commander** to order, command

960 **étudier** to study

961 **déterminer** to determine, find out, specify

963 **fonder** to found, set

966 **exercer** to exercise, exert, practice, carry out

968 **manifester** to show, demonstrate, display

969 **menacer** to threaten

970 **conseiller** to advise

981 **rejeter** to reject

984 **coûter** to cost

989 **autoriser** to authorize

990 **effectuer** to carry out, undergo

999 **retourner** to return, go back

1004 **inscrire** to register, write down

1007 **rejoindre** to rejoin, reunite

1014 **confirmer** to confirm

1017 **contribuer** to contribute

1018 **attaquer** to attack

1020 **remonter** to go back up

1027 **susciter** to arouse, provoke

1031 **lutter** to struggle, fight

1033 **contenir** to contain

1034 **déposer** to deposit, put down

1035 **modifier** to modify, adjust

1040 **traverser** to cross, traverse

1041 **transformer** to transform

1047 **renvoyer** to send back, dismiss

1048 **regretter** to regret

1051 **consister** to consist

1052 **réagir** to react

1053 **surprendre** to surprise

1056 **améliorer** to improve

1058 **réfléchir** to reflect

1061 **apprécier** to appreciate

1069 **contrôler** to control, check, inspect, monitor

1078 **contenter** to satisfy, please

1082 **citer** to quote

1088 **destiner** to intend, be used

1089 **causer** to cause; to chat

1093 **interroger** to question, interrogate

1095 **provoquer** to provoke

1097 **ramener** to bring back, return, take back

1100 **concevoir** to conceive

1101 **procéder** to proceed

1104 **acquérir** to acquire

1106 **convenir** to agree, be suitable

1108 **examiner** to examine

1110 **mesurer** to measure

1113 **impliquer** to imply, implicate

1118 **combattre** to fight

1120 **comporter** to comprise, include; to behave

1122 **mériter** to deserve, merit

1123 **emprunter** to borrow

1125 **traduire** to translate

1128 **emporter** to take, remove

1135 **doubler** to double, pass; to dub

1138 **tendre** to tighten; to extend, stretch, tender

1143 **évoquer** to recall, evoke

1144 **fonctionner** to function, work

1147 **accuser** to accuse

1152 **distribuer** to distribute, give out

1154 **prétendre** to pretend

1171 **entreprendre** to begin, start, undertake

1173 **étendre** to spread out, stretch out

1176 **décrire** to describe

1185 **entretenir** to maintain

1186 **habiter** to live

1189 **accueillir** to welcome, greet, accommodate

1190 **libérer** to free, liberate, release

1193 **rire** to laugh

1196 **commettre** to commit

1201 **enlever** to remove

1202 **jeter** to throw

1207 **prévenir** to prevent, warn; to notify

1209 **analyser** to analyse

1212 **témoigner** to testify

1213 **sauver** to rescue, save

1218 **remercier** to thank

1220 **réclamer** to ask for, call for; to claim

1230 **recueillir** to collect, gather

1231 **fabriquer** to manufacture, invent, make

1236 **vérifier** to check, verify

1238 **enregistrer** to record, check in

1248 **voter** to vote

1251 **nourrir** to feed, nourish

1256 **rechercher** to search for

1260 **garantir** to guarantee

1268 **pratiquer** to practice

1272 **bénéficier** to benefit

1274 **revoir** to see again, revise

1280 **renforcer** to reinforce, strengthen

1283 **qualifier** to qualify

1285 **dégager** to free, clear

1297 **surveiller** to watch

1301 **accomplir** to accomplish

1302 **décevoir** to disappoint

1314 **inspirer** to inspire

1315 **opérer** to operate, carry out

1320 **joindre** to join

1329 **rapprocher** to bring closer, get closer

1331 **fier** to rely on

1338 **manger** to eat

1339 **soulever** to lift up

1348 **survivre** to survive

1354 **gérer** to manage

1356 **informer** to inform

1358 **attacher** to attach

1359 **renouveler** to renew

1360 **asseoir** to sit

1363 **renoncer** to give up, renounce

1370 **plaindre** to pity, feel sorry for, complain

1377 **aboutir** to succeed, end up at

1378 **visiter** to visit

1383 **échouer** to fail

1384 **désirer** to desire

1389 **inquiéter** to worry, disturb

1396 **affecter** to affect

1398 **ressembler** to look like, resemble

1400 **supporter** to support, endure

1407 **favoriser** to favor

1413 **précéder** to precede

1415 **correspondre** to correspond

1419 **transmettre** to forward, transmit

1422 **associer** to associate

1426 **identifier** to identify

1434 **encourager** to encourage

1436 **dérouler** to unwind, enroll

1439 **signaler** to indicate, signal

1446 **attribuer** to award, grant, attribute

1447 **courir** to run

1450 **dénoncer** to denounce

1452 **échanger** to exchange

1454 **éliminer** to eliminate

1457 **exclure** to exclude

1465 **élire** to elect

1476 **sourire** to smile

1478 **suggérer** to suggest

1479 **interrompre** to interrupt

1483 **unir** to unite

1487 **franchir** to get over

1492 **écarter** to separate, move apart, keep away

1506 **investir** to invest

1507 **diminuer** to diminish, decrease

1508 **réfugier** to take refuge

1509 **entourer** to surround

1514 **communiquer** to communicate

1515 **prolonger** to prolong, extend

1516 **verser** to pour, deposit, shed

1519 **démontrer** to demonstrate

1523 **accroître** to increase

1532 **marcher** to walk

1535 **aborder** to reach, approach

1539 **tromper** to deceive

1541 **éloigner** to move away, take away, distance

1544 **évaluer** to evaluate

1553 **adapter** to adapt

1560 **comparer** to compare

1562 **provenir** to be from, come from

1565 **céder** to give up, give way

1567 **diviser** to divide

1576 **approcher** to approach

1581 **reprocher** to blame, reproach

1584 **peser** to weigh

1590 **supprimer** to remove, withdraw

1592 **douter** to doubt

1593 **ressentir** to feel

1595 **consulter** to consult

1601 **résumer** to summarize, sum up

1606 **hésiter** to hesitate

1610 **voler** to steal, rob

1611 **résister** to resist

1619 **avouer** to admit

1620 **saluer** to greet, salute

1630 **achever** to complete, finish, end

1634 **oser** to dare

1635 **rassembler** to gather together

1639 **corriger** to correct

1645 **prier** to pray

1648 **dominer** to dominate

1654 **critiquer** to criticize

1658 **évoluer** to evolve

1661 **percevoir** to perceive

1663 **approuver** to approve

1670 **relier** to connect

1676 **négocier** to negotiate

1678 **rêver** to dream

1682 **persuader** to convince, persuade

1683 **interpréter** to interpret

1686 **marier** to marry

1695 **introduire** to introduce

1705 **descendre** to go down, come down

1712 **baser** to base

1718 **déployer** to deploy, open

1721 **circuler** to drive, circulate

1730 **suspendre** to suspend, postpone

1749 **féliciter** to congratulate

1764 **intégrer** to integrate

1772 **financer** to finance

1775 **nier** to deny

1778 **étonner** to astonish, amaze

1781 **accéder** to access, reach, attain

1783 **récupérer** to get back, recover, recuperate

1784 **doter** to endow, provide

1787 **émettre** to emit, issue

1796 **pencher** to lean, tilt

1805 **mentionner** to mention

1807 **distinguer** to distinguish

1808 **exploiter** to exploit

1813 **faciliter** to make easier, facilitate

1816 **veiller** to look after, stay up

1820 **chanter** to sing

1823 **clore** to close

1831 **régner** to reign

1833 **ressortir** to go out again, come out again, take out again

1836 **dormir** to sleep

1842 **rassurer** to reassure, calm down

1853 **taire** to keep quiet

1856 **progresser** to progress

1858 **confronter** to confront

1864 **rétablir** to restore, re-establish

1869 **compliquer** to complicate

1870 **assumer** to assume

1872 **éprouver** to feel, experience

1879 **boire** to drink

1890 **foutre** to f*ck, shove off

1891 **apercevoir** to see, notice

1892 **refléter** to reflect

1893 **bouger** to move, shift, budge

1896 **isoler** to isolate, insolate

1900 **animer** to lead, conduct, animate

1903 **préserver** to preserve

1909 **exécuter** to execute, carry out

1920 **briser** to break

1922 **reculer** to move back, back up

1929 **transporter** to transport, carry

1930 **brûler** to burn

1936 **grandir** to grow, increase, expand

1937 **élaborer** to work out, develop

1939 **illustrer** to illustrate

1941 **affronter** to confront, face

1942 **éclater** to burst, explode

1946 **presser** to squeeze, press

1947 **mêler** to mingle, mix

1949 **formuler** to formulate

1950 **crier** to shout, scream, cry out

1956 **élargir** to widen, expand

1958 **plonger** to dive

1960 **fuir** to flee

1962 **varier** to vary, change

1964 **inventer** to invent

1971 **ordonner** to ordain, organize, order

1974 **contester** to contest, question

1979 **préoccuper** to worry, preoccupy

1982 **multiplier** to multiply

1987 **excuser** to excuse

1988 **recommander** to recommend

1995 **diffuser** to diffuse, broadcast

1998 **inclure** to include

2000 **combler** to fill, fill in, fulfill

2002 **annuler** to cancel

2004 **bloquer** to block

2008 **guider** to guide

2009 **spécialiser** to specialize

2020 **détourner** to redirect

2024 **blesser** to hurt

2028 **reporter** to report; to postpone

2034 **compléter** to complete

2038 **procurer** to get, bring

2039 **officier** officer

2041 **efforcer** to endeavor

2047 **éclairer** to light up

2048 **consommer** to eat, consume, drink, use, consummate

2051 **dépenser** to spend

2056 **détenir** to hold, detain

2061 **cultiver** to cultivate, grow

2063 **gouverner** to govern, rule, steer, helm

2064 **jouir** to enjoy

2065 **parcourir** to cover, travel

2070 **classer** to classify, file, grade, rate

2079 **renverser** to knock down, turn over, overturn

2081 **désoler** to upset, sadden

2082 **accélérer** to speed up, accelerate

2084 **résider** to reside

2086 **dessiner** to draw, design

2087 **rompre** to break

2091 **armer** to arm

2093 **bâtir** to build

2095 **résulter** to result

2098 **emmener** to take

2104 **dresser** to draw up, put up, raise

2106 **afficher** to display

2109 **survenir** to occur, take place, appear

2114 **sauter** to jump

2124 **orienter** to position, give advice, direct, orientate

2125 **reproduire** to reproduce, repeat

2128 **transférer** to transfer

2131 **croître** to grow, increase

2132 **tolérer** to tolerate, access, put up, bear, endure

2134 **enseigner** to teach

2135 **rédiger** to write, draw up

2144 **contraindre** to compel, force

2145 **trancher** to cut, sever, settle, decide

2147 **retarder** to delay, hold up

2148 **réjouir** to delight, rejoice

2149 **punir** to punish

2150 **repartir** to set off again, start up again

2152 **déclencher** to trigger, release, unleash

2155 **écouler** to sell, run off, flow out

2160 **coucher** to lie down, sleep

2170 **célébrer** to celebrate

2177 **hausser** to raise

2185 **casser** to break

2190 **croiser** to cross

2194 **voyager** to travel

2197 **répartir** to distribute, spread out, share out, divide up

2199 **réveiller** to wake up

2206 **songer** to dream

2211 **commenter** to comment

2212 **inciter** to incite, encourage

2214 **nécessiter** to require, necessitate

2219 **anticiper** to anticipate, foresee, look or think ahead

2224 **avertir** to warn

2228 **soigner** to treat, look after, take care over

2235 **débarrasser** to clear, get rid of

2251 **tarder** to delay

2252 **refaire** to redo, make again

2253 **pleurer** to cry

2254 **débattre** to discuss, debate

2257 **lâcher** to let go, release

2267 **remporter** to take away, win

2281 **recourir** to turn to, run again

2286 **engendrer** to father, breed, generate

2297 **ralentir** to slow down

2300 **requérir** to require

2303 **louer** to rent, praise

2315 **enfermer** to shut

2316 **abattre** to pull down, kill, beat

2320 **répandre** to spread, spill

2322 **adorer** to adore, worship

2325 **entamer** to start

2331 **calculer** to calculate

2334 **écraser** to crush, grind

2335 **enrichir** to expand, enrich, make somebody rich

2345 **invoquer** to call upon

2346 **compromettre** to compromise

2347 **arracher** to pull up, tear up

2351 **maîtriser** to control, overcome, master

2352 **violer** to rape, infringe

2354 **épargner** to save, spare

2360 **restreindre** to restrict, cut down, decrease

2364 **chasser** to hunt, chase away

2365 **dîner** to dine

2367 **fréquenter** to frequent, go around with

2368 **projeter** to plan, project, throw out

2370 **présider** to preside

2375 **soupçonner** to suspect

2385 **surmonter** to overcome, top, surmount

2399 **promouvoir** to promote

2404 **confondre** to mix up, confuse

2422 **sonner** to ring

2423 **protester** to protest

2425 **effacer** to erase, clean

2426 **débuter** to start

2427 **creuser** to dig

2432 **programmer** to program, schedule

2433 **traîner** to drag, pull

2442 **épuiser** to exhaust, tire out, wear out, use up

2448 **téléphoner** to telephone, phone, call

2449 **serrer** to tighten, squeeze

2450 **caractériser** to characterize

2453 **intituler** to entitle, call

2457 **avérer** to prove to be, turn out

2460 **gêner** to bother, trouble

2463 **accumuler** to accumulate, amass, store, stockpile

2477 **regrouper** to group together, regroup

2482 **privilégier** to favor

2486 **dater** to date

2487 **habituer** to accustom, get used to

2489 **recommencer** to resume, start again

2498 **influencer** to influence

2503 **délivrer** to set free, rid, relieve

2506 **aggraver** to worsen, aggravate

2508 **alimenter** to feed, supply

2510 **équilibrer** to balance

2515 **dicter** to dictate, lay down

2519 **solliciter** to request, solicit, appeal

2520 **convoquer** to call, summon

2526 **choquer** to shock, offend, shake, disturb

2536 **couler** to flow, run, sink

2538 **amuser** to amuse

2544 **glisser** to slide, slip

2547 **exagérer** to exaggerate, overdo

2551 **réviser** to review, revise, overhaul

2553 **rater** to miss, misfire

2563 **affaiblir** to weaken

2566 **envahir** to invade, overrun

2574 **négliger** to neglect

2576 **plaider** to plead

2577 **récompenser** to reward, recompense

2583 **réparer** to repair, fix, correct, make up

2594 **compenser** to compensate for, make up for

2597 **pénétrer** to penetrate

2599 **rouler** to roll

2601 **heurter** to strike, hit, collide

2605 **approprier** to adapt, appropriate, take over

2609 **surgir** to spring up

2612 **semer** to sow, scatter, spread

2619 **succéder** to succeed, take over

2623 **fumer** to smoke

2639 **déboucher** to unblock, uncork

2646 **grimper** to climb, go up

2649 **sacrifier** to sacrifice, give away

2652 **combiner** to combine, devise

2654 **ravir** to delight, rob

2667 **détailler** to detail

2675 **présumer** to presume, assume

2678 **exploser** to explode, blow up

2683 **mentir** to lie

2688 **revêtir** to take on, assume

2700 **repousser** to push away, postpone

2703 **nuire** to harm

2707 **repérer** to spot, pick out, locate, find

2710 **persister** to persist, keep up, linger

2719 **embarquer** to embark, board, take on board, load

2724 **déjeuner** to have lunch

2725 **disputer** to dispute

2730 **infliger** to inflict

2732 **déranger** to disturb, bother

2735 **consentir** to consent, agree

2749 **pointer** to mark off, clock in, clock out, aim

2750 **assassiner** to murder, assassinate

2752 **instaurer** to institute, introduce

2754 **revendiquer** to claim

2755 **secouer** to shake

2774 **ranger** to tidy up, put away

2783 **emparer** to seize, grab, snatch

2787 **trahir** to betray, give away

2789 **admirer** to admire

2797 **extraire** to extract, mine, quarry, pull out, remove

2799 **filer** to spin, run, get out

2801 **accrocher** to hang up, hang on, put up

2812 **planter** to plant, pitch

2822 **soucier** to care about, show concern for

2829 **déplorer** to deplore

2830 **mobiliser** to mobilize, call up

2831 **encadrer** to frame, train

2837 **séduire** to seduce, charm, captivate, appeal to

2838 **précipiter** to quicken, hasten, precipitate

2840 **piloter** to fly, pilot, drive

2849 **vider** to empty, vacate

2851 **démarrer** to start up

2852 **coordonner** to coordinate

2858 **différer** to differ, vary

2859 **honorer** to honor, do credit to

2866 **découler** to ensue, follow

2869 **prédire** to predict

2870 **enterrer** to bury, lay aside

2872 **recouvrir** to cover, hide, conceal

2883 **siéger** to sit

2889 **redevenir** to become again

2897 **amorcer** to bait, prime, begin, initiate

2898 **détester** to hate, detest

2903 **simplifier** to simplify

2904 **briller** to shine

2909 **calmer** to calm down

2912 **soulager** to relieve, soothe, ease

2916 **bouleverser** to upset, distress, disturb, turn upside down

2919 **vaincre** to beat, defeat, overcome, conquer

2921 **renseigner** to give information, get information

2928 **promener** to take for a walk, go for a walk

2932 **arranger** to arrange

2934 **danser** to dance

2936 **passionner** to fascinate, grip

2939 **généraliser** to generalize

2946 **défaire** to undo, dismantle, strip, break up

2950 **vouer** to devote, dedicate to, vow to

2962 **pardonner** to forgive, excuse

2963 **collaborer** to collaborate, contribute

2965 **tester** to test

2966 **proclamer** to proclaim, declare

2973 **coller** to stick, paste

2975 **approfondir** to deepen, make deeper, go further into

2981 **hériter** to inherit

2984 **souffler** to blow, puff

2989 **mélanger** to mix, mix up, confuse

2991 **enfoncer** to ram, drive in, hammer in, sink in

2996 **deviner** to guess, solve

2997 **tracer** to draw, write, mark out

2999 **baiser** to kiss

3000 **user** to wear out, wear away, use up

3008 **relancer** to throw back, restart, relaunch

3011 **poster** to post, mail

3019 **dispenser** to exempt, avoid

3021 **aligner** to lign up, align

3022 **absorber** to absorb, remove, take up, take over

3025 **dévoiler** to unveil, reveal, disclose

3027 **freiner** to brake, slow down

3028 **rattraper** to recapture, recover, catch up, make up for

3030 **régir** to govern

3033 **éteindre** to extinguish, put out, turn off

3037 **débarquer** to unload, land, disembark

3040 **respirer** to breath

3043 **équiper** to equip, kit out, fit out, tool up

3051 **agiter** to shake, disturb

3055 **impressionner** to impress, upset

3060 **loger** to put up, accommodate, stay, find accommodation

3063 **stimuler** to stimulate

3071 **déborder** to overflow, boil over, go out, go over

3077 **dissimuler** to conceal, hide

3086 **spécifier** to specify

3092 **imprimer** to print, print out

3093 **abuser** to abuse, mislead, take advantage

3096 **jurer** to swear

3102 **embrasser** to kiss, embrace

3106 **décrocher** to take down, take off, pick up, lift

3107 **rembourser** to reimburse, pay back, pay off, repay

3108 **adhérer** to stick to, support, join, be a member of

3112 **retomber** to fall again, fall down again

3113 **pourvoir** to provide, equip, supply, furnish

3119 **émaner** to issue from, emanate from, come from, radiate from

3123 **prévaloir** to prevail

3127 **effondrer** to collapse, cave in, fall down

3128 **apprêter** to prepare, get ready, dress

3130 **cibler** to target

3136 **épouser** to marry, wed

3156 **accentuer** to stress, emphasize, become more pronounced

3157 **rattacher** to attach, join, tie

3159 **contracter** to contract, take out, tense

3161 **subsister** to subsist, remain

3169 **allumer** to switch on, light up, turn on

3171 **disperser** to scatter, spread, disperse

3172 **déchirer** to tear up, tear, rip

3178 **contourner** to bypass, go round

3191 **conquérir** to conquer

3194 **motiver** to justify, account for, motivate

3195 **plier** to fold, fold up, fold back, bend

3204 **explorer** to explore, investigate, examine

3209 **abaisser** to pull down, lower, reduce

3213 **étouffer** to suffocate, smother, muffle

3225 **acquitter** to acquit, pay, settle, pay off

3229 **fatiguer** to tire, get tired

3231 **abriter** to shelter, shade

3235 **décourager** to discourage, dishearten, lose heart

3239 **détacher** to untie, detach, remove

3257 **applaudir** to clap, applaud

3267 **référer** to refer, consult, refer to

3268 **obéir** to obey, comply with, respond to

3270 **taper** to beat, slam, bang, type

3275 **fêter** to celebrate

3281 **préconiser** to recommend, advocate

3288 **vanter** to vaunt, boast, brag

3289 **coincer** to jam, hinder, get stuck

3297 **convertir** to convert

3300 **atténuer** to lessen, diminish, dim, subdue, reduce

3310 **brancher** to plug in, connect

3319 **redonner** to give back, return, give more

3320 **assortir** to match, accompany

3326 **restaurer** to restore, feed

3335 **moquer** to mock, make fun of

3336 **allier** to ally, match, unite

3342 **vieillir** to grow old

3351 **emprisonner** to imprison, jail, put in jail, trap

3360 **redouter** to dread, fear

3364 **contredire** to contradict

3368 **redresser** to straighten, set right, redress, turn around

3370 **ramasser** to pick up, collect, gather

3372 **acheminer** to forward, dispatch, transport

3380 **recruter** to recruit

3381 **conformer** to model, conform

3384 **délibérer** to deliberate, debate

3388 **puiser** to draw, take

3391 **ajuster** to adjust, alter, aim, aim at

3392 **œuvrer** to work

3406 **conférer** to confer

3409 **interpeller** to call out to, question

3416 **troubler** to disturb, disrupt, cloud

3427 **dériver** to divert, derive

3428 **évacuer** to evacuate, clear

3431 **fouiller** to search, frisk, go through, rummage through

3435 **cerner** to surround, encircle, delimit

3440 **induire** to infer, induce, result in, lead to

3444 **boucler** to fasten, loop, resolve

3447 **déléguer** to delegate

3449 **miner** to mine, erode

3451 **gonfler** to inflate, blow up, swell

3456 **comparaître** to appear

3461 **instituer** to introduce, impose, establish, institute

3472 **administrer** to manage, run, administer; to give

3474 **démissionner** to resign

3475 **racheter** to repurchase, buy back, redeem

3480 **ennuyer** to bore, worry, bother

3483 **manipuler** to handle, manipulate

3484 **peiner** to toil, labor, struggle

3491 **regagner** to win again, regain, get back, make up

3496 **méfier** to distrust, mistrust

3503 **laver** to wash, clean

3505 **faillir** to have almost, fail, fail to

3514 **coter** to quote, rate

3526 **geler** to freeze, ice over, suspend

3527 **défiler** to unthread, parade

3536 **aspirer** to breathe in, inhale, aspire to

3541 **énoncer** to state, set out, express

3552 **peindre** to paint, depict, portray

3561 **déceler** to discover, detect

3564 **acharner** to go at fiercely and unrelentingly

3571 **assimiler** to assimilate, take in

3574 **incarner** to embody, incarnate

3575 **opter** to opt, decide

3576 **habiller** to dress, get dressed

3580 **reconstruire** to rebuild, reconstruct

3589 **décréter** to declare, decree

3595 **coïncider** to coincide, correspond

3597 **ménager** to handle, arrange, domestic

3602 **guérir** to cure, heal, get better

3605 **contaminer** to contaminate, infect

4070 **envoler** to fly away, fly off, take off

4072 **activer** to activate, speed up, stoke, get moving

4076 **naviguer** to navigate, sail

4079 **alerter** to alert, inform, warn

4099 **émerger** to emerge, rise up, come out

4100 **instruire** to teach, educate, inform

4104 **déguiser** to disguise

4109 **soustraire** to substract, remove, shield, escape from

4115 **téléviser** to televise

4116 **consolider** to strengthen, reinforce

4121 **coder** to code, encode

4139 **découper** to carve, cut,

4142 **dégrader** to degrade, debase, damage, erode

4155 **inverser** to reverse, invert

4160 **stabiliser** to stabilize

4162 **centrer** to center

4166 **corrompre** to corrupt, bribe

4169 **couronner** to crown, award

4170 **relire** to reread, proofread

4171 **perpétuer** to perpetuate, carry on

4177 **omettre** to leave out, miss out, omit

4184 **massacrer** to slaughter, massacre

4187 **attarder** to linger

4188 **englober** to include, encompass, incorporate

4189 **grossir** to get larger

4198 **ratifier** to ratify

4202 **aviser** to notice, advise

4205 **parier** to bet

4211 **sanctionner** to sanction, punish, approve

4213 **détendre** to release, slacken, loosen, relax

4217 **défavoriser** to put at a disadvantage

4223 **pêcher** to fish, go fishing

4225 **trembler** to shiver, tremble, shake, flicker

4227 **civiliser** to civilize

4232 **octroyer** to grant, bestow

4241 **contacter** to contact, get in touch with

4245 **chier** to sh*t, piss off, get pissed off

4256 **replier** to fold, roll up, fold up, withdraw

4261 **avaler** to swallow

4270 **mépriser** to scorn, look down, spurn, disdain

4280 **chiffrer** to put a figure to, assess, quantify, number

4292 **mordre** to bite, overlap into

4313 **ébranler** to shake, rattle

4315 **anéantir** to annihilate, wipe out, ruin, vanish

4319 **économiser** to save, save on, conserve

4320 **tisser** to weave

4329 **bombarder** to bomb

4330 **éveiller** to arouse, stimulate, awaken

4343 **symboliser** to symbolize

4344 **substituer** to substitute

4347 **chuter** to fall

4349 **basculer** to topple, fall over, knock off

4354 **alourdir** to weigh down, make heavy

4356 **sévir** to act ruthlessly, be rife

4358 **piéger** to trap, booby-trap

4360 **pendre** to hang down

4368 **incliner** to tilt, tend towards

4370 **révolter** to revolt, rebel, outrage

4378 **bannir** to banish, ban

4382 **miser** to bet, stake

4386 **déformer** to bend, distort, deform

4390 **parer** to adorn, put on; to ward off, parry

4392 **handicaper** to handicap

4393 **filmer** to film, shoot

4397 **imputer** to impute to, attribute to

4398 **plaisanter** to joke

4400 **desservir** to clear, go against, harm, serve

4405 **ôter** to remove, take away, take off, take out

4412 **purger** to purge, bleed, drain

4413 **fâcher** to anger, make angry, get angry

4414 **repasser** to cross again, retake, show again, iron

4425 **dissoudre** to dissolve, disband, break up

4434 **relâcher** to loosen, release, let go

4441 **goûter** to taste, snack

4442 **renier** to disown, repudiate, go back on

4448 **entraver** to hinder, hamper, get in the way of

4449 **sous-estimer** to underestimate

4465 **véhiculer** to transport, convey

4466 **répliquer** to reply

4469 **advenir** to happen that, happen to

4470 **immigrer** to immigrate

4488 **contrarier** to annoy, bother, thwart

4489 **nouer** to knot, tie

4492 **improviser** to improvise

4503 **initier** to initiate, introduce

4509 **dissiper** to dispel, disperse, clear away

4511 **liquider** to liquidate, sell off, clear

4517 **entrevoir** to make out, catch a glimpse of, foresee

4518 **stipuler** to state, stipulate, specify

4519 **remédier** to cure, remedy, put right

4520 **flotter** to float, hang, stream

4528 **éclaircir** to brighten up, clear up

4532 **bosser** to work, bash on

4533 **articuler** to articulate

4537 **amplifier** to amplify, magnify, expand

4546  **restituer** to return, restore, refund

4548  **balancer** to swing, sway

4565  **appréhender** to dread, apprehend

4575  **borner** to limit, confine

4576  **triompher** to triumph, beat

4577  **concrétiser** to materialize

4580  **dérober** to steal, hide

4586  **pleuvoir** to rain

4587  **déplaire** to displease, be unhappy

4593  **diversifier** to vary, diversify

4597  **pénaliser** to penalize, punish

4604  **envelopper** to wrap, surround, veil

4608  **baigner** to bathe, wash, get a bath, go for a swim

4611  **déménager** to move

4613  **photographier** to photograph

4615  **moderniser** to modernize

4617  **incomber** to be incumbent upon

4619  **équivaloir** to be equivalent, amount to

4620  **différencier** to differenciate

4623  **gâcher** to waste, spoil

4627  **relater** to relate, recount

4631  **rayer** to scratch, streak, stripe; to erase, strike out

4634  **enchaîner** to chain up, connect, string together

4637  **copier** to copy, reproduce

4638  **inculper** to charge

4646  **harmoniser** to harmonize, harmonize with

4648  **rouvrir** to reopen

4656  **venger** to avenge, take revenge

4663  **obséder** to obsess, haunt

4673  **réconcilier** to reconcile

4676  **emmerder** to bug, bother

4682  **brouiller** to mix-up, confuse, scramble

4686  **hanter** to haunt

4689  **lasser** to tire, weary, grow weary

4690  **influer** to influence, have an influence on

4693  **stopper** to stop, halt

4702  **supplier** to beg, implore

4704  **camoufler** to cover up, conceal, camouflage

4708  **figer** to clot, coagulate, congeal, set

4717  **escompter** to discount; to expect

4724  **épanouir** to bloom, blossom

4725  **minimiser** to minimize, play down

4730  **murmurer** to murmur

4732  **décerner** to award, give, issue

4733  **replacer** to replace, put back

4734  **vêtir** to clothe, dress, put on

4738  **enchanter** to delight, enchant, rejoice

4744  **taxer** to tax

4753  **dévouer** to devote, sacrifice oneself

4754  **hâter** to quicken, hasten

4757  **boucher** to fill in, get clogged up

4766  **exiler** to exile

4771  **droguer** to drug, take drugs

4772  **connecter** to connect, go on-line

4777  **intimider** to intimidate

4779  **forger** to forge, contrive, make up

4780  **périr** to perish

4791  **réprimer** to suppress, repress

4796  **rémunérer** to remunerate, pay

4797  **fasciner** to fascinate

4801  **décharger** to unload

4802  **excéder** to exceed

4803  **blâmer** to blame, reprimand

4810  **concéder** to grant, concede

4811  **retrancher** to deduct, remove; to entrench

4812  **renfermer** to contain, shut, lock, enclose

4824  **inaugurer** to unveil, open

4837  **maltraiter** to manhandle, ill-treat, misuse, slight

4847  **réitérer** to reiterate, repeat

4848  **énumérer** to enumerate

4852  **guetter** to watch over, watch out for

4853  **frustrer** to frustrate

4856  **questionner** to question

4857  **injecter** to inject

4861  **caresser** to fondle, caress

4865  **écrier** to exclaim, cry out

4890  **militer** to militate

4893  **craquer** to creak, squeak, crackle, give in, strike

4894  **clarifier** to clarify

4906  **claquer** to flap, bang, slam, snap

4908  **buter** to stumble, trip, run into, prop up, score

4914  **exciter** to arouse, waken, excite, turn on

4921  **capturer** to capture, catch

4923  **allouer** to allocate

4924  **scandaliser** to shock, scandalize

4927  **empresser** to bustle about, hasten to do

4928  **inonder** to flood

4929  **réglementer** to regulate, control

4930  **sonder** to probe, poll, sound out

4939  **ravager** to ravage, devastate

4942  **ensuivre** to follow, result, ensue

4944  **ajourner** to adjourn, defer, postpone

4951  **ancrer** to anchor

4952  **raccrocher** to hang up

4956  **confiner** to confine

4957  **agrandir** to enlarge, extend

4958  **occasionner** to cause, give rise to

4963  **cuire** to cook, bake, roast

4964  **raser** to shave, raze

4966  **revivre** to live again, come back life, revive

4974 **hisser** to hoist, raise up

4975 **agréer** to accept, approve of

4979 **décoller** to take off; to loosen, unstick

4982 **dépouiller** to skin, strip away, deprive; to analyze

4984 **aménager** to develop, plan, fit, adjust

4994 **rigoler** to laugh

4997 **expérimenter** to experiment

4998 **détériorer** to deteriorate

5000 **écrouler** to collapse, tumble

**Related titles from Routledge**

# Developing Writing Skills in French

*Graham Bishop and Bernard Haezewindt*

Designed for intermediate to advanced students, this text equips readers with the necessary skills to write confidently in French in a range of situations. Suitable for use as a classroom text or as a self-study course, it is carefully structured to ensure a better understanding of the effect of choice of words, register and style.

Each chapter contains a selection of model texts, activities and clear notes on the format, style and language demonstrated. Every activity also has a model answer in the key, which also offers advice, explanations and further examples to support the student's learning.

Features include:

- key learning points clearly indicated at the beginning of each chapter
- a rich selection of model texts from a variety of different media.

Based on a well-reviewed Open University course and written by experienced teachers of the language, *Developing Writing Skills in French* has been trialled with non-native speakers of French to produce a valuable resource that will help students write appropriately for a variety of contexts.

PB: ISBN-13: 978–0–415–34897–3
EBK: ISBN-13: 978–0–203–02383–9

Available at all good bookshops
For ordering and further information please visit:
www.routledge.com

**Related titles from Routledge**

# Modern French Grammar

Second Edition

*Margaret Lang and Isabelle Perez*

This new edition of the *Modern French Grammar* is an innovative reference guide to French, combining traditional and function-based grammar in a single volume.

Divided into two parts, Part A covers traditional grammatical categories such as word order, nouns, verbs and adjectives and Part B is organized around language functions and notions such as:

- giving and seeking information
- describing processes and results
- expressing likes, dislikes and preferences.

With a strong emphasis on contemporary usage, all grammar points and functions are richly illustrated with examples. Implementing feedback from users of the first edition of the Grammar, this second edition includes clearer explanations and greater emphasis on areas of particular difficulty for learners of French.

This is the ideal reference grammar for learners of French at all levels, from beginner to advanced. No prior knowledge of grammatical terminology is assumed and a glossary of grammatical terms is provided. This Grammar is complemented by the *Modern French Grammar Workbook* Second Edition which features related exercises and activities.

HB: ISBN-13: 978–0–415–33482–2
PB: ISBN-13: 978–0–415–33162–3
EB: ISBN-13: 978–0–203–39725–1

Available at all good bookshops
For ordering and further information please visit:
www.routledge.com

# Savoir-Faire Plus
# Le Français á l'Université

*Géraldine Enjelvin*

Written by an experienced tutor, *Savoir-Faire Plus* is specifically designed to meet the requirements of today's generation of language undergraduates. Focusing on the life of an Anglophone first year undergraduate studying French in the UK and sharing a house with four francophone students, this engaging textbook provides:

- a clear, logical structure
- a blend of communicative, research-based and traditional exercises
- a wide range of activities covering the four key linguistic skills as well as intercultural skills
- authentic texts (with extracts from Le Monde, L'Express, Le Nouvel Observateur and Libération )
- guidance and practical tips for effective and independent learning

Each of the 10 chapters consists of 4 topics-based sections which provide students with a wealth of diverse material allowing them to gain an in-depth knowledge of relevant topical subjects such as regional languages, sustainable development and fair trade, amongst others. Digestible grammar points are integrated throughout and a range of additional exercises are available on the accompanying website allowing students to perfect their language skills.

Suitable for both self-study and class use *Savoir-Faire Plus* is the ideal course for all advanced students of French, consolidating knowledge gained at A-level while supporting the transition to undergraduate study.

PB: ISBN-13: 978–0–415–44475–0
CD: ISBN-13: 978–0–415–44476–7
MP3: ISBN-13:978–0–415–54985–1

Available at all good bookshops
For ordering and further information please visit:
www.routledge.com

**Related titles from Routledge**

# Thinking French Translation

Second Edition

## *Sándor Hervey and Ian Higgins*

*Thinking French Translation* is a popular course in translation from French into English. The course offers a challenging and practical approach to the acquisition of translation skills, with clear explanations of the theoretical issues involved.

Translation is presented as a problem-solving discipline. A variety of translation issues are considered, including:

- cultural differences
- register and dialect
- genre
- revision and editing.

This second edition features material from the fields of business and law alongside literary texts. The course now covers texts from a wide range of sources, including:

- journalism and literature
- commercial, legal and technical texts
- songs and recorded interviews.

*Thinking French Translation* is essential reading for advanced undergraduates and postgraduate students of French. The book will also appeal to a wide range of language students and tutors through the general discussion of the principles, purposes and practice of translation.

PB: ISBN-13: 978–0–415–25522–6
HB: ISBN-13: 978–0–415–25521–9
EB: ISBN-13: 978–0–203–16712–0

Available at all good bookshops
For ordering and further information please visit:
www.routledge.com